Warwickshire County Council

This item is to be returned or renewed before the latest date above. It may be borrowed for a further period if not in demand. **To renew your books:**

- **Phone the 24/7 Renewal Line 01926 499273 or**
- **Visit www.warwickshire.gov.uk/libraries**

   Discover • Imagine• Learn • *with libraries*

THE GHOSTS OF LANGLEY

Also by John Prados

Storm Over Leyte: The Philippine Invasion and the Destruction of the Japanese Navy

The U.S. Special Forces: What Everyone Needs to Know

A Streetcar Named Pleiku: Vietnam 1965, a Turning Point (longform e-book)

Operation Vulture: America's Dien Bien Phu (e-book)

The Family Jewels: The CIA, Secrecy, and Presidential Power

Islands of Destiny: The Solomons Campaign and the Eclipse of the Rising Sun

In Country: Remembering the Vietnam War (written and edited)

Rethinking National Security (longform e-book)

Normandy Crucible: The Decisive Battle that Shaped World War II in Europe

How the Cold War Ended: Debating and Doing History

William Colby and the CIA: The Secret Wars of a Controversial Spymaster

Vietnam: The History of an Unwinnable War, 1945–1975

Safe for Democracy: The Secret Wars of the CIA

Hoodwinked: The Documents That Reveal How Bush Sold Us a War

Inside the Pentagon Papers (written and edited with Margaret Pratt Porter)

The White House Tapes: Eavesdropping on the President (written and edited)

Lost Crusader: The Secret Wars of CIA Director William Colby

America Confronts Terrorism (written and edited)

The Blood Road: The Ho Chi Minh Trail and the Vietnam War

Presidents' Secret Wars: CIA and Pentagon Covert Operations from World War II Through the Persian Gulf

Combined Fleet Decoded: The Secret History of U.S. Intelligence and the Japanese Navy in World War II

The Hidden History of the Vietnam War

Valley of Decision: The Siege of Khe Sanh (with Ray W. Stubbe)

Keepers of the Keys: A History of the National Security Council from Truman to Bush

Pentagon Games

The Sky Would Fall: The Secret U.S. Bombing Mission to Vietnam, 1954

The Soviet Estimate: U.S. Intelligence and Soviet Strategic Forces

THE GHOSTS OF LANGLEY

INTO THE HEART OF THE CIA

JOHN PRADOS

AMBERLEY

First published 2017

Amberley Publishing
The Hill, Stroud
Gloucestershire, GL5 4EP

www.amberley-books.com

British Library Cataloguing in Publication Data.
A catalogue record for this book is available from the British Library.

ISBN 978 1 4456 6792 8 (hardback)
ISBN 978 1 4456 6793 5 (ebook)

Typesetting and Origination by Bookbright Media.
Printed in the UK.

CONTENTS

So do we pass the ghosts that haunt us later in our lives; they sit undramatically by the roadside like poor beggars, and we see them only from the corners of our eyes, if we see them at all. The idea that they have been waiting there for us rarely if ever crosses our minds. Yet they do wait, and when we have passed, they gather up their bundles of memory and fall in behind, treading in our footsteps and catching up. . . .

—Stephen King, *Wizard and Glass*

To Marilyn Young,
friend and colleague over these many years

PREFACE

DONALD J. TRUMP MADE THE FIRST OFFICIAL STOP OF HIS PRESIDENCY
on January 21, 2017, at Langley, the Central Intelligence Agency's Virginia headquarters. The agency is headed into its seventieth year of existence. One can only imagine what was going through Trump's mind as his
minions took him there. This bold visit showed chutzpah, for President
Trump had taken office having already picked several fights with America's spooks.

Rather than articulating any well-considered perspective on the Central
Intelligence Agency (CIA), other U.S. spy outfits, or even the general subject of espionage, Mr. Trump had accused its director of being a leaker,
the officers of behaving like Nazis, and the agency of being as hopelessly
wrong as it was when George W. Bush wanted to know if Saddam Hussein had nuclear weapons. Its cherry-picked appreciations had helped Bush
lead the nation to war. Now the agency—in combination with the director
of national intelligence (DNI), the National Security Agency (NSA), the
Federal Bureau of Investigation (FBI), and others—was saying that Russia
had intervened in U.S. electoral politics. Russian spies and cyberwizards
had infiltrated the computers of American politicians and staffs, collecting
embarrassing information, some of which had been used to smear Trump's
Democratic opponent Senator Hillary Clinton. What the Russians might
have held on to for the purpose of directly manipulating Trump remained
unknown, but the intelligence agencies had some illustrative examples that
they showed the president-elect before his inauguration.

Donald Trump had already displayed an extraordinarily thin skin for
an aspirant to the presidency. His standard tactic had been to deny every
charge, even when documented on paper or film or tape, while attacking
those stating or reporting the information. Trump's routine tactics were to
attack right back and do so without regard for the truth. Thus he had ruth-
lessly exploited allegations that Hillary Clinton, who had used a private

e-mail server while secretary of state, had been guilty of revealing secret information.

When the FBI could find no evidence of that but reported some of Clinton's messages missing, Mr. Trump had outrageously *invited* the Russians to hack her. Trump's differences with U.S. intelligence began when the DNI and others started to warn of Russian intervention. After his election victory, Mr. Trump strongly criticized the CIA when officials went to brief him, and he refused to receive the President's Daily Brief, one of the nation's foremost intelligence products. Soon Trump was insulting U.S. "intelligence," saying they needed extra time to concoct phony stories before meeting him, then demanding the resignations of the leaders of the principal U.S. agencies.

On January 21 there was already bad blood between the new president and his spy agencies. On one level, Trump's gambit in going to speak at the CIA was like walking into a den of vipers. Indeed, the president wore an overcoat and never took it off, and he left after just fifteen minutes. Trump could have been wearing a bulletproof vest under the greatcoat. More likely he never intended to make more than a whistle-stop, a political stunt to distract attention from the massive Women's March going on outside at that very moment, in hundreds of cities and towns in the United States and across the world, not least the U.S. capital, Washington, D.C., where the crowd matched those of the greatest protests in the 1960s and 1970s against the Vietnam War.

President Trump's appearance at CIA headquarters took place while the protesters gathered. The bad blood meant the president had an opportunity to mend fences. But the event took on an odd character. One of the main features of the Old Headquarters Building at Langley is what is called the Memorial Wall. The Wall has a star chiseled on it for each CIA officer who has given his or her life for the nation. Some of the stars have no names, for the persons they represent are considered undercover even in death. At the moment, there are 117 stars chiseled there. The Wall has special meaning for America's spies. President Trump entered the building and stood in front of the Wall to make his speech.

Trumpian bombast soon sent the president off on tangents, boasting of his "intelligence," his inaugural crowds, and denouncing the media. Some CIA folk were angered by Trump's use of the Memorial Wall to stage what was essentially a political event. His only reference to the Wall was to his standing in front of that "very, very special" monument. As if nothing had happened between the spooks and their leader, Trump called his spies "very, very special people." He implied a peace offer. The president made the point that he'd selected the CIA for his very first public event, accused the media of making up the feud between him and the spooks, and declaimed, "I just want you to know, I am so behind you." Or again, "I love you, I respect you, there's nobody I respect more." Trump intoned that he would give the spies so much backing, they would want less, and he presumed that most of them—at one of America's less political agencies—had voted for him. The jocularity seemed awkward, but it was pure Trump.

But more important are the bits and pieces of what President Trump said that truly concerned the CIA and U.S. intelligence. Great things, of course. In terms of concrete aims, there was one, "radical Islamic terrorism." In a clearer hint, he spoke of Iraq and Syria and the group called ISIS, oil, and how the United States should have kept it when we fought there before, but "maybe we'll have another chance." The wars had gone on for longer than any America has fought before. More generally the president said, "We have not used the real abilities that we have." Equally ominously, "We have to start winning again."

For what does President Trump want to use those capabilities? His modus operandi, on subject after subject since announcing his plans to run for president, had been to assert that he had a strategy but refuse to reveal what it might be. Off-the-cuff remarks promising one thing or another substitute. His cry of "America First" implied a withdrawal from the world scene. Conversely, at various times the new U.S. leader has promised to put more of the CIA's operations officers into the field, to smite enemies harder than ever—in particular in Syria and Iraq as indicated above. Not long into his presidency he answered Syrian government chemical attacks against citizens with American cruise missiles. Trump promised tortures even more severe than those of the CIA under George W. Bush, to the degree that former spy chieftains warned Trump he'd have to bring his own pail to interrogation sessions. Since his CIA speech, President Trump has told an interviewer that he will defer to the views of his agency director and his secretary of defense but that he, personally, thinks torture works well. The president *repeated* that formula at the press appearance marking his first meeting with a foreign leader, Prime Minister Theresa May of the United Kingdom, even as the British leader rejected torture.

Meanwhile, President Trump reached outside the intelligence establishment for his CIA director, appointing Michael Pompeo, a West Point graduate and Tea Party supporter who, as a congressional representative from Kansas, had sat on the House Intelligence Committee and called for the execution of Edward Snowden. His first director of national intelligence, Dan Coats, was another politician cut from similar cloth. In an expression of incoherence, Trump prohibited the top U.S. spy (Coats) from the National Security Council, while putting the CIA boss (Pompeo) on the guest list. That lasted only a few weeks, but it is anyone's guess where this is headed.

Though Trump stumbled through his visit to the CIA and told the crowd he loved them, the "reconciliation" seemed hollow—deserving of those demeaning quotation marks. Thus the Trump presidency began with a contradiction: a cleavage between the spies who populate Langley and the man who inhabits the White House. How deep that chasm remains will be revealed by events.

The agencies in this troubled relationship are going to be called upon for even greater efforts on covert operations. Mr. Trump saying the CIA had been "restrained" could only have reminded many of those gathered by the wall of heroes that the agency had baggage of its own. There are ghosts stalking the halls at Langley. At the moment of Trump's visit, the CIA was still in the throes of waves of recrimination resulting from the tactics—including secret overseas prisons and torture—that it had resorted to in the war on terror. Its leaders had attempted to evade responsibility for those acts. Senior officers had had to give up ambitions for top jobs because of their links to these projects. Contract psychologists who had helped administer the torture were being sued at that very moment. Yet President Trump wanted more.

The things Trump wants from the Central Intelligence Agency are very much like what the agency has done in the past. Before exploring what the future may hold, we need to delve into those times. *The Ghosts of Langley* excavates that past. It is a history of the CIA viewed through the eyes of key figures, focusing particularly on covert operations. It tells how the agency, over seven decades, has resisted—and finally decoupled itself from—government accountability. Slowly at first, but with increasing momentum, officials have broken fetters of all types. The pace reached a breakneck speed with torture and black prisons in the war on terror. A climax came when the Senate intelligence committee tried to investigate those things. Efforts to defeat outside attempts to enforce accountability, in the recent past, have escalated to highly troubling and even criminal acts.

This is the first book to relate the agency's current behavior toward authority to its founding and earlier history. *The Ghosts of Langley* puts fresh light on classic agency covert operations from Poland to Hungary, Indonesia to Iran-Contra, the Bay of Pigs too. It also lifts the veil covering the CIA's role in the war on terror, going beyond the actions to the cover-up. The account here follows the covert operations and shows how CIA lawyers have enabled them.

Even the CIA's own lawyers believed its original charter did not permit covert operations. Top agency officials found themselves defending against former supporters, even as early as 1952, when Russian adversaries tore off their cloaks and revealed themselves behind the fictive anti-Soviet partisan movement the CIA had been duped into supporting. Spies and stratagems have failed repeatedly, at times spectacularly. The CIA's secret funding of the National Student Association became a big scandal during Lyndon Johnson's presidency. In the mid-1970s, the inquiries by the Church and Pike committees in the U.S. Congress deeply embarrassed the spooks, an embarrassment exceeded only by the controversies swirling around alleged obstruction of justice flowing from the CIA's secret prisons in the past decade. In their memoirs, agency insiders largely focus on their own careers or on one or a few episodes in this story. Outside observers and analysts most often narrate one striking project or campaign among the secret wars. Historians covering the agency's entire history have so much ground to cover, they tend to tread lightly on deeper examinations.

But America's spies have a heritage, one that is missing from these accounts. Intelligence agents work for an organization that looks back as well as forward. The CIA honors its heroes, laments its fallen, regrets its dupes and disasters. The examples of past spooks are always there to encourage—and to warn—the current generation of CIA officers. For this reason, *Ghosts of Langley* follows the exploits (or misadventures) of the great, the good, and the misguided. Instead of adopting a straight chronological approach, this account groups the spies by character types and presents their stories as lenses showing the larger picture of the agency's evolution.

I have employed the metaphor *ghosts* quite deliberately. The ghosts that inhabit Langley headquarters may not be corporeal, but these individuals and others like them are exemplars. The legends of the forebears furnish illustrations for today—and tomorrow. They are both good, like Jennifer Matthews or Eloise Page, and bad, say Dewey Clarridge or Jim Mitchell. Some—like Robert Ames, perhaps—are sad, heavy with potential unfulfilled. Langley has seen them all. Its halls echo with the footsteps of past spymasters and their henchmen—and henchwomen. The CIA used to picture itself as America's primo Cold War agency. Had it not reached so far and endeavored so much, it would have fewer ghosts. Spymasters have tried to lighten the atmosphere, speaking of headquarters as a "campus," as if this were some university and not an agency practicing dark arts. The image of a haunted house fits much better. Indeed, every day that the militarization of the CIA increases, the agency is haunted even more by its drift away from the classic arts of espionage and intelligence analysis. Those who advocated a peacetime intelligence agency for America would themselves be haunted—by what their offspring has become.

Chronicles of the Central Intelligence Agency have conventionally focused entirely on the derring-do of operatives. A major theme here is how the operations, especially the failed ones, have driven the spies to contrive arguments and explanations they have relied upon—repeatedly—to escape from criticism and accountability. The narrative will show that in the most recent period the CIA reached new heights in this art of rationalization. You will encounter spy chieftains and operators but also visit little-known nooks of agency history. The growing power of lawyers at the agency is manifest. The oversight and control of covert operations have been critically dependent on a regulatory framework interpreted, in the first instance, by lawyers. In *The Ghosts of Langley*, you will see the operatives in their relation to the Delphic interpreters of regulation. The agency's treatment of women officers is an exemplary case. It is critical to identify the framework under which the CIA labors, and the ghosts give us new eyes to glimpse the stages of its history.

When Dick Cheney, George W. Bush's vice president, talked about walking on the dark side, he was referring to the Central Intelligence Agency, as well as the U.S. military's Special Operations Command. Mr. Cheney hinted obliquely at what the Central Intelligence Agency had been put up to—reaching past long-understood norms of behavior. As *The Ghosts of Langley* documents the Bush era, it reveals how the arguments developed in the past have been employed in new contexts, sometimes even in reverse, to deflect charges of torture (criminal assault, assault with deadly weapons, assault with or without intent to kill), conspiracy, obstruction of justice, evasion of legal oversight, and more. Those charges threatened the CIA's existence. The arguments and actions deployed to excuse failure, misadventure, and worse have been used to get past the monitors, disarm their objections, and avoid penalties. Each time the CIA skirted its overseers, the fabric of discipline, both within the agency and among the politicians who try to control it, has been weakened. The most recent and dramatic of the agency's disasters is clearly the CIA's torture program and the fallout from it. The torture program lay at the heart of U.S. actions in the war on terror, and with it this book begins.

Originally I aimed at a more conventional account. However, the writing took place amid a fierce struggle between CIA figures and congressional monitors on the oversight committees over the progress of, and even the principle of, an investigation of the agency's actions in its detention and interrogation projects. Egregious enough to trigger the investigation in the first place, the agency's actions that emerged steadily became darker, while its success at evading scrutiny grew ever more stark.

I have written a number of previous books on the Central Intelligence Agency, and one of my concerns has been to track the CIA's relationship with its overseers. As events of the war on terror unfolded, I began to see how central the fight over investigation of this agency project was becoming to the entire oversight enterprise. That understanding reshaped this book. A central point in *Presidents' Secret Wars*, my earliest work on this subject, was to argue that White House controls over the intelligence agencies offered an alternative to congressional oversight. More recently, in *Safe for Democracy*, the emphasis, at least so far as this element is concerned, showed an ebb and flow of White House versus congressional controls. In *The Family Jewels*, one goal was to demonstrate that the Central Intelligence Agency had erected a fortress of secrecy. Here I think the ghosts will tell us that the CIA has effectively broken free of congressional oversight, under conditions where White House control mechanisms have become increasingly ineffective and in which the agency, assuming a defensive posture, has used its fortress of secrecy in a way that will set up its next failure. If a new president with an itchy trigger finger embroils CIA in waters over its head, the impending disaster becomes ever more likely.

This record is not made up or based on journalistic speculations. To the greatest extent possible, I use sources that are entirely from the agency—official documents and releases, CIA histories, memoirs of former spies, and congressional hearings and reports bearing on agency activities. Press stories document some individual points, appearing where they figure as leaks the spooks seek to plug or where they denote media revelations that became part of this chronicle. The declassified annals, you will see, are quite sufficient to make this a stunning story, and I have made the narrative as tight as I can.

This book could not have been written by a CIA insider. If it had, either the text would be stuck in the limbo that nearly sank the Senate torture report, or you would see a sentence here and there surrounded by pages of blacked-out text. It is a sad commentary on how far our system has fallen that outsiders must say the things that intelligence persons cannot.

I have been studying the CIA for four decades. Along this lengthy road, I have been helped by people in many places. I want to specially acknowledge the Truman Library Institute, which assisted with a research grant. I owe a debt, too, to the staffs of the CIA and other government agencies, who have, however grudgingly, declassified material at my, and others', request. The records declassified by Freedom of Information Act and other requests, the CIA's own historical review initiatives, expiration of secrecy authority, and legal proceedings are all indispensable to making this authoritative record. Former agency people who have spoken to me at various times have been very helpful too. Librarians and archivists at the presidential libraries and the National Archives, the air force and army war colleges, the Naval Operational Archives, the libraries of Columbia University, New York University, the City of New York, George Washington University, and Montgomery County have all been vital to the completion of this project. At the Lyndon B. Johnson Presidential Library I've not until now had the opportunity to specially acknowledge the late Ted Gittinger, or the recently retired Regina Greenwell. Lara Hall continues to handle my declassification requests there very ably. At the Harry S. Truman Library I am recently indebted to David Clark, Sam Rushay, Randy Sowell, Tammy Williams, Jim Armistead, Jan Davis, and Lisa Sullivan. At the Dwight D. Eisenhower Library my thanks go to Mary Burtzloff, Nicole Beck, Deanna Kolling, and Michelle Kopfer. To all of these people, my great thanks. I owe a special debt of gratitude to Ellen Pinzur, my first reader, who has saved me from many pitfalls. At the New Press editor Carl Bromley, managing editor Maury Botton, and copyeditor Gary Stimeling saved the manuscript from many faults.These persons have all contributed things of value to this narrative. I alone am responsible for its errors.

—John Prados
Washington, D.C.
January 2017

A NOTE TO THE READER

LANGUAGE IS CRUCIAL IN DEALING WITH THIS SUBJECT. THE CENTRAL Intelligence Agency is a security service that includes among its functions propaganda and psychological warfare.

In these endeavors, the precise use of words is important, and the CIA had developed a certain expertise in it. It is expert at spin-doctoring, *and* it controls the declassification of secret documents as well as the content of writings by former agency employees who have held security clearances. In creating its action programs of recent years, the CIA developed a set of euphemisms to *avoid using* words conventionally employed to describe certain acts or things. By insisting on the use of these euphemisms in discussions of the behaviors and actions described here, the agency, its life in danger, subtly shaded the conversation in a direction more to its liking.

There were no prisons. There were "black sites." There were no prisoners; there were "detainees" and "high-value detainees." There were no beatings; there were "attention grabs," "wallings," and the "facial slaps." Near-drowning was "waterboarding." These were "enhanced interrogation techniques." Central Intelligence Agency officers—with exceptions, thankfully—strenuously protest characterization of any of these things as torture. Many approved of "legal" explanations from senior officials at the Department of Justice, which defined torture as something that begins only at the point of organ failure.

The Ghosts of Langley will not hide horror behind euphemism. It will call things by their real names. That will aid in understanding the true stakes at issue, because the specifics of the latest debate on torture are but one element in the larger dilemma of democracy choosing whether or not to permit unfettered activity by its security agencies. There will be no effort here to play the CIA's word game. If that is not acceptable, you can put this book down right now.

ACRONYMS

ACLU	American Civil Liberties Union
AGM	air-launched guided munition (as the Hellfire missile)
APA	American Psychological Association
AZ	Abu Zubaydah (Al Qaeda helper, CIA prisoner)
CAT	Civil Air Transport (proprietary CIA airline, later Air America)
CBS	Columbia Broadcasting System (television network)
CIA	Central Intelligence Agency
CIG	Central Intelligence Group (CIA predecessor)
COB	chief of base (CIA)
COS	chief of station (CIA)
COPS	chief of operations (early CIA/DO job title)
CTC	Counterterrorist Center (until 2004, thereafter Counterterrorism Center, CIA)
DCI	director of central intelligence (director of CIA plus all of U.S. intelligence, until 2004)
DCIA	director of Central Intelligence Agency (CIA only, since 2004)
DDCI	deputy director of central intelligence (deputy to DCI)
DDEL	Dwight D. Eisenhower Library
DDO	deputy director for operations (of the CIA, previously DDP)
DDP	deputy director/directorate of/for plans, or "that directorate" (usage avoided herein)
DI	Directorate for Intelligence (CIA)
DIA	Defense Intelligence Agency
DNI	director of national intelligence (director of all U.S. intelligence since 2004)
DO	Directorate of Operations (previously Plans, subsequently NCS, then DO again)
DOJ	Department of Justice

DP	displaced person (post–World War II refugee)
DPD	Development Projects Division (CIA, previously Development Projects Staff)
DS&T	Directorate of Science and Technology (CIA)
EITs	enhanced interrogation techniques
EO	Executive Order (a form of presidential directive)
FBI	Federal Bureau of Investigation (the Bureau, Justice Department)
FE	Far East Division (CIA/DO)
FOB	forward operating base (military and intelligence term)
FOIA	Freedom of Information Act (declassification law)
GID	General Intelligence Directorate (Jordanian spy unit)
GITMO	Guantánamo Bay (U.S. military prison in Cuba)
GS/G.S.	Government Service (civil service rank)
HPSCI	House Permanent Select Committee on Intelligence
IC-21	Intelligence Community for the 21st Century (HPSCI future study)
IDF	Israeli Defense Forces
IG	inspector general
IOB	Intelligence Oversight Board (White House watchdog unit)
ISI	Inter-Services Intelligence Department (Pakistan)
ISIL	Islamic State of Iraq and the Levant
ITT	International Telephone & Telegraph (multinational corporation)
JAG	judge advocate general
JCS	Joint Chiefs of Staff
JFK	President John F. Kennedy
JFKL	John F. Kennedy Library
JOT	junior officer in training
KGB	Komitet Gosudarstvennoy Bezopasnosti, Committee for State Security, Soviet intelligence service
LBJ	President Lyndon Baines Johnson
LCI	landing craft, infantry (medium-capacity amphibious ship)
MI-6	Military Intelligence branch no. 6, British secret service
NATO	North Atlantic Treaty Organization
NCS	National Clandestine Service (previously and subsequently DO)
NESA	Near East and South Asia Division (CIA units with this

	name exist in both the operations and intelligence director- ates)
NIA	National Intelligence Authority (Turman umbrella intelligence board)
NIC	National Intelligence Council (board of analysts who assemble NIEs)
NIE	National Intelligence Estimate
NIO	national intelligence officer (top analysis manager on the NIC)
NLF	National Liberation Front (of South Vietnam)
NSA	National Security Agency
NSA	National Student Association (private voluntary association, CIA front group)
NSC	National Security Council
NSPG	National Security Planning Group (NSC subcommittee)
NYPD	New York Police Department
NYU	New York University
OCB	Operations Coordinating Board (Eisenhower-era NSC subcommittee)
OCI	Office of Current Intelligence (CIA)
ODNI	Office of the Director of National Intelligence
OGC	Office of General Counsel (CIA)
OIG	Office of the Inspector General (CIA)
OLC	Office of Legal Counsel (Justice Department)
OMS	Office of Medical Services (CIA)
OPC	Office of Policy Coordination (CIA)
OS	Office of Security (CIA)
OSO	Office of Special Operations (CIA)
OSS	Office of Strategic Services (World War II predecessor of CIA)
OTS	Office of Technical Services (CIA)
PBCFIA	President's Board of Consultants on Foreign Intelligence Activities (Eisenhower-era predecessor to PFIAB)
PDB	President's Daily Brief
PFIAB	President's Foreign Intelligence Advisory Board
PKI	Partai Komunis Indonesia, Indonesian Communist Party
PLO	Palestine Liberation Organization
PRB	Publications Review Board (CIA)

PRU	Provincial Reconnaissance Unit (in South Vietnam)
PSB	Psychological Strategy Board (NSC subcommittee and staff)
QT	quiet (slang); on the QT: quietly
RDG	Rendition and Detention Group (CIA)
RDINet	Rendition Detention Interrogation Network (CIA computer monitoring unit)
RFE	Radio Free Europe
RIAS	Radio in the American Sector
RL	Radio Liberty
SEC	Securities and Exchange Commission (United States regulatory body)
SERE	Survival, Evasion, Resistance, and Escape
SIS	Senior Intelligence Service (CIA supergrade ranks)
SMO	support for military operations (jargon term)
SOCOM	Special Operations Command (or USSOCOM, or JSOC, Joint Special Operations Command, U.S. military unified command)
SRT	Special Review Team
SSCI	Senate Select Committee on Intelligence
SSU	Strategic Service Unit (Pentagon spy entity after World War II)
SUV	sport utility vehicle
UAV	unmanned aerial vehicle (drone)
U.K.	United Kingdom
UN	United Nations
UP	United Press (wire service, later United Press International)
USAID	United States Agency for International Development
WCR	Weekly Case Reports
WH	Western Hemisphere Division (CIA/DO, predecessor of Latin America Division)
WIN	alleged Polish underground group
WMD	weapons of mass destruction

THE GHOSTS OF LANGLEY

PROLOGUE:
GHOSTS IN THE MACHINE

GRAYSON SWIGERT COMPLAINS OF BEING CAUGHT IN SOME KAFKA STORY. He's not even allowed his own name. Courtesy of the Central Intelligence Agency (CIA), Swigert, who has been discussed under his real name for years, must have a pseudonymous existence in official reports, allegedly because terrorists endanger his life. In the meantime, James Elmer Mitchell, to give the fellow back his identity, lives near Tampa, Florida, and goes kayaking to pass the time. Franz Kafka, the Czech author, wrote tales of horror and weirdness. Jim Mitchell, a former Air Force psychologist, perhaps engages in the classic maneuver called projection when invoking Kafka, for the CIA paid him millions, built a Get Out of Jail Free card into his contract, and labors to keep Mitchell from any forum where he might implicate others. The psychologist insists *he* is the victim, but what he did has been condemned by politicians, the public, and the American Psychological Association.

Swigert asserts himself a patriot, solicited by people at the highest levels of the United States government. He only tried to help, Mitchell would say. Now Dr. Mitchell finds himself in enforced retirement, his license pulled, reporters—and lawyers—yapping at his heels. His retirement may be genteel, but jeopardy hangs in the air.

THE ATTENTION GRAB

On September 11, 2001, terrorists of the group Al Qaeda hijacked four airliners and crashed them into buildings in New York City and Washington, D.C. These mass-casualty attacks, now collectively known as 9/11, killed nearly three thousand persons. The attacks also led to work for Dr. Mitchell. The Counterterrorist Center (CTC) asked Mitchell, a former Air Force officer, to help its secret counterattack. Kirk Hubbard, chief of research and analysis in the Operational Assessment Division and chairman of a CIA psychological advisory committee, introduced him around the CTC. The 2009–2012 Senate intelligence committee investigation into torture establishes that Swigert worked with the agency's Office of Technical Services (OTS) from late 2001, doing applied research, at times in a high-risk environment, to help "shape the future" of a project "in the area of counter-terrorism and special operations." The psychologist was to earn $1,000 a day, $1,800 daily if sent abroad.

In the Air Force, Swigert/Mitchell had taught pilots and aircrews to resist enemy interrogation. His lessons formed part of their survival-and-escape training, with scenarios subjecting airmen to conditions of captivity, including harsh treatment and repeated questioning. Mitchell then reprised the scenarios, educating airmen on how they might preserve their persona—and secrets. By Swigert's own account, he had spent more than fourteen thousand hours observing military personnel in this training, watched hundreds of other instructors doing the same, and conducted more than 215 of the post-role-play debriefs for classes of ten to over one hundred persons. The captivity and interrogation training amounted to an extreme form of the game. CIA people needed training like this too. But here the CTC wanted the psychologist to *reverse* the logic and technique. Rather than train individuals to preserve their personalities and private knowledge, Mitchell would help the CIA break down detainees by exploiting the Stockholm syndrome—reducing prisoners to dependency upon their inquisitors. Along with Swigert/Mitchell came his sidekick Hammond Dunbar—real name John "Bruce" Jessen. Both participated directly, observing interrogation sessions and devising novel applications when their strong-arm tactics failed. More than that, Swigert and Dunbar collaborated with hard-ass CIA spear carriers to override the objections of the squeamish, namely the field operatives or officials who expressed concern that their methods violated international and U.S. law, morals, and agency regulations or were just plain wrong or ineffective.

James E. Mitchell, under his CIA-demanded pseudonym, Grayson Swigert, designed and supervised the program. It sought to break down the prisoners' personalities and make them "compliant," by means of "learned helplessness." Mitchell suggested methods to be used. Officials of the George W. Bush administration hid them under the euphemism "enhanced interrogation techniques." Many see those methods as torture.

As Swigert and Dunbar, Mitchell and Jessen were part of Project Greystone, a top-secret operation that created a series of "black sites" or "black prisons," CIA dungeons spread across the globe to which captives were taken, where they were held. Secrecy barely started with the code name. Everything about the project involved doublespeak. Prisoners were "high-value detainees," or "high-value terrorists." Moving them was "rendering." The black prisons themselves were "HVD detention facilities." There was a High Value Terrorist Group, for "rendition and detention." Torture had its own doublespeak. "Enhanced interrogation" included "waterboarding," "rectal hydration," "walling," "slapping," "hard takedowns," the "attention grab," "suspension," sleep deprivation, extremes of temperature, noise and light, and much more. One captive was threatened with a power drill and mock executions. A director of the CIA publicly dismissed "rectal hydration" as if it were innocuous, not torture.

Swigert and Dunbar strategized on how to disorient captives and make them dependent on their captors, how to teach them "learned helplessness." This treatment was a *preliminary* to questioning, although further actions could be taken during interrogation. In other words, victims were to be roughed up *until they were judged sufficiently tenderized for interrogation.* There should be no doubt that the people who truly lived in Kafka's twilight world were those whose lives Swigert and Dunbar touched. Detainees' days passed in a surreal place of dark menace, pain, and oppression—all of Kafka's classic ingredients. Yet the torturers were rookies, for neither Swigert nor Dunbar had ever interrogated anyone.

The captors denied their prisoners the most fundamental humanity in service of a nation that lauds itself as an exemplar of human rights.

Some among the public, when these excesses stood revealed, comforted themselves with the notion that the prisoners were all terrorists who deserved what they got and that their torture made citizens safer. Neither is true. Victims include people who were *CIA agents* as well as some complete innocents. To this day, the CIA *does not even know how many* captives passed through its black prisons. Confronting a necessity to report the number of prisoners, the same CIA director who claimed "rectal hydration" was not torture told an aide to pick any date he wanted so the number reported would be less than a hundred.

In the heyday of Greystone immediately after 9/11, the CIA had so little direct knowledge of its terrorist enemies that it simply thought that its captives *must* know things the spooks wanted to discover. Captives were tortured because they *might* know something, not for any specific information bearing on what the CIA already knew. The boundary case is that of Khalid Sheik Mohammed, the self-acknowledged Al Qaeda mastermind of the 9/11 plot. The CIA tortured him—including waterboarding the man

183 times—to delve into the plot, whereas the agency's ostensible purpose had been finding "actionable intelligence" about *future* terrorism.

This was about revenge as much as intelligence work.

How this desire for revenge unfolded is important. The history begins in the 1990s with terrorist bombings of two U.S. embassies in Africa, then metastasizes on September 11, 2001, with the horrific 9/11 attack destroying the old World Trade Center in New York City and gravely damaging the Pentagon in Washington. Extensive investigations established that, but for brave passengers who overcame hijackers to crash their own plane, there would have been another Washington building attacked, perhaps the Capitol Building (Congress) or the White House. It was a paroxysm of mindless violence. The CIA had long fought terrorism, had redoubled its efforts after the embassy bombings, and truly showed its wrath following 9/11. Mobilizing friendly security services across the world, sweeps of known or suspected terrorists nabbed real or imagined enemies for months. The United States also invaded Afghanistan, where Al Qaeda had its home base and where the CIA spearheaded the entire Bush effort. Many Al Qaeda militants were killed or escaped across the mountains into Pakistan. A few were captured.

The security sweeps and the Afghan campaign crystallized the question of what to do about terrorist prisoners. There had already been discussions at the CIA. Through the 1990s, when courts approved American authorities operating abroad, apprehending suspects named in foreign warrants, there had been a steady stream of roundups pursuant to either U.S. law or foreign warrants. The word *rendition* came into use to describe the capture and remand of prisoners to other countries. The State Department's annual reports on international terrorism actually contained lists of prisoners "rendered" the previous year, with the countries they were sent to. The CIA often cooperated with other intelligence services. For example, CIA contract agents in Khartoum, Sudan, tracked Ilich Ramirez Sanchez, better known as Carlos the Jackal, until 1994, when Sudanese police and French spies apprehended him. Imprisoned in France for a murder early in his terrorist rampage, Carlos became the exception, his name not listed.

The CIA station chief who presided over the Carlos snatch, Cofer Black, by 9/11 headed the agency's Counterterrorist Center, Langley's "fusion center" specializing in measures to combat terrorism. On Black's watch, CTC's first big challenge had been the "Millennium Plot," a kind of frenzy induced by vague fears that enemies would make coordinated strikes worldwide as 1999 turned to 2000. One terrorist was apprehended crossing the Canadian border with the idea of exploding a bomb at Los Angeles International Airport. Another plot was foiled in Jordan. That was all; the expected terrorist offensive never happened.

The next big development was the Bush administration's decision after 9/11 to make rendition secret. Many prisoners were sent to countries that practice torture, have shaky legal systems, suffer authoritarian regimes, or all three. Over time a certain disquiet evolved. Early thinking considered detention by the United States on boats or islands; some suggested "black" prisons in foreign countries. At first, officials felt that U.S. military bases offered the better option. Those had fine security but were subject to United States courts. After 9/11 spooks deemed the black prisons better, although the speed with which U.S. forces overran Afghanistan resulted in a hybrid system, since prisoners needed to be held immediately, in places that became bases. But black sites were desirable because they lay beyond legal writ.

The first prison was a CIA safe house in Chiang Mai, Thailand. The chief of station in Bangkok cleared this with Thai authorities when the agency faced an immediate need—a place to take the initial "high-value detainee." The torture investigation by the Senate intelligence committee calls this place Detention Site Green. Site Green was approved by the Thai government during four frantic days in March 2002, when the CIA considered its need so urgent and so secret that the approach was made without reference to the U.S. ambassador, traveling at the time. The station chief went to the Thais. Only afterward did he inform the U.S. deputy chief of mission. The Thais insisted on overall security control, but they authorized the CIA to hold prisoners there.

All this began with the detainee. In Pakistan there were CIA field operations, FBI physical and technical surveillance teams, and, of course, the allied security service, Inter-Services Intelligence (ISI), often called a state-within-a state in Pakistan. The agency worked with ISI to identify and raid terrorist safe houses. Pakistanis executed the raids, with the CIA and FBI on hand to examine the places—and suspects—once security pronounced the localities safe. The Pakistanis agreed that the Americans could spirit away individuals to third countries. One suspected Al Qaeda member the CTC focused on was a man named Abu Zubaydah.

Toward the end of March 2002, the spooks had enough data to plan a simultaneous strike on not just two or three safe houses but seventeen. The idea was that Abu Zubaydah might be at one of them. The op took place the evening of March 28. At the Shahbaz Cottage, a brightly painted house in Faisalabad, Pakistan, security agents captured Zubaydah after a shoot-out that moved from a second-floor apartment to the stairwell and then the roof. Confusion developed. Teams reported capturing the man at two different locations. The individual identified as Abu Zubaydah did not look much like his picture. A photo taken at the scene and sent to CIA headquarters by satellite got a verdict of 85 percent certainty that the captive was *not* their man. Dave Falco, an FBI special agent in Pakistan, insisted he was and ultimately was proved right. (Operatives in Afghanistan had shown the picture to a source not familiar with using photos, leading Black's people to distrust the identification made on the ground at the time of capture.)

John Kiriakou, the CIA case officer in charge, found that a Pakistani Punjab Ranger had wounded Abu Zubaydah gravely in the thigh and lower abdomen. Kiriakou stanched the bleeding long enough for local doctors to stabilize his wounds. The CIA sent a response team overnight with a doctor to treat the prisoner—a noted surgeon from a Johns Hopkins medical center, arranged by agency executive director A.B. "Buzzy" Krongard, who happened to be on the center's board. The agency also sent an anesthesiologist and a CIA trainee with a medical background, but it had no interrogators ready for immediate departure. The FBI did. Having participated in the raids, the Bureau also had an interest in what was learned, so its team crowded onto the plane. Ali Soufan was team leader. With the team still en route, early CIA questioning took place at the hospital and in an agency safe house in Pakistan. But as soon as Zubaydah could travel, he was moved to Thailand and held at Site Green.

The CIA's first interrogation plan for Zubaydah closely followed FBI practice, namely that the subject should be engaged by an inquisitor who bonded with him. The plan for Zubaydah merely suggested that if conventional methods failed, *foreign* government operatives could be introduced for a "hard approach." Within a few weeks, the CTC substituted a plan for coercive interrogation. At first Swigert/Mitchell only gave advice. The offer to participate in the interrogations followed. Mitchell accepted. Ali Soufan and his FBI colleague protested.

At headquarters, under standing orders George Tenet put in place even before he became CIA director, there were periodic gatherings where counterterrorism specialists updated senior officers on evolving threats. After 9/11 these "threat matrix" sessions took place every afternoon at

5 o'clock. A mood of satisfaction and pride prevailed the day after Zubaydah's capture. It seemed like the first big win. President George W. Bush personally approved Zubaydah's rendition to Thailand after CIA deputy director John McLaughlin put in the request. When Bush next convened his National Security Council (NSC) on April 1, the Zubaydah capture was a major subject. President Bush drawled, "We need to hustle to come up with a strategy to deal with this person." As the Thais approved Site Green, Cofer Black sought greater control. Black's operations chief, Jose Rodriguez, wanted Zubaydah at Site Green, which the spooks did not tell the Thai government when it considered approving the facility.

A few weeks earlier, according to CIA lawyer John Rizzo, CTC officials told George Tenet they needed to do something to "shift the dynamics" if the agency captured Zubaydah. Overheated, breathless analysts had crafted a psychological profile of Zubaydah that made him out to be a relentless psychopath. The answer would be the torture methods of Swigert and Dunbar. (However, White House lawyer Alberto Gonzales insists that when he saw the president on April 18, George Bush said he had instructed Tenet *not* to torture the prisoner.)

Only days after the capture, Rizzo opened his office to CTC lawyers and operatives. They named torture methods and demonstrated some. Rizzo, the deputy general counsel, at the time acting as the senior CIA lawyer, asked few questions, "mostly because a lot of what they were telling me was so alien to anything I had ever thought about before then that I was left largely speechless." Acting counsel Rizzo writes that his first reaction was to tell CTC, at a minimum, to forget about waterboarding. Rizzo thought he could suppress the most aggressive methods.

Director of Central Intelligence George J. Tenet, delighted with Zubaydah's capture, ordered the stops pulled out on interrogation. After one of the threat-matrix sessions in early April, Tenet kept CTC aides and general counsel Rizzo for private deliberations on the "enhanced interrogation techniques." Rizzo knew what this portended and told Tenet that some methods seemed all right but others were harsh, even brutal. Cofer Black's people insisted that they would never do anything that was torture.

"You're damn right!" the CIA director shot back.

John Rizzo, rather than pare back the proposed techniques, volunteered to take the whole lot to the Justice Department for a legal opinion. The CIA had sought official opinions dozens of times over the years. Next, Rizzo involved the National Security Council (NSC), whose own lawyer, John D. Bellinger III, had been an agency man in the late 1980s. On April 16,

Rizzo and Bellinger met at the White House with John Yoo, the deputy chief of the Justice Department unit that would craft the opinions, and Michael Chertoff, who headed the Criminal Division at Justice. Rizzo and a pair of CTC lawyers presented the interrogation techniques. A follow-up meeting took place on July 13, when the Office of Legal Counsel (OLC) at Justice had begun drafting its response. Rizzo learned that Justice was going to approve *all* the techniques. The CIA lawyer writes, "Above all, I wanted a written OLC memo in order to give the Agency—for lack of a better term—legal cover. Something that we could keep, and wave around if necessary, in the months and years to come."

Meanwhile, the Thais demanded their pound of flesh, obtaining CIA support for some of their budget and activities. Langley acquiesced.

When the Americans started the Zubaydah debriefing, the FBI unit—Ali Soufan and special agent Steve Gaudin—took the lead. According to Soufan, the CIA did not just miss the boat on having an interrogation team ready; it stalled deliberately because Cofer Black and his colleagues in the CTC didn't think the prisoner really was Zubaydah. Nevertheless, the FBI inquisitors soon connected with the Al Qaeda man and built a rapport that they used to question him. Soufan had worked the terrorism account for the FBI for some time. Fluent in Arabic, he had worked on the investigations of the 1998 African embassy bombings and the explosive boat attack on the USS *Cole* in 2000.

Soufan used the same principles enshrined in the CIA's own manual— gain the subject's trust, be authoritative in what you seem to know, *challenge* the subject to prove you wrong, and believe that all things are possible. Using those methods, Soufan had convinced one of the *Cole* attackers to reveal information that identified seven (more than a third) of the 9/11 hijackers.

The FBI had been looking for Abu Zubaydah since the Millennium Plot and were keen on questioning him now. Ali Soufan reports that when he began speaking to the captive, a Palestinian, at the Pakistani safe house, Zubaydah had an eye turning green from infection. There were cuts on his face and splotches of dried blood. Soon after his capture, the prisoner fell into sepsis and required heroic medical treatment to survive. Inquisitors posing as military officers kept up the questioning even then. Zubaydah explained that he was a facilitator, a sort of combination travel agent and logistics expert, and Soufan reported his statement to Langley. Zubaydah yielded the key information that Khalid Sheik Mohammed was an Al

Qaeda operative, not an independent terrorist, as the CIA had thought. Zubaydah also named an American Al Qaeda wannabe, Jose Padilla, in good time for Padilla to be arrested in Chicago.

George Tenet sent commendation cables to the FBI team. But Cofer Black, not convinced of the Bureau's discoveries, remained skeptical. For him the terror war was personal. In the Sudan, Al Qaeda had targeted Black for assassination. He'd been yanked from Khartoum, brought home, and promoted to counterterrorism chief. Black became the general of the secret war. The field marshal, leader of the clandestine service, was James L. Pavitt. Whereas Black looked like a gopher, and Jose Rodriguez, operations chief, like the Latino he was, Pavitt, with his magisterial bearing and shock of silver hair, could have stepped through the doors of central casting.

They were less than enamored of the FBI inquisitors, disputing Soufan's account, grudging of their success, as some CIA people are in almost every account of the war on terror not invented by agency loyalists. In this case, Rodriguez brings Grayson Swigert into the legend. Rodriguez insists in his memoir that within two days of Zubaydah's capture—that would still be late March 2002—the CTC went to Swigert to ask him to accompany an agency team to Chiang Mai where Zubaydah would be held.

Coercive interrogation started even before the psychologists became involved, on April 13, 2002, when an agency officer warned the prisoner that if he were not compliant by the time the Americans moved him, things would get very uncomfortable. Inquisitors held medical treatments over Zubaydah's head to exchange for cooperation, a violation of international conventions. The date is important because the agency, as well as CIA officers, have insisted that all their torture was legal under the Department of Justice (DOJ) approval. But as we have seen, John Rizzo's first contact with Justice officials took place in a White House office three days later. CIA hostile interrogation began before *any* DOJ legal memo. The efforts to evade accountability begin here. The problem with them starts with the fact that legal opinions do not have the standing of statutes—and laws and international treaties prohibited the CIA torture. Moreover, Justice's opinions were flawed on their face. It should not be a matter of having a mere paper to wave. To be truly responsible, the agency should have evaluated Justice's arguments.

The weakness of the legal opinions was recognized as soon as they were issued. Between 2003 and 2009, the Department of Justice revised the memoranda again and again. Amendments corrected flawed argumentation or tried to extend the umbrella of approval over more torture techniques. Multiple book-length studies, by DOJ itself as well as legal professional organizations, have analyzed the flimsy arguments and the flawed process. Suffice it to say torture is against the law. Equally eye-opening is the fact that both principal authors of the original legal memoranda—Jay S. Bybee and John Yoo—have since (in 2010 and 2014, respectively) observed that the agency went beyond anything they "approved." The role of CIA lawyers *in soliciting the opinions* has hardly been touched, and the palaver about "authoritative" Justice Department opinions skirts the defects revealed by the repeated DOJ revisions.

The Bureau team based at Site Green protested the CIA's interrogation plan. No effect. The inquisitors continued to employ techniques suggested by the CIA contract psychologists. Grayson Swigert went to Thailand in April with a large agency team including support people, inquisitors, and senior agency psychologist R. Scott Shumate. On April 27, with Zubayda at Chiang Mai for barely a week, Cofer Black's unit sent Bangkok Station a cable asking when videotapes of the interrogations would arrive at headquarters for cataloguing and official records.

At first Swigert/Mitchell was asked only for advice. The offer to participate came later, in June, when the psychologist returned to the United States at CTC request for a round of meetings. Jose Rodriguez, newly promoted CTC chief, huddled on methods to get more from the Al Qaeda prisoner, and Mitchell offered his own version of the hard approach. Rodriguez took him to see George Tenet late one afternoon following a threat-matrix session. Together with lawyer John Rizzo, they sat around a coffee table in Tenet's outer office. The CTC operative explained that he needed psychologist Mitchell and his coercive interrogation plan. Mitchell executed a new contract with the CIA and returned to Site Green as chief interrogator.

Figures for reports based on the interrogations illuminate the shabbiness of CIA behavior. In April, with Zubaydah on part-time life support, thirty-nine reports circulated based on his information. During May another fifty-six bulletins appeared. On May 6, the CTC thanked Bangkok for overcoming difficulties installing videotape equipment and warned the station not to record over or edit any of the tapes.

During May CIA lawyers put on the table the argument that Zubaydah was withholding information and that "novel interrogation methods" should be introduced, including the simulated-drowning torture called waterboarding. These proposals went to Attorney General John Ashcroft,

National Security Adviser Condoleezza Rice, her deputy Stephen Hadley, and National Security Council lawyer John Bellinger. The CIA's representations were those of officers who wanted approval and would say anything to obtain it.

"REFRAIN FROM SPECULATIVE LANGUAGE"

This is when Grayson Swigert enters the story for real. Swigert and a CIA team went to Bangkok in June. A day after their arrival at Chiang Mai, on Swigert's instructions, handlers stripped the prisoner naked and put him in a room with no windows, kept brightly lit 24/7, with blaring music (or noise) and cold air blasting. Tracks from the Red Hot Chili Peppers figured among the musical selections. His chair was permitted or taken away, or switched for one more comfortable or less, depending on how captors judged Zubaydah. The FBI's Soufan watched in horror as the psychologist, whom he calls Boris, kept making new demands to oppress the prisoner, dismantling the cooperation interrogators felt they had already achieved. Swigert wanted Zubaydah to see his jailor as a god. When Soufan objected to his methods and told CIA colleagues that Boris had no experience, he was stunned to learn that Swigert was actually controlling the CIA team. Mitchell charges Soufan with bollixing up the questioning, leading Zubaydah to clam up.

From June 18 until August 4, 2002, jailers kept Abu Zubaydah in complete isolation and asked no questions at all. Zubaydah kept a journal. He recorded, "One month or [a] little over a month went by during which no one came to interrogate me." During that period, the CIA distributed thirty-seven bulletins based on his intelligence. As a justification of its need to resort to torture, the agency represented, both secretly and to the public later, that Zubaydah had stopped talking and needed to be broken. As the Senate torture report comments drily, "CIA records do not support this assertion." The agency, by *avoiding* any questioning of Zubaydah, endowed its demands for strong-arm methods with some plausibility.

Work on legal memoranda began with John Rizzo's follow-up confab in July, which included Jonathan Fredman, a lawyer who worked for the CTC, the NSC's John Bellinger, and Justice Department lawyers. The CIA outlined proposed methods, requesting a formal opinion. Two days later, Bangkok Station received a CTC cable outlining next-phase procedures. Only the Chiang Mai base chief would have authority to stop an

interrogation in progress. Questioning would take precedence over medical treatment. If the captive died, he should be cremated.

A crucial encounter took place in Washington on July 17. That day
Director Tenet met National Security Adviser Rice to further Project
Greystone. Officials concerned about the legality of torture had asked
Rice for advice. She had been feeling around the issue since the spring.
Now she wanted Attorney General Ashcroft to review the advice—those
notorious memos—under preparation at his Office of Legal Counsel. John
Yoo headed that unit, and presidential counsel Alberto Gonzales met with
him that same day. Gonzales had been wrestling with dilemmas of how
much to tell President Bush about interrogation strategy, and in addition
to discussing with Yoo the form his legal memorandum should take. Gonzales also wanted to avoid tying the president to this discussion. Gonzales insisted that Yoo's memorandum should be addressed to the CIA,
not the chief executive. Over the following days, Gonzales confirmed the
approach with Mr. Ashcroft on the phone. On July 23, Gonzales reported
to President Bush, who agreed that he did not need to know specifics. The
next day, the Justice Department informed the CIA that Ashcroft would
find several methods lawful. Late in the afternoon on July 26, after phoning Ashcroft again, Gonzales met with Director Tenet and White House
chief of staff Andy Card. After that he briefed the president. On the last
day of July, Rice told Tenet's deputy that if Ashcroft approved, the agency
could go ahead with its stepped-up coercion. At headquarters, Tenet's staff
prepared talking points to seek presidential approval. Instead, NSC's John
Bellinger informed the CIA that it could proceed.

Things were beginning to move quickly. The agency had reviewed Bruce
Jessen's résumé in March and now brought him on board to back Mitchell. They became the on-site scientific authorities. Indeed, when Ali Soufan complained that taking away Zubaydah's chair would hardly make
him compliant, Mitchell shot back that he was using "scientific" methods. Never mind that he had never conducted an interrogation nor, for
that matter, used a waterboard. The original interrogation plan, described
in an April 12 cable, had intentionally provided for the FBI men "TO
ESTABLISH A RELATIONSHIP WITH [ZUBAYDAH] THAT CON-
VEYS RESPECT AND TOLERANCE TO HEAR SPECIFIC AND
REVEALING INFORMATION THAT COULD BE SHAMEFUL AND
DIFFICULT FOR [HIM] TO DISCLOSE." The spooks had already begun
talking about learned helplessness, but at that time mentioned only bright
light and sleep deprivation.

Then came advance word the harsh methods would be approved. On July 23, Site Green's chief, Gina Haspel, cabled headquarters. She would do her best to be careful, but a danger of death existed. On August 3, immediately after the White House approvals, headquarters instructed field operatives that only Mitchell and Jessen were to have contact. Others—except security men in black costumes and masks, restricted to using hand signals—could only observe. A cable recording the first "aggressive" session, in which Mitchell and Jessen appeared as "IC SERE Psychologists," "ISCPs," or simply "Interrogators," reported that the prisoner had been sealed in a box during final preparations, immediately given an "attention grab" when brought out of it, and then laid on the floor and told to furnish "DETAILED AND VERIFIABLE INTELLIGENCE ON OPERATIONS PLANNED AGAINST THE U.S." The inquisitors wanted names, phone numbers, e-mail addresses, weapons caches, and safe houses. Referring to the FBI agents, Abu Zubaydah said that "HE HAD ALREADY PROVIDED THE REQUIRED INFORMATION AND DENIED HAVING ADDITIONAL INFORMATION." Zubaydah would say that dozens of times under interrogation. Before the first session ended, the CIA contract psychologists resorted to administering an "insult slap" and pushing the prisoner up against the "walling wall" each time Zubaydah repeated his litany. The reporting cables for days two through six of the interrogation have been declassified, and they reveal the interrogators' steadfast refusal to believe what the subject said, their introduction of ever harsher methods, and, of course, the waterboarding—four times the first day alone.

The Federal Bureau of Investigation refused to have anything to do with this business. It brought its team home. CIA inquisitors proceeded to beat on Abu Zubaydah almost 24/7 for nearly three weeks, hardly questioning the naked man but making every effort to break him. The first waterboarding took place at about 6:20 p.m. on August 4.

Inquisitors introduced a big box and a small one. They shut Zubaydah up in one or the other for arbitrary periods of time. It was the prisoner's only time in darkness. Training the victim to be helpless, they made him climb into the boxes, march to the waterboard, to the walling wall, prompting Zubaydah with the command "You know what to do." The Pavlovian conditioning was constant. Mitchell and Jessen brought medical personnel into the interrogation cell disguised as security guards. They kept the detainee naked. Zubaydah wrote frankly of his shame when CTC officers visited and participated:

The hood was lifted and I saw two other individuals: a man and a woman in civilian cloth[e]s. It took minutes before I realized that I was completely naked in front of a woman. For moral and religious reasons I rushed to cover my genitals with my hands with expressions of anger on my face. The guy [. . .] said to me: "don't start getting angry again, otherwise we'll start again from zero. Understood?" He said this while shoving me several times to the wall and then he put me in a standing position. At this point the woman starting reading questions from a paper she was holding.

Afterward they sent the prisoner back to the big box.

Within a few days, agency officers watching this decided that the prisoner really wasn't withholding information at all. In a week, it was judged "HIGHLY UNLIKELY." Chiang Mai officers asked the Counterterrorist Center to send people out to see for themselves. They warned of breaching legal limits. This marked the beginning of a fairly bitter dispute within the CIA itself, for and against torture. At Chiang Mai, officers who thought the interrogations were getting out of hand found the captive "COMPLIANT"—the state the psychologists supposedly sought—only for headquarters to order the torture to continue without letup. Legal issues seemed to sharpen. On August 12, CTC operations chief Rodriguez replied, "STRONGLY URGE THAT ANY SPECULATIVE LANGUAGE AS TO THE LEGALITY OF GIVEN ACTIVITIES . . . BE REFRAINED FROM IN WRITTEN TRAFFIC." In a cable found to have been authored by the psychologists, Site Green proposed to CTC that Zubaydah's interrogation become the template for all future inquisitions.

Grayson Swigert and Hammond Dunbar had their way with Abu Zubaydah. The captive presumed terrorist became their guinea pig. Zubaydah endured eighty-three waterboardings. The psychologists noted their prisoner's reactions, then proposed their techniques to headquarters, whereupon the agency listed them for DOJ lawyers to consider. Approved tortures were then applied. Some that were used, including the "abdominal slap" and the use of diapers to clothe captives for prolonged periods, were not even reviewed at Justice. Line officers and specialists disliked the strong-arm measures.

Langley first began a training class for prospective interrogators only after several months of torture. Already by November 2002, a gun and a power drill had been used to threaten one detainee; another had died of hypothermia under interrogation. A Rendition Detention Group (RDG) at CTC assumed all responsibility for the program in December. On January 28, 2003, Director Tenet issued a formal directive. He added medical guidelines. Tenet continued to doubt the extent of presidential support. White House officials interceded for President Bush each time Tenet sought to sound out the top leader, preserving Bush's deniability at the expense of widening CIA vulnerability. Doubt became a continuing theme, *except* for the zealots, like Jose Rodriguez, and their confederates, such as Swigert and Dunbar.

By late 2002, discomfort regarding Greystone had already reached such a level that Terrence DeMay, the CIA's medical services chief, filed a complaint against James Mitchell's involvement. Rodriguez, recently promoted CTC chief, decided to seek an opinion on psychological ethics. Mel Gravitz, another member of the agency's advisory committee, considered ethics for a psychologist participating in interrogations. He completed this report in mid-February 2003, emphasizing national security as part of personal ethics. The review satisfied Rodriguez. He continued using Swigert and Dunbar, although narrowing their involvement after the summer of 2003 to advice more than fieldwork.

Psychologist Mitchell has provided his own account, acknowledging his differences with Ali Soufan, whom he portrays in a negative light. But Soufan is only the first with whom the psychologist wanted to settle scores. He clashed with Counterterrorism Center lawyers who found that some techniques that *didn't* involve strong-arm methods would still violate laws against torture, with security officers who refused to let him carry secret documents on an airplane, with the agency's director of Medical Services, and with a chief interrogator for the agency's Rendition and Detention Group (RDG), plus the base and station chiefs in Afghanistan. At one point, the contract psychologist maintains, he, too, agreed that Zubaydah had become compliant and recommended that Site Green *stop* strong-arming him. Headquarters sent people to check. Later, at a different site, CIA interrogators (*not* Swigert/Mitchell, he insists) used harsh (but not violent) methods on Zubaydah. Insisting that he is no Islamophobe, Swigert describes the terrorists' goal as "replacing our freedoms with a draconian medieval way of life that stopped evolving fourteen hundred years ago." The sense in which the CIA psychologist believes he exists in a Kafkaesque world is that he succeeded in his interrogations but was defeated by the agency's inner doubts and the former victims who took him to court.

The thorny question of torture videotapes also reared its head. In September 2002, officials debated what to do with the ones documenting Zubaydah's torture. Some argued that the tapes were a security risk, that enraged terrorists would endanger "all" Americans if they were revealed. This notion of invoking hypothetical security threats rather than CIA's legal jeopardy for torture came to dominate explanations for why the tapes were handled as they were, but the officials involved were the same ones who ordered Site Green to keep mentions of legality out of its cables—i.e., off the record.

Just a month later, in October, CTC's top lawyer, Jonathan Fredman, briefed U.S. military authorities at Guantánamo Bay on his unit's approach to interrogations. Fredman maintained that vague statutes and international law left room for coercive techniques, that the CIA had lobbied against affording prisoners any of the protections of the Geneva conventions, and that the agency made its own decisions on many interrogation techniques but sought outside approval for some. Of the videotapes Fredman said, "even totally legal techniques will look 'ugly.'" Notes made at the October 2 meeting indicate participants discussed how smart it would be smart to curb harsher methods when the International Committee of the Red Cross visited Guantánamo. The CIA lawyer expressed views on a version of waterboarding (the "wet towel"), death threats (not as effective as friendly approaches), and identifying and using prisoners' phobias against them. He reportedly argued torture was a matter of perception—"If the detainee dies you're doing it wrong."

When the Senate Armed Services Committee publicized harsh methods in the summer of 2008 it revealed this discussion among inquisitors. Mr. Fredman denied making those statements. In a November 18, 2008, memorandum sent to the committee by the intelligence community's top legislative liaison, Mr. Fredman admitted attending the meeting but insisted Project Greystone had been classified at the time "and so I was not at liberty to discuss any details of that program." The lawyer said he had simply reviewed legal matters at a more general level. He also insisted he had repeatedly offered his resignation to successive CIA general counsels. Fredman reportedly wanted to meet with the senators but made no move to do so. In November, a week after the Armed Services Committee announced a vote on release of its report, on the eve of that vote Fredman circulated his memo disputing the committee's account. But investigators asked other participants in that same 2002 Guantánamo encounter what they remembered of Fredman's remarks, and most of their replies confirmed the meeting record.

In an October 25, 2002, dispatch, meanwhile, the CIA's top covert operator, James L. Pavitt, reversed policy on the videotapes. Instead of preserving them, black prisons were to use a tape to chronicle the record long enough to write a summary, then record the next interrogation session over it.

Meantime, the presence of the words *CIA* and *torture* in the same sentence was so explosive that operatives found their claims of interrogation successes difficult to sustain. The ghosts of the hostile interrogation applied to certain Soviet spies in the Cold War and to enemy guerrillas in Vietnam stood in the wings to fuel fresh charges. Detention Site Green became the first casualty. State Department officials were uncomfortable having a black site in Thailand in the first place, and their objections had had to be overcome. Within a couple of months of creation of the base, a Thai newspaper had discovered Chiang Mai and its purpose. Only strenuous appeals induced the Thai press to keep silent. Next a major U.S. paper learned what was happening, and the CIA begged it to suppress the story. The *Washington Post* confined its reporting in December 2002 to hints that the CIA had begun questioning captured terrorists, without mentioning locales other than Afghanistan, remarking that the agency defended interrogations while decrying harsh methods.

For reasons that remain obscure, the Thai government withdrew its support for the secret prison. In any case, the CIA had more prisoners and needed more space. A new system evolved. Black prisons were prepared in several countries simultaneously and prisoners were moved from one to another, with Afghan sites as a constant. Recruiting the host nations, finding suitable facilities, and prepping them became a major task for the CIA executive director. Until 2004 this was Buzzy Krongard; after that, it was Kyle D. Foggo. The latter became the prime action officer starting from March 2003, when he was still with the Office of Technical Services. The next series of foreign prisons included one in Stare Kiejkuty, Poland, a three-hour drive north of Warsaw, called Site Blue. Next, two line officers met with Foggo to recommend Romania and Lithuania. Afghanistan was secure—the CIA eventually had four black prisons there—but Langley worried about legal entanglements. Site Orange, supposed to be a quantum leap in terms of plumbing, lighting, and whatnot, did not open in Afghanistan until 2004.

Nevertheless, when Site Green shuttered its windows and Station Bangkok tried to move tapes, Jose Rodriguez came down hard, firing off precise instructions to log and store tapes of one type and destroy those of another. In that cable of December 3, 2002, the counterterrorism chief added that he was prepared to send a trusted officer to Bangkok to help if necessary. He ordered the station chief to reply, using the priority grade "immediate," that she had read and understood these instructions.

After a week, Langley had a complete inventory of materials from the interrogations of Abu Zubaydah and another detainee, 'Abd al-Rahim al-Nashiri. A lawyer with the agency's general counsel undertook a comparison of the tapes and the reporting cables about them. On June 18, 2003, he told investigators he had found nothing unusual. Later, in an official interview with the CIA inspector general, he mentioned discrepancies in tape numbering, tapes with inaudible content or fuzzy visuals, tapes during which the camera had clearly been repeatedly started and stopped, and tapes that were all snow, re-recorded, or partially or totally blank.

"MORE STRINGENT THAN GENEVA REQUIRED"

The Counterterrorist Center began pressing to destroy the tapes almost immediately. Subordinates worried that both the White House and congressional overseers would oppose it. They were right. On January 10, 2003, Director Tenet convened officials to consider the matter. Sensitivity about tapes was one reason Tenet decided Project Greystone needed a more formal directive. Operations director Jim Pavitt and CTC chief Rodriguez told Congress of the tapes and their desire to destroy them in early February. On the House side, both chairman Porter Goss and vice chairwoman Jane Harman warned the agency not to do any such thing. So did presidential counsel Alberto Gonzales.

Equally significant, rather than relying exclusively on the John Rizzo formula of a DOJ memorandum to wave in an emergency, the CIA continually touted the legality of torture, elevating Justice Department opinions to the level of law, all the while declaring the (tortured) legal arguments a secret so precious that even congressional leaders were not entitled to see them. The secret was that the emperor had no clothes. That stance continued for years.

Langley's frustration that President Bush had not directly signed off on Project Greystone had everything to do with the legality of torture and imprisonment. Not only was torture illegal by multiple statutes, but also the CIA was prohibited from acting as a Gestapo, or secret police, by its original founding law, the National Security Act of 1947. On torture, Bush posed questions; Gonzales answered. Thereafter, the NSC carefully restricted discussions to lawyer Gonzales or security adviser Condi Rice. This continued through the winter and spring of 2003, when CIA Inspector General John Helgerson began looking into Greystone as a result of the death of Gul Rahman, a captive in CIA hands in Afghanistan.

Concern rose so high that, in late June, George Tenet ordered a halt. At this point, agency officials were already looking ahead to moving prisoners to an "Endgame Facility" at Guantánamo Bay. Here officials seemed to be viewing the end of a "resistance to interrogation" protocol. CIA's Medical Services office commented on the contract psychologists Mitchell and Jessen. The agency conceded weaknesses in its ethics policy for the program, and one official cautioned, "Just hope our myopic view of the interrogation process doesn't come back to haunt us." Ambivalence on the torture project is apparent in CIA documents, as RDG operatives were preparing to assign the psychologists to assess detainees for suitability for long-term incarceration. Medical staff believed the psychologists could help design the prison regime but knew no more about long-term assessment than they did about coercive interrogation. They should not be in charge of anything, the medical staff said. There were also fears that the psychologists had blown the CIA's cover, telling military colleagues about the waterboarding while the agency still pretended that "our interest in these techniques related only to evaluating them for possible use within a training program."

On July 3, Director Tenet sent Condoleezza Rice a memorandum explaining that his agency, worried about presidential commitment, wanted reassurances. Rice might have countered that plausible deniability required these matters *not* be aired before President Bush, but she went ahead to convene officials as high as Vice President Cheney and Attorney General John Ashcroft, along with White House, NSC, Justice Department, and CIA lawyers. Their meeting took place on July 29, 2003.

While the White House was willing to convene a high-level meeting to comfort the CIA about topside backing, it wanted nothing on paper. As Vice President Cheney later told a group at the Gerald R. Ford Museum— only half in jest—"I learned early on that if you don't want your memos to get you in trouble someday, just don't write any." Cheney notoriously declared that the vice president of the United States, who chairs a house of

Congress and sits at the side of the president, is neither of the legislature nor of the executive and is therefore not subject to federal law on the preservation of records.

In any case, Cheney led the White House group, along with Alberto Gonzales. Rice represented the NSC staff, accompanied by John Bellinger. Attorney General Ashcroft brought a full array of Justice Department officials. Director Tenet's CIA team included top agency lawyer Scott W. Muller and CTC deputy chief Philip Mudd. Tenet began, emphasizing that the CIA wanted an affirmation that President Bush supported its "enhanced interrogation" policies. In the heat of controversy over the military prison at Guantánamo, the White House had made several statements asserting compliance with the Geneva Protocols or else denying that the United States ever did what the CIA was, in fact, doing. General counsel Muller then briefed the others on the interrogations. The declassified slides demonstrate that the CIA claimed credit for obtaining by torture information that Abu Zubaydah had given the FBI voluntarily. Ashcroft, according to Scott Muller's record, "forcefully reiterated the view of the Department of Justice that the techniques being employed by the CIA were and remain lawful and do not violate either the anti-torture statute or U.S. obligations under the Convention Against Torture." Dick Cheney declared—and both Rice and Ashcroft concurred—that the CIA had faithfully executed administration policy. They decided *not* to convene the full NSC Principals Committee and told Tenet that Cheney, Rice, and Gonzales in "some combination" would carry word to Bush.

John Ashcroft exhibited doubts regarding the use of waterboarding when a CIA official mentioned that detainee Khalid Sheik Mohammed had already been subjected to 119 of these near drownings. Mohammed, captured on March 1, 2003, in Rawalpindi, Pakistan, had so far been in custody for less than five months (150 days), at Site Blue in Poland. The CIA explained that the waterboardings were different than Ashcroft understood. Another round of legal memos papered over those discrepancies. Near the end of 2004, an inspired leak to the *New York Times* reported that Tenet had issued an order on August 8, 2003, prohibiting officers from even being present at military interrogations where strenuous methods were employed. Here the agency did the same thing the Bureau had done to it, keeping its people safe from dubious legality. Tenet's order lends weight to the picture of agency discomfort that summer.

White House officials asked if Congress was in the picture. Tenet and his people said it was, that legislators had been introduced to Project

Greystone, and that new briefings would be held when Congress returned from summer recess. There *was* an NSC meeting that same day in the Situation Room, but officials kept the subject of torture out of it. Gonzales notes that the CIA told the group that Al Qaeda remained intent on carrying out another 9/11-style attack during the summer of 2003. No specific target was mentioned, but discussion centered on securing domestic flights as well as those of foreign airlines.

In view of the dispute over the quality of CIA congressional notifications on torture, one has to wonder if Tenet's crew actually believed what they were saying. When agency officials told the White House that there were going to be more congressional briefings, they meant they would tell only the chairperson and vice chairperson of the House and Senate intelligence committees, each attended by only a single staff person or none at all. The CIA minimized the information flow. Equally problematic is *what* Congress was told. For example, early in 2004, when the Supreme Court accepted a case for decision that involved whether Guantánamo qualified as U.S. territory for legal purposes, Langley consulted the NSC, White House counsel, and the Justice Department. Agency general counsel Scott Muller informed operations chief Jim Pavitt that DOJ "recommended that CIA move the detainees (except al-Libi) out of GITMO at this time." However, agency records indicate no briefings of Congress at all between September 2003 and July 2004. No one thought it worth consulting Congress on whether a large-scale relocation of prisoners was a good idea.

Some weeks after the congressional briefings in the autumn of 2003, Inspector General (IG) Helgerson issued a report on how one of the CIA inquisitors, *not* any of the contract psychologists, had intimidated a prisoner with a power drill and mock executions. No one went to Capitol Hill to inform legislators.

That IG report and, for that matter, the broader report Helgerson released on May 7, 2004, quite critical of Greystone, were both held back. The May 2004 IG report came at the height of the firestorm over U.S. military torture practiced on detainees at Abu Ghraib prison in Iraq. On May 6, CIA personnel met Senate committee staffers and, keeping the conversation focused on Iraq, avoided mention of Greystone. In a followup briefing four days later—*after* the IG report had been issued—agency general counsel Scott Muller had the chutzpah to contend that "some of our rules might be described as more stringent than Geneva required." Then the rash of matters that the CIA needed to justify overcame Muller's stamina. He resigned that summer, making John Rizzo again acting general counsel.

Congress—but still only the so-called Gang of Four—was told of the IG's inquiry in July 2004. Stan Moskowitz, agency congressional liaison, waited until late November to record that event. In fact the memos recording conversations at *all* these CIA briefings, going back to the first one, seem to have been created only on November 30, 2004, suggesting some after-the-fact massaging of history.

That spring, career CIA psychologists, still uncomfortable at the way military survival and evasion training had morphed into agonizing interrogations, complained to the American Psychological Association (APA). That set the organization on course to create explicit ethics standards. The ensuing debate quickly entangled others, including Kirk Hubbard, the CIA psychologist who had first introduced Swigert and Dunbar to the clandestine service. At the APA conference in the summer of 2004, a selection of psychologists met on the side to craft ethics guidelines. The group, also influenced by the Pentagon—for whom psychologists do a lot of work—adopted very permissive standards. Within months Mitchell and Jessen created a company, which hired retired CIA and private psychologists, plus retired agency line officers, especially former interrogators. In turn the company furnished the black sites with consulting psychologists, inquisitors, and strategic advice.

Meanwhile George J. Tenet reached the end of his rope. Observers, assuming Tenet would stay through the fall of 2004, speculated that he stood to become the longest-serving CIA director, outlasting the "Great White Case Officer," Allen Dulles, spy chief during the Eisenhower era. That did not happen. The White House embroiled the CIA in a very public dispute over blame for egregious errors in speeches President Bush had used to drive the nation into war with Iraq. Director Tenet dutifully fell on his sword and left CIA that July. It was a time of change, with a new director of national intelligence (DNI) to serve as an umbrella authority for the entire community, the CIA chief being reduced to leading only his own agency. The shrinkage in authority no doubt also played some role in Tenet's decision.

Tenet's replacement would be Porter J. Goss, formerly chairman of the House Permanent Select Committee on Intelligence, representing a case of sheriff turning cattle rustler or vice versa, since Goss, before becoming a politician, had been a CIA case officer. The guard changed in other ways, too. Jose Rodriguez, promoted to head the Directorate of Operations, would begin to lead it into the new DNI era as the National Clandestine Service. It took Bush much longer, until the spring of 2005, to fill the position of director of national intelligence. He brought in John D. Negroponte, then the U.S. ambassador to Iraq.

Evidence of the CIA's sensitivity about its torture mounted steadily. Slumping morale led President George W. Bush to make the drive out to the agency to buck up the officers himself. "I wanted to assure the people here that their contribution was incredibly vital to the security of the United States," Bush declared. "Together, we've achieved a lot in securing this country." Director Goss, giving Congress a routine annual evaluation of the threats facing America, left observers thinking that the CIA had been strong-arming prisoners. The *New York Times* wrote it up that way. Uproar followed. Spokesperson Jennifer Millerwise responded with a public declaration, accusing the newspaper of creating "the false impression that US intelligence may have had a policy in the past of using torture against terrorists captured in the war on terror." Of course that was precisely correct. Millerwise thundered that it was not so.

Driven by the excesses of military inquisitors at Abu Ghaib in Iraq, Senator John McCain proposed legislation to restrict all United States agencies, including the CIA, to using interrogation methods in the U.S. Army field manual. Even in these days of intense partisanship, the legislation looked to be sailing through. In an attempt to sustain CIA interrogation, Goss got White House permission to break security and tell the senator what the agency was doing. Goss led McCain through a welter of subjects—the terror threat, legal authorities, foreign clients, and such multilateral monitors as the International Committee of the Red Cross. Dick Cheney attended to lend the authority of the White House—and make sure Goss didn't give away the store. Robert Grenier, a new CTC chief, attended the preparatory session and came away worried—Goss did not have a thorough grasp of Greystone. It didn't matter.

Director Goss extravagantly asserted that *half* of *all* U.S. intelligence on terrorism came from torture. Goss had been McCain's friend on Capitol Hill. He returned to Langley stunned. "I got nowhere," he told Rizzo. "I don't think John even heard a thing I told him. He just sat there, stone-faced and looking straight ahead, like he didn't know me. No questions, no comments, nothing. When I was done he just said, 'It's all torture,' and got up and left." Senator McCain, a Navy pilot who had been captured in the Vietnam War, had direct knowledge, being the only member of Congress who had actually been tortured.

Then Vice President Cheney showed up with top CIA officers in tow to brief senators Ted Stevens and Thad Cochran on agency methods. In October 2005, these politicians were the Armed Services Committee managers for the Pentagon appropriation bill, to which McCain had attached his anti-torture provision. National security secrecy suddenly became a very relative thing. Methods so "secret" that knowledge of them was being withheld from oversight committees were extolled to outsiders as particularly effective. Cheney tried but failed to get a CIA exemption written into the new law. McCain didn't budge. The Detainee Treatment Act passed Congress in December, and President Bush signed it a week later, on New Year's Eve. The clock had run out on CIA black sites and the Greystone torture program.

When the president signed the new anti-torture law, the denizens of CIA's Langley headquarters were already backpedaling fast. The top-secret project had been blown. Media had previously reported bits of the story—that the CIA had been holding prisoners, deaths of two detainees in separate incidents in Iraq and Afghanistan, agency "snatch" teams kidnapping suspects right off the street or taking prisoners from one country to another. But by late October 2005, *Washington Post* reporter Dana Priest had Greystone all teed up: black prisons, torture, a German national mistaken for a terrorist and rendered to Syria, the lot. The *Post* followed protocol and asked the Bush administration for its reaction. Frantic efforts to suppress this news followed.

First up would be Jose Rodriguez. Director Goss asked him to have a go at Priest. The reporter came out to Langley for a private meeting with the spymaster. They sat on a couch in his office. Priest handed Rodriguez a signed copy of a book she had written. He glanced at Priest's work on the U.S. military. It did not please him. Priest, having taken the book along to introduce herself, not butter him up, recalls thinking that Rodriguez did not know her.

Priest remembers that the CIA man hardly followed talking points. He divulged real information in hopes of convincing her to drop the story. She was worried, but gamely outlined what she intended to publish. Rodriguez grimaced at the *Post*'s uncomfortably clear picture. The spy pitched the idea that Priest's story endangered CIA lives and damaged national security. She disagreed. Rodriguez rejected bringing terrorists to trial on the grounds that they would lawyer up and the CIA wanted information. Priest stood her ground.

Next came the big boys. This time the White House summoned *Post* executive editor Leonard Downie to the Oval Office. President Bush, Vice President Cheney, and John Negroponte, the director of national intelligence, the newly christened top American spy, all confronted the nonplussed editor. Negroponte took the lead. He made the same arguments as Rodriguez. Downie dismissed them. The *Post* agreed to suppress names of countries where black prisons were located, but it would publish.

With the boom soon to fall, the Bush people initiated damage control. On Halloween, CTC chief Robert Grenier and Joseph Wippl, the agency's latest congressional liaison, briefed the Senate leadership on Project Greystone, relying upon the Justice Department legal memos to argue that everything was awesome. Senate leaders wanted a wider conversation. The next day featured a regular Tuesday lunch of Republican senators. Suddenly Vice President Cheney strode into the room. He demanded that all staff persons leave. After the room cleared, Cheney introduced CIA briefers and supervised. Again the tight secrecy surrounding Greystone went by the boards for political expediency. On November 2, the *Washington Post* led with Priest's story, headlined CIA HOLDS TERROR SUSPECTS IN SECRET PRISONS.

Once the story appeared, Langley joined Republican congressional leaders in asking the Justice Department to probe the leak and prosecute those responsible. But leak investigations are difficult in principle, and in the climate of that time, rife with charges that the Bush administration had manipulated intelligence to start a war in Iraq, the move to lock up the messenger went nowhere. Instead Dana Priest's story won the Pulitzer Prize.

The story had much more concrete results. Condoleezza Rice, secretary of state in George Bush's second term, embarked on a trip to Europe. Priest had revealed that the CIA had located secret prisons in several eastern European lands. Secretary Rice's trip devolved into a journey of atonement. Reporters dogged Rice at every stop, asking hard questions. The European leaders and diplomats she met pursued more confidential inquiries. A couple of U.S. ambassadors demanded that Rice assure them that the black prisons had been authorized. Goss wanted the State Department's counterterrorism coordinator, Henry Crumpton, to call the ambassadors. One element of the tale that had become known earlier, the use of CIA airplanes to shuttle prisoners, had been protected by European countries refusing to make official inquiries. Now the gloves came off. There were probes into both the transfer flights and the black sites. Several U.S. partners in the war on terrorism, afraid of their own exposure, protested vociferously. One country instructed the United States to close its black site and demanded that the CIA get out within hours. Another rescinded its previous agreement allowing the CIA to obtain medical help for detainees at local hospitals. A third nation proscribed any CIA use of torture. Others wanted more money. Within months the prisoners remaining within this Kafkaesque world would be crammed into just two CIA black sites.

So began a lengthy denouement. Shadows fell across Greystone. Grenier of the CTC attended countless sessions of high-level Bush administration NSC units like the Principals Committee or the Deputies Committee, all supposed to hash out the endgame. At a Principals meeting on October 28, for example, the CIA complained that it had been attempting to obtain an administration decision on one matter for over a year. Then there were "tiger team" meetings chaired by the deputy national security adviser J.D. Crouch. Bob Grenier and CTC lawyer Robert Eatinger represented the CIA. Crouch begged Grenier to keep the interrogations going despite the McCain anti-torture bill. The agency man objected that his people would have no protection.

A few days later, White House chief of staff Andrew Card suddenly appeared at the center, which Grenier had renamed the Counterterrorism Center. Card gave a pep talk to CTC's senior people.

"I'd like to know if there is anything I can say that would increase your confidence," the president's man said. "Is there anything you would like to hear from me? You should know that I begin every day the same way: I walk into the Oval Office and say, 'Pardon me, Mr. President.'"

Grenier recalled, "The words rolled out on the table, as though daring someone to pick them up." George W. Bush's father, of course, had pardoned CIA, NSC, and Pentagon officials in the Iran-Contra affair. Bob Grenier thought instead of Gerald Ford's pardoning Richard Nixon.

The CIA man distrusted the proposition. It seemed underhanded. Rather than fight McCain's legislation, President Bush postured himself as close to Senator McCain in principle; the administration wanted both the high-road spin and the low-road interrogations. Grenier said nothing. A week later, President Bush and Senator McCain posed for a photo opportunity, shaking hands. Bush signed the bill into law on December 30, 2005.

—— ✧ ——

On December 19, CIA lawyer John Rizzo queried the Justice Department as to whether McCain's Detainee Treatment Act would affect the agency's methods. Uncertain, he took the problem to Director Goss. In view of the Detainee Treatment Act, on the same day that Andy Card held his séance for the CTC, Porter Goss suspended CIA use of strong-arm tactics. The paper explaining that decision left Langley on New Years' Eve. It angered national security adviser Stephen Hadley, who had sought to keep the interrogation program intact. Goss would be booted out of the agency four months later, convinced that suspending Greystone, and his memorandum announcing that decision, had been his undoing.

Also out would be Bob Grenier. The Bush people may have demanded Grenier's head. Jose Rodriguez could have gone after him for allegedly lacking aggressiveness. This remains unclear. His successor, Michael D'Andrea, would be aggressive indeed, with a drone offensive.

General Michael V. Hayden followed Goss. If the Bush administration wanted to pretend that it remained pristine while continuing torture in the shadows, Hayden stood for that. He solicited more DOJ memos, made more vague claims for torture's "effectiveness." Since the media had put black sites on the table, there could be no more question of confining contacts with congressional overseers to a Gang of Four or Gang of Eight. One major change would be that Hayden recognized the need for public relations. A week after taking the CIA helm, General Hayden told the chairman of the Senate intelligence committee that he wanted the agency out of the business of being the nation's jailer. He said no one was being tortured, but he continued to argue the need to maintain his authority for hostile interrogation and did his best to carve out a CIA exemption from the Detainee Treatment Act.

Hayden had been on the job less than a month when the Supreme Court cut the foundation out from under the CIA program with its decision in *Hamdan v. Rumsfeld*, specifying that all prisoners were subjects of international and U.S. law. On July 11, 2006, six weeks into his tenure, Hayden met with top leaders of the Senate committee to extol the potential offered by reviving the hostile interrogations. In September the full intelligence committees in both houses of Congress received their first briefings on Project Greystone, by then under way for five years.

The September briefs coincided with President Bush's answer to the quandary of the not-so-secret black sites and the *Hamdan* case. Bush publicly acknowledged the CIA had had black sites and had conducted interrogations. He shut down the prisons, Bush said, and was sending all those left in CIA custody to Guantánamo Bay. His speech, vetted by the agency, contained exaggerated and misleading information as to the successes of Greystone, according to the Senate intelligence committee's extensive later study.

The last prisoner subjected to CIA methods, Muhammad Rahim, taken in Pakistan in June 2007, would be interrogated for nearly a year. The vaunted techniques did not produce a single report. At one point, even Jose Rodriguez had had enough, and he refused to recommend extending the interrogation. Michael Hayden overruled him.

On December 7, 2007, while General Hayden served as cheerleader for Greystone, the other shoe fell when journalist Mark Mazzetti reported in the *New York Times* that CIA officers, two years earlier, had collaborated to destroy videotapes of agency interrogations. A firestorm followed—congressional hearings, subpoenas, a federal grand jury, a federal independent prosecutor. Jose Rodriguez's name immediately came up. The controversy spilled over into the Obama administration, but the new attorney general, Eric Holder, decided not to prosecute anyone.

Intrepid psychologists James Mitchell and Bruce Jessen continued collecting money from the CIA through their corporation. Despite the on-again, off-again character of Project Greystone, the agency maintained its torture capability after September 2006, and even then sought to preserve it as a contingency option. Plus, there was still advice to give on the prisoners moved to Guantánamo. In June 2007 under their aliases, Grayson Swigert and Hammond Dunbar, they went to brief Secretary of State Condoleezza Rice in an effort to gain her support. Another time they appeared before the Senate intelligence committee. The CIA provided security certification for a Mitchell Jessen office, equipped it to handle top-secret documents, and detailed an agency officer full time as liaison. When press reports blew the psychologists' cover, their company engaged a security service to protect them. Langley received a $570,000 bill for that.

The larger aspect is the effect on the Central Intelligence Agency. For all its coming years, Mitchell and Jessen will stand out as bad examples. John Dolibois, a legendary interrogator at the Nuremberg war crimes trials, who obtained his information by getting close to his subjects, has the opposite spot well filled already—Dolibois's light to Swigert/Dunbar's shadows. Each time a future project involves capturing and interrogating enemies, CIA officers will remember Project Greystone for making the agency vulnerable and exposing its officers to criminal liability. However, there is no question but that agency people saw the danger going in. That's why John Rizzo wanted a legal paper and George Tenet sought the president's explicit approval.

In January 2003, Langley's chief interrogator, seeing the plan for what he was supposed to do with a prisoner, told Jose Rodriguez he'd decided to retire. He informed colleagues, "This is a train wreak [*sic*] waiting to happen and I intend to get the hell off." David Ignatius is a newspaper columnist with extraordinary access to the spooks. Shortly after the black prisons story emerged, a senior officer, watching Greystone's collapse, confided, "We all knew it would." In April 2009, when President Barack Obama, George W. Bush's successor, declassified the now notorious Justice Department legal memos, another retired CIA man told Ignatius why he had avoided joining the inquisitors: "We all knew the political wind would change eventually." Four months later, a top spook added, "The agency is glad to be out of it."

They knew. Future generations of intelligence officers will remember. In this way, to cast a shadow is to be a ghost. Many ghosts populate the hallways of CIA headquarters in Langley, Virginia. The most familiar is Nathan Hale, whose statue adorns the lobby of the old headquarters building. His was the spirit of the American Revolution, evoked by the Office of Strategic Services (OSS), the World War II predecessor of the agency, carried over into Cold War years. Not all figures in CIA lore were bad ghosts. There have been good ones too.

There have been dreamers and schemers, idealists and rogues, problem solvers and empire builders, political-action specialists and paramilitary types, scientists mad and sane, lawyers and shysters, dedicated officers and those who would go wherever the wind blew. What follows is the story of men and women who built an institution, so influential in so many ways, and became its ghosts. The future of the CIA will be a product of their past.

1

THE HOUSE THAT ALLEN BUILT

THE MOST EXTRAVAGANT DREAMERS TO HAVE HEADED THE CENTRAL Intelligence Agency are those who sparked its creation. Bringing a peacetime intelligence agency into being required resuscitating an instrument of war, the Office of Strategic Services (OSS). One of the dreamers, William J. Donovan—"Wild Bill" to his acolytes—had headed the OSS in World War II. He continued to lobby for a similar entity. Without Bill Donovan the road to a peacetime agency would have been longer and rockier. But if you want someone who not only advocated but actually played a major role in setting up the agency, and then led it during the Cold War, that man has to be Allen Welsh Dulles. Without exaggerating, you can say that Allen Dulles built the house that is the CIA.

You could have expected it. This man filled the mold of the quintessential spy. Although Dulles had a career as a Wall Street lawyer, he found his true calling as a spook. Some might say Dulles played his international contacts for espionage purposes; others, that he used his intelligence role to shield foreign friends. Either way, he immersed himself early, kept up his interest in clandestine affairs, became Donovan's quick and willing ally at the OSS, and fought alongside Wild Bill for the new agency. Dulles imagined himself as the Great White Case Officer, luring agents the way Moby-Dick lured whalers.

A SPY OF QUALITY

After World War II, fame came to Allen Dulles. He had been OSS station chief in Switzerland, probably the best known OSS person besides Wild Bill himself. Dulles was renowned for two achievements. One had been spying. Agents reporting to Dulles had friends and relatives among, or were members of, the German high command. Some plotted against Adolf

Hitler. The Dulles pipeline into the inner thinking of the Nazis had been a vital source, unmatched among the Allies, even the Russians, who had a well-established spy network but one a layer more remote from the centers of Nazi power. Dulles's other signal success, the negotiation known as Operation Sunrise, had brought about a German-Italian surrender in northern Italy.

The OSS outpost in Bern, Switzerland, became Dulles's to run throughout his active service in the war, partly because of the difficulty of reaching Switzerland. Allen had crossed the border from Vichy France under the noses of the Nazi Gestapo. Just after that, the Germans took over Vichy, in November 1942, closing that access. Partly due to those conditions, partly to his success, there could not be any question of recalling Mr. Dulles, or officer 110, as he was known in OSS messages.

The neophyte station chief sought out business associates from prewar days and also put out a welcome mat for anyone who wanted to walk in with significant intelligence. One of his contacts was an agent for Nazi SS chief Heinrich Himmler. Years later the Soviets would publish that spy's reports on the talks, which had Allen speaking disparagingly of bankers, politicians, and Jews. A German mining executive gave Dulles better data. So, despite the OSS man's alleged opinions, did his banker friends. Mary Bancroft, American expatriate, femme fatale, and Allen's mistress, also furnished information and ideas. Noel Field, a former State Department colleague working with refugees and resistance groups, afforded Dulles access to networks beyond his own. An old acquaintance, Gero von Schulze-Gaevernitz, became the first important German; for Dulles he ran an entire ring of subagents.

There were other agents, many of them anti-Nazi Germans. Two became stars. One, Fritz Kolbe, served as personal assistant to the liaison officer between the German high command and the country's foreign office. The other, Hans Bernd Gisevius, an official of the German interior ministry, opened a window into the inner sanctum of anti-Hitler resistance, even in the Abwehr, Germany's intelligence service. Dulles's wartime reports to Washington became a prime source, the kind protected with an exclusive access list. By early 1944, the White House had begun conveying the Bern material to President Franklin Delano Roosevelt. Some challenged the authenticity of Dulles's reports, but the drumbeat of incredible intelligence spoke for itself.

Not only did Allen Dulles provide key information during the war; as it ended, a Dulles feeler helped simplify the German surrender, taking a mass of troops off the board. Station chief Dulles worked through trusted lieutenants. One was C. Tracy Barnes, an OSS captain who made his mark with Dulles by quietly making a copy of the diaries of the former Italian foreign minister Count Galeazzo Ciano, convincing Ciano's wife—the daughter of Italian dictator Benito Mussolini—that the material would be safer with the Americans. Another key spy was Schulze-Gaevernitz, who could speak to the German generals. Dulles brought them together with American field commanders and opened talks that turned into Operation Sunrise. Senior Germans agreed on April 29, 1945, to surrender three days later. Some 225,000 German and Italian troops stopped fighting. Dulles, hobbling on a crutch in those days due to a flare-up of his gout, secured the largest surrender of enemy forces accomplished by anyone at the OSS.

Allen Welsh Dulles, born to a family of distinction, had paths smoothed for him but nevertheless became a high achiever. Born in the spring of 1893, Allen was the third of five children of Allen Macy Dulles, a Presbyterian minister in Watertown, New York, and his wife, Edith Foster Dulles. The three a.m. birth revealed a baby with a clubfoot, but the family had been well enough off, in this age without health insurance, that Allen could have an operation to correct that condition. Sister Eleanor recalled the pack of children as being "like a pride of lions." Allen's father's uncle served as U.S. ambassador to England from 1877 to 1879. His maternal grandfather, John W. Foster, had been secretary of state to President Benjamin Harrison and was the author of books on world affairs. His mother's sister was married to Robert M. Lansing, "Uncle Bert," a Watertown lawyer who became counselor to the U.S. government in international maritime negotiations while Edith was pregnant with Allen. On and off, Lansing engaged in U.S.-foreign legal dealings right through Allen's childhood, and by the time the latter left for college, Uncle Bert was counselor to the State Department. Clearly, forebears established a strong tradition of government foreign service.

Uncle Bert adopted the custom of bringing the Dulles children to visit at his vacation home on an island in Lake Ontario. Older brother John Foster went first, but Allen followed at age seven. It was an important moment in world affairs—the British were fighting a war against the Boers in South Africa, and there were fears that Germany, whose emperor favored the Boers, might use its fleet to smuggle arms or obstruct shipping. A stream of American and foreign diplomats and public figures paraded through Uncle Bert's parlor. Young Allen saw them when coming in from swimming or bass fishing. He showed early interest in foreign policy a year later, writing an essay, soon expanded to a veritable book, on the Boer War.

"Allie" began making international contacts. Having been educated at home by reading and exchanges with parents and governesses, he found the public schools in Auburn, New York, disappointing. His parents sent Allen to boarding school, the École alsacienne in Paris. By 1910 he was matriculating at Princeton University, where older brother John Foster had already gone. Allen graduated on the eve of World War I. He toured East Asia, spent a year in India teaching English, then went back to Princeton for his master's degree, obtained in 1916.

By then the future spymaster had already drunk from the espionage well. His first sip occurred courtesy of Uncle Bert and the State Department, where Lansing first figured as a high aide and then became Woodrow Wilson's secretary of state. Both Dulles boys whetted their swords on the intricacies of diplomacy. John Foster, having secured his law degree in 1911, joined the Wall Street firm Sullivan and Cromwell and then consulted with State on legal aspects of negotiations. Then the department hired Allen as a diplomat. After receiving his master's, Dulles went to Vienna as legation secretary. In early 1917, Washington broke diplomatic relations with Austria-Hungary as the United States entered World War I. American diplomats withdrew, first to Switzerland. Whereas many continued to France, Allen Dulles wound up at the Bern embassy.

After a couple of weeks with no portfolio, Dulles's superiors drafted him to handle intelligence matters. In World War I, the United States had no spy service other than specialized branches of the armed forces. Responsible for all aspects of foreign affairs, the State Department created a small code-breaking office in Washington, and sections for espionage at various embassies, Bern being one. So Allen Dulles participated in an enterprise that took him away from dreary visa and passport duties. Though not especially productive as a spy, Allen came away with at least one whopper of a story. That first summer he was seeing a woman, daughter of a Swiss industrialist, who liked to play tennis. One Sunday they had a match scheduled when Allen got a phone call from a Russian. Of all people, Vladimir Ilyich Lenin, about to leave exile for his native Russia, wanted to see someone from the U.S. embassy. Dulles had no idea who Lenin was and no intention of standing up his girlfriend. He never saw the Bolshevik. Lenin left the next day, crossing Germany in the famous sealed train, on his way to igniting the Russian Revolution. Allen W. Dulles dined out on that for decades. That story made him the Great White Case Officer.

At war's end, the young diplomat, seconded to the American delegation to Versailles, reunited with his brother, whom familiars had begun calling Foster, in Paris as legal counsel for the United States. Allen continued dabbling in espionage, picking up bits of gossip and insider tips. Once the peace treaty had been signed, he went to Berlin as first secretary.

Allen married in late 1920. Martha Clover Todd had met him only months earlier, when he was between diplomatic posts. The attraction is not clear. Preoccupied, self-doubting, a devotee of psychoanalysis, Clover, as she was known, showed genuine emotion. Allen stayed aloof, only superficially interested unless he thought someone useful. Sadly, this detachment extended even to their three children. Clover did not accompany Allen on his next posting, to the American Commission in Constantinople, and perhaps that was a mistake. Her husband began to step out with a succession of mistresses. In addition, Dulles exhibited behaviors of a classic manipulator, uninterested in anyone not useful to him, heaping attention on a small number of associates, showing his temper in a calculated way. He returned to Washington in the spring of 1922 and led the Near East Division at State for four years.

Dulles followed his brother to the law, studying after hours and taking courses at George Washington University. He earned his law degree in 1926. Allen then resigned from the State Department. He had been offered the post of counselor at the Beijing embassy, a promotion but no more money than he already earned. That led to the break. Foster had made partner at Sullivan and Cromwell, and he brought Allen in as a starting lawyer. For over two decades, except the time Dulles spent with OSS, he functioned as an international lawyer alongside Foster. More than that, he used contacts made as a diplomat to further Sullivan and Cromwell's fortunes. German bankers Swiss and Austrian nationals became Sullivan clients. One of Germany's big problems that stemmed from the Treaty of Versailles was the need to pay war reparations. With a crippled economy and inflation rampant, reparations were a major headache. Allen Dulles's law firm not only supervised German bond sales to meet these expenses, but also suggested ways to make the reparations scheme more tolerable.

The German account suited Allen Dulles. He had other legal dealings in South America. His travels took him in many directions—away from Clover. Allen and Clover seem to have had an open relationship; they exchanged letters and conversed about his encounters, adventures, and liaisons with other women. Allen, quite the rake, conquered hearts at every turn. At the height of World War II, with Allied forces battering their way across France, Clover managed to reach Switzerland, volunteering as an ambulance driver to join her husband. In Bern she became a close friend of Allen's mistress Mary Bancroft. Clover seems to have taken her husband's adventures in stride, and Allen appears to have used his personal affairs to further his spy work.

SPOOKS AND ASHES

When World War II ended, the world was a mess. Smoke rose from the ruins of Berlin. German and Japanese industrial plants and cities had been carpet bombed or, worse, attacked with incendiaries. Atomic bombs had been dropped. American official Henry Morgenthau had had a scheme to punish Germany by reducing it to a pastoral economy. Though wiser heads prevailed, reality proved not very different. Soviet conquerors, eager to replace economic engines devastated by war, were carting away much of the German industry that had survived. Germany collapsed into a barter system in which potentates dealt in cigarettes, women's nylon stockings, clothing, wood, and other things that might get you through the winter or the night. Italy had been worked over too. The victors were scarcely better off. Britain and France both continued food rationing. Russia had lost somewhere between 18 and 31 million people.

All this merely scratched the surface. The fact that Soviet armies now stood on frontiers far from the motherland, having gained a wide protective belt to shield it, offered the West little comfort. Soviet territorial changes in eastern Europe included absorbing the Baltic States, plus parts of Poland, Germany, Hungary, and Romania. Russia awarded German land to Poland and Romanian territory to Hungary. Citizens of German lineage had property seized and were expelled. Other eastern Europeans simply fled the Soviets. "Displaced persons" (DPs) became the label for a vast human migration, comparable to the sea of Middle Eastern refugees escaping the troubles in that region in the 2010s. In 1945–46 alone, there were more than 14 million DPs, about half from former German lands suddenly made into Poland or Russia. Even as some settled in new places, others languished in DP camps in the occupation zones of Germany and Austria. As might be expected, Soviet agents infiltrated the flow, taking advantage of the chaos to enter the West. Weeding out Soviet spies quickly became a concern. The DPs also represented a pool from which intelligence services could find people to send east.

Denazification—a deliberate effort to extirpate the National Socialist ideology—framed a second issue. The Allied powers arrested former Nazi leaders and prosecuted them for war crimes. (In the Far East, Japanese were prosecuted too—some of them for waterboarding.) Lesser Nazis were barred from positions of official responsibility, denied work permits, or simply ostracized. This treatment became an intelligence problem in several ways. The security services sought to track and apprehend suspected war criminals, but they also wished to recruit German scientists, technocrats, and others with particular skills. In those cases, demonstrating that some former official had *not* been tainted by a Nazi past assumed great importance. Both the American and Russian guided-missile programs would be jump-started by former German scientists.

Allen Dulles entered the German stage here. As the war wound down, Dulles watched from Bern. One by one, starting with Tracy Barnes, his best operatives had gone home. Dulles hoped to be OSS chief for Europe, but instead General Donovan assigned him to head a new German mission. A different unit was looking for scientists. Dulles arrived in Berlin six weeks after the German surrender, visiting his old haunts but at length setting up shop at the Henkel, a former champagne winery near Wiesbaden. Bases subordinate to the station were established in Frankfurt, Munich, and Berlin.

At the village of Biebrich, Dulles lived in the Horn Rabbit House, so named because its owner had decorated the walls with the mounted heads of rabbits. As common for quasi-military billets—and this one had been furnished by the Army's Quartermaster Corps—Dulles shared the quarters with a cross section of individuals who became the first generation of CIA leaders. Richard Helms, officially a U.S. Navy officer, served as chief of the espionage branch. Frank Wisner, also of the Navy, headed special operations. Wisner had returned from service as OSS chief in Turkey and then the so-called Hammerhead mission to Romania. He was the tenant most comfortable with the rabbit heads—the Romanians had entertained him with weekend duck hunts. Helms writes that Wisner, at Biebrich, still seemed shaken by what he had seen in Romania. In residence as well, indeed responsible for the critical daily ration of Glühwein, the cinnamon-flavored warmed red wine that is a European treat, was Harry A. Rositzke, a philologist by trade, who served as the mission's top planner.

In July Allen returned to Berlin and focused on the base there. The OSSers helped find evidence for war crimes indictments and created lists of Germans suitable for employment, as well as those who ought to be proscribed. Some believe Dulles had a burning party, finding and destroying documents implicating his prewar German business associates. It is certainly true that Allen openly advocated favorable treatment for "Good Germans," by which he meant people who had resisted the Nazis, people like those who came to Bern to tell the OSS of Hitler's doings. About the time the Great White Case Officer began this advocacy, President Harry Truman abolished the OSS. Dulles left Germany then. In December 1945, Allen put in separation papers to leave government service. Richard Helms affirms that money played a role. Helms notes that brother Foster, who had stayed at Sullivan and Cromwell, earned several times what Allen could expect. And Foster had a job for him. So the younger sibling returned to Sullivan and Cromwell.

So far as the Good German issue is concerned, among the truly good and the great were plenty motivated by self-interest. And there were at least two sides to the issue, since Western interests changed with the onset of the Cold War. Denazification abruptly became a lesser priority. Former German generals helped Americans understand Soviet military practices, so suddenly they were afforded special treatment in the prisoner-of-war system. Soon former German intelligence people who had worked against the Russians offered to help the U.S. military. This unit became the nucleus of a new German intelligence agency. All the groups of Germans who helped the West in the Cold War later turned out to have members who concealed Nazi pasts, some quite atrocious. But such a résumé had yet to become a problem while Allen Dulles, at Sullivan and Cromwell, lobbied for a peacetime intelligence agency. As time passed, the younger Dulles stayed active in foreign affairs, serving as a consultant when the House of Representatives considered the Marshall Plan. He went beyond advocating for "good" Germans and put an oar into espionage waters.

The Office of Strategic Services had too many enemies. The unit formally existed as an appendage of the Joint Chiefs of Staff (JCS) but administratively lay within the War Department (the U.S. Army). The Army had its own intelligence section, the G-2, a loose espionage unit nicknamed the Pond, and a Counterintelligence Corps with other spooky functions. Army people looked askance at the odd ducks Wild Bill Donovan had gathered under his wing. President Franklin D. Roosevelt supported Donovan, but he passed away in the spring of 1945. Harry S. Truman, who succeeded, had no special esteem for the OSS. He instructed the Army, Navy, and the State Department to propose postwar arrangements.

President Truman abolished the OSS by executive order that September. A rally at Washington's Riverside Stadium, where OSS heroes were honored at a mass ceremony, was almost its last official act. Donovan's suggestions for a new entity, his appeal upon learning Truman's intentions, did not sway the president. Within the War Department, Donovan's insistence that the JCS be consulted was met by a paper showing the Joint Chiefs fully cognizant of the plan to demobilize the OSS.

State already had a recommendation to create an Office of Research and Intelligence, duplicating the OSS Research and Analysis Branch, while its covert operations components were judged not useful in peacetime. The Army and the Navy both had intelligence units that gathered information by technological means (radio intercept, aerial photography) as well as special operations forces, so the OSS seemed redundant. The actual running of spies seemed the only function neglected. Here the War Department (Army) grasped the reins to run a Strategic Services Unit. Truman created a National Intelligence Authority (NIA) to supervise the spooks, and a Central Intelligence Group (CIG) as a small operating unit.

On January 24, 1946, Mr. Truman staged an amusing ceremony at the end of a White House meeting in which he outfitted his new CIG chief, Sidney Souers, and his newly designated personal representative on the NIA, Admiral William D. Leahy, with black cloaks, highwaymen's hats, and wooden daggers. The photos of this scene, sadly, do not survive. White House aides proclaimed the new spooky supervisors looked splendid.

Sidney Souers had been a rear admiral in the Naval Reserve, a player in the JCS intel arena during the war, and a man too easily overlooked in American spy lore. He had sound instincts and, more important, the president's ear, for Souers was a Missouri businessman and a figure in the Kansas City political circles that Truman had inhabited as senator from Missouri. Not only did Truman make his Missouri acolyte a superspy, but also, when the president went on to create the National Security Council, he coaxed Souers back to help there too. Director Souers's key accomplishments came in laying down a CIG structure, beginning with three persons in a two-room office up the street from the White House, and in selecting the right people to fill it. Eager to mend business relations he had ignored during the war, Souers stayed only a few months. When he left, the agency had swollen—to fifty-five people. Ten of them monitored intelligence collection, twice that many worked on reports, the rest did everything from disseminate papers to planning to security.

In April 1946, Souers secured the future of the Central Intelligence

Group by absorbing the Strategic Services Unit. The SSU organization furnished the bulk of CIG staff through the next year. Souers also zeroed in on his replacement, Army Lieutenant General Hoyt Vandenberg, a dynamic go-getter who had led a tactical air force in Europe and who happened to be a nephew of the powerful chairman of the Senate Foreign Relations Committee. Vandenberg pressed for additional personnel and new spy functions. He revamped the Office of Reports and Estimates, the agency's first analytical unit, and he supported upgrading the entire CIG. By the winter, State Department counterparts were considering with Vandenberg how to keep their respective analysis shops from tripping over each other. "Co-ordination"—of both information collection and report production—consumed much attention through the first half of 1947.

Others, not least William J. Donovan and Allen Welsh Dulles, were unhappy with the system. Co-ordination be damned. They pressed for a new spy agency. Wild Bill had not taken lightly the dismantling of the OSS. From before it happened, he fought back. OSSers who had been journalists were fed information for articles recounting its exploits, others were quietly given material for more ambitious projects. So long as the articles and books lamented the absence of a robust peacetime agency, Donovan did not much care that wartime secrets were spilled. Allen Dulles took the opportunity to pen a piece for the *Saturday Evening Post* with the story of his Operation Sunrise secret negotiations. That led to a book contract, and Dulles used *Germany's Underground* to argue there had been "good" Germans, including those who plotted to assassinate Hitler, a subset of them being his spies at Bern.

Like Allen, Wild Bill Donovan had a Wall Street law firm, and from there he agitated for his spy agency. Senator Vandenberg, the CIG chief's uncle, became one target. Donovan hosted regular meetings of the old OSS crowd, using them to press too. Through a joint committee, Congress meanwhile investigated the surprise attack at Pearl Harbor, delivering its report late in 1946, with conclusions that offered a natural platform to advocate a peacetime agency.

Before Christmas, Director Vandenberg had readied a draft of possible legislation and forwarded it to the White House. There, Harry Truman already had a project for unification of the armed services on his desk, and he added the intelligence agency language to it. The president sent Congress this proposal in January 1947. By spring enough momentum had developed that legislators asked Dulles, who was president of the prestigious Council on Foreign Relations, to comment on the spy agency's shape. In August Dulles joined a small outside group advising Vandenberg. Dreamer that he was, Allen could not help being mesmerized by the CIA, the National Security Act, and all that went with them.

Most of Allen's comments were workmanlike suggestions regarding the powers this law would afford an intelligence chief and his organization. He agreed with those, eager to prevent the creation of a Gestapo-like entity, who opposed placing active military officers in CIA positions. Another item deserves mention. Dulles recommended that language be inserted to create an "official secrets act" prohibiting unauthorized disclosures, by both agency employees and anyone else in government. This disturbing proposal—odd coming from someone who had recently revealed secret OSS negotiations—Congress rejected. But it shows how the sirens of secrecy moved in on the ground floor of the fledgling spy entity.

Hearings and debates continued through the summer. Along the way, the "national defense act" morphed into the National Security Act. When passed, it became the most extensive realignment of government powers prior to creation of the Department of Homeland Security in 2002. It popularized the very term "national security"; until World War II, this had not existed as a formal concept. It created the National Security Council, an NSC staff to serve the president, set up a unified military command (called the "National Military Establishment," but soon enough transmogrified into the Department of Defense), provided for a peacetime draft, made the Air Force a separate armed service, outlined a formal charter for the Marine Corps, *and* created the Central Intelligence Agency.

A major concern in the debates revolved around fears that the agency could become a secret police like the Nazi Gestapo, which used torture to extract confessions in Germany. Those concerns were expressed in both houses of Congress. Allen Dulles agreed, and related this to the parallel concern over military officers leading the agency. The very first point made in describing CIA authorities in the National Security Act of 1947 is that "the Agency shall have no police, subpoena, or law enforcement powers or internal security functions." While the 1947 act provided for a CIA, it described an entity oriented to intelligence analysis, said next to nothing about other agency functions, and—aside from the domestic-operations and secret-police prohibitions—almost nothing was mentioned about permissible versus prohibited agency activity. The act was no real charter.

During all the to-and-fro, Vandenberg departed the CIG, his place taken by Rear Admiral Roscoe H. Hillenkoetter. In answer to the fears over military persons Hillenkoetter readily volunteered to resign his commission.

Congress did not oblige him to do so. Hillenkoetter established a tradition that was largely honored until the 1990s.

The admiral at least had the right formal qualifications. The fifty-year-old had been a quasi-professional intelligence officer before that military specialty existed. As a young officer in Panama in the mid-1920s, Hillen-koetter set up a spy network. The task whetted his appetite. The admiral had no fewer than four tours as a naval attaché, collecting information. In Vichy France before America entered World War II, he had conducted special operations too—helping the French underground smuggle individuals between German-occupied France and safe areas in Vichy territory and North Africa. During a crucial period of the Pacific war, 1942 to spring of 1943, Hillenkoetter helped set up the original "all-source fusion center" at Pearl Harbor. His assignment immediately before CIG had (again) been as naval attaché to France. More than that, Admiral Hillenkoetter had actually *been* at Pearl Harbor, so he could refer to that incomparable experience. Executive officer of the battleship *West Virginia*, Roscoe stood in his cabin dressing when the Japanese attack began on December 7, 1941. He headed for the bridge, but in the few minutes it took to reach the quarter-deck, torpedoes hit and *West Virginia* started sinking. He had a personal reason for wanting a crackerjack spy agency.

Hillenkoetter's watch brought significant developments. The Soviets successively installed Communist-led governments in the eastern European nations. They kept a huge army poised there. Refusing cooperation with the Western Allies, the Soviets stopped attending foreign ministers' conferences. In 1947 they completed taking over Czechoslovakia. The pro-Western prime minister leaped out a window—or was thrown. People spoke of the "captive nations" of eastern Europe. British allies informed Washington they would be pulling out of their commitments in Greece, where a Communist insurgency fought the government. There were places—in the Ukraine, the Baltic states, more quietly in Romania, to some degree in Poland—where nationalists opposed the Soviets. Greece demanded U.S. attention. Next the United States began a sustained foreign aid program under the Marshall Plan.

The launch of the Central Intelligence Agency took place at this moment of burgeoning hostility. An Office of Research and Evaluation had already been created. Absorption into CIG of the Strategic Services Unit created a fledgling clandestine service. CIG christened this its Office of Special Operations (OSO), with two-thirds of its personnel.

Demands for active Cold War measures grew to a drumbeat and led to the inception of CIA covert operations. It happened during the mad rush to make the CIA's potential a reality. The National Security Act of 1947 assigned the agency five roles, four of which concerned either producing intelligence estimates and reports, carrying out activities of common concern, or coordinating information collected by the broader community. The law barely mentioned espionage, much less covert operations. The early meetings of the new National Security Council (NSC) hammered out a series of NSC intelligence directives to guide CIA efforts. The fifth role, a simple catchall, in its current form provides that the agency shall conduct "such other functions and duties related to intelligence as the President or the National Security Council may direct."

That vague language eventually opened the door to a host of CIA actions that took the agency far from its roots. Covert operations were among the newfangled activities. President Truman had already changed the gameboard by declaring his doctrine—the United States would help countries that could not help themselves, starting with Greece and Turkey. In the wake of the Czech coup, particularly, came demands that the CIA conduct psychological warfare. Unlike wartime special units conducting ad hoc activities, here a peacetime agency acquired a permanent mission. The road would not be smooth, but it transformed the Central Intelligence Agency.

The top CIA lawyer, general counsel Lawrence Houston, argued in official opinions that the National Security Act did not authorize covert action. Director Hillenkoetter followed suit, agreeing with the need for "psychological warfare"—as these activities were then known—but ceding the playing field to the military. This encompassed all kinds of measures to affect the will or beliefs of target populations and countries, bending them to CIA purposes, or at least to an affinity for United States policies. Senior diplomats—among them the renowned George Kennan—and military men kept up pressure for action under the Truman Doctrine. President Truman approved a scheme to make the State Department responsible for "psywar" and covert action, but Secretary of State George C. Marshall rejected that proposition. Marshall's prestige and power were such that Truman backed off. In December Truman approved directive NSC-4A, making the CIA responsible for psychological warfare after all.

Secretary Marshall did not mind the State Department furnishing policy guidance for psywar but he wanted no operational role, for he wished to preserve a distinction between action programs and diplomacy. The

American military felt similarly. Suddenly political developments in Italy threatened Washington's interests. In late 1947 Truman's NSC, fearing that the Italian Communists—easily the largest political force in the country, its ranks swollen thanks to the prestige the party had gained from its leading role in fighting the Nazis—might win elections there, requested CIA intervention.

Intelligence officer James J. Angleton, with many contacts in Italy, warned that the Italian Communists were cornering the market on newsprint, the cheap paper used for newpapers. Defense Secretary James Forrestal worried that the budget had no money in it to book radio ads or recruit influence peddlers. Allen Dulles stepped in, circulating collection plates at a couple of his social clubs. Within days CIA operatives were throwing cash around in Rome. After the new year, the president set aside over a million dollars (equivalent to more than $10 million in 2016) for the Italian project.

The Italian election turned out the way Truman wanted, with the Christian Democrats victorious. Similar operations followed in France. The Communist challenge seemed to mushroom in February 1948, with the Czech takeover and new tensions in Germany. Cobbling together operations on the fly would never work. Not long afterward, George Kennan proposed a new covert activity framework, with an entity under general supervision from the State Department but not formally part of it, the CIA, or the military. A panel drawn from all those agencies would guide the new unit. Covert operations expanded tremendously. Meanwhile, Marshall Plan aid involved steady dealing in foreign currencies, and that trading could be tapped to launder—and increase—CIA funding for covert action. President Truman liked the idea.

In Italy there would be plenty more elections—with the CIA backing the Christian Democrats for decades. On the global stage, the NSC preferred a permanent covert action unit anyway. Dulles advised combining covert action *and* espionage in a single CIA entity. He did not mind its taking guidance from State but stipulated the unit should have considerable autonomy, that it be permitted to appeal to the NSC if the CIA's director's decisions went against it, and that it be headed by an outsider, presumably himself.

The National Security Council, meeting on June 3, 1948, mulled over the proposals. The council approved most of them, in its directive NSC 10/2, but rejected placing espionage and covert operations within a single unit. Mr. Kennan became the initial chair of the board of directors, called the Operations Advisory Committee (eventually the 10/2 Panel, launched as the interagency covert-operations approval authority).

Officials called the new unit the Office of Policy Coordination (OPC). The OPC became the covert action arm of the United States government. It had little to do with either policy or coordination. Kennan offered the OPC post to Dulles, but 1948 was a presidential election year, and Allen, out campaigning for Republican candidate Thomas Dewey, turned down the job. He anticipated heading the entire CIA in a Dewey administration. So Kennan turned to Frank Gardiner Wisner, a friend and, at that point, a fellow diplomat, to be OPC's first head. Allen Dulles became the godfather.

In 1948–49 in Washington at the birth of the CIA, it was too soon to speak of ghosts, but now in the lengthening shadows of seven decades of agency history, it is clear the ghosts rose even then, and they stayed. Sigmund Freud, the patriarch of psychological theory and psychiatry, once elaborated a concept of the "uncanny," in which the Viennese mentalist included ghosts. Analysis of the uncanny, Freud postulated, inevitably led to an animistic view of the universe as one populated by human spirits. Allen Dulles laid claim to a place among the spirits when he labored so hard to revive the OSS, his American spy agency. As Freud noted, among the commonplaces of fairy tales and religions are the false semblance of death and the raising of the dead, if only as disembodied spirits. Later we will see how Mr. Dulles ended his career in a way that ensured true ghostliness.

The links of psychological DNA were very clear. In February 1946, George Kennan had authored the so-called Long Telegram, in which he had foreseen Soviet hostility and advocated "containing" Russia. Allen Dulles had worked against the Russians in Germany at the end of the war. Frank Wisner, a Dulles subordinate, ran a section of the State Department that dealt with the displaced persons, had been shocked by the Russians' brute force, and wanted to combat them. Harry Truman, believing Soviet dictator Joseph Stalin to be installing a Communist empire, agreed. America's wartime ally Winston Churchill famously charged that Russia had brought down an "Iron Curtain" along the borders of eastern Europe from the Baltic Sea to the Adriatic. OPC's mission would be to roll it back.

A hiring campaign staffed the OPC quickly. Recruits gained higher rank than they would have elsewhere, including at CIA. More came from the military. Benefiting from temporary-duty assignees from both the agency and the military, the OPC within months had several hundred people and seven overseas stations. Wisner's first budget totaled $4.8 million. Officers were divided into functional groups for psychological warfare, political warfare, economic warfare, preventive direct action, and one for everything else. Half a dozen regional divisions paralleled those of the Marshall Plan. Operations were called projects.

Allen Dulles acquired a new quasi-operational role, drawing up legal papers for New York State certification of the National Committee for a Free Europe (later the Free Europe Committee), incorporated in June 1949. The CIA and State Department had agreed on the outlines of this scheme four months earlier. Dulles became a senior official and joined its board of directors. He would be executive secretary too. The National Committee became the umbrella for "black"—secret—psychological operations, in the first of which the CIA launched balloons across Eastern Europe with propaganda or reconnaissance payloads. It also ran Radio Free Europe, a quite elaborate effort to broadcast propaganda into the new Soviet satellite states. Project Umpire, begun even before the formal creation of the OPC or the National Committee, was the CIA's name for the use of broadcast and print media to influence events behind the Iron Curtain. This was among America's first covert operations.

Dulles's role mushroomed. Sid Souers, the erstwhile spy chief, had returned to Washington as executive secretary of Truman's NSC. The president's national security adviser, for that's what Souers had become, convinced Truman that the performance of the intelligence services needed review. Dulles became one of three principals—and the chairman—of the survey panel. In this role he had his greatest impact. With William H. Jackson, a psychological warfare authority, and Matthias Correa, representing secretary of defense James Forrestal, Dulles rummaged through CIA activities for nearly a year. Director Hillenkoetter considered Allen an antipathetic and obnoxious character sticking his fingers in every pie. During the survey, rioting broke out in the Colombian capital, Bogotá, while Secretary of State George Marshall attended a conference there. This crisis, known as El Bogotazo from the city's name, shook Truman's administration. Congressional committees questioned the failure of the intelligence agency to foresee the discontent. Allen's survey took that line, coming in widely critical of the CIA. The survey group's report drew two major conclusions: first, that the agency had failed to fulfill its mission of producing estimative intelligence and, second, Allen Dulles's hobbyhorse, that the OPC covert operators and the spies of the OSO should be combined.

When the survey went to Truman's NSC at the beginning of 1949, the CIA and other agencies rebutted its criticisms. Director Hillenkoetter accomplished the notable feat of securing passage of the CIA Act of 1949, with some positive but more negative effects that persist to this day. This law endowed the agency's director with powers to protect vaguely defined "sources and methods," to spend money off the books, and to fire employees at will. The Office of Policy Coordination and the Office of Special Operations continued to go their separate ways. No unification occurred. Some thought the new Defense Department opposed consolidation. Others blame the FBI, smarting at the CIA's taking over its Latin American networks. Hillenkoetter always maintained that infighting between the Pentagon and State delayed the move. The Pentagon rejected OPC's Frank Wisner as chief of a merged unit; State opposed OSO's Colonel Robert A. Schow, an Army officer.

Feuding dragged on for many months. Within the CIA the competition had consequences. The interagency OPC, having bigger budgets and higher ranks, offered greater salaries for the same work. It poached OSO people, dangling before veterans, nostalgic for their wartime roles, prospects for daring covert projects. OSO officers considered themselves the professionals, OPC the upstarts. Though many on both sides had OSS roots, the OSO operatives had stayed on through the lean years until the advent of the CIA. Their OPC colleagues had left for private life. They were the amateurs. In overseas embassies the OPC and OSO chiefs were direct competitors. But the OPC station chiefs, with their higher ranks, were senior to chiefs of the parallel CIA espionage unit. Meanwhile, at headquarters, the Operational Aids Division, responsible for cover identities and technical support, belonged to the OSO, not Frank Wisner. It had no clear duty to serve the OPC. The problems remained intractable. In the autumn of 1951, when Joseph B. Smith joined the OPC as a young psywar planner, so far as rank and file knew, a merger of OPC and OSO remained just a rumor.

By then Allen Welsh Dulles had come onstage himself. For a time, his primary role had been in the shadows with the National Committee for a Free Europe. Soon enough, Radio Liberty (RL), intended to broadcast directly into Russia, joined RFE as an operating unit. The committee and the Radios, as the CIA soon knew them, were Wisner's creatures, among the first agency "proprietaries," supposedly private entities that in reality were wholly or substantially funded by the agency and responded to its instructions.

Another proprietary coming online in this period was Civil Air Transport (later renamed Air America), a private business the CIA took over by investment. Within a year, an ostensibly private trading concern on Taiwan called Sea Supply complemented it. The advent of these entities arguably introduced new words into the CIA lexicon, starting with *radio* and *proprietary* but soon extending to the notion of CIA contract employees (as opposed to the agency's officers) and to the question of who could be trusted with knowledge of a true situation, that is, persons who were "witting" versus "unwitting."

The degree to which individuals knew about their CIA links is an intriguing question, especially in the context of Europe's intellectual Cold War—Allen's first battleground. Mr. Dulles was certainly witting, as was DeWitt C. Poole Jr., president of the National Committee and also an OSS veteran. Indeed, seven of the thirteen directors of this period had had wartime experience in intelligence or psychological warfare. Dulles and Poole met with Wisner once the group had formed and been recognized by the State Department. Allen pushed for direct National Committee fundraising to increase public awareness of the group and serve as cover for covert CIA funding. The "Crusade for Freedom" would function as the fund-raising arm. Dulles took Wisner to see Dwight D. Eisenhower, at the time president of Columbia University, who had agreed to chair the crusade. George Urban, an RFE broadcaster, later head of programming, and ultimately the director, felt the links were "subtly consultative and mutually enriching rather than of an order-taking kind."

However, there was indeed CIA guidance to RFE/RL on what to emphasize. The CIA referred to the National Committee by the cryptonym QK/Ivory*; there were other code names, for the Radios, for the people, and for ancillary elements. Agency pundits nicknamed DeWitt Poole the Little Napoleon. Senior CIA officials debated terms under which they would permit the Free Europe Committee to conduct its fund-raising, tailoring them to CIA money flows. Crowdfunding never financed more than a fraction of the committee's budget, which reached $10 million in its first year ($100 million in 2016 dollars) and tripled over time.

---

* There is confusion regarding CIA code names. A cryptonym is a code word or phrase used to refer to something in messages or documents. Agency cryptonyms had two parts and were called "digraphs." The first part was usually a two-letter couplet that classified the subject, place, or person referred to by regional or functional category. The rest would be a presumably nonsense word making the identification unique and completing the digraph. In agency documents, digraphs are usually rendered in all capital letters with no distinctions. Here, for clarity, the text will separate the parts of a digraph with a slash mark ("/"). In other instances it will skip the letter couplet and give the code word (the project name) in roman type.

The 7.5 kilowatt shortwave radio with which Radio Free Europe began broadcasting had been procured by the Office of Policy Coordination from U.S. Army surplus. Most early RFE/RL equipment derived from the CIA, and U.S. Army officers were the first heads of the enterprise. RFE began broadcasting on July 4, 1950. It was an index of the homogeneity of American opinion at the time that Radio Free Europe won the Peabody Award in 1950, an important journalism prize, for contributions to international understanding. The psywar mafia *loved* that.

In June 1950, North Korea crossed the 38th Parallel, invading the south and triggering the Korean War. The CIA had given a few days' warning of the northern capability to act, but not of its intentions. Dulles had gone to Europe to mark the start of RFE broadcasts. He came back to take up the implications of North Korea's moves at the Council on Foreign Relations. Allen was determined to agitate for sacking Hillenkoetter, already in the crosshairs for El Bogotazo.

No lobbying was required, however. The admiral had already asked the Navy for an active command at sea.

President Truman offered the CIA job to establishment stalwarts who turned him down, and then to General Walter Bedell Smith, former ambassador to Moscow and, during the war, Dwight D. Eisenhower's chief of staff. Bedell Smith, with a sharp sense of duty, accepted. Without much knowledge of intelligence work, he wanted a skilled deputy. Smith turned to William H. Jackson of the NSC survey group. Peter Grose, a Dulles biographer, attributes the suggestion to Sid Souers, but the idea is far more likely to have been Smith's own or to have come from Eisenhower. Jackson had been with them as a top psychological warfare leader under General Omar Bradley, surviving many bureaucratic ambushes designed to cut down the psy warriors. Bedell Smith, dyspeptic and sharp-tongued, conventionally minded but a brilliant judge of men, had seen Jackson up close. So Bill Jackson came to the CIA. He would knock heads together and make a start on unification. As an Eisenhower associate he had connections in the military; as a former partner at law with Frank Wisner at the firm Carter Ledyard & Milburn, he had an in with the OPC chieftain. Jackson was uniquely qualified.

Allen Dulles got a place too. Not above some dissimulation, Dulles would say in his book *The Craft of Intelligence* that "writing reports for the government sometimes has unexpected consequences. You may be asked to put your recommendations into effect." The truth is Mr. Dulles had long been positioning himself for this. Bedell Smith took over the CIA on October 7, 1950. Allen Dulles started as a consultant the same day. In *The Craft of Intelligence*, he maintains that he intended to stay for just six weeks to help Smith get acclimated. In fact Allen angled for a job—and he succeeded. On December 21, Bill Jackson's morning staff meeting took up the matter of the announcement of Allen Welsh Dulles as an agency deputy director responsible for a new Directorate of Plans unifying the Office of Policy Coordination and the Office of Special Operations—the unit of which Allen had long dreamed.

ATOP NAVY HILL

America's clandestine service in those days inhabited wood-frame "temporary" office buildings denoted by letters. Building I, known familiarly as Quarters Eye, housed the front office. Others included J, K, and L, and ran the length of the Reflecting Pool on the Mall. They were across from other wartime "temps" erected at the foot of Navy Hill, beneath the CIA's main headquarters, built on the western face of the height in 1904 at 2430 E Street, Northwest. As Allen soon learned, Quarters Eye and the others were drafty and cold by winter and dreadfully hot in the summer. They also blocked the view to the Lincoln Memorial. Dulles arrived there in January 1951. He approached the job cautiously at first, thinking himself a consultant, taking a per diem but no salary, committed for only six months. But Allen would not have been the Great White Case Officer if the Great Game had not enchanted him.

The deputy director for plans (DDP) hastened to make himself useful and before long indispensable. Almost his first act as DDP was to pass on a series of CIA papers that proposed principles for control of intelligence operations in peace and war. The proposals were for the NSC and the new North Atlantic Treaty Organization (NATO) command led by General Eisenhower, recalled to active service. The papers, with code names like Magnitude and Demagnitize, became enduring headaches. Dulles approved a draft NSC directive, delayed a paper on guerrilla warfare, and wanted the NATO study reworked. The proposition that CIA would control covert operations in peacetime and the generals take over in a war became problematical when war was "limited," like in Korea. Dulles received a paper on psywar issues from the Army's General Robert McClure. After briefings from OPC's Wisner and OSO's Schow, the deputy director accompanied Director Smith on an inspection of CIA stations.

By April the new DDP confidently presented regional and single-country accounts of his activities. Dulles had begun to review all covert projects. He prepared fresh clandestine activity procedures for NATO and reached out to foreign leaders and intelligence officials. One of them, former Polish general Władysław Anders, came from a place where OPC had swung into clandestine action. The biggest venture took place in Albania, where the CIA and the British were launching a joint effort to overthrow the Communist regime. At the end of April, the DDP gave his take on the twenty-odd OPC projects under way, promised not to start anything new, and declared he would close out others as they completed. It didn't happen.

Deputy director Dulles prepared to receive delegations for an international spy conference, where, among other things, the CIA and the British MI-6 reviewed the Albania plan. On April 27, at Director Smith's morning staff meeting, Dulles no doubt delighted discussing how the CIA might exploit the Peabody Award given to RFE. The next day he took a victory lap, going to New York to address a dinner of OSS veterans.

The Radios were an initiative the CIA never gave up, at least on Dulles's watch. Indeed, the agency expanded and multiplied the effort, widening covert political influence efforts to include a publications arm, quietly distributing the Bible, other religious tracts, and a variety of Western books behind the Iron Curtain. Secret funding of youth groups and labor unions followed. In Italy and France, these tactics had been utilized to influence specific elections. Now Allen Dulles and Frank Wisner regularized and globalized the technique for an open-ended campaign. When Congress held hearings on the public dispute between President Truman and former Korean War commander General Douglas MacArthur, whom Truman had fired for insubordination, the CIA entertained a suggestion from Robert McClure that the hearings be used to plant false information to deceive the Soviets. In short the advent of the Directorate of Plans and the coming of Allen Dulles did nothing to circumscribe CIA covert operations.

Mr. Dulles strove to make himself indispensable. Whether the issue was arrangements for secret warfare in NATO, stationing a small CIA staff at Pearl Harbor to liaise with the Pacific Command, or the prospective agency role in "electro-magnetic warfare," Dulles furnished advice and volunteered his directorate.

Walter Bedell Smith suffered no fools and never really warmed to Dulles. Allen had been DDP for just a couple of months when Smith instructed Bill Jackson to conduct a fresh survey, this time *only* of the DDP, and with only himself as judge. Supposed to be Jackson's legacy—he had promised Smith just six months and had already stayed longer—the survey threatened

Dulles's rice bowl. Still classified. Director Smith convened CIA's assistant directors as a "projects review committee" to pass on OPC's schemes. That made Allen's a minority vote. But Dulles won some too. With "electromagnetic warfare"—then a euphemism for the Radios—the director tried to squelch the CIA role, but Radio Free Europe and other organs of propaganda fit Truman's idea of psychological warfare so well the CIA chief struck out. General Smith also approved a suggestion that spy missions or project proposals with relatively small costs could be approved within DDP, avoiding the more cumbersome agency-wide project review.

There were other signs of discomfort—and of "Beetle" Smith's pain too. The director had ulcers, had had stomach surgery in the summer of 1950, and had lost about forty pounds, nearly a quarter of his bulk. He lived on soda crackers and mush, consumed all day long, not just at mealtimes. Beetle could be cold and distant. Pundits cracked he was the most even-tempered person in the world—always mad. One time General Smith declared a meeting ended the moment Dulles arrived and apologized for being late. Another time the director demanded that the DDP fix a gasoline leak that bothered the Air Force. Smith thought little of Dulles as an administrator. Once, when the DDP suggested some management massage, the CIA boss stopped him cold. "Allen," Bedell Smith shot back, "you don't know how to run *anything!* What's the biggest thing you've ever run?" A top aide records Smith on another occasion: "Allen isn't a *bad* administrator. It's just that he's entirely *innocent* of administration."

Another time General Smith harangued his assembled deputies, then challenged them to see who could write up what he had said in directive form. Administration chief Lincoln White accepted the challenge. He did it right away. White showed the paper to covert ops boss Frank Wisner, who refused to sign off even though he had not opposed Smith's challenge. Then White handed the directive to Allen Dulles, who said he would take care of it. In the hallway next day, White ran into General Smith, who demanded to know what had happened. White explained that he had completed the directive but left it with Allen. "You gave it to Allen Dulles, for God's sake?" the CIA chieftain exclaimed. "He won't understand it! Get it away from him right now!"

Director Smith wanted staff to stand to attention when he entered—the Army way. Mr. Dulles was willing to stand but refused to do Army drills. Once Beetle chewed out a senior official who gave him a precise answer when he'd asked for an approximation. In the privacy of his office, Allen laughed off Bedell Smith's quirks as the antics of a martinet. A standard Dulles quip would be, "The General was in fine form this morning!"

William Jackson, eager to return to his business affairs, resigned as Smith's number two. The director needed a new deputy director of central intelligence. Jackson recommended Gordon Gray, a North Carolinian. Gray had been secretary of the army, a university president, was a tobacco and broadcasting magnate, and had served alongside Bill Jackson in World War II. He'd been a candidate for CIA director but had refused. Now he rejected the deputy position too. Harry Truman prevailed upon Gray to come to Washington as staff chief of the Psychological Strategy Board (PSB), a novel new NSC unit to manage the Cold War. Director Smith, instead of getting him as deputy, rushed to find office space for PSB, a supervisory unit, which Gray preferred be on "neutral" territory. The Strategy Board became the 10/2 Panel's covert operations staff.

Next Smith hoped to entice General MacArthur's ex–intelligence czar, Charles Willoughby. He even speculated on ex-employees of the FBI. Smith got close to Willoughby, close enough to look for a plane to bring him to Washington, but the former Far Eastern person slipped away.

At mid-July, Dulles, using his agency pseudonym Robert A. Ascham, set off on a weeks-long inspection of the CIA's European stations. Re-energizing the political actions in Italy and France was key. Agency officials estimated that Communist party sources in those two countries fabricated half of what they gave CIA. On the trip, Dulles took aboard explanations and helped his officers brainstorm fresh ploys. This kind of monitoring of field activity became known in early CIA idiom as cruising, and it became a favorite activity of agency higher-ups. Nicely descriptive, it will be used that way in this text. Meanwhile Director Smith, pressed to find someone, turned to Allen after all. Shortly after his cruise, in August 1951, just as President Truman created the Psychological Strategy Board, Allen W. Dulles ascended to second-in-command of the entire U.S. intelligence establishment.

Reporting on his cruise to Director Smith, Allen Dulles led an extended discussion of what would become one of the CIA's most haunted initiatives, its support for an intelligence service in Germany. The Germans were a mixture of former Nazis and, only slightly less suspect, German military professionals. Efforts were sponsored by the U.S. Army at first, under the code name Rusty. The Army accepted German officer Reinhard Gehlen's initiative to bring together a circle, first simply to recount wartime experience against the Soviets, then to create an actual spy service. The Americans, desperate for knowledge of Russia, had already enlisted hosts of German officers to recount their experiences. The spy project seemed a simple extension. Gehlen and his associates went to Washington in August 1945. They were code named Bolero. Some others, called Keystone, stayed in Germany, where they laid the groundwork for a new service starting early in 1946. That summer the Americans united Bolero with Keystone to create Rusty. Gehlen took charge, his unit gradually becoming known as the Gehlen Organization.

The Americans had nothing like it. If the Army or the SSU, the CIA's progenitor, had more than a handful of spies outside the occupation areas at that time, it would have been surprising.

Gordon M. Stewart, then the top spook in Germany, believed it more important to spy out the Russians than hunt down Nazi war criminals. He trolled DP camps looking for recruits. Those who agreed, given several months training, were assigned to a network. After a while Stewart had one net of seventeen agents, plus a penetration that ran into Soviet-occupied Lithuania.

"The Org," as Gehlen's familiars knew it, claimed to have six hundred agents behind the Iron Curtain. But the Army, out of money, repeatedly tried to pass Rusty along to the SSU. That agency felt the Gehlen enterprise to be overambitious, expensive, and bedeviled by poor security and management. Another appeal, to Hoyt Vandenberg once his Central Intelligence Group had taken over SSU, also failed. Americans felt that the Org drew overly broad conclusions from inadequate evidence. Rusty cost more than the CIG's entire network in Germany, which had started making progress on sources. Even empire builder Vandenberg knew enough to steer clear.

Attitudes changed as Truman gravitated toward creating the CIA. Fresh reviews of German espionage accorded it more value. Watching from the wings, believing "good Germans" were good friends, Allen Dulles supported the change. His book *Germany's Underground* appeared as the Rusty debate swirled. A momentary setback occurred that summer, when the Army reversed itself, blocking its bid for the spooks to take over. Just weeks later, the CIA materialized and, equally important, the Gehlen Organization moved out of the U.S. military compound that had housed it, opening a headquarters at Pullach, near Munich. Opinion soured at the newly formed CIA as officers stationed in Germany reported doubts.

Richard Helms, chief of the OSO division that spied in central Europe, got warnings of the Org's security weaknesses. This theme always repeated. It could not have been otherwise in a milieu in which Nazism had tainted Germany, and a portion of Gehlen's people had been Nazi operatives. Not only was there a possibility that war criminals would be revealed; there were risks the Russians might discover such evidence and use it to blackmail the spies.

The boundary case was that of Heinz Felfe, whom the CIA knew as UJ/Drowsky. Born in eastern Germany in 1918, Felfe had joined the Nazi party, become a policeman, then an SS officer affiliated with the Nazi foreign intelligence agency. Nazi spymasters assigned him to Switzerland. Here was somebody Allen Dulles might have known. More than that, Felfe became known elsewhere. British soldiers captured him at the end of the war, and Felfe admitted his Nazi ties. He worked for British intelligence during the Rusty era, but MI-6 dropped him, suspecting that he also worked for the Soviets, which he did. Some believe Drowsky was motivated by anger at the West for the 1945 firebombing of his home city, Dresden. He joined the Gehlen Organization in 1951. Within a few years, Felfe had risen to chief of counterespionage, making him the best-informed German regarding CIA activities in his country. That occurred despite fears about Drowsky's loyalty. Arrested in November 1961, Felfe is believed to have compromised sixty-five CIA operations.

American suspicions never evaporated. General Vandenberg's resistance has already been noted. Division chief Helms told OSO boss Dan Galloway in 1948 that the Russians were aware of U.S. military support of the Gehlen Organization even if they had some details wrong.

Admiral Hillenkoetter rejected having anything to do with Rusty. Opposition began to crumble when Gehlen got a new American defender, James H. Critchfield. Working for the Army in Germany and Austria, Critchfield moved over to the CIA in 1948 and had been sent to Munich as chief of base. He arrived in a beat-up black Chevy carrying a typewriter in his front seat and a secretary in back. Critchfield's review of the Org impressed observers as the most thorough yet, and he argued that Gehlen's unit would be the most important influence on a German intelligence service. The agency would be left in the cold if it refused to get on board.

The CIA became Gehlen's keepers in the summer of 1949. The German spy boss resented the spooks, who proved more intrusive than the U.S. military. In 1950 Critchfield cut the guts out of the Org's planned operations, slashing projects from 150 to 49, then to a mere 10. He told Reinhard Gehlen that the German agency, in terms of sophistication, remained second-rate. Germany established an internal security service in 1950, yet in foreign intelligence Gehlen had another half decade to wait. But things were moving. Allen Dulles told General Smith in August 1951 that the best opportunity to obtain intelligence on the Soviets lay in the eastern zone of Germany, and that the Org had been the prime source to date. There were several penetrations under way, and the deputy director for central intelligence wanted them coordinated. A month later, Gehlen, invited by CIA's Critchfield, made his first visit to America as a spy chieftain. Allen Dulles was on a roll. But the Russian spies moved quickly, and right through until the unification of Germany at the end of the Cold War their agents and penetrations bedeviled the West.

Deputy Director for Central Intelligence Allen Welsh Dulles. The title had a certain ring to it. Administrator or not, Dulles had become second-in-command of the CIA. More than that, in the early years—indeed until past 9/11—the director of central intelligence (DCI) and deputy director of central intelligence (DDCI) functioned as heads of the entire United States intelligence community—the military agencies, the FBI, the State Department's small analytical unit, to some extent the Secret Service—everybody. For Allen the DDCI post, one divorced from operations, in one sense represented a step down, compensated by the community-wide leadership role. Dulles no longer just had charge of the spies. Now he could keep an eye on them while nosing into everything else, too.

Records of Walter Bedell Smith's meetings, as well as notes made by the DCI's executive assistant, reveal that DDCI Dulles did just that. First came the war scare of 1951. War scares, periods of heightened tensions triggered by real or imagined threats, occurred several times during the Cold War. The first, a real scare, had come in 1948, the year the Russians blockaded Berlin and took over Czechoslovakia. The American commander in Germany issued a warning that war might break out. In 1950, coincident with the Korean War, the Soviets began mobilizing military forces in all the satellite states of eastern Europe, stoking more Western fears. Moscow threatened invasion of one of its own satellites, Yugoslavia, for insufficient fealty to Soviet policies. The CIA took to drafting weekly and monthly reviews of the troop mobilizations but never issued a war warning. In 1951 the fears returned. Harry Truman ordered fresh appraisals of Russian capabilities for a surprise attack. While cruising that summer, Allen Dulles evidently heard things that worried him, too. Soon after Dulles ascended to DDCI, he and Smith mulled over the possibility of a crisis, perhaps as soon as that fall, considering a special code word access compartment for intelligence on Soviet intentions.

Nothing happened, but the episode led CIA to set up a warning apparatus in the form of an Intelligence Watch Committee whose entire purpose would be to alert the government of imminent crises, especially ones involving the main enemy, the Russians.

The list of innovations Allen Dulles initiated, supported, or resisted is really the record of the CIA's organizational evolution. Dulles served at a time of changes. They begin with the burgeoning unattributable CIA psychological warfare machine, including the Free Europe Committee, RFE/RL, and new links with labor unions and youth groups. A CIA International Organizations Division was formed in the DDP to spearhead these black projects. Merging the operations side of the agency was a proposal with which Dulles was identified. Yet there was no rush to accomplish it. Merger had been on the books since the creation of the OPC, was reemphasized in each survey, and was a management goal for Walter Bedell Smith, yet it remained a pipe dream. Dulles made a beginning in June 1951, integrating the Latin American units of OPC and OSO.

The DDI added an Office of Current Intelligence (OCI) to monitor day-to-day events. The Olympian Board of National Estimates looked for long-term trends and issued its National Intelligence Estimates (NIEs). OCI's intelligence reports in the *Central Intelligence Bulletin*, inaugurated in 1952, long served as the staple of U.S. secret reporting. An existing Office of Research and Reports kept its eye on the Soviet economy. The Office of Scientific Intelligence covered all manner of technical issues. By 1955 there were over nine hundred analysts in these entities and the Board/Office of National Estimates. The DDI became an information machine larger than some countries' entire security services. At the DDP a Technical Services Division was formed to support operations with gadgets, drugs, cover documents, and the like. A counterintelligence staff gained increasing importance. New technology like the U-2 spy plane, plus the need to manage proprietaries, led to creation of a Development Projects Division. The CIA created a series of logistical bases in forward locations including Germany (Frankfurt), Okinawa, the Philippines, and so on, and training bases in Germany and on the island of Saipan. More than a thousand people in the agency's administration directorate worked just on functions that supported DDP operations.

At the opposite end of the spectrum the agency dragged its feet cooperating with Truman's Psychological Strategy Board. Despite the fact that General Smith chaired the 10/5 Panel (which supervised the PSB)—with Allen his stand-in as necessary—and that CIA provided a number of its staff, the agency danced only reluctantly with the president's fancied Cold War command post. CIA security clearances for PSB personnel were delayed, requested documents slow to appear, and agency appointments to Strategy Board working groups were often held up. At one point Loftus Becker, CIA's chief of analysis, refused, on secrecy grounds, even to tell PSB how much the agency spent on reports. In September 1951 General Smith ordered up a summary of CIA covert operations across the globe. The Strategy Board would review and approve it. More than half a year passed before the report existed, even in draft, and weeks more until the PSB luncheon where the briefing took place.

POLITICAL TERRAFORMING

Allen Dulles's tenure as DDCI lasted only a year and a half. Late in 1952, Dwight D. Eisenhower won election as president. Eisenhower ("Ike") brought in John Foster Dulles as secretary of state and appointed Walter Bedell Smith his deputy. Smith could keep an eye on Allen's brother. Beetle warned Ike of Allen's poor administrative ability. Wild Bill Donovan still wanted the job. But President Eisenhower gave Dulles the nod for DCI. Donovan made do with an appointment as ambassador to Thailand. Allen held sway at the agency through the first year of John F. Kennedy's presidency. When Dulles took over the front office, there were roughly fourteen thousand people working for the CIA.

Much as Bedell Smith had done with William H. Jackson and Dulles himself, Allen liked to work through lieutenants. General Charles Pearre Cabell, a former chief of Air Force intelligence, functioned as his DDCI and did most of the heavy lifting of management. Lincoln K. "Red" White, deputy director for support, handled administration. Robert Amory led the Directorate of Intelligence and, alongside him, Sherman Kent skippered the NIE effort. Dulles kept up his engagement in espionage and covert operations. Frank Wisner remained chief lieutenant there, but Dulles built channels to subordinates such as Al Ulmer, the SSU's first postwar station chief in Vienna, who had migrated to the agency. He brought Tracy Barnes over from the Psychological Strategy Board. Richard M. Bissell became technology man, at the forefront of creating novel spyware. Within his community, Allen Dulles became an inspirational figure. He gave loyalty back, nowhere more apparent than when the notorious Wisconsin Republican senator Joseph R. McCarthy, whose persecution of alleged "Communists" in government ruined many careers, came after the CIA. Just when Dulles reached the director's office, McCarthy startled everyone by picturing the agency as full of Commies. On March 21, 1953, Director Dulles appeared on Capitol Hill to defend the CIA. McCarthy singled out William P. Bundy, an analyst and special assistant to Bob Amory. Bundy had married a daughter of Dean Acheson, which made him brother-in-law to Alger Hiss. He'd contributed to a legal defense fund that helped defend Hiss against espionage charges. Dulles knew it and told Bundy not to worry.

As it happened, Bill Bundy needed the kind of security clearance that involves nuclear weapons data. Naturally the information about Hiss and Bundy formed part of the investigative file assembled to decide on the clearance. It seems McCarthy had the FBI wired. Within forty-eight hours of Bundy's file going over to the Bureau for review, a McCarthy aide had the information and the senator slung new charges at the agency. On July 9, Amory told Bundy to get out of town. He went home to Massachusetts to play golf with his dad. Walter Pforzheimer told McCarthy's office that Bundy was away and could not answer a subpoena.

While Senator McCarthy and his henchman Roy Cohn raged, agency lawyer Pforzheimer asserted that they could subpoena anyone they liked but only Allen Dulles would answer. When the summons came, Allen sought President Eisenhower's help to knock it down, but the president refused to obstruct a congressional investigation. Dulles next turned to Vice President Richard M. Nixon, who happily did the favor. Director Dulles met Senator McCarthy on July 16 to smooth his ruffled feathers, and he testified at the Government Operations Committee on August 3. They exchanged correspondence. McCarthy moved on to target the U.S. Army.

Over the years, Allen Dulles's gout gradually worsened. Agency officers would not be surprised, entering the DCI's office, to find it steamy as a Turkish bath, humidifiers running incessantly, while the boss sat in slippers, swaddled in blankets. Dick Helms had seen Dulles like that back in Germany at the end of World War II. Ray Cline observed him this way on Navy Hill in the mid-1950s. Cline, a senior analyst with the Office of Current Intelligence, accompanied his boss Huntington Sheldon when they went to the DCI's office for Dulles to review briefing drafts to be presented at NSC meetings.

It would be late in the day. Dulles, tired, his glasses pushed up on his forehead, held the papers in gnarled hands about nine inches before his nose. Darkness gathered. Sometimes he would have a swath wrapped about his head. The image is of a swami with his crystal ball. The spy chieftain typically rejected more than half the material, complaining about quality, and rambled on. DDCI Cabell, national estimates chief Sherman Kent, and DDI Bob Amory often sat in on these séances, which sometimes lasted into the night.

But here, in 1956 to be precise, Cline witnessed Director Dulles at a key moment in Cold War history. At the Twentieth Congress of the Communist Party of the Soviet Union, Russian leader Nikita Khrushchev denounced the methods of his predecessor, Joseph Stalin, most especially Stalin's personality cult. Khrushchev spoke privately to an audience of top Communist leaders in February, even as Allen circled the globe on one of his most celebrated cruises.

When he got back, Dulles demanded that his operatives search high and low for the Khrushchev speech, of which the CIA had heard only rumors. Clandestine service work brought in the explosive text. Director Dulles recalls the episode as one of the high points of his CIA career. Suspecting there must be a prepared text, that Khrushchev's denunciation had been too long and too detailed to have been an extemporaneous sally, Allen ordered a hunt for the document. Different versions—not necessarily conflicting—claim that the text came from a Polish Communist official, from a senior member of the Italian Communist party, or from the Israeli secret service Shin Bet. Jim Angleton had sources in both Italy and Israel, and many Polish Jews had immigrated to Israel but still had ties in the old country. Israeli historians offer yet another version: the journalist Philip Ben of *Le Monde* obtained the text from Warsaw Communist party chief Stefan Staszewski, passed it on to a different Israeli spy service, the Mossad, and Israeli intelligence gave it to the CIA.

You can almost hear Dulles whistle.

In some versions, Allen's Turkish bath was going when he decided to push a political warfare button. Ray Cline had been senior manager for the national estimates analysts, work that brought him into contact with CIA directors and eventually White House aides. That led to his post at the head of the agency's current intelligence shop and, because of his expertise on the Russians, the assignment to help authenticate this speech. Spooks were torn between saying nothing, preserving the security of their source, and revealing the speech to score propaganda points. Frank Wisner and

James Angleton insisted on secrecy. They wanted to "exploit" the speech, leaking portions at key moments. Cline argued for opening it up.

On Saturday, June 2, 1956, with Cline in the DCI's office helping Dulles with a speech, the director probed him on his views. Cline recited them. With a twinkle in his eye, Allen suddenly exclaimed, "By golly, I am going to make a policy decision!"

This sounds dramatic—the CIA is not supposed to make policy—but Allen had not been candid. Long before Cline remembers this happening, Mr. Dulles sent a full copy of the Khrushchev speech to presidential staff secretary Andrew Goodpaster. Indeed, he had sent an advance copy on May 17 and a revised version at month's end. It is unthinkable that Dulles would have made a decision of this importance without consulting President Eisenhower. Moreover, the form that the revelation took—publication of the full Khrushchev text in the *State Department Bulletin* plus an attention-drawing prior leak to the *New York Times*—could not have been done without Ike's approval.

Weeks later, the fact that the British Broadcast Corporation had put passages of the speech on its airwaves occasioned comment at Dulles's staff meetings.

Deception in this simple recounting of an historic incident, unfortunately, is something that became endemic. Justified in the first instance by appeals for necessary operational security, and enshrined by a law known as the Central Intelligence Agency Act, which awarded the CIA director a mission to protect "sources and methods," over time legitimate purpose became distorted. Deception misled enemies, but it also cloaked faults. The inclination to report events in ways that reflected favorably on U.S. intelligence became overwhelming, substituting for protection of national security.

Keeping to this predilection for predigested "history," in 2011 official agency historians produced a review of covert operations that purported to analyze the record. It concluded that nearly *80 percent* of CIA interventions had had the goal of promoting and protecting democracy. Both the Iran and Guatemala operations—Allen Dulles's signal successes—produced dictatorships. The half-assed Congo intervention also led to dictatorship. No CIA action on Dulles's watch installed a democratic system. The interventions in Japan and the Philippines had the effect of *preventing* democratic movements from exercising political rights. In France and Italy, the CIA actively manipulated existing democratic systems to obstruct the emergence of leftist sentiment. Those covert ops were about *restricting* the political spectrum in foreign lands, not fostering democracy. The United Nations charter, to which the United States subscribes as treaty law, prohibits intervention in the internal affairs of other nations. The most charitable observation is that CIA historians must have focused simply on advocates' goals articulated, not substantive outcomes; or perhaps they employed a highly contrived notion of "democracy."

For now, the important point is that Dwight Eisenhower relied on the CIA for political intervention more than any postwar president until Ronald Reagan, so a substantial proportion of the instances analyzed took place on Dulles's watch.

In the 1970s, the agency attracted considerable criticism for its handling of journalists. The critics focused on the CIA's "Wurlitzer"—its use of the media to plant stories to orchestrate global deceptions. The Khrushchev speech is one example. Another facet was use of media to lend "cover," or identity protection, to covert operatives. Almost ignored, the agency's massaging of its own image through relations with journalists, columnists, and editors is equally insidious. This, too, began under Allen Dulles. What the media said about the agency became a frequent topic at the deputies meetings where Director Dulles held forth. For example, on Halloween 1956, the DCI complained of a "scurrilous" profile of him and commentary on the CIA that had appeared in a British magazine. Someone noted that the American general Claire Chennault, who had sold the CIA one of its proprietaries, sat on the magazine's executive council. Dulles promptly ordained that the next time anyone saw Chennault, he ought to be told, "He is in bad company," referring to the offending writer. Likewise, Allen's associate Frank Wisner was notorious for wanting to get out a reply anytime he saw something annoying, and Wisner would personally telephone journalists and tell them off. He spent long hours laboring over the texts of releases the agency might promulgate to counter bad publicity.

The temptation to curry public favor by selective revelation was seldom resisted, and a habit of deep, reflexive secrecy became engrained. The deceptive approach is also apparent with respect to CIA covert operations—as Mr. Dulles well knew. It extended even to phone conversations with his brother Foster, in which they commonly parsed their language in referring to locales of CIA projects (for example, that "matter on the other side of the world" for Indonesia).

Agency projects were often of indeterminate value. One such would be the WIN fiasco in Poland. WIN stood for Wolność i Niepodległość, or

Freedom and Independence, and represented the rump of the secret army of World War II. General Anders, with whom Allen had met, led the Polish veterans association, WIN's supporters in the West. A London office claimed five hundred full-time fighters in Poland, another twenty thousand semi-active partisans, and a hundred thousand sympathizers. These partisans would take to the field if war came. They just needed money, weapons, radios—the usual stuff. The British were WIN's first patrons but gave up the game. Frank Wisner took over in February 1949. OPC knew WIN as BE/Duffy. In Berlin the CIA made arrangements to smuggle people and small consignments into Poland under the cryptonym BE/King.

WIN exfiltrators arrived with specific requests. The Pentagon loved the idea of a Polish underground to contest the westward march of Soviet reinforcements in war. But the entire operation, front to back, had been a Soviet intelligence snare. The Russians had rolled up the real WIN years earlier. They kept some Poles around for just this kind of lure, played out into 1952. By then the CIA had furnished more than a million dollars in gold coins, revealed NATO war plans, and handed over state-of-the-art spy gear. When the CIA asked its WIN agents to nominate key choke points for NATO air bombardment the Soviets decided the game was up. Give true targets and they'd be baring their own plans; listing phony ones would unmask the deception, for the locations of transportation hubs could be verified. In late December, the scandal blew wide open when Radio Warsaw broadcast "confessions" from its fictive CIA agents and Poland opened a show trial.

This outcome plagued the secret warriors, Allen Dulles especially. In OSS days, back in Switzerland, he had worked with the leftist do-gooder and accused Soviet spy Noel Field. Fast forward to the late 1940s: Soviet security arrested Field, living in Prague, accusing him of being a CIA spy, making him the basis for trials Stalin used to impose new leadership in the Czech and Hungarian Communist parties and to wipe out Russian competitors for political power. The WIN disaster had all those features.

Fallout did not end there. State Department official Robert P. Joyce drafted a memorandum that amounted to an indictment of the whole covert ops technique. Joyce, witting because he had long served as the State representative or alternate on the 10/2 Panel, approving covert ops proposals, knew the drill. More than that, Joyce had been a friend to CIA. He'd been a housemate of Allen's in the Wiesbaden champagne winery and an OSS operative in Yugoslavia. Joyce had gotten an education in secret warfare.

At this moment, New Year's Eve 1952, State had yet to learn whether the United States would be able to keep its Warsaw embassy at all. Poland could have broken diplomatic relations. Joyce conceded the U.S. military interest in disrupting Russian reinforcements, attributing to this much of CIA's effort in WIN. But OPC had begun the game in 1949—before NATO existed—and officials at CIA and State, too, had warned against wishful thinking. Yet in the heat of action, State had not done enough to turn back pressures for continuation. The Psychological Strategy Board had never crafted a major plan for Poland, and its supervisory panel had looked at the WIN project only as part of its broadbrush review. Joyce analyzed tactics too: the Soviets had Eastern Europe so well wired that, given available contacts and techniques, operating there had become impossible. No resistance organization could survive.

Bob Joyce had been an early proponent of OPC action, a supporter of the Albania failure, but the WIN fiasco completed his turn to opposition. A month later, Joyce filed an even more scathing indictment. He argued that CIA operations were less and less geared to diplomatic strategy or policy objectives, receiving insufficient guidance to support national interests. More than that, Wisner's unit had tried to do too much, too quickly, with inadequate staffing, and with characteristic American impatience.

Evident failure plus internal criticism put the CIA in jeopardy. Allen Dulles wanted victories to make his case. Whereas Bob Joyce believed them overemphasized, President Eisenhower wanted even more covert ops. In 1953–55, Eisenhower's first years, a succession of these occurred, in Iran, Guatemala, and South Vietnam. In each, the project fell apart in key respects. Yet shaping up as failures, they suddenly succeeded. For TP/Ajax, the scheme to overthrow the legally constituted government of Iranian prime minister Mohammed Mossadegh, mounted in conjunction with the British MI-6, agency-recruited crowds failed to move the Iranian military. In PB/Success in Guatemala, the CIA-organized rebel army largely ran away. In both operations, however, the targeted enemies lost their nerve and were swept away. Allen Dulles framed the results as unalloyed victories. The next year, 1955, the agency engineered devastation in Saigon as part of a series of armed political maneuvers that cemented the power of South Vietnamese leader Ngo Dinh Diem. The CIA coups, in effect, were acts of political terraforming.

Kermit Roosevelt, the CIA's Iran mastermind, received the National Security Medal, the spy's equivalent of the Medal of Honor. To shape the picture reaching the public, Director Dulles prevailed on the *New York Times* to recall its own correspondent from Guatemala and had other journalists report doctored news from Iran. Later Dulles gave interviews to reporters preparing an article on the agency for the *Saturday Evening Post*. Both operations entered CIA lore as glorious. Both came back to bite.

The president empaneled an outside review under General James Doolittle to look specifically at covert operations, and the Doolittle survey gave the agency a clean bill of health. The appraisers wanted the agency to be as tough as they imagined the Russians to be. In private, with Eisenhower, Doolittle questioned keeping Allen Dulles. After all, Foster was secretary of state, and that smacked of undue influence. Ike replied that he would keep Allen, warts and all.

Not about to start a hot war with the Russians, Ike sought to disrupt their control mechanisms and turn back Soviet expansion. But the tool created to fight the Russians in Europe was turned against the Third World. Iran and Guatemala were only the first wave.

The Eisenhower years saw CIA operations aimed at Syria, Iraq, Lebanon, Indonesia, Tibet, China, and the Congo. None succeeded. There were political actions in the Philippines, Italy, and France. Psychological Strategy Board plans for Japan barely got off the ground, but CIA operated there too. It accumulated a spotty record, relatively successful in Japan and the Philippines, but with varying outcomes elsewhere.

Upheavals in the Soviet bloc, when they occurred, were spontaneous. In East Berlin in 1953, the CIA refused help to anti-Soviet rioters. Eisenhower approved a policy on disrupting Soviet influence—and his NSC machinery churned out reports on what had been done to further these goals. Radio Free Europe started Operation Veto to foment long-term resistance in Hungary. Operation Focus succeeded it. The agency periodically issued directives to RFE on broadcast themes. But when Budapest rose against the Soviets in 1956, RFE denied that it had had any role, and the Eisenhower administration insisted that no one had encouraged the rebels, whom the Russians repressed brutally. Internal CIA reports admitted a handful of minor infractions only—all related to the personal views of RFE broadcasters or to misinterpretation of their remarks. Here CIA had served policy, but Eisenhower's goals far exceeded practical capabilities.

This is a good place to dispose of the fiction that the CIA does not participate in policy making. Director Dulles made a joke of that in the matter of Khrushchev's speech, but the assertion is both oft-reiterated and wrong. The agency does more than speak truth to power, the standard articulation of its role. Once begun, any covert operation becomes a feature of U.S. policy, and the agency wants a say in strategy. In addition, obtaining, preparing, and maintaining the bases to mount operations requires arrangements with foreign nations and necessarily entails policy measures. The mere existence of and desire for such bases drives policy too. Here are examples from Allen Dulles's time: CIA's success in planting a pro-U.S. government in Guatemala led to the idea that a country could be used as base for CIA-armed forces to overthrow Fidel Castro. The agency planned to do so, and the president went along.

The U-2 spy plane furnishes another example. This overhead reconnaissance program required regional main bases (in the United Kingdom, Turkey, the Republic of China, and Japan) and temporary operating bases elsewhere (Norway, West Germany, and Pakistan). Access to, and overflight rights from, all these places were matters for diplomatic negotiation, success of which directly concerned the CIA. Aid money, military assistance, private information, and other special arrangements accommodated the foreign allies that the CIA required.

Dulles's very important bureaucratic advantage—his brother John Foster as secretary of state—usually trumped the opposition. The brothers privately arranged for many sorts of mutual support, conversed informally at each other's homes, and came to each other's aid at NSC meetings. This extraordinary circumstance endured through most of the Eisenhower years, until 1958, when Foster developed cancer.

Allen never seemed so engaged as when he dealt with clandestine service matters, though there, too, he did not prove especially prescient. Once, with a CIA covert operation under way, he bet Treasury Secretary George Humphrey $3 that Egyptian leader Gamal Abdel Nasser would be ousted within a matter of months. In the fall of 1957, Dulles had to pay up. Nasser remained at the head of Egypt for another decade. No matter. It would be under Dulles that the CIA acquired the shape and missions that sustained it into a distant future. Every cycle he could, Allen would address those graduating from CIA spy training. He told them the story of missing the contact he might have made with Vladimir Lenin. The point was constant vigilance. All of them should be Great White Case Officers.

LANGLEY OR BUST

Allen Dulles built a real house for the Central Intelligence Agency. Long before he moved up Navy Hill to the DCI's office, Dulles knew the deleterious effects of officers' scattered existence in seedy buildings. The "temps" down by the Reflecting Pool were awful. Wags cracked that even the repairs needed repairs. And the walk up Navy Hill could take ten minutes or more. In the rain or with snow, that could be miserable. Beetle Smith's people told him that agency personnel were scattered among twenty-seven buildings all over town. In Vandenberg and Hillenkoetter's day, it had already been ten. As early as 1951, cramped office space had made OPC reluctant to hire more people.

General Smith set out to do something. Congress appropriated a bit of money. The old-timers' tale is that a cost-conscious legislator, seeing an unidentified budget line item, cut it. Meetings on a new building took place in 1952, but with the demands of the Korean War Director Smith put aside the issue, and he soon left.

Allen Dulles got a wake-up call one morning when President Eisenhower became lost on the road to CIA, hardly a ten-minute drive from the White House. It had been a spur-of-the-moment thing. Ike volunteered to drop brother Milton at the agency. He gave his Secret Service detail no notice, and his driver had no inkling that the CIA building lay behind a fence with a sign reading Government Printing Office. Despite its nearby location, and the fact that Washington tour buses routinely stopped in front of the "Printing Office" to proclaim it the most secret of agencies, Ike had to telephone Allen for directions. For the short term, Mr. Dulles ordered a new sign that actually identified the Central Intelligence Agency. The larger solution would be a new building. Director Dulles hoped Ike would be a supporter. He was.

In *The Craft of Intelligence*, Allen tells that story to make the point that he favored openness, a minimum of secrecy for the CIA. But the immediate problem was a new home. Early one Saturday morning, Ike summoned Dulles, who took Red White with him. It was May 7, 1955. At the White House, the president told his spy chief that the District of Columbia was absolutely off limits. He wanted agency headquarters located in the direction the government planned to relocate in case of a nuclear attack—to the west. Ike and Dulles discussed one tract in Alexandria (technically, south, not west) and another in Falls Church as the most promising alternatives.

Under Washington urban design rules, the National Capitol Regional Planning Council had to approve land use. In April 1955, after opposition from local residents, the CIA announced it had given up on the Falls Church tract. The agency looked at a property that had belonged to the defunct Heurich Brewery, now occupied by the Kennedy Center for the Performing Arts.

But Allen discussed the Falls Church site with Eisenhower anyway, as it conformed more closely with Ike's preferences. Suddenly, in late June, the CIA reversed itself.

Citizens excoriated the agency's sudden reversals, arguing that Fairfax County was already challenged in providing water, sewer and other services. In the summer of 1955 residents of the Langley–Great Falls area protested to the Speaker of the House shortly after Mr. Dulles appeared to testify in behalf of a $54.5 million ($492 million in 2016) appropriation. According to Dulles, in July 1955 the boards of Fairfax and Arlington counties, the Falls Church City Council, and the Fairfax County Planning Commission all endorsed the plan. But that spring the McLean Citizens Association not only had voted against any CIA complex, it had defeated an alternate resolution making approval contingent on the United States paying every bill entailed in creating the support infrastructure. Agency inspector general Lyman Kirkpatrick lived in that neighborhood, and folks gave him an earful.

Among urban planners, National Capital Regional Planning Council chairman Max S. Wehrly dissented from the majority report approving the McLean site. Wehrly, executive director of the Urban Land Institute and an authority on land use and taxation, believed the CIA's complex would have a greater local impact on McLean than building it anywhere else in Fairfax. Among other things, the county would have to rewrite its just-completed master plan. Counting service workers, the CIA facility could be expected to bring in more than 22,000 new people daily. Estimates were that less than a tenth of them lived in the Virginia suburbs already. The water treatment plant then being funded was designed to service only 7,500 residents. There were legal complications relating to Arlington furnishing more water to Falls Church. In addition, accommodating CIA headquarters required extension, improvement, or both, of the George Washington Memorial Parkway and two other roads. Government spent $8.5 million ($76.6 million in 2016) to extend the parkway from Sprout Run to Langley's Route 123.

Wehrly lost the fight. Toward the end of the year, a regional council member from Alexandria passed away. That left an alternate delegate from Falls Church, who liked the idea, to cast his vote in favor of the McLean location. The plan passed the planning commission, a local group that worked with the council, on December 5. The national authority approved the final plans on February 3, 1956. Had one vote changed at either level, the outcome would have been a tie—with the plan rejected.

The land that became Allen's "campus" had belonged to Joseph Leiter, a Chicago tycoon who died in 1932. The Treasury seized his thirty-two-room "country" house, abandoned a few years later, in settlement of tax debts. The house burned down in 1945. About a hundred acres in addition to the Leiter property completed the CIA complex, in the place called Langley, Virginia.

Red White recalls that Allen and he spent long hours making arrangements. The new building would have central heating and air-conditioning. It was Dulles who shielded Red from the wrath of Wild Bill Donovan, whom he first met here. Donovan lobbied White to select a particular builder and a site in southeast Washington. Deputy director White knew Wild Bill had once headed the Public Buildings Service and well knew the contracting procedures, which precluded the end run Donovan proposed. The badgering continued until Allen rebuffed his old boss.

To avoid more shenanigans, Dulles selected Harrison and Abramowitz as lead architects. They worked with an inside unit of the Office of Support under Anthony T. Zaia, who could interpret design and engineering-ese for the other spooks. An agency committee made wish lists. Walter Jessel, DO officer and records specialist, convinced the architects to provide a system of pneumatic tubes to carry paper—and later punched cards—throughout the facility. The advent of the computer rendered that quaint very soon but, more important, he won the day on including conduits to carry future electric and electronic cables, which made all the difference when computers came. Dulles often began staff meetings with progress updates. Dick Helms, who attended them, recalled, "We sometimes thought he was trying to build it with his own hands, brick by brick."

The Cold War continued at high intensity as construction began. The Soviet Union launched Sputnik, the first space satellite, in October 1957, the same month that ground clearing commenced at Langley. The country's leaders were consumed by the "missile gap" intelligence dispute in the summer of 1958 when grading and drainage site preparations were finished—in the face of some of the worst snowstorms and summer rainfall in Washington in many years. Around that time, a C-118 aircraft (the same that had carried Allen on much of his world tour a couple of years earlier), pressed into service for a reconnaissance mission along the Russo-Turkish border, blundered into Soviet airspace and was shot down.

Construction arrangements were completed at the end of 1958. The contract, awarded in March 1959, came within a week of the day the CIA helped spirit the Dalai Lama out of Lhasa, a part of its secret war in Tibet. Harrison and Abramowitz had designed the United Nations complex in New York. The Tibetans and their American sympathizers pushed for a UN hearing. Superstructure work began in May; the missile gap had grown worse by then. Lincoln White faced repeated prodding from Pentagon potentates to install deep bunkers and shelters underneath Langley headquarters. But practically no one at the CIA believed in surviving a nuclear war. White stood his ground, and here, too, Director Dulles's interventions proved vital.

The design for the Langley building provided for 1,400,000 square feet and facilitated CIA secrecy. Open and clandestine services employees transited the same lobby but entered a half of the building dedicated to their own work. Officers hardly ever crossed cultures. Even at meals, the cafeteria had been arranged so that a central kitchen served the DDP people on one side, and the rest of the crew on the other. No one crossed over to lunch together except by arrangement. Exchanges between the open and clandestine sides of the agency were strictly monitored. The building would be completed in 1961. By then Allen Dulles was in crisis.

Deputy Director Lincoln White anticipated that the Central Intelligence Agency would build its headquarters and then have a gala opening. Director Dulles wanted a cornerstone laying instead. Several times the boss returned to this. His deputy for administration, shuddering at the work he'd have to do for that, dragged his feet. After doing this dance a few times, White openly suggested the combined cornerstone and dedication ceremonies. Dulles nixed that.

"Red," Allen exclaimed, "you know you have to have a cornerstone to hold up the building."

"The cornerstone doesn't really hold up anything," Lincoln White riposted.

But White really stirred Allen up when he suggested that, once the headquarters had been finished, they could put up a bronze plaque with everyone's name on it.

"You have apparently forgotten that we are about to have a presidential election." Dulles loomed, very serious. "After [that] I may not be director. I want my name on that cornerstone and I don't want it on some bronze plaque that somebody can take down."

The part about Allen Dulles mulling over his legacy may not, or may, be accurate—Lincoln White's reputation was as an honest man to a fault—but it has to be true that by this point Dulles worried about top cover for the CIA. There was lingering anger toward the agency over the Hungarian uprising, either at the presumed U.S. role in stirring up trouble and then standing aside or at the feeble efforts made to help simple people uprooted by tragedy. In Venezuela in 1958, Vice President Nixon had been ambushed by rioting much like El Bogotazo. An ambitious CIA gambit to overthrow Indonesian leader Sukarno failed miserably. Eisenhower now had a watchdog group monitoring U.S. intelligence, and it was scathing on the planning and conduct of the Indonesia project. Soviet leader Nikita Khrushchev came to America for a visit in the fall of 1959, encountering Allen in the receiving line at a White House dinner. Even Khrushchev could throw subtle daggers, and he countered Dulles's sally about CIA reports on Russia with the quip that, "I believe we get the same reports, and probably from the same people."

The dynamic duo of Allen and John Foster Dulles had broken, however, ruptured by Foster's cancer. The secretary of state made his last foreign trip in January 1959; by April he felt so sick, he had to resign. Foster died on May 24. Christian Herter replaced him. That changeover proved less detrimental to CIA interests than it could have been, because Herter had long been Allen's friend. They had met as far back as 1919, during the Versailles conference, where they worked in close harmony. Later, in 1947, with Herter a congressman from Massachusetts, he had Allen consult with his committee on the Marshall Plan. Dulles and Herter were not what Allen and Foster had been, but they were mutually helpful all the same. However, Herter lacked the bureaucratic base to protect the CIA, and worse, whereas Foster had been a crusader willing to overlook peccadillos, Herter was a stickler for rules.

Dwight D. Eisenhower enjoyed the Dalai Lama rescue. CIA operatives had included a cameraman of amazing dexterity in their special team, sent to assist the holy man's exfiltration to India in 1959 during a revolt against Chinese rule. His film had been edited into a movie screened at the White House. Ike now spent most of the time he devoted to intelligence on the U-2 flights—approving flight plans, reviewing the take. The mercurial president expressed fury at the continual delays and disasters in the CIA's development of a photo reconnaissance satellite. As Director Dulles saw it, an event that brought Eisenhower to the CIA amid pomp and ceremony, with Ike expected to strike a positive chord, had to be helpful.

Allen got his way. A cornerstone laying took place at Langley on

November 3, 1959. The Central Intelligence Agency proposed that the president should preside over the event, and it soon appeared on his calendar. Accounts differ on Ike's enthusiasm. There is evidence that he insisted on no speech, but naturally that didn't fly. His remarks, directed more at CIA officers' roles than at the agency's achievements, recognized that although "the work of this agency demands of its members the highest order of dedication, ability, trustworthiness and selflessness, . . . their reward can be little except the conviction they are performing a unique and indispensable service for their country."

Ike meanwhile wrestled with the question of what to do about Cuba, whose pro-American dictator, Fulgencio Batista, had been overthrown at the outset of 1959. The revolutionary government of Fidel Castro exhibited amorphous tendencies toward socialism. The question on officials' minds became "Is he communist?" Vice President Richard Nixon met Castro during the latter's visit to America, slightly ahead of Khrushchev. Nixon decided that Castro *was* communist and circulated a memo arguing the case.

Director Dulles's line is disputed. Historians like Stephen Rabe and Bevan Sewell portray the CIA director as taking a more moderate position throughout 1958–59, maintaining that Castro was a pragmatist even though figures surrounding him might be communists. Agency officer Victor Marchetti, on the other hand, recounts Dulles personally intervening in intelligence analysis to rewrite reports, painting Castro's victory as unnatural and predicting a slaughter that would go beyond that of the French Revolution. Eisenhower refrained from acting until Cuba nationalized American businesses and property. In March 1960, when a cargo ship mysteriously blew up in Havana harbor, Washington accused Cuban communists of sabotage. Eisenhower broke diplomatic relations. He also ordered Dulles to craft a plan to topple Castro.

For one more brief moment, the Central Intelligence Agency rode on top of the world. Then, on May Day, one of its U-2 spy planes disappeared over Russia. The foolish cover story held that the plane, collecting weather data, went off course and fell apart. The Russians, who had shot it down, captured and exhibited cameras, film, spy gear, and pilot Francis Gary Powers. The Soviets had a propaganda bonanza. Premier Khrushchev used the occasion to break up a summit conference about to take place in Paris. May 1, 1960, became another CIA fiasco.

—— ✦ ——

After that, Allen Dulles rode a bucking bronco. The spooks were blessed in August when their spy satellite Project Corona finally produced a workable photo platform. But that same month came rumbles in preparations for the Cuban operation, now too big for the agency to handle alone. President Eisenhower agreed to involve the U.S. military, providing Green Beret trainers to whip Cuban exile recruits into shape. A special program also canvassed the Air National Guard, eventually focusing on the Alabama air guard, for pilots and crewmen to help the Cubans learn to fly the B-26 bombers the CIA had obtained for the exile air force.

The new resources brought confidence, but for a sharp observer they should also have raised doubts. Throughout the 1950s, the agency had done best when reliant on its own resources. In those projects where the Directorate of Plans had had important inputs from the U.S. military—Indonesia, Korea, the Chinese offshore islands, Burma—the operations turned messy with reduced or no impact. On its own, the CIA had flubbed too, but at least there were also the "successes" of Iran and Guatemala.

Through the summer and into the fall, the CIA made efforts to get a partisan resistance going inside Cuba. Various exile groups were mobilized. Some sabotage took place. But the Castro security forces were vigilant and no resistance took hold. The CIA-supported infiltration program repeatedly failed to connect with any internal networks. In November, on the verge of that presidential election Director Dulles so feared, President Eisenhower suddenly demanded a recasting of the whole Cuba project—as a conventional invasion in support of partisans, who remained elusive. That should have raised doubts. Dulles simply moved ahead.

The 1960 election would bring John Fitzgerald Kennedy to the White House. Contrary to Allen's fears, JFK asked him to stay on at the agency. In fact, the defeated candidate, Richard Nixon, had he won, might have fired Dulles. Nixon expressed deep anger at the CIA in later years, believing that it had accorded Kennedy an unfair advantage in briefings while he, the vice president, fully aware of the covert operations, held his tongue in their televised debates where Kennedy advocated doing something about Castro. "I was faced with a heads-he-wins, tails-I-lose proposition," Mr. Nixon wrote in 1964. Had he revealed the covert op, "and point[ed] out that I had been one of its strongest advocates, I would pull the rug out from under Kennedy's position. But if I did so, the project would [have been] doomed." It is ironic that a Republican might have fired the Republican, Dulles, while a Democrat invited him to stay on. Allen happily agreed.

The Cuba operation, reframed as an invasion, had reached the top of the list—poised to destroy Dulles's leadership. The exile troops, now styled a "brigade," were ready to go. Nicaraguan and Guatemalan leaders who had made bases in their countries available to the CIA were restive and ready to be free of the foreign troops. Growing evidence from Cuba indicated that Castro had become aware of Project Ate and had begun taking countermeasures. Then came protests among the Cuban exile fighters, and troublemakers were isolated and confined while the operation took place. A covert ops planner in 1960–61 could plausibly have concluded that the Cuban project, cryptonym JM/Ate, had gone off track.

President Kennedy asked for reviews of Ate and got them. The reviews sounded optimistic but were subtly conditional. The Joint Chiefs of Staff were lukewarm. Kennedy, fearing diplomatic consequences, opted to reduce the invasion's "visibility." He tailored it in several ways that also reduced potential. At this point, CIA and military participants in this scheme really did entertain doubts. Allen Dulles might have too, but no one said anything. Nor did anyone say much when notices of the plot—still vague, but anticipating the use of Cuban exiles in an attempt to oust Fidel—began appearing in the press. The fact that news was out there did not provoke Kennedy to rethink CIA's entire scheme.

All this ended with the exile invasion on April 17, 1961. It took place at the Bahía de Cochinos, the Bay of Pigs. The beach, Playa Girón. Historians have dubbed it "the perfect failure" for a multiplicity of reasons. The question is, why did Allen not appreciate that? Instead, he helped contribute to the deception surrounding the operation, traveling to Puerto Rico with Clover to catch some rays and address the annual conference of the Young Presidents' Organization. While the trip had some value, it also made the CIA chief unavailable at the height of a key covert operation.

Details belong elsewhere, but there can be no doubt that the failure stripped Allen Dulles of his luster. Kennedy spoke of breaking the agency into a thousand pieces. He complained of CIA perfidy. He ordered a full-scale review of the flop, appointing Allen as one of the review group, partly to ensure that CIA security concerns were taken into account, but also to require Dulles to redo his sums, to sit through an exhaustive waltz through every imaginable aspect of this horror. Robert F. Kennedy, the president's brother, along with General Maxwell D. Taylor, the chairman—and JFK's special military assistant—ensured that White House interests were protected.

Later Mr. Dulles squirmed on the hook. The appearance of insider accounts from Arthur M. Schlesinger Jr. and Theodore Sorensen, plus Dick Bissell's July 1965 riposte to them, got Allen off the bench. But he split hairs to contrive some explanation for the mishap, only to leave multiple drafts on the cutting room floor. Instead, in *The Craft of Intelligence*, Allen wrote, "I have not commented on any details of the 1961 Cuban operation and do not propose to do so here." This refusal did not keep him from saying, in a different passage, that an account of the disaster based upon extended interviews with four of the key Cuban exile commanders had created a "new crop" of myths about the CIA. In fact the Cuban exiles' rendering had been on the money—and the agency had attempted to suppress it.

This botch terminated Allen Dulles at the CIA. The White House watchdog group known as the President's Foreign Intelligence Advisory Board, which Jack Kennedy had abolished but now brought back, recommended on July 18, 1961, that the CIA consider locating its clandestine service somewhere other than the new Langley headquarters. President Kennedy did not do that. He sought a replacement for Dulles and came up with John A. McCone. The president made one more concession to the long-serving spy chieftain. Kennedy agreed to take part in Langley's dedication. That took place on November 28, 1961. John McCone entered on duty the next day. Allen Dulles took home the National Security Medal as consolation prize. The cafeteria opened only in February 1962, the seventh-floor director's suite needed another month, and the last construction would be completed in November 1963. By then Allen Dulles was long gone.

So Allen Dulles the dreamer helped conceive a United States intelligence agency and breathed life into its form. Mr. Dulles built the house in which the CIA lived. But the detritus of disastrous operations gradually loomed over the glory of successful ones until the Bay of Pigs completed the undermining. Dulles's ghost seemed to teach "lessons"—most important for the CIA's future, that the mission was the thing, that anything else, including outside efforts at regulation, posed obstacles to be bypassed. That lesson proved misguided. Had JFK moved the agency's operations unit away from Langley, he might have avoided or reduced the impact of this lesson. On the personal level, the Dulles ghost reminds us that in spy work, as in few other arenas, one mistake can wipe away a lifetime of achievement. (This is *not* a claim that everything else Allen Dulles accomplished *was* an achievement, at least not in the positive sense.) Mr. Dulles learned that lesson too late. He may have been the first to inhabit the new headquarters, but his ghost moved in before Langley's doors ever opened.

On another level, it needs to be said that spying will always be a sensitive area, easily distorted by corruption—whether of the moral, material, or political variety—or stymied by inherent limitations of method, the difficulty of attaining goals, or indeed the unrealism of the goals themselves. A people really have no defense against repressive or renegade security agencies save for enforcing accountability, and that starts with personnel.

Unlike what Allen Dulles wrote about the secrecy of agency headquarters, his campus still operated under a cloak of deception. Until coming out of the closet in 1973, the George Washington Memorial Parkway exit that led to the back gate at CIA had a sign variously identifying it as leading to the Bureau of Public Roads, the Fairbanks Highway Research Station, or the Federal Highway Administration. It became an index of the rising controversy surrounding the agency that these phony road signs were stolen and exhibited on mantels all over the nation's capital. Indeed the cost of replacing highway signs became significant. Meanwhile, over time there developed a small group of intrepid CIAers, who lived on the Maryland side of the Potomac, commuting to work by canoe. That fulfilled a dream of another sort.

2

ZEALOTS AND SCHEMERS

"The social side was very important to Allen," observed Walter Pforzheimer, an early agency envoy to Capitol Hill. "Occasionally," Pforzheimer went on, "it warped his judgment." This was emblematic of an agency that well-connected journalist Stewart Alsop saw as run, in its infancy, by the Eastern establishment. The right schools, the right clubs, suitable World War II experience made all the difference. One CIA warrior who rose to command an important station captures the ethos in describing his own recruitment interview. His interlocutors asked him only three questions—describe the layout of the driveway at a certain elite school, identify the girl who had pursued everyone who went there, and reveal his favorite brand of scotch. Frank Gardiner Wisner was very much of that class and character—and in the end he could have benefited from Allen Dulles's exercise of prudence. Sometimes the contradictory forces overwhelm the individual. True believers labor in danger of permitting their yearning to override the essential moral compass. In Dulles's time, the danger rose from Frank Wisner's zealotry.

Officers cutting corners to achieve their ends—scheming—created equal peril. On the one hand, zealotry often flowed from purpose—in Wisner's case, saving innocents from the Communist hegemon. On the other, the zealotry could be more about a sense of superiority or superpatriotism or maybe just plain arrogance. These spies were both eager and ardent, displaying impressive fanaticism. For all his faults, Mr. Wisner had more good sense. Let's start with him.

THE SECRET WARRIOR . . .

In the war, Frank Wisner had served the OSS in Africa, Turkey, and Romania. Wild Bill's boys got in on the Middle East late, setting up only as Allied armies pursued a defeated enemy, so there was never that much to do out of Cairo, except try to gain a foothold in Turkey. The young Wisner, who clawed his way into the OSS because he hated pushing paper in a propaganda operation, pressed for the Turkey assignment. Istanbul and Ankara, though, had similarities to Cairo—less and less to do as the war became more remote. But Wisner stumbled into opportunity. While he cast feelers about, a Romanian delegation arrived with instructions to contact the West. Romania lay suspended between the belligerents, with Soviet armies smashing their way in, its alliance with Nazi Germany suddenly a liability. The Romanian plenipotentiaries sought a separate peace that might save them from the Russians. Frank Wisner correctly concluded that the Romanians were open to Western contacts.

The OSS operative obtained permission from Caserta, Italy, now agency headquarters for the Mediterranean, to infiltrate Romania. Wisner ingratiated himself with the Romanians in Turkey to cadge passage to their capital, Bucharest. He arrived there after the Germans had fled but before the Soviets arrived. For a few precious days, Frank found himself the senior Allied officer in a former enemy capital. All the Romanians dealt with him. Even more so because King Michael, chief of state, feared that the Russians would end his monarchy. So Wisner played potential savior, and when the Soviets arrived he postured as senior Allied representative. He and the small OSS team, who appeared later, sat in on Soviet interrogations of captured Germans and picked up Romanian information, including court gossip.

Wisner's network became one of the best in Donovan's agency. Robert P. Joyce, a future friend, then antagonist, who met Frank in Turkey, was among those impressed by the take. From Caserta, he and other OSSers expressed wonder at the reporting.

Frank Wisner enjoyed the time of his life. Connected to both the Romanian government and the royal family, even collecting pillow talk from royals and lovers, the OSS man truly had the inside scoop. It couldn't last, especially given Russian intentions. Early in 1945, the Soviets began rounding up Romanians of German extraction, even ethnics who might have been Romanian for generations; they were now sent to the Soviet Union. Everyone knew someone who needed saving. Wisner did what he could. In the spring, the Soviets moved against the royals. They emplaced a Communist government, then cracked down hard against spies. Wisner watched despairingly as the Russians loaded trains and sent them to the motherland. His wife Polly observed that watching the trains bound for labor camps probably shook Frank more than any other thing in life. Leaving Romania for Germany, for weeks after the surrender Wisner worked for Allen Dulles. In Paris he first met Richard Helms, another spook who would become a key colleague.

Later, in the United States, Frank returned to private life. Like Dulles and Donovan, Wisner briefly went back to the law, among a group of American spooks whom historian Hugh Wilford has dubbed the "Park Avenue cowboys." Wisner often lunched with one or another of the old OSS crowd—not just Allen Dulles, but also Donovan, William H. Jackson, William E. Colby, Gordon Gray, and others. Several were colleagues at his firm, Carter Ledyard & Milburn. Before the war, it was Gray who set up the interview at which Frank landed that job. But Wisner went to Washington in 1947 as assistant secretary of state for the occupied areas. There he joined George Kennan and Allen Dulles advocating for a unit to specialize in covert operations.

Wisner stood at the epicenter, personally responsible for the displaced persons (DPs), the whole diaspora from the East. One of his last acts at State, before moving over to CIA to take charge of the Office of Policy Coordination, had been to chair a review of policy for making use of Soviet refugees in the U.S. interest. At the CIA, the resulting program became known as Operation Bloodstone. In some ways, that effort encompassed a genuine bid to enlist Eastern Europeans and disaffected Soviets, but in a distressing array of cases, Bloodstone served to cover collaboration with former Nazis. In this respect, the project paralleled Operation Paperclip, in which the U.S. Army imported scientists who had worked in Nazi secret weapons programs to duplicate and improve those technologies for the United States.

Among the DPs, there were fewer Soviets than Nazis. Indeed, many "Russian" émigrés were really minorities, say Ukrainians, Balts, or Belorussians, restive under Soviet rule. A Ukrainian partisan army carried out active resistance against Moscow's forces. The famous Soviet marshal Georgi Zhukov commanded a postwar military campaign against them. In 1947 U.S. Army counterintelligence corps detachments in Germany were startled to encounter Ukrainians who had crossed Eastern Europe to make contact and beg for help. British intelligence already had an active project assisting partisans from the Baltic states—Latvia, Lithuania, and Estonia—which the Soviets had swallowed up at the end of the war.

Another strain among the *resistants* were the White Russians, remnants of the Whites who had fought the Reds (Communists, primarily of the

Bolshevik faction) in the Russian civil war of 1918–1921. White Russians played a role in the Far East and China, where they were of some peripheral importance. In Europe a plethora of émigré groups hustled their wares, with extravagant claims of intelligence knowledge or access to the homeland. The groups competed with one another for Western support. OPC came late to the scene, and before Frank Wisner could gear up, the chance to accomplish anything had evaporated even with active émigré groups.

This did not keep the CIA from getting into the game, however. Italy was its first important battlefield. Officer James McCargar, recently returned from work in Genoa for a shadowy military spy unit, wrote the twenty-page working paper that sketched the project, carried out by CIA's espionage unit. That impressed OPC chief Wisner, who recruited McCargar to be southeast Europe branch chief. When he began at headquarters, the OPC consisted of ten people—the director, a few officers, and some secretaries. The OSO, much bigger, resented the upstarts. Competition between them highlighted the early years, with the continued existence of the OPC hinging on its covert operations.

The first big move on Eastern Europeans at OPC came in Albania. The secret war that the CIA conducted there tottered, not halted even when Albania's Communist government captured OPC operatives and staged show trials late in 1951. That operation, Project BG/Fiend, had been betrayed to the Russians by Kim Philby, erstwhile Washington representative of Britain's MI-6, which was allied with the CIA in this paramilitary effort. Efforts to insert agent teams into Russia, in both the Ukraine and the Soviet-occupied Baltic states, were also joint ventures with MI-6 and also betrayed. The Polish project had been penetrated by Soviet security from the beginning. Mr. Dulles did not terminate it. Instead he sought to remedy the headaches of these failed projects with better preparations. And the OPC worked to expand resources for the paramilitary program by creating in Germany a supposed "labor" unit of displaced persons and recruits from all the "captive nations" who could be called upon for CIA operations.

When Allen Dulles joined the Central Intelligence Agency, a range of covert operations were already under way, not least his own Radios. A comparable effort in the Far East took form covered by the Asia Foundation, with Radio Free Asia and CIA funding under DT/Pillar. The "Wurlitzer" projects—the cultural Cold War—enjoyed some success. Agency programs funded intellectual journals like *Encounter,* a movie version of George

Orwell's *Animal Farm*, and later the publication and smuggling into Russia (and assistance in placing an edition in the West) of Boris Pasternak's novel *Doctor Zhivago*. Political actions worked sometimes and at others merely served to enrich politicians and influence peddlers. There were unilateral political actions and black propaganda missions aimed at the East German zone and East Berlin under a variety of cryptonyms.

Then there were the secret wars. With MI-6 again, in addition to Albania, the DDP, through Wisner, had ones under way in the Ukraine (AE/Carthage), Belarus (AE/Quor), Romania (QK/Broil), the Baltic states (AE/Freeman), and Russia itself (AE/Saurus and QK/Droop). The CIA, in conjunction with the Gehlen Organization, ran ops against Soviet intelligence in East Germany under the rubric of AE/Nidus.

There were projects for "stay behind" networks—advance recruiting and provision of equipment for agents who promised to act if the Soviets overran their countries. Known today as Gladio, after the Italian offshoot that was among the first revealed, these virtual secret armies had other code names then (TP/Apluck). They worked to an element at North Atlantic Treaty Organization headquarters called the Clandestine Planning Committee. The Italian secret service collaborated with the CIA in setting up this network, starting in 1951 with American weapons and training in Britain. Counterparts were formed in other western European countries. The Italian branch, built to exclude those with leftist tendencies, later became a reactionary hotbed. But in early Cold War years, the networks functioned because the prospective agents were doing little more than collecting stipends for staying in touch with agency contacts. All those were OPC initiatives.

Walter Bedell Smith grated on Wisner much as on Allen Dulles. But being further down the food chain—and serious rather than avuncular—Wisner couldn't afford Mr. Dulles's cavalier laughter. Within a week of coming on duty on October 7, 1950, Smith was cognizant of OPC's cozy suspension among State, Defense, and CIA. He did not put up with it. Smith simply announced that the Office of Policy Coordination belonged to him. The secretaries of state and defense kept mum. It was done. Agency officers were aghast.

Early on, General Smith created an Office of Training that became a jewel, giving the CIA the reputation of having the best junior officer program in government. OPC trainees went through it like everyone else. Smith did that without reference to Wisner. Then the general discovered that an OPC officer monitored the cables flowing into the director's office and left out the unflattering ones. Smith ended that quickly. "The operators are not going to decide what secret information I will see or not see," the boss declared. Bedell Smith and Wisner clashed during the director's reorganization of the intelligence directorate, with Wisner—alongside Allen Dulles—holding out for DDP folk to have as little to do with the analysts as possible.

General Smith pictured OPC as a sieve, spewing secrets to the press, if not the enemy. Agency people on the Georgetown party circuit were a particular irritation. Smith demanded a list—"I don't care if they are blabbing secrets or not." This was aimed squarely at Frank Wisner, who partied incessantly. In the summer of 1951, Willard Wyman, the latest OSO chief, thought DDP integration might be fine—if done by folding OPC into the Office of Special Operations—not the other way around. Frank Wisner might then be out of a job. But the Army man read the tea leaves. Toward the end of the year, Wyman returned to his service, taking up a combat command in Korea. Wisner emerged as winner of the OPC/OSO competition—as well as successor to the mantle of DDP. He had managed to evade the fire, but dozens of others left the CIA because of the merger. It became the biggest purge of operators until the middle 1970s, when James R. Schlesinger ordered a "drawdown" following the Vietnam War. When Wisner ascended to DDP, direct command at OPC went to another Army colonel, Kilbourne Johnston.

Integration was finally completed in August 1952. Bedell Smith still had the reins at CIA.

By that time Truman's Psychological Strategy Board had been working at inserting itself for a year. One of its most urgent projects dovetailed with Wisner's anti-Soviet efforts by looking at how "defectors" (displaced persons) might be mobilized for the Cold War. The Ford Foundation expressed an interest in helping to fund that, PSB passed it along to the agency, and the channels CIA used subsequently to help fund the Radios, the National Student Association, and some other activities were first established here. The PSB defector plans themselves were not quite finished when Dwight Eisenhower succeeded Harry Truman, but ultimately ended with the labor unit, called a "volunteer freedom corps" of émigrés, plus a provision for defectors to enlist in the U.S. military. Among PSB's more amusing sallies into straight psychological warfare, a pair of its experts read the script for CIA's projected animation *Animal Farm*. Both psywarriors found the movie's theme confusing and its story sequence nebulous. These objections failed to stop Wisner and the CIA.

Some board projects were much more consequential. Under code names "Clydesdale" and "Midiron" (parts of the "D-15" series of PSB schemes) there were operation plans aimed at reducing the power of Communist parties in Italy and France. The plans included encouraging the Italian and French governments to crack down on those parties themselves, measures for American operatives to directly discredit the foreign Communists, and provisions to utilize U.S. contracts extended under the Mutual Defense Assistance Program—the successor to Marshall Plan aid—to preferentially fund factories where non-Communist labor unions held power. Some suggestions for smearing local Communists were so offensive the State Department, when approving these plans, made its assent conditional on agreement of the U.S. ambassadors in Rome and Paris. That meant formation of backstropping units in those embassies to oversee implementation. The PSB plans were largely complete before the end of 1951, and a "Cloven" working group supervised field activity. Italian local elections late that year showed Communist strength, so the secret warriors knew more needed to be done. Frank Wisner represented the CIA when the Strategy Board met on these matters, with Gerry Miller, the operations directorate's European division chief, as his alternate.

With Wisner's electricity sparking fresh projects like an arcing circuit, General Smith worked on operational control. At one point, the balloon leaflet programs, uncontrollable, with unmeasurable impact, became ubiquitous. Smith rasped to OPC managers, "Kindly do not bring in here any more of those goddamned *balloon* projects of yours!"

The DCI's creation of a Project Review Committee was aimed at Wisner as much as Dulles, but Wisner's promotion had little impact on the burgeoning project list. General Smith countered with a new viceroy system: there would be five "overseas action centers"—in effect, fiefdoms—each with the director's "special representative." As proconsul for Europe, Bedell Smith tapped Lucian K. Truscott, an Army comrade he had known more than a decade. Truscott, who had met Smith at Fort Leavenworth, distinguished himself in Italy and France during World War II. He reined in some of OPC's more extravagant schemes.

Truscott and Bill Jackson exemplified a stream of personnel flowing into CIA in those days, as did Beetle Smith himself. The military lent officers who ran the OSO, led divisions and branches in OPC, and were up for all manner of things. Another was Lyman B. Kirkpatrick Jr. "Kirk" had been General Omar Bradley's OSS briefing officer during the northwest Europe campaign of 1944–45. He introduced Bill Jackson to the woman Jackson later married. Another Army buddy brought Kirkpatrick into what became the agency, but Jackson was his booster and Bedell Smith liked him too. Kirkpatrick and Allen Dulles were both members of Washington's exclusive Alibi Club. The thirty-four-year-old New Yorker—and Princeton football star—helped create a reports procedure at the CIA and a rudimentary electronic intelligence element. Kirkpatrick was leading an agency division when the director tapped him as executive assistant, serving as front man for the CIA chief. Kirk got one day to make the transition.

This is important because Lyman Kirkpatrick became Wisner's competitor. Controlling the OPC/OSO merger seemed deadly serious. Director Smith thought so. But Beetle also thought it unseemly to have the chief of either entity supervise their integration. He gave the job to Kirkpatrick, making him deputy assistant director under Willard Wyman. Merger began with DDP's Latin America Division, which had the fewest active projects. Kirkpatrick found himself in the soup, with the OPC/OSO feud raging around him. There were conceptual problems, and the primacy of the sides' detachments and stations in various places all had to be considered. As a first step, Kirk suggested consolidating common elements, like communications and clerical work. Kilbourne Johnston and Kirkpatrick agreed, and set off on a "cruise." At each station, the two explained how the new directorate would function. After they returned to Washington, General Smith reinforced the message, after which Kirkpatrick made another cruise, this one to Europe.

Suddenly, in the middle of it all, on July 20, 1952, Kirk woke up to nausea and a splitting headache. It developed he had been struck by poliomyelitis, and a week into the sickness progressive paralysis engulfed him. It is thought but not known that he might have contracted the disease in Thailand during his initial cruise. A stay in the hospital marked the onset of a lengthy sickness and rehabilitation that left Kirkpatrick in a wheelchair and partially crippled. He returned to duty in late March 1953. By then Dwight D. Eisenhower had become president and Beetle Smith had answered Ike's call to go to the State Department. General Smith recommended Lyman Kirkpatrick for DDP. But Allen Dulles, now director, insisted on his own people, and President Eisenhower had no problem with that. Dulles chose to leave Frank Wisner at the head of the directorate. As consolation prize, Dulles made Lyman B. Kirkpatrick inspector general. The fates put Kirk where his presence would have consequences.

Director Smith wrote to Willard Wyman in the Far East. Wyman had gone to command troops in Korea. Smith asked if he'd seen Kirkpatrick and Johnston, then cruising his neck of the woods. Wyman's reply is unrecorded, but the DCI's letter and his officials' cruise there signify intense CIA interest. Wisner had the helm. The deputy director for plans had arrived at a moment the United States found itself embroiled in the Chinese civil war, and war in Korea followed the nationalists' withdrawal from the mainland to Taiwan.

East Asian operations were stock in trade for OPC. In mid-1949, the Office of Policy Coordination had had 450 personnel; a year after that, 584. In 1951 there would be 1,531. By 1952 OPC had 2,812 officers on staff, another 3,142 contract personnel overseas, and a budget of $82 million, with forty-seven stations abroad. Most of that growth had been in paramilitary slots in the Far East. Put differently, following the outbreak of the Korean War, the OPC tripled in size—and then tripled again. It also acquired the proprietary called CAT (Civil Air Transport, later known as Air America). After the DDP integration, resources actually increased because the operators could now pull in money from the former espionage arm.

The Pentagon suggested that the Chinese, who had intervened in Korea, could be distracted by CIA-supported raids elsewhere. At the National Security Council, Director Smith spoke against that proposition, but he had no vote while Dean Acheson and Louis Johnson, the nation's top diplomat and the Pentagon chief, were in favor. Harry Truman gave the CIA its marching orders. Directive NSC-101 provided for vigorous assistance to anti-Communist guerrilla forces; NSC-118, for disruption of Chinese supply lines.

At OPC one of the military crowd, Colonel Richard W. Stilwell, led the Far East Division. He had joined after a stint as military attaché in Italy, seeing CIA's Italian political action up close. Stilwell conducted the first big Korean War support operation. He started largely from scratch. A fresh OPC station chief reached Tokyo to discover that his whole force consisted of half a dozen guys living out of a hotel room, in contrast to the much more numerous OSO station run out of Yokosuka. Stilwell recruited from his old Army unit, the 90th Infantry Division, so his China Branch chief, William DePuy, had been an Army comrade too. Other stalwarts included Desmond FitzGerald, division deputy chief, a vet of the Army's war in Burma; Carl Eifler, who had led the OSS detachment there; and Robert Barrow, a young officer who rose to Marine Corps commandant. Hans Tofte, OSS supply organizer for Yugoslavia, established a CIA compound at Atsugi Air Base, Japan. It employed a thousand people.

Stilwell devised a two-part scheme. One was to have Nationalist Chinese troops who had fled to northern Burma (Myanmar) invade China from the south. Southeast Asia Supply Company, or SEA Supply, which supplied activities in Burma and elsewhere, backed the forays from Bangkok. The Nationalist leader Li Mi had lengthy meetings with U.S. Marine General Graves B. Erskine in Bangkok in September 1950 to arrange arms shipments. But the Li Mi mission's radioman turned out to be a spy. Nationalist incursions from Burma were smashed.

Another prong was to give Nationalist troops and Koreans CIA weapons and training and have them launch raids along the coast. Western Enterprises on Taiwan, controlled by Colonel Eifler, sparkplugged the effort. The pattern in Korea was for the CIA or military special operations forces to recruit locals and make bases on offshore islands from which they mounted the raids. A parallel CIA operation on Taiwan replicated this formula. The American spooks flung raids at the mainland, this time from Chinese offshore islands, but with little visible effect. The raids reached the size of small-scale conventional invasions—a few thousand troops at a time. They were abandoned in 1951 after the collapse of the largest one yet.

Branch chief DePuy believed Nationalist Chinese claims that there were a million anti-Communist partisans on the mainland. Wisner and Stilwell— and George Aurell after them—first thought that the Nationalists had half a million guerrillas who needed only weapons to take the field. The agency spent $152 million (some $1.4 billion in 2016) on arms and ammunition. Another $28 million ($255 million today) went for a CIA training base on the Pacific island of Saipan. From 1951 to 1953, the CIA infiltrated 212 Chinese Nationalist agents onto the mainland. Every one was captured or killed. Two CIA operatives alongside them, John T. Downey and Richard Fecteau, captured during an air landing, spent decades in Chinese prisons. None of the raids or spy missions was ever connected with anyone. They achieved nothing. Director Smith—and Frank Wisner—learned painfully that amateurs are not suited for large-scale military operations. It was a lesson that Wisner and the CIA would need to learn again.

Relations between the Central Intelligence Agency and U.S. military commands remained controversial throughout the war. At the Washington level, NSC and the departments labored over command relationships for peacetime, limited war, and global conflict. In the field, a succession of CIA entities tried to either lead the effort or coordinate between spooks and soldiers. In Tokyo there appeared the euphemistically named Documents Research Division. With the OPC/OSO merger came the North Asia Command. Stilwell went back to the military, his place at the integrated Far East Division taken by George Aurell, a CIA professional. By then a unit called Covert Clandestine and Related Activities Korea (CCRAK) controlled operations. The CIA assisted the military in creating partisan bands to fight behind Chinese and North Korean lines, and it ran a similar activity on its own plus a project to infiltrate spies into the enemy camp. None of it proved very successful.

Washington regarded the Korean and Chinese projects as a species of guerrilla or counterguerrilla warfare. Guerrilla warfare became an NSC preoccupation, resulting in policy papers and Psychological Strategy Board attention. The PSB plan for a Southeast Asian strategy, "D-23," became one of those crippled by disputes over definitions and goals. The board's "I" panel wrestled with the planning. Insurgencies then raged in several places. PSB staff had to intervene to preserve a role for covert operations in the policy paper. The United States chose to intervene in French Indochina. One year to the day after Washington announced its diplomatic recognition of the French "associated states" of Indochina—later approving military aid for the French war—Allen Dulles read Director Smith's staff the text of a letter from Secretary Marshall on guerrilla operations. He forwarded it to Wisner for comment. The OPC soon concocted a scheme to fund Vietnamese nationalists' publication of anti-Communist magazines. The first issue of this covert propaganda outlet appeared before the end of 1951.

Agency officers were also very active in helping to counter a peasant rebellion in the Philippines, but by far the largest paramilitary effort under way remained the Chinese project. This indeed provided the primary impetus for the CIA's acquisition of the Civil Air Transport proprietary and creation of the aforementioned Western Enterprises cover organization on Taiwan, soon employing six hundred persons. The CIA remained in the thick of counterguerrilla operations. Psychological warfare lost its cachet after mid-1953, when President Eisenhower abolished the Psychological Strategy Board and replaced it with a unit more concerned with policy implementation.

. . . AND HIS SECRET WAR

Under Mr. Wisner, the Directorate of Plans assumed the shape it retained for several decades. The diminishing importance of psywar is reflected in its contraction into just one part of the business of the Political Psychological Staff of DDP. The other important functional staff in the directorate covered paramilitary operations. The staffs combined with regional offices and some technical support units. Chiefs of the offices were the paladins of the secret wars, the generals—"barons" to insiders. In the field, the CIA's contingent in a country would be run by a station—the local command—housed in the American embassy. Important subordinate units, if permanent, were called bases. Extra officers sent on temporary duty usually reported to the station chief, but spies under deep cover might be working directly for headquarters or a specific controller located somewhere else.

The deputy director of plans himself (the acronym DDP was used for both the organization and its chief) was the field marshal. Aside from reorganized staffs, changes among support units, and the creation of a separate Africa Division in 1959 (carved out of the Near East and South Asia units), plus occasional changes on Soviet coverage (by a single division for the USSR and its allies, or by one for the Soviet Union plus a separate one for Eastern Europe), there were no significant changes in the DDP until the Reagan administration. In 1973—after Wisner's time—the entity would be renamed more accurately as the Directorate of Operations.*

Frank Wisner continued his frenetic pace. He started News Highlights, a DO daily media summary, something that could be used to respond to what he thought scurrilous reporting. Wisner liked his nickname, the Wiz. Aside from his hard partying, propaganda interventions, and the administrative drudgery that goes with any job like being DDP, there was cruising—and the CIA projects that cruising aimed to manage. Colleagues saw a man driven by mission. He displayed tension, most noticeably when struggling to frame responses, when Frank would clench and open his fist, making the muscles ripple in his forearm. Wisner could be met at

---

* To eliminate confusion between the DDP as a person and DDP as an agency unit, from here on the narrative will uniformly employ "Directorate of Operations" (DO) to refer to the unit, and DDP or DDO (deputy director for operations) to refer to the person. Note that this conforms to usage that appears earlier in portions of the text that refer to the modern-era CIA.

the homes or farms of Paul Nitze, Chester Bohlen, or others, and heavy-weights like George Kennan or Richard Bissell were among his circle.

Central to the DO mission were its operations in Europe. The locus remained in Germany. There the CIA station grew to as many as 1,400 officers—the largest in the world and a huge fraction of DO effort. The agency's Berlin base became the front line of the Cold War. In Germany, too, the U.S. military sustained CIA projects, and a military spy apparatus further augmented agency resources. Next to Germany, the CIA station in Vienna also had special importance. Until 1955, Austria was occupied by forces of the Four Powers (the Soviet Union, the United States, France, and Great Britain). Agency stations in London and Paris held the next tier, for American spies had allied most closely with the spy services in those lands. Italy retained its status as playground for political action.

Switzerland and Sweden were significant neutrals who could be induced to cooperate but in any case represented platforms from which operations could be mounted into the East. The CIA found it so difficult to recruit spies in Russia, China, and some other places that intelligence officers called them "denied areas." While Wisner remained DDP the agency would not even *have* a station in Moscow. The spooks put great reliance on outsiders—journalists, tourists, diplomats of allied nations—persons who had legitimate reasons to be in denied areas. Upon returning to the West, they would be asked about what they had observed. These casual spies, if approached in advance and asked to look for specific things, were said to be on "mounted" operations. "Mounted" became an espionage term of art. Neutrals like Switzerland and Sweden had warmer relations—plus better transit access—to the denied areas. In the People's Republic of China, with which the United States had no diplomatic relations until the mid-1970s, there was no embassy, hence no CIA station. At lot of the intel came from "paper mills"—émigré groups claiming sources behind the Iron Curtain, which produced anything they wanted. As late as 1951, a third of all CIA effort in Austria aimed at nothing more than running down fabrications.

For all the resources the DO devoted to Europe, the Soviet target remained elusive. The Russians' success at infiltrating the CIA's Polish project, with its embarrassing denouement, had to be very painful. Here Wisner lost longtime comrade Franklin (also called "Frank") Lindsay, the central European baron. Lindsay decided he'd had enough and quit. Frank Lindsay had worked for OSS on partisan warfare in Yugoslavia, ending World War II as chief of the U.S. military mission. At OPC he had been a

major player in the creation of Radio Liberty and on the Albanian operation, where the enemy had broken up the CIA teams and staged show
trials too.

Wisner felt the heat from State Department complaints about covert
operations, sparked by Bob Joyce's distress. Joyce had been a close OSS
associate and Wiesbaden housemate, and here he was, running off the
reservation.

Upheavals in the East took place spontaneously, not as a result of CIA
subversion. Massive riots out of the blue rocked East Germany in June
1953, beginning with building workers marching in protest in the Fried-
richshain district of Berlin. There existed a military-affiliated local outlet in West Berlin, Radio in the American Sector (RIAS), which encouraged passive resistance to the Soviets along with labor activism. Rioters
expected RIAS to serve as a mechanism to keep the different bands up to
date. They also thought the Western garrisons in Berlin would invade the
East to restore order, thus holding back the Russians. Neither happened.
Officers at CIA Berlin Base wanted to provide weapons to the protesters,
but Washington knocked that down hard. The Russians sent in tanks and
troops to quell the riots. Wisner felt more pain.

After the event, the Eisenhower NSC demanded a fresh appraisal of
America's "psychological effort." The study observed that psychological
operations had been hampered by a requirement that they be keyed to
political action. Early in 1954, Allen Dulles and presidential adviser C.D.
Jackson disputed the thinking that CIA should be bound in this way. Mr.
Wisner commented "higher levels" had no inkling of the seriousness here
and insisted the CIA had received no guidance on planning for covert operations. For Dwight D. Eisenhower and John Foster Dulles, who had spoken during the election of "rolling back" the Iron Curtain, that amounted
to a real fault. For Frank, who had been a source of CIA's foot dragging
with the Psychological Strategy Board, the charge seems more than a little
disingenuous.

Wisner discussed matters with top aides, he told Director Dulles in a January 8, 1954, memo. They included two of Allen's lieutenants—Richard
Helms, former spymaster for Germany, and Tracy Barnes, now heading
the psychological-political staff—and they agreed. "Present governmental
policy does not provide for or support the stirring up, or the provision of
significant quantities of support to satellite uprisings." He did not understand, the DDP went on, how support for an uprising could be possible
without armies "prepared to march to the active assistance of the revolu-

tionists." No top authority, Frank insisted, had ever given "authoritative policy guidance" of a sort enabling the DO to develop generic plans to whip up or exploit local uprisings. In the days leading to the first anniversary of this futile revolt, Allen spoke to his brother about marking the event, which Foster considered doing. The CIA director held him back. Frank Wisner telephoned to reinforce the message: the DDP had talked to Allen, and to the working-level CIA officers, and all agreed, the less said the better.

President Eisenhower took a hard look. That spring he promulgated NSC-5412, the latest presidential directive governing covert operations. Here Ike established a 5412 Group and gave it formal responsibility for operations approval, dethroning the Psychological Strategy Board.

That summer Ike empaneled a blue ribbon commission led by James H. Doolittle, a wartime comrade and Air Force general, to do a top-to-bottom review of the DO. Wisner rode that out, pressing the point that no one had told the spooks what to do. Allen Dulles pulled out the stops to impress panelists. They went to visit the DO's training facility near Williamsburg, Virginia—"the Farm" or, more formally, Camp Peary. General Doolittle himself, with White House minder J. Patrick Coyne, made a whirlwind cruise to CIA stations at Frankfurt, Vienna, Athens, and Rome. Wisner appeared before the commissioners twice—on July 14 with Allen Dulles for a *tour d'horizon*, and August 17 to extoll the CIA victory in Guatemala. One after another the DDP trotted out nearly all his barons, too.

The attention yielded fruit. General Doolittle reported to President Eisenhower at the end of September. They met a couple of weeks later. Doolitle warned of Allen's emotional streak, far worse than appeared on the surface. Ike rendered an oft-quoted judgment on Dulles when Doolittle questioned retaining him: "I'd rather have Allen . . . with his limitations than anyone else I know." By contrast the general made no complaint regarding Wisner. Eisenhower commented that intelligence operations were "peculiar" and that it took an "odd kind of genius" to run them.

Logic in Doolittle's report ran to the circular—so long "as it remains national policy," the panel concluded, an "aggressive covert psychological, political and paramilitary organization" remained necessary. No one ought to be permitted to stand in the way of that objective, and indeed the apparatus must be "more unique and . . . more ruthless than that employed by the enemy." The report skewed toward operations, but it also argued that a strong covert program could be sustained with less money. Doolittle felt the DO could cut a thousand people, getting rid of deadwood, officers who'd not attained full potential. The Doolittle study implicitly criticized Wisner's apparatus—his directorate had half a dozen principal staffs, two of them with subordinate staffs, while the seven regional divisions were under five DO staffs. Contrary to Wisner's insistence, the Doolittle report found NSC policy guidance to have been adequate—and that some episodes during actions like that in Guatemala indicated a need for better DO coordination, not White House instruction. All in all, this mild wrist slapping didn't bother Wisner and there is no evidence that the Directorate of Operations was actually cut back as a result.

The commissioners saw a bright spot regarding the CIA and defectors. Whereas espionage had shed little light on Soviet intentions or capabilities, a stream of defectors had begun trickling out of the East. The agency had started Project Redcap to create uniform procedures for handling disaffected former enemies. These were not people who might enlist in secret wars against the communists, but former enemy operatives. Western services quietly put out welcome mats.

There were several important defectors in the months leading up to Doolittle's review. Yuri Rastvorov changed sides in Tokyo. A colonel in Soviet service, Rastvorov first approached the British but finally went to the CIA instead. Wisner surfaced him around Thanksgiving of 1954, as the ostensible author of an article in *Life* magazine revealing the bitter power struggle in the Kremlin following Stalin's 1953 death. Rastvorov married one of his CIA debriefers and was set up with an alias as a tennis pro. He could have been the real life model for the Robert Culp and Bill Cosby characters in the 1960s television show *I Spy*.

In Vienna, still under Four Power occupation, KGB major Peter Deriabin crossed the line. He had to be smuggled out of a city that, like Berlin, lay inside the Soviet occupation zone. Deriabin became an important CIA propaganda asset. He served as ghostwriter for the early 1960s book *The Penkovskiy Papers*, purporting to be the reflections of one of the West's most effective Soviet agents. In Germany the defector was Nikolai Y. Khokhlov, a man who could not bring himself to obey Soviet orders to assassinate a leader of the anti-Soviet Russian émigrés. CIA officials considered that scheme embarrassing enough to the Soviets that after just two months they had Khokhlov give a press conference detailing the plot. In Australia Vladimir M. Petrov, another senior Russian spy, switched sides too. He became a professor. All these spies were very well treated.

Eisenhower headed off a push on Capitol Hill to create a joint committee for intelligence oversight. Rather than acquiesce to the Congress becoming involved, Ike created a White House watchdog, the President's Board of Consultants on Foreign Intelligence Activities. He appointed skilled scientists, technologists, and men of affairs. They proved especially useful on technical collection issues—nudging the last ounce of value from National Security Agency intercepts, affirming the utility of radars in Turkey to observe Soviet missile tests, that kind of thing.

The board did not neglect covert operations. In 1956 chairman James R. Killian had the members split into two groups and conduct a field trip. Killian's party visited one country where the ambassador had fewer diplomats than the CIA station had operatives. The agency had closer ties with local politicians than the embassy. The agency spent money, the ambassador had none.

The other traveling party visited a country where the CIA busily involved itself infiltrating political parties in adjoining friendly nations. Killian expressed alarm.

Robert Lovett and David Bruce of the board were compiling a review that compared foreign intelligence with political action efforts. Bruce, who had headed wartime OSS operations in western Europe, complained of the CIA barging around in friendly countries, buying up newspapers and doling out money to political parties. Lovett and Bruce discovered that half the DO's personnel and 75 or 80 percent of its funds were focused on propaganda, political or psychological warfare, with little outside monitoring. The 5412 Group, supposed to review ongoing operations twice a year, lacked the time to get into much detail. The Operations Coordinating Board, an NSC subcommittee charged with monitoring policy implementation, on which Director Dulles sat, concerned itself mostly with pushing for action. Either way, Eisenhower's NSC units were limited to the information the CIA brought them. They had practically no capacity for independent fact-finding.

As Lovett put it, a CIA director could "navigate, fly, drop the bomb, get back and say what he had seen and everything else." Young, enthusiastic officers flush with cash were being let loose to manipulate the internal politics of countries. The board recommended measures to ensure that approved projects really were consistent with U.S. policy, efforts to coordinate more closely with the U.S. Information Agency and other propaganda organs, selection of more mature and experienced personnel, and closer NSC monitoring.

"EMOTIONS INVOLVED . . . DIDN'T PROVIDE A SOUND BASIS"

The Doolittle study was still winding toward completion when the NSC Operations Coordinating Board (OCB) took up the question of rolling back the Iron Curtain. At its August 25, 1954, meeting, the unit agreed on overt and covert measures to discredit the Russians and weaken communist parties. Ideas included damaging Moscow's reputation at the United Nations and the International Court of Justice, distributing several films (like the agency-funded *Animal Farm*) to "demonstrate the Communist technique of takeover and control," and giving fresh broadcast orders to the Radios.

The NSC board said the CIA's mission should be to "encourage and assist the satellite peoples in resistance to their Soviet-dominated regimes"— while avoiding incitement to "premature revolt." The United States should "be prepared to exploit any future disturbances similar to the East German riots." A lot more could be added, but the essence is, Washington intended active subversion, much of it by spooks. At the outset of 1955—a year after Frank Wisner's doubts—the Operations Coordinating Board followed up with an analysis of "detaching" one of the Eastern European nations from the Soviet orbit. OCB decided that Russian controls were too strong and American capabilities too limited to liberate any captive nation. Nevertheless, the United States must eschew "soft" policies, increasing pressures wherever suitable opportunities appeared. So Wisner's psywar should go on. This activity illustrated the precise faults Robert Lovett had found.

The Free Europe Committee had a big role. There were four propaganda balloon campaigns between 1953 and 1955. In Munich the Radios used powerful transmitters and had seventy thousand square feet of offices. The agency had loose control over RFE/RL but the Radios were necessarily populated by nationals of the captive nations, who had the credibility and language to broadcast into their homelands. RFE presented itself as the "Voice of Free Hungary," or Czechoslovakia, and so on. Since December 1951, standing RFE policy warned speakers not to yield to their impulses to give hope to compatriots by promising Western intervention. But a secret memorandum from the State Department office responsible for coordinating intelligence activities complained in August 1954 that RFE, though supposed to function with U.S. guidance, was increasingly charting an independent course. A 1955 internal review for CIA found, similarly, that controls over scripts and actual broadcasts were not sufficient to enforce a propaganda line or detect deviations from U.S. policy.

That conclusion soon became sensitive. Eisenhower's policy was contradictory—encourage resistance but *not* if Soviet tentacles were too deeply embedded. Naturally the Radios had been broadcasting incessantly about Khrushchev's secret speech—whose release Allen Dulles had pushed. The Radios harped on differing roads to socialism, emphasized Moscow's mild response to Yugoslavia's deviationism, and, when protest bubbled in Poland in June 1956, reported that throughout Eastern Europe. The airwaves rang with calls for reform.

A month later, in NSC-5608/1, Eisenhower's NSC reiterated its conflicting strategy. At an OCB meeting called to discuss that policy, Foster Dulles made the contradiction explicit in his language for an addendum, approved and duly issued on July 18. All those Radio Free Europe broadcasts and all those cultural Cold War investments aimed precisely at encouraging resistance. On October 23, 1956, Hungary erupted. Several hundred thousand citizens marched in Budapest, demanding that Russian occupiers leave the country.

The Russians crushed the Hungarian uprising. Events became a trauma for Hungarians but also a tragedy for the CIA—and for Frank Wisner personally. His OPC had begun planning for operations in Hungary as early as September 1948. A few years later, the agency's contingent in Germany started recruiting Hungarians for the "labor unit" whose name disguised a paramilitary force. Plans were made in the expectation that the CIA would need to intervene inside Hungary. But agents were unable to cross an increasingly impermeable border. The low point came when espionage missions were canceled with prospective agents still training. Later, Projects Zodiac and Zombie used legal travelers for casual spying or "mounted" missions. Hungarian specialists in the DO suffered cutbacks. By the mid-1950s, there were just two full-time officers in the field working against Hungary. Only one was in-country. At headquarters the entire branch consisted of half a dozen officers and two clerk-typists. When the uprising actually happened, after all that seeding the CIA had zero capability—and President Eisenhower no intention—of acting.

By dint of frantic file reading, canvassing of agency assets, and emergency summonses, by Halloween the DDP had assembled a pool of *seven* CIA officers able to speak the language. There was also the Vienna station, where the other Hungary field officer worked. But the Directorate of Operations had no contingency plan for the crisis or for deployment of its officers because no one knew enough even to assign tasks.

As the rebellion began, Wisner, beginning a cruise, had just reached

London. A dinner with a British counterpart evaporated in an MI-6 emergency—plotting with the French to invade Egypt (of which the United States was told nothing). The allies kept their secret as Frank passed through Paris and NATO headquarters, but then they attacked the Suez Canal on October 29.

Eisenhower, who had attempted to mediate between Egypt and his allies, was infuriated. Wisner felt betrayed too. Then, on November 4, Soviet tanks rolled into Hungary. The next day, the DDP arrived at Frankfurt, where base chief Tracy Barnes hosted him. Barnes tried to calm Wisner, in a terrible fury, letting him play with electric trains.

After a few days, Frank moved on to Vienna. Cruising always had a major goal of feeling the pulse of the myriad projects and—too often—obtaining arguments to excuse their failure. But Hungarian refugees were already beginning to flood into Austria. Vienna station chief Bronson Tweedy found his boss in a funk, convinced the Soviets, to ensure loyalty, were employing troops from the Russian Far East. Vienna had no such evidence. Officers there, like William B. Hood and John Mapother, thought this a delusion. Wisner demanded to see the station's reporting, all of it routine. If Wisner used the Far East blather it would not wash.

Then the DDP went to the border to bear witness. It reprised his shock at the 1945 Soviet crackdown in Romania. Colleagues heard Frank denouncing RFE, which the agency had funded to the tune of $16 million—60 percent of its budget—for 1956.

Vice President Richard M. Nixon also came to see the diaspora. Americans in Vienna were chagrined. In Washington, Allen Dulles initially favored CIA action but found the president steadfastly opposed. Then just as October drew to a close, the murder of a senior security official of the Cuban dictatorship made him worry—accurately—that revolution had broken out on the Caribbean island, further filling his plate.

In the meantime, RFE broadcasts swelled Hungarian hopes for help from the West and told of compatriots standing against the Russians. Once the dust settled, Eisenhower demanded reviews. Both the CIA and Radio Free Europe assembled reports. Both concluded that, except for isolated episodes featuring excited broadcasters, no one had misinformed or promised anything. Historical opinion remains divided. One view is that even without CIA orders RFE's reporting of hopeful Western statements, Hungarian secret police excesses, and exciting protests combined to give false hope. (A. Ross Johnson, a later RFE director, has a most detailed analysis that, in contrast, exonerates the Radios.)

Many fleeing Hungarians were funneled through Camp Kilmer, in Piscataway, New Jersey, which acted as a new Ellis Island. Major General Sidney C. Wooten commanded this receiving point for more than 35,000 (of some 188,000 Hungarians who made their way to Austria and 18,000 to Yugoslavia). Poor refugees flowed into Camp Kilmer from November 21, 1956, through May 1957. Some visited Western embassies in Vienna to impart advance information. In December at Camp Kilmer, Dorothe K. Matlack of Army G-2 set up the Armed Services Prisoner Intelligence Committee to debrief arrivals. After screening, roughly 6,000 Hungarians were asked to be interviewed, somewhat more than half agreed, and about a third became subjects of preliminary interrogation reports. In January another office, staffed jointly by the CIA, the State Department, and the armed services, started more extensive debriefs. Despite deep language difficulties, the unit produced another 1,500 intelligence reports. Hungarians dispersed throughout the United States. Judging from refugees met in New York and Boston, the Hungarians were *very* bitter—at both Radio Free Europe and the United States, even many years later.

After Vienna Frank Wisner continued to behave with manic fury. He kept it up at the next stop, Rome, where Gerry Miller, now station chief, could not get him to lighten up. Known for his sense of humor, style, and Mark Twain–like stories, now Frank chewed Miller out instead, right in front of his operatives. William E. Colby, Miller's deputy, sat through a dinner with the DO chief at which Wisner railed at Ike for sitting out the Soviet intervention. Colby saw Frank drinking himself into a stupor. So did the ambassador, Clare Boothe Luce. Later the DDP went on to Athens, domain of John R. Richardson, where disaster multiplied—Frank ate a dinner of spoiled clams. A month later, it turned out he had hepatitis. On December 4, Allen Dulles accorded Deputy Director Wisner the rare privilege of meeting the assembled directors of U.S. intelligence agencies to describe what he had seen of the Hungarian revolt and on the rest of his cruise, which had ended in the Middle East—also in crisis as the British and French, with Israel, fought Egypt. The clandestine service wizard then went on sick leave.

Mr. Wisner returned to headquarters months later. He acted more and more erratically. One day Frank stormed into the offices of FE Division, the barony that covered the Far East, and told its chief, "I think it's time we held Sukarno's feet to the fire." The DO boss seemed to threaten mayhem at those who didn't carry out his intention. That was typical Wisner. He would give the same order to half a dozen different people, then wait to see who produced results. At staff meetings, he upbraided those who didn't perform. He left the Sukarno matter in the hands of division chief Al Ulmer. The baron, mastermind of the CIA's intervention in Greece in the late 1940s and 1950s, and recently station chief in Madrid, numbered among Allen Dulles's favorites.

Wisner balanced on the razor's edge. The Cold War continued. He advocated a project to liberate Czechoslovakia. "No one was listening to Wisner by then," related the DO East Europe baron, now James Critchfield. "He was pretty sick." The cockpit of conflict had moved to the Far East. Even Wisner saw it, judging from his sudden interest in Sukarno, the president of Indonesia. There was also an election in prospect in the Philippines, plus a continuing struggle to prevent expansion of the Communist party in Japan. Heavy political action in the Philippines resulted in the triumph of the U.S.-favored candidate Diosdado Macapagal, for which Dulles took credit in a November 29, 1957, letter to President Eisenhower.

Indonesia was less a problem than a phenomenon. Comprising thousands of islands in a vast archipelago stretching from west of Malaysia on the mainland to the western half of New Guinea, it had been a Dutch colony until World War II. The islands were vastly different in economic and social development, many inhabited by tribes, but with dense settlements on Java and important oil production on Sumatra and Kalimantan. Islam had long been the majority religion. Governing such a mélange could only be a headache. Sukarno maneuvered among assorted parties and factions, staying on top by co-opting different ones. Complicating this situation were divisions within the army, an uneasy amalgam of veterans of the former Dutch colonial forces plus the postwar anti-Dutch resistance, overlaid by social differences imposed by the regions of the archipelago. The CIA understood. National estimates of the 1950s spoke constantly of them and repeatedly postulated that the PKI, the Indonesian Communist Party, would gain strength. It seemed routine until November 1956, when Wisner collared Al Ulmer and told his Far East baron that it was time to put Sukarno's feet to the fire. Then came February 1957, when Sukarno proposed a united front to include the PKI. Opposition from other factions precluded that, although in Javanese local elections that summer the PKI emerged as the only political movement that increased its following.

Suddenly Allen Dulles's briefings to the NSC acquired a darker hue. Indonesia was disintegrating, the region falling apart, the island military commanders breaking away from the central government. Allen used the "disintegration" line at the NSC in March 1957, but averred that Sukarno had negotiated adroitly, and that events "could not be described as an irrevocable revolt." By summer, the CIA had begun saying Indonesia had passed a point of no return. The razor's edge lay in the consequences of a breakaway of the outer islands.

It is true that on March 2, 1957, some dissident officers had issued a charter of struggle, declaring martial law on the outer island Sulawesi. A regional commander on Sumatra had asserted his autonomy at the end of 1956. But Sukarno's government continued functioning, even participated in a mediation designed to placate the dissidents, and the Indonesian leader went forward with his program of "guided democracy." Soviet leader Kliment Voroshilov visited Indonesia in 1957, raising hackles in Washington. A State Department paper suddenly materialized that found advantage in the breakup of the country.

President Eisenhower told a White House meeting that August that "the best course would be to hold all Indonesia in the Free World." A search for action options began. Eisenhower deputized an ad hoc group to brainstorm alternatives. A month later, they advocated no change in relations on the surface but quietly adjusting to support the dissident officers. That meant a CIA operation. The National Security Council approved it on September 23. The secret war in Indonesia would be known as Project Haik. America's ambassador John Allison, flabbergasted at this casual aggression, fought the decision. No shrinking violet where it came to covert operations, Allison had sparkplugged one of those PSB working groups in Truman's day. When the NSC ad hoc group made its recommendations now, the ambassador disputed those too, along with the CIA estimate that buttressed them. When Eisenhower refused to sell Indonesia military equipment, driving Sukarno into the arms of the Russians, Allison objected anew, and so did the entire corps of U.S. attachés in Jakarta. Allison had replaced Hugh Cumming that spring, and the latter had gone home to lead State's intelligence unit, where he egged on the Project Haik activists.

In December an eruption of anti-Dutch sentiment in Indonesia sealed the deal. When Allison expressed concern, Foster Dulles was instantly on the phone to Allen reporting—and making too much of—the ambassador's supposed change of heart. Washington ordered the Pacific Fleet to send a task unit into area waters, keeping out of sight of land, entering no port, telling no one—ready to protect American citizens and property or do anything else. Orders were for an aircraft carrier force to hold in readiness to augment the secret fleet. Eventually the Navy's warships berthed at Singapore to escape the rigors of the blue sea.

Meanwhile DDP Wisner became Eisenhower's executive agent for Haik. Where the United States refused to sell arms to Sukarno, the CIA wanted to *give* them to the separatist colonels. An agency officer, with cover as American consul in Sumatra, became envoy to one rebel wing, asking what they needed. Operatives with the same mission landed on other islands from submarines. The nearest major port was Singapore, then still a British possession. The CIA had liaison there with British MI-6 but suddenly sought to expand its presence. MI-6 base chief Foster Collins resisted, but after Secretary Dulles, on the sidelines of a NATO meeting, spoke to senior British representatives, reluctance wilted. A Far East joint liaison group met five times in the next month. CIA's Singapore presence expanded.

Frank Wisner left for the Philippines on a cruise. Many of Haik's supplies originated there. The agency also began creating an air wing to fly support. In the fall of 1957, the CIA took over several U.S. Air Force B-26 Invader bombers, part of a mass of seventy-three planes at Clark Field; they were written off Air Force lists, reconfigured for ground attack, armed with a dozen machine guns. In March 1958, three P-51 Mustang fighters were added. The CIA proprietary Civil Air Transport and the Philippine air force were canvassed for volunteer pilots.

American spooks cast rosy pictures of the possibilities. Al Ulmer had made a scouting trip to the East nearly a year earlier. More recent surveys were optimistic too. A paper the CIA sent to the White House at the end of January 1958 foresaw that the rebels, who had no military assets on Java, and no navy or air force to get them there, could conduct widespread guerrilla warfare right in Sukarno's stronghold. How that might happen the CIA did not say. Agency analysts also anticipated that the Indonesian leader would negotiate, not fight, once the rebel colonels issued an ultimatum. The Americans had at least five days' notice of their February 10 demand that Sukarno relinquish power.

Even the Indonesian rebels knew better. Doctor Sumitro Djojohadikusomo, in Singapore as a rebel envoy, said as much. "Some CIA men exceed their authority," he told journalist William Stevenson. "They get too excited. They believe anyone who says President Sukarno is a communist; and then they make wild promises."

Sukarno had a navy *and* an air force. He had an army and marines too. Government forces began bombing rebel radio stations, then made amphibious landings on their islands. Ulmer and Wisner, who agonized at Manila, had put their reliance on a rebel movement that was neither cohesive nor unified. As rebel troops began melting away, the CIA doubled down, tossing out its previous security restriction to a single team in the field. Weapons deliveries came by submarine and aircraft. The CIA's secret air force deployed to rebel airfields and began to fly from them. John Foster Dulles wanted to buck up morale by recognizing the rebels as an independent state.

But you could follow the rebel collapse in the newspapers, not to mention the *Central Intelligence Bulletin*. One after another, the bases were bombed, abandoned, captured; the islands fell. On March 23, a U.S. Navy plane on a scouting mission got shot up by Indonesian interceptors.

The next day, the CIA Development Projects unit, which ran the U-2 spy planes, moved its Detachment C from Japan to Cubi Point Naval Air Station in the Philippines, there to begin Operation Robin Hood—reconnaissance over Indonesia. Richard Bissell, the staff chief, and General Cabell, Dulles's deputy, both became quite involved. Cabell appreciated Bissell's abilities and pulled him into the planning. At the DO, Desmond FitzGerald had become the point man on Indonesia, but he remained an underling in Far East Division and needed an executive with clout. Bissell filled the bill. The first flight took place on March 28, and thirty U-2 missions were flown before Project Haik fell apart. The rebels on Sumatra were overrun at the beginning of May. A CIA team needed emergency extraction.

Two rebel aircraft were shot down, and the Jakarta government claimed to have destroyed half a dozen planes on the ground. Desperate for fresh pilots, Wisner's Covert Action Staff asked the U-2 unit to lend some. The request went up to Richard Bissell. The CIA pilots were critical to a top-secret program, highly trained, and the loss of any of them would risk the security of the entire program. Bissell OKed the request anyway.

Pilots Carmine Vito and James Cherbonneaux went to a rebel base on the island Morotai. Vito had never flown the P-51, but Cherbonneaux had. He explained the plane's peculiarities as the two sat at a nearby bar. Only Vito was present when rebels spotted a flight of Indonesian bombers. The CIA pilot got a Filipino mechanic to start his engine, and he got the P-51 into the air. Vito fired a single burst of machine-gun fire before the Indonesian warplanes scattered in every direction. The U-2 pilots were taken off this dangerous duty.

Allen Lawrence Pope proved less fortunate. Flying B-26s since March, Pope had his bomber over Ambon on May 18 when it was hit. The plane crashed near a village market where people were on the way to church. Pope and his rebel bombardier bailed out and were captured. The B-26 had been sanitized to preclude any link to the CIA, and crews endured strip searches before flights for the same reason, but Pope, unwilling to be taken as a spy, had concealed documents in the airplane. The Indonesians exhibited his Air Force and Civil Air Transport IDs, his contract for this operation, even a post exchange card for Clark Air Force Base. President Eisenhower and Secretary Dulles had both claimed U.S. neutrality and blamed "mercenaries" for the rebel air activity—the United States had no legal obligation to control American soldiers of fortune, Foster insisted. Sukarno caught them both in a lie.

The fiasco alarmed the President's Board of Consultants on Foreign Intelligence Activities. When the board demanded explanations, the CIA assembled a paper describing how Project Haik had originated. Robert Lovett filed a follow-up to the board's post-Hungary critique. The overseers believed ardent CIA officers had rooted for one side, filed "intelligence" that declared the rebels ready to fight and the government rotten to the core. With a little CIA help, as Lovett reconstructed the agency's group-think, the United States would get a government favorable to the West. Eisenhower's consultants came up with a pair of "crystally-clear facts," Mr. Lovett reported: "First, the emotions involved in this political fight didn't provide a sound basis on which to plan a paramilitary operation, and, second, every proposed flight had to be cleared in Washington."

Frank Wisner's manic depression took control. In June, Sam Halpern, aide to Far East baron Ulmer, met Frank at the airport on his return from Manila. Wisner seemed hyper, talking a mile a minute. Halpern knew something was wrong. For Wisner, Romania in 1945 had been heart-breaking. Hungary stung. When push came to shove, the CIA had nothing up its sleeve.

Project Haik added complete failure. One day at headquarters Frank boiled over, blasting his secretary, incoherent to colleagues. Finally he went home, where he deteriorated further. Wife Polly called Desmond FitzGerald, a close colleague, and Gordon Gray, now a key presidential aide. They mobilized CIA psychiatrists to examine Frank. Toward mid-September he checked into a psychiatric hospital, the Sheppard-Pratt Institute in Baltimore. Rehabilitation this time involved electroshock therapy. When Frank returned to duty after a year, he became chief of station in London. There Wisner would have one more inning—when the CIA enlisted the British in yet another joint project, one aimed at the leader of British Guiana. But the

Cold Warrior was played out. One day in 1965 he took a shotgun, put it in his mouth, and pulled the trigger. A few years later Frank Wisner's colleagues undertook a private collection and used the money to commission sculptor Heinz Warnecke to craft a bronze plaque with Frank's likeness to commemorate him. Richard Helms presided at the dedication early in 1971. The plaque went up on Langley's seventh floor, in the outer office of the director of operations. Wisner's ghost took up residence.

ILLUSIONS OF ZEALOTRY

Frank Wisner typified one CIA character type, the kind of officer who believed in the mission but was frantic to obtain results. He would follow the first subordinate who came up with a practical solution. There were other types too. Some who professed to be zealots were more the scheming kind. *They* knew the path—and, by God, anyone else had better get out of the way. These were officers who, once decided, battered down obstacles, scheming a course of action, holding operatives' shoulders to the wheel. Jose Rodriguez was such a man. Called to account, Frank Wisner—as he did in 1954—would craft a defense of his field agents. In a similar situation, Mr. Rodriguez would question the propriety of the inquiry—after intriguing to destroy evidence of the actions at issue.

The image of zealotry, quasi-religious and all Manichean, permeates this approach. By its measure, complaints about CIA torture trample values. Jose Rodriguez is tired beyond belief of being labeled a torturer. In the compendium *Rebuttal,* thrown together in 2015 to discredit the Senate intelligence committee's investigation of the agency's transgressions, Rodriguez titles his contribution "Broken Covenants." In it he expresses disgust at the label of torturer, and writes of feeling abandoned as his own government investigated him. Rodriguez charges those on the Senate committee who looked into Project Greystone with confecting revisionist history.

This is the fellow who, as chief of operations at the CIA Counterterrorist Center (CTC), dispatched operatives to take down the suspected Al Qaeda mastermind Abu Zubaydah in early 2002. Just months later he would maneuver to turn Swigert and Dunbar loose in the black prisons. As chief counterterrorist, Rodriguez rejected protests from officers he thought squeamish in the face of torture. And he encouraged a CTC lawyer to remove language from a memorandum recording a September 2002 briefing of senior House intelligence committee members that indicated congresspersons questioned torture's legality. Rodriguez admits leading the CIA team to that meeting. No record of it has been declassified. No matter.

Nearly a year and a half had passed since Alberto Gonzales, elevated to attorney general, and Cheney aide David Addington had instructed the CIA to preserve the tapes. The new White House counsel Harriet E. Miers expressed the same view. True, the Bush administration had muddied the waters in the fall of 2004, telling Langley that the NSC need not be involved in any decision about tapes, that the approval authority should be the CIA, in particular the National Clandestine Service (NCS), a new name for the Directorate of Operations that Jose Rodriguez had been promoted to head. Legal opinions or not, measures afoot in Congress to restrict interrogation methods demonstrated that spin control could not best the public's revulsion.

Rodriguez saw no sense in permitting the tapes to exist. He plotted to demolish them. In March 2005, the *New York Times* ran an exposé on the interrogations. The *Post*'s black prisons story that November became the last straw. The prohibitions against destroying tapes that were issued by White House lawyers and the agency's general counsel were aimed at him. They did not stop Rodriguez for a minute.

In the case of Zacarias Moussaoui, accused of being a left-behind 9/11 hijacker, the trial judge had issued a court order for the CIA to preserve evidence, including tapes. The court had subpoenaed any videotape, but the agency denied that this material existed—a legal transgression—most recently just a few days before the tapes were actually burned. The 9/11 Commission had also asked for tapes and been told they'd been given all the evidence the agency possessed. The American Civil Liberties Union (ACLU) had filed a Freedom of Information Act request for all records concerning interrogations—to include tapes—and the CIA had denied that tapes existed. The ACLU then filed suit in federal court. It would be a presumption in a lawsuit in which these very materials were at issue that an agency holding the records would preserve them. In all, seven court orders were in force requiring preservation of this evidence. None of this stopped the man who thought himself the pointy tip of the spear.

Director Rodriguez construed White House instructions to be only advice. But agency chief Porter Goss was himself on record opposing tape destruction. So was Director of National Intelligence John Negroponte. Top CIA lawyer John Rizzo concurred. In short the senior echelons of the intelligence community and the Bush administration agreed with the courts and with congressional opinion: the torture tapes must be preserved. The clandestine service chief's orchestration suggests a long-considered plan—designed to keep his fingerprints off it. Rodriguez pictured himself "getting rid of some ugly visuals that could put the lives of my people at risk."

On November 4, 2005, Mr. Rodriguez reached out to the CTC, now headed by Robert Grenier, and asked for a staff officer to draft cable language to be sent to Bangkok. It would say that cables described the activity in the tapes, which the IG no longer needed, so could they be destroyed? The station chief would pick up that language and paste it into a front channel cable to headquarters. CTC lawyers Robert Eatinger and Stephen Hermes told acting general counsel John Rizzo of the idea. He agreed they could help with the drafting. There are conflicting versions of whether they did so. Rodriguez maintains he sent the draft cable to Rizzo for review at the same time it went to Bangkok. Of course, "review" for a cable already sent is moot. All this happened on a Friday.

A day after the back-channel message, on the fifth, a request for approval to destroy the tapes duly appeared in a Bangkok cable. Rodriguez now asked his chief of staff, Gina Haspel, to prepare the approval. Haspel, the very spy who had led the black site at Chiang Mai when the first CIA torture occurred, had a clear interest in this dispatch. Sent EYES ONLY, the message pretended that headquarters accepted Bangkok Station's logic. Rodriguez released this early in the afternoon on November 8. As the fateful message went out, CTC chief Grenier and congressional liaison Joseph Wippl—summoned to Congress—were describing the interrogation methods for senior legislators.

General counsel Rizzo expected to take the "Bangkok" request to the White House once it arrived, and consult DNI Negroponte. Instead, the next Rizzo heard would be an information copy of the November 9 dispatch in which the station chief reported the deed done. Furious, Rizzo ran to Rodriguez's office, down the hall on the seventh floor. Rodriguez feigned surprise that the lawyer felt blindsided and said, "I understand your lawyers chopped on it."

Head spinning, Rizzo then confronted Eatinger and Hermes, both of whom denied seeing the message, pointing out it contained different text from what they had worked on. The CIA cable form has a line to record the individuals approving a message before transmission. None of the CIA lawyers' names appeared there.

"In my thirty-four-year career at CIA," John Rizzo would write, "I never felt as upset and betrayed as I did that morning."

Jose insists it had been "extremely important," in exchanges among agency higher-ups, to destroy the videotapes. Out of context, in the public domain "they would make us look terrible; it would be 'devastating' to us." Rodriguez volunteered to take any heat that resulted. Porter Goss laughed. "Actually," the director corrected, "it would be he, PG, who would take the heat."

Mayaguez, Puerto Rico, is known for the Indians, its winter-league baseball team, and for the University of Puerto Rico–Mayaguez. When Jose A. Rodriguez Jr. was born there and returned to live as a child, the university specialized as UPR's engineering school. Mayaguez was a textile and manufacturing center. Starkist, probably the largest employer, canned nearly 80 percent of the packaged tuna consumed in the United States in Mayaguez. But Jose spent only a few youthful years there. An agricultural expert for the United Nations and later USAID, his father moved the family around. Young Jose lived in Colombia, briefly in Bolivia, and then in the Dominican Republic. The family arrived in Santo Domingo in 1965, as a U.S. intervention sought to forestall an alleged communist takeover. Rodriguez spent his formative high school years on Hispaniola and was startled to learn that the parents of some of his friends had been involved in the assassination of dictator Rafael Trujillo. The moving around inclined Rodriguez to a foreign affairs career, and his Dominican interlude perhaps brought Jose to the notion that America, as a powerful nation-state, could do no wrong, and the U.S. government would always back up its officials.

Jose A. Rodriguez Jr. should have known directly that that view is as false as the one of which he accuses opponents. Indeed, in the Trujillo assassination, about which Jose found out at school, there were links to the Eisenhower-and-Kennedy-era CIA. The agency did nothing to shield those involved. Mr. Rodriguez joined the Central Intelligence Agency in 1976. That's just after the Church Committee finished its investigation of the agency, including assassination plotting—one of the most controversial issues. The report on that, released in November 1975, laid bare the details, and its release had to be fought through frantic CIA and Ford administration efforts to suppress it. The lesson was that defense of the CIA is inherently political. Agency officers will be thrown under the bus if government interests require.

After attending the University of Florida, both college and law school, and after an interval with his brother in San Juan selling apartment time shares, Jose A. Rodriguez entered the world of spooks. In junior officer training at Camp Peary, the young Latino did adequately but no more. His first tour took Rodriguez to a country that does not speak Spanish. Except for that tour, until the September 11 attacks, Rodriguez spent his entire career as an operations officer in the Latin America Division. That meant he had a front row seat when Ronald Reagan tossed the CIA to the wolves to protect his own skin in the Iran-Contra Affair. In fact, Rodriguez was deputy chief of station in El Salvador at the time. Director William Casey; the DO and its chief, Clair George; the Latin America Division chief, Alan Fiers; the agency station chief in Costa Rica, Joe Fernandez—*all* were figuratively consumed in the flames. Casey literally died, of a brain tumor. Another resident ghost for Langley.

James L. Adkins, a field officer who served as base chief at Aguacate, the airfield supporting a ring of Contra encampments in Honduras, had been a mentor to Rodriguez. He fell also. The dragon slayers of Iran-Contra, as per the official report of lead prosecutor Lawrence Walsh, refrained from indicting Adkins only because doing so would have distracted the larger investigation. His alleged offense turned on "hard rice," something Adkins had been familiar with as a paramilitary officer in Laos in the 1960s. There "hard rice" became the euphemism for military supplies (prohibited under the 1962 Geneva agreement) disguised as permitted comestibles ("soft rice") also carried by the CIA proprietary Air America. According to Walsh, Adkins knew and approved of Contra resupply missions by CIA pilots, gave the Contras fuel that he charged illegally to CIA accounts, and lied about it to investigators.

There is another version of the Aguacate story. Supporters say Adkins encountered a measles epidemic in the Contra camps and used agency helicopters because they were the only way to get vaccine there. Only one flight involved "hard rice." Later, congressmen came to the area on a "cruise" of their own, to see the progress under a new CIA Contra funding program, and Adkins overheard Sandinista radio talk about shooting down choppers transporting U.S. lawmakers. Adkins asked Contra leaders to send patrols to drive the enemy away, and the CIA's allies demanded the use of agency choppers in return. Adkins approved. An investigator for the agency's Inspector General (IG) questioned him about these episodes in March 1987. (Walsh asserts that Adkins lied.)

That May, Adkins was hauled before the IG in Washington—then John H. Stein. Livid, Stein accused the field agent of disloyalty and endangering the entire CIA operation. Adkins insisted he'd done only what he had to. The agency put him on leave for months. Then, in the storied "Holiday Party Massacre," on December 17, 1987, Director William Webster fired both Adkins and Joseph Fernandez, the agency's former chief of station in Costa Rica. Rodriguez could not have missed what Webster did to his mentor. He says nothing good about Webster as director.

Fast forward to the middle 1990s, and another purge followed the excesses of CIA allies in Guatemala. Langley's misrepresentations to congressional overseers regarding exactly what had gone on contributed. Agency director John Deutch swiftly dismissed Terry Ward—another DO Latin America Division chief—and Guatemala station chief Fred Brugger. Jose Rodriguez actually replaced Ward. The lesson he had to have learned is the Iran-Contra story all over again—that political daggers cut just as deeply as the ones behind spy cloaks.

Christopher D. Costanzo, a predecessor who, like Rodriguez, put in multiple tours as station chief in addition to jobs at headquarters, affirms that long before Jose there were no illusions in the Latin America Division. Costanzo saw agency officers as under siege from within and just as much from the outside. "The anti-CIA mood in government," Costanzo writes, "was evident whenever we sought cooperation outside of the service."

If observation were not enough, Rodriguez the baron *would be drummed out himself.* In his case, a friend from Dominican days had been busted for drug trafficking. The agency baron intervened, through his station chief, to obtain decent treatment for the man, who Rodriguez says was not, in fact, a trafficker, and who ultimately was released. A subordinate, recalled from the station, he supposed on the baron's orders, blew the whistle, revealing Jose's intervention. Agency IG Frederick P. Hitz investigated. Rodriguez, relieved as division chief on Halloween 1996, took a demotion. The deputy director for operations, Jack Devine—the man in Frank Wisner's chair—reviewed Hitz's report and one from an accountability board that reached a similar conclusion. He confirmed the recommendations. Rodriguez had been done in by someone far down the food chain. The daggers beneath spies' cloaks could wound deeply indeed. Jose says he would still have done the same thing, even knowing the cost to his career.

Bottom line: Mr. Rodriguez postures when he speaks of solemn covenants between government and its intelligence officers. He *knew* how the game was played. Ghostly apparitions loomed everywhere over his career. One more thing—Jose A. Rodriguez Jr. needed 9/11, or something like it, just like Allen Dulles needed the Langley headquarters project. After losing his baronetcy, Rodriguez kicked around a bit, did odd jobs with the CIA security office, finally to be offered the station in Mexico City. His second tour there—and the fourth as station chief, after Argentina, Panama, and the Dominican Republic—the CIA man had reached a limit. Mexico City represented an emeritus assignment, a career ender. Indeed, he named his riding horse Business, so associates could tell callers Jose was "out on Business." When he returned in 2001, Rodriguez had no posting. Operations chief Jim Pavitt told him, "We'll find something for you to do."

Rodriguez was lounging at home the morning the World Trade Center fell. He dashed to Langley, to the Counterterrorist Center, and pitched in alongside Cofer. In those challenging moments, the CTC chief needed the help. Black pulled people in, brought more from other parts of the agency, converted the conference room to a makeshift office, put desks in the halls. After about a week, when the CIA had finalized its plan to infiltrate Afghanistan, Black assembled everyone for a pep talk in the center's main vault, warning that they were going to war, CTC would do things its way, and some comrades would not be coming back. Rodriguez understood that.

For some time, the CTC had been the fastest-growing CIA unit, yet that proved nothing compared to the growth spurt now. An element of a hundred or so in the 1990s, by 2002 the center boasted three hundred officers, but a year later the count had swollen to 1,500 people. In time, the center couldn't even be housed at Langley. Doing things CTC's way took every moment for Jose Rodriguez.

Cofer Black would be preoccupied connecting to foreign intelligence services and organizing allied efforts to sweep terrorist suspects off streets across the globe. A 2013 study by the nongovernment group Open Society Foundation identified fifty-four nations that helped the CIA after the terrorist attacks. The pace became frenetic. With the capture of Abu Zubaydah, renditions became the pipeline to the black sites.

Meanwhile Director George Tenet deputized Henry Crumpton, Black's deputy, to lead the covert CIA campaign in Afghanistan. His top seer, Philip Mudd, had made a career as analyst, not operator. Rodriguez filled in to manage operations—organizing the field teams and the black prisons. Black retired in 2002, and Tenet elevated Rodriguez to CTC chief near the end of that year. Rodriguez energized the rendition and detainee program, by some accounts originating the idea (at one of Tenet's threat matrix meetings) of housing prisoners at Guantánamo Bay. He pushed CTC associates for action. The burden was enormous. The fusion center was designed to absorb information and convert it into instructions for field operatives. But in CTC's case, that meant 120 databases and ten to twelve *thousand* pieces of intelligence every day.

The black prisons were a constant preoccupation. Rodriguez deplored it when the inspector general opened investigations into torture allegations. Sure enough, right away John Helgerson, the latest IG, saw questionable activities. Rodriguez shrugged him off. *That* became the sword of Damocles that hung over CIA heads—and the real reason for destroying the videotapes.

Other booby traps were sown too. A CTC snatch team entered Italy in February 2003 and, with the help of Italian security services, kidnapped a Muslim cleric right off the street in Milan, speeding him to the NATO airbase at Aviano, where a proprietary plane flew Hassan Mustafa Osama Nasr to Egypt. There Egyptian security organs tortured Abu Omar, as he is also known, for seven months, seeking answers to questions provided by the agency. The CIA is reported to have sent officials to witness this travesty. Ingeniously tracing orders for pizza delivery and use of cell phones, Italian prosecutors identified twenty-three Americans involved in the kidnapping. They were charged along with Italian intelligence officials who collaborated with the CIA in this affair.

The American defendants included Langley's station chief in Rome, its base chief in Milan, other CIA officers, plus contract goons and aircrews. The agency's people and their henchmen were convicted, and in 2012 their convictions were upheld by the Italian supreme court. In 2016 the European Court of Human Rights condemned the Italian government for permitting the CIA kidnapping and ordered it to pay Omar damages for knowingly exposing him to risk.

Agency officer Sabrina DeSouza sued the United States after the government refused to acknowledge any relationship or pay for her legal defense—another instance of the real standard (which Rodriguez claims so unusual). Italian courts sentenced DeSouza, whose offense had been no more than to translate at meetings where CIA's team, its managers, and the Italian secret services blocked out the mission. DeSouza got four years in prison. Her appeals failed. At this writing, she is in Portugal.

Robert S. Lady, CIA base chief in Milan, also on the run from an Italian prison sentence, had already gotten off the hook. The United States, in 2014, petitioned the president of Italy to pardon a passel of agency officers and contractors, including Lady but not DeSouza. The Portuguese courts accepted Italian extradition requests. In the spring of 2017 Italian police officials were reportedly on their way to take DeSouza into custody when President Sergio Mattarella of Italy reduced her sentence enough to permit her to work it off remotely and in community service. If reports are accurate that President Donald J. Trump intervened to help DeSouza that would be an indication of his desire for better relations with the CIA.

The Milan case is the first time in history that agency officers on agency business in an allied country have been indicted and convicted for criminal actions; it is also the first time a friendly government and its own intelligence services have suffered criminal consequence for a CIA operation. Jose Rodriguez engineered these projects. He is directly responsible for inflicting grave damage on American national security. Just to cap the point, Rodriguez has been notably absent from the legal defense of the CIA officers. Covenant? That's how the game is played.

THE POINTY TIP OF THE SPEAR

Jose relished travel of a different sort—"cruising," and now the world seemed hardly enough. He spent about a quarter of his time on the road, often with just one aide, and mostly on commercial flights. There were trips twice a year to meet with the Russians. He himself did the heavy lifting of liaison with allied security services. In 2004 the Olympic Games were scheduled for Athens. The CTC chief went there too, selected as the CIA's lead man for Olympic security. After he left and the Olympics ended, Greece erupted in the "Vodaphone scandal," in which it turned out that American and Greek intelligence had begun spying on a wide swath of locals—not just political activists, but also businessmen, politicians, even military figures. Washington, hard-pressed to make explanations for these excesses, watched the scandal blow open in February 2005. This led to parliamentary and criminal inquiries, as well as one by Greek intelligence. As late as the spring of 2008, when former NSC lawyer John Bellinger visited Athens in his new capacity as counselor to the secretary of state, the Vodaphone scandal remained as the top item of the agenda. The ambassador reminded Bellinger that the issue "could resurface . . . given press speculations of an alleged U.S. involvement."

Meanwhile, Jose Rodriguez adverts, even as the first chief of the National Clandestine Service, he could never seem to avoid being scrutinized closely by Immigration and Customs whenever reentering the United States. Jose compensated for the annoyances he suffered from border officials by riding a Harley-Davidson motorcycle on weekends and driving a Corvette other times. He loved the Vette and rued the time, visiting a CIA outstation, when the security gate malfunctioned and bollards rose from the ground to crumple his front bumper.

Rodriguez moved among agency stations, from one secret place to another. The black prisons, fashioned from whole cloth, had to be succored. Dusty Foggo, at first head of the agency's logistics base in Frankfurt, Germany, helped the spy chief create a new roster of black sites when the Thais, increasingly terrified of leaks, ordered the agency to empty its prison there. Rodriguez and Foggo toured some of them. Later Junior—as Rodriguez was familiarly known—took Langley lawyers on similar visits. In the spring of 2003, Foggo approached officials in Poland, Romania, and Lithuania about sites on their territory. Foggo arranged for a full-scale prison to be built in Morocco. Rodriguez visited there when he had ascended from CTC to head the entire Directorate of Operations, renamed the National Clandestine Service (NCS) in the 2004 reorganization. He loved his Athens visits for the 2004 Olympic consultations. On his watch, the spy chief claimed to have doubled the number of CIA espionage sources among the terrorists. That could have meant going from one to two. It was certainly not a large number.

His successor, Robert Grenier, learned that in two years Rodriguez had never held a "town meeting" or other mass morale-building session for CTC officers. Hosting one himself, Grenier quickly discovered, did not open the way to Junior's heart. Jose's time on the road put extra pressure on his deputy and other senior aides, including those at Alec Station, and Rodriguez bore some responsibility for the lax supervision that facilitated problematical Alec Station interventions in detainee cases. Air support for renditions needed to be routinized, another function made more difficult while the chief traveled. Rodriguez bristled when subordinates like Grenier, when still a station chief abroad, sided with George Tenet, who perceived a weakening in White House support, and suspended operations to seek renewed commitment from President Bush.

By spring 2005, the differences between Rodriguez and Grenier were the stuff of rumors at Langley. The NCS director seemed to have it in for the CTC chief, his primary field commander. The troubles weren't about cruising. In 2005 alone, Grenier made a lengthy trip to Afghanistan and Pakistan, one to Europe, one to coordinate with Central Command in Tampa and Doha, another to the Middle East, and two to East Africa. As near as Grenier could figure it, Rodriguez deplored the time CTC spent ironing out problems with the White House, Pentagon, and Congress. The degree to which Rodriguez had successfully evaded Congress magnified his later explosion at Grenier's efforts to resolve issues. The NCS boss wanted CTC run the way he had done it. Even changing CTC's name from Counterterrorist to Counterterror*ism* Center grated on him.

The NCS hit-team concept showed Rodriguez the schemer. While still at CTC, he had dreamed up Project Cannonball, nothing less than a resurrection of the CIA's notorious on-the-shelf assassination squad—a permanent operational capability—called ZR/Rifle in John McCone's time, to carry out "executive action" on short notice. In Cannonball, a commando team would be on call for a mission at any time. Personnel reportedly included individuals from the private security firm Blackwater, though that cannot be confirmed, because Congress would be kept in the dark, allegedly at Vice President Cheney's instigation, though surely with Rodriguez's full accord. The Cannonball concept seemed harebrained. The capability would be automatically controversial, while post-attack recovery of agents would be tricky. Plus, there was no good target intelligence (where is Osama bin Laden?), and the unit faced stiff competition from the military's Special Operations Command (SOCOM), whose Joint Special Operations Command already did the same thing. George Tenet put Cannonball on hold, but Rodriguez kept it on the back burner, demanding progress reports and occasional reviews. He convinced Porter Goss to revive it. Once Michael Hayden took over Langley, the DCIA made activation contingent on acquisition of usable intelligence. Over a million dollars disappeared into Cannonball, stopped only after Rodriguez went into retirement. When CIA director Leon Panetta discovered the hit-team project in 2009, aghast that Congress had never been told, he rushed to disclose the scheme.

Meanwhile back at CTC, Bob Grenier juggled his feelings, on the one hand believing the center's activities were going quite well, his operators terrific; on the other, acutely conscious of his boss's enmity. At meetings Rodriguez exhorted Grenier to detain more terrorist suspects. Over a hundred individuals disappeared into the CIA maw during Jose's watch; the number under Grenier could be counted on the fingers of two hands.

Unlike his predecessor, Grenier felt the changing political pulse. He repeatedly explained that the agency could not simply "disappear" people. In February and May 2005, new versions of legal opinions approving torture extended the paper trail if not the legitimacy of the action. With wavering support for the CIA program, knowing that secrecy could not be maintained much longer, the Bush National Security Council even created a "tiger team" to consider what to do upon disclosure. Rodriguez simply wanted to forge ahead.

Jose thought of his wife, Patti, as chief of station at home. He felt it necessary to keep her in the loop, as she did so much for the family. Patti remained supportive throughout. But that had its trying moments too. Naturally the agency labored hard to discover the whereabouts of Al Qaeda's Osama bin Laden and very frequently had to describe the status of the hunt. One time the NCS director swore to a colleague that he'd blast the next person who asked with a "Fuck you!" That night at dinner Patti asked, "So why haven't you guys got bin Laden yet?"

At the head of the Counterterrorism Center, Robert Grenier noted that no strategic plan underlay its growth. CTC had simply mushroomed. One of Grenier's long moves was to craft such a concept, but he frankly notes the clandestine service chief would never accept a plan coming from him. Grenier finessed this by gathering his senior people—many, officers who had worked under Jose—and let his subordinates advocate what mattered to them. Director Rodriguez approved the CTC strategic plan.

The commission that examined all aspects of the 9/11 attacks passed Rodriguez by to fasten on Black and Tenet, but among its central conclusions would be that terrorists had achieved surprise because security services built walls keeping one another from knowledge of key data, something at which Rodriguez excelled. Enhanced cooperation became the watchword. Jose made proper genuflections. His center, an amalgam of operations officers and analysts, consumed intel but still walled off the detainee program. The CTC became an odd "fusion" center, where information came in the door but not so much went out.

The 9/11 Commission advocated fusion centers, and before long these were created for every major metropolitan area in the United States. This effort became CTC business too—the joint task forces (as most of these were called) brought together local authorities with federal ones. The push began while Cofer Black remained chief, but Rodriguez soon took center stage, designating officers to work with task forces and deciding what intel the locals could access. This initiative created sparks in New York City, where the New York Police Department (NYPD) set up an Intelligence Division. The unit became a sort of mini-CIA—accused of illegal surveillance of Muslim Americans, among other things.

More than once Mr. Rodriguez styled himself as among those at the pointy tip of the spear. One of the pointiest elements put the National

Clandestine Service up against the military. The Department of Defense, through its Special Operations Command, was sticking its nose more and more into classic intelligence. This was not just a matter of military covert ops but of espionage and other spooky functions. Much like Langley with local police, in the Rodriguez era the CIA rushed to play. *It* became more military, adopting similar procedures for drone attacks. The agency controlled all drone flights inside Pakistan. In other regions, SOCOM alternated with it. Officials began speaking of "Title 50" versus "Title 10" operations—a shorthand for the looser legal restrictions applying to intelligence versus military initiatives. The difference between spies and soldiers suddenly turned on how to get around war powers laws.

Rodriguez left the agency in the fall of 2007, and his era ended only a couple of months later, with the *New York Times* revelation (on Pearl Harbor day) that the torture tapes had been destroyed and the NCS chief had engineered the deed. Rodriguez refused to testify before Congress, hinting he would invoke Fifth Amendment rights. Some saw Junior as falling on his sword to protect associates; others accused him of obstruction of justice. Jose Rodriguez stridently proclaimed torture saved lives, while insisting in the next breath there had been no torture, and in the following one that those who disagreed were armchair critics. The ironies seem to have been lost. Defending himself, the CIA man invoked constitutional rights denied to those targeted in U.S. drone attacks and in the black prisons. Equally poignant, the intelligence committee's investigation of the torture and black prisons *began* when Senate staff realized the program they saw in the cable traffic differed from the one Rodriguez had described to Congress.

The Department of Justice assigned a federal prosecutor to look into obstruction of justice allegations and ultimately decided not to pursue them. Attorney General Eric Holder in the Obama administration reviewed that decision and decided not to go ahead either. Jose Rodriguez construes this as being investigated twice. Whatever the merits of that perception, the truth is that prosecution would have bumped into classic dilemmas of accountability. He could not have been tried without the CIA revealing much more than embarrassing facts, namely moral transgressions and breaches of international and national law. The Justice Department prosecutor, incidentally, concluded that CIA lawyers Robert Eatinger and Stephen Hermes had erred in advising Rodriguez that he had the authority to destroy the tapes.

In the end, the Central Intelligence Agency convened an internal "accountability board" review of Jose A. Rodriguez's action. By now it was 2011, and the CIA director was David Petraeus. He asked Michael Morell to chair this board. Thinking of what Rodriguez had already endured, Morell decided to do the job by himself. He joined Jose for a drink at a hotel and broke the news. The former CIA man, stunned, nevertheless answered questions and left Morell with food for thought. Morell determined from the written record that the NCS chief had known that his bosses and the White House had ordered the tapes preserved. Morell felt confident that Rodriguez himself would not have tolerated a subordinate doing the equivalent.

The endgame played out in Morell's office on December 21, 2011, when Rodriguez returned to Langley to hear the verdict. "I told him," the CIA's accountability reviewer writes, "although I knew he believed he'd done the Agency and its officers a service by ordering the destruction of the tapes, I believed his action had been inappropriate." But a letter of reprimand proved the worst result. Jose A. Rodriguez Jr. stood ready to jump on the bandwagon attacking the Senate committee's investigative conclusions on CIA torture. Nevertheless Junior had been a key character, perhaps *the* major impetus, setting in motion the investigation that so threatened the Central Intelligence Agency, as Jacob Marley's spirits and the Flying Dutchman will show us.

There are times when the contradictions between goals and conventions lead a person to jettison morality. The ghost of Jose Rodriguez dwells there. In his case, demands for action made social norms go by the board. Arguably, discipline followed. Those who abandon moral compasses remain in jeopardy of criminal prosecution and public condemnation for the foreseeable future. Like the French army officers after the Algerian war, or the Argentine and Chilean spooks from the dirty wars of the 1970s and 1980s, pardons or amnesties, even when granted, do not wipe away the stain.

Convictions can also lead the individual to presume the transcendence of her or his own morality. Frank Wisner's ghost could tell that story. Here moral anguish led to temptation to exceed orders. In the 1950s, Wisner's covert operations placed time bombs that exploded later, again with immense damage to American security.

The CIA suffers both ways. The zealots were more dangerous than anyone realized. None of them were rogue elephants. They did what they were asked, performed efficiently, and obtained short-range successes. Their ghosts demand that intelligence officers think of long-term consequences, not only the immediate moment.

The ghosts have equally disturbing lessons for an agency striving to avoid responsibility. The zealot of Eisenhower's secret wars fended off criticisms by asserting that his warriors never got guidance from high authority—the president—to know what they should do. How could it be otherwise in a schema of "plausible deniability"? That same reasoning applied when associates resisted having George W. Bush directly exposed to the torture program. George Tenet was right to perceive the CIA being left out on a limb.

The ghosts teach the spooks another sinister lesson. Operations that straddle legal boundaries have better chances of survival in a high-threat environment. The Cold War CIA needed little help to portray the Soviet threat as supreme, but the present is highly curious. No matter how many terrorist organizations are busted up, cells taken down, or individuals rendered or killed, our intelligence agencies describe the threat level only as high, even increasing.

3

STARS AND METEORS

THE ZEALOTS LEAD, COMMANDING A FIELD FORCE OF STATIONS AND bases scattered around the world, staffed by agency officers and contract personnel, who run networks, recruit agents, and conduct operations. At headquarters the regional divisions—and lately the mission centers—manage this global activity. But the bedrock upon which the system depends is composed of dedicated officers working their hearts out to achieve the goal. Many are skilled and competent. Some are not. And some excel. Those stars are the agency's heroes, though some, like meteors, burn up passing through the atmosphere, signaling the dangers that face all spies.

Jennifer Lynne Matthews was almost second-generation CIA. Her uncle had been an agency paramilitary officer in Laos. During this war on terror the secret armies from the Southeast Asian war of the 1960s and 1970s have only been duplicated in Afghanistan. Elsewhere the agency has relied upon its alliances with foreign intelligence services, backed up by kidnapping crews and—the ultimate weapon—drones. The most important drone targeteers at Langley worked for the Counterterrorism Center. Jen Matthews stood among them. Indeed—as the drama critics say of the first to play a particular character—she might have originated the role.

Formally known as unmanned aerial vehicles, the drones started as robotic scouts and evolved into hunter-killers. The very name Predator, which identified the first generation of missile-armed drone, gives the flavor. Armed with a laser-guided Hellfire missile, its cameras scanning the ground, linked by satellite communications to a pilot and support crews thousands of miles away, the Predator can circle over a target area for many hours, loitering until the prey appears. One of the biggest difficulties using drones is intelligence—the data to know whom to target, and the problem of watching figures on the ground, following them long enough to make positive the crosshairs center on a true enemy. That's where Jennifer Matthews took center stage.

Such a role seemed unlikely. From the South, deeply religious, the product of Cedarville College, a small Christian college in Ohio, Matthews majored in broadcast journalism and political science. A year after graduation, she married a chemist, equally religious, a few years older. They met at college. She jogged for exercise but debated theology for fun.

Matthews joined the CIA in 1989. Her first assignment—to tease data out of aerial photos taken over Iran—helped provide the visualization skills that became so crucial. Matthews became a reports officer, extracting intel from sources like photos, agent reports, or open sources and putting it into a form useful to analysts. Not much distance separated reports officers from expert analysts, and Matthews, who read people well and managed to be diplomatic even while being outspoken, was soon counted among them.

In 1997 the CTC created what it called Alec Station, named for the baby son of its chief, Michael Scheuer. Jennifer Matthews won assignment there. Alec Station specifically focused on Osama bin Laden. The agency's field stations had always been situated geographically. Alec Station became the first to exist functionally—and at Langley. The 1999 covert operation against bin Laden that Tenet is accused of blowing had been designed by Scheuer and Alec Station.

Beyond bin Laden, their writ targeted all of Al Qaeda. After the Islamists detonated car bombs at American embassies in Kenya and Tanzania in 1998, Alec redoubled its efforts, but failed to prevent the boat bombing of the U.S. destroyer *Cole* at Aden in 2000. There would be criticism after the September 11 attacks too. Alec Station had perceived something big but could not put its finger on what. One day in August 2001, the President's Daily Brief, based on Alec's reporting, had warned of Al Qaeda using airplanes as weapons, but the threats were not connected to New York or Washington. On 9/11 Jennifer Matthews happened to be on vacation in Switzerland. Like Jose Rodriguez and others, she rushed home to help.

Matthews took criticism from 9/11 investigators who discovered that she was among a small number of CIA officers aware that some of the Al Qaeda plotters had entered the United States. They had failed to pass along that intelligence. The internal inquiry by CIA Inspector General John Helgerson singled out Matthews and some others for disciplinary action. Others argued that Alec Station had been understaffed and overworked, and no reprimands were issued. But the events of 9/11 haunted Matthews. She soon displayed encyclopedic knowledge of the Islamist foe.

Enter the drone. The first weaponized CIA drones were deployed to Pakistan just a few months after 9/11, in time for the covert campaign to topple the Taliban in Afghanistan. Predators forced the pace, both deepening knowledge of Al Qaeda and requiring development of positive control mechanisms. Two episodes in the Afghan campaign of 2001–2002 show the spectrum. In one, the Al Qaeda operations chief Mohammed Atef was killed when a Hellfire missile collapsed the house in which he sheltered. In the other, a senior commander fighting the Taliban, and his CIA minder, were nearly killed when Predator controllers mistook them for Osama bin Laden. These episodes illustrate not only the ease of Predator attacks but also the dangers of error.

Jennifer Matthews stepped in to pioneer photogrammetric methods of comparing overhead imagery with standard pictures, contextual analysis of ground movement, and amalgamation of motion pictures, file date, electronic intercepts, and other information to verify targets' identity. She had a few temporary duty stints in Kabul but always as an analyst. Matthews assembled targeteers and taught her methods. Soon CTC drone operations attained new sophistication. Michael D'Andrea, the officer who followed Rodriguez as CTC chief of operations and then succeeded Robert Grenier as director, thought highly of Jennifer and became her mentor.

In 2005 came a dream assignment—to London Station as CIA's top terrorism liaison to MI-6. Matthews lived in an attached house near Hyde Park, close to the embassy on Grosvenor Square. Her husband, two sons—a toddler and a preschooler—plus a daughter in second grade stayed home in Fredericksburg, Virginia. Jennifer indulged a taste for science fiction, watching the BBC television series *Dr. Who*. As the Bush administration gave way to Obama's, Matthews felt restless. She saw a notice for an Afghan posting and put in her buck. Her husband thought Matthews would be good at the job. He sent her a silver Celtic cross for Christmas. She wore it always. Her uncle, the CIA paramilitary vet, warned Jennifer against the assignment. He didn't think she had the right training for a war zone.

Some other agency veterans suspect the demons of 9/11 were what drove Matthews to Afghanistan, but there she went. A friend would recall that Matthews, who loved the actor Tommy Lee Jones in the movie *No Country for Old Men*, espoused the credo, perhaps a bit fatalistic, that while you cannot stop what's coming you still have to try. And a war zone tour was sure to help her stock at the agency and CTC. All of which led to Forward Operating Base (FOB) Chapman in Khost province. Jennifer L. Matthews became the CIA's chief of base.

An FOB is an interesting place, a point of departure for missions radiating into hostile territory. In the Vietnam War, the FOB had been a place at the edge of Indian Country, where special operations forces held sway. For example, Khe Sanh had had an FOB. In Afghanistan the CIA and military shared the FOBs—and participation became especially important because the agency went into Pakistan while the military could not. (Rules of engagement prohibited cross-border military operations.) FOB Chapman, named for Nathan Chapman, the first American soldier to die in the war—a Green Beret detailed to the agency for the campaign—dated to the original U.S. intervention and now housed, in addition to the CIA unit, a provincial reconstruction team, a security force, and some Afghan troops.

Base chief Mathews, in-country only since June 2009, received a short course in the secret war. Recruiting Soviet spies had been difficult enough in Cold War days. Espionage in the war on terror was harder by orders of magnitude. For starters, after cutbacks in the 1990s, the CIA did not even have stations in some of the African and Central Asian lands that were now hotbeds of fundamentalism. Equally problematic, Westerners attempting to contact locals were obvious. And the jihadists didn't have tank armies or missile silos for satellites to track. Electronic intercepts of cell phone traffic dried up after 9/11 when the terrorists realized how much the spooks were getting. Tortured or not, detainees were a limited source. By definition their knowledge extended only into the past. Direct observation—of what the jihadists put on the Internet and what the CIA could discover or see—became the main sources.

At FOB Chapman, the forty-five-year-old Jennifer Matthews became a casualty of the CIA's desperate need for data. There are at least two versions of the backstory, or perhaps the story has nuances that are not immediately apparent. In one, Pakistani spooks, the shadowy Inter-Services Intelligence (ISI), had an ongoing relationship with a Taliban band led by Salar Haqqani, who engaged a double agent to strike the Americans, while the ISI supplied $200,000 to bankroll the op. Since Pakistan is allied with the United States in the war on terror, there is no obvious reason for ISI to have done that, at least theoretically, but deep motives have always been at the heart of the Great Game. In any case, this information comes from reports the U.S. Defense Intelligence Agency (DIA) compiled over the following weeks. The ISI had been the CIA's major ally in Afghanistan since the anti-Soviet war there but had always kept private its hand of cards. It had played favorites among insurgent groups and had backed the creation of the Taliban itself.

In the other version, unbeknownst to Matthews, Jordanian intelligence approached the Americans about the prospective double agent, a doctor named Humam Muhammed al-Balawi. The Jordanian General Intelligence Directorate (GID) had been close to the CIA for years. Langley officials trusted the Jordanians. Al-Balawi showed a lot of potential, supplying inside information the likes of which the agency had hardly ever seen. Langley could confirm some of his tips. Other data suggested that he might be able to supply the whereabouts of the Al Qaeda number-two man, Ayman al-Zawahiri, whom the CIA had long been eager to get at and who was believed to be in Pakistan.

Barack Obama had focused on Pakistan in his successful 2008 presidential campaign. Leon Panetta, his CIA director, followed suit, and the agency racked up drone attacks in unprecedented numbers. Good intelligence is food for the Predators, and a Jordanian agent who could access Al Qaeda at the top level seemed heaven-sent. Sharif Ali bin Zeid, the spy's GID case officer, asked al-Balawi to come to FOB Chapman for a show-and-tell with the CIA. Chapman lay close enough to Pakistan that the spy could get away and return without his Al Qaeda hosts noticing, and it offered safety from enemy discovery. Headquarters, the Kabul station, and the FOB jointly decided on a meeting at Chapman.

The spy at first preferred meeting inside Pakistan. Finally he agreed to come to Chapman.

Base chief Matthews agreed to host. Unconfirmed reports indicate that the CIA station chief in Afghanistan also came. The Afghan provincial border-guard boss drove al-Balawi to Camp Chapman. According to the DIA reports, that commander had been offered half the ISI spy money to do so. Several weeks before the meeting, a Jordanian operative had told a GID officer that al-Balawi might really be a *triple* agent—someone working for Al Qaeda while pretending to be working with the GID and CIA against terrorists. This warning apparently didn't make it into the system. Nor did anyone suspect the border-guard commander. For his part, al-Balawi actually made a videotape denouncing CIA drone attacks, ending with "Don't think that just by pressing a button and killing mujaheddin, you are safe." Balawi's tape made no mention of ISI or the Haqqani network.

Everyone wanted in on the first get-together in memory with an actual human source on Al Qaeda. The CIA people even baked a cake, expecting to celebrate al-Balawi's birthday. Director Leon Panetta personally briefed President Obama on the spy. Obama wanted to know more, yet another reason for the FOB Chapman encounter, which took place on New Year's Eve 2009. Washington was already in pandemonium. On Christmas Day, there had been an incident on an airliner in which a terrorist, having concealed an explosive device in his underwear, was overpowered before he could detonate it. Panetta and others were still dealing with the fallout when his telephone rang. A senior aide came on the line, her voice trembling. She asked for the secure line. "There's been an attack in Afghanistan, and some of our officers have been hit."

Panetta called in his deputy Stephen R. Kappes, and they began reviewing the dispatches. By afternoon the situation had clarified. Al-Balawi, driven into the CIA compound at FOB Chapman, had detonated a suicide vest just as he was about to be searched. A dozen people were nearby, including his GID case officer, his Afghan driver, CIA personnel, and private security company guards. Seven people died, and there were varying injuries among others. The most senior were Jordanian major bin Zeid and Jennifer Matthews. Bin Zeid died immediately. Jennifer Matthews, wounded in the neck, had also been so badly burned on one leg that the bone was exposed. The base chief expired on her way to the hospital.

Director Panetta went to the White House. "This guy turned out to be a double agent," he told President Obama. "We lost seven people." One of them, CIA officer Darren LaBonte, had also raised questions regarding al-Balawi's loyalty before the meeting.

Langley's chief ordered a review. Charlie Allen, one of the agency's Grand Old Men, the one who believed that Matthews had been haunted by 9/11, led the review on the CIA side. By the fall of 2010, Director Panetta had approved twenty-three recommendations from the review panel, including provisions for more intense counterintelligence, creation of a "war zone board" of senior officers—another way for the National Clandestine Service to control the CTC—and formation of a "surge cadre" of senior officers for counterterrorism. The last-named initiative brought back George Tenet's idea of more than a decade earlier for a clandestine service reserve. In all the history of the CIA, there had been just one occasion of greater loss—in Beirut, in April 1983, when a truck bomb destroyed the U.S. embassy. Another CIA meteor perished there.

STAR-CROSSED SPOOK

Beirut has been a storied and sad place for the Central Intelligence Agency for many decades. In the days of the infant CIA, it served as playground for assorted misadventures with MI-6, French spies, and schemes with Turks, Egyptians, Saudis, and Syrians. Agency figures Kermit and Archibald Roosevelt, Miles Copeland, Edgar Applewhite, and Wilbur Crane Eveland operated with some panache. Former British spy (and Soviet agent) Kim Philby resided in Beirut for nearly a decade. Later the Israeli Mossad, then the Soviet KGB, got involved too. After the Iranian Revolution, Tehran's agents influenced the creation of the Hezbollah fundamentalists.

With the Lebanese civil war in the 1970s, Beirut morphed, becoming very dangerous but still a spy haven. The Palestine Liberation Organization (PLO) took refuge in Lebanon after the October War of 1973, and its camps on Beirut's outskirts were hotbeds of plotting. An American ambassador was assassinated, Soviet diplomats were held hostage, and a variety of others were kidnapped. Israel destabilized the country with its 1982 invasion, and by encouraging Christian militias to massacre Palestinians in the refugee camps it pretty much swept the board clean of moderates. Beirut became a city at war.

When Gerald R. Ford lived in the White House, the United States sent Marines, evacuating Americans after the June 1976 murder of Ambassador Francis Meloy Jr. and his economic counselor Robert O. Waring. Under the Reagan administration, the United States acted, it thought, to defuse some of the Lebanese travails, sending troops as part of a multinational force. That set the stage for the embassy tragedy, and the losses that went with it. One was highflier Robert Clayton Ames.

In a very real sense, Bob Ames represented a bridge between the classic age of Allen Dulles and the era of Bill Casey and Ronald Reagan. He also was among the small circle of CIA people—like Jennifer Matthews—who worked both sides of the street: operators one day, analysts the next. Moreover, Ames had the distinction of making it in the early days, when Ivy League pedigrees were a step up at the agency, although he had none. What he did have was a love of basketball. George Tenet would have approved. Born and raised in Philadelphia, son of a steelworker, Ames played college ball for LaSalle University. LaSalle was the National Collegiate Athletic Association champion in 1954 and a runner-up the following year. On those teams, Bob Ames scored points with later CIA recruiters. Graduating in 1956, he was drafted into the Army—America had a peacetime draft then—and sent to Kagnew Station in Asmara, Ethiopia (now the capital of Eritrea).

Kagnew not only happened to be in a country where Arabic was spoken (in addition to Ethiopian), but also it held a special place in United States intelligence as one of the National Security Agency's radio intercept stations. Working at Kagnew exposed Ames to the intricacies of the spy world, while living in Ethiopia challenged him to learn Arabic, especially when, participating in the military's basketball league, he hopped over to Saudi Arabia to play ball. By the time Ames completed his service in July 1958, he wanted to do something international, so he tried for the State Department, with the Central Intelligence Agency as plan B. The Foreign Service examination proved too formidable, so he went for the agency. Clandestine service recruits went through the general CIA course, in ancient buildings along the Potomac, then on to operations training at the Farm. There were forty-four men and one woman in the courses Ames attended. He was at the Farm when the CIA attempted its disastrous Bay of Pigs invasion.

Bob Ames entered on duty when the most sought-after clandestine-service jobs aimed at the Soviets and their Communist satraps, but he preferred the Arabic world, so he volunteered for that. James H. Critchfield, the Allen Dulles lieutenant who had cemented the CIA's alliance with the West Germans, headed Middle East operations then. Ames completed a jungle training course in November 1961, and the twenty-seven-year-old officer stood out among the graduates. Moreover, he actually spoke Arabic, making him a rarity. Critchfield snapped him up. Sent first to Saudi Arabia for four years, Bob worked under the cryptonym Orrin W. Biedenkopf. He married Yvonne Blakely, and they had two children—the first of six. Highly security conscious, Ames kept his work and family separate. Son Kevin knew nothing of his dad's occupation until the fifth grade, when Bob attended his school career day—and then "Biedenkopf" told the kids that he labored in government on foreign affairs. Daughter Cathy learned her father's true employment only in the 1980s, when she was twenty years old.

The young spy proved an adept talent spotter and recruiter. In the mid-1960s in the Yemeni port city of Aden, then a British possession, he enlisted a young revolutionary who went on to be president of South Yemen. Ames found more sources during tours in Kuwait and Tehran and a first tour in Beirut. But he had already met the man who became his most notorious agent, the "Red Prince," Ali Hassan Salameh, who became the

CIA's MJ/Trust/2. Salameh happened to be the intelligence chief and a bodyguard for PLO leader Yasser Arafat, heading a shadowy unit known as Force 17. Ames, who affected a casual air and often appeared in cowboy boots and lightly tinted aviator glasses, developed MJ/Trust, as well as another PLO agent, during his late-1960s Beirut tour. Through Salameh, Langley had access to the most important Palestinian leader of that age. More than that, the Red Prince could deliver action as well as shrewd judgments on PLO internal politics, and Arafat could use the Salameh channel to send messages to Washington.

Robert Ames grew to understand the Middle East better than almost anyone. He believed Israel engaged in a zero-sum game with its Arab neighbors, a situation that became increasingly evident after the Six-Day War, when the Israelis captured the West Bank, and then after the October War, when Tel Aviv continued resisting UN Security Council resolutions aimed at getting the sides to live together in peace. Israeli sources credit Ames with facilitating certain peace feelers between moderate Jewish leaders and Jordan's King Hussein—who was on the CIA payroll too. PLO leader Arafat came to New York in 1974 to address the United Nations. At a side meeting between Salameh and CIA officers at the Waldorf Astoria Hotel, the Red Prince forswore terrorism against Americans—and Force 17 protected the U.S. Beirut embassy during the troubles there.

Ames's great trial came with the Red Prince and the Israeli Mossad. During the 1972 Olympics, held in Germany at Munich, a dozen Israeli athletes were massacred by PLO militants. Israel swore revenge and for years pursued those responsible. Mossad judged that Salameh's Force 17 had helped in the murders. Mossad wanted him dead. It is reported that the CIA prevailed on the Israelis not to carry out their intentions once, but in January 1979 a Mossad car bomb killed the Red Prince after all. Robert Ames, who'd been ignorant of the plot, could hardly believe what Mossad had done. Here was a case where a CIA alliance with a foreign service came with a very steep price tag.

Actually, "Biedenkopf" had been in no position to prevent Salameh's killing even if he had known in advance about the Mossad hit. Admiral Stansfield Turner, CIA director for President Jimmy Carter, shifted Bob Ames over to the agency's analytic side. At this point, Turner, struggling to understand the Iranian Revolution, depended on Ames to clarify the bewildering factors involved. As a senior analyst, he became a national intelligence officer (NIO), one of the small panel of CIA experts, each holding a special portfolio, responsible for the National Intelligence Estimates (under a scheme introduced in 1973). Director Turner promoted him to the Senior Intelligence Service, the top ranks of CIA officers. In the Iranian hostage crisis, as Carter moved toward a commando raid to free the American prisoners, Operation Eagle Claw, Bob Ames furnished intel. The hostage rescue failed, Ronald Reagan won the 1980 election, and his campaign manager, Bill Casey—one of the old OSS crowd—became the new director of central intelligence. Casey liked Ames. As an agency operator-turned-analyst, Casey took the NIO along on his first "cruise" to the Middle East. There, and on a subsequent trip of his own, Ames widened his contacts with the Israelis, whom he had previously kept at arm's length. Casey's executive assistant, brought back from the NSC staff, was Robert Gates. Ames impressed him too. Before the first year of President Reagan's administration had ended, Casey decided to replace the chief of Near East and South Asian (NESA) analysis in the Directorate of Intelligence. He gave Bob Ames the job.

As a clandestine-service man seconded to the DI, Ames knew that people would question his knowledge and purpose. He enlisted a renowned analyst, Robert Layton, as deputy. Ames had known Layton on the National Intelligence Council, the board of NIOs, where the latter had been deputy on the Southeast Asian portfolio. They agreed that Layton would review NESA papers first. Ames involved himself only if there were problems. Layton appreciated the fact that the boss stood up for his analysts, even against Robert Gates, whom Casey had made deputy director for intelligence and who was notorious for riding herd on analysts. For his part, Gates, aware that Ames had deep experience in the Middle East, rarely contested NESA reporting.

The Israeli-Palestinian confrontation stayed hot even though the Lebanese civil war temporarily cooled. Tel Aviv recruited Lebanese minorities as an auxiliary force for a buffer zone in southern Lebanon. The PLO fired rockets into Israel. Then the Israeli air force bombed Beirut.

The CIA struggled to predict what might happen. Bob Ames had kept up the PLO contacts he'd developed in the clandestine service. One day that spring, 1982, Ames brought together several top analysts with Mustafa Zein, a friend and former PLO operative who had once been his link to the Red Prince. To escape Langley's atmosphere, they met for lunch in downtown Washington. Ames asked the group to debate the probability of another Middle East war. His NESA people felt that Israel would continue its subterranean battle against the PLO without open conflict. Zein argued that Israeli defense minister Ariel Sharon wanted to smash the PLO and stood ready to pounce. Zein had even anticipated the Israeli military plan. The CIA analysts disputed how far the Israelis might go, but Ames, impressed, got Zein to put his arguments into a paper for PLO leader Yasser Arafat. Ames gave Zein leave to tell Arafat that he, the CIA's expert, *wanted* Arafat to see this analysis. In early June, a different Palestinian faction attacked the Israeli ambassador to Great Britain. Tel Aviv retaliated, invading Lebanon. The Israelis were on Beirut's outskirts in three days.

The Israeli invasion of Lebanon marked the beginning of a volcanic time. Ronald Reagan got swept up in the conflict, and American policy was tied into knots. This vicious circle spun on to the Iran-Contra Affair and the kidnapping of CIA Beirut station chief William Buckley—plus other U.S. citizens, as well as foreign nationals—but it started with a Western effort to separate Israeli forces from Lebanon's myriad armed factions. President Reagan appointed George Shultz his new top diplomat. Told he needed to speak to Bob Ames for the real lowdown, the secretary quickly called on him. The spook's PLO contacts bothered Shultz, but having that channel proved crucial to a three-way negotiation some weeks later, ending Israeli bombing with a July 1982 truce and leading to a PLO evacuation to Tunisia.

To monitor and protect the PLO withdrawal, Yasser Arafat asked for a multinational force. There were repeated violent outbreaks, including Israeli artillery shelling and threats against the Palestinian refugee camps Sabra and Shatila. Western leaders agreed to a force of U.S., French, and Italian troops. Working with Shultz, Ames pushed for a new U.S. policy, but the ship of state turns very slowly. As a practical matter, Reagan's changes were quite modest. Meanwhile pressure on Arafat to evacuate increased. There were some who preferred to fight it out, mounting a Stalingrad-style defense. A bodyguard named Imad Mughniyah overheard one of these appeals, which—like the others—Arafat rejected. Starting in late August, some eleven thousand PLO fighters left for Tunis. Claiming that thousands more PLO fighters had stayed, Israeli forces moved into Beirut.

Diplomatic appeals brought only grudging concessions. A more forceful measure was a bomb that Syrian operatives planted to blow up the headquarters of the Lebanese Christian Phalange militia, killing twenty-six, including the leader of the Phalangists, Bachir Gemayel, who had been recently elected president. In retaliation, Christian militia entered the Palestinian refugee camps of Sabra and Shatila during the night of September 16. Over a period of hours they massacred between one thousand and four thousand civilians. With the PLO gone, the role of Palestinian fighters went to a new fundamentalist force, the Amal (which later morphed into the group known as Hezbollah). Imad Mughniyah, Arafat's bodyguard, joined Amal.

With Washington in a quandary, Robert Ames briefed several NSC meetings over the next few months. Reagan proposed a vague plan for Arab states and Palestinians to recognize Israel's right to exist, with Tel Aviv to acknowledge it had to make true peace. Some credit Robert Ames with inspiring that. With maneuvers impending, in any case, Ames felt he needed better perspective. In April 1983, he planned a cruise to the Middle East, first to Israel only, then Beirut also. Friends in the DO told Ames that if he visited Lebanon without stopping by the CIA station, brethren might feel snubbed. Langley's passport office expedited his documents to enable Bob to leave sooner. So Ames widened his itinerary and reached Beirut on April 17. That evening he dined with station staff. They met the next morning to talk substance.

No one took Imad Mughniyah into account. Of the CIA station, many of them recent arrivals, mostly post-Vietnam transplants to Mideast operations, no one even knew who Mughniyah was. The Amal operative organized an attack with a truck bomb, two thousand pounds of explosives that detonated when the panel truck crashed into the U.S. embassy shortly after one p.m. on April 18, 1983. Floors of the building pancaked over the entrance. The blast killed 63 people, 17 of them Americans; 120 persons were wounded. One of the dead was Bob Ames, his body discovered many hours later. Seven other CIA officers also died. Robert C. Ames had been a star—still rising. Or was he a meteor, flaming out?

Mustafa Zein had argued that there were but two sides to the Palestinian movement, the leftists, represented by the PLO, and the Islamic fundamentalists. Zein believed the defeat of the PLO would benefit the fundamentalists. That proved to be true.

Director William J. Casey, as it happens, decided his expanding Central Intelligence Agency had outgrown that enormous house that Allen Dulles built. Casey wanted to add a whole new wing just as big—and he got the money to do it. The appropriation requests went more easily when the agency let it be known that the new headquarters building would be named for its hero Robert Clayton Ames. Construction began just over a year after the embassy bombing. It was completed in 1991. Perhaps it is of a piece with the CIA of this era that the Ames Building proved to have a leaky roof, which after a few years had to be entirely replaced. When the

CIA rededicated the new headquarters, it was renamed too, for George Herbert Walker Bush, once director of central intelligence. Star or meteor, Robert Ames had been extinguished.

THE MAN WHO HAD IT ALL

Tracy C. Barnes had been a favorite of Allen's since those heady days at the Bern consulate. Theirs was the romance of the hunt. Dulles once called Barnes the bravest man he had ever known. The OSS station chief, slightly disabled by gout, admired the buff paratrooper who jumped out of airplanes for fun, and who had made *two* combat drops into France with the famous Jedburgh teams. When the Allies broke out, finally opening the Swiss border so Allen's outpost could obtain reinforcements, the blond, thirty-four-year-old Captain Barnes arrived among them.

Tracy had received all the sacraments. Private school at Groton. Alumnus of Yale College, where he had managed the glee club and played on the hockey, rugby, *and* baseball teams. Graduating at the height of the Depression, family money insulated Barnes from that. He went on to Harvard Law School, where in 1937 Tracy made law review, then moved to the New York firm Carter Ledyard and Milburn, becoming friends with the ubiquitous Gordon Gray. Barnes returned to Harvard Law for a year of graduate study, but the day Japan attacked Pearl Harbor found him back at the firm. Like many others, Tracy heeded the call, though at first for civilian service. He became an attorney for the War Production Board.

However, the Washington stint soured. Barnes wanted action. He joined the Army and got a commission and a posting to London as assistant air attaché. No gunsmoke there, either. Barnes finagled an attachment to the OSS and immediately went out for the Jedburghs, a project that trained three-man teams of British, American, and European commandos who helped prepare the D-day invasion by parachuting in to join western European resistance bands, becoming their advisers, sometimes leaders, and their links to outside help. The French government awarded Barnes its Croix de Guerre medal for each of his forays into occupied France.

In Switzerland the paratrooper had a key role in one of Allen Dulles's great coups, one that foreshadowed the search for the Khrushchev secret speech. In late 1944, American intelligence became aware that Italian dictator Benito Mussolini's foreign minister Galeazzo Ciano had kept a diary right up through the demise of the Fascist regime. Married to Mussolini's daughter, Ciano had been in on all the encounters between Mussolini and

Hitler, and his diary served as a record. Furthermore, Ciano disliked the Germans and had gone out of his way to itemize their outrages. With the Allies looking to prosecute bad guys for war crimes, the Ciano diaries sounded like a splendid resource. The Germans arrested Ciano soon after Mussolini's fall in 1943; he had played a crucial role in Mussolini's downfall and was executed for that in early 1944. Before his shooting by firing squad, his wife, Countess Edda Ciano, tried to use her husband's papers, which a confidant of hers had smuggled from Rome, to bargain with the Germans for her husband's freedom, but that didn't work. After Ciano's death, Countess Edda fled from German-occupied Italy to Switzerland with five volumes of Ciano's diaries.

Dulles approached Edda through intermediaries, then met her in person in December 1944. The OSS emissary made some promises about use of the materials and safeguarding of publication rights but refused to pay any direct bounty, and the countess agreed to let the diaries be photographed. Dulles worried that she might back out. The countess sat at the center of a vortex—pressures from Italian friends, German enemies, and other Allied supplicants. The OSS chieftain sent his handsome, well-spoken paratrooper to head the photo team. There was at least a chance that Captain Barnes might sweep the countess off her feet for even better terms. That didn't happen, but events were amusing enough. Barnes and a photographer slipped past Swiss security guards watching the sanatorium where the countess lived. Two men on a social visit, they said. Inside they set up photo equipment. Turning on the lights blew a fuse, fraying their cover even more, but they walked away with 1,200 photographs of the Ciano diaries. Washington officials later discovered that their set was incomplete, and Captain Barnes had to do it all over again.

That made one hell of a story for the grandchildren, but Barnes soon built another, around his forays across the front lines, arranging palavers between German generals, Italian fascists, and Allied representatives. He set up Operation Sunrise, the surrender of Axis forces in northern Italy, which became the biggest feather in Allen's cap. For that, Barnes received the Silver Star. Meanwhile, all the danger earned Tracy a huge pile of the points that American authorities used after the war to decide who had priority to go home. Barnes left first.

For a couple of years in civilian life, Mr. Barnes served as an attorney for the National Labor Relations Board. Then he moved to Rhode Island as partner of a law firm and president of the state's Urban League advocacy group. He came to Washington in 1950 to be special assistant to the secretary of the Army, his old associate Gordon Gray. His mentor left but returned in late 1951 as Truman's director for the Psychological Strategy Board (PSB). Gray offered Barnes the post of deputy. Tracy took it immediately.

And so it began. Intensely concerned to establish the PSB as America's Cold War headquarters, Gray went everywhere in search of the best people. Tracy ran the shop—and pulled at his hair as CIA dragged its feet. Meanwhile, Gordon Gray had only a short leave of absence from the University of North Carolina, where he was president, and left at the end of the year. Reflecting its tenuous grip on power, the PSB went through four successive directors before President Eisenhower abolished it. All that cascaded onto Barnes's head. Early in 1952 he tried to compile a board procedures manual only to face barriers everywhere. Staff meetings revealed the series of obstacles Frank Wisner threw in the face of the board and its strategy working groups. The big briefing on CIA covert operations—at the agency they called this "the packet" because it surveyed over a hundred projects and involved huge investments of staff and money—reached the PSB only in May 1952. Barnes thought historic the luncheon where the agency presented the data but then weeks passed before the 10/5 Panel approved the packet. The PSB lost its second director about then. Meanwhile the board's defector planning had stalled, its Middle East plan lacked substance, and the one for Southeast Asia seemed to be unraveling. Tracy thought he knew a sinking ship when he saw one.

Allen Dulles attended 10/5 Panel meetings when Director Smith could not. Pleased to encounter his old lieutenant, Allen renewed their friendship. Frank Wisner had been a colleague at the Carter Ledyard firm. The CIA dangled a job before Barnes and poached him away from the Psychological Strategy Board in late 1952, just as the agency completed the merger of its old espionage and covert operations units into the newly strengthened DO. Tracy became a senior assistant to Wisner for psychological and paramilitary projects.

His first big fling was Central America, PB/Success, the overthrow of the democratically elected leftist government of Guatemala. Eisenhower's minions decided on that in August 1953. It took place in the territory of the Western Hemisphere (WH) Division, Joseph Campbell King its chief. King was fearfully known as Jesus Christ and honorifically called a colonel, which he was not. He was a former FBI capo who had come over to the agency when Roscoe Hillenkoetter grabbed the Bureau's Latin American operations. King set a record for longevity as baron of this fiefdom. But

Colonel King held no brief for Success, wanting to pursue a diplomatic track instead. Albert Haney, the field commander, had been a special-ops guy in the Korean War and wanted to take off the gloves in the fight against Latin American independence. The two remained at odds.

Frank Wisner took a hand. Both operators reported to him as DO chief. But "J.C." soon fastened on Wisner, casting him as an enemy. The project task force, nominally under WH Division, floated on the tides. No one thought this a road to Success. Wisner solved the problem by removing the task force from WH Division, putting it under direct control. But soon enough, Haney squabbled with Wisner, too. Dulles decided to make Tracy Barnes the action officer.

Barnes supervised the creation of Lincoln, a CIA forward command post set up at Opa-locka, Florida, entirely for the purpose of ejecting Jacobo Arbenz and his government. Planners expected the project to have an important aerial-operations component, so the field commander, Haney, was made familiar with the Civil Air Transport proprietary. Haney had about thirty officers with him in Florida, forty more in Guatemala or scattered elsewhere, and a certain number with the air unit. Tracy personally selected E. Howard Hunt, one of the agency's psywar people, to head Sherwood, the propaganda apparatus. Frank Wisner visited Opa-locka only a few times. Tracy spent a lot of time there. By the end of 1953, the agency judged Success ready to roll.

The CIA recruited a disaffected Guatemalan military officer and helped him assemble a private army of several hundred. More than eighty were chosen for special training as troop leaders, demolitions men, radio operators, or support experts. While preparations progressed, the Arbenz government tried to shore up its position by obtaining arms from Czechoslovakia, carried aboard a merchant ship named *Alfhem*. Sherwood had been spewing allegations about Soviet control of Guatemala when suddenly the fact that Arbenz sought weapons against the inevitable American attack seemed to Sherwood's officers as evidence for the charge. Agency operatives had planted an arms cache to be "found" to confirm their propaganda. This was better, but the agency also freaked out that weapons might actually reach Arbenz. On May 16, 1954, Allen Dulles and his Intelligence Advisory Committee, terrified that Arbenz would seize the Panama Canal, asked the NSC to set a date for the CIA and its allies to invade Guatemala. Headquarters and Lincoln discussed a commando raid to destroy a train transporting the arms shipment from port to the Guatemalan forces. Al

Haney assigned paramilitary officer William ("Rip") Robertson Jr. to the mission, which failed.

Operation Success began with a lengthy psywar program designed to soften up Arbenz officials, making them fear public upheaval. Official American displeasure was demonstrated by a change of ambassadors. The new man toed a distinctly anti-Arbenz line. When the Guatemalans temporarily suspended constitutional guarantees in early June, the project went into its operational phase. The "rebel army" entered from Honduras on June 17. Many deserted. Agency field teams were horrified. The op seemed to be falling apart when a CIA bomber demoralized the Guatemalans by dropping empty Coca-Cola bottles over the capital. These sounded like falling bombs, sowing confusion with limited damage.

Meanwhile, Nicaraguan dictator Anastasio Somoza, the CIA's main local ally in this scheme, learned of another merchant ship supposedly coming to help Arbenz. This was a British-flagged vessel, the *Springfjord*. Somoza called in Rip Robertson, who had become a friend, demanding that the CIA destroy the ship. Tracy Barnes and Al Haney, in Opa-locka, got Robertson's request to go after the *Springfjord* one morning at two a.m. The idea made no sense to them. Arbenz seemed on the verge of folding.

Somoza, enraged, demanded the bombing: "You use my airfields, you take my orders!"

Robertson decided to ignore Lincoln's rejection and have one of his contract pilots make the strike. The napalming and sinking of the ship—loaded with coffee and cotton rather than delivering weapons—marked the beginning of a two-year dispute, highly damaging to the United States, which first pretended that the Guatemalan rebels were responsible. The episode embarrassed Tracy, but it hurt the CIA. Washington ultimately tabulated the cost to Norwegian and British insurance companies at $1.5 million (nearly $20 million in 2016 dollars).

Meanwhile, Barnes had reached the end of his headquarters tour. "William D. Playdon," as his alias made him out, got a plum assignment, chief of base at Frankfurt, Germany, one of the agency's most important centers. Playdon liked the action but knew how to game the system. When Frank Wisner showed up cruising, Barnes dropped everything to squire him around. Many liked Tracy, who affected loafers, plaid sport jackets, and oxford shirts with old school ties. He had a pleasant demeanor, concerned himself with "decent" action, and prided himself on civilized behavior.

However, others despised Barnes or did not trust his judgment. Richard Helms and John Bross, two of the agency's Old Men, both held Tracy in less esteem than Dulles. And Barnes earned no friends at Frankfurt toward the end of 1956 when, promoted chief of station in London, he just walked away, leaving unfinished business behind. Bross succeeded Barnes and had to clean up the mess. Helms noted the director's boosterism for someone he considered lacking in tradecraft skills, writing that Barnes was "a man of Allen Dulles's imagination."

In London there were mixed reviews too. Chester L. Cooper, a CIA analyst there to liaise with British intelligence, thought Playdon an improvement over the outgoing chief, Norman K. Kriebel Jr. And in an inspired bit of personnel handling, Tracy happened to be a cousin of John Hay "Jock" Whitney, who had just arrived as ambassador. The CIA lost out with another Barnes cousin, however. Decades later, Michael Straight confessed to having been a Soviet spy, one of the notorious ring the Russians recruited at Cambridge in the 1930s. Straight long wrestled with the weight of what he had done. When Barnes was in town, they went to lunch, where Straight *invited* Tracy to ask him questions about Cambridge. Barnes refused to do so. Counterespionage be damned. Perhaps Helms had a point.

Actor Douglas Fairbanks Jr. began showing up at London station, spending an inordinate amount of time with the spooks. Cooper couldn't decide if the movie star had been hooked by Barnes as a CIA recruit or if he was simply chatting up the girls. Either way, Mr. Playdon made no move to stop him. The ill-fated Indonesia covert operation took place in 1958, with Barnes in London talking to MI-6. That brought about the downfall of Frank Wisner, who was succeeded by Richard Bissell. For Playdon, another career change.

Bissell appreciated Tracy Barnes. They had been friends since private school at Groton. Barnes went through both Groton and Yale a class behind Bissell. On the Guatemala coup, for which Bissell had supervised air ops, they had worked well together. Once Bissell became DDP, he wanted Barnes at his side and, content to let Bissell bask in the limelight, Barnes/Playdon proved to be a loyal lieutenant. Bissell appreciated Barnes's salesmanship. At a civil service rank of GS18, the equivalent of a CIA general, Barnes became associate DDP "for action."

So Tracy Barnes held sway in March 1960, when President Eisenhower told Director Dulles to craft a plan to oust Fidel Castro. In fact, at the meeting where the agency's top boss brought back Ike's marching orders,

Tracy gossiped with Dick Helms about a Georgetown party while Dulles took Ike's follow-up call. Barnes and John Bross, at the home of Senator John F. Kennedy just a few days before, had had cocktails with the star attraction, British novelist Ian Fleming, author of the James Bond spy novels. Asked what he would do about Castro, Fleming expounded on Cubans' fascination with sex, money, and religion and said he would use those interests to discredit Fidel. Barnes, a James Bond fan like Allen Dulles, passed along Fleming's advice.

The plan for the Bay of Pigs invasion started there. As active as during the Guatemala project, "William Playdon" traveled to Florida, Louisiana, Guatemala, and Nicaragua to make arrangements. Agency scuttlebutt held that after a Castro takedown, Richard Bissell would become CIA director, and Tracy Barnes, chief of the clandestine service. Lots of folks positioned themselves with that expectation. Others distanced themselves. David Atlee Phillips, who had run the Sherwood radio in the Guatemalan coup, reprised that role as Cuba propaganda chief and told his friend Joseph B. Smith that this was the time to get in. Smith, coming to WH Division from the Far East, doubted it. Dick Helms, Bissell's chief of operations, absented himself too. Later reviews established that DO captains, asked to contribute officers to the Cuban venture, sent their goofballs and misfits and got away with it. As chief of the Psychological and Paramilitary Warfare Staff, Tracy had had responsibility for personnel and ought to have caught them.

At first, JM/Ate, the Cuba venture, provided that the CIA would back a Cuban rebellion against Castro. Significantly, Eisenhower's order coincided with Castro's move to nationalize American businesses in Cuba. Early in June 1960, Barnes went to State Department working sessions that set economic sanctions. A CIA covert project faced difficulties. Planning alone would consume six to eight months. Fidel, very popular, did not appear vulnerable. Cuban exiles outside the island had weaker political support than the revolutionaries. By July, agency planners wanted to expand the exile force. The DO did find anti-Castro militants on the island, but getting supplies to them involved stupendous headaches. The agency drew on its proprietaries to create an exile air wing. But crews lacked navigation skills and night-flying experience. Supply flights mostly failed. In July 1960, the CIA created a new proprietary, oriented to the Western Hemisphere, called Southern Air Transport. The idea of an exile ground force started well enough, with the U.S.-installed government of Guatemala agreeing to a CIA training base, but soon the Cuban unit grew larger than the agency could handle with its own resources. Jake Esterline, leading the Cuba task force, argued for U.S. military trainers. Tracy Barnes agreed.

On August 18, a day after the 5412 Group had approved the latest plan, principals hashed out their differences at the White House. Gordon Gray, now returned as Eisenhower's national security adviser, worried about the lengthy preparations. There was no alternative, agency officials replied. Secretary of Defense Thomas Gates complained of the danger that the U.S. military might end up fighting in Cuba. Richard Bissell answered that the trainers CIA needed were mostly military men already on assignment to the agency—except for some additional Green Berets—and would get no closer to Cuba than the third-country bases. The exile force should be ready by November. Measures should be taken to neutralize Fidel Castro. When Gates refused to back down, Allen Dulles interposed that the danger to American participants could be reexamined by the CIA together with the Joint Chiefs of Staff. Gray warned that an abortive Cuba operation would be worse than none at all. Sitting along the wall as a backbencher, Tracy could see quite clearly that the Cuba project had raised hackles.

When the agency terminated its operation many years later, Cuban officials claimed that their leader had survived as many as 634 assassination attempts, most by the CIA. Initial contacts on the first of these followed this August 18 meeting. Mr. Bissell brought in CIA security director Colonel Sheffield Edwards, instructing him to arrange contact with the Mafia, which owned hotels in Havana and had huge gambling casinos there. The thinking was, the Mafia would be happy to ally with the agency in this affair.

After 5412 Group, Director Dulles also visited Ike's budget director, Maurice Stans, to ask that the JM/Ate money be incorporated into the CIA budget request for the 1962 fiscal year. The agency had priced the project at $4.4 million ($35.2 million in 2016), but Stans could already see a price tag of more than $13 million ($104 million). Dulles refused to supply documentation supporting his demand. When Stans objected, Allen shot back, "It's none of your damn business!"

He told Stans to go see the president.

Stans did just that. Ike reassured him: he had authorized spending but not a specific military plan and would not do so unless he thought it essential and foolproof.

There is little point speculating on where the Cuba venture went off the tracks. The better way to think about JM/Ate is that it never reached stride. Agency paramilitary staff who had worked in the Far East conducted training that had to be repeated. The Army dragged its feet on assigning trainers. The exile air unit, grandly dubbed the Cuban Volunteer Air Force, couldn't put a supply drop where it was needed. CIA's Development Projects Division, managing air operations, couldn't say no to General Charles P. Cabell, CIA deputy director. Cabell notoriously ordered that some shipments be larded with rice and beans, not restricted to necessary equipment. The pooh-bah earned the nickname "Old Rice and Beans" Cabell. One militant, his finca compromised by the airplane circling and a heavy load he could not move, actually left Cuba to tell off the CIA. The air operation strained the Cuban exiles.

In November 1960, the fundamental strategy shifted, from an outside support apparatus for resistance within to an intervention from outside Cuba supposed to spark an uprising against Castro. Just a couple of weeks later, Guatemalan leader Miguel Ydígoras Fuentes, who had permitted the CIA to base its Cuban paramilitaries in his country, demanded and obtained their help to put down a revolt against him. When the CIA shifted to an invasion scheme, planners failed to notice the offshore reefs at the Cuban beaches they would assault. Barnes and Bissell increased the size of their Cuban force. The Opa-locka command post, shuttered after the Guatemala coup, reopened.

The agency frantically mounted a search up and down the U.S. East Coast for suitable small boats and outboard motors. Matching boats with motors and performance were problems never solved. Castro's security forces wore down the opposition. No one listened to analysts' assessments of Castro's military or his popularity.

After the 1960 presidential election, which resulted in a Democratic administration, that of John F. Kennedy, the Cuba plan entered stasis. Eisenhower set Tracy Barnes up with a proprietary aviation expert, Whiting Willauer, to oversee progress. With each successive decision, the anti-Castro operation became more visible, and its link to the United States less deniable. Cuban exiles in Miami and elsewhere quickly learned that the CIA was behind the recruiting. Photos that E. Howard Hunt took of Camp Trax, the exile base, ended up in the *Miami Herald*. The American aircrews were a giveaway. Intervention in Guatemalan politics became another.

Castro's government had an efficient spy service, which discovered the project. So did the *New York Times*. Reporter Tad Szulc had the story about when Eisenhower's administration gave way to Kennedy's. One of the new president's first encounters with JM/Ate was to convince the *Times* not to run Szulc's story of an impending Cuban exile invasion. Kennedy enjoyed some success. The newspaper moved it to an inside page, giving the story less prominence.

A week after Kennedy was inaugurated, he ordered the Joint Chiefs of Staff to evaluate the JM/Ate plans. Security concerns drove poor coordination; asked to brief the plan for a military evaluation, the CIA put nothing on paper at all. Barnes provided a purely verbal briefing.

Barnes's Cuban exiles were now called the 2506th Assault Brigade, after the ID badge number of one who died in a training accident. They had never rehearsed an invasion landing. The concept featured coming ashore on the Caribbean coast of Cuba at the town of Trinidad. The CIA expected its Cuban exile brigade to swell with volunteers, doubling and redoubling in size. The U.S. military felt less confident. The lead officer on the Joint Chiefs' panel gave Ate only a 30 percent chance of success—but that detail was kept out of the report sent to President Kennedy.

Perhaps because of his near miss with the *Times*, Kennedy cut the plan back to reduce its "visibility." The target area was switched from Trinidad to the Bahía de Cochinos, the Bay of Pigs, in the middle of nowhere, sparsely populated, with few to swell exile ranks. (As an index of how much Castro knew about the CIA invasion, it would later be noted that he concentrated troops and artillery at the Trinidad site.) Next, Kennedy halved the number of exile B-26 bombers scheduled to hit the Cuban air force in a surprise attack.

The agency's deception scheme provided that one exile aircraft, specially marked in the manner of Castro's air force, would fly to the United States rather than bomb. Its pilot would be represented as defecting from Castro. Adlai Stevenson, American ambassador to the United Nations, needed to be prepared for the inevitable UN debate. Bissell told subordinates that Tracy would brief him. Task force chief Esterline and his deputy traded glances with a sinking feeling. They were sure Barnes would lie to Stevenson. To make it worse, just before Barnes left for New York, Bissell privately told him, "Don't be too specific on briefing Adlai."

Tracy Barnes thought of Adlai as an old family friend—society connections were ramified then—and he'd known his deputy Francis T.P. Plimpton, again from the law firm Carter Ledyard and Milburn. Stevenson's aide Charles P. Noyes had been a Yale classmate and a wartime roommate in London. Barnes told them a secret operation was about to begin, that the United States had helped with training, but that the invasion would be all Cuban. Then they lunched at the Century Club. Stevenson opined that Kennedy was boss. It could be all right.

Deceptions are tricky. This one was falling apart. The pretend Castro B-26 turned out to be one like those the CIA had acquired for Indonesia, not the older type in Fidel's air force. The pilot neglected to fire his guns somewhere on his flight to Florida. The plan had been that the guns' partially emptied magazines would be evidence that the alleged deserter had fought, attacking Castro's airfields. But his gun barrels, to prevent tropical moisture accumulation, had been taped over, and that oversight exposed the ruse. When Stevenson mouthed the CIA cover story, he would be revealed a liar. On April 14, 1961, Assault Brigade 2506 hit the beaches at the Bay of Pigs. Tracy Barnes, already in hot water, might have suspected that his meteor was fading.

The Bay of Pigs involved lots of CIA muscle. Secretary Gates had been right to fear that Americans would be pulled in. While landing, the Cuban exiles ran into Castro militiamen, who summoned help. Fidelista forces responded urgently, and their opposition built quickly. Castro's troops presently contained the beachhead and began grinding it down. Fidel's air force—not neutralized after all—made strong attacks and sank two of the CIA flotilla's vessels. The CIA's exile pilots, only seventeen crews, quickly exhausted themselves flying the long approach and return missions from Nicaragua. Alabama Air National Guard crews were drafted to supplement them. Four Americans, crews of a pair of exile B-26s, perished during strike missions. Fidelistas recovered one of the bodies.

Over the horizon, the U.S. Navy held an aircraft carrier and its escorts ready to intervene. When the situation became hairy, President Kennedy agreed to let the Navy fly (but not fight) support for a single mission. Navy jets buzzed the beaches and Fidelista interceptors for about an hour. As the CIA landings collapsed, U.S. destroyers stood just offshore in hopes that some exiles might escape. Washington's hand, only slightly less visibly, showed in the very presence of American-type landing craft and an amphibious force in the style of World War II invasions.

THE COWBOYS

Secretary Gates, the public, and the Fidelistas would have been scandalized to know that Americans were among the very first to land at the Bay of Pigs! Two men were involved, paramilitary operators, one the CIA cowboy from Guatemala, William A. ("Rip") Robertson Jr., already controversial after the *Springfjord* affair.

In the Good War, Robertson had been a Marine officer, leading a company of the 2nd Battalion, 9th Marines. Another "junior," Robert E. Cushman Jr., battalion commander, took Rip under his wing. During the first big wave of military detailees in the CIA, Cushman went to the Far East Division and brought Robertson in after him. Rip became a trainer at the agency's secret base on Saipan. That's what made Robertson attractive to Al Haney, field commander in PB/Success, who named Rip his man for pulling together the troops supposed to fight the Arbenz government. Robertson led the commando raid that failed to derail the trains carrying Czech arms to government forces.

A big, boisterous Texan who favored Hawaiian shirts, Rip Robertson also served as the key intermediary when it came time to induce Nicaragua's Anastasio Somoza to allow CIA planes to fly from his airfields. He imagined the *Springfjord* a Guatemalan supply ship. For Robertson, top commanders were feather merchants, and headquarters—city hall—rife with politics. Robertson sought out one of the CIA pilots, Ferdinand Schoup (a former air attaché), who dutifully dropped a napalm bomb on the ship.

Agency lawyers recorded that either Robertson or Schoup, in their cups in Central American bars, had bragged of sinking the hapless merchantman. "With Rip you could never be sure," Richard Bissell told an agency historian. "I am very fond of him and a great admirer of his, but the niceties of consultation with political authorities was not one of his strong suits."

Robertson would be drummed out of the agency's paramilitary corps. He bummed around Central America for several years. Rip drilled water wells and prospected for Nicaraguan gold, occasionally trading on his friendship with Somoza. When JM/Ate began and the CIA needed a new training base in Guatemala, plus airfields in Nicaragua, Robertson, already on the scene, had the right contacts. In addition, within the Eisenhower administration, Vice President Richard M. Nixon exerted particular influence on the Cuba project, and his national security adviser happened to be Major General Robert Cushman, Rip's old mentor. Near as we can tell, Cushman went to Cuba task force director Esterline and had the latter put in a special bid for Robertson's services. Rip regained his CIA position. Investigation disclosed that Robertson had been reemployed at Esterline's request.

The CIA also hired Grayston Lynch, a Green Beret captain, wounded in Normandy, who had fought in World War II and Korea and was called while serving on a special CIA mission in Laos. Lynch met Rip on his fourth day working for the agency. They were sent to Key West as case officers for the exile "navy." Ate planners understood that the brigade needed landing ships and arranged for the purchase of two Landing Craft Infantry (LCIs), a type very familiar from the Normandy invasion. Although the ships had third-country skippers responsible for navigation, as "operations officer" Rip effectively controlled the one named *Barbara J*, and Lynch the *Blagar*. On the night of the invasion, the Americans left their LCIs to accompany the exile beach teams in rubber boats. They were to mark the landing zones for the main landing. Rip's frogmen fired the first shots, at Fidelista militiamen on the beach.

Details of the Bay of Pigs landings are not so important as what came afterward. In security sweeps before the invasion, Castro had swept away many of those who might have sided with the exiles. His air force survived. His militia arrived in time to seal up the Brigade 2506 landings at Playa Girón. The ships loaded with the brigade's ammunition and communications gear sailed away. Only the *Barbara J* and *Blagar* remained off the beaches. The Cuban exiles fought until they were overwhelmed or ran out of bullets. In four days of hard fighting, the exile brigade went down to defeat. More than eleven hundred CIA-recruited soldiers marched into Cuban prisons. President Kennedy ordered an investigation. This led to a panel headed by his special military representative, General Maxwell D. Taylor, and composed of his brother Attorney General Robert F. Kennedy, Allen Dulles representing the CIA, and Admiral Arleigh A. Burke for the U.S. Navy. On April 27, Rip Robertson and Grayston Lynch, summoned to appear before this Taylor panel, began a ride that was truly meteoric.

4

CRISES

RIP ROBERTSON ARRIVED IN WASHINGTON WITHOUT SO MUCH AS A change of clothes. He and Gray Lynch holed up at the Shoreham Hotel to await their moment before the inquisitors. Robertson had little more than Navy-issue khakis and coral-cracked paratrooper boots. He had a few hundred dollars, so he enlisted his sidekick to distract their security detail while Rip slipped away to buy a suit. On the street Robertson ran into a businessman he knew from Central America, who looked at Rip's shabby clothes and immediately volunteered to set him up with some work contacts. He handed Rip his card with a $20 bill wrapped around it. When Robertson returned to the Shoreham wearing a new suit, he panicked the CIA minder by pretending to be a reporter. Panic there would be aplenty, for the CIA had orchestrated a disaster. And the more the public learned of it, the worse it would become.

President Kennedy, as Eisenhower had done for the U-2 affair barely a year earlier, stood up to take the blame. "I am the responsible officer of this government," JFK said to reporters two days after the exile collapse. But Kennedy very much believed that he—and other officials—had been victims of a CIA con job. Only Senator J. William Fulbright and, to a lesser degree, White House historian Arthur M. Schlesinger Jr. were in the clear—though JFK thought Fulbright, at least, might have succumbed too if he'd been exposed to as much honeyed talk as the president's circle.

To Rip Robertson and Gray Lynch, the shoe was on the other foot. They, especially Lynch, were completely convinced that Ate failed only because air strikes that might have disabled Castro's planes had been canceled. To Lynch it remained a certainty that the preplanned bombing *would* have destroyed all the Cuban warplanes.* In all these CIA scandals, it is striking how often participants seize on one claim—usually unconfirmable—among a welter of issues, to insist Langley had really been right. With Cuba the canard concerned the air strikes. However, so little went smoothly with the CIA scheme—and the plan itself became so Byzantine—that it is difficult to see how JM/Ate could have led to anything but defeat.

Rip Robertson and Grayston Lynch were the only CIA people actually on the scene. A DO debriefing before the operatives met Taylor's committee was the first time headquarters learned the realities at the front. "Tears came to their eyes," Lynch writes, "when we told them of the last hours of the brigade, and of the suffering of the pitiful group of survivors that we had brought out of the Zapata swamp."

Rip and Gray first went before the Taylor committee on April 28. Before his statement, the meeting record shows, Lynch tried to lay down a series of stipulations: the CIA plan had been sound, Brigade 2506 was winning, and it would have inflicted tremendous damage on Castro had it had the requisite ammunition and air support. "The men in this force fought as well as any he had ever seen." Robertson then described the incident in which he and his team fired on Cuban militia. Here the CIA had been in direct combat with a nation with which the United States remained at peace. Robertson and Lynch returned the following week. Lynch's testimony paralleled Robertson's so closely that watchers noted only when he said something different. The lack of microphones or recording devices—even stenographers—in the meeting room disturbed Lynch. Later he learned that the transcripts for each day were constructed by General Taylor and Bobby Kennedy afterward.

Agency on-scene commanders may have been biased as to their prospects, and they were wrong to suppose the Kennedys were insincere on wanting to "get" Fidel, but they were right to perceive this inquiry as designed to shield perpetrators. Still, their vision stopped with Bobby Ken-

---

* Lynch reports of his testimony that General Taylor, fair and efficient, kept alluding to the curtailed exile air strikes, saying, "It all goes back to the planes." He thought that good and deplored Bobby Kennedy's direction—questions to support the idea that "the invasion would have failed even without Castro's air strikes," adding that Kennedy's proposition "was something that was impossible to prove." Lynch passes by the point that it was equally impossible to prove the proposition that 1,400 exiles of Assault Brigade 2506 could have beaten the Cuban army of 200,000 no matter how successful the exiles' air strikes.

nedy. Jack Kennedy's scope ranged more widely. Allen Dulles sat on that board to protect the CIA, the main culprit. Note taker for the first session had been none other than Jesus Christ King. The early meetings took place at CIA headquarters. Admiral Arleigh Burke attended for the Navy. The fleet's vulnerability centered on the possibility that its intervention could have saved the exiles. Max Taylor may have appeared efficient, but he, too, worked directly for JFK. Taylor had put those cards on the table at the group's second gathering, when he told them all that President Kennedy did not consider this *either* an "investigation" *or* an "inquiry." Just what it might be, he left to the imagination. In the hot seat that day was the high command, C. Tracy Barnes and Richard Bissell. For the CIA, in a crisis that threatened its being and purpose, the presence of gladiators to take its side would be crucial. More often than not, those individuals added their spirits to the Ghosts of Langley.

THE NERD WHO SPIED

"I'm your man-eating shark!" Dick Bissell proclaimed to Jack Kennedy. The two were at an evening affair at the Alibi Club, on I Street a couple of blocks west of the White House, where Allen Dulles had gathered his minions to regale the Kennedyites with tales of their derring-do, building rapport with the new president. The Alibi Club is a storied Washington institution. Its members pledge to answer the telephone ready to offer explanations—especially to spouses—for why husbands, their fellows, cannot come to the phone. The club had long been Dulles territory. This occurred before the Bay of Pigs, while the CIA labored to sell its plan. Mr. Bissell, out of character, perhaps remembered a Chicago childhood when his older brother kept a pet alligator in the sunroom.

Bissell didn't look like a shark or an alligator. He looked exactly like who he was, an economist. Severely cross-eyed at birth, he had worn thick glasses from the age of six months. Summers in Maine, life in Chicago, then Hartford, where his father moved to pursue a career as an insurance executive, Groton, Yale—you've heard it here already. At Yale Richard went on to graduate school, became an instructor, and initiated a course on model building that became part of the economics core curriculum. His PhD thesis explored capital as a variable under static versus dynamic conditions.

With the approach of World War II, Bissell went to work with the Department of Commerce, moving to the War Shipping Administration.

There he proved so successful that by the last year of the conflict the White House was calling for advice. The thirty-five-year-old economist went to Yalta as part of the U.S. delegation to one of the last wartime summits.

None of this had anything to do with international affairs, much less the world of spooks. In fact Bissell's first "foreign" involvement was the opposite. Before the war, he helped organize a chapter of the isolationist America First Committee at Yale. Bissell warmed up the crowd for an October 1940 appearance by Charles Lindbergh. The road from that to CIA's top covert operator had to be long. Years later, on an agency "cruise," Bissell impressed the political action chief at one of his Far East stations as a college professor, not a man of action. Different from a shark, Richard Mervin Bissell Jr. became the accidental spy.

He begins as the fellow who keeps trying to return to his calling only to be summoned for another service. After the war, Bissell returned to academia as associate professor of economics at MIT. But in 1947 Averell Harriman called on him to create a staff for the President's Committee on Foreign Aid. At congressional insistence, Harry Truman created this entity to review European requests for international help under the Marshall Plan. As a former governor and ambassador, Harriman had both the political skills and foreign service credentials to function as quasi-diplomat. He'd solved problems with Bissell when the governor headed the London embassy during the war, and he'd seen the economist again at Yalta, which Harriman attended as U.S. ambassador to Moscow. Harriman asked Bissell to be his executive secretary. In due course, Congress passed the Economic Cooperation Act in the spring of 1948, providing Marshall Plan aid. To implement this, Truman set up an Economic Cooperation Administration. Its deputy chief, Paul Hoffman, a member of the Harriman committee, prevailed on Bissell to assist. He had not completed an academic year before returning to government.

Exposure to the world of spooks began then. One friend, Frank Lindsay, rejected an employment offer, telling Bissell he was joining the Office of Policy Coordination. A good friend from Groton, the columnist Joseph Alsop, happened to be Frank Wisner's cousin. Bissell and his wife, Ann, were soon part of a social circle that included Wisner, former OSSers Paul and Julia Child, good friend (and soon agency economist) Max Milliken, and top CIA wise man Sherman Kent. Groton friends Tracy Barnes and John Bross also materialized in their CIA incarnations. One day Wisner turned up in Bissell's office in his official capacity. To fuel its activities, the agency needed to access funds in foreign currencies. Could the OPC piggyback on the Marshall Plan, receiving a portion of its "counterpart funds"? Told that Harriman agreed, Bissell approved. Soon, 5 percent of what the European nations furnished in their currencies went to pay for CIA activities in those countries. Bissell never learned how the agency used Marshall Plan money.

When the Truman administration promulgated its famous Cold War policy paper NSC-68, Bissell joined a group translating its prescriptions into budget proposals. One consequence of sharpening conflict, replacement of the relatively benign foreign aid program with one aimed specifically at defense assistance, led Bissell to leave government toward the end of 1951. He followed Paul Hoffman to the Ford Foundation and headed its Washington office. At this time Ford approached the PSB about helping fund Eastern European "defectors." The swan songs were never far away. Max Milliken, an intimate since before the war, had been instrumental in inducing the CIA to fund an MIT institute, the Center for International Studies (CENIS), and create the Princeton Group, a circle of outside consultants with whom it tested perceptions. Gordon Gray attended some of their sessions. Dick Bissell joined this group. Ford Foundation money then found its way to CENIS. Bissell consulted for them. The Cold War was tightly wound indeed. Years later, the foundation would be exposed as having served as an agency conduit.

Meanwhile, Mr. Bissell developed an expanding portfolio of agency work. One project he liked brought in Frank Lindsay. Together they brainstormed ways the CIA could encourage anti-Soviet resistance in Eastern Europe. Bissell never recorded his feelings regarding the East German upheavals in 1953 or those in Hungary and Poland three years later. In any case, he attracted Allen Dulles's increasing attention. Dulles offered a job that Bissell rejected, but the CIA chieftain kept at it. Again Bissell wanted to return to academe. Dulles brought him on as a consultant for five months. Bissell accepted because it meant he could delay moving his family, now with four children, until after the school year. He started at the CIA on February 1, 1954.

Immediately Richard Bissell became swept up in the swirl of agency operations. The Guatemala coup, hampered by differences between headquarters and the Lincoln field station, needed special attention. Director Dulles made Bissell his watchman. In a quandary over how to make effective the supposed rebel air force, which never seemed to have more than four planes able to fly, Bissell suggested increasing their psywar role, but the agency had practically no way to measure Guatemalan public opinion.

When one of the aircraft ran off a runway, Dulles put Bissell in charge of getting a couple of replacements down to Nicaragua. He had a hell of a time. Headquarters understood the weakness and poor quality of the CIA armed band. Agency radio jamming contributed to its own communication problems. All hands breathed sighs of relief when President Jacobo Arbenz threw in the towel and left for exile.

It remains unclear when exactly Dick Bissell became Dulles's fair-haired boy, but before the year was out he would be the director's special assistant, working permanently for the CIA. His gifts were great—and widely perceived. The historian Arthur Schlesinger, when he arrived at the White House in 1961, had known Bissell for a decade and a half. He described Dick as "a man of high character and remarkable intellectual gifts. His mind was swift and penetrating, and he had an unsurpassed talent for lucid analysis and fluent exposition."

Mr. Dulles put Bissell in charge of the agency's most secret venture, Project Aquatone, the U-2 spy plane. The economist performed brilliantly. This program had been so tightly held that no one had thought about the mechanics of development. Bissell understood line items and realized that if the CIA had something called a reserve or contingency fund, things financed out of it might enjoy extra secrecy. He went to Allen for permission. The CIA contingency fund, with all its mischief, is Dick Bissell's invention.

The special assistant set up a small staff in Washington—originally two rooms on Navy Hill, plus an even smaller technical management team at the Lockheed "Skunk Works" plant. He implemented very tight security. With the Pentagon, Bissell negotiated an arrangement to share costs—CIA would pay for airframe and cameras; Air Force would finance engines. When it became time for test flights, Bissell arranged for CIA use of Groom Lake, a dry salt flat in the region of Edwards Air Force Base and the now notorious Area 51 in New Mexico (Groom Lake itself is actually Area 53). An agency pilot perished during the flight test program. Bissell handled that quite discreetly. Tight security continued (though this is disputed—Lyman Kirkpatrick visited Watertown, the name of the airstrip, and returned to tell Allen Dulles that security had been virtually nonexistent). The U-2 flew over the United States to test its stealth characteristics—very successful. As proof of concept, Bissell staged a mission directly over Washington. Photos of the White House and Congress that Dick showed President Eisenhower convinced everyone they had a winner.

Ike thanked the briefers. The next day aide Colonel Andrew Goodpaster phoned with Ike's OK of a ten-day window to fly over the Soviet Union.

Pilots were recruited from the Strategic Air Command. "Sheep-dipped," they went through pretend retirement, resignation, and hiring by cover organizations. The first detachment trained at Groom Lake and deployed to Europe, initially to the United Kingdom. When the British got cold feet, Richard Bissell and Colonel Goodpaster made a trip across the pond. The British eventually returned to the fold, but for the moment they wanted no overflights from UK soil. The Americans moved to Germany, where Chancellor Konrad Adenauer allowed the U-2s to use an airfield at Wiesbaden. Early Russia missions flew from there.

This happened in the summer of 1956. The routine called for a morning flight briefing in Washington for a mission to take off in Europe the next morning. A final afternoon confab corresponded to when the European base began readying the aircraft. In Washington there would be a go/no-go decision about eleven p.m., when the U-2 pilot would be completing his prep. Flights typically launched at five thirty or six a.m., Central European Time, while Washington slept. The first day, the weather proved awful. Bissell scrubbed the flight. The second was worse. That evening, the European forecast looked much better. Bissell authorized the mission.

At about eight forty-five or nine a.m., Dick returned to headquarters and encountered Dulles, who asked about the U-2 flight.

"It's in the air now," Bissell said.

"Where is it going?" Allen asked.

"Going over, first Moscow . . . then Leningrad," Dick answered.

"My God," Dulles erupted. "Do you think that was wise, for the first time?"

Bissell had considered that. "It'll be easier the first time than any later time."

By midmorning he was able to phone to say the flight had landed, and pilot and film were safe. The flight series proved so successful that Bissell called it off after five days and half a dozen missions. The CIA had obtained photos of all the Russian heavy bomber bases. The numbers in their force were way less than some, in particular the U.S. Air Force, had expected. The so-called Bomber Gap stood revealed as a fabrication.

That marked the beginning of a long run—and a feather in Dick Bissell's cap. He got the Soviets' attention for sure; within a month, they had filed a diplomatic protest. Soon they stationed a KGB team outside Wiesbaden base. Under Bissell the CIA expanded its U-2 program, purchasing several dozen aircraft, forming a second detachment, stationed in Japan (Lee Harvey Oswald would be assigned there later, as a Marine radar operator). The agency began launching flights from additional locations, including England, Norway, Cyprus, and Pakistan. The British and Nationalist Chinese contributed pilots, and the latter formed their own U-2 unit.

After the U-2, Dick Bissell became pretty much unassailable. When Frank Wisner got in trouble, Allen Dulles had a close choice for a new operations chief. Richard Helms, who had served faithfully since the beginning; Lyman Kirkpatrick, still soldiering on as inspector general; or Bissell. Not only did Dulles choose Dick; he heaped even more work on him, while continuing the deputy's role as aerospace technology wizard. An entity called the Development Projects Division (DPD) coalesced around Bissell. The agency wanted an even more sophisticated follow-on to the U-2, and it sought cameras and satellites to accomplish the same overhead photography from space. Bissell and DPD rode herd on both programs.

Eisenhower's intelligence watchdogs, the President's Board of Consultants, were up in arms over the operations directorate even as Bissell took it over. They had been highly critical of the CIA fiasco in Indonesia. Allen Dulles begged for time. Bissell got a few months after taking over in January 1959. Then he reported to the President's Board that he had reviewed DO projects, useless ones were being phased out, new procedures adopted for approval, and so on. With experience on Guatemala and in Indonesia, Dick found his way forward. While this delicate dance went on, Bissell's other portfolios boiled over. At almost precisely this time, DPD made the design selection for the advanced spy plane, code named Oxcart, and gave Lockheed four months to build a full-scale mockup. In January 1960, the CIA went ahead to contract for a dozen of the aircraft, by then called the A-12 (and still later the SR-71).

Meanwhile the reconnaissance satellite brought huge headaches. The project, code named Corona, would be disguised as a scientific satellite program dubbed Discoverer. It suffered one failure after another, beginning in January 1959, when the upper stage of the Thor-Agena rocket began firing with the booster still on the pad preparing for launch. After a month of repairs, the rocket took off successfully but simply disappeared from the radar screen. Eight successive launches of the Thor-Agena booster each failed in some fashion. Only one rocket, Discoverer 3, actually carried a science payload. In that case, the mice who were to ride the rocketship poisoned themselves, eating paint on the interior of the capsule. Supplied with new crewmice, Discoverer 3 launched on June 3 but suffered an inertial guidance failure and pitched into the Pacific Ocean. Failures continued almost monthly until August 1960, when Discoverer 13 succeeded in carrying out all portions of a mission profile from launch to de-orbiting a film capsule. On August 18, Discoverer 14 returned the first actual overhead photography.

Each mission involved Bissell in elaborate secrecy, with the spy satellites secretly assembled in Palo Alto, California, at a plant of the Hiller Helicopter Corporation and then moved to Vandenberg Air Force Base for launch. It seemed somehow fitting to be orbiting spy satellites from a base named for a general who had once headed the CIA.

The Corona satellite entered service in the nick of time, for on May 1, 1960, a CIA U-2 piloted by Francis Gary Powers had been shot down over Russia. Agency plans for this eventuality assumed that the aircraft had been destroyed, so the CIA could claim the U-2 had been on a weather data–gathering flight. But the Russians captured not only the pilot, but also the cameras and other espionage paraphernalia, making it completely clear that this had been a spy mission. With the collapse of DPD's cover story, the CIA stood exposed.

Worse, the U-2 affair obliged President Eisenhower to take responsibility for the spy missions (giving John Kennedy his precedent). The Russians canceled participation in a long-anticipated summit conference that could have reduced global tensions. Equally distressing from Ike's point of view, the shootdown led to a congressional investigation of national security affairs, including the spy plane fiasco. Operationally, uncertainty over the capabilities and distribution of Russian air defenses led the president to halt all overflights of communist territory.

That brought disaster for another of Bissell's ongoing covert operations, ST/Circus, the secret war raging in Tibet, where the CIA had helped the Dalai Lama flee Lhasa early in 1959, then continued furnishing arms to anti-Chinese Tibetans. The agency had had the foresight to send along a camera crew to make a movie out of the Dalai Lama's rescue, which Bissell showed to a much-impressed President Eisenhower. But without overflights, the CIA arms deliveries inside Tibet diminished to practically nothing, ensuring the rebels' defeat. Overflights of Cuba also had to end, hampering preparations for the JM/Ate project too.

It's a wonder the U-2 affair did not derail Dick Bissell at the CIA. Its consequences were that dramatic. Yet despite it, people spoke of Bissell as heir apparent. With the Cuban operation in high gear, Dulles may have been reluctant to relieve him. The agency's operations chief also benefited from credits piled up in exploits from the U-2's development to the Guatemala coup and the Dalai Lama rescue. Most striking is that President Eisenhower's showdown meeting on the Cuba project took place on August 18, 1960—the same day the Corona satellite made its first successful launch, inaugurating a new era in spying. So Bissell kept his job. But with so much on his plate, it is not surprising he delegated to Tracy Barnes.

Except for one thing: the assassination plotting. Within days of that White House meeting, Dick Bissell began moving on several fronts. He quietly took security chief Sheffield Edwards aside to ask him to open a channel to the Mafia. Bissell had already had a conversation with J.C. King on going after Fidel. Now he became serious, and the Mafia had interests in Havana.

By late September, Bissell saw enough movement on the Mafia channel that he took Colonel Edwards around to Director Dulles and General Cabell. About this time, the idea of getting rid of Congolese premier Patrice Lumumba was added to the mix. When the Church Committee in the mid-1970s probed these matters, Bissell testified that he received the green light in October or early November 1960, just prior to the election. In a different place, Bissell insisted he had no knowledge that the president had, in fact, ordered anything.

"The planning for this operation," Bissell related, "was conducted in a manner completely different from that of any other operation that I ever knew of." CIA Security kept the approach out of standard channels. Edwards hired Robert Maheu, a former intermediary between CIA and FBI, now a Las Vegas private investigator, as go-between. Shef's deputy accompanied Maheu to meet the Mafia don. According to Bissell, the CIA understood that the syndicate would move unless the agency called it off. The decision to enlist the Mafia in this assassination, in terms of operational security, represented probably the worst choice of all. Sure to come back and bite when some mafioso wanted to manipulate the U.S. government, the collaboration would be explosive no matter how it came out.

In any case, the JM/Ate planners for the Bay of Pigs were completely out of the loop on any assassination plots. After President Kennedy entered office, a White House official did tell Bissell that the agency should create an "executive action" capability. Within the DO, Bissell eventually sanctioned the creation of ZR/Rifle, supposed to provide an in-house capacity for murder.

All this went on while the Cuba invasion scheme ground ahead. And Bissell manned his ramparts. After the election, a Kennedy talent scout, a former agency person, visited Joe Smith, recently transferred to the Western Hemisphere Division. "After the President," the fellow ruminated, "the DDP is the most important man in the U.S. government." The operations deputy could actually initiate CIA activity and spend unvouchered funds. Dick Bissell had done both. Smith's visitor, an old college friend, finished his thought: "He could easily get the country so deeply involved in a situation that started out as a simple covert action activity we couldn't get ourselves out of it." Despite pious words to Ike's consultant board, Bissell had made no substantive changes to the way the DO did business. And he was deeply invested. "There will be no Communist government in Latin America while I am DDP," he had said.

In Palm Beach, Florida, a few weeks after the election, Bissell and Dulles gave John F. Kennedy his first detailed glimpse of the Ate plan. Almost instinctively, Kennedy began chipping away at its margins. Bissell followed the president's cancellation of some preinvasion air strikes by scaling back some others. The final mission, itself cut in half, would be the only one left. A program of more than forty bomber flights had been pared back to just eight.

Allen Dulles told a March 11 meeting with JFK that there would be a "disposal problem" if the exiles simply disbanded. He had also impressed JFK during a sit-down in the Oval Office, telling the president he had more confidence in the Cuba plan than he'd had in 1954 during the Guatemala coup.

Meanwhile, several of the top CIA operators, including task force chief Jake Esterline and the agency supervisor for the exile brigade, Marine Colonel Jack Hawkins, were threatening to resign over the cutbacks. In the middle of preparations for the Cuban venture, a coup against the Guatemalan leader occurred. The CIA's Cuban exile troops actually took part in suppressing the coup. CIA-sponsored forces intervened in the domestic affairs of another nation for the purpose of preserving U.S. bases for a covert operation to destroy the government of a third nation. Bissell repeated what Dulles had said about disposal—it would be worse than an invasion—and he assured his operatives that Kennedy, having OKed the landing, would not leave the exiles in the lurch.

Robert F. Kennedy, attorney general, learned of the invasion only four or five days ahead of time. Bissell went to the Justice Department to brief him. According to Bobby, the CIA wizard put the chances of success as two in three.

The estimates were obviously flawed. When the weakened air attack proved less than a total success, Bissell, with Deputy Director Cabell, appealed for reinstatement of the original plan. President Kennedy happened to be at his weekend home in Hyannis Port, Massachusetts. The two CIA men went to see Secretary of State Dean Rusk, who listened to their arguments, then turned them down. He offered to phone the president and let them brief him directly. The CIA officials, feeling it wouldn't do any good, desisted. Brigade 2506 went down in defeat. No one actually attempted to assassinate Fidel Castro.

HIGH STAKES FOR THE CIA

General Taylor's committee initially met at the main CIA building on Navy Hill, barely a week after the exiles waded ashore at Playa Girón. Taylor ran a tight inquest in the way one might say a Navy skipper ran a tight ship. After lunch on April 22, five top agency people sat for the first hearing. Led by Old Rice and Beans Cabell, they included both Dick Bissell and Tracy Barnes. Allen Dulles led off, speaking from the bench to describe Eisenhower's 5412 directive, the special group it sanctioned, and its authority for covert ops. The CIA brass then revealed a couple of abortive, last-minute attempts made to head off Fidel before he took power. Havana station chief William Caldwell had tried to induce Fulgencio Batista to resign in favor of a picked successor. Bobby Kennedy wanted to know when Washington had ruled Castro politically unacceptable, a question for which the witnesses had no ready answer.

Mr. Bissell described the CIA's March 17, 1960, project proposal, Ike's approval, and the concept of a "catalyst" force infiltrating in small teams. Max Taylor scratched at the central abscess—the question of how the plans related to officials' understanding of the capabilities needed to unseat Mr. Castro. Dulles admitted that they had little to offer on that score. From there Bissell took the conversation back to infiltration teams, asserting that the idea had been to build large groups to facilitate airdrops. Not until several hours later did a CIA witness—Tracy Barnes—mention the transformation of the CIA infiltration concept into an invasion. Bobby Kennedy spoke up then, asking what purpose a strike force served. Bissell argued that the invasion would strike a blow leading to a general uprising.

A couple of days later, the same group gathered at midmorning in Allen Dulles's conference room. This time they went all day. Richard Bissell confirmed that there had been no formal policy paper on the shift to an assault force. He went on to survey the plan's evolution through the three months of Kennedy's administration. Bissell and Dulles made up a tag team, each handing off to the other to read excerpts of records noting JM/Ate's progression. In one session, on February 18, JFK had been presented with a paper described as "Bissell's View." That had argued for the invasion option, even advocating a single beach landing as an optimal way to "infiltrate" guerrilla fighters and asserting that Castro's military had little (but daily improving) effectiveness. In six months, Bissell insisted, the Fidelistas would be unassailable, implying the need for rapid action. Taylor's group mulled over the lack of a paper trail for the move from Trinidad to the Bay of Pigs, and focused on cutbacks in the air strikes intended to neutralize Castro's air force.

Toward the end of a long day, Mr. Bissell reflected on the CIA's most serious miscalculations. First, the agency had underestimated Castro's organizational ability, reaction speed, and will to fight. Those were rookie intelligence errors, and some of them had been discussed in CIA analyses that the DO had ignored. Second worst had been the inadequate air capability—especially in crews—which would have avoided the exhaustion that quickly led to committing American pilots. A related error, Bissell admitted, had been "unnecessary concessions" to favor plausible deniability over military effect, namely the reduced attacks on Fidel's warplanes.

Exactly like Grayston Lynch, Bissell implied that a fully executed bombing campaign would have meant victory on the ground. Years later, the journal *Diplomatic History* sought Bissell's commentary on the paper a scholar had written based on Allen Dulles's draft manuscripts containing his detailed defense of the Bay of Pigs—material that never went into *The Craft of Intelligence*. In that commentary, Richard Bissell *accepted* the Taylor committee's criticism of him: "The Taylor Committee was probably correct in concluding that Cabell and Bissell [note his use of the third person] were negligent in failing to make a last attempt to persuade the president by telephone to reverse his decision."

However, the myopic reductionism by which the CIA equated beating up Castro's air force with "victory" is just the first error. To Mr. Bissell's list we can add others.

Assault Brigade 2506 simply lacked the firepower to beat Castro's ground troops. Moreover, Allen Dulles had told the White House that there would be a "disposal problem" and that the best solution would be to send the exile unit into Cuba. That decision, too, could be laid at the CIA's feet.

The idea that Cubans, after a decade of impoverishment under a corrupt

American-sponsored dictator, would rise up to join an exile brigade that represented the Cuban oligarchy was absurd. It seemed inherent in the CIA plan, yet Dulles *later* wrote in *The Craft of Intelligence*, "I know of no estimate that a spontaneous uprising of the unarmed population of Cuba would be touched off by the landing." If that is so and the CIA's real working premise had been that the exile brigade would win on its own, defeating Fidel's entire army, the plans were utterly foolish. They were incoherent too: the ships contained thousands of weapons to arm expected volunteers.

The exile political leadership also lacked unity despite lengthy agency hand-holding, a sure disadvantage. In fact, the CIA contributed to the problem when top political operative E. Howard Hunt walked away from the *frente* because it had enlisted moderates and leftists, not just right-wingers. Without presenting themselves as a unified movement, the exiles had no chance.

That shortcoming, too, traces directly back to the Central Intelligence Agency. Jake Esterline, CIA's task force chief, told the Taylor committee that around mid-March the 5412 Group had given him clearance "to attempt to set up an acceptable alternative to Castro." Esterline took immediate action *"to establish a covert mechanism, through which we could . . . get rid of Castro."* At first hearing, this sounds as though the Special Group was ordering a plot to assassinate, even while the CIA had a *different* plot to murder Fidel already under way. A close reading suggests that Esterline spoke colloquially, that he was simply referring to the provisional leaders of the Frente Revolucionario Democrático. Still, the statements raise a question: with the NSC's covert-operations decision unit and the CIA task force leader both recalling plans to "neutralize" Fidel, wasn't it time for Mr. Bissell to say something? As a matter of fact, he *did not even tell the Taylor inquiry* about the Castro murder plot. He left that to Allen Dulles. A decade later, Bissell told the Church Committee he thought that Allen was responsible for the murder contract and that Dulles would at least have hinted about it to Taylor. But by his own account, Bissell did nothing to verify his suppositions. All those errors went beyond stupid invasion planning and all led to Richard Bissell.

When Taylor's group consulted Robert A. Lovett, Eisenhower's former consultant told them that the Bay of Pigs reminded him exactly of the Indonesia affair, Project Haik, which the CIA had bungled. President Kennedy had abolished Ike's board of consultants, but following the Cuban fiasco JFK turned around. He set up the President's Foreign Intelligence Advisory Board (PFIAB). In just a few months, the CIA would be telling

PFIAB that efforts to oust Fidel were dragging because its people were spending so much time on Bay of Pigs inquiries. In Eisenhower's day, the agency had actually tracked staff hours consumed responding to the Doolittle inquiry and a later review led by Herbert Hoover, complaining that these efforts impeded its work.

Max Taylor would be kind. No criticism of individuals appeared in his final report, rendered in June, but the DDP already knew where he stood. Within weeks—while the Taylor committee still met, Bissell recalled later—President Kennedy told him he would not be moving into the top floor office suite at the new Langley headquarters. Kennedy is said to have spoken of "splintering" the agency "into a thousand pieces" to "scatter it to the winds."

Instead, as he had made Allen Dulles do studies poring over his failure, so he put Dick Bissell in charge of an interagency paramilitary review. Bissell resisted the work—senior staffer Jim Cross, who helped assemble the paper that became the starting point for the review, repeatedly failed in efforts to get an appointment to see his chairman. The study concluded that paramilitary operations should be the domain of the U.S. military. Mr. Bissell also avoided the CIA inspector general's examination of his actions. Lyman Kirkpatrick got his interview with Bissell only after three tries.

National security adviser McGeorge Bundy told associates that he could no longer trust Bissell's judgment in an operational situation. Bundy thought Allen had had more misgivings than he had let on but had kept his counsel out of loyalty to Bissell.

General Taylor and his colleagues sat with Kennedy to discuss their report on June 13. Next day at the agency, the Deputies Committee mulled over how to proceed. Dulles explained JFK had decreed that there should be just one copy of Taylor's report and that he would keep it. Dick Bissell implored the DCI to try to obtain a copy anyway, or at least to ask Kennedy to put the report in a file that the agency could see after a few months. Halfway through, the DO chief talked himself out of his idea; it would be better if the CIA had no access. That way, when the inevitable leaks came, they couldn't be blamed on the agency.

Bobby Kennedy said that President Kennedy and he were both very fond of Allen, but that JFK was determined to see Dulles go. The president accepted his resignation on September 27, 1961. At one point, perhaps facetiously, Kennedy suggested Arthur Schlesinger as successor. The president also spoke to Bobby about succeeding the Great White Case Officer. His brother refused. Robert Kennedy recommended having a member of the opposing political party (the Republicans) as CIA chief. President Kennedy settled on John A. McCone, a millionaire industrialist who had been head of the Atomic Energy Commission in Eisenhower's time.

Richard Bissell's greatest challenge came from within the agency. Allen Dulles, as he pretty much had to do, assigned his inspector general to review the Bay of Pigs operation. That put Kirk on the hot seat. Kirkpatrick said nothing at the Deputies Committee meeting just mentioned, for he already had the assignment. He put his best people to work on it, led by his deputy David McClellan. Three more investigators read every file. In addition to Bissell, the IG inquisitors interviewed Tracy Barnes, Jake Esterline, J.C. King, and 124 others. Considering that there were roughly 450 people in all assigned to JM/Ate and that a goodly number were radiomen or aircraft mechanics—not much help—investigators heard from a healthy slice of the entire project staff, certainly its top people. The investigation, Kirkpatrick later wrote, amounted to "one of the most painful episodes of my entire career in intelligence, both personally and officially."

The content of his report is familiar to anyone who has read histories of the Bay of Pigs. Themes like "perfect failure" or "brilliant disaster" are ubiquitous in the histories, and the IG found flaws everywhere. From the way agency components assigned underperforming staff to the task force to exile training, communications, operations, air efforts, and decision making, it was all a mess. It's more interesting that Kirkpatrick's report kicked over a hornet's nest. "Rather than receiving [my report] in the light in which it was produced, which was to ensure that the same mistakes would not be repeated in the future, those that participated in the operation resented it and attacked it bitterly."

His actions make clear Inspector General Kirkpatrick anticipated something like that reaction. The finished report bears an October 1961 date, but Kirkpatrick did not hand it over to Allen Dulles, who had commissioned it. Instead he waited until November 20, just a few days before the dedication of the Langley headquarters, when Dulles went into retirement. The IG handed his report to John McCone, and he did so just as the newly anointed DCI left for California to attend to last-minute personal business.

Kirkpatrick's tactic ensured that Dulles could not bury the IG report. The way the Taylor committee's inquiry had trailed off might have suggested that move. The CIA's Cuba historian links Kirk's motives to his long competition with Richard Bissell. In half a dozen conversations with Allen

Dulles over the months in which the IG report was crafted, Kirkpatrick practically volunteered to take Bissell's place at the head of the operations directorate. The agency's official biographer of John McCone concludes that Kirkpatrick breached protocol and angered the new director.

Evidence cuts both ways. On the one hand, McCone employed Kirkpatrick again, on some rather serious business. On the other, the DCI's correspondence with Dick Bissell indicates sympathy for him. McCone, who eschewed his given name and preferred to be familiarly known as "Alex," signed his private correspondence "Jack." That is the form he used with Bissell. Moreover McCone sided with the reductionists who insisted that only curtailment of the CIA bombing had prevented victory at the Bay of Pigs.

In the event the report would be battered and bashed. On November 28, John McCone's first day, General Charles Pearre Cabell—familiarly referred to by his middle name—instructed Kirkpatrick to restrict circulation to those who had already received it. Explicitly kept at arm's length would be the PFIAB. McCone himself told Kirkpatrick that his report conveyed a false impression of CIA responsibility.

Pearre weighed in again on December 15, claiming that detailed comment would result in a paper almost as long as Kirkpatrick's. Bissell went ahead to do that, in a fifty-plus page exegesis that disputed nearly every point. However, even the persuasive Bissell had a hard time—as he had had before the Taylor committee—explaining the shift from infiltration to invasion, here attributed primarily and improbably to the difficulty of successful air drops. The DO analysis reached past the IG to aim at the president and NSC. Allen Dulles, as well as Cabell, complained they had not been consulted for the investigation.

Tracy Barnes did much of the writing on the DO response. By his lights, the IG report had been incompetent, biased, malicious, and released without informing affected individuals of its conclusions. That persuaded later agency historian Jack Pfeiffer. Barnes held that in the future no IG ought to be permitted to investigate the operations directorate without specific instructions approved by the CIA's director, and that, in such a case, the concerned chief should actually be monitoring the inquisitors. This precisely parallels the CIA–Senate committee argument over the torture report.

Lyman Kirkpatrick protested in vain that the IG's job was contained within the agency's walls and that he had confined himself to examining the efficiency of the CIA project. Kirk never lived down the experience of being shunned by his colleagues. Shortly before retiring, Kirkpatrick had a revealing encounter with a Cuban exile writer, Mario Lazo, who had compiled an article he hoped to sell to *Reader's Digest*. The piece, which Lazo sent to Kirkpatrick for his reaction, had commented favorably on the CIA at the Bay of Pigs. Kirk had said nothing until Lazo followed up in May 1964, when the CIA man asked that the author give up on the article. Lazo protested that he was a friend of the agency. "This was indeed part of the problem," Kirkpatrick replied, adding that "I had been actually accused of writing the article myself." Lyman Kirkpatrick couldn't gain favor at the CIA even if he reversed his entire position.

If there had been a disposal problem with the Cuban brigade, an even bigger one existed with the CIA officers who had worked with them. Rip Robertson and Gray Lynch became lieutenants in the secret war against Castro, specialists in "maritime operations," sometimes using those same ex-Navy LCIs they had at Playa Girón. Robertson had been singled out by the IG as a specific example of a poor officer. He and Lynch registered as agents for "Ace Cartography" and were responsible for the LCIs. Robertson, one exile relates, would feel sick or angry when missions were scrubbed. He once offered $50 for a *miliciano*'s ear. When the exile fighter brought him a pair, Robertson shelled out a hundred bucks and took the Cuban home for turkey dinner. How one might establish that the ears had belonged to a Fidelista as opposed to anybody else went unrecorded. Robertson later served in Southeast Asia, where he participated in more CIA operations and eventually died from malaria in Laos.

Grayston Lynch was given a medal, the Intelligence Star, the CIA's second-highest decoration. Lynch, whose dislike for Robert Kennedy ran so deep that some JFK assassination theorists include him among their candidate conspirators, may not have known that Bobby was a cheerleader for Project Mongoose, the long-running series of plans to assassinate Castro. He left in 1971 after a hundred maritime operations; he passed away in 2008. Jake Esterline hated Bobby too; he refused to tell a CIA historian, even off the record, what he thought of RFK. Co-author of the CIA's original March 1960 project proposal, Esterline got medals too and ended up running the Miami station from 1967 to 1972, shutting down Cuban operations once and for all. Lyman Kirkpatrick retired in 1965 and became a professor at Brown University. Richard Bissell went into the aviation industry, working for the corporation that became United Technology as a sort of government liaison.

Tracy Barnes gets a special place. Director McCone found him a sinecure as chief of the DO's Domestic Operations Division, a unit that handled some procurement programs, "mounted" operations, contract agents such as Robertson or Lynch, and the rehired Cuban exiles. His division also took care of survivors' benefits, including those for families of the Cubans killed at Playa Girón. Howard Hunt went to work for him. A couple of times Barnes tried to get Dick Bissell back with him, once on an initiative to manufacture underwater sleds like those the SEALs use, another time on an international investment gambit.

As deputy, Barnes got the naturalized Dane, Hans Tofte, whom he had known since Guatemala. Tofte fancied himself larger than life. He talked as if he had single-handedly won the Korean War for the CIA, and turned out to have exaggerated his exploits in the "blockade" of China, faking movies of Chinese Nationalists supposedly making combat landings. He also had tales of bouncing back and forth between British intelligence and the OSS during the war, stories that ranged from Singapore to Burma, Yugoslavia, and Germany. Tofte overreached when, asked to recommend a security policy for Colombia, he delivered one to President Kennedy that extolled the value of covert ops too soon after the Bay of Pigs.

In July 1966, a young CIA recruit looking to rent a basement apartment in Tofte's home opened a closet and found three cartons of secret documents. The new officer dutifully reported the stash to the deputy division chief, after which the Office of Security sent a team and found more. Tofte insisted—as CIA chief John Deutch did in 1996—that he had the materials at home for work. Unlike Deutch, Tofte claimed that the security men stole his wife's jewelry. He sued. Courts dismissed Tofte's case. He resigned.

That embarrassment finished Tracy too. Barnes retired in 1967 to work for Yale University president Kingman Brewster as a community relations specialist. The job was perfect for the unctuous Barnes. He died in early 1972, too soon to see how a bunch of his exile Cubans had signed on for a White House dirty tricks campaign, becoming notorious as the Watergate "Plumbers." Barnes's ghost shows the danger of a spy elevated beyond his competence level; there have been a depressing number of them. Robertson and Lynch are even more sinister, illustrating the damage done when operators unthinkingly forge ahead.

The CIA headquarters at Opa-locka continued in service as JM/Wave. Before its eclipse by agency activities in Vietnam, JM/Wave would be the largest CIA station in the world. It had never been true that the Kennedys weren't serious about getting Fidel. Under JFK a whole new CIA project, Mongoose, would target Castro with more assassination plots, more sabotage, more team infiltrations, more deception operations—more of every-thing. One JM/Wave infiltration mission right in the middle of the Cuban Missile Crisis might have started World War III; the Russians could have misinterpreted it as scouting for a U.S. invasion. The Kennedys repeatedly revamped their arrangements and changed the names of the CIA's field unit, but they were serious about Castro.

President Kennedy also felt a debt to the exiles of Brigade 2506. Bobby Kennedy recruited law school classmate E. Barrett Prettyman Jr., plus New York lawyer James B. Donovan (no relation to the general, but he had been general counsel to OSS), the man who negotiated with Russia and East Germany for the return of U-2 pilot Francis Gary Powers, to bargain with Castro to free the exile prisoners. The Powers exchange, made familiar by the movie *Bridge of Spies*, had involved an actual spy trade. This time Washington had no such trading material, but it could offer Cuba $53.5 million worth of medical equipment and medicines ($422 million in 2016), which had been denied by the U.S.-imposed trade embargo. Shortly after the missile crisis, Cuba released most of the prisoners. Donovan bargained for a few remaining exile frogmen and twenty-two Americans still rotting in Castro jails. They were released in the spring of 1963.

In Miami, at the Orange Bowl, the president came to inspect Brigade 2506 on December 29, 1962. Handed a replica of the exile battle flag, Kennedy promised to return it in a liberated Cuba. That never happened, but he opened up U.S. military ranks to the Cubans, paid compensa-tion, and continued Mongoose and its successors. Lyndon Johnson did too, through 1965. The Cuban exiles became a CIA recruiting pool. The agency brought some back for service in the Congo, Vietnam, Bolivia, and Central America, among other places. Exile factions conducted their own plots against Castro, participated in assorted mayhem in Lat-in America, and according to Kennedy assassination scholars conspired against the president of the United States. Some of them were recruited by minions of another president, Richard Nixon, for the Plumbers. Their excesses in Watergate helped bring down his presidency. The agency had opened Pandora's box. The Reagan-era CIA operation in Afghanistan, where agency mobilization of Islamist tribal resistance to the Soviets led to formation of the Al Qaeda terrorist network, is just another example of the evils let loose by these kinds of operations.

THE CRUSADERS

"Sticks and stones may break my bones, but the pitiful, feeble evidence of my alleged crimes presented in the Walsh report will *never* hurt me." Thus wrote CIA baron Duane "Dewey" Clarridge, upon reading the final report of independent counsel Lawrence R. Walsh, who filed a criminal indictment against Clarridge in November 1990, based on his alleged perjury in multiple venues during investigations of the 1980s Iran-Contra Affair, when the CIA man participated in the sudden epidemic of amnesia that afflicted agency officials implicated in those events. One can sympathize with Clarridge's frustration at the perjury accusations, never adjudicated because President George H.W. Bush, the first President Bush, preemptively pardoned him among a group of Iran-Contra figures. More interesting is Clarridge's colorful rejection. He went on to say that he hoped the prosecutor would *not* seal the documents and to issue the veiled threat that "I will deal with Walsh's allegations in the fullness of time and on my own terms." The truth is, Dewey Clarridge had been a central figure in CIA projects which led to a crisis that nearly consumed Ronald W. Reagan's presidency. Clarridge and the other amnesiacs faced the greatest crisis yet in the new era of intelligence oversight.

As delicate as Tracy Barnes but a lot more effective, Duane Ramsdell Clarridge had come up through the Near East and South Asian (NESA) Division. Clarridge, who went by the nickname Dewey, made his reputation as Barnes's went into eclipse. In 1964 he was the base chief in Madras, India. His first encounter with the new house at Langley would be a year later, as headquarters desk officer for India and Pakistan. He'd been prescient when colleagues could not foresee Pakistan's foolish 1965 war with India over Kashmir. Clarridge followed with a very successful tour as chief of station in Turkey. Later it became embarrassing that Aldrich Ames, the agency's greatest traitor, served under Dewey there, but this occurred before the betrayal. Ames, on his first overseas assignment, underperformed, and Clarridge finally decided he lacked the skills to be a case officer. Not so Clarridge himself, who notably recruited a Polish couple by helping his prospective spies determine whether the wife was pregnant.

From solid New England farm stock, Dewey had been just old enough, when World War II started, to follow what his family and neighbors were saying. His grandmother's election to the New Hampshire state legislature opened his eyes some, and Dewey aspired to more, while his family wanted him to go to private school and an Ivy. He did, in fact, attend a New Jersey private school, graduate from Brown, and do advanced study at Columbia, where an agency talent spotter collared him. Clarridge offered an interesting mixture of predatory talents. He sharpened his observational skills by watching the people go by at Grand Central Station before taking the train to Boston, and at Brown he developed a sense of the importance of memory.

As a spy, Dewey showed adaptability but naiveté, too. He was several years into a CIA assignment in Nepal before he realized that the agency had health and pension plans. Fulfilling a male citizen's military service obligation, required in the 1950s, Clarridge joined the Army Reserve and passed through officer candidate school together with another agency fellow, John Stein, who rose to head the DO. Whereas Stein hated the Army interlude, Clarridge mastered tactics so well that he taught them in basic training and extolled them to CIA case officers. He was a quick study. In Nepal Dewey learned polo and used the sport as an entrée to the nation's elite, as he did also in India. That led to an assignment as escort officer for a Nepalese general visiting Washington in 1960—and a first encounter with Allen Dulles.

When Beirut erupted in 1975, Dewey had been NESA's chief of operations. No longer the powerful number-three position in a CIA unit, as it had been when Richard Helms held that job for the entire directorate, the chief of operations slot had morphed into a staff position with no command responsibilities, merely tasks sloughed off by the deputy division chiefs now controlling regions. Clarridge blames Jim Critchfield. The agency's German enthusiast had switched to the Middle East beat before being drafted as top oil expert for the National Intelligence Council. Critchfield left behind a newfangled organizational structure that frustrated Dewey. He didn't like the job, yet held it for a year and a half. Then Clarridge became one of the regional deputies, responsible for Arab countries. The Lebanese civil war took center stage on his watch. Clarridge managed Bob Ames and his agent the Red Prince, and he traded places with Clair George, who had been the deputy chief of NESA and relinquished that for the prestigious slot of Beirut station chief, only to have the post become a nightmare.

Dewey played musical chairs with George for a decade. Like others before and after, Clarridge went on "cruises." He saw George again in Beirut, but CIA staff were soon evacuated to Athens, awaiting a moment for safe return. There were other headaches. NESA's boss detested the men in the DO front office. He had Dewey take care of any business with them. The "Year of Intelligence"—1975, with its multiple investigations of the CIA—came and went. Dewey thought the revelations were the fault of agency director William E. Colby. He would later reflect that the twin traumas of Vietnam and the Church and Pike committees had led to skittishness at the agency.

The rules of the game had changed. On Capitol Hill, Congress created oversight committees in both houses, a formal structure for covert operations approval, and a new source of worry for agency officers. President Gerald R. Ford fired Colby, and for a year George Herbert Walker Bush headed the CIA. Bush saw Clarridge often because the NESA officer frequently accompanied DO brass to explain Arabs to the CIA chieftain. Dewey had little good to say about Stansfield Turner, whom President Carter brought in to lead the agency. He considered Turner a moralist—he was a devout Christian Scientist—and paranoid. But Clarridge could get away. After a stint of broadening as a southern European deputy, he headed to Italy as station chief in Rome, a primo CIA ticket.

Palestinians, Libyans, and homegrown extremists of both the left and the right were active in Italy then. Langley deliberated whether Dewey should get an armored vehicle. The leftist Red Brigades had kidnapped and murdered former Italian prime minister Aldo Moro in the spring of 1978. Moro had been a moderate who favored compromise with Italy's giant Communist Party. Forty deaths a year were being attributed to terrorism. Not long after Clarridge completed his tour, new discoveries linked right-wing Italians, including Masonic lodges and some of the old "Gladio" networks, to some of the murders and bombings of this age.

Both Dewey and his wife, Helga, did a two-week course on firearms and defensive driving at Camp Peary before leaving for Rome. Clarridge seemed a target. An Italian magazine published a piece about him soon after his arrival. His flamboyance—he was notorious at Langley for pastel jackets, white shoes, kerchief, and cigar—made him very identifiable. Plus, Dewey did a lot of entertaining. He developed a reputation as a risk taker but, curiously, never ran into trouble.

Until Bill Casey, that is. Ronald Reagan rewarded his 1980 campaign manager, William J. Casey, with appointment as director of central intelligence. The assignment wasn't farfetched, since Casey had been with the OSS and on Gerald Ford's PFIAB. He wanted to fight communists, and the CIA had the ideal tools. On a get-acquainted cruise to Europe early in 1981, squired by Alan Wolfe, Casey had a pleasant dinner with Clarridge. According to Dewey, that was the end of it. But a few months later, his wife done with Rome, Dewey returned to headquarters. A succession of assignments were proposed, until the Latin America Division suddenly opened up, the post emptied by its chief, who left for the Pentagon. At this point, the head of the DO was old comrade John H. Stein. He recommended Clarridge. Casey approved. That marked the start of a disturbing passage.

Never accuse the CIA of being a rogue elephant. Bill Casey with his "private, off-the-shelf covert operation" and even the Castro assassination plots were products of someone's idea of what presidents wanted. In the spy business, plausible deniability is rooted in the notion that covert operations are by definition secret. The hand of the United States, like that of God, must remain invisible. By extension, a president should not be seen approving the plots. This classic way has since been turned on its head, starting with the Bay of Pigs, where the Taylor group understandably concluded that it had been fantasy to suppose that America's hand could be hidden. There were more of those ventures. There was a *new* Cuban exile air force, this time in the Congo. For a time, the CIA spent $1 million a day ($7.6 million in 2016) there. There was the "secret army" in Laos, where the price went higher. There was the Phoenix death-squad program in Vietnam, not to mention the whole Vietnam secret war. There were Air America's proprietary CIA operations throughout the world. There was Track II, to depose Salvador Allende in Chile.

The sea change occurred in the mid-1970s when Congress passed laws defining procedures for covert operations approval and created oversight committees in both the Senate and House of Representatives to monitor spy work. Under the new system, Congress was to be informed of covert operations, and the oversight committees could supervise and monitor them. The legal instrument for telling Congress became known as a presidential finding or, more formally, a memorandum of notification. As is typical of complex mechanisms, this one lacked precision when installed. Throughout the CIA's subsequent history, even into the present, the struggle over putting meat onto those bones has continued. The *size* of operations to be approved by a finding (too small is not worth it), the *scope* of a finding (which delimits the operation), the *timing* of filing with the oversight committees, the *extent* of notifications (how widely is Congress to be informed?), and the *content* of findings have all been matters of dispute.

Gerald Ford became the first president to be bound in this way. His

officials complained vociferously of the number of congressional committees required to be informed and blamed the system for the failure of the
CIA's Project IA/Feature, its 1975 paramilitary adventure in Angola, in
which agency-funded indigenous fighters chalked up an ignominious failure against Marxist government forces and were saved for the short term
only by South African intervention. Jimmy Carter ran afoul the system
with his 1980 Operation Eagle Claw, attempting to rescue the American
hostages in Iran. Carter worried that informing Congress too soon might
compromise the op. But it would be his successor, Ronald Reagan, who
pushed back hard. His instrument was Bill Casey, who frequently acted
through minions like Dewey Clarridge.

On the verge of his sixty-eighth birthday when he started at Langley,
Director Casey left booby traps everywhere. When he sat for confirmation hearings before the United States Senate, it emerged that Casey had
acted as a representative for foreign nations and interests without regis-
tering with the State Department, a crime under U.S. law. He'd failed to
list two foreign governments and seventy other clients. His past business
dealings were smelly. Casey had not mentioned nearly $500,000 in debts
and $250,000 in investments. In the Nixon era, when the International
Telephone and Telegraph Corporation (ITT) collaborated with the CIA to
prevent the advent of Allende as Chilean president, Casey had been head of
the Securities and Exchange Commission, and Alex McCone on the board
of ITT. Suspecting corporate shenanigans, the SEC had had ITT under
investigation. Someone quashed that investigation on Casey's watch. Dozens of cartons of ITT documents were returned to the company. A Senate
intelligence committee inquiry led to the odd verdict that "no basis has
been found" to conclude that Mr. Casey was "unfit to hold office."

There were also allegations that Casey, as head of Reagan's campaign,
had convinced the Iranians to delay releasing American hostages until
after the election. This "October surprise" rivaled the political dirty tricks
Richard Nixon had resorted to in his 1968 election victory. The Senate
Foreign Relations Committee looked into this scandal but reached no
conclusion.

Hardly even vexed, Casey promptly appointed another businessman,
Max Hugel, to lead the CIA's Directorate of Operations. Hugel's appoint-
ment dissolved amid a welter of controversies as bad as Casey's. To reas-
sure the now doubtful troops, Bill asked old pro John Stein to lead the
DO instead. That did not end controversy. Two years later, a Jimmy
Carter briefing book from the 1980 presidential debates, which had been

purloined, turned up in the DCI's safe. By then Mr. Casey had become well established and "Debategate" proved only a passing frenzy.

An Irish Catholic swashbuckler, Bill Casey had been in charge of prepping OSS teams to infiltrate Nazi Germany. The war ended before more than a handful were in play. You wouldn't hear that from Casey, though. He'd written a history of the OSS in Europe—a good one—full of Wild Bill Donovan, David Bruce, and the French Resistance, but there had not been much to say about the OSS in Germany, except to relate Allen Dulles's exploits. In Casey's words at his Senate confirmation hearing, "Intelligence and counterintelligence capabilities that were brought to bear against the enemy were worth many German divisions." No one caught him, but if pressed Mr. Casey would no doubt have shifted his ground to explain that he had really been referring to the Ultra codebreakers or the aerial photographers. Assert, then change the subject—that remained Casey's modus operandi in the 1980s.

After the war, Casey had gone back to his business, the law, capital ventures, and the Research Institute of America. That organization advised on tax shelters. Casey invested himself. Within a few years, he had scored big, selling a start-up microfilm records company to the 3-M Corporation. By 1948 he could buy an estate in Roslyn Harbor, Long Island. Before the 1980 campaign, he tipped the scales as a millionaire. Reagan tapped Casey early enough for the confirmation fracas to blow over. Bill took up the reins a week after the inauguration.

Another part of Bill Casey's m.o. was encouraging opponents to underestimate him. Director Casey frequently mumbled and spoke unintelligibly. President Reagan turned to aides after one early NSC meeting to ask if anyone had understood anything Bill had said. Casey combined that with seeming to eat his tie. The overseers on Capitol Hill didn't know what to make of him. *Newsweek* magazine wrote of Casey's "chronic inarticulateness." Wags called him the Mumbler. Senator Barry Goldwater, alternately chairman or senior member of the intelligence committee through the first half of the decade, called him Flappy. Journalist James Conaway in a 1983 profile found a former lawyer colleague who said quite openly, "It's a tremendous advantage to Casey to have people underestimate him. They hear him mumble and ask, 'How bright can this man be?' The next thing they know, Casey's eating their lunch."

Mumbling and unintelligibility were indeed unexpected from this gentleman lawyer and author. Besides his OSS history, Casey had written one on the Revolutionary War. His reading of history remained deep, even while ensconced at Langley. Aides and CIA line officers have recounted how the director would run off to Washington or New York bookstores, or ones in London or Paris, even in Cairo while cruising, and purchase armloads of history books. He would then *consume* them like lightning.

Mr. Casey absorbed what he read, too. In 1984, the CIA op in Nicaragua had gone off course and the sharks were circling. The Nicaraguan government had brought suit against the United States at the International Court of Justice, while the Senate intelligence committee spat fury over the CIA's failure to notify on its activities in Central America. With all this going on, *Diplomatic History* published its critique of Allen Dulles's Bay of Pigs confessions. No one had to tell Bill. It was *he* who sent full-length photocopies of the journal article to interested friends. Both in general, about the controversies surrounding business interests, and in particular, about those arising from spy work, Bill Casey had been forewarned.

MARCHING AS TO WAR

The Sandinistas were to Ronald Reagan what Fidel had been to the Kennedys. The Nicaraguan revolution brought to power a political movement named for Augusto Sandino, a nationalist and socialist leader from the 1930s. During the Carter years, the Sandinistas had overthrown the Somoza family, the same one that the CIA had worked with in its Guatemala coup and at the Bay of Pigs. President Carter initially had been friendly toward the new government, but propelled by advisers who emphasized the dangers of Russian and Cuban ties in Central America he became more guarded. Sandinista leaders spoke of revolution as an international movement, and indeed a civil war between socialist and right-wing forces raged in neighboring El Salvador. With U.S. aid in the balance, the Nicaraguan government talked of opening to all political tendencies but accepted whatever aid it could get, which amounted to the Cubans and Russians. President Reagan halted all U.S. aid. Bill Casey's CIA assembled intelligence alleging Nicaraguan arms aid for the socialist rebels in El Salvador.

Reagan relied on Casey. This president made more use of covert operations than anyone since Eisenhower. There were efforts in Angola, Madagascar, Mozambique, Cambodia, Poland, the Soviet Union, and more. Only some stayed secret in the classic way. The Reagan administration innovated the "overt covert operation" for the bigger ones. Far from studied secrecy, Reagan openly lobbied for ostensibly "secret" actions. The CIA's war in Afghanistan, contrived to put a thorn in Moscow's side, turned out like Iran and Guatemala in the far gone past. Apparent success evaporated afterward, when the op became the fountainhead for the Islamic extremism that fuels today's war on terror. But the open-secret war against Nicaragua, controversial at the time, almost destroyed Reagan's presidency.

The first presidential finding governing a Nicaragua operation came from the White House in March 1981. Wasting no time, Mr. Reagan justified war against Nicaragua as an effort to block shipments of weapons to El Salvador. Funding of $19 million ($54.6 million in 2016) went to create an antigovernment Nicaraguan force. Built around members of Somoza's former National Guard, the partisans called themselves counterrevolutionaries, or *contras*. Later other political factions joined, but the name Contra stuck.

Casey brought in Dewey Clarridge when Nestor D. Sanchez, chief of the DO's Latin America Division, moved over to the Pentagon. Clarridge worked alongside spy chief John Stein until the director made Stein the inspector general. Following service in Southeast Asia, Stein had been in Middle Eastern operations. Later Casey introduced Clair George as DO chief. The Central America task force, initially led by an East Europeanist, went to an officer who had divided his time between European and Middle Eastern assignments. His replacement, Alan K. Fiers, also hailed from the Middle Eastern tribe. Thus top leadership in the Central American secret war had largely been drawn from CIA's Middle Easterners. This may or may not have had an impact on what happened, but it is suggestive.

Dewey Clarridge threw himself into the work. Using the pseudonym Dewey Maroni, he cruised the front lines and set up strong CIA stations in all the countries surrounding Nicaragua. At home Dewey drove a Ford Bronco with the vanity license plate I'M A CONTRA TOO. In El Salvador, the CIA's effort focused in-country on the civil war, but elsewhere attention centered on Nicaragua. Dewey had a simple plan: get people into the country and have them kill Cubans.

Casey loved it. Clarridge presented his plan to interagency councils and ultimately the NSC. In November 1981, President Reagan approved it in a decision document.

Clarridge immediately visited Argentina. At first the CIA acted through them, but the Argentines dropped out in 1982 when Washington perched uncomfortably between the sides in the Falklands war. The embattled Latin America baron made his last visit to Buenos Aires that November. Taking the Argentines out of the equation quieted some critics of their "dirty war." Clarridge felt he was in a two-front war, not just in Nicaragua but in Washington too, and he believed that CIA unilateralism might just improve the Contras. Unlike Jose Rodriguez with his cant about covenants, Clarridge had no illusions: "If the operation blew up or if Congress came down hard on the Agency and the division once again, somebody had to be the scapegoat . . . I could afford to take the fall."

Despite money and technology, the secret warriors found themselves stymied. The Contras ate money but didn't accomplish anything. A few partisan bands hiked into Nicaragua and blew up some bridges. Mostly they killed peasants, thousands of them. There were no Cubans to speak of, except for Cuban teachers in Nicaraguan primary schools, so Clarridge's plan wasn't going far. This became the pattern. Contra leaders claimed bigger forces, but these didn't translate into action. By then the CIA had 180 officers on the project, mostly in Honduras and Panama, that many more in El Salvador, plus over a hundred Green Berets and various U.S. military personnel on temporary assignment for "exercises." Honduras became the central station in the secret war, and the American ambassador there, John Negroponte, its proconsul.

An intelligence committee member, Senator Patrick Leahy, scheduled his own trip to Central America in January 1983. He cleared it with CIA deputy director John N. McMahon, emphasizing that he wanted real info from frontline agency stations. In Honduras Leahy heard a briefing that sounded like conspiring to overthrow the Managua government—going further than permitted by the presidential finding, now embodied in a congressional amendment restricting CIA expenditures. In Panama City, the station chief stonewalled altogether. Leahy sent word back to Washington that he would not budge until he got information.

Dewey, who had been in Panama and left the day before Leahy's arrival, dashed down from Washington to bail out station chief Jerry Svat, an episode that goes entirely unmentioned in Clarridge's memoir. Also obscured is the real status of the Contra "army." The largest faction, the FDN, claimed seven thousand troops in 1983, when their true number was less than a third of that, and fifteen thousand in the spring of 1984, when strength had risen—to about six thousand. The CIA baron is also silent about the Contra numbers game.

Frustration led the CIA to new initiatives. Clarridge enlisted disaffected former Sandinistas to operate from Costa Rica, a southern front. The Miskito Indian minority living along the Atlantic coast joined in too. The baron worked to endow the Contras with rudimentary air assets. An airplane attacked the airport at Managua, Nicaragua's capital, in September 1983. With the lame luck that characterized this covert op, two U.S. senators arrived at the airport just as Contras bombed it.

The Nicaragua project faced strong headwinds on Capitol Hill. The first $19 million came from agency contingency funds. Congress appropriated $21 million, and then $24 million, but it had slashed that madly, down from an $80 million request. It also passed the Boland Amendment, named for Massachusetts Representative Edward P. Boland, which prohibited the use of funds for the overthrow of the Nicaraguan government. Director Casey agreed to a new presidential finding to bring operations within the stipulated boundaries.

The September 1983 finding, according to top CIA officer Robert Gates, enabled the agency to support Contra efforts but *not* to conduct paramilitary operations of its own. Casey admitted as much to the National Security Planning Group. With a wink and a nod, the DCI and Clarridge pretended not to be doing any such thing while conspiring to hurt the Sandinistas. Scandals complicated the CIA's project even more. The promulgation of a fresh presidential finding led to strategy reviews that included two fateful decisions: to close Nicaraguan harbors by mining and attacking them, and to commission a training course and a subsequent instruction manual titled *Psychological Operations in Guerrilla Warfare.*

Mining harbors amounted to a step-level escalation. To accomplish that required a maritime capability CIA completely lacked. Clarridge thought of Q-boats, heavily armed patrol vessels disguised to look like fishing boats or merchant ships. Instead, U.S. Customs donated a couple of speedy vessels called cigarette boats. These were then armed with Bushmaster machine guns. The CIA acquired a larger vessel as mother ship and to serve as platform for an armed helicopter. The crews for the attack boats, called Piranhas (after the carnivorous fish), and for the mother ship were contract agents called unilaterally controlled Latino assets. Clarridge speaks of sea patrols to stop boats traveling from Nicaragua to El Salvador, but the truth is the basic choices were made above his pay grade—at Reagan's National Security Planning Group (NSPG) meetings in the spring of 1983.

The Clarridge memoir is again misleading here. The idea of mining had actually been mentioned at the NSC, in the very dawn of the Nicaragua program, as early as 1981, in the same meetings that led to Reagan's first directive. It had been brought back to the White House in May and December 1983 for the decisions to create the naval force and then to use it.

Clarridge's version in his memoir is that he thought up the mining over gin and a cigar at home, one evening late in January 1984. That should not be believed. Langley had already begun marching deeper into the Big Muddy.

Director Casey explicitly told the National Security Planning Group at the time of the September finding that it prohibited unilateral U.S. activity, yet the maritime attacks relied on this. The first harbor attacks took place in October. The first mine exploded under a ship on January 3, 1984. Two days later, Contra official Edgar Chamorro would be awakened in the night and handed a "press release." In it, the Contras were to claim credit for the CIA attacks against ports and coastal targets. More strikes followed. Mines damaged a dozen merchant ships belonging to six nations. There were Q-boat raids on ports on both the Pacific and Atlantic sides of Nicaragua; the CIA mother ship transited the Panama Canal to switch coasts. One port, struck half a dozen times, left the Nicaraguan government in no doubt as to its adversary. In at least one raid, the CIA operational commander Rudy Enders personally flew in the helicopter gunship supporting the Piranhas.

On January 12, 1984, Bill Casey informed Congress that he intended to empty the CIA's Contra program accounts, suggesting large-scale procurement. Langley's obfuscations started when the Senate Select Committee on Intelligence, intrigued by Bill Casey's intent of draining the Contra aid fund, asked for a briefing. Clair George, still the CIA's congressional liaison a few months before his elevation to deputy director for operations, tried for a postponement. The committee insisted. Director Casey then phoned chairman Senator Barry Goldwater (R-AZ) and got the date pushed back to March.

Meanwhile, CIA witnesses and briefers kept to their Contra-attacks cover story. By March the harbor attacks and mining were front-page news. But when Casey appeared at the SSCI on March 8, he focused on a new agency budget request for another $21 million. Clair George and Dewey Clarridge spent half an hour that morning prepping Casey for his appearance, and both ducked in later with last-minute details. Clarridge would be the last person to see the director before Casey left for Capitol Hill. Langley later claimed that the committee was fully briefed at this session. In fact, Casey referred to the mining in one sentence—twenty-seven words in an eighty-four-page text. That sentence presented the cover story: mines placed by Contras.

Next, the DCI attempted to bypass the Goldwater panel completely, appealing to the Senate Appropriations Committee for a direct grant. The chairman had been a friend to the agency and might have agreed, but his vice chair insisted on enforcing the Senate rule that whatever committee had substantive jurisdiction had to approve money requests. Senator Goldwater became enraged when he learned that Director Casey had tried an end run.

More holes opened in Langley's wall of silence. The CIA chieftain went to the House intelligence committee on March 27 to request the new money. Members there pressed him on *who* was *controlling* the maritime attacks. Casey admitted, "We are."

A few days later, an SSCI staffer, veteran of a decade as a DO officer, saw a letter in which Casey used the term "unilaterally controlled Latino assets" and instantly realized that the CIA had sunk up to its ears in this operation. Mention of "firecrackers" clearly referred to mines, and Rob Simmons, the staffer, knew a mine packed with plastic explosive had far more power than a holiday noisemaker. "The CIA was directly involved in the mining," he angrily told Goldwater. "Casey withheld the information from us. The President personally gave the go- ahead . . . in the fall of 1983." Chairman Goldwater's anger came through in the letter he sent the director on April 9, saying, "I am pissed off!" and "This is no way to run a railroad!" At Casey's Capitol Hill appearance the next day, congressional overseers were frustrated and the CIA director truculent. Goldwater had to be dissuaded from dumping CIA secrets in a Senate floor speech. After a closed-door debate, the Senate passed a resolution rejecting the mining by 84 to 12, and the chairman issued a statement insisting that the committee had been deliberately misled.

Instead of contrition, Langley offered defiance. Casey denounced the complaint in a newsletter to employees, asserting that the CIA had met both the letter and spirit of the law. Spooks went to the *New York Times* to claim that Goldwater must have forgotten the briefings or that he was too old (a fateful accusation in Ronald Reagan's time). Casey went so far as to ask the committee's vice chairman, New York Democrat Daniel Patrick Moynihan, what the problem was with Goldwater.

Langley officers also averred that the delay of the January briefing to the SSCI had been at the committee's behest. White House officials told cadets at Annapolis that every detail of the mining had been shared. Rob Simmons observed that the spooks' behavior "can only be described as a domestic disinformation campaign against the U.S. Congress." Senator Moynihan announced on April 15 that he would resign: "This appears to me the most emphatic way I can express my view the Senate committee was not properly briefed." Notification, Moynihan insisted, had not been full, current, or prior, all of which were required by the Intelligence Oversight Act of 1980.

Moynihan made his promise on a weekend, in fact on a Sunday morning talk show. Bill Casey, as he often did, had gone home to New York. Moynihan's action brought the developing crisis to a head. Staffer Simmons insisted that the CIA, not the intelligence committee, had sought to delay its briefing—twice, in fact. The Monday at Langley proved frantic as a succession of officials marched through Casey's office in an effort to quiet the flap. The spy boss met agency lawyer Stanley Sporkin first thing. There was no way to wiggle off the notification hook. Section 413 of the act required the committee be "fully and currently informed of all intelligence activities which are the responsibility of, are engaged in by, or are carried out for or on behalf of the United States." That included "significant anticipated" actions by the CIA *plus* all other branches of government. The congressional committees should have been told of the CIA mother ship, Piranha boats, and attack helicopter months earlier. When CIA personnel planned and participated in the attacks, the committee ought to have been informed of that, too.

No chance the Hill-ites were going to get that, at least not from the Casey-era CIA. Dewey Clarridge expressed contempt—for Moynihan specifically and the oversight committees in general. At one briefing, Clarridge draped his leg over an adjacent chair when Moynihan arrived late. The CIA man's casual air offended the senator, who said something. Other CIAers sat aghast. On their way back to Langley, the baron quipped, "Moynihan was probably drunk."

Another time, using a pointer to emphasize items on posters, Clarridge set up the easel in the senators' faces and slapped the pointer hard each time he waved it, making the overseers cringe. The spook tickled his colleagues by saying, "It felt good." If Langley wanted war with Capitol Hill, it could have begun over Nicaragua, long before the CIA torture.

Casey huddled with John McMahon, his deputy, and with Clarridge and George. Spokesman George Lauder tried to thread the waves. He was in Mr. Casey's office five times that day. Lauder cobbled together an official statement declaring that the CIA had been fully responsive. Citing promises made at Casey's confirmation hearing, Lauder asserted that the director or his deputy had met Congress on Nicaragua thirty times since 1981, with other staff responding to nearly two dozen requests in just the past six months. About briefings on mining, the statement asserted that Congress had been told eleven times. There was nothing about delays. When pressed and given the particulars of Rob Simmons's account, Lauder checked. He called back to admit that the Senate's version was exactly correct.

Widespread leaks sprung, and they revealed yet more CIA shortcuts. These disclosed creation of the maritime force, the nature of the mines, and the fact that agency officers had helped plan the project and had participated in attacks. Langley's extravagant denials disintegrated. Casey spent hours on April 24 and 26 traipsing between offices, making private apologies to SSCI members. On the twenty-seventh, at an open hearing, Casey added his act of public contrition. Senator Goldwater convinced Moynihan to stay and withdraw his pledge to resign. An official CIA history of the agency and the Hill concedes that Director Casey's apology had been "grudging."

A few years later, under oath at the Iran-Contra hearings, former national security adviser Robert McFarlane admitted that Congress had not, in fact, been informed of the mining, as required by law.

Dewey Clarridge insists that the distinction between Contra mining and CIA mining is specious. The mining was *consistent* with a finding, Clarridge argues, so additional notice of it was absurd. He does not explain how this would be, if the September 1983 presidential finding prohibited CIA participation in paramilitary action, as its declassified scope paper specifies. Moreover, Clarridge insists, Congress *was* informed. He picks up the same number George Lauder had used (eleven times). Breaking that down, two mentions had been given to individuals who'd asked the right questions, four were part of the original deception, two concerned the budget end run, and several more were Casey's after-the-fact explanations.

Laying mines is an act of war under the 1856 Treaty of Paris and the Hague Conventions of 1899 and 1907. The CIA went beyond flagrant violation. Its mines obstructed freedom of the seas and specifically targeted merchant (civilian) ships—two more breaches of international law. Worse, the CIA issued no danger notices to mariners, also required under law, even when the mines began exploding (the Contras were supposedly laying them). Most absurd is the position that a direct CIA action that had both domestic and international legal implications required no special mention to overseers (and in Dewey's version, in which *he* dreams up the campaign of mines and Piranha attack boats, no approval from higher authority). For the Contras' creators, legality amounted to no more than an annoying side issue.

Clarridge maintains that another month of mining would have driven

Managua to the negotiating table. The assertion is disturbingly reminis-
cent of U.S. officials' claims about the bombing of North Vietnam during
the Southeast Asian war.

Of course, in his memoir, the CIA baron was responding to prosecutor
Walsh in a place and by means of his own choosing. But his account also
betrays his attitude at the time—and no one had Mr. Casey's ear on the
Contras more than he. Director Casey's schedules show that Dewey cast
a giant shadow. He saw the director, in the latter's office, almost every
day. Charles Cogan and Bert Dunn, fellow barons who ran the Near East
Division and the Afghan war, hardly ever sat with Casey one-on-one.
Afghanistan remained in the hands of DDO John Stein and his deputy Ed
Juchniewicz. Stein mostly kept his hands off Nicaragua. Perhaps he knew
something Dewey did not. The baron's private time with Director Casey—
just in the first quarter of 1984—came to over nine hours. Clarridge also
accompanied Casey to a couple of dozen larger meetings and brought key
figures to see "the boss," including John D. Negroponte, proconsul of the
secret war, and General Paul Gorman, commander in chief of the U.S.
Southern Command. Clarridge reinforced Casey's aversion to congressional oversight.

Apparently more sensitive than Casey or Clarridge to Capitol Hill tides,
the White House demanded a fix. That meant specifying more detailed
reporting requirements to Congress. After the mining of Nicaragua, the
CIA agreed to furnish prior notice for actions beyond a finding's limits,
for anything requiring presidential or NSC approval, and for any plans
about which oversight committees expressed interest. The so-called Casey
Accords were committed to paper in January 1985. President Reagan then
issued a directive recognizing the arrangement, affirming that all covert
operations were to be authorized by finding and periodically reviewed.
Langley would be in control unless Mr. Reagan decreed otherwise. But
actions already under way completely trampled these new rules.

BILL CASEY'S ENTERPRISE

The travesty of the mining, especially in an overt covert operation, ought
to have led to disintegration of the Contra project. For a moment, it seemed
that it would. Only Dewey Clarridge paid a price. Clearly he could not
remain the baron for Latin America. Casey suspended him between the
DO's European Division and the agency's newly forming Counterterrorist
Center. Then, just as the Nicaragua project budget came up for a vote, the

press revealed a CIA manual covering assassinations and psychological operations.

More controversy. The field manual had been crafted by a CIA contract officer under the pseudonym John Kirkpatrick. Ostensibly produced to inculcate standards of human rights and prevent new Contra atrocities, the manual actually advocated deliberate terrorism, the creation of "martyrs" (even arranging deaths of Contra fighters if necessary), and such selective violence as the assassination of Sandinista leaders. In it, "neutralization" and murder were equated. About a dozen CIA officers had reviewed the draft; none objected. When a couple thousand bound copies reached the office of Contra politico Edgar Chamorro, he had them locked away and assigned young recruits to razor out the offensive pages and substitute more innocuous material.

Psychological Operations in Guerrilla Warfare represented a time bomb primed to explode. Its exposure brought renewed investigations. These showed that Casey and top minions had never approved the text, suggesting that, at best, they had been asleep at the switch. The Congress not only refused the extra money; it defunded the Nicaragua account. So as to send a crystal-clear message, Congress that October passed an even more restrictive version of the Boland Amendment. The staff lawyer at the DO, John Rizzo, watched Casey react and thought the director "had taken the action as a personal repudiation." Under the new Boland prohibition, both the CIA and the Pentagon were prohibited from spending money for direct or indirect support of military action in Nicaragua by any government, agency, movement, group, or individual.

The spy chieftain had anticipated this. In March, at the height of the mining fracas, Casey sent a paper to the White House warning of an imminent funding crisis and recommending exploration of foreign alternatives. At the time, Casey thought of the Israelis. Robert McFarlane of the NSC soon met with Saudi ambassador Prince Bandar. Riyadh responded with a flourish. Promising $1 million a month, the Saudis made eight deposits before the Reaganites took the game further. This covert aid came on top of matching funds the Saudis were already putting into the CIA's operation in Afghanistan, so Reagan owed them quite a debt.

President Reagan crossed the Rubicon when he gathered his National Security Planning Group at the White House on June 25, 1984. Officials were brainstorming ways to keep the Contras in the field in the face of the Boland prohibition. Director Casey suddenly construed the September 1983 presidential finding as encouraging third-country support. Presidential aide James Baker warned that obtaining third-country money would be an impeachable offense, but Vice President George H.W. Bush speculated that doing this was reasonable and no one should object. Others, too, talked around Baker. Ronald Reagan had the last word on soliciting Contra funding: "If such a story gets out, we'll all be hanging by our thumbs in front of the White House."

Mr. Reagan really worried about leaks, but his meditation described exactly what did happen. Casey had already sent Clarridge to solicit South Africa. The Pentagon, on the CIA's behalf, asked Israel to donate captured Soviet-type weapons. McFarlane had solicited the Saudis. The line had been crossed. More followed. When the Saudi king came to Washington in the spring of 1985, President Reagan entertained him, and McFarlane subsequently made a money pitch. The Saudis increased donations substantially. The Reaganites got money from Taiwan, South Korea, Brunei, and private citizens. Israel and South Korea gave weapons. South Africa leased aircraft. The Contras made their first arms deal in late 1984.

In a burst of misguided creativity, William J. Casey created a private, off-the-shelf covert operation. To evade prohibitions, which he woodenly supposed applied only to the CIA, Casey ran the op out of the White House, using the NSC staff. Marine Lieutenant Colonel Oliver North, assigned by McFarlane, became Casey's primary operative. Reagan's administration had been bedeviled by events in the Middle East. In Lebanon, the barracks of the Marines in the multinational force were truck-bombed after the embassy. Then CIA station chief William Buckley and a succession of other Americans were kidnapped by fundamentalists controlled by Iran. To this day, it is unclear where the idea of intertwining Iran with Nicaragua came from, but by 1985 Director Casey had begun tapping CIA analysts for reports suggesting the desirability of an opening to Tehran. This effort turned into a project to sell weapons to Iran, primarily antitank and antiaircraft missiles, with the understanding that Tehran would instruct Hezbollah to free the Western hostages. Using the weapons-sale money to fund the Contras completed the circle.

This arrangement became the Iran-Contra Affair. Several points are important. First, this represented official United States business, not Mr. Casey's private scheme. The arms sold were *American* weapons, taken from U.S. stocks or forwarded by Israel from American-furnished inventories and then replenished by the Pentagon. In November 1985, Israel sent a plane to deliver the weapons but couldn't obtain landing permits. At that point, the CIA substituted a proprietary aircraft. Dewey Clarridge, now the agency's counterterrorism chief, stepped in to arrange transit and landing rights in Portugal. (Clarridge disputes the nature of his activity here, along with the charge that he perjured himself in accounting for it.) Deputy director John N. McMahon demanded that a presidential finding be created to authorize this action, which had already occurred. Because the finding *was* retroactive, it was especially sensitive. Never returned to the CIA or briefed to Congress, White House officials destroyed the finding when Iran-Contra exploded.

In broad outline, U.S. allies donated or were induced to give money to Nicaraguan rebels, while U.S. weapons were diverted to sell to Iran for the ostensible purpose of obtaining freedom for American hostages in Lebanon. Monies from these transactions were also given to the Contras, who used these and other funds to buy guns. Several Contra factions dealt in drugs for some of that cash, as later agency investigations confirmed. Casey's vest-pocket covert operations unit set up a proprietary arms network with CIA assistance, and those "private benefactors" not only carried the arms to Iran, but also sold some to the Contras, shuttled Contra supplies around Central America, and parachuted them into Nicaragua. Meanwhile, pro-Iranian militants in Lebanon seized more hostages for ransom.

The CIA provided proprietary aircraft for these functions, excepting the actual airdrops (although in March 1986 Southern Air Transport flew at least one in-country mission). Langley also furnished bank accounts in which Contra funds were deposited, good offices in Honduras, Costa Rica, and El Salvador, packets of intelligence for Contra operations, encryption devices and sophisticated communications equipment for the private benefactors, and full intel backing for the Iran side of the project. The Pentagon declared surplus some of its antitank and antiaircraft missiles, so as to give to Israel or sell to Iran, and also gave the CIA powerful machine guns for its Piranha boats.

Wink-and-nod tactics were very much in evidence. On October 1, 1984, Langley sent a cable to area CIA stations. All were to cease any actions that could be construed as providing any kind of support to the Contras. Seventy-three operatives were recalled. Analysts predicted declining Contra capabilities anyway, and certainly the rebel field forces had little to show. Efforts to energize the rebels, in particular by creating a southern front, were very much a Langley concern. Top floor, as field officers knew the high command of the secret war, wanted victory.

Alan Fiers, the new Central America task force chief, had been set to

take on the Afghan project until Casey pulled him off. Fiers knew nothing about Latin America—"I didn't even know that British Honduras had
become Belize." Clair George, who had been handling congressional relations when Casey switched him over to lead the DO, like Fiers, came from
the Near East Division. Al Wedemeyer, Clarridge's successor, at least had
a background on Latin America. Jerry Gruner, another Latin Americanist,
soon replaced him.

Bits and pieces of the private benefactor activity started to reach the
public, including the fact that Oliver North had been cooperating with
the CIA to help the Contras. The Boland Amendment restrictions applied
to "all agencies" of the federal government, including the NSC. One Saturday, George called in Fiers and Wedemeyer and took them to Casey's
office, where they found Ollie North sitting next to the director. Through
Wedemeyer, Fiers had reported discovering North active in Central America. Now, in front of both of them, Casey asked North if it were true. North
denied it. In high dudgeon, the CIA director then told the NSC staffer, "I
don't want you operating in Central America. You understand that?"

When the meeting broke up and they were safely away, Clair George,
who had a reputation for wisecracking, turned to Fiers. In the hallway, he
explained that they had just seen a show staged for their benefit: "Some-
time in the dark of night, Bill Casey has said, I will take care of Central
America, just leave it to me." They had witnessed a charade.

"Jesus Christ, Clair!" Fiers exclaimed. "If that's true, then this will be
worse than Watergate!"

While the CIA mining did not survive its revelation, the Iran-Contra
project went on for more than two years, unraveling in spectacular fashion in October–November 1986. First, on October 5 a private benefactor
transport crashed inside Nicaragua, downed by a government antiaircraft
missile. Everything about the incident smelled of CIA. The plane, a Lockheed C123K, was of a type favored by the agency proprietary Air America. The pilot and copilot, dead in the crash, had flown for Air America
in Laos. The pilot's personal logbook, captured by the Sandinistas, confirmed his CIA links. The plane's loadmaster, Eugene Hasenfus, survived,
and *he* told the Nicaraguan government the plane belonged to the CIA.
The aircraft, tail number N4410F, had actually been used by the United
States in a drug-entrapment scheme against the Sandinistas. Once journalists traced the aircraft to the private benefactors, its co-owner turned
out to be Richard Secord, a U.S. Air Force general who had worked with
the CIA in Laos. Felix Rodriguez, in El Salvador as a facilitator for the

benefactors, happened to be a former CIA contract officer who launched at the Bay of Pigs, worked in Bolivia against Che Guevara, and deployed in Vietnam, too.

Congress sought explanations. Nothing had been briefed to the intelligence oversight committees as having gone beyond the September 1983 finding. Clair George and Alan Fiers told SSCI that they knew nothing. Robert Gates, who had succeeded John McMahon as deputy director for central intelligence, seconded their denials. George went so far as to say that he knew only what he had read in the newspapers. Wrong answer. Both George and Fiers were eventually prosecuted for perjury. Bob Gates lost a promotion to CIA top dog.

Congressional overseers started probing the extent of CIA activity with the Contras, to Langley's intense discomfort. A few weeks later, the Lebanese newspaper *Al-Shiraa* (The Sail) reported that the United States had been supplying weapons to Iran, trading them for hostages, and that Reagan's former national security adviser Robert McFarlane had been in Tehran to make that deal. The speaker of the Iranian parliament confirmed the account, evidently leaked by the Syrian foreign ministry after Iranian operatives roughed up one of its diplomats. The *New York Times* picked up the report, which contained the irresistible detail that McFarlane had brought a cake baked in the shape of a key, plus a Bible inscribed by President Reagan.

As *Al-Shiraa* printed the weapons-for-hostages story, American David Jacobsen was released in Beirut. The Reagan NSC had thought all three Americans being held by militants were to be liberated, not just Jacobsen. Oliver North held center stage. On the surface, White House officials insisted that an arms embargo against Iran remained in effect. Reagan denied the *Al-Shiraa* report, claiming that discussion of these machinations made it harder to free hostages. But the cover-story bucket sprang leaks everywhere. Israeli media reported that Tel Aviv had helped the U.S. by sending military spare parts to Iran in exchange for hostages. American sources added that Washington sent spare parts too. Next, officials admitted the truth of McFarlane's oddball cake-to-Iran overture.

By November 8, 1986, silence had become untenable, and Director Casey privately briefed top senators of the intelligence committee on the Iran project while still holding out on the Contra side. Similarly, when SSCI staff went to Langley to hear a presentation regarding the Iran arms deliveries, the facts of the abortive Israeli shipment a year earlier and the consequent retroactive finding were hidden from them. When they asked to see NSA intercepts, these were denied. The project, supposedly, was too secret. That month's issue of *Reader's Digest* had an article, "Congress Is Crippling the CIA," by Rowland Evans and Robert Novak, who attributed agency failures to congressional oversight. The senators were certain that Bill Casey had been a source.

Capitol Hill committees decided to investigate the breaches of covert operations restrictions while officials conceded that the United States *had* actually engineered the arms transfers. President Reagan personally admitted U.S. participation when he met congressional leaders on November 12. In a nationally televised address the next day, Mr. Reagan insisted the weapons were defensive, supplied only in small quantities, and would have fit in a single airplane.

In a meeting at the White House on November 10, Secretary of State George Shultz first learned that a January 1986 finding had approved arms transfers to Iran. Reagan held a press conference to insist that no laws had been or would be broken. His pledge was deceptive on its face, because *any* deliveries to embargoed Iran required notification to Congress under the Arms Control Export Act. That had not been given. Congress had been denied the opportunity to reject proposed deliveries. Lawmakers had also been kept ignorant of multiple presidential findings, breaking the very promises Reagan had made after the Nicaragua mining controversy.

Beginning with the *Al-Shiraa* disclosures, NSC staff, anticipating having to mount a goal-line defense of White House actions, started compiling chronologies of this exploit. The "chrons" were designed to mislead and conceal. CIA people were dragged in to the drafting. But James McCullough, who directed Casey's executive staff, remembers the Iran operation as barely intruding into the director's suite. Because the op had been so tightly held, Casey, Robert Gates, Clair George, and a few others had dealt directly with the White House.

The unraveling began with Iran. A businessman friend of Casey's, Roy Furmark, came to warn him that individuals who had provided short-term money to cover cash transfers in the arms deals, and had not been repaid, were about to blow the whistle. In a series of eyebrow-raising encounters, Casey's suite suddenly rang with exclamations. Something would have to be said. Even to someone as close to Casey as McCullough, however, the moment the director ordered key people to contribute to the false chrons is obscure. Instead Mr. Casey left for a weeklong cruise to Central America. He remained there when the Senate and House oversight committees scheduled a hearing on the Iran initiative for Friday, November 21.

While Casey was traveling, Bob Gates had a couple of DO officers draft testimony the DCI would use to tell the story for Congress. Gates advised Casey that he should return to prepare for his appearance. On the morning of November 18, Clair George held a session for oversight committee staff in which he ran down a list of actions taken under the January 1986 presidential finding, of which Congress had just been informed. Jim McCullough attended. He found the Hill people irritated they had been excluded. Then DDO George swung into his litany.

"We were transfixed," McCullough wrote. "No one in the room except Clair and his staff officers had ever heard any of this before."

David Gries, Clair's successor as Hill liaison, proved as ignorant as the rest. More than one of the committee people warned McCullough that Casey could expect a tough grilling on the CIA's violation of agreed notification procedures.

In the hallway, George's assistants stunned McCullough. They told him the DDO had failed to mention the November 1985 arms shipment. No doubt Clair had kept silent because *that* shipment had been carried out without *any* finding at all. Equally bad, the reincarnated Dewey Clarridge had arranged for that shipment to transit Portugal. Barely out of the starting gate, and against Gates's instructions, DDO George had put the CIA in the position of holding back on events at the heart of the very matter that angered the overseers.

To make things worse, Ollie North's doctoring of the NSC chronology represented the November 1985 shipment as a full-on CIA op. Langley staff fought North on that. But in chrons compiled over at the White House, North repeatedly made changes, both excisions and inserts, designed to show that the NSC had had nothing to do with arms trading. North's efforts notwithstanding, the heat on the president had grown so fierce that on November 19 Mr. Reagan admitted that the United States had broken its own embargo to ship arms to Iran, and—after denials at that press conference of things already established—the NSC and State admitted that a third country had been involved. The next day, taking advice from Attorney General Ed Meese, President Reagan approved a Department of Justice (DOJ) investigation of the particulars.

Director Casey returned on the day of Reagan's news conference. An early draft of testimony had been hand-carried to him in Central America and he had failed, both on paper and by tape recorder, to articulate thoughts for a rewrite. Now Casey came to work at 8:45 a.m. of November 20. Deputy Robert Gates spent most of the day with him, either alone or with others. The director's first meeting included both Clair George and Dewey Clarridge. After lunching with Gates, Casey spent several hours at the White House, ending with Ollie North. Returning to Langley, Casey amended his proposed testimony to drop a direct acknowledgment that the NSC staff had asked the CIA for an airplane back in 1985. Now, he simply noted receipt of an "outside request."

Mr. Casey met with officers who had worked the Iran deals. Their conversation went in circles. Many in the room had no idea what they were talking about. The agency's comptroller first learned of money sent to the Contras while working on this testimony. Gates tried to lead a line-by-line shakedown of the text, but there were too many interruptions. People spoke out of turn. Staff chief McCullough and agency lawyer Rizzo agreed the director seemed exhausted, uninterested in what would clearly be a crucial event. The "murder board," convened to prepare Casey for his testimony in Congress, basically disintegrated. Both Casey and Gates went home, leaving Jim McCullough to finalize the statement, now being sought all around town. Casey deleted a sentence that referred to antiaircraft missiles. This version became the testimony he delivered.

Director Casey appeared before the oversight committees, starting with the House, on the morning of Friday, November 21. His description of the Iran initiative attributed the idea to Israel, saying that Tel Aviv offered channels for Americans to reach alleged Iranian moderates, who wanted weapons as a token of earnestness. CIA participation, according to Casey, began when someone asked Langley to recommend a reliable airline for bulk cargo. Clarridge's extended maneuvers to obtain right of passage through Portugal and the aircrews' talking their way past transit and flight clearances in several countries were passed off with obscure anodyne references. Casey said nothing about the NSC covert operation, his role in it, the CIA activities unauthorized by finding, the retroactive finding, or the one withdrawn in early January 1986. In connection with the (later) finding of January 17, 1986, which ordered that Congress be kept in the dark, the spy chief asserted that the president "does have the authority to withhold prior notice of operations."

Casey went on to fuss about CIA lawyers, "extraordinary circumstances," and the legislative history of the Intelligence Oversight Act of 1980—which had *confirmed* the statutory requirement for covert operations to be authorized by presidential finding—as permitting Langley to *refuse* prior notice. House intelligence committee chairman Lee Hamilton instantly engaged on the notification issue.

"The Congress so far as I know, and certainly this committee, has not recognized a constitutional basis for the President to withhold information," Hamilton declared. "Such an interpretation of the statute very severely undermines the oversight role of the intelligence committees."

The Iran operation as Casey explained it—at that moment yet to be connected to Contra activities—had been a long-term policy initiative in no way meeting the secrecy and urgency criteria claimed to justify blackout. In any case, Hamilton said, Congress understood that *even under secret and urgent conditions*, the CIA and government were obliged at a minimum to inform the Gang of Eight—the senior leaders of the intelligence committees of the House and Senate. Both the post-mining compromise and the national security directive President Reagan issued in January 1985 affirmed this requirement. "If the President were free to make some arbitrary determination of his own in each case," Hamilton went on, "then the statute is meaningless."

Director Casey yielded no ground, invoking the legal opinion of the CIA general counsel ("a consistent view between the successor general counsels and the successor directors") and the precedent of President Carter's Iran hostage rescue operation, of which Congress had also not been informed. Member after member came back to focus Mr. Casey on notification. The only possible conclusion is that the CIA's interpretation of the notification requirements was rejected by the overseers, Republicans as well as Democrats.

Later that day, a colleague confided in McCullough. He worried about what would happen when it became known that Ollie North had given Iranian weapons-sales money to the Contras. Meanwhile a State Department counselor who had seen Casey's draft presentation and smelled a CIA cover-up expressed his concern to DOJ officials. Justice investigators were already searching NSC records. They found discrepancies in the White House chronologies, which led to digging deeper, revealing a memo about diverting cash to the Contras. That disclosure occurred during the weekend, *after* Casey's testimony. Like Clair George, the CIA director had already gone on record with a false narrative, repeated in both House and Senate.

Over the weekend, and while Justice sleuths were plowing through NSC papers, top intelligence community officials convened for a periodic management conference at an off-campus center in Airlie, Virginia. Casey's talking points included claiming that the different agencies had worked together well during Reagan's administration. His point that there had been no scandals must have stunned officials. Nicaragua had been one scandal after another, and there had been controversies over Angola, Mauritania, Afghanistan, estimates of Soviet military spending, alleged Soviet directed-energy weapons, and more. Just before this event, the DCI had met with a Justice Department investigator. What truly boggled the mind was Casey's declaration that the Iran affair was over, thanks to his November 21 testimony.

Storm clouds gathered quickly. The first notorious "diversion memo" had now been discovered. Attorney General Edwin Meese heard at lunch that Saturday. Charles Cooper, the DOJ official who saw Casey Sunday morning, had been there. Director Casey, rather than preparing defenses, defiantly shook his fists.

He phoned Ed Meese and tried to deflect suspicion onto middlemen in the arms sales. First thing Monday, Casey wrote a letter to President Reagan demanding that he fire George Shultz, the secretary of state, with whom the CIA boss feuded. When Jim McCullough saw the letter, he tried to stop it, only to discover the missive had already been sent. That afternoon White House chief of staff Don Regan came to Langley and closeted himself with Casey for fifteen minutes. The DCI left shortly afterward for a reception at the Heritage Foundation. McCullough thought the director looked pale and seemed distracted. The next day the staff chief realized why—Regan must have come to Langley to tell Casey the jig was up on Iran-Contra.

Bill Casey enjoyed one last night of fun. That evening he went to Washington's Metropolitan Club for dinner with Edward Hymoff, a fellow OSS veteran and the author of a highly regarded history of the cloak-and-dagger agency.

Beginning on Tuesday, November 25, strong blows fell, hard at first but with increasing weight and quickening pace. On Tuesday President Reagan announced that a diversion of proceeds from Iran sales had benefited the Contras. Reagan insisted he had not been fully informed and had not approved any diversion. He introduced Ed Meese, who delivered the rest: a diversion of $10 million to $30 million ($21 to $63 million in 2016). National security adviser John Poindexter resigned; Oliver North was fired. Next day the president empaneled a commission under former senator John Tower to investigate the scandal. Intense media scrutiny produced a continuing stream of revelations, adding to the political firestorm.

In mid-December the Senate, followed by the House of Representatives, created special committees to investigate the Iran-Contra Affair. A few days later, a former federal judge, Lawrence E. Walsh, was appointed special prosecutor to establish whether criminal activity was involved. The investigations and legal prosecutions that flowed from these covert operations continued through the remainder of Ronald Reagan's presidency and all of George H.W. Bush's. Pundits cracked that the officials called to testify suffered from the widest epidemic of mass amnesia in U.S. history. That proved especially true of CIA people. Investigations would have gone on longer except that, in his very last days, Bush pardoned the officials in prison or in criminal jeopardy, including Dewey Clarridge and Clair George.

By then William J. Casey was no more. The day of Meese's soon infamous Iran-Contra news conference, Director Casey called in some senior people. One of them, Jack Devine, ran the DO task force conducting the Afghan secret war. Casey wanted opinions. "Boys," Devine recalls Casey asking, "this will blow over in a few days, right?" Devine thought that proposition ridiculous, but the querulous tone represented a step back from the erratic exuberance of Airlie. James McCullough saw Casey as exhausted and uncharacteristically passive. John Rizzo, now with the congressional liaison office, felt Casey looked older and seemed unfocused. Bob Gates had seen him falling over or bumping into things.

Meanwhile, the CIA's problem had escalated. Eugene Hasenfus, Air America, and Laos were birds of a feather. The private benefactors of the Contras were the same people as the arms dealers to Tehran. Rather than explain a blackout of Congress on a controversial arms-for- hostages initiative that involved relatively small CIA involvement, now the agency had to show it *was not* behind an operation that supported rebels dear to Reagan's and Casey's hearts, utilizing classic CIA methods (plus former and even current agency personnel), situated in a region the agency had wired, and in a country where it *had* started a secret war. Adding another layer, the senior officers directly responsible (Clair George and Alan Fiers, plus Casey) had given Congress false testimony in their strenuous denials of knowing anything about the Contra resupply apparatus.

Bob Gates, in retrospect, thinks the evidence supports the view that the spy chief had not sponsored the diversion, even though he concedes that Casey stoood behind the push to solicit third-country funds, and also (separately) undertook to support an Iran mission, due to his guilt that Langley could not directly accomplish release of the hostages.

By the first week of December, Casey's executive staff focused on new testimony. Naturally, the overseers had now scheduled multiple hearings and were loaded for bear. Casey fell out of his usual routine of days packed with his spooks consulting on one venture or another. At the first of the new hearings, with the House Appropriations Committee on December 8, the DCI repeatedly deferred to aides for answers, rather than pushing ahead himself. With the House Foreign Affairs Committee, Casey had his aides right with him at the witness table. Then the director punted for the House Permanent Select Committee on Intelligence, arranging a conflicting engagement that left *only* staffers to answer questions after his brief opening statement. By the Friday, Mr. Casey had declined so far that he was barely coherent when interviewed by *Time* magazine.

The ax of doom hung over headquarters that weekend. The Senate Select Committee on Intelligence (SSCI) had scheduled its hearing for Tuesday, December 16. Jim McCullough got an upbeat telephone call from the director Saturday night, but Monday morning he saw a pale, gaunt Casey, late for work and unusually dressed. Deputy director Gates found Casey had a cut on his forehead and walked unsteadily, putting hand over hand to move along furniture. Security told Gates the director had done that over the weekend. The agency's medical director, Arvil Tharp, came to monitor the DCI's blood pressure because Casey's personal doctor had changed his medication over the weekend. McCullough handed Director Casey the *Time* magazine he had interviewed for, plus a copy of his Senate committee opening statement, which included a politic mea culpa with which the DCI could appease the senators.

"Jim, I'll look at it," Casey rasped. "But I'll tell you right now I'm not apologizing to Congress."

Minutes later Director Casey had a seizure. McCullough ran into Gates's office and they summoned emergency services, which took Bill Casey to Georgetown University Hospital. Tests showed a brain tumor. Surgery took place on December 18. Within a month it had become clear that William J. Casey could not resume his post. Mrs. Casey summoned Bob Gates on January 28. The director resigned the next day. The following morning, President Reagan appointed Robert Gates the next director of central intelligence. Bill Casey passed away on May 6.

In the meantime, in its examination of Mr. Casey's November testimony, issued the day he resigned, the Senate intelligence committee determined that he had given false testimony. A draft report predictably accused the CIA of violating the Intelligence Oversight Act. In their legal defenses, Oliver North, John Poindexter, and the private benefactors all fingered

Bill Casey as their leader and inspiration, undoubtedly an exaggeration, though we cannot establish by how much. What *is* demonstrable is Langley's aversion to congressional oversight, as well as the clear damage that that arrogance inflicted on U.S. national security and the agency itself.

One of the last public functions Director Casey attended, little more than a week before his seizure, had been a memorial dinner in Philadelphia for Robert C. Ames, a Casey favorite and a brilliant intelligence officer. The new headquarters wing at Langley, named for Ames, would be completed in 1987. Bill would not be there to see it.

Casey's may be the real ghost of Langley. For the most part, the others are men and women who see their careers explode in one excess or another. Dewey Clarridge left a ghost of that sort.

Casey had blown into Langley as the fresh wind going to invigorate CIA operations. He left the agency condemned to five years spent trying to prove that it had not become a criminal enterprise. Obstruction of justice, perjured testimony, illegal operations—that's the same menu as the subsequent war on terror.

Alan Fiers, senior operations officer, copped a plea. Joseph Fernandez, chief of station in Costa Rica, reprimanded for the Contra psychological warfare manual, then fired, would be indicted on four counts in the Commonwealth of Virginia, but the case was thrown out because it couldn't be prosecuted without revealing classified information. Declared guilty on four felony counts of filing false income taxes, Thomas G. Clines, former DO officer and active among the arms traders, went to prison. Clair E. George, CIA deputy director for operations, indicted on ten counts of perjury and obstruction, had a mistrial. A second trial on lesser charges led to conviction in December 1992, but he received a pardon before sentencing. Donald H. Winters and John Mallett were reprimanded for the Contra psychological warfare manual. Dewey R. Clarridge, CIA baron, relieved, demoted a pay grade, received a reprimand. Mr. Clarridge would later be indicted on seven counts of perjury and making false statements. He had a trial date when the CIA officers (except Clines) were pardoned by President George H.W. Bush on Christmas Eve 1992.

Dewey Clarridge went off to do risk analysis and security work, as do many former agency folk. He worked for aerospace corporations at first, but later missed the fieldwork. In the era of "private military contractors," Dewey worked for a private intelligence agency and then formed his own. The *New York Times* hired his agency at one point to help search for a kidnapped reporter. The private firm obtained a Pentagon contract to run agents in Afghanistan and Pakistan. The flamboyant Clarridge made a renewed appearance in the primary season of the 2016 presidential election as a foreign policy adviser to Republican hopeful Ben Carson. By then Dewey stood on his last legs. He passed away that April.

This sorry record shows exactly and very concretely why Jose Rodriguez fantasizes when he talks about a compact with the American people. Agency operations are acceptable so long as they proceed under proper legal statute, authority, management, accountability, *and* within moral boundaries. Juicy-looking operational proposals float past all the time. Zealotry makes them all the more attractive. Smart fish don't bite. They stop to think how projects will appear in the white glare of public knowledge. Smart fish don't become ghosts.

5

THE CONSIGLIERI

WHEN BEING INTERVIEWED BY JOSEPH PERSICO, BILL CASEY'S BIOGRA-pher, Stanley Sporkin quoted the boss a lot. The top spook's constant refrain, his general counsel related, had been simple. "Don't tell me it can't be done legally," Casey would say. "Find me a legal way to do it." Sporkin left the CIA's Office of General Counsel (OGC) with the Iran-Contra ventures at their height. President Reagan nominated Sporkin to the federal bench. He spent the next fourteen years as a judge for the U.S. District Court for the District of Columbia, then went into private practice. General counsels, Sporkin felt, play to their chief executives—in the CIA's case, to the director. Or for them. That's precisely what Mr. Sporkin did for Mr. Casey.

When Iran-Contra exploded into national trauma, Stan Sporkin had been confirmed to the bench and had a year as a jurist under his belt. Out of respect, congressional investigators never deposed Judge Sporkin, and special prosecutor Lawrence Walsh used him only as a cooperating witness at trial. But in actuality this denizen of the OGC was crucial to misdirecting the inquiries: Sporkin helped deflect scrutiny of the violations of law in the presidential findings. The retroactive finding, on its face, was not lawful. Another had been defective because it admitted a goal of freeing hostages, for which arms deliveries seemed inherently illegal. The law provides a narrow range of purposes for weapons sales and a specific schema for notifying Congress and obtaining approval thereof. The legality of the arms deals turned on which statute one cited. Either way, for covert ops, "timely" notification was built into the Oversight Act and affirmed in the Casey Accords.

As general counsel, Sporkin had actually written those presidential findings. On June 24, 1987, the joint committee conducting the official investigation had Judge Sporkin as witness. It fit with the amnesia suddenly afflicting so many that Sporkin held to very strained legal interpreta-tions. "In a perfect world," the former general counsel offered, it would be "important" for presidents to approve covert operations in writing in advance. But what had been done in Iran-Contra, Sporkin maintained, "I believe . . . was a correct thing to do." He insisted that what had been done was *not* an abuse of the law. When committee lawyer Timothy C. Woodcock pointed to the matter of principle and the fact of post hoc "ratification" as inconsistent with the concept of a finding, Sporkin shut him down. "I'm not going to debate that with you," the judge declared flatly. They moved on.

Had the congressional oversight committees, the special prosecutor, or both, moved at the time to enforce the statute by something more than naming and shaming, it is likely that management of U.S. intelligence would have been considerably enhanced. Instead, the Congress and the executive have fought, for more than four decades now, over the mean-ing of "notification," the nature of "timeliness," and the consequences of violation.

Some took away lessons that have done harm. One person listening to this very discussion was Richard Cheney, then a Wyoming Republican congressman. When his turn came at questioning, Representative Cheney zeroed in on executive refusal to notify. Sporkin referred obscurely to the Nicaragua harbor mining as a "partial non-notification" where the agency went to the Gang of Eight only and House intelligence committee chairman Lee Hamilton "decided he didn't want to hear it or something"—turning the history of that incident on its head. Cheney asked the CIA lawyer why he hadn't recommended that Casey inform the Big Eight of the Iran ploy.

"I can't recall whether that even crossed my scope," Judge Sporkin replied.

A little later, after some repartee, Representative Cheney came back, "I am not one of those members who insists or believes that it would even be unwise to require the President to notify the Congress in advance. I think lots of times demands for notification are overdone." Cheney conceded that Sporkin—and others after him—had made "a very big decision" with a finding providing for non-notification. In his minority report at the end of the Iran-Contra inquiry, Mr. Cheney inserted a rec-ommendation that the circle for notification be reduced even further—to a Gang of Four (the party leaders in the intelligence oversight commit-tees), as the document put it, "on the principle that notifying fewer peo-ple is better." As vice president fifteen years later, Mr. Cheney stood for refusal to notify in nearly every instance, typically approaching the Gang of Four under circumstances that made honest oversight impossible, at most the Gang of Eight, almost never the full committees. The history of the CIA torture program demonstrates how that practice abetted abusive behavior. Had the Intelligence Oversight Act been enforced at the time of Iran-Contra, it is possible some horrors of the war on terror might have been avoided.

Be that as it may, here you had a CIA general counsel functioning as operational aide, finding some "legal" way to get it done, whatever "it" might be. That was but one piece of the brief. Agency lawyers *do* need to tell bosses from time to time that no authority exists for something they want to do. The counsel is supposed to act as consigliere too, going beyond law to advise on what feels or seems right—or not. At the height of the Watergate scandal, a United States attorney called in CIA deputy counsel John S. Warner to ask him what he knew about the agency's help for former employees now working for the Nixon White House. Warner took the matter to then director Richard Helms. The DCI, in a fog, had no idea what to do.

Warner told the boss that, until he knew more, he couldn't even make suggestions. Helms finally put William E. Colby in charge of getting to the bottom of Watergate, as least so far as it concerned Langley.

Counsels dealt with other agencies. They performed legal chores outside the CIA, like arranging for the incorporation of proprietaries or working with employees on and off the reservation. When outsiders investigated the community, counsels safeguarded agency interests. Indeed the lawyer at the end of Casey's watch, David P. Doherty, had had his people sit in on all the depositions that preceded hearings like Sporkin's. To make just one example, the OGC lawyer who accompanied Afghan task force chief Jack Devine to his deposition frankly told him the legal function was to protect CIA, not Devine. If Jack got in trouble, he would be on his own.

"DON'T TELL ME IT CAN'T BE DONE"

Stan Sporkin and Bill Casey were good friends. They first met at the Securities and Exchange Commission (SEC), the government's Wall Street watchdog, where Richard Nixon appointed William J. Casey commissioner. Sporkin had been a twenty-nine-year-old lawyer when he joined the SEC as an enforcer in 1961. By the time Commissioner Casey arrived, a decade later, Sporkin had risen through the ranks to associate director of enforcement. During that time, he had investigated bond schemes, been a branch chief, chief enforcement attorney, assistant, then associate director. Bill Casey impressed him mightily. Over the years, SEC chiefs had erected barriers of one kind or another. Instead of that, Casey came to him—an unusual act from someone at the top—to ask what he could do to make Sporkin's job easier. The enforcement attorney's litany enumerated the earlier barriers. Casey made them go away. His reputation at SEC was as a strong watchdog, ready to prosecute. Part of that rested on Stan Sporkin's achievements. But the boss did not always join the hunt.

As Sporkin's team investigated a shady New Jersey financier named Robert Vesco, Casey promoted the lawyer to deputy director of SEC's enforcement unit. Among other self-protective measures, Vesco had allegedly funneled cash into a Nixon presidential campaign slush fund—a charge Sporkin's investigators documented sufficiently to include in a draft SEC complaint. It disappeared, thanks to quiet political pressure, when Casey filed the civil suit in late November 1972. Casey left the SEC after Nixon's reelection, hoping for the top CIA job, but he ended up in the State Department. A year later Nixon appointed him to head the Export-Import Bank. At his confirmation hearing Mr. Casey dismissed the Vesco matter as a minor issue—a small amount of money within a much larger enforcement effort, where he contented himself with arrangements made by subordinates, Sporkin among them.

Casey was confirmed at the Ex-Im Bank. His SEC successor's career fractured on the Vesco case; he had lied under oath regarding exchanges with one of Nixon's minions. Vesco fled to Central America—Costa Rica mostly. For a time during Bill Casey's CIA campaign against Nicaragua, Robert Vesco lived there, and in 1982 he relocated to Cuba—Bill's bête noire—where he lived the rest of his life. That must have rankled. Meanwhile Casey took a seat on yet another watchdog group, the White House monitors of the President's Foreign Intelligence Advisory Board (PFIAB), courtesy of Gerald R. Ford. The PFIAB papers contain news clips regarding Vesco—Casey continued following the story.

At the Export-Import Bank, Bill Casey reached out to Stan Sporkin. He offered Sporkin the general counsel job. Both men enjoyed chess, and Sporkin played the long game. At the SEC, he had more bad guys he wanted to pursue. As Stan put it, "I hadn't had my fill of chasing the wrongdoers on Wall Street." So in 1974 he turned Casey down. Sporkin rose to the top of the SEC Division of Enforcement the same year. He remained there as deputy director in 1981 when Bill took the helm at the CIA. The Vesco case still haunted—it came up again at Casey's confirmation. Sporkin wrote to the SSCI supporting the nomination.

One day that spring, Stan Sporkin emerged from a friend's funeral to see a limousine pull up. A couple of brawny security men materialized, one taking the lawyer by each arm. They marched Stan to the car. Sporkin relaxed when he saw Bill Casey in back. They drove around a bit and went for a drink. The CIA director said that Sporkin had turned him down for a general counsel job before, but here he tried again. Sporkin wanted to think about it but decided quickly enough. He replaced Daniel B. Silver at the OGC on May 18, 1981.

Arriving at Langley, Stanley Sporkin knew nothing about spying, absolutely nothing about the CIA, and had spent virtually his entire working life—nearly two decades—immersed in the arcana of insider trading and other SEC concerns. Casey, a lawyer too, had not only an agenda but also greater knowledge of the playing field, from OSS, from PFIAB, and from his friend Leo Cherne, whose long association with CIA started with the International Rescue Committee, as well as from study of the law. Another agency lawyer, called to Casey's office that spring, found the DCI with a copy of Title 50 of the United States Code (the part that covers the Central Intelligence Agency) at his side, and a pile of those infamous presidential findings in front of him. The lawyer, who served in the operations directorate and had drafted some of those findings, was brusquely informed that he would be writing stronger ones in the future.

Stan Sporkin called in that same lawyer, John Rizzo, and drew on his knowledge to get established. The neophyte also counted himself lucky that previous GCs were around to help. He created a consulting panel of former top lawyers. This high-powered group included chiefs Lawrence R. Houston, John S. Warner, Anthony A. Lapham, and Daniel Silver. Together they had led the OGC from its inception to the moment Stan took charge. He convened them four times a year. The counsel's office had come a long way since Larry Houston's day, when it consisted of *two* lawyers. In the Carter era, there had been eighteen. By 1982 there were fifty, so many that Director Casey decided the entire OGC would have to move. Sporkin kept an office at Langley and his big crew went to a building in Tyson's Corner, Virginia. It took just a couple of days for Stan to realize he couldn't manage the OGC from his space, so he worked at the OGC office, shuttling to Langley only when necessary. Sporkin's routine would be to see Casey every week or ten days. In Tyson's Corner, because he hadn't moved in with the crowd, the top lawyer had to take a little, closetlike room.

John Rizzo thought Stan Sporkin a lot like Bill Casey. Both were perpetually rumpled, their clothing something the fastidious Rizzo always noticed. Both gobbled their food and scattered crumbs. Where Casey mumbled, Sporkin was excitable, larding his speech with sports metaphors. At meetings, no matter how obscure the conversation, Casey and Sporkin each seemed to know precisely what the other one meant. Sporkin recalled, "We reached a point where we communicated by not communicating. Nothing needed to be said." The general counsel would put staff to work on something. "Nine times out of ten, he would ask for the thing I'd already put in the pipeline," the lawyer said. "It was the only way I could stay ahead of him."

Thus Stanley Sporkin made himself indispensable. At the very outset, the DCI antagonized many by refusing to put his money in trust. Sporkin defended the action, assuming the role of monitor, warning the boss when some financial move seemed smelly. Casey's appointment of business crony Max Hugel as DDO—equally fishy—Sporkin excused.

The OGC became a major player during Reagan's first year, when the lawyers fully vetted language for a fresh executive order to govern all intelligence activities. This was President Reagan's gambit to avoid a statute regulating the agencies. Issued in December 1981 as E.O. 12333, it remains the basic "charter" document today.

The executive order anchored one end of the spectrum, but to prevent any repeat of the Carter-era efforts at a law regulating intelligence, the political mavens decided there *needed* to be a law, just one containing no charter. This led to the Intelligence Oversight Act of 1980, which spooks brag is just two pages long. Officials took to displaying smoke and mirrors—the executive order as a concrete charter, like a statute, and the oversight "act" as subject to agency interpretation. Stanley Sporkin became the interpreter. The 1980 law set the presidential finding requirements, which Casey's CIA immediately found so onerous. President Ronald Reagan traded an arrangement under the Hughes-Ryan Amendment, by which many congressional panels had to be informed, for one in which only the Senate intelligence committee and its House counterpart needed to be told. The executive would continue, as under Hughes-Ryan, to present formal documents called Memoranda of Notification, or "findings." Throughout Jimmy Carter's administration, there had been heated complaints from Langley about how the reporting requirements set by Hughes-Ryan tied agency hands. The blackout for the Iranian hostage rescue led to a stipulation in the 1980 act that Congress be kept "fully and currently" informed. Sporkin told the Iran-Contra investigators he had been a stickler for requirements. Actually, he strove to find ways to stretch them.

Legislation became a big part of the OGC portfolio. There was the Intelligence Identities Protection Act of 1982, which the agency quickly interpreted to permit much more than the withholding of names of clandestine service officers during and for a short time after their covert assignments. The OGC followed with a strong effort to amend the Freedom of Information Act to exempt operational files. Sporkin's assurances notwithstanding, Langley soon construed everything from official histories to project proposals as "operational files."

One thing Mr. Sporkin tried but failed to secure was a modification of the federal criminal code that would shield CIA people from *any* criminal prosecution in U.S. courts so long as they were embarked on approved projects outside the country. Mr. Casey's top lawyer characterized this as "strictly a technical matter." Had the ploy succeeded, the CIA's terror-era torture and black prisons would have been legal. Equally significant, Sporkin's failure objectively meant there was no "covenant" of the sort Jose Rodriguez desired.

Agency lawyer John Rizzo reports himself the drafter of covert project findings. But a change occurred around the time of the Nicaragua mining. Sporkin dreamed up an arrangement under which the CIA, rather than provide detailed notification and briefings on all presidential findings, would supply written "advisories" to committee chairpersons. The DCI would reserve the right to restrict the real information to oral briefings, when he deemed the project sensitive, to restrict notice to the Gang of Eight when the president so ordered, and to withhold notice altogether when desired.

With the ink hardly dry on the Casey Accords, the DCI proposed this procedure early in 1985. Congress rejected it, though later, in 1986, the SSCI accepted the principle of notification confined to the Gang of Eight. Nowhere did Congress accept a restriction to the Gang of Four. Investigations of Iran-Contra make quite clear that all the findings involved in that affair came from Sporkin, at times in concert with NSC staff, but always OGC. Department of Justice investigators' notes record Mr. Sporkin disclosing a previous presidential finding that had provided for withholding notification—one concerning a covert activity aimed at Libya. The OGC chief reported that President Reagan decided the withholding would have been improper. That provision disappeared from the draft finding. There had, in fact, been such an operation, Project Flower, in 1985–1986.

The findings show Stanley Sporkin at work. He called the November 1985 retroactive finding on a missile shipment to Iran "prudential"—an insurance policy in case the CIA was called on the mat. Though he told the Iran-Contra committee he saw the finding as not required by law, Sporkin admitted elsewhere that it *was*, because in its absence the agency could not legally spend money except to gather intelligence. Historian Theodore Draper, one of the most careful observers of Iran-Contra, concludes that "this draft raises troublesome questions about the comportment of General Counsel Sporkin." By explicitly providing for withholding notification, Sporkin's finding committed the president to a course violating both the 1980 law *and* the Casey Accords. In his Iran-Contra testimony, Sporkin showed that he understood the project's purpose as trading arms for hostages, in contravention of U.S. law on control of weapons exports and a declared policy of never "dealing" with terrorists. Draper also argued that Sporkin's text ranged far more widely than what his superior, DDCI McMahon, had demanded. In short, the general counsel had acted as enabler, not as guardian.

Stan Sporkin understood the guardian function well. Central America task force chief Alan Fiers recalls Sporkin's warning that he ought to have a lawyer with him as watchdog as "the best advice anybody ever gave me." Sporkin himself reflects that he consistently held the line against anyone at CIA participating in fund-raising for the Contras. That seems overdone. An August 1984 OGC review, anticipating the Boland Amendment, left the door open for CIA solicitation of third countries *provided that* personnel did not participate directly, there was no recompense from the United States, and the third countries contributed at their own expense. In early 1985, when Contra fund-raising needed fresh impetus, Benjamin B. Wickham Jr. suddenly resigned from the agency with the avowed intention of helping raise money for the rebels. Wickham, one of Bill Casey's two special assistants, had been station chief in Managua from 1982 to 1984.

With the tighter 1985 Boland Amendment, Sporkin counted angels on the heads of pins and advised the CIA that it could still deal with third countries on plans *they* might have for the rebels, because that was "intelligence gathering." The agency merely had to keep detailed records to prove it was not doing something more.

Sporkin often played the consigliere. The year of the Nicaragua mining, 1984, gives the example. Director Casey spent twenty minutes closeted with general counsel Sporkin the morning of January 4, the day after the first ship was mined. For the CIA, the international legal implications were important. The instruction to the Contras for *them* to claim responsibility—using a release written at Langley and handed to a Nicaraguan rebel officer by the CIA's Honduras deputy station chief—shows OGC's impact. Another long session with the lawyer (March 6) coincided with the Nicaraguan government's charges that the coordinated air and sea attacks exceeded rebel capabilities. On March 23, when Moscow saddled Washington with responsibility in the mining of the Soviet tanker *Lugansk*, Sorkin and Casey had another long encounter. The general counsel met with the DCI the morning after Senator Moynihan threatened to resign. During Director Casey's late April pilgrimage of apology to the Hill, consigliere Sporkin met with him on April 24, just before the DCI began his sessions with individual senators, and again on April 27, when Casey reviewed results with Sporkin and DDO Stein.

The pattern is even more pronounced with the Contra murder manuals. On October 15, 1984, both the *New York Times* and the Associated Press revealed the CIA-authored *Psychological Operations in Guerrilla Warfare*. The contract officer's CIA link formed part of the initial disclosure. Langley passed the point of mere denial days later when media reported a related Contra comic book. The rebel manuals talked of "neutralization" and anticipated overthrowing the Managua government—clear violations of Boland restrictions. On October 17, Senator Goldwater demanded a briefing. The next day, President Reagan ordered an investigation. For more than an hour on the nineteenth, counselor Sporkin and Director Casey worked with Clair George, recently appointed head of the DO, his deputy, the agency's executive director, and its spokesman. Their strategy had Casey order newly minted inspector general John Stein to do the inquiry.

This time the director got no New York weekend. Casey went to his office at Langley both days. Counselor Sporkin saw the DCI for nearly an hour on Sunday afternoon, then accompanied Casey nearly the entire day on Monday, October 22. That day a CIA team tramped up Capitol Hill to speak at a closed SSCI session while a shifting constellation of senior officials huddled with Casey at Langley. Sporkin sat in for more than four hours. John Stein presented his preliminary results. The top brass were thrilled to learn records confirmed they had never personally handled or approved the manuals. *That* information Langley gave to the media immediately. On October 23, Casey ordered all copies of the offending field manuals destroyed. Inspector general Stein formally presented his results on the twenty-fifth, the same day Nicaragua filed a diplomatic protest and

Casey sent a letter covering copies of the IG report to the House and Senate intelligence committees. On the twenty-seventh, Mr. Sporkin brokered an exchange between Casey and Goldwater to deal with the latter's final questions, and on the Monday, Sporkin plus other officials helped Casey with Moynihan. In some respects, OGC activity in this scandal appears more intense than in the harbor mining.

Friends of Casey described him as anxious to profit from associates' skills, but not someone to stand in their way. In Stanley Sporkin's case, the lawyer's father had been a federal judge and he had that same ambition. Bill put in a good word and, in June 1984, Ronald Reagan nominated Sporkin for the Federal District Court. The Senate held up this nomination for many months. Except for that, Sporkin would not have been there for the findings muddle on Iran-Contra or the psywar manual fracas. Indeed the delay went on long enough that the general counsel, in the winter of 1985, could preside over the CIA approach to the Justice Department to exempt agency personnel from having to refer drug smuggling allegations to DOJ, normally required under legal understandings. Mr. Sporkin's nomination hearing took place late that October. Confirmed, he received his commission in December. Sporkin's last day at the CIA was February 7, 1986.

TIMELY NOTIFICATION

The general counsels continued to labor in the vineyard—or perhaps the thickets and minefields—of the law. Thorny issues of authorization and notification were raised by the Nicaragua project. Even before Iran-Contra demanded attention, Senators Goldwater and Moynihan had both declared the need for "timely" notification. All hell broke loose when Iran-Contra revealed that precisely what the congressional overseers feared had happened.

General counsel David P. Doherty spearheaded a fresh compromise with the Senate intelligence committee in June 1986. As a Casey Accords addendum, the formula defined things that require notification. The previous arrangement had specified that the CIA would report significant changes and developments. Given what had happened in the harbor mining, the latest version added that for paramilitary operations "significant" would include the initial decision, the first provision of military equipment, modifications in quality or quantity, and changes in the level of activity of the United States, a contractor, or agent personnel, as well as unusual foreign participation. Doherty fought for—and secured—an "exceptional circumstances" exclusion.

Stanley Sporkin had written those findings. Far from providing full and current notice, he and his staff kept secret the arms trades with Iran, made retroactive findings for previous actions, and even resorted to "mental" findings that were not written down at all. David Doherty had to deal with the fallout. Notification issues built to another climax. They remained contentious. The SSCI innovated a covert action audit staff and began reviewing projects every quarter. In August 1987, President Reagan, under pressure to reform, explicitly accepted Senate committee suggestions that findings should be in writing, should not be retroactive, should include anything that relied on means outside the CIA, and should be timely except under exceptional circumstances.

Two aspects dominated the next stage of the fight: foreign participation and the "exceptional" circumstance. As Doherty knew, timely notification had not been guaranteed at all.

In 1983, Senators William S. Cohen and Gary Hart, on a fact-finding mission, arrived at Managua airport hours after it had been bombed by CIA-Contra aircraft. In January 1988, the Maine Republican Cohen championed a bill to make notification within forty-eight hours a matter of law. The White House wanted no such statute on the books. This bill died in the spring of 1988 when the House of Representatives took no action, but it had passed the Senate in March by a veto-proof margin. Director William H. Webster, Casey's successor, and national security adviser Frank Carlucci both threatened a presidential veto anyway.

Sustained by a new general counsel, Russell J. Bruemmer, Webster spoke darkly of constitutional defects. Behind that verbiage lay the exceptional circumstances exclusion. Law or no law, the executive branch was determined to hold open the possibility of *not notifying Congress* of covert operations. Fortunately for the White House, it did not have to go to the mat, because the House of Representatives failed to act on its version of the legislation.

The impasse continued into the presidency (1988–1992) of George Herbert Walker Bush, still the only chief executive to have been a CIA director. The SSCI took its forty-eight-hour rule and made a tighter definition of notification terms an action item. When the intelligence committees sought to obtain a sense of how the president intended to implement notification, the former top spook got his chance. Bush tried to finesse the headache by giving temporal definition to the exclusion. With Webster and Bruemmer's encouragement, Bush *intended* timely notice. The general counsel and NSC officials then palavered with congressional staffs about what that might mean. The Senate committee's top negotiator, its staff director George J. Tenet, would one day be on the opposite side of this issue. In October 1989, President Bush fleshed out the concept with a letter declaring that prior notice would be standard and, when withheld, would come within a few days. But Bush, too, could not let go, tossing out the compromise with the assertion that he would rely upon his constitutional powers when withholding notice for longer than the stipulated period.

Happy to obtain part of what it wanted, the Senate committee codified Bush's formula in a new oversight statute. This may have been George Tenet's finest hour with the SSCI. But it did not satisfy the House select committee, which passed different legislation. The final version dropped the formula. Meanwhile both houses of Congress moved to incorporate reforms they thought necessary in the wake of Iran-Contra, which they believed the agency's OGC and the White House had accepted. These went into the next intelligence budget appropriation. President Bush seized on language there providing for notice of third-country or third-party participation, rejecting the reforms. Bush pocket-vetoed the bill.

But Senate overseers plugged away, and President Bush subsided. George Tenet kept up his active role. Their efforts resulted in a 1991 revision to the Intelligence Oversight Act. In addition to slight refinements on the "full and current" theme, the amendment provided that the congressional committees be informed promptly of all illegal activities (and any corrective actions), and that nothing in the law, including intelligence sources and methods, could be construed as authority to keep information away from the overseers. Between 1995 and 1997 Congress received more than four hundred notifications of CIA activities. Later, during Project Greystone, at the instigation of Dick Cheney, that law would be repeatedly flouted.

GUNSLINGERS

Another role for the general counsel is as the director's gunslinger. It could take different forms, some quite damaging to individuals. Since the 1950s, the CIA has had an understanding with the Department of Justice (DOJ) regarding which potentially criminal matters had to be referred to Justice. General counsel Doherty made such a referral in 1987, involving nine employees who had used agency money to buy stamps at a post office. One noticed that some of the stamps had inverted printing. They replaced them and sold the misprinted ones to a numismatic dealer for a big profit. An easy call. But the closer wrongdoing came to operational activity, the *less* likely it was that a gunslinging counsel would make a referral. When CIA inspectors general found an illegal mail-opening project in the 1960s, discovered that agency officers had planned assassinations, and learned that contract personnel might have smuggled drugs, there were no referrals.

On the contrary, there were efforts to make problems go away. Leaks much more than criminal acts formed the basis for DOJ referrals. Counsel Doherty made at least one referral like that, involving the disclosure of findings by a joint CIA-DOD study group looking into whether the United States could verify a ban on mobile ballistic missiles. The leakers were never found. Of course such stories often came from officials pushing agendas, leaking to favor one policy over another. Director Bill Colby once asserted to a bright disgruntled analyst, Frank Snepp, that the CIA had a right to leak—it was like a pot and "pitchers should leak from the top."

Then there was the reverse-field play. The most prominent example of that came in the Green Beret Affair of 1969. This involved the murder of a Cambodian agent working for a U.S. Special Forces network whom some suspected of being a double agent. In their defense, accused Army personnel insisted that CIA officers had okayed or even ordered the killing. John K. Greaney, an OGC associate counsel, went to Saigon to look at the evidence and meet the CIA people involved. He found that one of the Green Berets implicated in the murder had past agency associations. That and other evidence could be cobbled into a CIA conspiracy. Langley declined to provide evidence for any prosecution, and the rejection eventually forced the Army to drop charges.

A few years later, the CIA repeated the ploy. Greaney refused background documents to DOJ on a Thai drug smuggler who happened to be a CIA agent. Same result. The spy, one Puttaporn Khramkhruan, had been enlisted at Chiang Mai, northern Thailand, in late 1969. In 1973 customs officers in Chicago found a package in the mail containing canisters filled with fifty-nine pounds of pure opium. An envelope led back to the spy. Greaney and other OGC lawyers verified his bona fides, and a CIA officer actually introduced authorities to the agent, who was then studying at Syracuse University. In a case that dragged on for more than a year, the OGC advised that it would reject a subpoena from the U.S. government, recommended that prosecutors use their drug smuggler as a prosecution witness instead, applied to the Justice Department to drop the charges, and rebuffed other DOJ requests. Justice dropped its indictment. The spy went home. The general counsel could deny as well as refer.

———— ✧ ————

Gunslinging lawyers are the key to building the fortress of secrecy that confines the agency's own. The rush to suppress whistleblowers began at the OGC. John S. Warner tells the tale. He had been deputy counsel from the inception of the agency until promotion to the top post at the end of 1973. His "lite" version is that a former officer, Victor L. Marchetti, a fifteen-year veteran who had spent the last few as executive assistant to the DDCI, had resigned, disaffected. Marchetti was going to press with a book full of CIA secrets, written with former State Department intelligence analyst John D. Marks. The publisher brought the manuscript to Langley and asked that its people take a look at it because it seemed to contain sensitive material.

Warner's version is phony. The truth is altogether more sinister. Marchetti put himself on Langley's radar with a novel he published in October 1971 titled *The Rope Dancer*, full of the moral dilemmas of spy work. Then he gave an interview to United Press International—the spooks had gotten too big, big enough that secret agencies could start covert wars, analysts were pressured on their reports, all of that. Langley went on the lookout. A copy of the book proposal turned up on March 12, 1972. Not the manuscript, the proposal for what became *The CIA and the Cult of Intelligence*. Later OGC took months to pore over the text and list things it wanted removed. That would not have been necessary if the lawyers had had the full manuscript, because that work would have been done before the spring of '72. The publisher, Alfred A. Knopf, opposed the CIA censorship. Knopf spent $125,000 (over $700,000 in 2016) defending this case, even though the American Civil Liberties Union took it pro bono. Whether the proposal was purloined or handed over may never be known.

John Warner and his boss, Lawrence Houston, the general counsel, had thought about censoring publications in a theoretical way. They considered the secrecy agreements employees sign to obtain security clearances as contractual commitments to protect information. Lots of CIA people had written books, starting with Allen Dulles. This had never been enforced.

Anyway, the Marchetti and Marks book was really a nuts-and-bolts tour of Langley and its lore, not so much a dive into the CIA's deepest secrets. The OGC lawyers were looking at the options when the executive director phoned to ask if they had thought about going to court. As a result they met with the director, then Richard Helms.

On secrecy grounds, Director Helms worried about pursuing a legal case. It would reveal sensitive secrets and invite negative publicity. Helms took his problem to the White House, where Richard Nixon approved action. On March 23, 1972, Helms ordered CIA security to surveille Marchetti. Warner prepared the DOJ referral. Irwin Goldblum handled the case at Justice. In April a court injunction prohibited Marchetti and Marks from publishing without Langley's review. The authors lost their appeal. The agency deleted massive swaths of text, much of it later restored because it hadn't been so secret after all.

The Marchetti case illustrates the work of OGC gunslingers in public. Behind the scenes, they can be even more devilish. The next whistleblower up would be a Latin Americanist, Philip Agee. Disgusted with the Vietnam War and the agency's operational methods, he resigned from a post in Mexico City in 1968. Agee went back to school and—by his account—got the idea of writing a critique of U.S. foreign policy as expressed in the CIA's work. This evolved into an exposé. He pursued research and writing in Mexico and Cuba, then Paris and London. Like Marchetti, Phil Agee put himself on the radar, writing a long letter to a Uruguayan political weekly that Langley naturally picked up.

At a certain point, a former colleague appeared at his door, pretending a social call but admitting that the agency wanted to know what Agee intended. Without doubt this had to be early on, because agents were put on Agee's trail. Fooled into accepting the loan of a bugged typewriter and showing manuscript pages to CIA operatives or agents, the former case officer bared his hand. It appears that, in the guise of gaining his confidence, CIA agents actually contributed to Agee's support. Surveillance teams followed him. Agee's book did not appear until 1976, but Joseph B. Smith, who retired in 1973, spent his last year helping shut down Latino networks and deactivate agents the agency expected Agee to blow. Langley had plenty of advance notice, which had to have come from Agee's text.

The disaffected CIA officer records that, in September 1972, he received a letter from his father wherein the latter reported a visit from an OGC lawyer, in fact John Greaney. The attorney told Mr. Agee that Director Helms worried about Phil, and presented a copy of the secrecy agreement Agee had signed when first joining, plus a copy of the Marchetti court decision. The elder Agee defended his son. Mr. Agee's tax returns, son Phil reports, were repeatedly audited for several years after this episode.

Greaney next appeared at the door of Phil Agee's ex-wife and, according to the former CIA officer, asked her to refuse permission for their children to visit the divorced husband, apparently a scheme to entice the renegade to return to the United States. The attorney, though he had trained at law, had been a long-service CIA officer (deputy chief of the task force running the secret war in Tibet) and had transferred into OGC to escape the harried life of a case officer and have more time for his half dozen children. Why Greaney should lend himself to a scheme like this is a puzzle. Later Agee enlisted legal help from Melvin L. Wulf of the American Civil Liberties Union, the same fellow who had defended Victor Marchetti. At a hearing, Wulf took Greaney aside to ask what business he had interfering with Agee's wife. Wulf reported that "Greaney's eyes almost popped out."

Phil Agee's fight with the Central Intelligence Agency ultimately assumed epic proportions. Langley did more than a little to spark this confrontation, and the general counsel's gunslingers were central to the action. Agency referrals led the Justice Department to seek revocation of Agee's passport, to contest his suit to regain it, oppose the Freedom of Information Act suit Agee brought for his own file, and so on. OGC attorneys sat behind the government table at every proceeding. The OGC itself served papers on Agee's publisher demanding the proceeds of books the former case officer subsequently participated in.

In the last-named instance, Langley relied upon a novel legal construction the gunslingers built. Greaney figured in that too, but top lawyers were ahead of him. This was the "constructive trust," new law made from prosecution of former analyst Frank Snepp. The case grew out of the disastrous end of the Vietnam War, when the United States, forced to evacuate Saigon virtually overnight, after weeks of stubbornly refusing to acknowledge any problem, left behind American allies, employees, records, CIA files, every kind of thing. Snepp experienced this trauma as lead intelligence analyst at the U.S. embassy. He raged at the U.S. ambassador and the station chief, both of whom denied the reality for political and public relations reasons, and Washington officials had gone along with them. Frank wanted to blow the whistle on this irresponsibility. Langley officials prevented Snepp from making his case in-house, leading him to resign and write a book.

As in both the Marchetti and Agee cases, the gunslingers had foreknowledge. John Greaney fired the opening salvo with an October 1976 letter reminding Snepp of his secrecy agreements and demanding to see the manuscript. Also like the gunslingers' action against Agee, the Snepp case wound on for years, with multifaceted complications. For one, Snepp had a more sophisticated understanding of his obligations under existing CIA secrecy agreements—with one exception, the ones he had signed demanded to review only "classified" material. The sole exception offered the employee an out—go to the agency inspector general—an avenue that superiors actually denied to him. The former officer simply made sure his narrative contained no secret information.

The gunslingers' effort to get Frank Snepp became more complicated when former U.S. ambassador Graham Martin, after an automobile accident, admitted that the trunk of his car was full of secret documents about the last days in Saigon. This left the CIA in the position of seeking to enjoin someone who had *no* secret information, while taking no action against another official who was up to his shoulders in classified documents. Lawyer Greaney had begun compiling the legal memoranda to solicit DOJ to obtain a court order against Snepp based on the assumption that Frank would use everything to which he had access. Once the book appeared and they could see the text, it became clear that the CIA could not prosecute on the basis of secrecy. When Martin's car trunk popped, that became even less feasible. Now the lawyers imaginatively argued that Snepp was "profiting" from *information he had learned in government employ.* The agency was therefore entitled to his earnings. This was a "constructive trust." Never mind that by statute the United States government is prohibited from *owning* information; now it would be permitted to *profit* from what it could not own, for the purpose of disciplining employees.

Proceedings in the case form a disheartening story of incomplete disclosure, overblown legal arguments, and judicial bad behavior. Frank Snepp lost at trial and would be denied at the appellate level. The Supreme Court turned down the case, leaving him in the cold. While those proceedings progressed, the Carter administration, spearheaded by White House lawyer Lloyd Cutler, completely revised Langley's secrecy agreements. These now formally acknowledge an obligation for manuscript review, contain a stipulation of government entitlement to proceeds, and threaten criminal prosecution for disclosures.

Former officers do not necessarily benefit from cooperation either. The illustrative case here is that of Kermit ("Kim") Roosevelt, long-retired mastermind of the 1953 Iran coup. Roosevelt considered the overthrow of Iranian prime minister Mossadegh a heroic chapter in CIA history and had no qualms about cooperating with agency censors. He approached John H. Waller early in 1977. Waller had been baron of the DO division for that region, and had transferred to become inspector general. Kim told Waller of his plans for a book on the coup. Waller warned Roosevelt the agency would want to vet the manuscript and would also want to know what the shah of Iran felt about the idea. He passed the matter along to general counsel Anthony A. Lapham. Roosevelt jumped through all the hoops. He discussed the book project with CIA director George Bush, Waller, and OGC attorneys. He got the shah's permission; the Iranian leader was pleased. Kim handed over draft chapters in advance of completing his full manuscript.

In the meantime, Langley created its Publications Review Board (PRB), directly responsible for approving manuscripts by former officers. The PRB performed a quick review of Roosevelt's partial draft, with the general counsel in the background. But by mid-1978 when the officer had completed his manuscript, PRB and OGC both had problems. They found 156 objectionable passages in the text, while the leader of the clandestine service, John N. McMahon, decreed that no book like this could appear. Langley's associate general counsel warned that McMahon's blanket edict would not stand in court, so the agency began negotiating revisions with the author. In December Kim Roosevelt, so angered at Langley's intransigence in the face of his cooperation, sent a letter to OGC announcing that he was going ahead with publication with or without CIA's approval. On April 30, 1979, agency officers at the other end of this transaction, reviewing the totality of the changes the author had made in response to its demands, exulted, "This has become . . . essentially a work of fiction." Agency lawyers were happy.

Despite all of this, Roosevelt's book, finally titled *Countercoup,* was recalled at the last minute because of *British* sensitivities regarding disclosure of the role of the Anglo-Iranian Oil Company in originating the idea for the covert operation. Four hundred copies had already gone out to stores and book reviewers, but the remainder of the print run went to the shredders. A version of the book that attributed actions to British intelligence appeared in the summer of 1980.

Ironically, Admiral Stansfield Turner, the CIA director who loosed his gunslingers against Snepp and Roosevelt, had a hell of a time getting his own memoirs approved. Turner ultimately resorted to hiring the attorney who had been his own general counsel, Tony Lapham, without much improving his chances. Turner's book emerged emasculated. Putting together the Marchetti decision, solidifying a right to review, the Intelligence Identities Protection Act, a product of Sporkin's OGC, and the exemption Sporkin carved out of the Freedom of Information Act to cover CIA "operational files," Langley had erected a true fortress of secrecy.

——— ✧ ———

The lawyers for a long time dominated the CIA's people. Today Langley issues press releases touting same-sex couples receiving employment benefits or gender minorities being accepted by colleagues, but back at the height of the Cold War, Carmel Offie, Frank Wisner's deputy, found himself shunted to the side for being gay. Section 102 (c) of the National Security Act of 1947 gave the CIA's director the authority to fire anyone he wanted, so long as he deemed it "advisable in the interests of the United States." There were other suitable exclusions also, and the gunslingers fought hard to keep them. In Director Webster's day, counsel David Doherty became the defendant of record when plaintiff "John Doe" sued because the agency fired him for being homosexual. Doe was told that the CIA would write him a good job recommendation unless he applied for something requiring a clearance, in which case Langley would tell the prospective employer that Doe was a security risk. He could not obtain redress in the courts.

In 1949, through the Central Intelligence Agency Act, Congress endowed the director with other summary powers. This law is usually cited when referring to the agency's ability to spend money "off the books," without specific appropriation, and later on from a slush fund controlled by the director. But the statute also gave the director a responsibility in law to "protect" sources and methods (which has been construed to mean nearly anything), and it charters the lawyers.

Mostly the gunslingers triumphed, but one they lost happened in 1952, when a Seattle travel agent told two CIA men at a party that American scholar Owen Lattimore had booked passage to Moscow. Recently (and falsely) denounced by Wisconsin politician Joseph R. McCarthy as Stalin's top spy in the United States, Lattimore was renowned for his studies of China. The travel agent, Harry A. Jarvinen, slipped nuggets to CIA's Seattle domestic contact office. The two officers, Miller Holland, the Seattle chief, and Wayne Richardson, a subordinate, were the only agency people involved. Jarvinen later recanted his story to the FBI, but not before Washington leaks disclosed its intent to prevent Lattimore from travel.

The Department of Justice got orders to prosecute Jarvinen for providing false information on matters within the jurisdiction of U.S. agencies. Holland and Richardson testified to the grand jury in closed session but then the CIA got cold feet. Agency counsel Lawrence Houston made a special appearance at trial to argue that his director could exercise executive privilege. Under the National Security Act, Houston maintained, the director could refuse to testify *and* order subordinates not to respond either. The court rejected that argument. When Holland and Richardson sat mute, the judge ordered a hearing aimed at them. He found the recalcitrant officers in contempt and sentenced each to two weeks in jail.

Counselor Houston, the DOJ, the Donovan law firm (Donovan Leisure Newton & Irvine were involved pro bono), and local Seattle lawyers all arrived at the same conclusion—the facts of the situation could not sustain a CIA appeal. In particular, Houston wanted to avoid any precedent of an appellate court judgment against the agency. The State Department made a public apology to Dr. Lattimore. Mr. Jarvinen, the evidence against him now suppressed, walked free. President Truman pardoned Holland and Richardson on December 17, 1952, without the CIA having actually filed any of the papers normally required for a presidential pardon.

The lawyers had better luck when it came to sustaining the director's firings under Section 102 (c). Thomas Parrott, a senior officer at Frankfurt base, had filed reports about Estonian émigrés that DO's Soviet Russia Division rejected as misleading. In April 1956, John Maury, its baron, enlisted clandestine service office John Torpats to solve the problem. According to Torpats, he not only smoothed the ruffled feathers but received several commendations. Yet before Torpats could write his report, Tom Parrott grumbled to Washington. Frank Wisner, DO chief, had recruited Parrott to the clandestine service. Rice bowls were at stake. Suddenly Wisner's sidekick Tracy Barnes, then base chief at Frankfurt, put Torpats under house arrest and shipped him home under a cloud. Accusation led to investigation. Torpats filed a claim within CIA channels, but by then Barnes had become entrenched in the DO front office. Torpats went to court when he got fired early in 1961.

The general counsel's office helped Dulles fashion letters he used in the case—one to Torpats relying upon a Civil War precedent to assert that agency officers had no right even to air their grievances in court, and one to the court, demanding that the case be dismissed. In July 1961 it was. Torpats appealed. On the eve of the Cuban Missile Crisis, the appeals court found that the CIA director had acted within his broad discretion.

John McCone himself became a target in 1962, when he terminated George S. Rhodes, who went to the Civil Service Commission. Langley's general counsel argued that the law exempts the agency from standard work rules, hence civil service regulations. Rhodes alleged wrongful termination and sued for damages, contending that he had been fired in contravention of CIA regulations, civil service rules, *and* preferences in law for employing veterans. The court backed the director, ruling that the 1947 act accorded "the absolute right to terminate any employee whenever he deemed it necessary or advisable." This power has remained, relocated to Section 104 (g).

For a very long time, the Office of General Counsel stayed ahead of the wave. Langley's sovereign immunity gradually dissipated under the assault of social changes, starting with the Civil Rights Act of 1964. Still, the gunslingers mostly prevailed. Their tactics included demanding secrecy agreements from opposing lawyers (plus restricting the number—and the plaintiff's choice of lawyers!), foot-dragging on furnishing evidence, exploiting secrecy to exclude evidence, out-of-control application of the concept of "sources and methods" to shield all information, denial of access to witnesses, acting as defendant (putting the burden of proof onto the aggrieved party being denied evidence), and more. They bolstered their chances by invoking the vague cloak of "national security" to overawe judges and dissuade them.

Right through Stanley Sporkin's time, the OGC maintained a high batting average. Frank Snepp would not be wrong to note that, within the agency's close moral spaces, "general counsel" amounted to an oxymoron. The function of the general counsel, its main purpose, Snepp wrote, "was to keep the CIA free of the law."

FASTEST GUN AT LANGLEY

Or not. The agency's first lawyer, whom some at Langley have called the father of intelligence law, had been Lawrence Reed Houston. The attorney had won the agency's top honor, the Distinguished Intelligence Medal. President Nixon awarded him the National Security Medal for a thousand legal maneuvers, all important to CIA evolution, right down to drafting the National Security Act. Houston had been chief architect of the Central Intelligence Agency Act of 1949 and a principal in developing the CIA retirement act in the early 1960s, further refining agency personnel policy. Houston did it all in the shadows, the public hardly aware of him.

Son of an academic, born in Saint Louis in 1913, Larry loved the sea and spent summers sailing off Cape Cod. His dad, David Houston, who had been chancellor of Washington University of Saint Louis until a few months after the birth, took the family to Washington to be Woodrow Wilson's secretary of agriculture. David sidled over to head the Treasury Department in 1920. Young Larry became an enthusiastic Washington resident.

Lawrence collected and prized the $5 and $10 bills David Houston signed when treasury secretary. Later they moved to New York, where the boy participated in regattas off Oyster Bay. As a Harvard College man, Class of 1935, young Houston chose the law and read it at the University of Virginia. There he met and wedded Jean Wellford Randolph, from a storied commonwealth family that traced back to colonial America, including one Peyton Randolph, a member of the Continental Congress. Substitute "spy agency" for "republic" and Lawrence Houston's role would be equally formative.

Like many, Houston arrived at CIA by way of the OSS. He had been practicing law in New York when World War II erupted, and in due course joined the Army, which rejected him for combat due to poor eyesight. The Army sent Houston to basic finance school. He learned that sight waivers were available for the Judge Advocate General (JAG) Corps. There were problems with the paperwork, though, and Houston and other finance students missed class while the Army sorted them out. Afflicted with pneumonia, he missed more classes. Finally it came together. As a lawyer Houston became a natural for JAG.

In the spring of 1944, the night before graduation, the prospective JAG found new orders assigning him to OSS. At the time, Houston had never heard of it. He went to Washington and reported to its general counsel, a lawyer named James Donovan (the man who negotiated with Castro for the Bay of Pigs prisoners, but no relation to Wild Bill), who told Houston he would be sent to OSS Mediterranean theater headquarters at the palace in Caserta, Italy, as the agency's counsel there. "OSS had all kinds of people," the lawyer recalled. "It had genuine heroes, it had outstanding academicians, it had princes and professional wrestlers and a few bums."

Caserta proved a madhouse—as Houston saw it, "Italy was not a very good example of the organization of OSS." His favorite stories had to do with the Anzio beachhead, where, while assigned to an OSS commando unit, the Italian Marines of the San Marco battalion, he helped save the pinned-down Allied troops; and, of course, Allen Dulles with Operation Sunrise.

The Greek civil war brought chaos, with British troops intervening there at the end of 1944. One night outside Athens, a British sentry shot a couple of OSS officers in the dark. Caserta sent Houston to its Cairo outstation, which had the direct link to Athens, to investigate. Larry found a muddle of jumbled reports and no real solution. He was about to head back when the Cairo chief told him to wait—Wild Bill Donovan was coming! Donovan was, in fact, doing his own "cruise," the one time he circled the globe visiting frontline detachments.

Cairo, a stop on Donovan's way to Karachi, then part of British India, had a base for the OSS chief to visit. Houston organized transport from the airfield to the OSS base. General Donovan used his stopover, in part, to elevate Cairo to a regional command and install a new chief. At one point, Houston found himself standing next to this man, a tall, imposing fellow, who asked him, "Well, lieutenant, how do you like your new assignment?"

"I don't know, sir," Lieutenant Houston replied.

The colonel shot back, "You are my deputy for the Middle East theater."

So Lawrence Houston stayed on in Cairo until September 1945. He witnessed World War II winding down, and was there when General Donovan issued verbal orders—no one dared write them down—for OSS stations to switch from the Nazi target to spying out the Soviets. The Greek fighting continued, but a cold war set in. Events educated Larry Houston on espionage and covert operations, and the spook bug bit him. Instead of returning to his law practice, Houston sought instructions from the general counsel. But staff fled the agency at a tremendous rate, and President Truman abolished the OSS, effective October 1, 1945. The rump of it became the War Department spy group called the Strategic Services Unit.

Pretty soon no one was left in the general counsel's office but Lawrence R. Houston. He stayed for twenty-eight years, while the SSU morphed into the CIG and then the CIA. The agency would be less flamboyant than its wartime predecessor, but Houston thought it an ideal combination of intellectual ability, imagination, dedication, and integrity.

General counsel Houston would have marveled at the resources of Stanley Sporkin's OGC, even more that of John Rizzo, where dozens, then hundreds, of lawyers pored over project proposals, cut paths to enable ops, filed necessary paperwork, and kept the agency, if not its officers, out of trouble. Houston had been the spooks' *only* lawyer. More than that, the job encompassed not just the legal work but also being the spies' congressional lobbyist. Soon lawyers John S. Warner, a former air force officer, and Walter Pforzheimer, another OSS veteran, joined him. Together, into the 1950s they constituted CIA's legal staff. It took the OGC more than a decade to expand to as many as ten lawyers. In 1975 the roster still numbered just fourteen—and only one came from outside the agency.

Walt Pforzheimer said of Larry Houston, "He was a can-do lawyer. He'd always try to find a legal way that you *could* do something."

The most notable instance of Houston's gunslinging had to do with

CIA's proprietaries. Counselor Houston negotiated the contracts and drew up the incorporation papers when the CIA bought its first airline, Civil Air Transport (CAT), in 1949. A decade later, when the agency realigned the unit's cover to create Air America, Houston's legal footwork disguised the CIA–Air America relationship behind no fewer than six layers of paper. The general counsel involved himself in creating nearly every agency proprietary—Southern Air Transport, Intermountain, Evergreen Aviation, St. Lucia Airways, E Systems, Air Asia, Radio Free Europe, Radio Free Asia, and so on.

In keeping with the role of air coordinator, Lawrence Houston negotiated the CIA's indemnity to the insurers of the *Springfjord* after the Guatemala operation. No money changed hands but Houston's craftsmanship showed in the device of routing the transaction through the Guatemalan government. Houston again served as the main man in drawing up contracts with Lockheed Aircraft for the U-2 and SR-71 and the reconnaissance satellites that Richard Bissell managed so well. When the Russians captured CIA pilot Francis Gary Powers, shot down in a spy plane over Russia, Houston handled the agency's end of the negotiation to get him back, and he—reaching back to OSS days—recruited Jim Donovan as lead attorney. When Powers did return, counselor Houston supervised the debriefing, where some viewed the U-2 pilot with suspicion.

In the Indonesia fiasco, when Civil Air Transport pilot Allen Pope was shot down and captured by the Sukarno government, Houston would be all over the case. He oversaw arrangements for the Cuban exile air force before the Bay of Pigs, as well as the employment of some of the same Cubans for CIA ventures in the Congo.

In the mid-1960s, the Portuguese government bought a number of the same type B-26 bombers the CIA had used, and contracted an American pilot to transfer them, after which the Portuguese intended to fly the planes against African rebels. The American pilot Richard Hawke went to trial on arms-smuggling charges and mounted a defense claiming the State Department and CIA had actually arranged the sale. Counselor Houston appeared at Hawke's Buffalo trial to insist that the CIA had nothing to do with these events, although he admitted the agency had known of one transfer five days in advance and at another point had had specific knowledge of how many of the aircraft had arrived in Portugal on their way to Africa. Houston kept Langley out of the hot seat, though Hawke and a co-defendant were acquitted. The jury was not overly impressed with the CIA's protestations of ignorance.

On the other hand, Mr. Houston could also speak his mind. Probably the most important instance was on the very issue of covert operations. The agency's chief lawyer *believed the CIA had no authority to conduct them!* The very first memorandum of legal opinion Houston crafted, on September 25, 1947, noted that in creating the CIA, Congress had primarily intended an agency for coordinating intelligence. It had not even endowed the organization with authority to conduct espionage. As for "commando type functions" and propaganda, the language always cited as the legal basis for those (that CIA should perform additional activities "of common concern" and that it carry out "such other functions" as presidents might direct) had all been clearly constrained by the phrase "related to intelligence." Covert operations and propaganda are not related to intelligence gathering; they are offensive missions.

Roscoe Hillenkoetter sided with Houston. One reason the covert operations function had been located in Frank Wisner's newly devised Office of Policy Coordination (OPC) had been that opinion. A few years later, OPC merged into the agency's Directorate of Operations, with no one (Houston included) objecting to the legal infringement. Houston continued to hold his view, however. Later in the 1950s, with Soviet spies carrying out assassinations of émigrés and the CIA plotting its own murders, Houston held such operations to be impractical, unethical, and immoral. After the Bay of Pigs, legislators, in particular Minnesota Democratic senator Eugene J. McCarthy, began questioning the CIA's authority to do covert operations. The Justice Department wanted Langley to mull over the "legal basis for Cold War activities." Counselor Houston became the contact person. He managed to lead with a different point—that nothing in law *prohibited* "Cold War activities," but he also reprised his stance from 1947—"there is no specific statutory authorization to any agency for the conduct of such activities."

Later Houston confronted this very point in 1975, when Congress undertook its Year of Intelligence investigations. Investigators deposed the lawyer, then called him to deliver testimony. Lawrence Houston spoke to questions on these memoranda. He talked his way out of the box: Washington in 1947 had been consumed with concern, right up to Harry Truman, that the situation had become desperate and the United States needed to counter "Russian subversive action." So, Houston recounted, "I came to the conclusion that in the innate, inherent powers of the president, both as commander-in-chief and head of a sovereign state, he could direct these actions to be carried out, and if we got such a directive and Congress provided the funds, . . . we could then undertake the action required." (In the war on terror, the commander-in-chief language became the basis for asserting that torture is legal in the face of laws criminalizing it.)

Mr. Houston reacted with incredulity when congressional inquisitors supposed the practice at Langley had been to *not* speak to the lawyers when operators wanted to do something, consulting the legal eagles only when they were uncertain. Houston protested. "Over the years," he shot back, "John Warner and I remember many things coming up . . . at a morning meeting, or someone dropping by the office, or maybe even a telephone call and saying, well, what do you think about this, and we would say no, no, don't get into that. . . . You won't find a memo, . . . but we were often consulted."

Yet Houston related he *was not* consulted on CIA assassination plots, and records showed him ignorant, too, of CIA dragnet surveillance (the mail-opening program), and its break-ins. John Warner told inquisitors he had not known of the dragnet either, of any surveillance of dissidents, of loans of equipment to local police, or of assassinations, and knew of the agency's Project Chaos only in the most general terms. Warner speculated, as his inquisitor recorded, that "many projects may have been discussed by Mr. Houston with the [director] without his ever being aware." The lawyers covered each other's backs. Records exist that show both men, in May 1962, briefing Robert F. Kennedy on the CIA-Mafia plot to kill Fidel Castro.

That would be Larry Houston, the can-do counselor. Another example is Langley's "executive privilege," of which Houston wrote in *Studies in Intelligence*, the CIA's secret in-house journal, in 1958. In an analysis ranging back to the American Revolution and the constitutional conventions—perhaps a nod to the Randolph family—counselor Houston avidly sought precedent to exempt the CIA from judicial review and argue for shielding it when considering new law. Some of these, applied in reverse, were employed later to silence critics like Marchetti or Snepp.

Besides helping draft laws shielding the agency from scrutiny, Houston also negotiated with the Justice Department to agree on the CIA-DOJ arrangement for criminal referrals, first articulated in a 1954 memorandum. Counselor Houston took with him to Justice a review of expenditures on a DO project, showing that a finance officer in the Middle East—in that era of paper accounts and funds transfers—had exploited delays inherent to the system to divert to himself money from a CIA transfer account. That case had almost certainly involved criminal violations, the lawyer told DOJ officials, but they couldn't be touched without exposing the underlying op. Houston further professed that the project itself would be incomprehensible to anyone who lacked a detailed understanding of CIA operations. The deputy attorney general reasoned that, given such circumstances, DOJ could hardly be interested in prosecuting. The CIA had made a hole big enough to drive a truck through. When Larry Houston, in the harsh light of the Year of Intelligence, testified about the CIA-DOJ "understanding," he conceded that officers had escaped criminal liability in just such shabby circumstances but, he feebly protested, that had not been the intent.

The general counsel wasn't always successful. The most notable early instance came in the *Jarvinen* case. Houston had relied upon the authority in the 1949 CIA act for its director to protect "sources and methods." The trial judge's rejection of the CIA's argument still stands as a chink in its armor.

Because prosecutors never filed indictments, the CIA never had to test its exemption. Much pleasanter to consider—from Langley's viewpoint—is the outcome of another of Houston's cases, *Heine v. Raus*. Again a legal proceeding revolved around émigrés, again Estonians. In this episode, one sued another for defamation. Eerik Heine, a naturalized Canadian and a kind of professional agitator common in the secret wars, made his living attacking Soviet brutality. Comrades suddenly denounced Heine as a Russian spy before the executive board of the Legion of Estonian Liberation. Four anonymous leaflets were distributed making these charges. One appeared mysteriously, placed up against a ceiling, suspended above balloons to be released at a party in such a way the leaflets would shower onto guests below. Though caught before it happened, that seems to have been the last straw. Heine considered his prime persecutor to be Juri Raus, the national commander of the Estonian league, and a resident of Maryland, where Heine filed suit in November 1964.

Heine's complaint put Langley on the spot. The CIA had been using all these émigré groups for years. Moreover, smear tactics against individuals had been standard procedure in such operations as the ones against the Italian and French communist parties. Larry Houston estimated the sheer numbers of aliens and ex-aliens with whom CIA still kept touch at tens of thousands. A lot of the energy had drained away, but the vestigial groups were still out there. The infighting had always been vicious.

The charges against Heine were hearsay—from several Estonians, true, but hearsay nonetheless. Langley counterintelligence had interviewed

Estonian acquaintances to learn the Russians had arrested Heine and made a deal with him in 1940. For whatever reason, it appears that Langley *ordered* its agent Juri Raus to defame Heine. Heine's suit actually charged Raus with being a CIA agent acting under instructions.

Counselor Houston organized the response. In November 1965, the CIA's deputy director, Richard Helms, filed an affidavit affirming that the agency had given Raus the information used against Heine. Meanwhile Houston invoked the vague legal privilege for "state secrets" to assert the CIA had no requirement to provide evidence to the court. Raus's lawyers argued that the suit ought to be dismissed because the defendant enjoyed absolute privilege—he *was* a CIA employee acting on instructions. In April 1966, Helms supplied two more affidavits affirming CIA links to Juri Raus, confirming that he had been ordered to defame the other Estonian. Helms asserted that further information would damage national security.

The credibility Eerik Heine lost among Estonians as a result of the Raus denunciations could easily have made all the difference to his livelihood. Soviet forces had gobbled up Estonia in 1940, long before the CIA existed, and citizens had had to make compromises to avoid the gulag, where thousands had been sent. The people who told the CIA that Heine was a spy had done the same.

While it is possible the Estonian *was* a Soviet spy, that could be said of any of his accusers, and one could question how much Moscow center stood to learn from an émigré network by this time in the 1960s. Langley's benefit in destroying Heine remains obscure. Mr. Helms situated CIA's acquisition of the derogatory information in the period before November 9, 1963. The responsible officials would have been James Angleton, chief counterspy; John Maury, in his last months as Soviet Division chief; or Richard Helms himself, at the time heading the Directorate of Operations. Any of them could have given the order. Alternatively, Juri Raus could have set out to destroy Heine and then blackmailed Langley into protecting him. At a later stage, Helms admitted that a counterintelligence officer on the Estonian account—not necessarily Angleton—had given Raus his marching orders and that he, Helms, had ratified the action in December 1964.

Meanwhile, Heine countered that CIA secrecy didn't matter because the National Security Act explicitly prohibited the CIA from acting within the United States. Larry Houston came to the rescue, taking advantage of the fact that this was a civil and not a criminal case (unlike *Jarvinen*), to reassert the CIA director's responsibility for protecting "sources and methods." This prohibited revealing more about Raus or specifying who stood behind the slander. National security required destroying Heine's reputation. On April 14, 1966, the trial judge ruled that Heine could depose a CIA witness in his presence. Two weeks later, at a hearing for that purpose, Mr. Houston stood in for CIA director William F. Raborn as the deposee.

A U.S. attorney moved to drop the case. On May 13, the judge ordered Houston to submit a paper on the CIA's legal authority within the United States. He brought back a document that merely referred to paragraphs of a secret directive. The agency had the Justice Department "certify" its veracity and hand over paragraphs for the judge to study in private. The conditions were so harsh that Heine's lawyers refused to look at material they were not permitted to tell their client about. Just before Christmas, the court ruled in favor of Raus and the CIA—a nice present.

The gunslinger got his way. Here the agency secured a precedent allowing it to use defamation as an instrument of policy. You can see the tactics employed against such whistleblowers as Philip Agee. Not only that, but Langley got away with legitimizing *domestic* action on the barest showing of authority, in obvious contradiction to its governing statute. Plus, Houston managed to keep CIA witnesses out of court. Eerik Heine appealed to the Fourth Circuit of the U.S. Court of Appeals, which effectively found against him in the oddest way, ruling that, yes, it was OK for CIA to refuse to provide evidence; but, no, the decision against Heine could not stand, because the trial record did not establish that the order to defame Heine came from an official at a responsible level (which would have been the CIA director or his deputy).

Author of this bit of legal cunning was Chief Judge Clement F. Haynsworth Jr., whom Richard Nixon appointed to the Supreme Court in 1969. In an example of bipartisan cooperation so rare today, both civil rights and labor organizations opposed the Haynsworth nomination. The former complained of his decisions supporting racial segregation. Republican lawmakers found him short on judicial ethics, revealing he had bought stock in a corporation in a suit he had ruled upon but had yet to announce. The Senate rejected Haynsworth by 55 to 45.

In *Heine v. Raus*, which the Fourth Circuit decided in the summer of 1968, the dissenting judge pointed out that Richard Helms, who became CIA's top deputy only in April 1965, had had no more privilege at the time than any other employee. Privilege belonged to the director and could not be delegated. "If the CIA must defame someone in order to protect national security," Judge James B. Craven Jr. wrote, "it seems to me it could be done more effectively by the Director himself than by a secret underling—and with far less danger to a free society."

Lawrence Houston emerged from the Heine case in a plum position. By now the leadership at Langley had changed again. He rose with the new director, none other than Richard Helms, the very person whose marbles he had saved in this court case.

6

THE SHERIFFS

The CIA had long had a problem with women. From the beginning, agency folk considered spying man's work. Women were not viewed quite the same as homosexuals, but they needed to fight for acceptance. The agency encouraged spooks to wed within its family because those unions joined people already vetted. Beyond that, women at the CIA labored at a disadvantage. What jobs should be open to them and how rapidly they might rise were questions seldom asked. The agency frequently hired wives of officers as clerical workers, especially when the husband was headed overseas. That practice simplified tasking and security in the stations. Throughout the CIA, any women often worked as clericals, or later sometimes as reports officers (in the DO) or analysts (in the DI).

Naturally women noticed, and of course they were restive. Men noticed too. Years later, a senior officer reflecting on the clandestine service culture of the 1950s remembered, "There were plenty of women in the dank, sloping halls of the temporary buildings below the Lincoln Memorial and later in Langley, but almost all were in the clerical category . . . the DO had some of the best-educated women in the country doing its filing and typing." That impression, published by a thirty-five-year DO veteran in the early 1990s, had its roots in the very first days of the Central Intelligence Agency.

In basic courses, women junior officer trainees (JOTs) were excluded from the explosives, weapons, sabotage, and parachute segments, leaving them unqualified for command functions. This continued to be the situation in May 1953, when the Great White Case Officer himself appeared at the JOT course for his soon-to-be-standard keynote speech. After reciting his great failure to enlist Vladimir Lenin before the Russian Revolution, Allen Dulles opened the floor to questions. Many could have been expected—on the CIA's role in the U.S. government, whether the agency would still be needed if the Soviet Union had a change of heart, on the need for a paramilitary capability, or on the danger of politicization in intelligence analysis. But several female JOTs put Dulles to the test. Did he think women were given sufficient recognition? Why were members of the fairer sex hired at lower grade levels than men? Was he going to do something about it? "I think women have a very high place in this work," the recently promoted CIA chieftain replied, "and if there is discrimination, we're going to see that it's stopped." Director Dulles promised he would put the agency's inspector general on the matter.

GLASS-CEILING DILEMMAS

Here the action illustrated another kind of role for CIA lawyers. The inspector general (IG), like a camp counselor, had a responsibility to keep the action within bounds. This applied to all aspects of spy work. One result of Dulles's encounter with the women trainees was formation of a task force of agency women. That group itself illustrated the depth of the problem. Agency officers were ranked from GS (General Service)-1 to GS-18; the top ranks—equivalent to Army colonels and above—started at GS-15. The Petticoat Panel, as the women's study group became known, met in the I Building. It had thirteen full members plus nine alternates, deliberately restricted to experienced officers, women who had served at least three years. One board member in World War II had commanded all Women's Army Corps personnel in the entire Mediterranean theater. Another had been a representative in the Vermont State Assembly. Several had doctorates, including an archaeologist, with one woman the daughter of a general. Many had been with the OSS or its precursor, the Office of the Coordinator of Information—by 1953 giving them a dozen years in service. At the agency, *none* of these women had risen above GS-14. *There were no CIA women of higher rank.* Few served in the DO.

When the Petticoat Panel asked to see data on CIA officers by rank and sex, the personnel boffins rebuffed them *on grounds it was classified.* An agency official review conducted by security-cleared, trusted officers would be denied information necessary for its work. The most they got was percentages—and that only after the IG's intervention. They did discover that the agency actually had done *better* than the rest of the federal bureaucracy, but that seemed small comfort. A year later, General Doolittle's study of covert operations found no females among the thirty-four top officers.

Director Dulles had said that his inspector general would take care of the problem. That job went to lawyer Lyman Kirkpatrick. Chairing the agency's Career Service Board, Kirk held the right position to effect change. But the board wrestled with a host of issues, from retirement policy to insurance and medical coverage, and women were just one item. Kirk proved to be of some help. It was he who squeezed the percentages out of the personnel goons, but the IG had his own limitations. "No supervisor in this Agency in his right mind is going to take a good stenographer or a darned good competent file clerk and say, well . . . we are going to make a Case Officer or Researcher out of you," Kirkpatrick said at the career board's November 1953 meeting discussing the Petticoat Panel recommendations. Needless to say, no women were present.

Thinking in the DO, very much the same, is typified by Richard Helms, at the time its chief of operations. "There is a constant inconvenience factor with a lot of them," Helms said at that same meeting. "You just get them to a point where they are about to blossom out to a GS-12, and they get married, go somewhere else, or something over which nobody has any control." Helms believed that able women had had "damn good opportunity and very fair treatment in this Agency." At the time, there were five women in the Directorate of Operations (and seven in the entire CIA) who ranked GS-14—the equivalent of Army lieutenant colonel. Women represented just 7 percent of DO's field force and a quarter of its headquarters staff.

A decade later, in December 1963, the directorate had exactly five women at the GS-15 level (colonel) and none higher. Of the three women in the JOT class who had confronted Dulles that fateful day in 1953, only one remained on duty. A new officer, Carla, who joined the agency in 1965 as a secretary (and eventually became a case officer), recalled later, "When I came in . . . the first assumption was that any female you met in the hallway was a secretary or a clerk. And the other big difference was when I came on board, we wore hats and white gloves every day. The gloves were inspected as you entered the office to be sure that your palms were white."

Women at the CIA were patient. Langley officials took that as license to put the problem out of mind. A July 1971 memorandum noted, "Recruitment Division has had few if any specific directives either encouraging or discouraging the recruitment of professional women." There had been notable advances, if not in the DO. By 1972 a few women had reached or passed GS-15. Nearly 2 percent of officers in the highest rank were

women, but progress comes slowly in the clandestine service. A 1976 study
of the field station of the future noted that younger women seemed optimistic about challenging jobs and advancement opportunities, while older
ones expressed pessimism regarding double standards and having to work
harder than men to reach the same place. In the 1977 DO, there were
6 percent *more* men ranked GS-14 than GS-12, but on the female side
the number *dropped* 77 percent. Worse, the drop-off between GS-14 and
GS-15 amounted to *another* 92 percent for women as compared to just
under half for males.

The first woman station chief came in 1978, when Eloise R. Page went
to Athens. After that, female COSes remained few and far between. Only
one, Carol A. Roehl, headed multiple, major stations. No woman headed
a DO division until 1994. Gina Haspel rose to deputy and briefly acted as
chief, but excesses in the war on terror tainted her and she did not succeed
to the position. A woman has been deputy chief financial officer. Women
have headed CIA science, analytic, and support units and served as agency
number twos and threes, but no woman has headed the Directorate of
Operations to this day. Haspel and Avril Haines have served as deputy
directors of the CIA. "I'm so sick of the deputization of women," says
Gina Bennett, a CTC officer who was among the first to warn of Osama
bin Laden. "Deputy is the worst thing you can be. You're carrying out the
vision of someone else. It's not a glass ceiling; it's a wall."

Whenever the Directorate of Operations needed to point to its successful
women, it trotted out Page, and a colleague, Virginia Hall Goillot. Both
had started with the OSS—Hall, in fact, earlier, with British special operations. Page had been Wild Bill Donovan's secretary, went to London with
OSS counterintelligence, and helped set up one of America's first stations,
in Brussels for the Strategic Services Unit. She turned to the CIA immediately when it was created, always with the DO.

"Miss Page," as she remained and liked to be known, led the DO's scientific and technical operations staff, and took on field assignments. She
also accumulated experience on committees and interagency groups. For
a decade starting from the mid-1960s, she helped staff the critical collec-
tions problems group of the intelligence community's board of directors,
the U.S. Intelligence Board. Pentagon colleagues began to call her the Iron
Butterfly. She chaired the unit for several years before promotion to GS-18.
Page became an early CIA expert on terrorism. With his penchant for history, Bill Casey enjoyed Page, an OSS colleague as well as a descendant of
the founders of Jamestown, Virginia. In Casey's day, Page dealt with CIA

budgets and held the distinction of being among those who spent time with him one-on-one. In fact, in 1986 Eloise would be among the last to see Mr. Casey still coherent, late on the afternoon of November 25, 1986. A few months after Casey's seizure, she went into retirement.

Virginia Hall Goillot's experience takes us back. Hall, like Page, started out as a secretary (in the State Department). She lost a leg in a hunting accident in Turkey. When World War II began, Hall volunteered as an ambulance driver for the French, then for *British* special operations, for whom she worked as an agent helping set up networks in Vichy France. When the United States entered the conflict and created OSS, Hall wrangled a transfer. She entered France for the OSS by boat because of her prosthetic leg (a more romantic version has Hall parachuting with the device—she nicknamed it Cuthbert—strapped to her body). She was on her way to assignment in Vienna when the war ended. Her bravery and resourcefulness earned the Distinguished Service Cross as well as high British decorations. Hall married Paul Goillot, another OSS man with the Resistance, a decade later while with the CIA.

Like Eloise Page, Hall stayed on in U.S. intelligence. She made the transition to the CIA seamlessly. She reported on both Yugoslavia and Italy and took a cover role in the National Committee for a Free Europe when it was formed as parent entity for Radio Free Europe. She returned to the OPC at the end of 1951 and headed its paramilitary desk for France, monitoring the Gladio secret army project as a GS-13. Then she did the same work for the Southern European Division and later the DO's Paramilitary Staff.

Virginia went on temporary assignment to Europe during the first half of 1956. Her mission was to find third-country agents to use in a political action contemplated by the Near East and Africa Division. She thought she'd done well, but her supervisor rated her average and had her cooling her heels for half a year—typical stuff then for a female operative.

Hall transferred to the Western Hemisphere Division to clear her path, and she did logistics for Jesus Christ King. Soon she was back at political action and psychological warfare. Hall needed eleven years to top the hurdle from GS-13 to GS-14. By then she had become an important player in the CIA's covert operation against Cheddi Jagan in British Guiana. Hall retired in 1966, unheralded at the time. Despite this stellar career, she never attained the GS-15 grade.

For every woman the agency touted, there were uncounted legions who went unmentioned. Their trajectories show the pattern. Martha D. Peterson met her husband in college. He became a Green Beret, fought in Vietnam. She studied for a master's degree. He joined the CIA, which sent John Peterson to Laos as a paramilitary officer with the Hmong secret army. Martha went with him and enlisted as a CIA clerical. John was killed in 1972. Martha returned to the United States. Some months later, she rejoined CIA as a trainee operations officer. Her first assignment: Moscow in 1975. The operations directorate sent very promising officers there on initial tours because the Russians would not yet have identified them. Peterson worked in support of a spy the CIA had recruited in Soviet military intelligence. Russian security caught her in July 1977, making a delivery for the agent, code named Trigon. Roughed up, Peterson kept her composure; she was declared persona non grata and returned to the United States. She became a CIA training officer, later a DO operative in the Middle East, and put in thirty-two years in all.

Then there was Linda C. Flohr, of the same generation, who joined in 1967. Flohr needed more than a decade to reach middle level, and in the early years of the Contra project she served as executive assistant to the task force chief. She produced the biopic the CIA filmed to laud "Comandante Zero," a Sandinista defector who joined the insurgents. On her own sewing machine, Flohr created a flag for the group, along with backdrops for the film. The CIA wanted to take over the network that Nicaraguan government broadcasters used and show its Contra film instead. In 1983, when Reagan invaded Grenada, Langley dispatched Flohr on a last-minute scouting mission, meeting officials as well as the imprisoned British colonial governor. Flohr's last assignment came with the Iraq Operations Group, whose op against Saddam Hussein after the First Gulf War fell apart. A year later, in the ferment to refashion U.S. intelligence for the post–Cold War era, she joined the staff of the Aspin-Brown Commission, an official effort to foretell the future. Later Flohr worked for the Rendon Group, which did public relations for Iraqi exiles, and for the NSC staff in the second Bush administration.

Robert M. Gates, as CIA director, created the Iraq Operations Group with which Flohr served. He looked past the demise of the Soviet Union and set up initiatives with the aim of recasting Langley in a new mold. One of those was the Glass Ceiling Study, in March 1991, which Gates ordered to review conditions for women and minorities. There had been some movement since Dulles's day. In contrast to the Petticoat Panel's struggles, the CIA not only did not assert that its demographic data were a secret; the Office of Personnel actually handed quantitative analyses to outside contractors hired to crunch numbers for the study. The contractors also administered surveys and had focus groups to explore the data in greater depth. The Glass Ceiling Study found that women were a constant in personnel terms—about 40 percent in 1992—but concentrated in lower grades than men, peaking at GS-12, dropping at the next rank, and diminishing rapidly afterward. Among the Senior Intelligence Service (SIS—an entity created to broaden the government's ability to offer perks at the highest levels, doubling for the old ranks of GS-16 to GS-18) women made up 10 percent of the force. Measured by bureaucratic clout, women represented just 6 percent of office directors or deputies. In the Directorate of Operations, there were fewer than ten women in those command positions.

A CIA management committee met to push reforms and devise ways to overcome barriers. Bonnie Hershberg, a major mover in this group, was recognized by a Trailblazer Award in 2007, but progress remained uneven. A year after the Glass Ceiling Study, aides could still poke fun at women in the Undercover Quilters, Langley's in-house quilt-making club. Data for Fiscal Year 2009 show that the number of women who had reached SIS rank had *diminished*, tumbling by half, though those of GS-15 rank climbed to 22 percent of staff. That includes minorities, a smaller fraction in every category. By 2012 the SIS women, according to recent CIA disclosures, had risen to 19 percent, and in 2016 female "senior leadership"—probably something other than SIS—stood at 34 percent, both figures difficult to reconcile with the 2009 data, especially because the overall proportion of women at the CIA has remained constant at 45 percent.

Operations officer Melissa Mahle found it difficult to pursue Middle East operations, with Langley simultaneously micromanaging and yet so skittish about vulnerabilities that she was told to get liability insurance. Getting the agency to extend maternity leave and honor personnel policies was another problem. Women interviewed for a *Newsweek* feature repeatedly described the social costs of intelligence service—children costing them promotions, barren relationships limiting them to adoption, inability to make time for dating. A woman analyst who labored on nuclear proliferation issues and eventually left for one of the weapons labs put it this way: working hard for her own promotions, each year she found fewer women colleagues, while less-skilled men were rising as fast or faster. One day she realized that the only two women still with her had been in the office for a decade. It was time to go.

For others it was time to sue. Hershberg's steering committee led to agency negotiations on equal opportunity, but stubborn bureaucrats yielded little. By 1994 the fever had run high enough that some two hundred women joined a class-action lawsuit. That brings us back to the Office of General Counsel. Ironically, at this moment, Langley's gunslinger would be a woman, Elizabeth R. Rindskopf, who had arrived by way of the National Security Agency and the State Department. Naturally, she happened to be the agency's first female general counsel. Rindskopf ran out of gas due to a related nightmare, a measure of the obstacles women face at the CIA.

THE SPOOK AND THE SHERIFF

Janine M. Brookner had been another of Langley's meteors. Born in upstate New York on the eve of World War II, she married young, her high school sweetheart, divorced at twenty-two, and raised a son while earning a master's at New York University. An NYU professor warned that if she followed her dream of joining the Peace Corps, she would starve. Janine followed Mom's advice. Brookner's academic focus had been Russia—perfect for the CIA, where her mom advised her to apply. In 1968 the agency hired Brookner, trained her, and promptly sent her to the Philippines. The twenty-eight-year-old case officer infiltrated the Philippine Communist Party. Sent to Thailand, she helped whittle down the insurgency in the northeast of that country. On a tour in Venezuela, Brookner became so critical to progress, she acted as station chief. In New York in the mid-1980s, Brookner managed CIA watchers of Soviet and other Eastern Bloc delegations at the United Nations. She noticed misbehavior among colleagues and reported one, Aldrich Ames, who might have been stopped before he became a Russian spy.

In July 1989, Ms. Brookner went to Kingston as station chief. Considered a backwater, Jamaica also had a reputation as a poorly managed station, but it had staff and conducted operations. She became the first female COS in the Latin America Division. Jerry Gruner, who had been Linda Flohr's boss on the Central America Task Force, led the division and proved supportive. Janine's efficiency ratings were superb, and graders credited her with energizing the station. Two years passed in a flash. The personnel gurus slated her for Prague in the Czech Republic.

Many elements of the assignment remained beyond the COS's control, but Brookner was given her choice for deputy. She picked an African American officer she'd met at Langley. A black, even an American, could pass more easily on Kingston's streets. The station chief's trouble began halfway through her tour when the deputy's wife telephoned, came to see

Brookner, and accused her husband of assault. Under questioning the offi-cer did not deny the incident but claimed the wife had started it. Feeling her way, anxious to avoid a repetition, Brookner told Langley. That was a judgment call. "I doubt I would have reported it," Eloise Page told a reporter working this story. "I maybe would have felt that I could have gotten it worked out, just to avoid ruining his career."

Ms. Brookner encouraged the deputy to report his version too. Not long afterward, headquarters recalled the officer. But Inspector General Fred Hitz investigated the station chief, not her subordinate. A month before her tour ended, a couple of IG inquisitors arrived in Kingston and dug out every bit of dirt imaginable. Someone alleged Brookner had improperly charged overtime. Others said she was an alcoholic, wore short shorts, thin T-shirts, and microscopic underwear, had sexually harassed a male subordinate at a Christmas party, and so on. Brookner suddenly found herself at Langley in a room with no phone, no window, and no work to do. Prague was out. She did not even discover the range of allegations until May 1992. She appealed to bosses. Dorwin Wilson, the Latin baron at the time, proved unresponsive.

A former boss, George Kalaris, who had been chief of station in Manila when Brookner served there, recalled, "She had a drive, persistence, and sensibility not normally found in male officers." Brookner displayed that now. Soon a stream of affadavits began flowing to Hitz. The U.S. ambas-sador from her time in Jamaica reported his admiration for Brookner. Col-leagues like Kalaris provided testimonials. The COS could show that the factual charges made against her were wrong. The IG asserted that every-thing was secret.

The IG's office apparently would not say when alleged conduct had occurred or identify witnesses. Its January 1993 report recommended that Brookner take counseling and repay overtime claims. A new CIA director, R. James Woolsey, professed that he did not interfere in personnel mat-ters. So in July 1994 Janine Brookner filed suit against the CIA. Now the winds blew against Langley. The Senate intelligence committee expressed its intense interest in the case of "Jane Doe Thompson," as it was filed, in SSCI's biennial report. The Christmas party sexual harassment, once that documentation surfaced, traced to a Drug Enforcement Administration officer who insisted he had made no such charge. The allegations about clothing related to someone else, a case officer Brookner had also reported. A claim that she had improperly used an agency helicopter proved to be without foundation. Indeed, a document that came to light during discovery proceedings demonstrated that Hitz's office, between November 1991 and September 1992, had investigated at least forty allegations of illegal or improper activity by male officers ranking GS-15 or above, only three ending in reprimands, while here the CIA persecuted a female station chief in the face of contrary evidence.

Watching all this, Elizabeth Rindskopf, the general counsel, collared Jim Woolsey. With the CIA already in talks to avert a glass-ceiling class action, the Brookner lawsuit represented the very vehicle that would show that suit to be precisely correct. In December 1994, the CIA settled out of court, paying Janine Brookner $410,000 ($659,000 in 2016) in arrears and damages.

Rindskopf chose this moment to take a leave of absence to recharge her batteries, teaching at Cleveland State University Law School. She returned for only a few months in 1995 to supervise a settlement of the glass-ceiling litigation. Brookner's case illustrated the workplace culture.

The DO had more than 2,000 officers. More than 250 of them saw themselves as did Brookner. Langley settled their December 1993 class-action suit in the summer of 1995, just as George Tenet came on board. The agency offered back pay, two dozen retroactive promotions, opportunities for women who had left in disgust to return as case officers, and more. It kept the monetary cost to $1 million. Rindskopf left for good. There has yet to be another female general counsel.

SHERIFFS IN SNEAKERS

The 1949 law granting extraordinary powers also governs both the general counsel and the inspector general, but those amendments were inserted much later. Where the language pertaining to the counsel consists of exactly one paragraph, simply providing that the top lawyer "shall perform such functions as the Director of Central Intelligence may prescribe," the text pertinent to the inspector general goes on page after page. The difference testifies to the transformation of the IG's role. There has yet to be a female IG, though it appears that the recent standard is to have one as deputy.

It is a long time since Lyman Kirkpatrick held the job. He focused on efficiency reviews. Kirk began to buck the trend with his Bay of Pigs study. "There are few who would argue that it wasn't a flawed operation," an inspector noted. "To have reported it differently would have been dishonest." But look what happened. The IG, condemned from all sides, found wide dismissal of his recommendations. No wonder Kirkpatrick considered this painful. It would be Tracy Barnes who continued, only to get in more trouble.

So the IG went on measuring efficiency. Just make sure the survey doesn't break any rice bowls. Ten years earlier, the IG's audit function had been split off and given to CIA administrative organs. Inspectors general were left with the surveys. The IG had a staff in mid- to senior grades (GS-14 to GS-17) and, for much of the period, very limited in number (fifteen inspectors and four secretaries). Teams formed for each review. They began at headquarters, requesting documents and interviewing officers. Then they went cruising. A team captain decided the method. Her/his crew varied with the importance of the assignment. Even in the 1960s, there were nearly *four dozen* components to inspect, so clearly coverage could not be constant or comprehensive, and many times surveys threw up sensitive issues requiring separate and private handling.

In 1962 the IG looked into the CIA's illegal mail opening, the equivalent of today's dragnet NSA eavesdropping. The inspector general found the operators' cover story useless, because U.S. law criminalizes tampering with the mails, so the surveillance was illegal on its face. Angleton's staff traded memos deploring the IG's conclusion.

One success came in evaluations of the CIA mind-control program, which had caused the death of unwitting test subject Frank Olson. The IG advised that the project should be terminated, but the scientists insisted that it continue. It was terminated.

Another survey covered the Western Hemisphere Division, which had conducted the Bay of Pigs, subsequent Cuban projects, the op against British Guiana, electoral interventions in Peru, Bolivia, and Chile, and more. Aside from compiling statistics, the IG accomplished little.

The agency had many proprietaries, ostensibly private businesses that existed to supply particular services for Langley's operations or cover for CIA agents. Its air proprietaries are the best known. Among them the IG review led to confusion, to Larry Houston's special task force, and to new umbrella management. Obtaining data from operators remained a problem. When inspector Scott Breckinridge complained to the IG, Gordon Stewart, the boss told him to drop the fight.

After leaks triggered charges on assassinations from columnist Drew Pearson, President Johnson demanded that the CIA review allegations that it had plotted to murder Fidel Castro. That 1967 review became most significant for the fact that it was on CIA letterhead and confirmed that the agency really had at least considered assassination plots. Details were limited—and the lawyers then sent all the agency records they'd consulted to the burn bin.

The war in Southeast Asia occasioned numerous IG reviews. One concerned the agency's own analysis of the size of enemy forces; in it an analyst named Sam Adams contested the numbers furnished by military authorities. The IG decided not to credit the CIA man's methodology or his argument that the United States might have avoided its surprise in the Tet offensive. But Adams had been right, and the military had manipulated the data.

For a major review of the Far East Division in 1971, the IG allocated a permanent staff of just five, though there were augmentations for different parts of the inquiry. One piece concerned Laos, where allegations persisted that Air America crews were trafficking drugs aboard CIA aircraft. The inspector general decided that aside from "bad apples" there was nothing to the charges. Other parts of the survey focused on the notorious Phoenix program, in which Washington and Saigon sought to eliminate the National Liberation Front (NLF) administrative network. The district, provincial, and national centers where prisoners were interrogated became a most controversial aspect. These were direct antecedents of the black prisons of the war on terror. IG inspectors actually visited some of them. The public heard torture charges. There is no indication that the IG filed complaints on either centers or interrogation methods.

The CIA paid and supported a paramilitary army in South Vietnam that formed the strike force of the Phoenix campaign. Individual platoons were called provincial reconnaissance units (PRUs). Charges were rife that the PRUs killed indiscriminately, were used as enforcers in corrupt shakedowns, and more. The inspector general's survey concluded that the PRUs were highly effective and that their professionalism was improving. When the PRUs transferred to South Vietnamese government control, IG officers expressed confidence.

Then the inspector general's field people discovered, during an inspection of the DO European Division, that a good deal of effort was being devoted to spying on Americans, dissenters against the war in Vietnam. Angleton's Project Chaos staff were the beneficiaries, the CIA's contribution to the war against dissent in America. The diversion from spy missions was obvious, even given the excuse that the spooks watched antiwar activists simply to see what enemy agents they might contact (none, other than official North Vietnamese or Liberation Front diplomats).

Part of the inspector general's difficulty no doubt flowed from the nature of those selected for the job. Lyman Kirkpatrick set the mold. He had been DO, tried and true. He had wanted to be the chief operator. Others were hewn from that stone. John Earman had been special assistant to Allen Dulles and executive aide to Dick Bissell. Earman had helped in the postwar race to utilize former Nazis for intel purposes. Like him, successor Gordon M. Stewart had a German connection, in fact an important role advocating for CIA support of a nascent German intelligence agency. He had been chief of station in Germany. William V. Broe had been in the Far East and Latin America. All of them were creatures of the DO. Donald F. Chamberlain, the IG under Colby from 1973 to 1975, hailed from the agency's technology side and was a plank holder in creation of the Directorate of Science and Technology. Changes under Chamberlain highlighted another reason for the IG's ineffectiveness. As if the small staff of the 1960s hadn't been problem enough, at this point the office was cut to just five investigators.

That was the situation in the Year of Intelligence, when the Church Committee looked into the inspector general's work. The congressional investigators recommended that the IG office be strengthened. Church Committee members found that the inspector general lacked objectivity, authority, and independence. The Church, Pike, and Rockefeller investigations led to creation of the congressional oversight committees. The Senate committee's projected CIA charter in law provided for a stronger inspector general, but the bill won little support from stalwarts. Langley went to its DO for Inspector General John H. Waller.

Needless to say, Bill Casey had little use for an inspector general, especially one whose job was to ensure legality. Of course, the paradigm cases were the scandals over the Contra assassination manual and the Nicaraguan harbor mining. As related earlier, John Stein (another DO officer posted as inspector general) excused agency activities in its secret war. The joint congressional investigation found that the inspector general "appears not to have had the manpower, resources or tenacity to acquire key facts uncovered by the other investigations of the Iran-Contra affair," failing to uncover those facts despite residing *inside* the CIA's secrecy envelope.

Inspectors general were watchdogs in sneakers, monitors who begged to be taken seriously. Congress decided to create an independent CIA inspector general like the IGs established throughout government by a 1978 law, which had exempted Langley. In 1987 Pennsylvania senator Arlen Spector introduced the bill. William Webster, Casey's successor, testified against it at hearings in 1987 and again the following year. Director Webster insisted that his post–Iran Contra reforms eliminated the problem. Webster had previously been FBI director and had a lot of support on Capitol Hill, so Congress deferred action.

Next the oversight committees asked the IG to undertake several particular investigations. The Senate committee saw results that varied widely in scope and competence and felt the office was floundering. By the summer of 1989, the overseers had decided a law had become necessary. By then George H.W. Bush was president. Politician Bush had shepherded the CIA through Ford's last year and had his own views on the balance between confidentiality and oversight. He spoke to Senate leaders several times while the legislation took shape. It passed Congress with an overwhelming Senate majority.

The new office of inspector general, appointed by the president, confirmed by Congress, with a duty to report outrageous activity to both, became a reality in 1990. For the first time, the office had a budget funded separately from the rest of the agency, authority to hire and fire its own staff, a renewed capacity to conduct audits, and a legal right to access Langley's contractors and employees. The inspector general could initiate inquiries, and previously existing channels for disgruntled officers to warn the IG of excesses remained in place.

The new IG had the advantage of no longer serving at the pleasure of the CIA director but still had important limitations. The inspector general had no subpoena power and so couldn't compel subjects to yield evidence, and he needed the DCI's approval to seek cooperation from other agencies. Under the legislation, which amended the Central Intelligence Agency Act of 1949, the IG also had a duty to inform the agency director of problems and deficiencies in CIA administration, preserving the old role of efficiency expert. The director could forbid inquiries. Obviously, good relations with the director remained important. Most reports went to the seventh floor for consideration, and the IG soon found it difficult to recruit CIA specialist staff if their return to agency posts was not secure. The inspector general, in spite of the statutory right to access, would need the CIA director on his side to break logjams over files and end foot-dragging by recalcitrant agency offices. This system went into effect in the fall of 1990 when President Bush nominated the first independent inspector general.

NEW SHERIFF IN TOWN

Frederick P. Hitz appeared before the Senate Select Committee on Intelligence on September 25, 1990. George J. Tenet, then the SSCI's staff director, sat among the listeners, as did as L. Britt Snider, then on the staff. (Hitz would ultimately sit opposite Tenet as CIA director, and Snider would follow Hitz as IG.) The senators were in a celebratory mood. They were rolling out an institutional change years in the making, one that promised to extend their reach and assist their oversight role. The refashioned IG could serve as a warning bell against repetition of anything like Iran-Contra. Ideally, such excesses could not occur because the IG would catch them first, investigate them to death, and bring them to both Capitol Hill and the White House.

Hitz represented a known quantity, or at least no surprise. He arrived with recommendations from former CIA director James R. Schlesinger and top agency lawyer Daniel B. Silver. Virginia senator John W. Warner, an old acquaintance, presented Mr. Hitz. The committee had private insights into the nominee. Fred Hitz had been something akin to a professional legislative aide, having worked on legislative affairs between bouts at the law. He was also the uncle of long-serving SSCI aide Natalie Bocock. He'd been on the Hill liaising for the State Department, the Pentagon, and the Department of Energy, as well as the CIA (from June 1978 to July 1982). Admiral Stansfield Turner had honored Hitz with a merit award and elevation to the Senior Intelligence Service at the midpoint of that tour.

Nearing his fifty-first birthday and acceptable throughout the agency, Hitz had not been just a lobbyist. He'd joined the CIA as an operations officer trainee in 1967, the same year as Linda Flohr. He'd served a tour in the Ivory Coast with State Department cover. President Bush, when he led the agency, knew Fred as the Pentagon's water carrier on the Hill. At that time, the Lebanese civil war embroiled both the CIA and the Department of Defense, and lots of congressional committees clamored for the executive agencies to answer their questions.

More than those of most successors, Fred Hitz's nomination hearing consumed itself with conversations on how he intended to act within the confines of the new law. It would be fair to say that Hitz originated the role of the "modern" inspector general. He recognized "the heavy seas upon which the legislation sailed." He had a clear perception that the IG and his staff must understand intel operations and procedures and build the trust of agency officers. For example, whereas the law provided that the IG should report to the committees (with comment) each time a spy chief shut down an investigation, Hitz stated his intention to stand down unless he and the CIA director differed on the validity of DCI's action. The lawyer also anticipated that he would not be called upon to report criminality to the Department of Justice, as required in the law, because the CIA was supposed to do that. Fred apparently thought there would be no more Bill Caseys. He was comfortable with the IG's lack of subpoena power.

Only Senator Howard Metzenbaum (D-OH), who believed a stronger candidate should have been sought, opposed the nomination. Hitz received confirmation from the full Senate. Feeling ran strong that the inspector general's office, which had gone unfilled for nearly a year, needed to be put back on track.

So there was Fred Hitz, facing the Senate inquisitors, at precisely the moment when Janine Brookner's troubles began in Jamaica. The misbehavior of the deputy that started the mess took place in September 1990. Just as Hitz geared up his new office, the complaint about Brookner floated up through channels. The inspector general opened an investigation. Hitz at least assigned a woman officer as team chief. Hitz continues to believe that the Brookner case had been handled properly but that comments elsewhere around Langley inflamed both sides, while press coverage made the thing appear botched.

But there *was* a learning curve. When allegations surfaced against Jose Rodriguez in 1996, Inspector General Hitz did his investigation and concluded that Division Chief Rodriguez should be disciplined. That result would then be reviewed again, by an "accountability board" responsible only to the CIA director. In the baron's case, the board agreed with the IG. Measures taken against Rodriguez did not, ultimately, prevent his rise to head the clandestine service. The process became standard procedure.

Inspector general investigations also evolved. Disciplinary inquiries like the ones regarding Brookner and Rodriguez remained the bread and butter of the Office of the Inspector General, along with audits of the operating units. Indeed, the audit staff became the largest part of the IG office. Hitz professionalized the practice by developing a mixed cadre of people hired directly plus officers seconded from agencies. He attempted to rely on insiders as much as possible, worrying that outside gunslingers would spook the workforce. Reflecting the IG's new independence, the staff grew beyond its previous peak. He had at least a dozen women in senior positions and recollects that all performed admirably.

A lot had changed since Fred Hitz served with Stan Turner. Fred felt the swish of turnover at the top during the Clinton era—five CIA directors in seven years. Agency officers were driven in different directions, then their bosses were gone. Hitz agrees with George Tenet's judgment that the collapse of the Soviet Union essentially triggered a state of bankruptcy at Langley. Rebuilding became everyone's job. The IG's part, Hitz decided, would be to articulate standards for oversight, be candid with and available to the CIA director, and to be straight with the rank and file. Hitz believed the CIA Act revisions creating his post gave him the jets for the job. If he needed more, he was ready to go to the president, Congress, or the CIA director.

Mr. Hitz tried to endow his unit with specific legal expertise, establishing a deputy inspector general for investigations. This was A.R. Cinquegrana, a fellow who had worked for the Department of Justice and also OGC. When Admiral Turner revealed the agency's MK/Ultra drug experiments back in 1978, it had been Cinquegrana who gave the University of Wisconsin the CIA documents revealing its role in that program. Liz Rindskopf, the IG's opposite number as general counsel, got along well with Hitz except for a few minor territorial skirmishes. Langley's barons, office and branch chiefs, and others took more time to realize that IG reports had consequences. When audits or recommendations came, the barons ignored them, only to have Tenet order implementation. Then even the cynics wised up.

The inspector general's major inquiries grabbed attention. On Hitz's watch, there were many. By far the best known centered on activities in Guatemala. The inquiry delved into the agency's relationships with Guatemalan intelligence and security units, but it started with the bulldog determination of Jennifer Harbury, whose husband had been tortured and killed by Guatemalan security forces in 1992. A Guatemalan officer who doubled as a CIA agent would be connected to these events in a January 1995 report.

True enough, Harbury's husband, Efraín Bámaca Velásquez, had been a rebel leader married to an American, but he was a heroic figure in a struggle in which the Guatemalan military were killing peasants and burning villages in what amounted to war on Mayan Indians. The CIA station reported the rebel *comandante*'s disappearance within days, as well as its expectation that his fate would be hidden. Harbury, a lawyer, went to Guatemala to discover what had happened and asked for U.S. embassy help.

Another death of an American, in 1990, had been reported to Langley at the time—and connected to the same CIA asset. In November 1991, the CIA, tentatively or not, had had general counsel Rindskopf prepare a referral to the Justice Department, and the Latin America Division had briefed a senior Justice official in connection with it. Thus the CIA station had known the situation from day one. But station officers stonewalled Harbury and reportedly lobbied embassy colleagues in the defense attaché's office, which had its own links to the Guatemalan military, to withhold their cooperation too.

Jennifer Harbury began a much-reported hunger strike. Media attention uncovered new angles. It turned out that at least a dozen Americans had disappeared into the maw of Guatemalan security forces since 1984. Primarily important by then to Washington's war on drugs, Guatemala was using its $3.5 million a year in CIA money for ethnic cleansing. In the Clinton years, the annual dole declined to about a million, but the place still crawled with CIA spooks, and most of them fought the government's war.

The human rights implications were clear, and Langley had had human rights directives on the books since the time of the Contra assassination manuals. These were strengthened in 1989, and a year later the Latin America Division had affirmed them. Then discovery of the murders put it all in question. Not only did the local station clam up, but also at Langley the DO failed to flag Guatemala for the congressional overseers.

Jennifer Harbury met with staff of the intelligence committees in 1995. By then she was convinced the CIA had been mixed up in Bamaca's death and said so. The Senate committee followed up and soon discovered rumors of the Guatemalan agent's involvement. Besides its own probe, the SSCI asked the inspector general to inquire. The IG probe ramified as it proceeded, eventually encompassing multiple elements, including one on the Bamaca murder, one on that of the American Michael DeVine, one on other allegations, another specifically on the agency asset implicated in these events, and one into whether documents had been hidden or destroyed.

The president's own Intelligence Oversight Board opened another investigation, but all of the inquiries failed to establish any deliberate intent to withhold information. And the veracity of reports linking the agent to the killings came into doubt. Some were hearsay, others were from unreliable sources, and so on. But the Guatemala City station had delayed a report connecting its asset to the Bamaca killing, a sin of omission that was real. Otherwise the slate seemed clean.

Nevertheless, Admiral William O. Studeman, acting CIA director, had been mousetrapped by his channels into inaccurate testimony. Director John Deutch, who took charge in the middle of this, was determined to sweep clean. A dozen officers were disciplined, including former division chief Terry Ward and former station chief Fred Brugger, who was forced into retirement. Deutch promulgated new regulations to make clear that he himself would take the lead in deciding what congressional notifications would be made. Deutch reaffirmed human rights directives and issued new orders requiring background checks into persons proposed to be put on payroll, with prohibitions against those with human rights transgressions.

It's worth pausing a moment for the Deutch "bad boy" prohibition. This brought a hail of complaints, to a degree sloughed off onto the inspector general. Some said the kind of people who know stuff you want to find out are bad boys by definition, and to prohibit them is to cut off your nose. Think about that. Of the top spies in CIA history—Popov, Penkovskiy, Tolkachev, Gordievsky, Kuklinski—none were bad boys. Even the knuckle draggers, say, Cuban exiles, among them the good ones were principled men and women in the fight, their aim to get Castro. Bad boys talking the talk but out for the buck are neither effective agents *nor* good investments. This kind of simplemindedness leads to trouble. After 9/11, when the terrorist attacks were examined by a commission and Langley was obliged to furnish evidence, the CIA disclosed that *no* agent recruitment had *ever* been prevented by the bad-boy rule.

Another argument takes the form that the prohibition and the IG have led to a risk averse CIA, an operations directorate reluctant to get its feet wet. That amounts to fear mongering. The risk aversion charge has actually been around nearly as long as the congressional oversight system. *Each time there is a push* to increase accountability on spy activity, the charge comes back from those seeking to avoid regulation. Spooks dreaded risk aversion when covert operations reporting mechanisms were under review, when Congress wanted the independent IG, and again when operatives refused to give lawmakers or the public access to the "legal memoranda" that "justified" torture or extrajudicial killing.

The truth is that, at the very moment the inspector general probed high-handed CIA refusals to apply rights norms in Central America, the DO had embarked on a high-risk, poorly conceived covert attempt to oust Saddam Hussein in Iraq, something called DB/Achilles. Squabbling Iraqi opposition and ethnic factions compromised the op. Jittery Washington officials let the project come apart.

Risk aversion comes from repetition of stupidity, not from accountability.

Agency officers involved in the Iraq fiasco were investigated by the FBI. The Senate committee and inspector general largely stayed out of it. In April 1996, after he'd spent a year on the hot seat, Justice dropped its probe of DO operator Robert Baer. Advice that operations officers should maintain million-dollar liability insurance policies flowed from proceedings like this—and not just to the women. Baer's troubles came not from risk aversion but from CIA *ghosts*—from the agency's contradictory tendencies to forge ahead, then run for cover when the institution seemed threatened. Agency lawyers protected the institution, not the man.

Another of Hitz's inquiries was more personal. That would be the IG's examination of the Aldrich Ames espionage case. Here the question became why it took Langley nearly a decade to expose the traitor, even though suspicions of a mole instantly deepened when the Soviets swept up virtually all the CIA agents in Russia over a short period in 1985. Aldrich H. Ames had been in Hitz's training class. It was also poignant, after the glass-ceiling suit and Hitz's misstep in the Brookner case, that CIA women led the counterspy team that caught Ames. Results of the IG inquiry leaked to the *New York Times*. Furious, Jim Woolsey, CIA director, ordered Hitz to undergo a polygraph test. Fred passed without difficulty.

On September 28, 1994, Hitz appeared before the Senate intelligence committee to discuss the Ames case. The IG had put a team of a dozen on it, acting on an unusual request from the SSCI, made directly to him rather than through the CIA director. For the first couple of months, for fear of tainting a criminal prosecution, the inquisitors had restricted themselves to background interviews with persons not likely to be witnesses. Once Ames pled guilty, the IG went to full speed but then had less time. Hitz also chose not to involve his deputy, Cinquegrana, except to compare the list of officials whose management of Ames was scrutinized, with a list of CIA awardees whose honors were held back due to the investigation. The major conclusion, that the sudden loss of virtually all agents in Russia did not receive enough attention quickly enough, appeared quite reasonable. Clair George, Richard F. Stolz, and Thomas A. Twetten led the DO during that time. George, of course, had been preoccupied by Iran-Contra, and Twetten by the Guatemala affair.

Bill Casey left Fred Hitz uncomfortable amounts of business. Cinquegrana knew where many of the bodies were buried. He had, for example, been involved in Casey's effort to exempt the CIA from reporting drug trafficking to the Justice Department. The Senate formed a special committee to look into the drug trade in the early 1990s, and its hearings made many charges that linked the CIA's Contra rebels to the flow of drugs into the United States The issue had already grown heated by August 1996, when *San Jose Mercury News* investigative reporter Gary Webb published a series of articles linking Los Angeles drug rings to the Contras, directly charging agency complicity. Director Deutch actually flew to Los Angeles to give a public press conference in November 1996—one of very few ever held by a spy chief—denying the charges.

Under pressure from California's congressional delegation, Director Deutch agreed to an investigation. That, too, became an IG assignment, and Cinquegrana conducted the detailed inquiry, which produced two volumes of reporting, one on the California side and another focused on the Contras, especially in Costa Rica, but also Nicaragua and Honduras. Where trouble gathering information from CIA operating divisions might have been expected, there turned out to be remarkably little. Perhaps that had to do with their story. The inquiry found no CIA misbehavior with California drug rings, conceded that (uncertain numbers of) Contras had moved drugs, and argued that the CIA had been generally aware but lacked direct evidence.

Since Casey's Central American wars already preoccupied the IG, Hitz went on to produce an investigation of agency activities in Honduras. In the Salvadoran civil war there had also been a single attack in which a number of U.S. Marines were killed, and the IG looked into what the CIA had known about that. By then Fred Hitz had decided his time was up. The controversy surrounding his investigations had been distracting, and he felt the IG office was now sufficiently established. Hitz left the CIA in the spring of 1998.

His successor was a natural. L. Britt Snider, long a lawyer and counsel to the Senate intelligence committee, had been an author of the legislation creating the independent inspector general, the annual intelligence authorization bills, and even the original Senate resolution creating the Select Committee on Intelligence. Britt had been a lawyer to the Church Committee back in 1975. The fifty-three-year-old graduated University of Virginia Law School, then joined the Army Signal Corps, serving as an officer in Vietnam. He returned as the war wound down, to work on constitutional rights for the Senate Judiciary Committee, and went from there to the Church investigation. Snider returned to his North Carolina home and set up a law practice, but Capitol Hill lured him back, and then he spent nearly a decade at the Pentagon as a civilian official in the intelligence field.

Snider joined the SSCI in January 1987 and stayed through February 1995, then directed the staff of the Aspin-Brown Commission. At the

SSCI, Britt had been friends with George Tenet, and a few months after the latter ascended to director of central intelligence he enlisted Britt Snider as special counsel. President William J. Clinton found Snider an attractive candidate for IG for the same reason he appointed Tenet to lead the agency—the Senate would certainly confirm, and Clinton had trouble getting approval for CIA appointees.

At his confirmation hearing, Britt Snider spoke of his closeness to George Tenet—with whom the senators were also intimately acquainted—and said he and George agreed the IG must be completely independent. That proved fortuitous, because almost the first item on Snider's IG agenda was an inquiry into Director Deutch's handling of classified information—and Deutch had been the man who brought Tenet to Langley, originally as his second. Snider's relationship with George Tenet endured, but the inspector general's health suffered, and he felt obliged to take several leaves of absence.

The office settled down again in 2002. Then for the first time in the era of the modern IG, a CIA professional was nominated. John L. Helgerson had learned the trade as deputy to Snider. Helgerson had come up through Langley's analytical side, a career analyst. His specialty had been North Africa and the Middle East, and he proved useful in the inquiries after 9/11. In the mid-1980s under Casey, Helgerson's Africa portfolio expanded to include Latin American analysis. During that period, the DI produced some notorious reporting, such as a paper claiming that the Sandinistas were about to field Soviet jet fighters, which they never did. Later, as a top DI official, he had refused to remove heavy-handed managers who terrorized their people. Shielding one senior Soviet Analysis (SOVA) Division officer, most of whose staff put in for transfer, he browbeat the disaffected analysts rather than disciplining their wayward boss. He had a reputation for tacking with the wind, perhaps starting from his time as assistant for policy support under Stan Turner. Ultimately Helgerson rose to deputy director for intelligence, leading the entire analytical apparatus.

Jim Woolsey, as CIA director in 1994, rewarded Helgerson with a plum posting to London to liaise with MI-6. After returning, John did that stint for Britt Snider, and after a tour with the newly created mapping and geospatial agency he took charge of the National Intelligence Council (NIC), the community's top analytical unit, responsible for the National Intelligence Estimates. In the months preceding the 9/11 attacks, the NIC did not read the omens. This was also the time the Bush administration began churning out phony charges that Iraq possessed nuclear and other weapons of mass destruction. Helgerson spent a good deal of his NIC period giving speeches. For all that, John L. Helgerson became a surprise as IG, rising to his calling.

On Helgerson's watch, Langley's directors came to dread the touch of the inspector general. No doubt some of them began to think nostalgically of the days when the IG, constricted, restricted, and carefully selected from friendly cadres, had been kept in a box. The last of Langley's bosses to enjoy those benefits had been Richard Helms.

7

THE HEADLESS HORSEMAN

ONE DAY TOWARD THE END OF 1958, ALLEN DULLES INVITED RICHARD Helms to lunch. In Helms's memoir, this is a shared sandwich in Allen's office. In notes Mr. Helms prepared for his co-author, it's an invitation to the Great White Case Officer's Georgetown home. Either way, Dulles wanted to let Dick down gently. That is, they both knew that the CIA could not continue with Frank Wisner as the head of operations. Richard Helms had already begun acting in his place, but Dulles had resolved to promote his protégé Richard Bissell, not Helms. The latter had been in the fight alongside Allen since 1945, when they shared quarters in Wiesbaden. Now, at the Directorate of Operations, Helms had put in his time, serving as Wisner's right hand for years. The quaintly titled "chief of operations"—in agency usage abbreviated COPS—filled either the second or third slot, depending on officers' personalities and whether a unit had a deputy director. Helms had succeeded Lyman Kirkpatrick in that post.

At the operations directorate, it had been Helms as de facto number two, and he had a legitimate claim to the top spot—COPS for seven years, *and* he'd been acting chief for months when Wisner had gone to the hospital. Equally important, like Dulles himself, Wisner had never been much of an administrator, so the COPS had done that too. Dick Helms had really been the glue holding together the DO. The least Dulles could do was give him lunch. Helms admits to genuine surprise and disappointment, to put it mildly.

Richard Bissell knew just a handful of the key people, and his knowledge of the clandestine service's global ventures remained strictly limited.

Helms decided the director thought him not enough of an activist, not sufficiently dedicated to covert operations, a holdover from the old days of competition, before the units had merged in the Directorate of

Operations. Helms *did* consider himself a primary exponent of spying and counterespionage.

Dick remembered another encounter with the boss. It had been mid-morning, years earlier, when the COPS trudged up the hill from the Reflecting Pool to get Allen's approval on an outgoing cable. This was not Dulles's close-of-business séance. Rather, Allen began expounding on the value of different types of activity. Dulles referred to the agency's purpose of avoiding another Pearl Harbor, then to its suddenly being thrown into covert operations. Allen recognized the paramount importance of spy work, but he said, "We have to face the fact that because espionage is relatively cheap it will probably always seem inconsequential to some of our less informed friends on the Hill."

A "bag of pennies"—a few hundred thousand dollars was a pittance for lawmakers who dealt in millions and billions. Helms could see the point. Accounting showed that the spy Pyotr Popov, one of the CIA's most successful Russian recruitments, ran on less than four thousand dollars a year. "What I'm getting down to, Dick, is that no matter how important collection is, in the short and even the long run, it just doesn't *cost* very much." Expensive covert operations, successful or not, added more to the CIA budget, in his view a *good thing*.

Director Dulles did not mention that, back in the war, he had favored the derring-do of secret missions. He had, after all, run an op that achieved the surrender of thousands of enemy soldiers.

Now Richard Bissell reaped the reward that could have gone to Helms. Bissell took over as DO on the first day of 1959. Helms thought of resigning, asking for transfer to some frontline station, or soldiering on as COPS. He decided to stay. He would be quietly ranged against Bissell for the entire time the empire builder ran the clandestine service. Like the mythical headless horseman, Helms kept up a relentless devotion to *mission*, always, in the face of any obstacle.

Richard Bissell brought in Tracy Barnes, and relations cooled. The COPS presumed Deputy Director Bissell would sit him down and delineate spheres of responsibility, but that never happened. Helms simply picked up whatever crumbs fell from Bissell's table. He was the professional, with the agency far longer, before there *was* a CIA. He bridged all the history from the heroic days of World War II to the moment the sea changed and the inquisitors came. More than that, agency officers backed up Helms, lionized him, and later arrayed themselves in factions for him—and against his fancied enemy Bill Colby. Helms's views on the agency, its relationship to presidential power, congressional authority, and its legislative charter, won the day at the time—and baited a trap into which Langley has fallen. The CIA had barely let the contracts for construction at Langley when the ghosts began settling in.

THE MAKING OF A MASTER SPY

Nothing was written in stone. But to take Helms at his own word, his devotion to foreign intelligence and counterespionage gave him a perspective denied the covert ops aficionados. The really big opportunity to shine—and not as a ghost—came with the Bay of Pigs, which a responsible operations officer should have opposed. Helms did, again by his own account. But he said nothing. A foreign intelligence specialist could have pointed to the softness of the CIA's data. *Why* did it think only a sprinkling of Castro *milicianos* would fight? *What* made the wishful thinking of the Cuban exiles acceptable as hard intelligence. A counterespionage devotee could have underlined the very high probability that Castro's spies had infiltrated exile ranks.

Those observations needed to be in the agency's calculus.

Not that this was all on Helms. Dick Bissell was aware of resistance to the JM/Ate project within the agency, including Helms's, even though the COPS never expressed an opinion.

Bissell writes, "I am sure his reluctance was a result of the cool relationship that had developed between us after I was appointed." The deputy director goes on, "I regret today that I did not take Helms's views more seriously and that I did not encourage sufficient discussion among my colleagues to allow their concerns to be raised." Robert King, a special assistant to the DDO, reported that Helms seemed to treat everything to do with the anti-Castro plot with an eleven-foot pole. Bissell discussed the situation with Allen Dulles, who regretted not having moved Helms elsewhere when Bissell took over. The deputy director also spoke to Tracy Barnes, functioning as number two man, and to John Bross, who had been a Groton classmate and whom Bissell summoned from Germany to be a DO planner. In the run-up to the Bay of Pigs, the two Richards sat in offices only thirty-five feet apart, but Bissell never consulted Helms, while the latter reports that once Tracy entered the picture the cable traffic never again crossed his desk.

Bross, an OSSer, could have been the intermediary between the two camps. He had taken British commando training during the war, acted as

an enabler ahead of the Bay of Pigs and, after it, helped rally the rejectionists against Kirkpatrick's IG report. He ended up as one of Helms's closest
advisers. James E. Flannery, another Bissell aide, finally decided things
were so out of kilter that he began to brief Helms, on the QT, once a week.
But as the project moved into the Kennedy phase, when it began morphing
by the minute, Flannery decided he couldn't ensure that his briefs were
accurate, so he went to Mr. Bissell, confessed, and argued that Helms be
read in. Bissell refused, dressing down Flannery for a quarter of an hour,
all about not working with deputies. "The wonder is he didn't throw me
out of his office, but I felt I had to do this." Bissell then ordered his assistant to continue briefing Helms.

General attitude remains in question. Mr. Helms avers he opposed this
project, and says elsewhere that he disagreed with the covert ops in Guatemala and Iran, but he signed many, many proposals that came to him, for
projects ranging from a few thousand dollars to sustain a friendly politician somewhere to subsidies for Western journals in the culture wars. He
supported the Radios too, as well as the agency's book program, which
had recently brought Boris Pasternak's *Doctor Zhivago* to the West, after
Pasternak received the 1958 Nobel Prize for literature. Subsidies for the
National Student Association, which enabled the CIA to compete with the
Soviets on the international youth stage, were also good. The sense is that
the master spy drew the line where political action gave way to paramilitary effort. Be that as it may, Langley would carry out covert actions of
both kinds when Richard Helms himself was its director.

The Cuba paramilitary op, though the biggest the CIA had yet attempted,
did not fill its plate. Others under way simultaneously included a proxy
war in Tibet, just then being reorganized to rely on mule trains over the
Himalayas from Nepal in place of aerial deliveries. A second, increasingly ramified, secret army project had begun in Laos. A spy infiltration
effort from South Vietnam into North Vietnam had entered its preparation
stage. It would eventually turn into a commando program. In Africa, in
the Congo, the CIA had begun another secret war. In both the Congo and
the Dominican Republic, the agency's activities included plots to assassinate national leaders.

All these carried over from Eisenhower to Kennedy. Dick Bissell lost
them after the Cuban disaster. "In a parliamentary government," President Kennedy famously told Bissell, "I'd have to resign. But in this government I can't, so you and Allen have to go." He gave Bissell the punishment
task of heading an interagency study of paramilitary and limited warfare,

and, after a decent interval, let him go. On February 17, 1962, Richard McGarrah Helms rose to head the Directorate of Operations.

Allen Dulles, child of privilege, found his vocation as the result of a posting in the diplomatic service and the instructions of an ambassador. Richard Helms had been born to privilege too, but of the corporate and banking elite. His granddad an international banker, his father a corporate executive, Helms had been born in Saint David's, Pennsylvania, on Philadelphia's Main Line, and reared in South Orange, New Jersey, a gaslight bedroom village for New York businessmen. Herman Helms, his father, was a district manager for the Alcoa Corporation. Believing in foreign cultural education and languages for their children, Herman and wife Marion took the family to France the summer after Richard's junior year in high school. Herman cashed out his stock accounts for the purpose, fortuitously just months ahead of the Black Friday crash that triggered the Great Depression. The economic terrors of the 1930s barely touched young Dick. Instead, he attended boarding schools in Switzerland and Germany, Williams College (editor of the school newspaper, Phi Beta Kappa, second in the class), and tried to decide between Harvard Law or becoming a journalist. Journalism posed the bigger obstacles, but some string pulling produced an interview with the head of the United Press (UP) wire service, who offered a job if the young man could make his way across the pond. Helms did, and worked briefly for UP in London, but without a work visa he moved on to Germany, where the service's chief correspondent gave Helms an assignment.

The high point of his United Press career came during the 1936 Olympic Games, held at Nuremberg, where Helms interviewed Adolf Hitler, already darkening Germany with his Nazi cloak. Dick felt himself lucky to be in the press box when African American Jesse Owen took the gold medal in the 200-meter sprint. This black man's achievement, in a place the Nazis were touting Aryan superiority, tore the cover off a disturbing vein of German sentiment. The story of Nazism's spreading tentacles and the final descent into World War II clearly would be huge—William L. Shirer, among others, a Helms colleague in Berlin, made his name with it—but Helms had visions of media management and craved exposure to the business side. In 1937 he moved to Indianapolis to join the *Indianapolis Times*, rising from messenger to advertising boss.

His dream of running a newspaper and working with reporters was regretfully dashed, though Helms's papers are replete with correspondence from journalists of many stripes. Cyrus Sulzberger, of the *New York Times* Sulzbergers, became so close that later he was accused of being an agent. Helms and Sulzberger often lunched. He kept up other journalistic ties too. Records of Helms's staff meetings in charge of the agency are replete with high-level talk on what the media said about the CIA and who said it. Helms didn't so much look back at his journalistic ambitions as build on them. They may have had something to do with the way the agency later relied upon journalistic cover to shield many clandestine service officers. Helms would have denied that—but he specifically credits the *Indianapolis Times* with teaching him frugality, and he claims to have been frugal with taxpayer dollars at the agency.

So Richard followed a different path to spyhood than Allen Dulles. His family was lunching with an Indianapolis lawyer friend one Sunday in December 1941 when they learned Pearl Harbor had been bombed. Richard's friend happened to be the brother of the man for whom Hawaii's Hickam Field was named. Like so many others, Helms volunteered after the Japanese surprise attack. He resigned from his newspaper to join the U.S. Naval Reserve. Wanting a commission, Helms filed for officer candidate school only to spend months waiting for acceptance. The papers had been wildly misplaced. Ordered to the training course at Harvard College, right after getting a first look at his son Dennis, Ensign Helms worked at a New York command center, updating the shipping plot the Navy used to help merchant ships evade rampaging German U-boats. He had not been at this long when his old Berlin UPI bureau chief asked Dick out for a drink. Frederick Oechsner told Helms of the supersecret OSS, adverted that Wild Bill Donovan had asked the ex–bureau chief to create a propaganda unit called Morale Operations, and invited Helms to join.

"You're a natural," Oechsner said.

Helms turned him down. But a few months later, Ensign Helms got orders to OSS anyway. After a couple of weeks' training, superiors put Helms to work preparing contingency plans for secret operations. Apart from knowing nothing about planning secret wars, Dick sensed that no one would even read his plans, much less carry them out. Salvation took the form of assignment to a staff section managing intelligence collection in Germany. This put Allen Dulles on the radar for Helms, since Dulles, from Switzerland, produced the best intel anybody had.

Too good. The British objected that the source, Fritz Kolbe of the German Foreign Ministry, must be a plant. Assignment to the OSS German Section plunged Helms squarely into the fight over Kolbe's bona fides.

Helms and his chief felt the stream of high-level information Kolbe furnished was too valuable for a phony. Had the Germans simply been trying to gain trust they would not have given up so much—ultimately over 1,600 documents. The British, after checking the Kolbe material against their ULTRA intercepts, finally stopped fussing. Kolbe's product, compartmented as the "Boston" series, ultimately got such high grades that the CIA—a successor that had nothing to do with any of this—awarded the German spy a pension.

Richard Helms benefited from the accelerating momentum that came as Nazi Germany crumbled. In January 1945, he went to London to work with the German branch there—under Lieutenant William J. Casey, with whom he shared quarters. The new mission involved preparing for an OSS station to be opened when the Allies bashed their way into Germany. Leaders had already slated Allen for chief. Within weeks the OSS nexus moved to Paris. Helms went too, then with an advance party to Luxembourg, finally on to Germany, where he roomed with Dulles.

Espionage thoroughly enchanted the spook from South Orange. After the war, it would be Dulles who departed. Richard Helms stayed and paid his dues. He led Foreign Branch M, the unit spying in central and eastern Europe, with an office in the Q Building, later given up. It is a commentary on U.S. agencies of that era that the spooks deemed the move to the Reflecting Pool ruins a step up. Not much though. "The heat absorbed by the tin roof of my second floor office taught me the difference between perspiration and sweat," Helms wrote. The paper in files stuck and had to be peeled apart; carbons disintegrated. The buildings leaked when it rained, froze when it snowed, and got so bad in summer that, as the thermometer soared, staff were sent home.

When Dulles, Wisner, Barnes, and Bissell arrived at the agency, Dick Helms had the old-hand chair and they were the amateurs. Yet those early years were the time of the amateurs. In the OPC-infused operations directorate, Dick Helms became the consummate deputy. Dick provided the perfect anvil to Wisner's hammer when the boss wanted to smash some story in the press. Wisner wrote rejoinders, but Helms actually knew reporters. Later, even when Bissell ignored him, Helms kept up DO's serious espionage work while the boss dug his hole in Cuba. Bissell's confession of error in not involving Richard Helms speaks loudly. It was winter, February 1962, when Dick Helms finally ascended to DDO. At least he'd not be freezing by the Reflecting Pool. The spanking new Langley headquarters had central heat.

TEACHABLE MOMENTS

Offices of the deputy director for operations were located on the third floor at Langley. The suite was nice, the job fantastic. Helms had not quite moved in when CIA chief John A. McCone called him to the seventh floor—director's country. Lyman Kirkpatrick had just handed in his Bay of Pigs report. McCone was setting up to deep-six it. But he still needed a field marshal for Cuba, and it could not be anyone mixed up in that benighted failure. Director McCone told Helms the Kennedys were set on getting Fidel and that he, Richard Helms, would now be the DCI's man. Dick Helms, who had so carefully kept hands off, would be on Cuba up to his eyeballs. "In the preceding weeks," Helms relates, "I had seen enough of the new boss to realize it would have been a mistake to ask for further guidance." The headless horseman *acts*.

So began an education. The peremptory, persistent John A. McCone blew through Langley like a hurricane. Agency accounts of the building blithely record that, although dedicated on McCone's very first day, Langley wasn't really finished until the spring of 1963. The real story is that Alex McCone, corporate tycoon and industrialist, looked at his office and demanded that it be completely redone. A large portion of the executive suite would be converted to a private dining room. The offices of the director and deputy director were both enlarged. Workers paneled the whole place in wood and furnished it in the style of a gentleman's club. *That's* what took until 1963.

John McCone subtly signaled CIA personnel that he, not a spook but a manager with a good eye, could get along nicely with them. Helms got a lesson there. Frank Wisner, station chief in London, had reached the end of his tour—and tether. A few months into McCone's reign, Wisner came home. Rather than put Frank out to pasture, the DCI made him a special adviser, given little work but permitted to bask in comrades' esteem. When Wisner reached mandatory retirement, McCone let him go but hired him back as a consultant. McCone's burial of the Kirkpatrick report was a huge favor to many. But President Kennedy exacted penance regardless. For Allen Dulles, part of that penance was taking Director McCone on his first cruise, a weeks-long journey to introduce the new top spook to the CIA's field operators.

As with his executive suite, Alex McCone complained about his airplane. The Directorate for Support found orders to buy a new aircraft and furnish it plush private-plane style. Similarly, McCone demanded and got a larger, armored limousine. He used both a lot. A February 1963 cruise took

McCone to Europe. Later he inspected South Vietnam on Kennedy's behalf. McCone made a 1964 European trip to brief allies on CIA evidence for a Chinese nuclear weapon. There were ten cruises in all, half to Europe, three to Southeast Asia, two to Latin America. The director's California trips were grist for agency gossips. He courted and married a California woman, Theiline Pigott, while leading the agency. The "Honeymoon cables," in which McCone responded to Cuba data even while on vacation, went down in Langley lore as his long-distance effort to guide reporting—and were instrumental in alerting the CIA to what became the Cuban Missile Crisis. No one could take that away, although some top Kennedy people deplored McCone as a Cassandra. His advice to bomb the hell out of the Cubans and Russians—and later the North Vietnamese—proved unwelcome. In the spring of 1963, for policy purposes, McCone played a central role in manipulating a national intelligence estimate on Vietnam. The consequent policy failure helped lead to the Saigon coup against Ngo Dinh Diem, which McCone opposed. Wow! Another teachable moment.

Crucial passages in Kennedy's presidency—when vital information arrived on the Soviets, before a coup d'état in South Vietnam, and on the day of Kennedy's own assassination—all found John McCone in California. A lesson lay there too.

Helms appreciated how McCone's demands turned heads, his top-floor leadership impressing the rank and file. Alex was credible because he had something on the ball. In the wake of the Bay of Pigs, President Kennedy ordered the director of central intelligence to exert stronger leadership over the flocking entities of the U.S. intelligence community. McCone promptly formed a new staff to monitor cooperation, and another to choose collection targets. He created a budget-review committee and brought the OGC gunslingers and the agency's Capitol Hill lobbying unit into his own executive office.

A novel organization, the National Reconnaissance Office, had come into being in the last months of Eisenhower's era. McCone presided over its consolidation. Within the CIA, he grouped disparate offices throughout the agency into a new directorate, at first for "research," but eventually the Directorate for Science and Technology, which it remained. On McCone's watch, the processes for development of spy satellites were regularized. The fight over who would control their development and operation became one of the most heated in U.S. intelligence history, and John McCone had the technology chops to manage it. Richard Helms, who became a great admirer of the "machine spies," watched in fascination.

As DO chief and point man for Cuba, Helms couldn't help but see McCone's success in the missile crisis, and then the increasing resistance to his policy advice. Dick, who had always been about getting the intel, no doubt concluded that policy intrusions should be avoided.

When director in his own right, Richard Helms would famously say, "I work for only one president at a time."

This is something else he might have learned from John McCone—or, more properly, from Alex's downfall. The spy chief prized his time with presidents. McCone had twenty-seven private sessions with JFK. After each encounter, he would note out, and often have aides note too, the salient points, which he turned into action memoranda. Many McCone exchanges put Helms in the catbird seat. For example, McCone generated eight action items from his May 7, 1962, meeting with President Kennedy; five of them were for Helms. They ranged from a demand for prepara-tory materials ahead of a 5412 Group meeting and one for more concise Cuba briefings, to specifying personal qualifications for a new assistant for paramilitary and air support operations and a special project on which Kennedy wanted operational details. JFK sometimes used McCone as an emissary to former president Dwight D. Eisenhower, though he relied more often on Air Force general Andrew Goodpaster, who had been an intimate in Ike's own White House and glad for opportunities to renew the friendship.

In Lyndon Johnson's first month, Director McCone saw him a dozen times. The CIA chief often brought over the report known today as the President's Daily Brief, and kept that up a few days, but Johnson preferred to do his reading at night or on weekends. The daily situation reports stopped being notices of hot news. Langley eventually changed its routine and assembled the briefs in the afternoon. Once McCone showed up just to talk about Radio Free Europe; another time, about Johnson's demand that the CIA put its "first team" into Vietnam. But frustration grew. At a session on April 30, 1964, McCone voiced concern that LBJ was not get-ting adequate intelligence. That disturbed the CIA director.

Johnson replied that he was always available, all McCone had to do was call up. Alex shot back that he had tried that several times recently to no avail. The president rasped that he did not care to endure briefings "just for the purpose of being briefed."

The next day, McGeorge Bundy, LBJ's national security adviser, sent the president a note jesting that he had run into presidential friend and adviser Clark Clifford and that both men agreed the "ideal method" of keeping

Alex McCone "really happy" was to play golf—"McCone is an energetic and agreeable golfer, and . . . he can pay his own Burning Tree Greens fee."

Like Bill Casey after him, John McCone had pronounced views on American foreign policy and saw no reason he shouldn't express them. McCone voiced his opinion that the United States should smash North Vietnam before the end of 1962. In LBJ's first month, the president, always concerned that Vietnam might trigger a bigger war with China, put that very question to his CIA director. Director McCone minimized the danger. He also dined out too often on his prescience before the Cuban Missile Crisis. By the spring of 1965, President Johnson had had enough; he had staff check his daily appointments. LBJ had had eighty-nine meetings and fourteen phone calls with John McCone.

"I'm sick and tired of John McCone's tugging at my shirt tails," Lyndon Johnson groused to McCone's successor at their first one-on-one session. "If I want to see you, . . . I'll telephone you!"

The president reached into the military for McCone's substitute, choosing Admiral William F. Raborn. The admiral, renowned for shepherding development of the Polaris submarine-launched ballistic missile, brought a technocrat's sensibility to Langley. The CIA needed a professional deputy. That opened the door for Helms, who moved from the third floor to the seventh.

Raborn took charge on April 28, 1965, the very moment the United States began to intervene in the Dominican Republic on the basis of flimsy claims that Communists were the driving political force there. The Caribbean intervention marked the beginning of a turbulent year during which LBJ moved to war in Southeast Asia, approved a new generation of dangerous nuclear missiles, finally shut down the Cuban operation, and escalated CIA support for the U.S.-favored Congolese faction. Admiral Raborn muddled through. Langley wags said, "Dulles ran a happy ship. McCone ran a tight ship. Raborn runs a sinking ship."

Lyndon Johnson might have taken his cue right from CIA denizens. The admiral received virtually no White House invites. Instead the summons went to Dick Helms. President Johnson altered the routine for national security decisions. Rather than the dry meetings of the NSC or its subcommittees, Johnson took to having what he called Tuesday Lunches— not always Tuesday, and not always lunch, but definitely confabs of the nation's top officials over drinks or a meal. Soon after Helms reached the top floor, LBJ invited him to a lunch. Thereafter the deputy director, not the DCI, typically represented the spooks in the president's councils.

Helms had lessons from both McCone and Raborn to take to heart as he exercised power. Before long Helms himself took the top slot, for Admiral Raborn lasted just over a year. In June 1966, the fifty-three-year-old Helms became the director of central intelligence.

Thomas Powers, Helms's biographer, titled his fine study *The Man Who Kept the Secrets*. Helms did precisely that. Congressional leaders who dealt with Helms marveled at his ability to seem open while volunteering nothing. The agency's venture with assassination plots aimed at Castro furnishes a fine illustration. The CIA's official history of John McCone as spy chief records that, in the summer of 1963, a Chicago newspaper first reported the agency had approached hometown bad boy Sam Giancana for help on Cuba. McCone demanded explanations that Richard Helms gave him. The operations man not only forwarded a memo in which Shef Edwards updated Bobby Kennedy, but also Helms added his own thoughts. A year after that, when the Special Group—Lyndon Johnson renamed it the 303 Committee—girded its loins to discuss the matter, Helms sent McCone another memorandum, discounting talk of murder as "Miami cocktail party chatter." Meanwhile, both as operations supremo *and* as McCone's field marshal for Cuba, Richard Helms had to be aware of the ZR/Rifle project, in which William K. Harvey—whom the DDO knew well—set up a unit with standing capability for assassination, involving operatives who had been enmeshed in CIA plots in the Congo. Plus, there would be the extensive report on the Mafia-based murder plots, which the inspector general compiled in 1967. The IG found that Helms had been informed on a current basis.

When these matters came under investigation in 1975, Helms told the Rockefeller Commission, "I don't recall anything about any plans to assassinate Patrice Lumumba." He confessed to have heard something about plots against Dominican dictator Rafael Trujillo (because President Johnson had asked him to look into it). On Castro his recitation was classic:

> The business about the assassination of Castro, I have read about this in the papers. I have heard about it from associates. It has been kicked around whether this was a viable proposition or not. I have no doubt it was written into various plans as one of many options but I don't recall any successful effort that was made in this direction and since Castro is alive and apparently

well in Havana, the extent to which this was serious I have
never ascertained.

   Like a champion debater, Dick Helms registered his personal distaste for
the idea—referring to his rejection of assassination in an episode of early
spy history—then turned the tables. He pressed his questioners on what
they knew. What was the evidence? Did they *have* the information? Were
the poison pills *delivered* in Cuba? How did they know? *Whose* idea was
it? Who authorized it? Had any CIA director *ordered* it? Who could say
all this was anything more than conversation? Who had returned to report
that they'd *done* it?

   Helms admitted to hearing about the scheme for using exploding sea
shells to kill Castro and called that another "nutty idea." He compared it
to an episode in OSS history when the propagandists fantasized about getting a herd of cows, grazing in France, to eat packets stuffed with leaflets
and then excrete them after wandering across the border into Germany.

   Under questioning Helms maintained he could not be sure about anything. He had had occasion to refresh his memory. The August 1963 Chicago newspaper story "could" have been the occasion (Helms correctly
identified its author) when he wrote about assassinations. "I am relatively
certain I must have seen it the day I sent it to the director," he said about
one of these items. Dick remembered conversations with Bill Harvey about
taking over the Mafia project, then, typically, objected, "I don't recall any
specific plan or proposal that was approved to assassinate Castro."

   The sharpster to whom assassination is distasteful clamps down at the
first word of it and, when the president asks about Murder Incorporated,
issues a prohibition and tells the boss. The headless horseman orders a pro
forma review and has the records destroyed.

   Mr. Helms later told the Church Committee that he opposed assassination and saw no wisdom in it, plus many practical disadvantages. Then,
referring to mafioso Johnny Roselli, Helms averred, "There is something
about the whole chain of episode [*sic*] in connection with this Roselli business that I am simply not able to bring back in a coherent fashion." Spooks'
amnesia did not begin with Iran-Contra.

   When Helms took over, there were fears that the operations directorate
would run the table. Analysts working for the Directorate of Intelligence
were especially concerned. But Dick had learned those lessons well. The
DCI marshaled *all* the spooks. Though not an analyst, Helms appreciated

good reporting. He often cited a Middle East special national intelligence estimate produced just before the Six-Day War as the finest piece of CIA analysis in his experience—a precise prediction of Israeli victory that proved exactly correct. Though not a technologist, Helms developed an appreciation for the engineering and development obstacles in the way of new machine spies. Under his leadership, the agency—and U.S. intelligence writ large—introduced a generation of new satellites with a steep shift in capability.

As for the DO, Helms did not ignore it either. But there were headaches. In 1965 revelations showed the agency had botched a project in Singapore during Ike's last year. A pair of officers made improper electrical connections for a portable polygraph and caused a major power failure. They were arrested. The CIA had offered bribes for their freedom. Editors at the *New York Times*, stunned at this news, began their own, wide-ranging investigation of the agency. The *Times* published its results beginning in April 1966.

Newly minted Director Helms rushed to respond, organizing an ad hoc working group to counter the stories. He sent cables to stations worldwide, instructing agency personnel how to respond to the charges, soliciting detail on specifics affecting individual countries. Cord Meyer, heading the covert action staff, actually accosted *Times* Washington bureau chief Tom Wicker at a cocktail party, poking his chest, shouting that Moscow must be pleased with him. That accusation would be reprised on other occasions by CIA black propagandists attempting to frighten American dissenters to the Vietnam War.

THE *RAMPARTS* WE WATCH

Helms didn't spend much time cruising. The center of gravity remained at Langley and that's where Dick Helms hung his hat. Time bombs were ticking for long-standing CIA operations and methods. One of the worst started with Texas congressman Wright Patman, who inveighed against tax loopholes and chaired the House Banking Committee. He held hearings in 1964 that disclosed certain ambiguous, possibly government, connections among select private foundations. Patman inadvertently revealed links between them and the agency. Spooks descended upon him and convinced Patman to disavow the remarks, but blood was in the water. Journalists began linking government money to foundations, verifying the hint.

Meanwhile, in February 1966, the magazine *Ramparts* published an article by former Green Beret Donald Duncan on Special Forces in the Vietnam War, where a number of their initiatives had involved the CIA. Four months later came another article in the same magazine that revealed the Vietnam role of advisers from Michigan State University. Langley had contracted Michigan State to help the Saigon government and also used it to furnish cover for CIA operatives.

Langley could find no identifiable foreign communist ties of *Ramparts* employees, although two of its staff were members of the Communist Party of the United States of America. The CIA went to the FBI to recommend that *Ramparts* be investigated as a subversive threat. Langley informed the White House of its failure.

Then Jim Angleton, Helms's counterespionage maven, set up a unit just to look into *Ramparts*. Under Richard Ober, an officer just returned from the course at the National War College, the unit had a dozen officers creating files on *Ramparts* reporters and editors. Later the agency assembled an action program focused on the magazine and carried out under another officer, Edgar J. Applewhite. This amounted to a prohibited domestic operation, further compounded in February 1967, when the CIA approached the Internal Revenue Service about auditing the journalists and the magazine's funders. Thomas Terry, special assistant to the IRS commissioner, was given CIA inside information on *Ramparts* staff and backers. Next Langley wanted to obtain copies of IRS tax returns. But the CIA action plan, completed in April, came too late—by then the chestnuts were on fire.

Richard Helms, in Albuquerque, New Mexico, with a couple of agency weapons experts, had gone to meet Atomic Energy Commission officials and visit the Los Alamos nuclear lab and the Nevada Test Site, where weapons were perfected. It was Monday, February 13, 1967. The director sought to familiarize his analysts with U.S. nuclear weapons developments, to educate them for projecting Soviet capability. After a long day of tromping around, the group had just reached their hotel when aides handed Helms a flash cable ordering him to telephone the White House and return to Washington.

It took time to get through, then hours for a callback. That became "one of my darkest days." There were no airline flights. Staff prevailed on the DO air branch to get an agency proprietary aircraft to carry him. In the hour that consumed, the director ate a sandwich and racked his brain for what he might have done to rouse Lyndon Johnson. Helms's fears grew with every minute.

His callback, in fact, did not come until Helms had reached Langley.

But Director Helms had done nothing wrong. Rather, President Johnson wanted his spy chief in place when controversy broke. This was about *Ramparts*—and a bolt of lightning descending upon the CIA. For years—decades—the agency had secretly funded the National Student Association. The students themselves had approached Harry Truman's Psychological Strategy Board toward the end of 1951 and the board had passed them along to CIA. Under Cord Meyer's covert action staff, student support had been part of the raft that included the Congress for Cultural Freedom and RFE, and was about contesting the Soviets in the cultural Cold War. CIA used identical channels to fund all these entities.

Langley's secret relationship with the National Student Association (NSA) enabled the agency to dictate much of the message Americans took to international youth gatherings. A few student association officials had always been witting of the CIA relationship—membership dues of $18,000 obviously could not cover annual spending of $80,000 ($570,000 in 2016)—but most members had no idea. In the mid-1960s, some of the witting NSA officials, restive at the CIA relationship, told others. They were scandalized. One, Michael Wood, NSA's director of development, tried to replace the CIA with some other funding source but struck out, even after going to a sympathetic Vice President Hubert H. Humphrey. Superiors fired him.

Wood began talking to editors of the San Francisco–based magazine. He had some documents and suspicions but not much more. *Ramparts* editors took the suspicions to Michael Ansara, a Harvard student who did occasional research jobs in Boston for the magazine. They gave him the names of a couple of foundations and asked him to look into them. Ansara started with the Wright Patman disclosures. The trail led to public IRS returns for foundations, and the researcher saw additional data that showed them getting plenty of extra money, from which they funded the NSA—*and* the Radios *and* CIA labor operations through the American Institute for Free Labor Development. Some of the channels were the same ones Congressman Patman had alluded to. Reporters and editors from *Ramparts*, stringers in Boston, New York, and Washington, and analysts for the Institute for Policy Studies all worked on the story, which appeared in the March 1967 issue under Sol Stern's byline.

Langley wasn't caught flatfooted. One day in the summer of 1966, coincidentally, Cord Meyer had brought Michael Josselson by the director's office. Josselson had been OPC's operative for the Congress for Cultural Freedom since the project's inception, but Helms had never met him. Had he waited a year, Helms reflected later, it would have been awkward because of *Ramparts*. In thinking about his memoirs, Helms termed the affair unexpected, but in writing them he noted, "the pending exposé did not come as a total surprise."

Branch 5 of Meyer's division handled the student association and swiftly learned of approaching danger. When Michael Wood left the NSA, Robert Kiley of Branch 5 heard there had been a leak. Later, when Harvard student Ansara researched the foundations, a lawyer he consulted, a former CIA person, phoned a friend at the agency. In January 1967 there were rumors from New York publishing circles that archenemy *Ramparts* had scheduled an article on the CIA and the National Student Association. Around that time the agency also learned of the denunciation, as a CIA agent, of an international student official by a Vienna-based organization suspected as a Soviet provocateur. Meyer actually sent his deputy Walpole "Tad" Davis to London to warn the Brits.

But this foreknowledge did not lead to warning the White House. That was on Helms. Douglass Cater, a speechwriter and one of Lyndon Johnson's political operatives, had been a founding member of the student association and kept an eye on it. His phone rang one day and it was the organization's current president, W. Eugene Groves. Cater presumed the NSA wanted a back channel to the president to protest about Vietnam. Instead, Groves told him that the following week *Ramparts* would be running an advertisement blowing the lid off the CIA-NSA relationship.

Cater informed President Johnson as soon as Groves left.

LBJ called Cater on the direct line. "Well, aren't you the lucky one," he drawled. "You let that fellow come into your office and lay a big, fat turd right in your lap."

The president turned to undersecretary of state Nicholas deBelleville Katzenbach, temporarily in charge over at Foggy Bottom. Katzenbach began wrestling with the issue even before Helms got back from Albuquerque. Katzenbach thought the State Department should make a statement at its regular noontime briefing, one attributed to the CIA, simply admitting the NSA subsidy. On February 14, *Ramparts* editors, with Sol Stern's article hung up in the production cycle but opinion already going viral, took out full-page advertisements in both the *New York Times* and *Washington Post* detailing the gist of their charges.

By then President Johnson, grilling Helms, wanted chapter and verse on Langley's decisions regarding the National Student Association. A frantic search of records showed that the Special Group had had seven discussions about the students since 1959. The early meetings featured Allen Dulles and Richard Bissell. Most had simply been reminders that the project was out there. But the students, by CIA's own account, had routed Soviet youth initiatives at the international meetings in Vienna (1959) and Helsinki (1962).

President Johnson's own initial denials, in addition, were refuted by the 303 Committee record of December 12, 1963, where John McCone told the group that he had reviewed *all* covert programs, twice, with "higher authority." Cord Meyer then briefed on the students. Helms had attended too. A year later, December 3, 1964, McCone had led the discussion when 303 approved a specific CIA plan to use the students at an upcoming world youth conference at Algiers. Helms misleads in his memoirs where he writes, "It would have been difficult to imagine a more cockeyed and convoluted picture of the Agency's relationship with the NSA than that published by *Ramparts*." To the contrary, the CIA's vigorous efforts to discredit magazine staff and create problems for the company were driven by how close *Ramparts* had gotten to the truth. If the journalists had been far from the mark, the spooks would simply have laughed them off the stage—Langley's usual method.

Director Helms saw the revelations as a chain of exploding firecrackers. The magazine's ads in the big newspapers set the ball rolling. *Ramparts* exposed the student links and the funding conduits. Other media jumped in to report more. The *Times* speculated on links to funds flowing to labor unions, publications, and broadcasters—all true, and traceable by following the money through the foundations. The CIA's director considered that what happened with the *Ramparts* affair dwarfed the agency's operational difficulties in the Vietnam War.

President Johnson ordered a halt to all projects aimed at students and a policy review on everything else. LBJ put Nick Katzenbach in charge of the inquiry, and made Richard Helms a member of the panel. The other principal, John Gardner, ran Johnson's social programs, but back in OSS days he and Helms had shared an office, and together they went to war. Now Gardner argued for abolishing the covert projects. Helms, ready to let the students go, fought to preserve the Radios and the Congress for Cultural Freedom. The latter did not survive, but the Radios did.

The Katzenbach committee agreed with one of Helms's proposals—that the CIA funding could be replaced by a public-private mechanism with all government aid given overtly. Secret funding, direct or indirect, by the CIA and other federal agencies should stop. By 1972 the United States had moved the Radios entirely to public funding, severing their CIA links.

When Helms moved up to the seventh floor, Desmond FitzGerald got the operations directorate. FitzGerald's background had been in Asia, and he had become a good wartime DDO. But the *Ramparts* thing was different. Here the "enemy" were American citizens. Both men were stunned by these events that cracked CIA's facade of secrecy. FitzGerald did not survive. That summer, a few months after the crisis, he collapsed playing tennis and perished from a heart attack. The director selected Thomas Karamessines, a Europeanist, to head the DO. Within weeks Helms found himself pushed into operations that irretrievably crossed the line of legality. Tom Karamessines traversed it with him.

FORDING THE RUBICON

Surviving this near-death experience, Langley struck back. Having crossed a Rubicon into illegal domestic activity, the headless horseman presided as the spooks retaliated. The agency recruited a source to report on inner workings at *Ramparts*. Discovering that journalists were about to interview a CIA asset, Langley primed him with material to feed the reporters.

There were efforts to defund *Ramparts*, by encouraging donors to drop it, attempts to mess with the subscriber base, and derogatory smears in articles planted in *Human Events* and the *Washington Star*. Richard Ober's unit continued its drive to discredit the *Ramparts* group.

Langley marched steadily further into the heart of darkness. In February 1967, just as the student association scandal began breaking, frightened by the increasingly hostile reception recruiters encountered on college campuses, the CIA surveyed potential challenges. At that time, Howard Osborn's Office of Security began Project Merrimac to secure agency facilities.

Merrimac furnished discreet assistance to local police, then began a broader effort to track four specific groups of civil rights and antiwar activists. *Every* move was illegal and each one more intrusive than the last. That September, DO chief Karamessines authorized Merrimac agents to infiltrate the National Mobilization Committee to End the War in Vietnam, which had planned a massive protest at the Pentagon for a month later.

In December the CIA added Project Resistance. That purported to study dissidence on the campuses. Within months Langley had so much data, it started a Targets Analysis Branch.

Targets? In World War II, "target analysis" is what planners did to decide which enemy city or factory should be devastated next. Now, this CIA branch opened files on between six hundred and seven hundred Americans, and put twelve thousand to sixteen thousand more on watch lists.

Although Resistance was not supposed to be infiltrating political groups, so many informants and local police agencies offered their services that the CIA entered that arena too. Spooks looked for financial information, photographed members, meeting places, and protests, collected license plate numbers, and attended meetings of activists. At least twice—in May 1968 and November 1969—Resistance was *ordered* to surveille particular individuals and groups. In October 1970, the project reported that the Weatherman faction of the Students for a Democratic Society was considering CIA headquarters as a target for its "fall offensive."

By January 1971, the stream of wannabe informants had broadened so much that security chief Osborn prohibited new agent recruiting. CIA also infiltrated its own operatives into antiwar groups. Long afterward, in 1993, Helms recounted to a Smithsonian Association audience that infiltration took place only a couple of times, and only for the purpose of creating suitable cover stories for agents Langley wanted to infiltrate in Europe. In fact the activity had been much broader. One of Helms's "couple" had to be the penetration agent sent to monitor Phil Agee. But just a single DO project utilized twenty-four agent sources, eleven of them in the way Helms recounted. The notorious Chaos project had forty agents referred to it, and used more than a dozen of them. The headless horseman of mythology tries the same thing over and over, never drawing the conclusions when schemes don't work.

Starting with the 1967 march on the Pentagon, hardly a major protest took place without some level of CIA countermeasures. At the Pentagon in October, Langley helped staff a command center. At the Chicago Democratic Party Convention in August 1968, the agency provided sophisticated communications gear and specialists to run it. Agency officers kept watch on African Americans preparing for Resurrection City, a 1968 Washington poverty encampment.

There was CIA counter-participation in the fall 1969 marches on Washington, the Cambodia protests of May 1970, and the May Day protests of 1971. When the Republican Party had its political convention in Miami in 1972, the CIA lent a safe house to other security services and provided false identities for disguises. All those things were on Richard Helms's watch. All were illegal domestic activities.

Bedeviled by Vietnam and the growing dilemmas of war there, Lyndon Johnson wanted greater effort. The president issued no order or directive. Richard Helms *interpreted* LBJ's constant demands for proof that the enemy secretly controlled antiwar activity. *Helms* took LBJ's concern and turned it into a CIA project. In August 1967, this led to MH/Chaos, the baby of Helms intimate and agency counterintelligence chief James Angleton. Director Helms, DDO Karamessines, and Angleton blocked out arrangements for a branch of the counterintelligence staff just to spy on Americans, tracking the antiwar movement, called the Special Operations Group. Its activity received a priority equal to espionage against the Soviets and Chinese. Helms brought over Richard Ober from the counter-*Ramparts* project to head the Chaos staff. It began with the *Ramparts* files. Quite a lot of fieldwork took place. Indeed, Chaos's downfall began with an inspector general survey of DO's European Division that showed Chaos consuming a substantial portion of the entire division's effort, which, based on faulty premises, generated no useful intelligence.

In the meantime, Chaos grew. Like some other CIA domestic activities, the dimensions of public distress and the size of burgeoning political movements constantly outran Langley's capacity. Chaos compiled over 13,000 files, including 7,200 on American citizens; listed names of 300,000 Americans, tracked both individuals and organizations, prepared 3,500 internal memoranda plus almost as many for broader circulation, and 37 for top officials. Ober always wanted more personnel. Jim Angleton never permitted it. He wanted to prevent the Ober unit from taking over. Chaos staff peaked at fifty-two, some 40 percent of Angleton's whole operation. On the other hand, Angleton defended the Special Operations Group against reductions. When Richard Nixon succeeded LBJ, he demanded CIA budget and personnel cuts. The Ober unit would be spared in the first round when Karamessines, backed by Helms, stood up for Angleton. But a year later, it was Tom himself asking to reduce Ober's unit. Helms overruled him. Only after the headless horseman left Langley did his successor reorient Chaos. In fact, Ober's domestic spooks became the ancestors of the fabled Counterterrorist Center.

President Johnson wanted to know if the Russians, Chinese, or North Vietnamese were subverting the antiwar movement. There, too, Helms involved the CIA, this time the analysts, who compiled two major reports.

The Ober staff coordinated information for the first, in October 1967, "International Connections of the U.S. Peace Movement," on which Paul Corscadden of the Office of Current Intelligence (OCI) was the lead author. The second paper, "Restless Youth" in September 1968, carried a cover sheet that openly declared that the content of the paper exceeded authorities conveyed by the CIA's charter.

After LBJ left, Richard Nixon continued demanding high-level reports on the movement. "Restless Youth" would be updated for him. Nixon also wanted more action against Americans, leading in 1970 to the "Huston Plan," named for White House staffer Tom Charles Huston, who did most of the legwork on an initiative to engineer a board of directors from the intelligence agencies to spearhead aggressive attacks on American dissenters. Helms had no objection. Opposition from FBI director J. Edgar Hoover scuttled Huston's Plan. The headless horseman does the same things over and again.

The public's anguish over Vietnam washed through Langley too. At a Helms staff meeting in September 1970, many months before Daniel Ellsberg's leak of the Pentagon Papers, agency baron John Bross asked that Ellsberg's security clearances be lifted. The leak actually appeared in June 1971. By then other irons were in the fire, and staff meetings deliberated on the memoir of notorious spook Edward Lansdale, the manuscript for which had gone to Harper & Row. CIA officials tried to get the publisher to let them read it in advance.

A little earlier, in January–February, columnist Jack Anderson had published a pair of stories linking the CIA to Castro assassination plots. More followed, leading to columns that December on Nixon's tilt toward Pakistan in the Indo-Pakistani war during East Pakistan's war of secession. In March 1972, Helms approved a memo, "Allegations of Assassinations," which he sent to prepare subordinates to deny the charges. Then Helms approved Project Mudhen, full-scale surveillance of Anderson's home, office, and associates. Twenty agency officers were on the chase teams. The columnist, tipped off, turned the tables; his children photographed the CIA security squads. On March 17, Helms actually had lunch with Anderson, wired for sound. All illegal. Project Mudhen collapsed of its own weight a few weeks later.

In February 1972, the *Washington Post* reported on a new spy satellite that would be all digital, so sophisticated that it could transmit pictures directly to earth. Langley promptly put the journalist who had worked the story, Michael Getler, under surveillance. The spooks went right down to renting space in a building directly across from Getler's office so he could be watched. Illegal.

Journalists discussed at the CIA director's staff meetings included Joseph Alsop, Roland Evans and Robert Novak, Stanley Karnow, John Crewdson, Sanford Ungar, Tad Szulc, David Kraslow, David Burnham, Thomas B. Ross, Seymour Hersh, and others. Deliberations over cooperating with reporters, versus investigating leaks to them, were not illegal, but the prevalence of the subject reminds us just how sensitive the agency remained.

FATEFUL DECISIONS

All this was in addition to the standard skullduggery at which Langley reveled. Many, many projects were under way in South Vietnam, where the CIA held primary responsibility for pacification, and in Laos, where it ran a secret army of Hmong tribesmen. Pacification remained sensitive because the CIA had originated the plans for an effort to target the guerrilla infrastructure known as the Phoenix Program. That became linked with assassination. Sensitivities about Laos focused on the fact the United States claimed it honored the neutrality of Laos while conducting military and paramilitary operations there.

One bit of chicanery in Latin America occurred in Chile, where Nixon insisted that Helms prevent the accession to power of Chilean socialist Salvador Allende. Allies—among them John McCone, now on the board of the International Telephone and Telegraph Corporation—teamed up with Langley to finance Allende's opponents in the Chilean election. When that didn't work, Nixon ordered a "Track II" that aimed physically at Allende, and took the agency back toward assassination plotting. Dick Helms famously observed that if he ever carried a field marshal's baton out of the Oval Office, that moment came with Nixon's Track II. The degree to which the CIA and the United States manipulated the Chilean economy against Allende would be sensitive. Langley had taken to the dark side with its domestic operations while also vulnerable abroad.

Toward the end of 1968, LBJ had taken Helms aside after a White House meeting, telling him Mr. Nixon had made inquiries about him. This surprised Helms and pleased him, because he understood Nixon did not like the Central Intelligence Agency. To keep an insider at its head, rather than bring in someone else, seemed like turning over a new leaf. But the original thought *was* the accurate one. In his first year Nixon demanded outlays be slashed ten percent. Overseas postings were to be reduced. On numerous occasions, speaking with national security adviser Henry Kissinger, with others, on the telephone or in the Oval Office, Nixon evinced disdain for the agency and expressed himself as having done favors for the spooks, at the Bay of Pigs and elsewhere. In 1971 Nixon and political aide John Ehrlichman considered that CIA had done them bad when Helms refused to produce documents on Cuba and the Diem coup that the president hoped would blacken his opponents' reputations. After that, Helms's days were numbered.

Nixon prevailed upon the head of his Office of Management and Budget, James R. Schlesinger, to shake down the spooks with a study he used to justify additional budget cuts. Some of the pressures to cut MH/Chaos flowed directly from this report and its consequences. In 1972 Nixon felt he had done Langley another favor, backing its effort to muzzle whistleblower Victor Marchetti. Oval Office conversations surreptitiously recorded Nixon telling associates he had protected Dick Helms from a host of things. Helms in his memoir quotes a September 1972 H.R. Haldeman note that has the president saying, "Helms has got to go. Get rid of the clowns—cut personnel 40 percent." Nixon felt the spy chief had let him down.

Mr. Nixon won the election. There were no celebrations for his minions. At the very next cabinet meeting, he asked everyone to resign. Helms considered himself different, that presidents handled CIA directors personally. So he did nothing. But on November 20, Nixon acolytes summoned Helms to Camp David for what he thought would be a budget review. Instead Nixon spoke of personnel changes and new blood. Director Helms noted that in March 1973, he would reach the CIA's mandatory retirement age anyway. Mr. Nixon skirted that and mentioned an ambassadorship. Without thinking, Helms said Iran. So it came to be.

As a newly nominated ambassador, Richard Helms had to pass muster with the Senate Foreign Relations Committee, charged with advising the full Senate on consent to any nomination. In early February 1973, he testified at a public hearing. There Helms fielded questions on Langley's relationships with corporations active in Chile—the previous year columnist Jack Anderson had charged that companies including ITT (John McCone again) had colluded with the agency to oppose Allende's candidacy. But senators framed their questions around espionage, not political action. Helms comfortably denied everything.

A couple of days later, on February 7, the former CIA director returned for questioning under oath at a closed session. Here the gloves came off.

Stuart Symington, a Missouri Democrat and longtime member of the intelligence subcommittee, posed the key questions. Lyndon Johnson, a sharp observer, once said he'd never met anyone who could turn on a dime faster than Symington. Helms had considered Symington a friend of the agency, if not him personally. Thomas Powers, Helms's biographer, casts them as friends too. Helms himself makes Symington a friend of John McCone's, and adds that the Missourian stopped talking to John when McCone asked why Stuart had put Helms on the spot the way he did.

The spook adds that Symington had been to Laos, twice, fully briefed on CIA activities. Perhaps Mr. Helms forgot what that meant: the CIA snowed Symington on a major paramilitary operation. In 1969, when the cover for the Laotian project wore thin, Symington led a Senate investigation of American military bases that zeroed in on the CIA in Laos. Langley dissembled and contrived to get Air Force and State Department officials to lie in parallel. The agency then claimed the right to censor the proceedings and gutted them in declassification.

No doubt Jack Anderson's Chile charges in 1972 rankled Symington, who considered the Helms nomination an opportunity to pin down the CIA on a covert operation, on the record.

Even in the autumn of his years, even with this episode in the public domain, Richard Helms could not bring himself to that straightforwardness. Helms repeatedly attributed his problem to Senate squabbles between Symington and John C. Stennis of Mississippi. Those, Helms related, led Symington to create the investigating committee that looked into Laos, implying it had all been about getting attention. Helms never linked *the agency's* behavior toward Symington on Laos with what happened on Chile. Referring to the latter, Helms wrote in his memoir, "Because Senator Symington knew the answers to the questions, I could not understand why he posed them. And in the decades that followed, I've yet to determine why he wanted my answers on the record."

Sometimes, headless horsemen don't learn. Sigmund Freud, in his theory of the uncanny, wrote of the unconscious mind having a compulsion to repeat.

So there it is. Stuart Symington asked, "Did you try in the Central Intelligence Agency to overthrow the government of Chile?"

Richard Helms, under oath, replied, "No, sir."

Senator Symington pursued. "Did you have money passed to the opponents of Allende?"

"No, sir."

"So the stories you were involved in that war are wrong?"

"Yes, sir," Helms reiterated. "I said to Senator Fulbright many months ago that if the agency had really gotten in behind the other candidates and spent a lot of money and so forth the election might have come out differently."

Total lie. Depending on when you start clocking the funds, the CIA secretly poured between $1.0 million and $1.2 million ($6.1–$7.4 million in 2016) into defeating the Chilean politician, with an extra $350,000 coming from ITT. Langley gunslinger Larry Houston looked at Helms's testimony and warned him this exchange posed problems. Helms declined to change it. To make an analogy to the recent past, in 2013 Director of National Intelligence James Clapper, asked under oath whether U.S. intelligence programs eavesdropped on hundreds of millions of Americans, made the same denial as Helms. His gunslinger, Robert S. Litt, also pointed to the danger. Clapper also rejected correction. Both men suffered consequences.

Langley saw the storm gathering. Director Helms had hardly driven out the gate when the president appointed Jim Schlesinger his successor. Schlesinger's background as an economist—even though he had spent most of the previous two decades as a defense intellectual—suited Nixon's idea of cutting the agency. The new boss spoke of clearing halls too crowded for him to walk. With the Paris cease-fire, the intensity of America's Vietnam War diminished rapidly. Schlesinger let go about a thousand people, mostly contract officers in paramilitary slots in Laos or South Vietnam. But soon Schlesinger left too. Mr. Nixon moved him over to the Pentagon as secretary of defense.

Langley learned of its peril before Schlesinger moved on—and the director took a step that made it worse. On the House of Representatives side of Capitol Hill, there was a new broom in charge of the secret subcommittee that monitored intelligence. Congressman Lucien Nedzi of Michigan, concerned to do a good job, had set up a "cruise" of his own. Nedzi planned to visit Finland, Russia, Bulgaria, and Greece. He asked for a CIA briefing. Legislative liaison John Maury plus Soviet Bloc division chief David Blee turned up to see him on January 18, 1973. During their conversation, Nedzi mentioned that journalist Seymour Hersh had spoken to him, already several months earlier, about CIA domestic operations. Hersh, who then worked for the *New York Times*, alleged the activities were extensive, and he had several examples. On January 23, Langley discovered that

Hersh had established that some government departments automatically supplied the CIA with data on officials' travel plans. Then Langley learned the *Times* had assigned Hersh to cover Watergate. That seemed good but actually boded ill for the agency. Watergate might keep Hersh off the CIA beat, but Watergate had its own agency angle, and investigating it might simply lead the reporter to more spook stories.

These were Dick Helms's final days. Schlesinger took over on February 2. At the January 18 staff meeting, Maury had volunteered to write a memo for circulation within the agency that discussed CIA domestic activity. Helms ordered staff to assemble a high-ranking team and brief Nedzi on actions inside the United States. The next day, Congressman Nedzi asked that his House Armed Services subcommittee get the full presentation.

Jim Schlesinger took charge. A few days later, Mr. Helms offered his fateful denials to the Senate. At the CIA's staff meeting on February 8, Maury reminded the group of pending business—the Nedzi domestic activities briefing. Ed Proctor, deputy director for intelligence, suggested an in-house review. This was the first mention of what became known as the Family Jewels. A week later, when Maury met with Nedzi, the staff meeting reprised the conversation, with Proctor repeating his recommendation. Schlesinger seemed reluctant at first, but his mission to scale back the CIA, known on Capitol Hill, resulted in repeated calls for his testimony, and at those appearances Schlesinger constantly faced questions on agency domestic activities he'd never heard of.

Late that April, the Justice Department revealed that the Cuban exiles who had worked for the CIA and then for Nixon's White House Plumbers unit and his political operation—they were the ones caught installing electronic eavesdropping devices at Democratic Party headquarters at the Watergate—had also burgled the office of the psychiatrist who treated Daniel Ellsberg. The admission blindsided Schlesinger. A few days later, he would be stunned again, by news that Plumbers chief and former CIA operative E. Howard Hunt had gotten agency assistance preparing for the Ellsberg burglary. Schlesinger summoned Cord Meyer, at that moment acting chief of the DO while the boss cruised, only to hear Meyer confirm the disastrous news. The DO's chief, William E. Colby, had been point man for Watergate, and now the carefully separated strains were intertwining. Colby, in Bangkok when he heard, rushed home. Director Schlesinger ordered him to craft a directive prohibiting domestic operations, telling officers who knew anything to come right to his office, and instructing

CIA barons and chiefs to compile reports describing past activities of their units that had flap potential. Schlesinger issued that directive on May 9. Bill Colby took the lead assembling the unit reports into a compendium— the Family Jewels. Then Schlesinger left. William E. Colby became the CIA's director in July 1973.

While the agency pursued internal inquiries, on the outside the investigative reporters plied their trade. Sy Hersh followed not only Watergate and the domestic spying story; at least two other scoops sat on his plate. One concerned naval spying. For years American submarines had secretly been trailing Soviet ones, picking them up outside their bases and sticking with them, sometimes for thousands of miles, in a highly classified operation code named Holystone. Hersh, on to that, wrote about it in the spring of 1974, only to uncover an even bigger CIA secret behind it—Project Azorian, nothing less than an attempt to raise a sunken Soviet submarine from the bottom of the Pacific Ocean. The agency had constructed a huge oceangoing recovery crane called the *Glomar Explorer*, ostensibly intended to vacuum mineral deposits lying on the ocean floor. A recovery attempt in July 1974 salvaged bits of the Russian sub.

Washington wanted to try again but had to wait a year for suitable weather. Director Colby, aware that Sy Hersh had part of the story, met with the reporter and gave him more, on condition that Hersh hold back revealing it until the agency had tried again.

By then Hersh had more on the CIA in Chile too. Project FU/Belt had involved forcing the Chilean economy to grind to a halt, manipulated by U.S. dominance of international markets, while Allende's political opponents were sustained by agency money. The Track II operation, even worse, involved a coup plot, botched, ending in the death of a top Chilean general. By the fall of 1973, the situation had worsened to the point that a real coup toppled Allende, who died by suicide in the presidential palace. Hersh had parts of that story and continued developing it. In Congress, Massachusetts representative Michael D. Harrington pushed for information in a way that told Hersh more. In September–October 1974, Hersh unleashed a series of articles in the *New York Times* that had President Ford and other officials scrambling to figure out how to get ahead of the news. At the White House, Henry Kissinger's aides drafted a false statement the CIA could issue, denying it had had anything to do with Chile. Langley couldn't bring itself to be that deceitful.

While the Chile story neared the surface, what Helms had said under oath about the CIA operation sparked controversy. The Central Intelligence Agency, pulled in different directions during this period, had its first big clash start right here. Helms stalwarts always represent these events as Bill Colby—somehow an enemy, jealous, stopping at nothing—persecuting his predecessor. This same Bill Colby had worked amicably with Richard Helms for *two decades* while the latter ran ops for the DO, led the directorate, then the agency; Colby rose through the ranks of station chief, then division chief. The two were competitors, but more like Tracy Barnes and John Bross, not Dick Bissell versus Lyman Kirkpatrick. The truth reflects the essence of the Watergate era—events forced Colby's hand.

In this case a middle-ranking officer used the word *perjury* to describe the Helms testimony. Another fellow, reviewing Latin American activities for the IG, saw that and raised doubts. General counsel John S. Warner rejected the charge. The inspector general, William V. Broe—himself a creature of the DO—viewed the matter as too important to drop. He bucked it up to the top floor. Director Colby went back to Warner, who set up a panel—like an accountability board—to review the charges. They split, unable to decide whether Helms had perjured himself, recommending that the choice be left to the Justice Department. *Even then*, Colby held the line against referring the Helms affair to DOJ. But the counsel's panel rebelled. Director Colby made one last try at suppression. He met with the acting attorney general to clarify CIA options under the 1954 agreement. The Justice official, Laurence Silberman, saw the political ramifications and insisted on the referral. Colby ran out of options.

So did the Central Intelligence Agency. The Colby-Silberman meeting took place on a Saturday. The next morning, December 22, 1974, emblazoned across the top of the *New York Times,* came the startling headline HUGE CIA OPERATION REPORTED AGAINST ANTI-WAR FORCES, OTHER DISSIDENTS IN NIXON YEARS. The story, by Seymour Hersh, contained many of the charges that were in the Family Jewels CIA report (though Hersh lacked access to that digest). In the next few days, more eye-opening revelations about CIA domestic abuses followed.

Thus began a political firestorm that nearly swept away the CIA. At the White House, deputy staff chief Dick Cheney held the fort. His boss, Donald Rumsfeld, and President Ford were in Vail, Colorado, on a ski vacation. Cheney spearheaded Ford's response, creation of a presidential commission headed by Vice President Nelson A. Rockefeller, designed to preempt any congressional investigation of the charges. But White House staff who hoped to head off deeper inquiry were dreaming, especially after January 16, 1975, when Gerald Ford himself dropped a bombshell, telling reporters he had drawn careful limits around Rockefeller's inquiry to keep it from getting into CIA assassinations. What? That guaranteed an inquisition.

The Senate set up a special committee under Idaho Democrat Frank Church. The House also created an inquiry, initially under Representative Nedzi. It is typical of the political turmoil of 1975 that Nedzi's foreknowledge of the Family Jewels became public and, once it did, drove him out of the House investigation, which finally coalesced under Representative Otis Pike (D-NY).

Richard McGarrah Helms became a principal target. After all, Helms had been CIA director when the most egregious domestic abuses occurred. Two things happened at once—a Justice Department criminal inquiry aimed at him, while various investigations sought him intensely as a witness. On December 27, Helms asked to see President Ford. Naturally Gerald Ford had a keen interest. Aides immediately made the arrangements.

Their encounter took place on January 4, 1975.

"You and I have known each other a long time," President Ford told Helms. "I have only the most admiration for you and your work. Frankly, we are in a mess."

Former director Helms agreed that the mood in the country had become ghastly.

The president told the spy chief that the White House would shortly create a blue-ribbon panel to look into intelligence abuses. Helms countered that such an entity ought to investigate the FBI, not just the CIA. Ford promised to consider that, and hoped the Rockefeller panel would stay within its charter, but—ominously—"in this climate we can't guarantee it."

Richard Helms, not pleased, put a threat on the table. He didn't want to "foul the [president's] nest if he could help it." Helms referred to the perjury charge: "If allegations have been made to Justice, a lot of dead cats will come out. I intend to defend myself. I don't know everything which went on at the Agency; maybe no one really does. But I know enough to say that if the dead cats come out, I will participate."

Gerald Ford, Helms's one president at that time, reiterated that the White House would try to complete the probe while protecting the CIA. "I hope you understand my position," Ford said. "You have my pledge that everything I do will be straightforward."

The ambassador went back to Tehran by way of a safari in Kenya. During the trip, Sy Hersh struck again, telling a State Department official he knew Helms had been in town "blackmailing people." Frantic messages passed back and forth about the ambassador's testimony and his plans.

Langley's Nairobi station set up an aircraft and crew to pick Helms up whenever he came out of the bush. By February 21, the former DCI, considering asking the Justice Department to represent him, traded cables with the CIA's John Warner, trying for wiggle room by disputing the validity of a summons served on him at the Tehran embassy, not in person.

Alas, the spectacle of the Justice Department indicting Helms with one hand while defending him with the other did not occur. Even Dick Helms could appreciate the absurdity. He finally hired the famous lawyer Edward Bennett Williams. Between Gerald Ford's promises and Dick Helms's threats, the perjury investigation stalled for more than a year.

On the agency's side of the Potomac, Helms had done little to restrain Angleton's counterintelligence staff from tearing the DO inside out, with its misguided hunt for a Soviet spy inside the CIA. Director Helms had met Angleton's lodestar, the Russian fabulist Anatoli Golitsyn, and had spent many hours listening to Jim's paranoid theories. Congress wanted to talk about Vietnam, the Diem coup especially, about estimates of Soviet forces, and about the Chile coup.

At Langley one facet of Helms's practice had been to keep himself out of ops he considered doomed, like the Bay of Pigs. But the other side of the coin had been how he relished the business of spies and counterspies, which happened to encompass many of the domestic abuses.

The mail-opening project, cryptonym HT/Lingual, in which the addresses of millions of Americans were recorded and the mail of tens of thousands tampered with? Richard Helms was the only senior CIA official whose signature appeared on an authorizing directive, and the only one other than Allen Dulles who had met with the postmaster general.

Hostile interrogation of prisoners—the "enhanced interrogation techniques" of the day, practiced on KGB defector Yuri Nosenko? Helms had met with Nick Katzenbach, then a Justice Department official, to get immigration rules waived for the Russian. Then he'd followed the inquisition from his perch on high.

Interference with American domestic politics? Helms had set the DO loose against *Ramparts* and had at least been aware of the scheme to send the IRS after the journalists. Under Helms the CIA had created projects Merrimac and Resistance, and Helms had let Jim Angleton set up MH/Chaos. Thousands of files were illegally created on citizens and hundreds of thousands of names put on illegal lists. Helms had protected that project from budget and personnel cuts. Langley's agents, invoking Helms, had interfered with CIA dissidents. When Nixon's White House tried to set up a high command for domestic repression, Helms had not objected. Headless horsemen trap themselves in time loops.

Had the 1975 investigations concerned criminal acts rather than just figuring out what the CIA did for a living, Richard Helms would have had a lot more to answer for. Nevertheless, his perjury on the Chile covert operation still loomed, potentially prosecutable.

In the meantime, the Rockefeller, Church, and Pike investigations took their courses. Mr. Helms would repeatedly be called to testify at one or another. There were hearings and depositions, but the shadowy spy chief could not bring himself to deliver on his threat to Ford. Perhaps Helms held his secrets in reserve; that would probably have been his lawyer's advice. Equally possible, Dick appreciated that letting out the cats would sharpen the public's rage at CIA abuses, reports of which swirled through the media.

Agency director Colby sympathized, though he is regarded as a Helms enemy. Successor George Herbert Walker Bush, on the other hand, is considered a happy shipmate. Yet Bush understood that no CIA attempt to stand in splendid isolation could succeed. The forces in play were too powerful. In March 1976, Director Bush sent Helms a cable that said,

ONE OF THE BASIC REASONS FOR THE LACK OF SUPPORT, THE ATTACKS, AND THE UNHELPFUL BOASTS IS THAT WE IN INTELLIGENCE HAVE NOT BUILT THE FOUNDATION WITH THE CONGRESS AND THE AMERICAN PUBLIC NECESSARY TO WITHSTAND THE GENERAL DECLINE IN THE PRESTIGE OF INTELLIGENCE. THIS DECLINE IS PART OF THE DISRESPECT FOR AND SUSPICIONS ABOUT GOVERNMENT IN GENERAL. THE SECRECY ABOUT VIETNAM AND WATERGATE TOGETHER WITH THE NATURAL SECRECY OF INTELLIGENCE ARE AT THE ROOT. NO MATTER HOW MUCH WE COULD WISH IT OTHERWISE I DO NOT BELIEVE WE CAN GO BACK TO COMPLETE SECRECY.

Bush states what the headless horseman, like his present-day counterparts, had difficulty appreciating—that *no compact* existed between the CIA and the American people. Failure to understand that took away the incentive to forge one, and made sand castles of the agency's pious rationales for excessive actions.

The Justice Department inquiry, at a standstill for more than a year, reignited in 1976 when the former ambassador to Chile Edward Korry supplied evidence confirming that what Mr. Helms had said under oath had been a lie, thus perjury. Korry, worried that he'd been left to take the fall for Nixon and the CIA, wanted no part of that. From then on, the wheels of justice ground ahead, slowly but inexorably. Justice Department investigators identified 55,102 pages of CIA documents relevant to the perjury—enough to fill four four-drawer file cabinets. Langley eventually declassified 152 of 758 documents, denied 87, and issued more in redacted form. In December 1976, a grand jury began considering the case, and a month later authorities formally advised Helms that he was the target of federal investigation. Indictment followed in the spring.

In November 1977, Richard Helms solved his criminal dilemma in classic CIA fashion, entering a plea of nolo contendere—not contesting the federal criminal charges but not pleading either innocent or guilty. In court Mr. Helms delivered a statement designed to appeal for leniency. If he had made a plea deal, the statement would have been his allocution. What happened in court *was* the product of a deal, hammered out by lawyer Williams and the DOJ, approved by the attorney general, reviewed by President Carter. The notion that Helms had not allocuted was a fig leaf.

His statement argued that the congressional hearing at which Helms had perjured himself had not been held for oversight of intelligence and that testifying had placed him in a position "of total conflict." He felt legally bound to protect classified information, had been given no authorization to reveal information, and was not a spokesperson for the United States. Therefore it would have been wrong for him to assume the responsibility for revealing secret information. "If I were to contest these charges," Helms declared, "I believe that grave and perhaps irreparable damage to the United States would result."

Sentencing was scheduled for November 4. Judge Barrington D. Parker of the federal district court convicted Richard Helms of a misdemeanor and levied a fine of $2,000. Parker declared that no public official could be allowed "to disobey and ignore the laws of our land because of some misguided notion and belief that there are earlier commitments and considerations they must observe."

Mr. Helms went directly from the court to the Kenwood Country Club in Bethesda, Maryland, where a luncheon of the Central Intelligence Retirees Association was in progress. Members rose for a five-minute standing ovation as Helms entered. Former agency officer Benton Lowe thought him "obviously very drained by his experience." Someone put a pair of waste-baskets atop a piano, and spooks began to fill them with cash, checks, and promissory notes. Agency rank and file paid Richard Helms's fine. He wore his conviction as a badge of honor.

President Carter declared, "A public official does not have a right to lie." Carter had already told a press conference in June that he hoped a statutory charter would be among the achievements of his presidency, but he did not persevere. At first promoting such a statute, Carter's administration lost interest. Congress initially debated the issue, then turned away too. Walter Mondale, the vice president and Carter's point man for intelligence issues, told this author that the White House really had lost interest. He couldn't even put his finger on why.

Gerald Ford's executive order at the end of the Year of Intelligence, which Carter broadened and renewed, reluctantly acknowledged a duty to keep Congress in the loop, and Senate Resolution 400 set up the Senate Select Committee on Intelligence as a way for the executive branch to furnish Congress information on all of its intelligence activities. The *Washington Post* editorialized that these two developments "have effectively shredded both of the rationales that Mr. Helms invoked to justify his decision. . . . No longer can a CIA official claim that he is bound by an oath of secrecy not to inform Congress." The *Post*'s editors anticipated that Carter would shortly resolve any remaining differences and propose a formal charter for the intelligence agencies. Their successors are still waiting.

8

A FAILED EXORCIST

THE NEED FOR A CHARTER THAT THE YEAR OF INTELLIGENCE HAD RAISED has returned as a concern. The Iran-Contra Affair, with its operational-izing of measures to evade controls, ended by raising those basic questions anew. By the mid-1990s, when Republican lawmakers were furious at alleged CIA activities in Bosnia-Herzegovina, the same fears showed from the other side of the Hill. The politics of intelligence were in flux. Since the summer of 1991, when the Soviet Union effectively collapsed, following a praetorian coup against its political leadership, there had been four CIA directors—five if you counted Vice Admiral Studeman, acting boss for sev-eral months in 1995. One director joked he might get the president's atten-tion if only he could crash an airplane on the White House lawn. Morale was shot. The agency, which prided itself on never having been penetrated by enemy spies, suddenly discovered that Aldrich Ames had been selling out for a decade. In opinion polls, the American public had less confidence in the CIA than it did in the tax collectors of the Internal Revenue Service. That was 1997. Post–Cold War ennui overshadowed current activity.

Ghosts stalked the halls at Langley. Spies were so yesterday. Searching for missions, the CIA had fastened on support for military operations—soon its own acronym, SMO—accelerating the militarization of the agen-cy. In this climate, President Bill Clinton appointed the agency's top depu-ty, George Tenet, as the new director. Tenet led the agency through much tumult and became the poster boy for new controversy. It took a very par-ticular sort of person to endure these trials. Also determination—poised to lead, Tenet understood the need to forge an actual covenant with the American people.

Had he succeeded, Tenet might have exorcised the ghosts. He faced a huge challenge. During the just-ended Obama administration, there had been three CIA directors, two acting directors, and two directors of national intelligence (DNIs). Over the full period, from Clinton through Obama—in which Tenet became spy chieftain and held that job for more than seven years—six men had the helm at CIA and four acted in that capacity. There have been four DNIs. In terms of steady leadership, Tenet is it.

George Tenet's watch began a time of troubles. Make no mistake about it. Tenet, the last CIA director responsible for *all* U.S. intelligence agencies, had every imaginable headache. Merely listing things that happened on his watch shows the immense terrain of spying and its considerable impact on American foreign policy. As he took up the reins, of course, the Bosnian crisis—with alleged arms dealing, Serbian intervention, confessional politics, and more—consumed a great deal of attention. But that was one leaf, on the surface. The water was much deeper. The CIA's espionage capabilities, bad as they were, atrophied. The agency had trouble in Latin America with projects assisting counterinsurgents in Colombia and anti-drug actions in Peru. When the Peruvian air force shot down an American missionary family as part of a CIA-guided operation, the bankruptcy of U.S. spy missions in the southern cone of South America stood revealed. Americans could hear the radioed pleas of the missionaries and the agency contractors begging the Peruvians not to shoot. It was Tenet's worst day— until September 11.

Starting while Tenet was still deputy director, what became the war on terror began to dominate the CIA's playbook. An Air Force barracks in Saudi Arabia was truck-bombed in 1996. U.S. embassies in Kenya and Tanzania suffered the same fate from Al Qaeda militants two years later. Thousands were injured and hundreds died, including dozens of Americans, among them agency employees. The American retaliation, a cruise missile strike against Al Qaeda training camps in Afghanistan and a chemical plant in the Sudan, derided for its ineffectiveness, accomplished nothing more than Donald J. Trump's April 2017 initial attack on Syria. The Clinton strike seemed especially ridiculous when the intelligence on the Sudanese factory turned out faulty. George Tenet's plans to mount raids against Al Qaeda leader Osama bin Laden kept falling apart. In 2000, with a boat bomb, Al Qaeda heavily damaged the U.S. destroyer *Cole*. Then came 9/11. It fell to Tenet to lead the detentions and imprisonments of Project Greystone. Investigation of those excesses, and the attempts to keep inquisitors away from them, have damaged the CIA as much as the post–Cold War doldrums.

A STREAK OF INTEREST

All this is a mouthful. Only someone with awfully strong commitment would be capable of stomaching some portion of these events, much less the whole of them. That person had to *want* to achieve, to reach beyond, to derive a new synthesis. Practical and pragmatic, but visionary at the same time, with thick enough skin to endure intermediate setbacks. A dreamer. George Tenet was such a person. Tenet pictured himself as the man who could fashion a consensus. He would preside over the recrudescence of the agency's suddenly obscure raison d'être. For the CIA to flourish, it needed fresh dedication and, equally important, actual links to Americans.

It used to be said that U.S. intelligence—and more specifically the CIA—was possessed by the denizens of elite Ivy League colleges. Later in the agency's seven-decade history, that no longer seemed true. George John Tenet's life tells a different story, perhaps a little of both. Mr. Tenet earned a degree from an Ivy, a master's in international affairs from Columbia University's School of International Affairs (today the School of International and Public Affairs), but he rose from shopkeeper's stock. His father, John, of Greek ancestry, grew up in what is now southern Albania, immigrating to France after an abusive parent threw the boy out. As a teenager, John worked seven years in a French coal mine before the Great Depression.

Moving to the United States, John settled in Little Neck, Long Island, on the edge of New York City, where he opened a diner in a converted railroad car and bought a house around the corner on Marathon Parkway. The home lay just a few miles from the rarefied lands of Jamaica Estates, where Donald Trump spent his childhood. John married a woman named Evangelia, also of Greek origin, who had fled Albanian Communists on board a British submarine. John went to Greece to court her. George and William Tenet were born nonidentical twins less than a year later, in early January of 1953. Donald Trump was six years old.

You wouldn't have marked George for America's top spy any more than you'd have seen Donald as president of the United States. George went to Public School 94, played stickball, and could hit a Spaulding two sewers—that's how those things were measured. Indeed he'd once shared the PS 94 stickball championship. In wintertime he and William played football, even with snow on the ground. George became a Yankees fan. The fact that his favorite was second baseman Bobby Richardson—known for coming through in the clutch—perhaps provides a clue to Tenet the spy chief. Both brothers were altar boys at Saint Nicholas, a Greek Orthodox church in Flushing, for which George played both softball and basketball.

At Benjamin Cardozo High, there was soccer. The sports thing wove through Tenet's life. He became a big fan of his college basketball team, the Georgetown Hoyas. Tenet would be the only CIA director known to dribble a basketball in his office and down the halls at Langley.

A streak of interest in international affairs pervaded the Tenet household. That became the torrent that swept George away. Papa Tenet devoured newspapers, and around the dinner table the family debated world affairs, especially events in Greece. When French president Charles de Gaulle came to New York in 1960, Papa Tenet took both kids to witness the Manhattan parade for the French leader. When it came time for college, George gained admission to the Georgetown School of Foreign Service. After the undergraduate degree, it was on to Columbia's SIA, one of the nation's top international affairs programs. Colleagues at SIA remember him in the sixth-floor lounge, saying over coffee that he was going to head the Central Intelligence Agency.

It wasn't a beeline progression. George first acknowledged his Greek roots, working as research director for the American Hellenic Institute. Then it was an international technology job for a trade association. His big break came in 1982, when Pennsylvania Republican senator H. John Heinz brought George onto his staff. A couple of years later, the young staffer moved over to Vermont senator Patrick J. Leahy's crew. At the time, Leahy sat on the Senate Select Committee on Intelligence (SSCI). Each member nominates one person to the staff. Leahy appointed Tenet, who took to the staff work like a duck to water. These were days of such controversies as Bill Casey's covert operations in Central America, Africa, and Afghanistan; the Iran-Contra Affair; and the question of Soviet compliance with arms control treaties. The thirty-two-year-old staffer would be assigned to follow arms control.

By 1988 Tenet had established a clear primacy. At that point, a new chairman, Oklahoma Democrat David Boren, asked George to be staff director, a position he held for more than four years. The most important developments Tenet orchestrated were the 1991 revisions to the Intelligence Oversight Act and the hearings after the first President Bush named Robert M. Gates to be CIA director. Mr. Gates had been Casey's deputy and some CIA officers were convinced he had played crooked, not only with intelligence on the Soviets, but also with key knowledge about Iran-Contra. Tenet organized a review process that screened prospective witnesses for and against, took private testimony, and then held public hearings, after which Mr. Gates was given an opportunity to respond, and *then* the SSCI members and staff produced an extensive analysis, comparing charges to responses and drawing conclusions. Gates would be confirmed. That gave little comfort to opponents, yet the SSCI examination Tenet arranged turned into the most extensive review of intelligence since the Church and Pike committees.

In 1993 the White House called. Bill Clinton needed his own National Security Council (NSC) staff team. He appointed Anthony Lake, who had headed his campaign foreign policy shop, as security adviser. Lake asked Tenet to come on board, likely at Senator David Boren's suggestion. Quite often, NSC staff intelligence directors are detailed from the CIA or other agencies. George Tenet became the exception, so well versed on the issues that he could function at the NSC staff level. Tenet not only took the job, but before long he had the *top* job, senior director of the NSC intelligence cell. When the United States reached an agreement with Pyongyang to supply North Korea with food and other aid in exchange for a halt to the North Korean nuclear program, it was Tenet who told Capitol Hill doubters that he would supply weekly progress reports. That proved enough for Congress to agree to Clinton's initiative. Another issue that engaged Tenet, export provisions for encryption software and devices, showed his awareness of the cyber future. George Tenet became a loyal lieutenant. He stayed on subject and soon forged strong links with the national security adviser, Anthony Lake.

THE PRESIDENT'S CHOICE

Meanwhile, at the end of 1994, the serving CIA director quit. R. James Woolsey had been frustrated in the job and unhappy with his lack of access to President Clinton. Complaints about Woolsey's refusal to make heads roll in the wake of the exposure of Aldrich Ames irked the director. He resigned. Woolsey's number two, Vice Admiral William O. Studeman, had been in the deputy job nearly three years and felt it was time to leave too. He stayed briefly while Mr. Clinton recruited new leadership. The president nominated John Deutch, a figure from academia via the Pentagon. Tony Lake turned to Tenet to keep an eye on the director, appointing George as deputy director for central intelligence, replacing Studeman. Deutch lasted just over eighteen months, brought down by the CIA cocaine allegations scandal and a charge that he had handled secret information improperly.

Investigators probing Director Deutch's mishandling of classified information believed their inquiry had been blocked at a high level. That's worth a word because Tenet was Deutch's deputy and because charges related to secret documents have become an albatross hung around the neck of senior U.S. officials one after another in every presidency.

Moving into Clinton's second term, Deutch announced his retirement. At home the outgoing director had desktop computers that the agency owned, but he also used them for bank records. Authorities told Deutch he could continue using the computers if he were a consultant. Deutch also became a member of the commission on government secrecy that Daniel Patrick Moynihan headed. The CIA sent someone to check his machines for intrusions, and the specialist found that the desktops at Deutch's home contained agency documents, against the rules. Among them were forty-two complete documents and fragments of many others. Using the desktops for banking purposes required accessing the Internet via an unsecured connection, which meant that malware could potentially invade and compromise classified information. Deutch ran into difficulties trying to purge the records from the machines and called on CIA experts again. They carried away four memory cards containing many documents. It could never be established whether anyone, in fact, accessed Deutch's computers.

Security people began an inquiry. Nora Slatkin, the number-three person at CIA, and Michael O'Neill, the gunslinger (formerly Deutch's chief of staff), watched closely. In fact O'Neill took the memory cards and hung on to them for weeks. Slatkin and O'Neill also resisted the inquisitors' efforts to question Mr. Deutch. The investigation ground to a halt. A few months later, the Office of Security drafted a perfunctory report that, without the Deutch interview, essentially refused to take sides. The Deutch affair bridged George Tenet's arrival in the director's office.

Meanwhile President Clinton turned to Anthony Lake as the next CIA chieftain. His nomination instantly encountered trouble. Conservative politicians lashed Lake on issues ranging from allegations of a covert foreign policy in Bosnia to his views on American communism (in such historical spy cases as that of Alger Hiss). Opponents impeached Lake's political views and demanded access to the private background investigation the FBI conducts on appointees. Tony Lake withdrew, and he had not been the first CIA nominee who failed to obtain confirmation.

Bill Clinton needed someone bulletproof. Lake recommended Tenet, who had actually worked for the Senate committee. George proved just right. The nomination gained unanimous approval. Vice President Al Gore swore him in on July 31, 1997. Among his remarks that day, Tenet gave special thanks to Pat Leahy, who had started him down this road, and "the great" John Deutch, "one of the most remarkable people I have ever known."

Michael O'Neill left the agency as Tenet reached the director's office. O'Neill never referred the Deutch case to the Justice Department because the Office of Security had not completed its report when he left. Catch-22. Director Tenet later said he had not known the report *had* been finished. In the autumn of 1997, the Office of Security itself recommended that Deutch's security clearances be extended so he could serve on a blue-ribbon commission studying the proliferation of WMD that formed under Donald Rumsfeld. Months later, line officers, disgusted that the Deutch affair had been buried, complained to Fred Hitz.

The inspector general began an investigation. Hitz also notified the Intelligence Oversight Board, but being on the way out, he left any referral to his successor. Thus it fell to L. Britt Snider, a veteran of the renowned Church Committee, to refer the case to Justice, which considered filing criminal charges against Deutch. The former director retained lawyer Terrence O'Donnell. Some officials pressed for a special prosecutor, but legislation permitting this expired toward the end of 1998. A few months later, Attorney General Janet Reno decided not to prosecute. The IG report on Deutch was not issued until February 2000, months late.

Director Tenet suspended Mr. Deutch's security clearances in August 1999. He sent copies of the internal report to the congressional committees. At the end of his presidency, William J. Clinton pardoned John Deutch. At that point Tenet, not consulted, revoked the clearances.

George Tenet's roundabout path to the director's suite was merely the first unusual thing about him. There had been spy chieftains from inside the CIA, military officers given the job, and figures from outside government. John Deutch had been a chemist whose most important work related to forms of combustion, especially the creation of fuel-air explosives. Mr. Tenet was the first CIA director ever to have come from Congress, much less the congressional overseers, as well as being the first top CIA official to move over from the White House. Although he had brokered spy programs for Congress and for presidents, Tenet had no experience as an intelligence officer. Some anticipated his failure. Instead Director Tenet proved quite successful for a very long time.

Perhaps it came from his time on Capitol Hill, where politics is bread and butter, or in the Clinton White House, where the chief executive remained the quintessential political animal. The new top spook got it.

In the wake of the Cold War, the CIA needed a true compact with Americans, not the phony, self-asserted "consensus" claimed too often by spies, but a genuine understanding based upon actual dialogue. "We will honor always the trust you, the American people, have placed in us," Tenet said at his nomination hearing, "and we will serve you with fidelity, integrity and excellence."

The director bought the "intelligence community" line, whereby the primary role of U.S. intelligence, beyond warning of doomsday, is ensuring that the troops get maximum benefit from all the nonmilitary national intelligence programs. Tenet had been on the Hill after the First Gulf War. One of the big disputes in its wake, which came down to public hearings at SSCI, had been coalition commander General Norman Schwarzkopf's contention that intelligence had dragged its feet providing data from national systems, as opposed to the military's tactical intel. The CIA thought it had done quite well, but this argument could end only one way. Schwarzkopf had emerged the hero of the day, the conflict hailed as a huge military success.

INTELLIGENCE FOR A NEW AGE

Director Tenet told the Senate, "We've put in place a system of command alertness." James Woolsey, Clinton's first CIA director, was really the person who installed it. At that point, the CIA and the other agencies had a host of people who'd made careers watching the Soviet Union—and suddenly it was no more. Jim Woolsey famously said that America might *miss* the Soviet adversary—that America could be entering a forest of snakes—but his immediate problem was shifting intelligence capabilities away from the Soviet target. The CIA had no idea which snakes needed watching. Woolsey devised a sort of triage system. Issues were ranked and collection plus analytical resources were focused on the highest-priority matters. Langley experts periodically reviewed the rankings and changed priorities. At the height of the Cold War, the Soviet target absorbed 60 percent of CIA resources. By 1993 that figure had diminished by three quarters.

There were many entrants in the post–Cold War intelligence sweepstakes. Robert M. Gates headed the CIA when the Union of Soviet Socialist Republics actually collapsed. Gates more or less transformed himself. He had made his name in Soviet analysis but Bob Gates suddenly morphed into a polymath. Gates became the man who engineered the enormous redistribution of agency money. Whereas many had seen him as conservative to a fault, here Gates began a series of task force restructuring reviews, covering everything from the CIA's organizational template to the role of women to the degree of secrecy it really needed.

In addition to the Gates task forces, there were schemes proposed by other agencies, hearings in both houses of Congress, a proposed IC 21—intelligence community for the twenty-first century—courtesy of the House Permanent Select Committee on Intelligence (HPSCI). A measure of the growing pressures for militarization at the CIA was IC-21's recommendation that the second-in-command slot in the agency's clandestine service, the Directorate of Operations (DO), be reserved for a military officer minimally of two-star rank. HPSCI at least maintained that a DO professional head the directorate.

The Council on Foreign Relations, the Twentieth Century Fund, and the Institute for the Study of Diplomacy at Georgetown University did their own studies. In contrast to HPSCI, the Twentieth Century Fund found a need to make the intelligence services more responsive to the policy maker. It suggested doubling the budget for analysis and narrowing the scope of DO collection to areas where U.S. military forces are actually deployed, plus a few other carefully chosen targets of prime importance.

When the spycatchers unmasked Aldrich Ames in 1994, the Senate intelligence committee recommended a big review of the whole community, at that time comprising thirteen agencies and spending $28 billion a year. Director Woolsey opposed this as outside interference, whereupon the SSCI wrote a joint executive-legislative review panel into the budget authorization. Congress chartered it in October 1994.

President Clinton enlisted a former secretary of defense, Les Aspin, to head the panel. Aspin, Clinton's first Pentagon chief and current chairman of the President's Foreign Intelligence Advisory Board, appears to have been motivated by the mess that became of the U.S. humanitarian intervention in Somalia. The Mogadishu battle (detailed in the book and movie *Blackhawk Down*) took place on his watch and begged for critical examination. Others wanted to look at counterintelligence in the wake of Ames, at technical collection, at CIA's reporting methods, and more. There were a host of issues.

As it happened, Les Aspin had already agreed to participate in the Georgetown colloquium on the future of intelligence. Tenet, then still on the NSC staff, was a Georgetown alum and eager to participate also. Chaired by a CIA officer-in-residence, John H. Hedley, the colloquium had had two sessions before Congress created the Aspin Commission. Hedley and Aspin quickly decided the Georgetown inquiry could function as a sounding board, identifying issues the Aspin commission should cover. Hedley wrote up the results as a checklist.

Lots of straws were in the wind. And everyone agreed on some things but not others. The Georgetown study, HPSCI's IC-21, and the one from the Council on Foreign Relations, for example, all argued that the director of central intelligence needed more authority and that the CIA should make greater use of open sources—material in the public domain, not secret. The council study underlined the advantages of collaboration with foreign intelligence agencies. Studies differed on the value of so-called competitive analysis, the practice of deliberately asking organizations with opposing views to report on the same subject. The Georgetown colloquium, which included many current or former intelligence officers, wanted less; the council, more. The colloquium raised the issue of reconnaissance satellites, pointing out that the constellation in orbit was already much reduced from what had been available at the time of the Gulf War (1991). That group expected *more* spending on intelligence. They argued that folks wanting a "peace dividend" from intelligence were looking in the wrong place. The IC-21 advocates would take more money but aim it at intelligence analysis. The Georgetown colloquium anticipated reductions, recommending that authorities identify necessary baseline capabilities before looking at cuts, implying that a hard look would confirm the higher numbers. In partial compensation, the group advised that the figure for total U.S. intelligence spending be public, something CIA had been resisting since the Church Committee and Rockefeller Commission had recommended it.

The Aspin inquiry effectively began when staff first met, in March 1995, several weeks after principals held their initial meeting, at a building housing parts of the executive office of the president. Security adviser Tony Lake attended the first session. One staffer thought the spy Aldrich Ames was "the ghost in the room at many commission meetings." But the agenda remained quite close to the Georgetown checklist. Two months into the exercise, Mr. Aspin suffered a stroke and passed away. Vice chairman and former senator Warren Rudman filled in. Clinton appointed Harold Brown, a past secretary of defense, in Aspin's place.

The revamped Aspin-Brown Commission covered the waterfront. Like the Council on Foreign Relations, Aspin-Brown called for expanded international cooperation and more presidential leadership. In common with both groups, the commission held out for a stronger DCI, in this case by giving the director *two* deputies, one for the CIA, the other to manage the wider community. Aspin-Brown agreed with others in insisting on preserving a robust covert operations capability. The DO culture needed reform. Aspin-Brown joined the Georgetown group in backing creation of a new agency to handle overhead imagery. The new-generation reconnaissance satellite wasn't among its public recommendations, but it had wide support. The report, completed in the spring of 1995, went to a CIA with John Deutch at its head and George Tenet as deputy. Reforms were up to them.

George Tenet arrived on the seventh floor at the Central Intelligence Agency's Langley headquarters at a pregnant moment. The atmosphere of threat hanging over America had largely dissipated. Opportunity beckoned. There were apostles of change. Robert Gates had already started the ball rolling with his task forces, and Gates had appeared before Tenet's Georgetown colloquium, the Aspin-Brown Commission, and in public before groups of historians, speaking of openness. Langley began experimenting with new kinds of analysis and fresh ways to perceive data. The CIA had begun relating to the public in novel ways. Officers were being assigned to universities and other institutions to be "in residence," not only teaching about intelligence but serving as interpreters of the spooky world. Agency historians were producing monographs that were beginning to be declassified. Secret documents exploring the world as the CIA saw it began appearing in *Foreign Relations of the United States*, the official serial that records U. S. government actions. The CIA had started to host conferences on its role in various events, and on specific subjects also. While a proclivity to speak only about the Soviet Union remained, soon enough the conferences explored wider-ranging aspects, such as the development of the U-2 spy plane and the reconnaissance satellites, the CIA under Harry Truman, or events in Cold War Berlin. The agency was approaching its fiftieth anniversary. At the celebration, George Tenet honored fifty "trailblazers," people from every field who had contributed to the spy enterprise.

At these events, the director would play the field, walking up to people at random to pick their thoughts. I experienced that myself, during a break between panels at a conference the CIA held to reexamine the end of the Cold War and fall of the Soviet Union. It was in College Station, Texas, at the presidential library of the first President Bush, and I had stepped outside for a cigarette when the director of central intelligence came up with a cigar and his entourage. Tenet cut quite a figure. Insiders thought so too. Michael Morell, who served Tenet as executive assistant, called him "the most down-to-earth, approachable senior government official I have ever met." When, at the end of a meeting prepping Tenet for a session on Capitol Hill, Morell advised the boss to pull up his zipper, the director quipped, "Finally! A fucking piece of advice that's actually useful."

President William J. Clinton, together with Congress, also pushed Langley toward openness.

Several times Clinton signed legislation or promulgated executive orders mandating declassification of intelligence records. In this Clinton's administration followed on that of George Herbert Walker Bush, during whose presidency Congress had voted a John F. Kennedy Assassination Records Review Board, which actually labored through 1998. A Clinton-era mandate would be the Commission on Protecting and Reducing Government Secrecy, headed by Daniel Patrick Moynihan, which reported in 1997. That group considered general principles. Mr. Clinton also initiated action to improve the system for declassification of U.S. secret records, but there the mavens of secrecy defeated him. Another mandated group specifically mined the documentary record on CIA activities in Chile—and there Mr. Clinton apologized to the Chilean nation on behalf of the United States, handing over records on Nixon-era actions. A third panel reviewed records on U.S. postwar employment of former Nazis and Japanese fascists, including war criminals. Its work spilled over into the second Bush presidency.

When he reached Langley, George Tenet brought with him John Hedley, erstwhile chairperson of the Georgetown colloquium, and before that an analyst on prime CIA products such as the President's Daily Brief and the *National Intelligence Daily*. As chairman of Langley's Publications Review Board (PRB), John Hedley became Tenet's designated hitter on openness. The Georgetown group's report, which Hedley authored, found that spies often cling to myths. One was that the public understood spying and automatically endorsed it. Another one—paradoxical—is that *only insiders* could truly understand. The Aspin-Brown Commission's report rejected secrecy. Both implied the need for the CIA to reach out. The Moynihan report held that attempting to preserve complete secrecy creates a climate in which public trust disintegrates and secrets emerge anyway. The experiences of the Kennedy board, the Chile release, and the Nazi records release *all* demonstrated that records of even the most secret operations can be opened without damaging national security. Indeed, the CIA itself assembled and released an official history of one of its most closely held post–World War II projects, creating a new German spy service using former Nazi spooks, without bringing down the republic.

Since the Carter administration, the PRB had served as the mirror that showed CIA's face to the world. After the 1970s, and disastrous experiences with whistleblowers, everyone who worked for the agency and held a security clearance had to clear whatever they wrote about the CIA with the reviewers. The board consisted of the head and his deputy plus representatives of each agency directorate. Any of them could object to any element of a manuscript, after which it became the author's problem to convince the PRB that its fears were misplaced. Many former officers had had problems with the PRB in the past. John Hedley maintained that the agency could have it both ways—protect real secrets while being more open. Director Tenet saw that as part of his commitment. The PRB made a start by minimizing its interventions on a clandestine service memoir by Dewey Clarridge, and an account of spy wars in Berlin by David Murphy and a former Soviet opponent.

As director, Tenet did not feel bound by conventions, and he had a good eye for talent. From an agency point of view, John E. McLaughlin would be an inspired choice as deputy director of central intelligence. John Brennan, one of the people Tenet employed to head his staff, would lead the agency in his own right. The boss hired Alvin B. Krongard, a banker, for executive director. Tenet's appointments to agency directorates were excellent. These years also marked the moment that women effectively broke through Langley's glass ceiling. George Tenet became the first to have two directorates led by women. He had the first woman chief of staff, the first to serve as top intelligence analyst, and the first female baron in the DO too. There were more female case officers than ever and more women as station chiefs. In many ways it *was* a new age.

A few things were easy. Given a transformed Russia, the old Soviet Bloc Division of the clandestine service became obsolete. Collection shifted to Russia and Eurasia. The East European Division of the Directorate of Intelligence (DI)—the agency's analytical experts—merged with DI's European Division, and the division ultimately got the Russian portfolio as well. The DO also added an operational division to act against nuclear proliferation.

Langley also adopted a new organizational formula, the so-called fusion center. The idea was to laser in on a subject, bringing together intel from all sources in one place, while simultaneously breaking down walls between operators and analysts by having them work in the same office. Tenet's immediate predecessors had started the bandwagon rolling, creating fusion centers for counterterrorism, counterintelligence, and combating the illegal-drugs trade. Now more were added—for countering nuclear proliferation, for conventional weapons and forces, and for other purposes. The centers transcended the CIA's old structure of directorates, working directly under the DCI. This shift, well under way when George Tenet went to the NSC staff, was largely accomplished by the time he left Langley.

Much remained to be done. The operations directorate had deteriorated. "Special activities" of the paramilitary sort had suffered a black eye in the Iran-Contra affair and other Bill Casey ventures, still being unrolled when the Soviet Union collapsed. Traditional espionage seemed less important. A wave of resignations roiled the ranks, hitting especially hard at the cadre of midcareer clandestine officers, men and women with five years or so in service who stood to be the next wave of CIA leadership. Dozens of stations were closed, the core of DO collectors reduced by about 30 percent, and an average station typically left with five actual spies, including a chief of station focused on management, with most frontline people on their first or second tour. These developments proved so disturbing that the IG mounted a formal investigation, interviewing people who were leaving, looking at working conditions.

Morale remained iffy. The tradition had been that DO officers were asked to skirt boundaries and then were hung out to dry, abandoned. This was confirmed in the mid-1990s with the failed clandestine operation against Saddam Hussein. In France there were allegations of CIA economic spying against French corporations to benefit American ones. Station chief Richard Holm, declared persona non grata, left the country.

Another major upheaval concerned CIA actions on the world stage. Director Deutch had promised Congress he would take a hard line on notifications, and with Guatemala the CIA had misrepresented the human rights situation to Capitol Hill. In addition, Deutch knew that congressional overseers were furious that in the Ames espionage case the CIA had failed to discipline anyone. Now Deutch fired the responsible division and station chiefs and reprimanded others, including a former DO boss who had already retired. George Tenet watched all this as deputy director.

The DO's acting chief John J. "Jack" Devine disagreed with Deutch's decision. Deutch hesitated to make a new appointment to head the DO but now did so, giving the job to David Cohen, actually an analyst. Devine got a European post as station chief in a major power instead. Langley kept that quiet, but the Paris slot is known to have been open.

Deutch ordered a revalidation of CIA assets. By some counts more than a thousand CIA spies—not agency officers but local sources—were dismissed for transgressions of human rights strictures. Guidelines for agent recruitment followed.

Clandestine service officers took this as a rejection. When Terry Ward and Fred Brugger, the headquarters and field station culprits, were drummed out of the building, DO people lined the halls to shake their hands. Director Deutch assembled officers at the agency's outside auditorium, the Bubble, to explain his decision. This special auditorium Allen Dulles had had built beyond CIA's security perimeter so the agency could host outlanders. Deutch was heckled. CIA veterans asked what he had done to improve morale. Deutch insisted he had tried and added that subordinates—his deputies—also needed to address these issues. Jack Devine had tried that—with Deutch. At least some of the zealous probe of John Deutch for improper handling of secret documents should be traced to this lingering resentment.

These blows shook the DO to its foundations, in a climate where the spy's product, so-called human intelligence, remained a primary concern. *Every* review of intelligence collection over the years had found a need for more humint, as the cognoscenti knew it. That situation had not changed. In the mid-1990s, the security services attempted to produce empirical data about the contributions of information types. A panel under the National Intelligence Council, the top analytical body, tried to compile a comprehensive list of intel requirements, much as a collection manager might do. After identifying nearly four hundred subjects, it estimated which kinds of collection would be relevant to each. Humint was assessed as critical in 55 percent of questions, more than twice as many as the next nearest competitor (including the much-vaunted communications intelligence). As the CIA moved into the war on terror, it would be simultaneously true that humint became even more important and that the CIA failed miserably at acquiring it.

Following Deutch, George Tenet set out to rectify the mess at the DO. Achieving that, too, would have been a dream. As deputy director, Tenet had spent a lot of time on "hard targets," selecting a dozen and creating community-wide teams to pursue each. Now he redoubled that effort. Tenet found recruiting fouled up. Only twenty-five new officers joined the clandestine service in all of 1995. When the director looked into training at Camp Peary, he found barely half a dozen persons in the clandestine service course. At that rate, the DO couldn't replace officers lost to resignation much less increase strength. In his first budget request, Tenet appealed for extra money to rebuild the spy unit.

The director told Jack Devine he wanted him for DDO, but he later cooled to that idea, hinting at pressures to turn elsewhere. Instead Tenet coaxed legendary spy Jack G. Downing out of retirement. Downing fashioned a scheme to refurbish the Directorate of Operations, started the biggest recruiting campaign in its history, acquired Directorate of Science and Technology mechanisms that facilitated operations, and fashioned a new balance between technical collection and agent handling. A Clandestine Service Reserve was established to ensure important skills were not lost as officers retired. Here Tenet adopted a measure advocated in the House intelligence committee's IC-21 study.

The DO strategic plan and the evident responsiveness to Capitol Hill's recommendations became the basis for Tenet's funding plea. He favored creative but responsible risk taking, ruling out the use of clergy or journalistic covers, which John Deutch had refused to do. Tenet told a Senate committee, "risk-taking does not equate with recklessness." The director's watchword would be flexibility. The DO would be accountable, could not be insular, and must respond to its chain of command. He took nothing for granted. Jack Downing bragged that on his watch—also Tenet's—no one was hung from the yardarm for doing their job.

Director Tenet created a climate for recovery. In the summer of 1998 he presented the Director's Medal to a pair of CIA operatives long held in Chinese prisons. At a suitably quiet moment, Director Tenet invited the disgraced Terry Ward back to Langley to present him one of the CIA's top decorations, the Distinguished Intelligence Medal. After 9/11, as a Clandestine Service Reservist, Ward, like others, would be reemployed in the war on terror. A few months before, Camp Peary graduated its biggest class since Vietnam days.

Then there was covert action, which Tenet agreed was a critical instrument of U.S. foreign policy. However, he added a qualifier. "It should never be the last resort of failed policy," the director told Congress. "You should never ask us to do what cannot be achieved by other means."

The dawn of the terror war suggests the boundaries. Langley had been active in support of the military in the peacemaking operation in Somalia. The intel had never been good enough to pin down the top adversary warlord, and U.S. military action—even with Special Operations forces—failed. New enemies materialized. The Battle of Mogadishu started the face-off between the United States and Osama bin Laden, chief of the Islamic extremist group Al Qaeda. Bin Laden had earlier been active in the Afghan secret war the CIA fought against the Russians. But he had gone his own way.

In 1996 a serious truck bombing took place in Saudi Arabia at the Khobar barracks, a facility housing many American servicemen. Nineteen Americans were killed; nearly five hundred of many nationalities were wounded. Many believed Al Qaeda responsible, among them the CIA's station chief, John Brennan; others blamed Saudi dissidents. The two may have been one and the same; bin Laden came from a prominent Arabian family. In any case, Al Qaeda declarations lumped the United States with Israel as "crusaders" and infidels. While Tenet still held the deputy director's desk, Langley created its Alec Station, a special unit within CTC dedicated to watching bin Laden, whom it traced to the Sudan. Named for the son of chief Michael Scheuer, Alec Station strove for "virtual" focus—to exist in the field even while playing from northern Virginia. Some at CIA viewed this newfangled idea with a certain disdain. Scheuer also rose from the analytical side of the agency, not the DO. His unit suffered from the reluctance of operators to pitch in and support it.

Meanwhile the United States interceded with the Sudanese, who made Osama leave. Al Qaeda took refuge in Afghanistan, more powerful than ever, with bases, training camps, and even a conventional military unit brigaded with the Taliban government army. Alec Station crafted a plan for a paramilitary unit to attack Tarnack Farm, bin Laden's new headquarters, a complex in the high Afghan plains, using a tribal band who had earlier been CIA allies. The Covert Actions Review Group thought the plan had no better than a 30 percent chance of success. From Pakistan the CIA station chief rated it at 40 percent—but judged the planning tops. Jack Downing assessed low chances in a letter to Clinton's security adviser. Downing's deputy James L. Pavitt felt the DO could not afford the $3 million price tag.

Nevertheless the project reached the director's office, where Tenet supervised drafting of a presidential finding. Jeffrey O'Connell, chief of the Counterterrorist Center, briefed cabinet officials and Justice Department prosecutors who were pursuing terrorist cases. The hope had been to exfiltrate Osama and put him on trial. In late May 1998, the CIA held a full-dress rehearsal and decided the plan was feasible. As the rehearsal began, Director Tenet discussed it with national security adviser Sandy

Berger. They anticipated a final interagency confab, followed by execution of the raid that June. Instead the high-level approval never came. Tenet later told the 9/11 Commission that he had canceled on the advice of top officers—Downing and Pavitt.

At 5:35 a.m. on August 7, Sandy Berger had to wake Mr. Clinton with a phone call, telling the president that the American embassies in Kenya and Tanzania had just been truck-bombed. More than two hundred were killed, including a dozen Americans, two of them CIA officers. There could be no doubt of bin Laden's enmity.

Director Tenet put out an order naming Al Qaeda and declaring "war." The United States retaliated with cruise missile attacks. A serious error took place with a strike on a Sudanese factory the CIA wrongly thought was a bin Laden chemical weapons plant. Mary McCarthy, Tenet's successor in the NSC staff intelligence cell, had warned against it. The CIA resumed contact with partisan bands left from the Afghan war and hatched fresh plots to neutralize bin Laden, but the intel was never hard enough that President Clinton approved. This remained the situation when George W. Bush came to office and shuffled into 9/11.

Countering Al Qaeda in the 1990s illustrated Tenet's point that Washington could not substitute covert operations for foreign policies. A more proper approach to the Taliban government—which once offered to turn bin Laden over to an "Islamic court"—might have finessed the problem.

Bosnia, Serbia, and the former Yugoslavian lands, erupting into internecine warfare once communism collapsed, were another case in point. In 1991 the Bosnian confederation fractured into three mini-states. One became a satrapy of Serbia, with covert Serbian intervention to kill Muslim ethnics. The first Bush administration had backed a United Nations cease-fire and arms embargo, but in 1992 came the Bosnian Serb siege of Sarajevo. An index of CIA risk aversion would be that, before taking up assignment there, Langley's prospective Sarajevo station chief was asked to sign a paper indemnifying the agency if anything happened to him.

Clinton found little international support for lifting the embargo. Yet other nations did aid the Bosnian Muslims while the United States looked away. Later it emerged that Bosnian officials had been in contact with American diplomats on the arms traffic and that the Clinton White House had kept the matter outside diplomatic channels. This enraged those who considered Iran an American archenemy, because it had been a main weapons source for the Bosnians. The White House stood accused of giving a green light to the traffic. Congressional anger played a major role in the opposition to Tony Lake being appointed CIA chief.

In May 1995, during Tenet's final months as intelligence director for the NSC, the DO Covert Action Planning Group reviewed the project, the director-level Covert Action Review Group vetted it, and it then went to Tenet at the NSC Interagency Working Group for Covert Action, and finally to be approved by the NSC deputies—all in the space of one weekend. A horrified DO officer, a veteran of Middle East operations who had been one of the Iranian hostages in that painful crisis, found the price tag stunning—more than the gross national products of half the world's nations.

The arms traffic put Langley on the spot. Agency analysts warned that without weapons the Muslims could not hold, but the DO opposed cooperation with traffickers. When the U.S. ambassador brought in his station chief, asking him to estimate the impact of a certain amount of weapons, the CIA began keeping book on White House maneuvers. R. James Woolsey, then still the director, had once been a congressional aide and was a likely source now. In the House, a panel of the International Relations Committee probed the alleged green-light policy.

President Clinton ordered the Intelligence Oversight Board (IOB), his official monitoring group, to look into the affair. The board found no CIA project had actually gone beyond planning stages, and Clinton's enemies in Congress soon abandoned the Bosnia dispute in favor of the much juicier attractions of the Monica Lewinsky affair.

But a United States military contingent went to Bosnia as a "peacemaking" force. Under its rubric of "support to military operations," CIA involvement broadened. The miasma almost did in the future director—returning from a visit to the front, George Tenet's plane had to make an emergency landing after a bird struck and cracked the cockpit windshield over the North Atlantic. Some observers, historian David Halberstam prominent among them, argue that the Pentagon and CIA, familiar with the former Yugoslav officers who dominated Serbia's military, mistrustful of the johnny-come-lately Croats, Bosnians, and Herzegovinians, exhibited a pro-Serb bias. There is a CIA official history of the civil war (which is purely historical and excludes intelligence aspects) that does not seem to take sides. Declassified documents that may clarify are far from reaching the public domain. Wherever the truth lies, the fact remains that when a covert project materialized, it sought to aid those who fought the Serbs, not the other way. A decade later, when Islamists warred against America, the CIA's failure to build friendships with Muslims over their help for the Bosnians would have national security consequences.

President Clinton finally took the track of diplomatic mediation backed by the threat of force. A tenuous agreement emerged. The Serb Republic squirmed under an international spotlight, and the CIA sought to contribute to so-called force protection for the U.S. peacemakers inserted into the region. This resulted in operations in Bosnia-Herzegovina and Croatia, and in the death of a female officer. Scrambling to put personnel into the field, the Directorate of Operations discovered that its people fluent in Serbo-Croatian could be counted on one hand. This stunning realization became a benchmark argument for the need to build a Clandestine Service Reserve. Operations also resulted in an early use of private military contractors to train the minor states' armed forces and of unmanned aerial vehicles, or drones, at that time only for observation.

The Clinton approach of coercive mediation returned to the fore in the spring of 1999 when Belgrade sought to block independence demands by the province of Kosovo. Clinton obtained support of the North Atlantic Treaty Organization (NATO) for an air campaign to induce the Serbs to let Kosovo go. As part of this war, the U.S. military provided defensive assistance where necessary, and the CIA helped Kosovar rebels with weapons. By far the most controversial aspect of Langley's participation in the campaign would be the Chinese embassy bombing—its boneheaded failure to check Belgrade street addresses when preparing the target folder for bombing a Serbian supply headquarters.

The spies produced a major snafu in choosing this, the single target CIA nominated for bombing during the seventy-eight-day war. Three meetings at Langley reviewed target information, but the agency had no formal process for checking a nomination, no actual guidelines to follow. The Chinese embassy in Belgrade had moved a few years earlier. American diplomats visited it in the new location a number of times, but no intelligence or military database contained the correct address, and neither did the Serbian supply headquarters appear on any of the maps used to locate its address. The embassy and supply warehouse lay within a block of each other. In another version, the embassy's coordinates *had* been changed on CIA records but not in a military database intended to prevent attacks on unintended targets. One intelligence officer saw the discrepancy between the warehouse location and a notice he had previously seen that it had been misplotted. The officer not only warned the Pentagon bombing planners but checked the strike list a few days later and found the target marked for *that day.*

A call to the Pentagon planners revealed that a B-1 bomber, already in flight, aimed at the Chinese embassy. In Belgrade several Chinese spooks and diplomats were killed, at least twenty more wounded. The mess involved at least two agencies, the CIA and the forerunner of today's National Geospatial Intelligence Agency. Director Tenet barely held on to his job. An accountability review board in 2000 recommended written or oral reprimands for several CIA people. One retired military man working on contract was essentially fired—but the Pentagon disciplined no one. Of such things are dreams dashed. George Tenet approved reprimands but later changed his mind. He writes, "It wasn't the last time on my watch that CIA would take sole responsibility for errors in which other agencies shared the blame." For spooks the disturbing lesson made out wholesale denial as the best path to the agency's safety. The ghosts smiled.

The dust had barely settled from the embassy bombings when India, with a new right-wing Hindu revivalist government, after a fourteen-year gap, in May 1998 conducted a series of nuclear tests. The Indian bomb came as a surprise and heightened tensions with Pakistan; both nations tested weapons and came near open confrontation. On the phone with Richard Shelby of the Senate intelligence committee, Director Tenet admitted that the CIA hadn't had a clue. Senator Shelby promptly trumpeted Langley's colossal failure. President Clinton phoned the spy chief to assure Tenet of his support. America's top spook recalled this as his first big crisis. As the mud flew, it became clear that agency analysis had been dominated by assumptions and plagued by the need to digest massive amounts of raw data. In Surrey, Canada, a Sikh separatist group without the need to toe those lines had correctly identified the Indian test site, talked of nuclear test preparations, and predicted tests several days in advance. In Washington Director Tenet felt obliged to ask Vice Admiral David Jeremiah to probe how intelligence had erred.

Of course the joke was on the CIA. And some made light of it. John C. Gannon, chairman of the National Intelligence Council, the board of senior specialists responsible for the National Intelligence Estimates (NIEs), told an audience in early June of his rough couple of weeks. "It is a delight to be away from Langley for a few hours." Gannon recounted dozing off reading a book when his fifteen-year-old daughter came home and threw her sneakers into the closet. "I sprang to my feet terrified that I had missed another Indian nuclear test," the analyst teased.

George Tenet wanted to target investments at innovation. He believed the intelligence community, just as it had brought America the U-2 spy plane and the reconnaissance satellite, should be a center of technology advances. Tenet credits two women, Ruth David and Joanne Isham, with bringing him the concept for funding a private entity to bridge between CIA and the Silicon Valley computer geniuses. Executive director Buzzy Krongard encouraged the move. Officials canvassed technologists seeking advice, talking to more than two hundred industry experts.

One CIA unit, its Directorate of Science and Technology (DS&T), had long been the cradle for new gizmos, innovating everything from digital photography to facial recognition software for computer systems. But Director Tenet believed the private sector more flexible. His DS&T head, Ruth David, had come from the outside, from the Sandia Laboratory, and shared that view. David presided over abolition of the directorate's Office of Research and Development. She replaced it with a new Investment Program Office, enhancing the agency's ability to contract research outside government. At first the idea was to re-create the Skunk Works—the design outfit responsible for the U-2 Dragon Lady and A-12 Oxcart (later developed into the SR-71 Blackbird) spy planes.

Isham, David's deputy, became DS&T chief in her own right. In 1999 both women gave Tenet a plan to refashion CIA innovation, suggesting that Langley partner with a Silicon Valley start-up to spin off a subsidiary oriented to agency requirements. A related issue was that valley companies had begun poaching Langley's long-service technical specialists, often hiring them back under contract for more money. The Skunk Works model failed, because personnel would have been paid at federal rates and hampered by government contract requirements. With an affiliated technology company, one driven by the profit motive, the agency could both stem the brain drain and direct resources where it needed them. The venture, called In-Q-Tel, launched in combination with Gilman G. Louie and venture capitalists Norman R. Augustine and Lee A. Ault III. During Tenet's time, the shop reportedly produced more than a hundred solutions that Langley adopted, and over $37 million of CIA money fueled it. Naturally, secrecy makes impossible any precision as to how effective this public-private collaboration has been, but it fits George Tenet the dreamer.

INTO THE CAULDRON

Identifying trends in nuclear proliferation had been a major goal of CIA analysis for years. Not only that, but the agency had both a fusion center and a division in the operations directorate specifically aimed at countering proliferation. Tenet's counterproliferation unit had some success in Europe, secretly buying up critical items to restrict supply, and in Africa, with information sharing and joint action. The Republic of South Africa gave up its nuclear program. Libyan dictator Muammar Gaddafi, in a maneuver in which CIA officers Stephen Kappes and Ben Bonk played key roles, not only gave up his own efforts to create weapons of mass destruction (WMD), but permitted the equipment and raw materials to be crated up and taken away. CIA analysts provided the information for Operation Desert Fox, a December 1998 aerial bombardment against putative Iraqi WMD facilities. This action had indeterminate results and left the agency in the dark about Iraqi programs. The CIA's errors opened the door to Bush administration officials who wanted to transform the Middle East by invading Iraq.

Director Tenet's analysts further contributed to the disastrous Iraq invasion by producing intelligence to please, in this case an NIE that compounded previous misunderstandings of Iraqi programs and helped Bush hoodwink Congress, the American people, and to some degree the United Nations, adding to phony justifications for the invasion. Once that war began, disputes over whether the CIA had supplied language for some of the most outrageous Bush claims contributed directly to George Tenet's downfall.

No account of Tenet's stewardship would be complete without his part in the run-up to the attacks of September 11, 2001, and the Iraq invasion. By then Jim Pavitt headed the DO. In October 2000 at Aden, a port in Yemen, the American destroyer *Cole* suffered grievous damage from an explosive boat piloted by Al Qaeda militants. CIA and FBI officers investigated the incident, in which seventeen U.S. sailors died. Despite the notion the CIA had Al Qaeda in its crosshairs, Pavitt's operators tracked down the perpetrators only individually, over months and years. Meanwhile Al Qaeda prepared an even more devastating assault, with teams hijacking a number of airliners simultaneously and crashing them into major landmark buildings in the United States. President George W. Bush's incoming administration didn't take the threat seriously. In August 2001, the CIA report called the President's Daily Brief warned that Al Qaeda might use aircraft as weapons. George Tenet made a trip to Texas to give President Bush that warning, without effect.

Tenet may have had his hair on fire, but errors bedeviled CIA analysts, preventing them from making an undeniable case. Agency operatives learned of an Al Qaeda reunion in Malaysia that convened some of the *Cole* bombers with other militants, then discovered that some of those persons had entered the United States. Another skein of warning information came from Hamburg, Germany. Just the day before the attacks, the National Security Agency (NSA), Tenet's communications intelligence arm, intercepted a message referring to a major upcoming event.

None of the warnings were circulated, and on September 11, Al Qaeda hijackers took over four airplanes, crashing two into New York's World Trade Center and one into the Pentagon in Washington. The fourth plane is thought to have been intended for another Washington target, but it is impossible to know. This airliner crashed in rural Pennsylvania. In any case nearly three thousand Americans died in the 9/11 attacks. The intelligence failure was huge.

Bush administration officials responded with their scheme to attack Iraq. On the fly they invaded Afghanistan, spearheaded by CIA paramilitary teams and U.S. special operations forces. The presidential finding of September 17, 2001, with which Bush authorized these actions, became the bedrock authority for CIA's torture program and all its actions in the war on terror.

The Iraq venture, capitalizing on fictitious WMD claims, became the one on which White House hearts were really set. Vice President Richard B. Cheney visited agency headquarters at Langley, Virginia, a number of times to obtain the intelligence he wanted. Cheney's demands for "deep dives" helped pressure CIA analysts on both Iraq and terrorism intelligence issues. When Tenet's analysts held their ground, as they did against claims that the Iraqi government was colluding with the Al Qaeda terrorists, the Bush White House looked elsewhere for its "authoritative" intel. In March 2003, the United States invaded Iraq, overthrowing Saddam Hussein's government and searching for his alleged WMDs. Just a few months into the campaign, President Bush traveled to the region and trumpeted, "Mission Accomplished!"

Actually the wars continued. At this writing, in 2017, the Afghan War is America's longest and the defenses of the U.S.-backed government seem to be crumbling. The United States left the Iraq War in 2011, but returned three years later when fundamentalist insurgents sliced away portions of both Iraq and Syria. The full story of the CIA's wars in Afghanistan and Iraq is still to be written, but it began with George Tenet. The CIA director felt like a member of a Greek chorus, sitting behind Secretary of State Colin L. Powell, when the latter famously went to the United Nations Security Council to make a phony U.S. case that Iraq possessed weapons of mass destruction. Within a year, Tenet says, he had become afraid the U.S. war had failed.

A diplomatic issue current today—the attempt to rein in Iranian ambitions to possess a nuclear weapon—had already been a key intelligence question on George Tenet's watch. There were various appreciations of Tehran's progress, on both the enriched uranium necessary to craft a bomb and on weaponization, the design and fabrication of an actual device suitable to be carried by missile or aircraft. The CIA not only reported on Iranian weapon prospects; it also mounted a covert operation to restrain Tehran by feeding it false engineering information and suborning physicists who might labor in such a program. When NIEs revisited this subject, analysts saw evidence that Tehran had unilaterally stopped work on a nuclear weapon in about 2003, a time when Tenet's experts still saw a great Iranian threat.

One more nuclear proliferation matter needs mention, and that is the illicit trade in nuclear materials, technology elements for weapons, and platforms suitable to carry them. North Korea engaged in this trade. So did a network of traders run by a senior Pakistani physicist, Abdul Qadeer Khan, selling blueprints, design information, component items, and centrifuges. The CIA developed evidence that Khan helped Pyongyang on nuclear enrichment while acquiring North Korean missiles and other technology to sell elsewhere. With British help, the CIA traced elements of the A. Q. Khan network across the globe and built a full profile of its activities. In September 2003, Director Tenet met with Pakistani leader Mohammed Musharraf and laid out the case. A few months later, the Musharraf government dismissed Khan from his official positions in Pakistani programs and shut down his network.

Events triggered a season of inquiry the likes of which the CIA had never seen. Not satisfied with probes conducted by the U.S. Senate and the House of Representatives, in 2002 Congress created a national commission to investigate the 9/11 attacks. The Iraq invasion brought a CIA-led mission to find the elusive Iraqi WMDs. It came up empty. Oversight committees in both houses of Congress initiated investigations of the intelligence underlying the Iraq War. Not to be outdone, and seeking to control the action himself, President Bush ordered a presidential panel to conduct a broad inquiry into WMD intelligence.

The Iraq War ended the dreamer's run. George Tenet, on the verge of breaking Allen W. Dulles's record as longest-serving CIA director, was knocked out by the controversies that swirled around its origins. The director had buttered this piece of bread himself, telling President George W. Bush the case against Iraq was a "slam dunk." Afterward, the director objected that the CIA had simply been presenting an early version of intelligence that could be used to make a public case for Iraq's possession of weapons. Bush had been unimpressed. Tenet then enthused at how bulletproof they could make the evidence down the road. He insists that the agency did not go beyond conclusions to justify a policy—and Jami Miscik, his DDI, repeated during a Christmas Eve 2002 meeting with both presidents Bush that there had been *no* smoking-gun evidence for Iraqi WMD.

Were that the sum of it, the CIA might have got itself off the hook. But the "slam dunk" episode took place partway through a long series of Bush administration prevarications, *many* of them based on allusions to supposed CIA reporting. It's not worth going through the granular detail on this.* What is important is that Vice President Richard Cheney and other officials invoked the CIA as authenticator of their claims, that Langley continued to furnish the Bush White House the information it demanded, and that the agency made no effort to indicate to lawmakers a different fact situation than Bush officials represented. One of the "deep dives" that Mr. Cheney liked to make later revealed that the CIA *did* induce officials to tamp down some of their more extreme claims, but they were promptly inserted into another presidential speech. Study would also show CIA analytical errors in the NIE and other reports it made about Iraq. The intelligence failures on the Sudanese chemical plant, the Chinese embassy in Serbia, the Indian nuclear weapons, and the 9/11 attacks were eclipsed by the Iraq War, where the intelligence not only proved wrong, but those responsible for it effectively functioned as cheerleaders for the war party.

The immediate occasion for George Tenet's demise was one of the Iraq lies—the "sixteen words" claiming Baghdad had attempted to buy urani-

---

* For a detailed investigation of the specific allegations made regarding Saddam Hussein and WMDs, and a reconstruction of how various episodes in this tale occurred, see my book *Hoodwinked: The Documents That Reveal How Bush Sold Us a War* (New York: The New Press, 2004). This is more succinct than the seven volumes of official reports put out by the Senate intelligence committee on this subject.

um ore from Niger in Africa. The White House attempted to smear Langley with responsibility for this charge, enunciated in Bush's 2003 state of the union address. The CIA had already objected to the deceit in the draft of another speech, and it had succeeded in removing the language, only now to see it reappear in one even more important. But Langley had permitted the claim in a joint critique it made with the State Department. Evidence in the summer of 2003 showed that officials had ignored the falsity of this story. For the speech, the White House sourced it to the British.

The mess started a war between Langley and the White House. Director Tenet reluctantly issued an official CIA statement accepting responsibility. The statement went through seventeen drafts, coordinated among a CIA official traveling in Australia, George Tenet, giving a speech in Idaho, and senior White House officials, traveling with President Bush in Africa. Partway through the exercise, Vice President Cheney's office blew the cover of a CIA clandestine service officer, Valerie Plame, in an effort to discredit her husband, a critic of the Niger misinformation, who had gone on a fact-finding mission to Niger, based on recommendations from Plame's office, and found nothing.

Tenet ended up in Sawtooth City, Idaho, looking for a phone. His cell phones had no connectivity. The CIA director needed to know what was happening with the release of Langley's statement on the "sixteen words." He consumed a milkshake and fries as four people ahead of him used the single pay phone at the Smiley Creek Lodge. Things only got worse. Within a week, the CIA was fielding White House demands for selective declassification of language from the NIE and other reports that supported its version of the Niger story. On July 18 a "senior official"—no doubt presidential chief of staff Andrew Card—gave a press conference where he retailed the White House version and released the Key Judgments section of the NIE with its language on Niger uranium ore. Days later, having found copies of CIA memoranda dating from as early as October 2002, the Bush administration had to admit its carelessness.

The "sixteen words" destroyed George Tenet's standing at the White House. That September the president asked him to stay on, and he did, for the better part of a year. But in the spring of 2004, Bob Woodward's book *Plan of Attack* was published, recounting the run-up to the Iraq War.

Tenet could see that he and Langley were being scapegoated. At the Jersey shore over Memorial Day weekend, Tenet ran into a friend at the grocery store. Former FBI chief Louis Freeh gave George advice on how to cut free. On June 2, 2004, Tenet sat down with President Bush and chief of staff Card and declared he would be leaving. Afterward, George and his wife, Stephanie, sat at an obelisk behind the White House, watching the sun set. He set a departure date in July so as to leave Langley exactly seven years after arriving.

The intelligence embarrassment on Iraq convinced George Tenet that his time had come to leave, but it was the war on terror that left him in potential criminal jeopardy. Back on the Al Qaeda front, after 9/11 that war became generalized. Langley mobilized allies around the globe to sweep presumptive enemies off the street. Presently a framework to deal with captives became necessary. Director Tenet's operators created the whole black-site structure and the torture program described in the prologue. The psychologist ghosts, whose actions cast such a pall, were hired on George Tenet's watch, for a project he instigated. And the director would be nothing if not sensitive about it. Tenet returned to Georgetown University in February 2004 to give a speech enumerating CIA achievements, extolling its efforts against terrorism, its success at sweeping no fewer than 2,500 terrorist suspects off the streets throughout the world. Weeks later, in two appearances before the 9/11 Commission, Tenet took great pains to praise the agency's progress.

Behind the scenes, the cup had already run over. Agency officers had begun torturing internees almost as soon as they had them. Langley solicited flawed legal papers and used them to justify torture. The CIA videotaped the proceedings. The agency's contract psychologists had already begun practicing their dark arts. The FBI, horrified, had already pulled out of joint interrogations. Agency lawyers had gone to Guantánamo Bay and bragged about their "effective" techniques. Prisoners had died in CIA hands.

In January 2003, Director Tenet promulgated formal orders to govern CIA prisons, interrogation methods, and medical actions. Again he intended to set restraints, but the implication is that problems with Project Greystone were already apparent. Then there is Tenet's seeking reconfirmation of President Bush's approval and his suspension of Greystone in the spring of 2004. Both times the real issue had to be the CIA's jeopardy.

United States law and treaty law both make criminal the behaviors that occurred here. An international legal doctrine exists under which subordinates are not excused for these actions by virtue of orders from superiors. The CIA's own official interrogation manual states that this sort of strong-arm approach is ineffective, and that view is also articulated in the field manuals of the U.S. Army and Marine Corps and an official study by the Defense Science Board.

Langley's response came on multiple levels, first insisting that its actions were not torture. The so-called legal memoranda the CIA solicited were based on false representations of what the psychologist interrogators were actually doing. Langley's inspector general (IG) had already initiated several inquiries into activities in the detainee project. The most comprehensive wended its way toward completion just as Mr. Tenet wrestled with his future. A draft report circulated for comment from senior agency officials. The agency's director for operations, Jim Pavitt, responded on February 27, 2004. Pavitt admonished the IG for not crediting operators sufficiently. He forwarded a seven-page summary of claims in different cases, under a cover memo that asserted, "I would make it clear as well that the EITs (including the waterboard) have been indispensable to our successes," adding that the IG's review should not "shy away from the conclusion that our efforts have thwarted attacks and saved lives."

The assertedly neutral, nonpolitical Publications Review Board that was supposed to ignore personal proclivities became a hotbed of manipulation. Enjoined to weigh only national security, restricted from using classification to shield malfeasance, wrongdoing, or criminal activity (under both its own regulations and the executive order governing secrecy), the PRB threw away the rules. National security became the shield for criminality. Views that the interrogation methods were not legal or not effective were not welcome. More than that, PRB secret mongers *reached outside the agency* to demand a right to approve manuscripts by non-CIA authors. A year after Tenet had left, Michael Scheuer, the former Alec Station chief, by then also in retirement, said about the PRB's attitude, "I think it is going to be very difficult to publish a book on anything except cooking or Civil War history."

Agency officers became obstacles as well to general moves to declassify government records.

Langley had never had an especially good record here, but after 9/11 the agency descended to new depths. Innocuous information was deemed highly classified. Information already released was *re*classified. Agency officials substituted different documents for ones whose declassification had been requested and even stooped to "releasing" records they had *already declassified* in answer to legitimate freedom of information requests. CIA historical reviews and conferences ground to a halt, then resumed only slowly. Agency officials continued to obstruct publication of the official record volumes of *Foreign Relations of the United States* because of concern over CIA embarrassment. Langley effectively falsified its own historical record, both on general matters and specifically on its torture programs.

Here is one more thing Director Tenet said at his confirmation hearing: "Lying is not something that I will ever tolerate." If a person lies, he declared, "that means they're out." Again, "There's no room for anybody that lies at the Central Intelligence Agency."

The tragedy of George Tenet is that the demands of world events and the pressures of zealots to whom he owed responsibility drove him to take the CIA beyond the pale and then betray principles in defending improper actions. The conflict between desire to proclaim the CIA's achievements and the will to deny its horrible acts is what drove Tenet's disquiet.

Somewhere George J. Tenet morphed from spy hero to ghost of Langley. He knew it, too. When Mr. Tenet published his memoir in the spring of 2007, the CBS Television show *60 Minutes* hosted him for an interview. One question concerned whether the CIA had tortured detainees in its secret prisons, the existence of which had been revealed a year earlier. Tenet's denial was strident. He displayed that vehemence again in the 2015 film *The Spymasters: CIA in the Crosshairs*, wherein filmmakers interviewed Tenet at length. Instead of reflections, viewers saw the man attacking those who objected to torture. The exorcist not only failed; the ghosts turned him into one of them. In this persona, Tenet became doubly menacing.

All this had been prefigured in a way by a predecessor, William E. Colby. During the Vietnam War, Mr. Colby had been sent to Saigon to take charge of U.S. pacification efforts, which included something called the Phoenix Program. Intended to combat the insurgents' network of political control and guerrilla bands, Phoenix had involved interrogation centers and torture, target lists, and goals for "neutralizations." The goals lent themselves to manipulation, corruption, and excess. On several occasions, Colby issued directives or otherwise intervened to sharpen the regulatory framework. Of course, what impressed the public—and dogged Colby for the rest of his life—was Phoenix as a torture and murder operation. Mr. Colby's ghost stalks Langley for other reasons too, but the warning here is of peril, the danger of not listening to the ghosts. George Tenet's dreams were destroyed by the war on terror. Like Colby's, his ghost teaches that charges of abuse live forever and negate all good works.

9

JACOB MARLEY'S GHOSTS

In Dickens's *A Christmas Carol*, Jacob Marley's spirit appears to Ebenezer Scrooge in a late-night vision and tells him that he will come to perdition unless he gives up his greed, selfishness, and arrogance.

Marley warns that ghosts will visit Scrooge, who will end as a chained, tormented ghost himself if he doesn't heed the message. The past was childhood and that spirit was pleasant. The present is starker. For Langley, as for Scrooge, the ghosts change with the era. Of late, for Langley, there is even competition for ghost of the present. It seems appropriate to let both have their say. It sharpens our sense of how far the Central Intelligence Agency has migrated from its youthful ideals. This is a dark picture of a dark period, only slightly ameliorated by such CIA triumphs as the initial campaign in Afghanistan, which drove out the Taliban leadership in just a few months in 2001–2002; the shutdown of the nuclear-smuggling A. Q. Khan network; or, in 2004, the Libyan divestment of its entire nuclear weapons program. Had the story stopped there, the CIA would have looked good. As it is, there is a major problem.

THE CIA DOES NOT DO TORTURE

Porter Goss makes a good spirit to start with. When George Tenet tired of the Bush people using the CIA as punching bag for their incredible stupidities in invading Iraq, Goss followed him at Langley. Goss had assisted in that—he *was* the overseer at the time, chairman of the House Permanent Select Committee on Intelligence (HPSCI), and the Florida congressman made sure HPSCI failed in its oversight role by refusing to do any serious postmortem on the intelligence failures and the way intelligence was corrupted to support the Iraq invasion.

For the CIA, this was a time of transition, with the United States just creating a new supernumerary position, the director of national intelligence, to assume the task of boss over all U.S. intelligence. Goss became the last director of central intelligence, the job title of the official who headed both the CIA *and* the intelligence community as a whole. For six months, Porter Goss served as DCI, then for a little over a year as a diminished director of the Central Intelligence Agency alone. He had actually studied ancient Greek as an undergraduate at Yale. His time at Langley, appropriately, added up to tragedy.

The moment would be as turbulent as it was transitional. At his nomination hearing, fellow Florida politician Senator Bill Nelson declared that intelligence reform had become urgent and that Porter J. Goss could do it. The nominee himself estimated that rebuilding agency capabilities could take more than five years. Terrorism continued to be the most urgent task, good intelligence crucial; the agency must increase its take from spies, do better analysis, and protect and reinvigorate the machine spies. "You have my word," Goss promised when asked whether he and the CIA would cooperate in oversight inquiries into the interrogation programs.

From September 2004, when Goss took over the CIA, until July 2006, when he left, Porter J. Goss on his own *never* briefed Congress on interrogations—not the Gang of Four, not the Gang of Eight, no one—according to an official CIA chronology of agency congressional briefings released five years later. Lesser officials handled all contacts—except where Vice President Cheney entered the lists to overawe doubters—and *then* Goss might accompany him. In 2015 Director Goss contributed a piece to the *Rebuttal* compendium that former CIA persons put out to parry the Senate committee's report. There he claimed, "I briefed both the HPSCI and the SSCI . . . in 2004 and 2005. . . . Defenders of the SSCI Democrats might argue that the briefings were not in sufficient detail or that not every Committee Member was included." The deception is subtle and deplorable. The facts are as noted in Langley's official record.

In March 2005, a couple of weeks after President George W. Bush visited to laud CIA employees' dedication, the *New York Times* published a major exposé on agency torture. Jennifer Millerwise, a spokeswoman Goss had hired from the 2004 Bush-Cheney presidential campaign, countered, "The truth is exactly what Director Goss said it was: 'We don't do torture.'" At the time there was a CIA contract officer, David Passaro, on his way to trial for the death under interrogation of a detainee. Those things seemed antithetical. Naturally Congress wanted to know more. No briefing. In mid-April, after a generic counterterror update, the Senate intelligence committee sent Langley questions for the record. Goss's CIA waited two months before replying and then kept its silence on the worst "enhanced interrogation techniques."

Goss and the CIA often found themselves in reactive mode. The *New York Times* story triggered a debate within the agency about going public. Before long there were even talking points. But officials remained reluctant to speak openly, wanting to attribute comments to the proverbial unnamed source. Langley itself takes the position that only official acknowledgment ends secrecy, so that would have accomplished nothing. Nevertheless, the CIA spin doctors put together a four-page scenario for how to "roll out" the interrogations.

The CTC and the gunslingers all got into the act. On April 25, a CTC lawyer, aware that Goss wanted to defend Greystone in public, commented, "We need to have the 7th Floor confront the inconsistency in filing a [secrecy] declaration" in the case of David Passaro, and at the same time planning to reveal darn near the entire program. He finished acidly: "These goals are not obviously compatible."

Director Goss talked to the press, not Congress. Goss claimed neutrality in the congressional debate over John McCain's 2005 bill to ban cruel, inhuman, or degrading treatment of detainees, and to restrict interrogators to methods detailed in official U.S. Army field manuals. The spy chief commissioned a "blue ribbon panel" review of interrogation methods that reported to him that September. Results were divided. Some opined that there were no external standards for comparison and no objective way to measure efficiency, plus, due to secrecy, no way to compare Greystone with any other program. Others maintained that both DO operatives and DI analysts agreed they were getting more than half their information about Al Qaeda from hostile interrogation.

Mr. Goss spoke of misinformation deluding the public, refused to describe CIA methods, but repeated his mantra, "This agency does not do torture. Torture does not work. We use lawful capabilities to collect vital information, and we do it in a variety of unique and innovative ways." Goss wrote in the *Rebuttal* compendium, "Successfully fighting . . . brutal radicals will require capturing, holding, and questioning the enemy." His rejoinder—that if opponents (Goss mentions Senator Feinstein) had a better plan, they had not revealed it—both suggests that Goss really *is* talking about torture and implies that, so far as he is concerned, anything goes. Equally to the point, the logic of this argument is that criminal acts are the norm and that the burden for change should be on opponents of torture, not its perpetrators. That is certainly false.

Senator Thad Cochrane commented that he never learned what waterboarding really was until, a couple of days before the *Washington Post* blew the lid off black prisons, Dick Cheney attended a Republican congressional breakfast and presided over a briefing. At that point, of course, CIA and White House efforts to get the newspaper to quash Dana Priest's story had failed. Cheney knew what portended. In his later rebuttal to the Senate torture report, Mr. Goss *admitted*, "It is true that specific sources and methods were not generally spelled out in most CIA briefings on the Hill and that extra-sensitive intelligence was limited to the 'Gang of Eight,' the senior leadership." The same CIA briefing record referred to above discloses that, until the Bush administration found itself in the political fight against McCain's legislation, *only* members of the senior leadership were briefed at all.

Then came the Goss purge. Perhaps it began with Mary O. McCarthy. McCarthy had the reputation of a solid analyst who played by the rules. An Africa specialist, she had risen steadily, serving as national intelligence officer for warning and on the NSC's intelligence staff, where she handled the White House end of congressional notifications. McCarthy had been the one who tried to save President Clinton from ordering cruise missiles to attack an innocent Sudanese chemical plant. Later she took a sabbatical and attended law school, only to return to Langley in 2004 as deputy inspector general. In June 2005, she was startled to hear a senior agency official repeatedly insist that the CIA did not violate the international convention on torture or seek to do so. Of course, Helgerson's office had probed this very question and reported critically shortly before Porter Goss ascended to director. There existed a possibility that the oversight committees, not to mention the IG, would never get to the bottom of the story.

McCarthy became a target of the CIA's leak investigation after the *Washington Post* revelations. She had, in fact, spoken to *Post* correspondent Dana Priest, but it's impossible to know what role, if any, the CIA person had in the story. A wide range of associates agree that McCarthy had always been extremely scrupulous in her handling of classified information. Porter Goss fired McCarthy, a senior officer, in April 2006, ten days before she became eligible to retire.

The punitive nature of the top floor's treatment of McCarthy itself says something about the CIA and torture. It contrasts with Goss's failure to take *any* action on Jose Rodriguez, who put the agency in deep jeopardy by conspiring to destroy the torture tapes immediately after the *Washington Post* disclosure. An agency officer working for legality experienced censure while a bull-headed spy walked away.

Goss took charge of a CIA pushing hard on detainee interrogation, with Jose Rodriguez sending CTC snatch teams around the world. By the time Goss left, the spies would be destroying evidence. Along the way, the roadster careened from one disaster to another. With rhetoric going in that promised to unleash the agency for more vigorous operations, break the CIA out of risk aversion, and make it more effective, Director Goss accomplished the reverse.

That was a good trick even for an experienced spook. Porter Goss, a veteran agency operations officer, had spent a dozen years in the DO—in Miami with JM/Wave, on the covert action staff, spanning the Cord Meyer years of the *Ramparts* imbroglio, finishing in London. Both Goss and Jose Rodriguez had served in the Dominican Republic, and their friendship kept the heat down on the seventh floor when Rodriguez conspired against evidence.

His CIA career ended by a medical event in London, Goss retired to Sanibel Island, off Fort Myers in Florida, where he found a network of former spooks and grounded sailors and airmen. On top of his experience in the trade, Porter Goss learned politics, starting with that circle to make a second career at age thirty-four. He worked his way up through city council, mayor, five years on the Lee County Commission, then as Republican member of the House of Representatives from 1989 onward. All those skills finally came to nothing.

Porter Goss came to Langley with his own crew of aides, rousing more ire than anyone since Stansfield Turner appeared with his alleged Navy Mafia. An actual purge followed. Goss's henchmen looked at files, sized up officers, and made demands. Heads rolled.

The most notorious of these belonged to one of the CIA's top women, Mary Margaret Graham. When she took the clandestine operations course at the Farm in 1979, there were only five other women there, and as was typical, after two years, only a pair were left. Graham went on to great things, including the National Intelligence Medal in 1996 and the Donovan Award in 2001, when she headed the CIA station in New York. Graham had compiled the CIA's operations budget, and had been a senior counterintelligence officer. She crossed swords over Kyle D. Foggo, whom Goss had discovered on a cruise, as a logistics chief at the CIA base at

Frankfurt, Germany. Goss wanted to catapult Foggo up to the agency's number-three position, executive director. Graham and Jeanette Moore, chief of the Office of Security, looked at Foggo's file and found complaints. "Dusty" Foggo apparently had a reputation as a hard-drinking woman-izer. They took the issue to Goss aide Patrick Murray in November 2004. Murray, one of the "Gosslings" from HPSCI, upbraided the women for raising this issue and threatened them if there were any leak.

Graham went to the associate chief of the DO, Michael Sulick, and related Murray's over-the-top response. Sulick cautioned Murray against such treatment of employees. At that point, chief of staff Murray escalated, demanding of DDO Stephen Kappes that Sulick be fired. At a meeting with Director Goss in mid-November, the boss took his Gossling's side. Both Kappes and Sulick resigned. That was how Jose Rodriguez got his pro-motion to head the DO, replacing Kappes. Rodriguez handpicked Robert Richer as his associate, the kind of fellow you want with you in a foxhole, as Jose saw it. Fleeing Langley and Goss, with the brass, were thirty to for-ty top officers, including more than a dozen division chiefs, station chiefs, or department heads. Mary Graham became one; she joined the Office of the Director of National Intelligence.

As for Dusty Foggo, he turned out worse than advertised, leaving under a cloud in 2006, later convicted of fraud, conspiracy, and money laundering.

Director Goss ended the daily five p.m. threat-matrix sessions that George Tenet had used to tweak CIA strategy. Goss wanted only private briefings, a few times a week. That worked for him, but it missed the point. The threat-matrix huddles had become the main tool for senior officials to calibrate their efforts. Goss also objected to the ceremonial roles of a CIA director, disparaging the speeches and talks the spy chieftain typically makes.

The more Porter Goss cut back, the less feel folk had. Director Goss notoriously circulated a round-robin message to chiefs of station that, when planning for intelligence chiefs in their countries to visit the United States, meetings with the CIA director should be set for Tuesdays or Thursdays. The spy chieftain seemed unavailable. Agency programs floundered too.

Sidestepping Langley's constant rhetoric as to how well it was doing, and without saying the CIA had been broken, Goss had told Congress five years would be necessary to reanimate it. So clandestine chief Rodriguez began work on a five-year plan to double the size of the clandestine ser-vice. His associate Robert Richer headed the working group and labored on the details with the barons for months. At the end, CIA gathered its

station chiefs from around the world at headquarters for the firs
They conferred in the "Bubble." Rob Richer did not last long p
work on the strategic plan. A year into Goss's reign, the DO's principal
associate director, Richer, left too—with a blast at Goss delivered to a
Senate hearing.

The man from Sanibel had a certain hapless quality. On a European
cruise during which he visited Slovakia, Goss arranged for a meeting at
an organic farm because he was a big fan of natural food and wanted
to see how the Slovaks did organics. That raised eyebrows. More serious
would be the director's blurting out to the press, in the summer of 2005,
that he "knew" where Osama bin Laden was hiding out, but diplomatic
niceties prevented him from doing anything about it. In fact, agency operative Michael Morell records that Goss was so worried about one of the
Pakistani border regions, he ordered spooks to flood the zone. It became
the largest surge of CIA resources since September 11. This time the raised
eyebrows were at the White House, where officials were trying to keep a
positive spin on U.S.-Pakistani relations.

In Italy, on Goss's watch, the authorities issued arrest warrants for CIA
participants in the kidnapping of Abu Omar.

Representative Jane Harman, ranking member on the HPSCI when
Goss had been chairman, made her own Middle East cruise about a year
after her colleague moved to Langley. At a major CIA station, she asked
for a show of hands on who understood where Goss was taking the agency.
Almost no hands went up. Around this time Director Goss approved seeking a warrant extension of the bugs on an individual, reportedly an Israeli,
on whose phone Harman had been overheard. Though counterintelligence
framed the excuse, the action inevitably had its chilling aspect, especially
where Mr. Goss, at HPSCI, had torpedoed any investigation of the hugely
controversial intelligence purporting to justify George Bush's invasion of
Iraq. Harman had been a major proponent of that inquiry.

In June 2005 came the report of a presidential commission that had
studied U.S. intelligence on weapons of mass destruction. Goss flaccidly
announced that "at CIA, we are improving how we do our business," and
attributed the serious errors CIA had made on Iraqi weapons to agency
budget cuts from the 1990s. That fall, after digesting the investigative
report of the public-private commission that had investigated the failures
of 9/11, Inspector General John Helgerson released the IG's own review
focused specifically on agency accountability. Director Goss maintained
that the review unveiled no mysteries: "After great consideration of this

report and its conclusions, I will not convene an accountability board to judge the performance of any individual CIA officers."

Meanwhile Director Goss, who had spoken of new CIA stations in Latin America and of unleashing the agency, presided over an evaporation of recruiting. The President's Foreign Intelligence Advisory Board questioned the recruiting drought and blamed the decline on morale at Langley. Goss's witch hunt after the CIA black prisons leak, which involved a rare speech, an op-ed article in the *New York Times*, plus the firing of Mary McCarthy, did little to improve morale. Director Goss did not long survive the debacle. Barely a month later, he appeared at the White House with President George W. Bush to announce his departure. With typical Gossian aplomb, he spoke of record numbers of new agency employees, better training than ever, and Langley's "field forward" approach.

Under Porter J. Goss, the Central Intelligence Agency experienced its latest instance of a director hiring a crook to a top post (the jury remains out on Bill Casey's enthusiasm for Max Hugel), saw the director sanction obstruction of justice by a subordinate while firing an officer who objected to CIA prevarication, and witnessed the director deliberately refusing to apply accountability processes for officers involved in the greatest intelligence disaster of the age. Agents feared the director as he purged those who disagreed, worried as the duping of Congress continued, and shivered as Italian authorities issued criminal indictments for CIA officers. There is much to ponder in the ghost of Porter J. Goss. In Freud's disquisitions on the uncanny, he postulates the evil eye as one of the most recurrent superstitions.

THE CIA DOES NOT DESTROY TORTURE TAPES

Marching alongside the director was his gunslinger John A. Rizzo. John had been at Langley the morning of September 11, 2001, and like so many Americans he watched on TV as the horrors unfolded. Director Tenet and a few key officials, including his boss, general counsel Robert N. McNamara Jr., went to the printing plant, out by the perimeter fence and likely to escape destruction if a plane came at the CIA. The evacuation order created bedlam, so Rizzo decided to stay where he was, in the OGC office on the seventh floor of the old headquarters building. Anticipating that President Bush would demand a full-scale assault on Al Qaeda networks and that investigations would probe preattack intelligence failures, lawyer

Rizzo began listing possible covert actions. Later they could be compared with directives on the books to see what was permitted. His list included "capture, detain, and question." Following the day of carnage, Bob McNamara took Rizzo's list and collaborated with NSC officials to craft a presidential finding in less than a week. President Bush approved it the day he saw it.

As CIA officers knew it would, after the horror, Congress rallied to the flag. When the oversight committees were handed copies of the finding, on September 18, the day after Bush signed it, overseers asked if the agency needed more. John Rizzo described the finding: "Multiple pages in length, it was the most comprehensive, most ambitious, most aggressive, and most risky Finding I was ever involved in. One short paragraph authorized the capture and detention of Al Qaeda terrorists, another authorized taking lethal action against them."

Langley hustled, generating a heap of business for the gunslingers, furnishing legal advice on international security sweeps the CIA developed in concert with friends across the globe, negotiating details of arrangements with foreign spy services, and handling domestic aspects of CIA operations. For some time, Bob McNamara had been planning to depart, and in October 2001 he did. That left Rizzo the acting general counsel of the Central Intelligence Agency.

It would be an amazing time. The operational tempo—no matter what Tenet's successors claim—grew, peaked, and remained at that high level for months, all while parallel operations aimed at nuclear technology smugglers and the Libyan program. Acting counsel Rizzo found himself in uncharted waters, from skull sessions in the director's office puzzling over the choice of mystery ships versus deserted islands for black prisons to advising the CTC on permissible techniques.

Attorney Rizzo will aver that the CIA used interrogation methods approved by the Department of Justice (DOJ). Agency officers, particularly those at CTC, will agree. The senior people who banded together to rebut the Senate torture report will intone that its conclusions that the CIA resorted to unapproved techniques or that agency methods were harsher than it told Justice are wrong. That debate may never be resolved. But three things are beyond dispute. The CIA's enhanced interrogations began on April 13, 2002, whereas no DOJ legal memoranda existed until August. The agency's psychologists "Dunbar" and "Swigert" began plying their trade before the legal memos existed. And Langley *solicited* the Justice memos *and* supplied lists of methods it wanted approved. When

CTC first went to the general counsel for approval, John Rizzo, by his own account, volunteered to take the list to DOJ. Another way to put that is that Rizzo did not want his fingerprints on the decision. All of that was squarely within OGC's purview.

Imagine Mr. Rizzo's upset when, in 2003 and repeatedly thereafter, the crucial Justice Department memos were invalidated and withdrawn. The periodic fights to obtain new versions of the supposed justification became a theme over the remainder of Rizzo's agency career. There is another matter on which his advice remains shrouded. The security sweeps going on around the world got agency help. Some were unilateral. In numerous cases that involved aircraft and action teams, landing in foreign countries to take custody of people, conveying them to other places, sometimes CIA black prisons, sometimes elsewhere. How did the gunslinger advise? The Abu Omar kidnapping in Italy is a case in point. Some nations were cooperative and witting, the record on others remains obscure. Every one of those "renditions" meant dealing in some way with international and national laws on use of airspace, plus national laws on border control, customs and immigration, extradition, the carrying and use of firearms, and much more.

Until October 2002, when Scott Muller became counsel, Mr. Rizzo's voice dominated. The change relieved John Rizzo of the burden of answering all the late-night emergency phone calls, but there were still multiple headaches. Muller arrived just in time for the Bush administration's invasion of Iraq, which involved a manipulation of intelligence reporting and a White House attempt to cast the CIA as driving the issue, but the war in Iraq revealed the supposed threat as phony. Muller fancied himself a crisis manager, but Langley had ensnared itself in a host of unmanageable crises.

When Richard Cheney's aides blew the cover of clandestine service officer Valerie Plame in a gambit to discredit a critic of the Iraq deception, Langley swam in a poisonous fountain. Attorney Rizzo sent the obligatory notice to the Justice Department, but he saw the leak as minor, couldn't remember ever meeting Plame, and figured the likelihood of a Justice investigation minimal. That affair led to the criminal prosecution of I. Lewis "Scooter" Libby, the vice president's chief of staff. Cheney was the CIA's biggest White House customer. Then in the spring of 2004, the revelation of photographs of how military interrogators at Abu Ghraib in Iraq had mistreated detainees resulted in a public outcry, multiple new investigations, and charges that the CIA used similar tactics. The story was getting uncomfortably close. John Rizzo foresaw a "drip by drip" slow-motion disclosure of the truth.

Scott Muller had been on a cruise to the black sites, and Langley flung him into the soup with White House aides over the interrogations. Langley's inspector general weighed in with his own investigations at just this point. Muller, who had clerked for the Watergate special prosecutor's task force back in the day, had had a bellyful. Abu Ghraib became the last straw. One day in July, he told John Rizzo he was resigning, that day. Less than a week later, George Tenet resigned too. Stunning. When Porter Goss arrived, John Rizzo was the CIA's acting general counsel again. From his top-floor perch, the attorney watched the broad Potomac, where the distance to the White House daily seemed longer, and Capitol Hill, where congressional anger seemed hotter every day.

The most furious man at Langley when Jose Rodriguez had the torture tapes destroyed was not Director Goss but gunslinger Rizzo. Not only had the CIA's lawyer had to track each White House order to preserve the material; he'd had to listen to Congress say the same thing. Plus, the General Counsel's Office had certified to courts that the CIA had not destroyed evidence, which the tapes were. Plus again, Rizzo understood how Jose had gamed the system, collaring lesser lawyers on assignment to the Counterterrorism Center, people beholden to the National Clandestine Service (DO), less to the general counsel.

Rodriguez knew what Rizzo would have told him. At a meeting with Goss, the counsel had pointed out that the clandestine service chief really wanted a final determination on the tapes. Rodriguez heard Goss reiterate the advice he had given when still on the Hill—preserve the tapes at the station where the black site had been. But Goss failed to *order* that they be kept. Rizzo would have repeated Goss's advice and reminded Rodriguez of White House instructions that it be consulted prior to any action. The CIA operative needed to avoid that conversation.

Instead, through his chief of staff, Rodriguez asked CTC lawyers Robert Eatinger and Stephen Hermes if he had the authority to order the tapes' destruction by himself.

Mr. Rizzo argues that Rodriguez and others who sought destruction on security grounds were sincere and deserved a full hearing. On that basis, he permitted Eatinger and Hermes to answer the narrow question. They kept away from the weightier matter of legal constraints—more than twenty court orders were in effect requiring the CIA to preserve evidence in various cases, and neither the CTC lawyers nor Rodriguez had the authority to determine whether the tapes constituted evidence. Absent such a ruling, any action regarding tapes in potential evidence ought to have been prohibited.

Rizzo concedes he had been naïve. "I have often wondered," he writes, "whether I should have gone to Jose at that point and told him, 'Forget it, Jose. No one is ever going to agree to destruction.' I came to conclude that telling him that wouldn't have made any difference."

The action format offered one last opportunity to prevent the destruction. Jose Rodriguez no longer led the CTC. Its chief, Robert Grenier, would approve the cable too. Along with Jose's staff chief, lawyers Eatinger and Hermes drafted language so the Bangkok Station chief would frame the question just right. Grenier had a more evolved sensibility—one reason for his difficulties with Rodriguez—and he had been wrestling for some time with increasing inertia in the detainee program. But perhaps *because* of his problems with Rodriguez, Grenier did not object. Sent on the back channel, the cable asked the station to dispatch a routine request on the front channel. On November 8, 2005, a front-channel cable from Langley, 081855Z Nov 2005, mentioned the Bangkok message and approved the request to destroy tapes "FOR THE REASONS CITED THEREIN."

Rodriguez's maneuver aimed to make it seem like the initiative for destroying the tapes came from elsewhere. Like Richard Helms and the Bay of Pigs or John Rizzo and legal advice on interrogation methods, Rodriguez wanted to leave no fingerprints on the op. Chief of staff Gina Haspel posed the key questions to CTC lawyers. She and the attorneys wrote the message. The Bangkok Station asked for the destruction. Rodriguez widened the circle further with Grenier and Rizzo, to whom he sent a copy of the dispatch—too late to stop it.

Describing this sequence of actions to Congress in the aftermath, the next CIA director, General Michael Hayden, maintained, "It was an agency decision—you can take it to the bank."

John Rizzo watched with horror as this kabuki play unfolded. In Bangkok a bonfire took place. Videotapes melted. The station reported successful destruction. The Bush administration for months had privately been noodling over what to do with the CIA detainees. Pieces of their story had been emerging; host countries were restive. That had been one reason the agency had had to keep changing prison locations. After the *Washington Post* revelation, there were more demands to get out. White House officials queried CTC's Grenier whether the CIA would go on using "enhanced interrogation." The agency man answered no. The CTC chief would not budge. The McCain bill passed, and President Bush signed it.

Porter Goss wanted to continue the hostile interrogation program. He had written a letter to that effect late in December and structured a Power-Point briefing to threaten that the CIA would stop the interrogations if it couldn't use "enhanced" methods. Secretary Condoleezza Rice called out Director Goss right there. It was almost his last appearance at the White House. The same frosty winds buffeted Bob Grenier. On February 3, Jose Rodriguez summoned Grenier to the top floor at Langley to fire him.

Jose Rodriguez enjoyed a soft landing after the destruction of the tapes, as did John Rizzo, who failed to enforce the various holds placed on them. By then, however, the OGC's plate had been heaped with another weighty matter, the drone war, in which the CIA and the U.S. military, in particular its Special Operations Command, were on the offensive, using armed unmanned aerial vehicles—UAVs, or drones—to fire at enemies on the ground. For reasons that will become apparent, John Rizzo stood at the center of the drone war, much as he occupied that position in the struggle over the detainees.

Drone technology had been coming for a long time. The CIA had used drones in conjunction with its SR-71 spy planes, and the U.S. military had had a variety of them. Traditionally these were a form of reconnaissance aircraft, programed to follow a given flight path and to take pictures to be processed. Three things made the old-fashioned UAV into the modern drone. First, televised pictures relayed to the ground replaced still photography permitting real-time scouting. Second, the television sensors plus aircraft avionics, communications, and automation allowed a remote pilot to actually fly the aircraft. The UAV could then respond to situations, not simply follow a preplanned trajectory. The third element—missing until recently—would be remote-controlled weaponry for the warplane.

This kind of technology existed by the 1980s. The CIA first used it in Bosnia, where a small UAV called the Gnat, controlled from vans at local airfields, helped guide peacekeeping forces. The Gnat's ability to stay in the sky for long periods—twenty-four hours even—impressed Langley. A UAV called the Predator had already begun taking shape, made by California's General Atomics Corporation, designed by the Israeli inventor of the Gnat alongside American innovators. Predator was bigger, could carry more, and fly farther, higher, and longer. The craft could link through communications satellites for truly *remote* control from hundreds or thousands of miles away.

The agency experimented with Predators in the late 1990s, and the Air Force first made use of them in 1996. Some at Langley wanted in badly, and conceived of a mission nicknamed Afghan Eyes, in which a Predator detachment would be deployed to Pakistan and used to spy on Al Qaeda. A meeting in the director's conference room at Langley on Memorial Day of 2000 found the DDO plus George Tenet's deputy, Air Force General John A. Gordon, opposed to the idea. Briefed on it, Tenet also seemed resistant. But White House officials plus a cabal of CIA advocates kept pushing. Technologists had just perfected the remote links. Operatives arranged with Uzbekistan to base the Predators and controlled the mission from an American base in Germany. The CIA had a schedule of prayer times at Osama bin Laden's hideout and timed the Predator to orbit then. One noon in late September, the Predator pictured a tall robed man who had to be bin Laden. Langley was hooked.

Armament made the Predator UAV into the drone. The CIA and Air Force fought over who would fund this, with Langley pleading it had no money. In June 2000 higher authority ordered each to put up around $2 million for arming the UAV. The cost could be so low because a suitable weapon already existed—the AGM-114 Hellfire missile—originally created as a self-guided weapon to destroy enemy tanks. The only things required were to hang the missiles on the aircraft and install systems to transfer target information to the pilot and launch the missile. Experiments with the prototype drone took place at China Lake, in the Mojave Desert, long a U.S. weapons test center. By August 2001, Predator stood ready. Lieutenant General John "Soup" Campbell, another Air Force fellow detached to the agency, held political-military exercises centered on how to use the armed Predators.

By the summer of 2001, the CIA had begun asking for presidential approval to fly the weaponized Predator. Conversations were desultory. Director Tenet wavered, at times favoring an agency attack role, elsewhere pronouncing it a terrible idea. In fact, Tenet's last meeting with the NSC Principals Committee prior to 9/11 centered on this very subject. Bush's presidential finding after 9/11 suddenly incorporated "lethal" mission authority. That meant drone strikes. The CIA speedily got Pakistani agreement to a Predator detachment close to the Afghan target.

The legal headaches brought John Rizzo into this action. Flying scout missions from Uzbekistan, controlled from Germany, was one thing. A lethal mission flown from anywhere required German approval. Director Tenet broached many matters at his five p.m. threat-matrix staff sessions, but the really secret issues went to conversations held afterward. During one of these Tenet told Rizzo that no one wanted a CIA attack program subject to German veto. Rizzo agreed. The alternative would be to reconfigure the communications and guidance protocols to control the drones from American soil. The technologists took care of that. They also modified the Hellfire missiles to make them more dependable and effective, and they developed a larger, even more capable drone, the Reaper.

Other concerns included the principle of the thing. Israel had been making targeted strikes against Palestinians. Just months before 9/11, the United States had protested these as extrajudicial killings. Now Langley proposed to do the same. The arguments over that thorny issue are still secret today. Who should pay for crashed Predators the agency borrowed from the Air Force? Tenet argued the Air Force. It thought the opposite. And there was the chain of command—who should press the button in a lethal drone strike? Tenet felt most comfortable with the military handling those aspects. Buzzy Krongard, his executive director, and Predator advocate Charlie Allen were both happy with the CIA taking the shot. Rizzo's advice is not recorded. The White House told Langley to go ahead but ordered SOCOM into action too. The resulting parallel drone campaigns from *both* the military *and* the agency set up twin operating mechanisms. So began the CIA's notorious drone strikes.

The missions were ramped up in parallel with the CIA's covert campaign to topple the Taliban and its protected ally Al Qaeda. One strike, which alert CIA teams managed to abort at the last moment, would have hit Americans themselves and their Afghan allies. A more successful attack took place in mid-November 2001. It killed Mohammed Atef, thought to have been Al Qaeda's top military commander, at his home outside Kabul. The first deliberately targeted strike took place on February 4, 2002. The target is thought to have been Osama bin Laden, who had escaped from pursuers at Tora Bora mountain a month earlier.

After that, the drone program assumed a certain routine. Porter Goss told one interviewer that President Bush had no need to waive or modify the prohibition on CIA assassinations that had been in effect since Gerald Ford's time, because "lethal force . . . is a concept most Americans are fairly comfortable with." As did associates, including lawyer Rizzo, Director Goss fudged the distinction between combat and drone strikes. He justified killing "where you're trying to bring well-known criminals to justice," and they have been properly identified, a capture attempt is made, and "the person resists and tries to take a shot at our law enforcement people." In the CIA and military drone attacks, the targets are often not well known (at times they are not known at all), no capture is attempted, and there is no enemy shooting back. Like the CIA detainee project, secret Justice Department legal memoranda underlay the drone attacks.

Once the first few strikes occurred, Bush's White House wanted to hear only about results. Top leaders sought to preserve deniability. CIA directors were more directly involved, and they might participate in targeting decisions when the quarry was a sufficiently bad guy—and in the early days most were. But the day-to-day marshaling of files, compilation of "cases," and maintenance of the hit list—and, yes, there *was* a list—fell to John Rizzo. There were thirty or so names on the list at any given time. Field commanders, CIA stations, or Washington would "nominate" targets and explain why. Rizzo would open a case file, summarizing the pros and cons in a memorandum to higher authority. At times the lawyer himself acted as that authority. "How many law professors have signed off on a death warrant?" Rizzo rhetorically asked a *Newsweek* magazine reporter, knowing that "one" (Barack Obama) was the correct answer (Rizzo had never been a law professor). "I was concerned it be done in the cleanest possible way." Counsel Rizzo often joined the command team when CIA drone attacks were under way.

The offer John Rizzo couldn't refuse came near the end of 2005. By then, the videotapes episode notwithstanding, the lawyer had become increasingly close to his CIA director, and Porter Goss offered to make Rizzo a candidate for general counsel. The gunslinger was now on his *third* stint as *acting* counsel. Each time, directors left him in place for months or years. John wanted the formal title that went with the job. In his memoir, Rizzo notes that his appointment could inspire the 120-odd agency attorneys to think that they, too, might rise to the top. No career CIA legal person had ever been general counsel. (One reason was the law—Section 20 of the Central Intelligence Agency Act of 1949 provides for an individual "appointed from civilian life by the President.") Bush went ahead to nominate John Rizzo.

Here Mr. Rizzo fell into the black hole of the increasingly hostile relations between the Bush administration and congressional overseers, who believed they were being scorned. For a CIA officer who had come on board in the wake of the Church Committee crisis and had witnessed the bloodletting of Iran-Contra, the situation had all the same portents. Indeed his nomination was held up. It would be nearly eighteen months, until June 19, 2007, when Rizzo had his nomination hearing. He decided to face the bull head on and spoke the lesson he'd learned from Iran-Contra, lasting and indelible: "CIA courts disaster whenever it loses sight of the absolute necessity to inform the intelligence committees on a timely basis [of] what they need to know." Langley's lawyer averred that his service in the terror war—mentioning the Greystone detentions but not the drones— had been the most challenging of his career. He said he expected to discuss everything in closed, executive session. The senators hammered him in the open, so badly that Rizzo recalls a "public flogging." Senator Sheldon Whitehouse (D-RI) pressed Rizzo on whether there were *other* DOJ opinions, besides the ones justifying interrogation techniques, being withheld from Congress. That came uncomfortably close to asking about justifications for targeted killing.

"There are no other opinions . . . that fall into that category," Rizzo announced.

Michigan Democrat Carl Levin, who had apparently crossed swords at a prehearing private meeting, continued to pursue Rizzo on torture. Senator Ron Wyden (D-OR) engaged him on his own expression of respect for oversight, and listened as the gunslinger blew smoke to claim that the Bush notification practices had been full and current. Wyden also broached the matter of whether a president has legal authority to direct the CIA to capture and detain United States citizens overseas, an allusion to the American mullah Anwar al-Awlaki, on the drone hit list. Rizzo squirmed until the committee chairman moved that exchange into closed session. Senator Wyden eventually blocked the Rizzo nomination, which the Bush administration finally withdrew.

Under President Bush, the Central Intelligence Agency carried out its first targeted killing inside Pakistan in 2004. It was the only attack in Pakistan that year, followed by three each in the next couple of years. But then the program ramped up, with five drone strikes in 2007 and thirty-eight during Bush's last year. There are discrepancies in the publicly available data for the Obama years, but by any measure President Obama hurled more drone strikes during 2009 than in all the Bush era. In Pakistan alone the total is about 52. The number peaked at 128 in 2010, before President Obama formulated a new command framework, with key choices regularly brought to the White House, a Pentagon process for the military drone missions, and a CIA procedure to govern flights.

Recently Obama radically reduced attacks in Pakistan, but the SOCOM attacks continue, and the CIA has widened its role in such other theaters as Yemen. In July 2016, the director of national intelligence (DNI) released a fact sheet disclosing that from Obama's inauguration through the end of 2015 there had been a total of 473 drone strikes, eliminating roughly 2,500 enemy combatants while causing no more than 64 to 116 civilian deaths. That figure conflicts with other tabulations of civilian casualties and is absurdly low.

In the summer of 2011, human rights advocates filed information reports to Pakistani authorities as a first step in seeking an international arrest warrant to prosecute John Rizzo in that country. In August 2015, Buzzy Krongard, who had been ready to push the button on CIA drone attacks, was caught—by the hapless Transportation Security Administration—attempting to board a flight at Baltimore-Washington International Airport with a loaded 9mm pistol in his carry-on bag. Naturally Mr. Krongard explained that he had inadvertently grabbed the wrong suitcase in his rush to get to the airport, but the larger question is why the former CIA official feels he needs to travel armed. There are ghosts here.

The spirit of Rizzo has much to teach. Langley's gunslingers in the early years complemented the operatives, of whom many were also lawyers. They had common understanding and purpose. More recently, with the lawyers as gunslingers, the levels of arrogance and disdain have risen, and the legal advice appears to have deteriorated. The drive to be relevant, to keep the director's esteem, seems to have carried the spirits into stormy seas. Rizzo's role in the torture memos, in the detainee program, in the consultants' contracts, in the CTC snatch missions, and in the drone program were in each case objectionable for a conscientious lawyer. Meanwhile, in keeping with our increasingly apparent trend, John Rizzo suffered no ill effects from these ventures. He kept his job. Mr. Rizzo didn't need the title. The man who followed Porter Goss continued to rely upon him.

THE SAME KIND OF DRILL

On September 11, 2001, General Michael V. Hayden had been the director of the National Security Agency (NSA) at Fort Meade for two and a half years. The crisis of that day began with Hayden groggy, headed in after staying up late to watch the Denver Broncos beat the New York Giants 31–10 in a Monday night football game marking a stadium opening. At first, everything routine, the NSA operations center had nothing to note. Mike Hayden took time to get a haircut. Once he was in his office, an executive assistant appeared, breathlessly reporting that an airplane had crashed into one of the World Trade Center towers in lower Manhattan. When the other tower got hit too, Hayden realized he needed to do something, a thought only confirmed when yet another airplane smashed into the Pentagon. In Washington, false reports of explosions at the State Department pumped up the fear. Director Hayden ordered security to evacuate the headquarters complex.

Not long afterward, George Tenet phoned from the CIA to ask what intelligence Hayden's people might have on unfolding events. There were a couple of items on the NSA's intercept logs, with vague mentions of coming events, but no context or detail.

Even that much Hayden owed to the people in his counterterror unit, and *that* would be the one element Director Hayden decided to keep on the job. They were not evacuated. Later that day, Hayden went upstairs to visit. The story that far is clear. After that it starts to fragment. The general first recounted it on October 17, 2002, at a session of the joint inquiry into the 9/11 attacks held by the oversight committees of Congress. Hayden described them as "hard at work, they were defiantly tacking up blackout curtains to mask their location." By early 2006, in a speech at the National Press Club, Hayden changed this to "seeing the NSA counterterrorism shop in tears while we were hanging up blackout curtains around their windows." In his 2016 memoir, it morphed to Hayden visiting the counterterror shop, walking from one workstation to another, gripping a shoulder here or there, while the analysts labored and "the maintenance staff was tacking up blackout curtains over the windows."

These discrepancies are minor but characteristic. The same October 2002 joint committee appearance marks the starting point for a more consequential obfuscation. Director Hayden noted that just three weeks earlier, the NSA had signed contracts for a $300 million project, Trailblazer, which was "our effort to revolutionize how we produce SIGINT in a digital age." Bringing the electronic spy agency into the twenty-first century certainly preoccupied him, but far from accomplishing the mission Trailblazer became a huge morass.

By 2006, in Hayden's Press Club speech, he was acutely aware of the project's failure. When a reporter asked about NSA whistleblowers—a question that did not mention Trailblazer but zeroed in on officials who had complained about it, initially through channels—Hayden's reply changed the subject. At his nomination hearing, for the Office of the Director of National Intelligence, he conceded "deltas" (technospeak, using the mathematical symbol for change, to suggest cost overruns without having to say so) of several hundred million dollars. The general went on to say,

"We've had pretty good success with the front-end in terms of collection," that Trailblazer aimed at helping sort through those masses of data, and that when the NSA asked industry "for something that no one had yet invented, they weren't any better at inventing it than we were doing it ourselves." *But,* in terms of engaging industry, Hayden remarked, "A personal view, now—looking back—we overachieved." The other thing he'd learned was how to preserve a degree of cooperation between agency and industry. And "we don't profit by trying to do moon shots."

Later that year, after he was nominated for CIA director, senators at Hayden's confirmation hearing probed him on this very statement. By then the press was reporting *billion-dollar* cost overruns on Trailblazer, and both the *New York Times* and *Baltimore Sun* had investigative reports exposing the program, one appearing that very day. "What my memory tells me I said," Hayden replied, "was that a lot of the failure on the Trailblazer program was that we were trying to overachieve. . . . I can't ever think of my saying we were overachieving in Trailblazer." In his memoir, Hayden says, "We were also trying to do too much, too quickly. Trailblazer comprised multiple moon shots." The former NSA boss goes on to describe the agency whistleblowers as purveyors of a competing technology, engaged in guerrilla warfare by making end runs to HPSCI staff. Hayden doesn't mention the degree to which government authorities persecuted the whistleblowers, accusing them of leaking classified information, some of that beginning right after Mr. Hayden's congressional hearing.

The National Security Agency's notorious Stellar Wind scandal over blanket electronic eavesdropping contains many more examples. Michael Hayden's attitude seems to have been that facts are malleable in the service of goals, enough so to warrant thinking of him as a fabulist. Again and again, in locales ranging from congressional inquiries to speeches to media appearances, Hayden referred to the NSA eavesdropping as subject to the most rigorous oversight imaginable. But—just like CIA prisons and torture—until its cover disintegrated, notice of the bugging would be restricted to the Gang of Eight. The "oversight" amounted to the NSA's IG and its lawyers. In the kind of sports analogy Hayden loved, all of it was "inside baseball." The lawyers, it turned out, *never even wrote* an opinion on the surveillance. NSA's director satisfied himself based on comments from Bush presidential attorney Alberto Gonzales, another of those flawed DOJ memos, and conversations with his own gunslingers. Hayden himself *did not read* the Justice Department paper. He answered a question at the

Press Club thus: "I have an order whose lawfulness has been attested to by NSA lawyers who do this for a living." Inside baseball.

In a veiled allusion to the vast dragnet already eavesdropping on Americans, in October 2002 with the 9/11 Joint Inquiry, the general spoke of a need to "find the right balance between protecting our security and protecting our liberty." At the Press Club speech: "It is not a driftnet over Dearborn or Lackawanna or Freemont." Oregon senator Ron Wyden challenged him at the May 18, 2006, confirmation hearing. Having admitted to NSA eavesdropping, Hayden had insisted on six separate occasions that this was limited to domestic-to-international calls. The former NSA chief defended himself, saying that in 2002 he had been trying to be careful, while in his 2006 appearance he had been saying the most he could without crossing into classified territory.

When her turn came, California Democrat Dianne Feinstein put a series of more significant questions to the general. Without doubt this strategy had been discussed among committee Democrats, in hopes Hayden might be more responsive to Feinstein, who had long cultivated the spooks. On rendition, the general didn't know. Length of detention? The prospective CIA director wanted to keep that question for secret session. Utility of interrogation? The same. Was waterboarding a professional interrogation technique? Closed session. Had the CIA obtained new guidance since passage of the McCain Act?—which Hayden insisted did not apply to Langley. Closed session. A discussion of the agency's IG investigation into extralegal interrogations? It should be held for the secret testimony. Iran? Closed session. More on how the CIA could *not* be bound by the law on torture? Hayden wanted the closed session.

The microphone, still live when the chairman gaveled this hearing to a close, recorded Dianne Feinstein's peeved remark to a colleague: "He didn't answer *any* of the questions!"

Later, when questioning resumed after lunch, Wisconsin's Russell Feingold asked General Hayden for a pledge to provide the committee with information on intelligence activities, including covert activities, previously restricted to the Gang of Eight. Feingold quoted the language, right out of the National Security Act, wherein the executive—including the CIA, NSA, and all the other agencies—were prohibited from withholding from Congress any information necessary for it to fulfill its oversight duties.

"I'm sorry," Michael Hayden replied. "I'm just not familiar with the requirements under the law for that." It was bravado—or defiance. The general closed the briefing book in front of him. In his memoir Hayden writes, "This was getting to be pointless bantering."

Senator Wyden summed up the perplexities in one question. "What's to say that, if you're confirmed to head the CIA, we won't go through exactly this kind of drill with you over there?"

Ron Wyden posed the right question. General Hayden shot back that the senators were simply going to have to make a judgment on his character. And they did. The Hayden nomination passed out of committee. The full Senate confirmed him on a vote of 79 against 15. The general got a copy of the roll-call list, had it framed, and hung it on his wall. Mr. Hayden titles his memoir *Playing to the Edge*, a football metaphor referring to a strategy of aggression, where players employ tactics to the very point referees might call foul, hoping for every advantage. His time at Langley would be just like that.

Director Hayden initially concerned himself with ramping up CIA operations. Porter Goss had begun this. Hayden's reforms were essentially the same. He cut to four years the time envisioned to carry them out, but a little over a year had passed since Goss, his friend, had unveiled the program. Drone strikes held steady for a time but doubled in Hayden's second year, and increased exponentially after that. He sought to maintain the "operations tempo" and constantly exhorted CIA employees to keep up the pace. The general brought back Stephen Kappes, purged earlier, as his deputy director over the entire agency. The Gosslings were drummed out. Even the historians were to be put to work furthering operational objectives—the Center for the Study of Intelligence was tasked for "lessons learned" reports.

One of Director Hayden's first cruises took him to Iraq, Afghanistan, and Pakistan with Jose Rodriguez. Each country posed headaches that kept the spy chieftain occupied. The Shiite prime minister of Iraq never trusted his CIA-sponsored intelligence boss. Incessant car bombs, sectarian infighting, and the continuing disarray among Iraqi security forces were seeds of disaster. Director Hayden supported the "surge" of American troops into Iraq that helped short-circuit civil war. The military figures who controlled Pakistan remained reluctant to war against Islamic fundamentalists and refused to avert their gaze from India, the country's central conflict partner. In Afghanistan, where the CIA funneled more than $1 million a month to President Hamid Karzai, the Afghan chief proved quite pleasant, but spoke defiantly of America all the time. Karzai continued his dialogue with the CIA—as you might expect—even after Afghan relations with the United States soured.

President Bush wanted to be kept up-to-date on CIA covert operations, so on Thursday mornings he gave Hayden half an hour. Emphasizing high operational tempo, Langley's chief ranged the world. And he began using the sessions to push the line that Al Qaeda, already brazen, had become steadily more powerful in Pakistan's tribal territories. "The main point was that as bad as this might be for Afghanistan and our forces there, this was fundamentally becoming a threat to the *homeland*."

Michael Hayden had a lot more to talk about. John Rizzo observed Hayden closely and said he "loved being a spymaster, by which I mean he reveled in conceiving and running covert operations involving real people and back-alley intrigue." Hayden told Bush about everything from the agency's secret contacts with Libyan intelligence to its inability to detect a fully articulated Syrian nuclear weapons program to uncovering the efforts of convicted spy Harold Nicolson—one of the moles Russia had actually recruited inside the CIA—to get his own son to spy also. Then there was the disastrous Khalid El-Masri case, which began on Jose Rodriguez's watch. An innocent German with almost the same name as 9/11 terrorist Khalid al-Masri was swept up by Macedonian security on the last day of 2002. El-Masri would be handed over to the CIA, rendered to a black prison in Afghanistan, and tortured for months. Eventually the agency dropped him on a road near where he'd been taken, with nothing. When El-Masri went public, there were German diplomatic protests and another public relations disaster for CIA.

Naturally, Langley's inspector general mounted an investigation. John Helgerson issued the report on July 16, 2007. There were issues about El-Masri's treatment and the manner of his release. According to Michael Hayden, Helgerson's report improperly fastened onto one CIA official, by then the Alec Station chief within the CTC. Hayden thought her a splendid analyst with encyclopedic knowledge of the target. He wouldn't think of replacing her. The IG, in contrast, wanted the analyst hauled before an accountability board. Identified elsewhere as Alfreda Bikowsky, she had recommended the German be held without meeting CIA guidelines for detention, and once it had been established they had the wrong man, she opposed releasing him. Although Director Hayden pointed to the delay as one of his concerns with the Masri case, he refused any action against Bikowsky, who, even worse, had *also* been associated with a key CIA failure before 9/11—not informing the FBI that it knew an Al Qaeda operative, later one of the hijackers, had entered the United States. That omission had figured in a previous IG report.

Not very many CIA officers are implicated in multiple inspector general inquiries. In addition, Bikowsky had been involved in the torture in Poland of detainee Khalid Sheik Mohammed. The worst that happened to her was to be passed over for deputy chief of station in Baghdad. Instead she became deputy chief of the CTC. By the end of General Hayden's tour, the Counterterrorism Center comprised nearly a third of the entire Central Intelligence Agency.

Director Hayden notified congressional overseers of the El-Masri case, as well as his strong belief that it helped to accept mistakes. After one more of Helgerson's reports, an exhaustive inquiry into George Tenet's worst day—the 2001 shootdown of American missionaries over Peru—Mr. Hayden turned the tables. He had his special counsel, Robert Dietz, the former NSA lawyer who had certified domestic spying as kosher, investigate the Inspector General's Office on the excuse that *it* might be the source of the leaks that annoyed Hayden so much. He had told the SSCI that "the American intelligence business has too much become the football in American political discourse," and that the CIA needed to get out of the news, as either subject or actor. Nevertheless, the general ordered an action sure to leak as well as to chill everyone at Langley.

Officially, the Dietz inquiry, completed in October 2007, centered on eliminating the confusion for line officers between legal advice emanating from the inspector general versus the general counsel. Dietz pitched his recommendations to IG Helgerson the week before Halloween. General Hayden put out an all-hands bulletin to make sure everybody got the message. Officers could appreciate the outcome: IG interviews with subjects and witnesses should be videotaped; individuals who had undergone interviews would be given the opportunity to review (and dispute) reports based on them; a "quality control" officer would be placed in the IG's office; and an ombudsman would field complaints about investigations. The inspector general, for the trouble he had taken, was punished. Laden with so many details, Michael Hayden's memoir never mentions this chilling inquiry or, indeed, John Helgerson.

Credit the general for giving fair warning. Answering a senator as to his sense of the limits of permissible action in 2005, General Hayden had replied, "You should expect of me that I'm right up to that line." The line became something with real meaning for Michael V. Hayden. As candidate for Langley's top floor, Hayden reflected on the moderation of the

NSA since the mid-1970s and characterized it as it having "played a bit back from the line." The title of his memoir, titled *Playing to the Edge*, is another allusion to lines.

One aspect of playing to the edge was to extract something, always, for anything, from every situation. Never give anything away. Secrecy became one place he did that. General Hayden had problems on the declassification front. Two sets of documents were up for review under the Freedom of Information Act. One, the notorious Family Jewels, had been in the queue for a decade and a half. The National Security Archive, which had requested the set, was prepared to sue. The archive's director, Thomas Blanton, and its attorney Meredith Fuchs had been in conversations with CIA declassification officials, reminding them of the request, pointing out that release of the documents would give Langley something to talk about besides torture.

The other set were the documents known as the President's Daily Briefs (PDBs), the stream of daily intelligence reporting to the White House. They've been compiled on a near- daily basis since Jack Kennedy sat in the Oval Office. Many of these had great historical value, but only very recent ones are important from an intelligence standpoint. Hayden was desperate to keep the PDBs secret. He played the two ends against the middle, appearing in June 2007 at the annual conference of the Society of Historians of American Foreign Relations. There Hayden announced release of the Family Jewels. When the question period came around, he answered the inevitable queries on PDBs by declaring that these, essentially equivalent to newspapers, were really purveyors of CIA "sources and methods" and so-called predecisional documents, which had to be protected. Hayden gathered the declassification staff, the historians, the Publications Review Board, and the spokespersons into his executive office. Suddenly all aspects of CIA history and its documentary record were controlled by the spin doctors.

Just to cap this, a requestor, joined by the National Security Archive, ultimately *did* sue for release of the PDBs. The courts ruled that Langley could keep PDBs secret for the moment but no longer could it apply a blanket exemption. The agency would actually have to review documents for release. By 2015, some time after Hayden's tenure, it suddenly seemed desirable to declassify the PDBs, and the agency sponsored a conference at the Lyndon B. Johnson Library in Austin, Texas, where more than 2,500 were put into the public domain at once, covering the presidencies of Kennedy and Johnson. Later, another conference at the Nixon

Library heralded release of PDBs of the Nixon-Ford era. It became apparent immediately that, except for generic references, there were no "sources and methods" in these documents. When a former CIA officer who used to work on the PDBs reflected on the documents—full of facts—he quoted General Hayden: "If it's a fact, it ain't intelligence."

The top spook's concern back in the day had plainly been for show.

His speech to the diplomatic historians also featured Hayden's reference to what became his mantra of the "covenant" with the American people. Langley's chieftain said, "Here's an informal yardstick I use: if I could tell my brother back in Pittsburgh or my sister in Steubenville what CIA has done and why, would it make sense to them? Would they accept it as reasonable?" He recognized that the agency functioned on a grant of trust, not power, in keeping with the law. "The best way to strengthen the trust of the American people," Hayden said at his confirmation hearing, "is to earn it by obeying the law and by showing what is best about this country." That came close to plagiarizing George Tenet. But whereas Tenet had done something to further the goal of a compact, Hayden did not. Somewhere down the line, Hayden's covenant degenerated into the purely bureaucratic—the claim that an op ordered by the president and reviewed by the chain of command was automatically within bounds—a completely different notion and one that notably excluded Capitol Hill.

The general's antipathy for congressional oversight comes across in *Playing to the Edge*. Regardless of Hayden's boredom at lengthy disquisitions on congressional wisdom, its disturbing questioning as to whether he would have waterboarded his kids, and comparisons of detainee treatment with World Wrestling Federation bouts, the issues were real and the national security too important for a CIA chief to hinge them on personal antipathy. Hayden notes it had been a difficult time—an embattled president, both houses of Congress in the hands of the opposition, several members posturing to run for president. The former spy chief leaves unstated the implication that those persons might have gone after CIA to further their political chances.

So what? Oversight should apply only when the president is omniscient and his party is in control of Congress? (Wait and see the oversight under President Donald Trump.) Hayden's responsibility was to fit into oversight, not the other way around. Here is a good place to spend a moment on this. Professionals in the departments and agencies, well aware that politicians have their narrow, parochial interests, are reluctant to be patient. They are also anxious to protect favorite projects. But the authority is clear—congressional oversight of intelligence, like civilian control of the armed forces, is set by law and necessary for the functioning of the republic. Legislators stymied by the executive's playing to the edge are prone to react by adopting increasingly dim views of intelligence work overall. When party majorities switch in Congress, high-handed treatment of overseers is likely to result in investigations.

Michael V. Hayden actually gave subordinates permission to walk out on congressional hearings if they decided the sessions had become abusive. In another place, the agency chief attests he received more cooperation from the International Committee of the Red Cross than from Congress. What did matter, a lot, was that CIA aversion to oversight and contempt for politicians multiplied the impact of Bush White House arrogance. Hayden deplores what the Senate intelligence committee did with its torture inquiry, but he had a role in triggering it.

The director lost stature with Congress in particular with the revelation of the NSA eavesdropping, which President Bush acknowledged and dubbed the Terrorist Surveillance Program. Michael Hayden took hits as pitchman. When the general went up for appointment to the ODNI, Barbara Mikulski, a respected member, made a ringing endorsement when introducing Hayden to the Senate intelligence committee. With the CIA nomination, barely a year later, the senator stayed away. So did some others who had lauded him in the past. In commenting on the 2005 hearing, the general credits John P. Murtha (who had gone second) with introducing him, and does not mention Mikulski at all. Fabulism? Michael Hayden's tin ear? No matter.

For Director Hayden, who struggled to *preserve* Langley's hostile interrogation program, relations with Capitol Hill would be critical. He provides data on briefings given, reports completed, congressional testimony, letters answered, and so forth, as if the statistics, and not the quality of the interchanges, are the measure of merit. In fact, if the CIA were stonewalling, these metrics only indicate the intensity of congressional efforts to penetrate the cone of silence. In no way do they measure the CIA's responsiveness. Had the agency answered to the satisfaction of overseers, the numbers would actually be lower.

"It didn't take long to realize, as I began settling into the job, that the biggest immediate challenge would be dealing with what I came to think of as the elephant in the room—the CIA's program for detaining and interrogating senior al-Qaeda members."

Hayden knew Project Greystone could not go on as before. Only about

5 percent of terrorism intelligence was coming from detainees by now, and Langley had been forced to reject many reports produced under duress as fabrications. It had become like the bad old days of Cold War "paper mills."

The general nevertheless thought a reconfigured program might work—new Justice Department memos to carve out an exception to the Detainee Treatment Act (and deal with a fresh Supreme Court decision, *Hamdan v. Rumsfeld*, as well), a new list of interrogation techniques, confinement either at Guantánamo or in third countries, a commitment to hold detainees no more than sixty days without additional permission, and an actual move to bring in Congress by briefing the full committees. The CIA director went to the White House, explaining his idea to NSC staff chief Stephen Hadley. On September 6, 2006, President Bush formally acknowledged the CIA's black prisons, ordered them dismantled and the remaining fourteen prisoners sent to Guantánamo Bay. Bush also said the most aggressive techniques had been used on only three detainees—and Hayden followed, saying there had been only about a hundred prisoners and repeating the small number for those subjected to the harshest treatment.

Bush's order opened a new front, the home front, for the detainee program. Where previously the controversy had been hidden by confining it to the Gang of Eight, suddenly it was in the open. As the president spoke, Director Hayden went before the full oversight committees in each house of Congress—the HPSCI twice, plus a separate encounter with Jane Harman—and presented the first full briefs on Greystone. Hayden also met with Senate leaders. After that the pace and adversarial intensity increased. In February 2007, contract officer David Passaro received a sentence of eight and a half years in prison for killing a detainee in CIA custody.

Two months later, Director Hayden and lawyer Rizzo showed up to present the SSCI a detailed review of Greystone. This April 12 testimony apparently riled the committee. From records the CIA later censored and declassified, one could find questionable elements in this briefing, including Hayden's statement that neither FBI nor CIA inquisitors got anything out of Abu Zubaydah until after he had been tortured. Senate investigators later filled nearly forty pages with side-by-side comparisons of SSCI questions and Hayden's replies against facts established from CIA documents. Among the highlights was the account by one of Hayden's assistants of an order to find a date, any date, for which he could truthfully report that the number of detainees was ninety-eight.

This hearing represented the first appearance of Counterterrorism Center officials at an oversight meeting in more than two years. Equally perplexing was the presentation on *thirteen* CIA "enhanced interrogation techniques," because in the CIA's 2002 conversations with the Justice Department, John Rizzo had listed just *ten*, and those were the only ones John Yoo had considered in his infamous legal memoranda.

The discrepancy between what CIA said (in 2007) the approved techniques were, and what the Justice Department had actually considered in 2002, likely rang alarm bells at Langley. After this hearing the Senate committee asked for the agency's documents underlying the Yoo analyses. No answer. President Bush had refused to give Congress the legal memoranda themselves, affording the CIA a cloak to hide behind. The committee waited more than a year, then repeated its demand in a June 5, 2008, letter, followed by "numerous verbal requests." There had been no CIA response by late 2008, when the SSCI chairman wrote again.

Mr. Hayden dismisses the Senate committee's critique of his April 2007 testimony as small potatoes. His defense centers on having John Rizzo and a CTC interrogator with him, with whom he checked statements, and that, having come on board much more recently, he might "simply get a few things wrong." Actually, Senate investigators found fault with the testimony on more than two dozen issues, often in multiple instances—a clear sign of sticking to talking points. And the post-testimony refusal to provide requested documents or answer questions for the record cannot be attributed to misunderstanding or ignorance.

Meanwhile, the CIA took custody of another prisoner in July 2007. Hayden sent President Bush a letter requesting an executive order that interpreted the Geneva conventions in a way that carved out a CIA exemption from the latest laws prohibiting torture. The CIA chief dispatched a group including "Dunbar" and "Swigert" to brief Secretary Rice on a new menu of proposed interrogation methods. Condoleezza Rice curtly told them she would oppose anything that included nudity but that other techniques didn't bother her. Nudity disappeared from the CIA menu not as Mr. Hayden maintains—sometimes on, sometimes off—but as a specific device to gain the support of the secretary. Fabulism. Bush launched the executive order. Langley had its ducks lined up. In August 2007, General Hayden laid out his revised "Greystone lite" schema on Capitol Hill. Senators were beginning to sound skeptical when questioning the legal bases for the program. The House committee proved even more combative.

Then came the firestorm. On December 7, the *New York Times* reported the destruction of torture videotapes back in 2005. The *Times*, quickly followed by the *Washington Post*, linked Jose Rodriguez to this action. Other media outlets joined the hunt. Director Hayden issued a statement to CIA employees minimizing the event. He claimed the tapes were destroyed only when they were not relevant to any proceeding—including judicial—and maintained that the congressional committees knew all about it. That lie poured gasoline on the fire.

The very next day, the House intelligence committee protested. Hayden's account simply was not true. Chairman Silvestre Reyes (D-TX) had been Hayden's friend. He cited an offhand remark on one occasion and a brief mention in a letter to a single HPSCI member. That was not notification, Reyes and his vice chairman wrote. The vice chairman, Peter Hoekstra, a Republican who had saved Langley from much of the fallout of the Iraq debacle, followed up a couple of days later, telling Hayden it was unacceptable that Langley had not publicly corrected Hayden's statement. This was the Nicaraguan harbor mining fiasco all over again.

If Reyes was not satisfied, CIA adversaries among the public and on the Hill were even less likely to be. The Senate intelligence committee called upon Hayden for testimony specifically on the history of the tapes and opened the session by upbraiding the director for presuming to say the tapes were of no importance to any SSCI investigation. This hearing on December 12, 2007, led directly to the Senate committee's investigation of the CIA torture program, so it is just silly for our friends at Langley to insist, as many did, that the investigation blew up out of nowhere as a political attack.

Director Hayden discussed the history of the videotapes. Chairman Jay Rockefeller asked to be given all material the director referred to, including e-mails, cables, and legal opinions. Senator Sheldon Whitehouse asked about differences between the videos and their written summaries. Hayden replied that a set of operational cables constituted "a more than adequate representation of the tapes," and while CIA did not normally share cables, the tapes no longer existed. He claimed that the agency *would* have shared the tapes if SSCI had asked for them; therefore the committee could see the cables. A week later, the Senate committee sent a letter enumerating many items it wanted to see, with the tape messages heading the list.

The House intelligence committee was even more upset. Silvestre Reyes wanted a full investigation. Jose Rodriguez, the former operations chief, scotched that by threatening to invoke his Fifth Amendment right to silence. The maneuver there played on Iran-Contra, about which Congress had compelled testimony by overriding the Fifth Amendment with grants of limited immunity, which had ended up derailing criminal prosecutions of indicted suspects.

Peter Hoekstra complained that when he had been HPSCI chairman in 2005, Langley had never told him about any tapes. Hayden had still not corrected his statement to agency employees. At a follow-up grilling of John Rizzo in January, members from both political parties voted to have the room cleared of all CIA persons save the attorney. The House committee then told Rizzo documents they had seen portrayed an agency out of control.

When HPSCI staff went to Langley to review a summary of the torture cables, they were handed a two-page document. Staff members were insulted that the agency might think this would satisfy their need to see records, upset that the CIA would demand their presence to view such a small amount of such vague material rather than just send it over to their own secure vault, and outraged that House committee requests had already gone unanswered more than two months. They blamed agency congressional liaison Christopher Walker for the runaround.

At the end of January 2008, by letter, Director Hayden informed the Senate intelligence committee of his internal investigation of the inspector general's office, which raised eyebrows on the Hill. After this, the committee sent two of its own staff to look at the actual CIA torture cables. Daniel Jones put the most time into this research, which took place at Langley on nights and weekends. Like the House staff, Senate investigators rejected summary handouts CIA tried to foist on them. On April 21, Chairman Rockefeller wrote to General Hayden stating that many December requests remained unfilled, and others were censored in key places, even though Senate members had full security clearances.

In the summer of 2008, the committee finally secured access to the Justice Department legal opinions, and from those concluded that the torture methods described in CIA cables exceeded anything DOJ had authorized. The Senate committee posed questions for the record in September, noting that requested materials from the CIA's side—John Rizzo's side—of the Justice Department memoranda had gone unanswered for more than seventeen months. On October 17, CIA congressional liaison Chris Walker refused to supply the information.

More than a year passed before the SSCI review of the agency's cables had finished. Barack Obama had been elected president of the United States. Michael Hayden's time had expired.

Obama brought in a new CIA chief. The Senate intelligence committee got a new chairperson, Dianne Feinstein, a California Democrat. But the whole matter of CIA torture had become a raw sore, an open wound, hidden behind a fig leaf, the agency stonewalling congressional overseers and hiding that, too, behind curtains of secrecy.

All this while, Michael V. Hayden was on television and speechifying—on shows like *Meet the Press* and at venues like the Atlantic Council, saying publicly that the CIA does not torture but that it can because it is not bound by the Detainee Treatment Act—while privately asking the president for an edict to make that true. In secret he held the rampart against discovery. That also makes Hayden a fabulist. For this ghost, reality is imagined. To his way of thinking, congressional investigation started because people who wanted to be president needed to posture, *not* because Michael Hayden promised access to CIA documents, then tried to foist substitutes, then simply refused. Such ghosts encourage contempt that harms the Central Intelligence Agency.

And the stonewalling had everything to do with Hayden's *operational* goals. Pakistan remained the key front in the CIA's secret war, and it had been only the previous year that President Bush had approved a more aggressive posture, with less coddling of Pakistani political and especially military authorities. Bush had been feeling toward that, approving a cross-border SEAL mission late in 2005 and a huge scheme called Valiant Pursuit to get bin Laden in 2007. Hayden contributed to a National Intelligence Estimate that saw Al Qaeda as on the march again. As a result, Bush approved more drone strikes; there were thirty-eight in his last year, an increase of over 700 percent.

The strategy gave Director Hayden that much more incentive to preserve torture. He planned to pare down the menu, hold the prisoners for a limited time, and implicate Congress by drawing it into the circle. Had Hayden given up, those documents from before his watch would not have been so sensitive. A responsible investigation could have been devoted to them and to the program that had created them. Playing to the edge guaranteed that the Senate torture investigation would occur, would take place against an increasingly adversarial backdrop, and would come back to bite Langley. This ghost casts a shadow over the whole future of the Central Intelligence Agency. The spirit of Langley's future already had its hands full dealing with the consequences.

10

THE FLYING DUTCHMAN

As the parties swapped the presidency in 2009, changes loomed at Langley. Barack Obama had opposed the Guantánamo detentions, the renditions, the hostile interrogations. The public agitation for a "truth commission" inquiry had been growing for months. During the campaign, CIA lawyers thought, candidate Obama had been withering on torture. Obama had spoken against drones too, in the past, but he had lately been silent on that, and as president, Obama became the most prolific user of Predators. However, there was no doubt of his aversion to CIA strong-arm methods. Michael V. Hayden had been the face of those for nearly three years. He had to go, if only to signify President Obama's change of direction.

It's a measure of Mr. (no longer a general, he had retired from the Air Force the previous year) Hayden's character that, even now, he maneuvered to tie the hands of the incoming president. The general knew the Obama transition team had begun preparing executive orders terminating rendition once and for all and ending the interrogation project. Hayden wanted to preserve them. He took aside Gregory Craig, the president-elect's lawyer, to denounce the prospective orders. As the transition ground forward, Director Hayden pressed to make his case to Obama's incoming national security team. Langley got its chance. After a month of jockeying, the crucial encounter took place on January 9, 2009.

On the seventh floor at Langley, the DCIA's plush, wood-paneled conference room, the one John McCone had demanded, furnished the scene. Guests included General James Jones, a former Marine now designated national security adviser; Denis McDonough, his staff of chief; John O. Brennan, NSC counterterrorism director; presidential lawyer Craig; former agency attorney Jeffrey Smith; and David Boren, the former Oklahoma senator and SSCI chairman (and George Tenet's mentor). They sat around a handsome table of solid cherry. Receiving them were Director Hayden with John Rizzo sitting next to him, and CIA brass, including CTC chief Michael D'Andrea, plus backbenchers. It had been in preparation for this encounter that Hayden ordered selection of a day for which he could truthfully report a certain number of detainees—because Hayden had repeatedly insisted his spooks held fewer than a hundred prisoners.

Massaging the briefing had always been a key to his success, and Michael Hayden's reputation as a brilliant briefer attests to that. He wanted a real shot. The general quotes himself, at the outset of the Langley meeting, saying to Greg Craig, "If this was just theater, we would happily give him and his team their morning back." The lawyer reassured him. Hayden began by insisting that the CIA did not defend torture; it intended to promote a real program. The audience perked up, Rizzo noticed, when the presentation turned to drones and operations against Al Qaeda.

Hayden jabbed at his critics, especially the senators, taking offense at their use of the word *torture*, then "wondered aloud why . . . they would think they had to mischaracterize what we had done." Busy settling scores by the time of his memoir, Hayden, writing that, didn't pause to reflect on why, if the CIA were so sure of *its* position, it was so necessary to express its behavior in euphemism and then that all discourse be confined to the doctored terminology. Director Hayden made his pitch: "We believe that what you think you have to do, we actually took care of in 2006."

No reaction is recorded. According to Hayden, David Boren startled him, going beyond Dick Cheney's notorious aide David Addington in saying that in some extreme circumstance President Obama might order the CIA to do something on his authority alone. Director Hayden refused to support that. CTC baron D'Andrea declared that he would never issue such an order. Then the back bench spoke up: "It doesn't matter what those two guys might say; we're not doing it." The meeting did not end well.

On January 20, Barack Obama took office as president of the United States. Two days later, he issued an executive order requiring all U.S. authorities to enforce international conventions on torture and common understandings of humane treatment. President Obama issued a similar order on renditions. John Rizzo preserved a wedge there—at the moment of the inauguration—pointing out that if the CIA were not permitted to hold prisoners, it could have no role in handling them, rendition or not. The White House relented.

Obama still lacked his full team. CIA appointee Leon Panetta awaited confirmation. Panetta made his advance rounds—not just of the Senate intelligence committee but of former CIA directors. Mike Hayden begged him not to use the word "torture." According to Rizzo: "Criticize the program, say it is being scrapped, but avoid that word, Mike pleaded. He told Panetta it would be a gratuitous, crushing insult to hundreds of Agency employees." On February 5, at his first day of testimony, Panetta used the dreaded word at least twice, in the context of rendition, assuring Senators Dianne Feinstein and Ron Wyden that Obama's order prohibited rendering detainees for torture. Feinstein instead spoke of detention and interrogation. Wyden had not been so delicate. Director Hayden went ballistic, phoning his CTC chief, who agreed with him that the agency had not done what Panetta had said. Hayden heated up the phone lines to novice White House officials. The following morning, Panetta "corrected himself," saying, "It is my understanding that—and I want to clear up the record on this—there were efforts by the CIA to seek and to receive assurances that . . . individuals would not be mistreated and that they did receive those assurances."

Director Panetta had just left on his first cruise in early March when John Rizzo learned from Gregory Craig that the administration had begun to consider releasing the infamous Justice Department papers justifying torture. Rizzo hastened to inform Stephen Kappes, Langley's deputy director, who told him to touch base with former CIA chiefs. So Michael Hayden's telephone rang again. This time, after dropping his wife off for her book club, he called the NSC staff offices from a parking lot, looking for Jim Jones, who had been a neighbor when they both served in the military in Germany early in the 1990s.

Hayden told Jones that if the Obama administration let out the torture papers, there would be no CIA operations directorate worth the name for the rest of his first term. Hayden went to see Tom Donilon, Jones's deputy, and Craig. The White House tracked down Panetta and demanded to know why former agency directors were on the warpath. Panetta called Rizzo and ordered him to stand down, then spoke to White House chief of staff Rahm Emanuel and asked him to hold off until the current chief could have his say. The White House postponed action pending a meeting of NSC principals. That made time for Leon Panetta's return.

Deputy Director Kappes and CTC officers won Panetta over, and afterward he argued strenuously against releasing the memoranda. The NSC principals were divided. Dennis Blair, the director of national intelligence, predicted that it would be a one-day story. With President Obama about to leave on a trip to Mexico, Director Panetta phoned Emanuel again, this time to advise the president to at least hear out the people in the trenches. Obama agreed. Panetta filled a couple of SUVs with an assortment of his top officers, including D'Andrea of the CTC, his chief of operations; John Sano, deputy to the clandestine service chief; James Archibald, deputy to lawyer Rizzo; and others. The group rushed up the stairs from the West Wing basement. Outside the Oval Office, the spooks heard Obama say, "Come on in, fellas." However, they failed to convince the president, who released the documents on April 16, 2009.

One week before, the Central Intelligence Agency had announced publicly that it would close the last black sites. Release of the embarrassing Justice Department arguments for torture did not, after all, destroy the operations directorate. If anything it served as a plus for Leon D. Panetta, who had come to Langley as Obama's outsider but whose fight to keep the memos secret forged a bond with agency rank and file.

Even more important, the fight over the Justice papers shows how disconnected the CIA had become from the reality of American politics. Embarrassing for an intelligence agency, to be sure, but the controversy showed it incapable of reading the tea leaves. Agency officers *knew* they had a problem with Greystone because torture is illegal and immoral no matter what the Justice Department says. That was why Langley demanded that it be spoken of only as "enhanced interrogation" and other euphemisms. Somehow, though, CIA officers could not see through their own fears to the thought that Americans might be seriously upset by torture committed in their name. In the spies' looking-glass world, the spymasters rule the people, rather than the Central Intelligence Agency serves Americans. Michael Hayden, George Tenet, and Porter Goss all pretended that the agency had not tortured and acted as if questioning the spooks was improper.

The truth—what the CIA is supposed to speak to power—lay elsewhere. Obama entered office on a wave of political pressure for a truth commission to reveal the security services' actions. The Congress already knew of detainee interrogation problems. Staffers from SSCI were at the point of finishing their preliminary review. By 2009 the congressional committees had access to the Justice Department memos and could see the discrepancies between CIA action reports and what the DOJ papers supposedly justified.

Barack Obama *resisted* a truth commission. He wanted to move the intelligence war ahead, not dwell on the past. Obama's problem lay in how to placate Americans who wanted to blow the whistle, who demanded the commission. More than that, the American Civil Liberties Union (ACLU) had long since filed suit to declassify a wide range of secret documents pertaining to Greystone, including the Justice Department memos. In the spring of 2009, the courts were about to adjudicate that case. John Rizzo discovered that, unlike George W. Bush's lawyers, who'd been confident they could stonewall, Obama officials calculated that the ACLU stood on the verge of winning.

Suspended between releasing the Justice papers—and claiming credit, with "case closed" and all of that—versus the documents coming out at court, the administration chose the former. Stonewalling would gain no political points, with perhaps a greater firestorm in public opinion because of the continued intransigence.

Agency folk also despised other Obama decisions—one, to declassify more of John Helgerson's report on the detainee program (more, again, would be released under court order, to the ACLU in June 2016); second, in August 2009, to widen the scope of the Justice Department examination of Jose Rodriguez's decision to destroy the videotapes, expanding it to incorporate a wider inquiry into whether the torture had violated federal law. President Obama and Attorney General Eric Holder gambled that these cosmetic concessions might permit them to slide past the political dilemma.

Congress also remained alert to the politics of the CIA's problem. At his nomination hearings, besides the usual questions on whether he would be responsive to oversight, Leon Panetta had to field specific queries as to how he would treat the agency's inspector general. Early in March, the House intelligence committee had a full-scale session on the detainee program with Panetta and Michael J. Sulick, Langley's operations boss. About a week earlier, on March 5, the SSCI had voted to initiate a detailed investigation. This would not be a truth commission; it would be a closed inquiry, without the public testimony that had bedeviled Langley with the accountability threat during the Church Committee era. Arguments about secrecy and responsible oversight won the day at the Senate intelligence committee. Americans would have to be satisfied.

The story of the Senate torture investigation brings us to the Flying Dutchman, the ghost of CIA's future.

A FAILED RECONCILIATION

Director Panetta understood Langley's problem with Congress. He had been on both sides of the White House–Capitol Hill divide, as a California congressman and in several key posts in the Clinton administration. Feathers were still ruffled from Hayden's time at Langley. Legislators made hay from attacks on the agency. Hearings took the form of senators and representatives seated on high, bellowing questions at helpless witnesses. Panetta reminded the legislators he had been cut from the same cloth, having spent a decade and a half in the House of Representatives, starting in Jimmy Carter's day.

Langley's chief also took the advice of his congressional liaison and tried to sweeten the atmosphere, inviting the overseers to Langley to converse around a table over coffee. (Panetta's later deputy Michael Morell attributes this idea to Dianne Feinstein.) Senator Feinstein, for sure, brought the donuts—Krispy Creme glazed. A likable character with the air of a working stiff, Panetta was quickly on better terms with individuals, and because he hastened to brief the oversight committees on everything that came up, figures on the Hill gradually relaxed. So did Panetta, who soon matched Alex McCone's weekend trips to California, playing golf with associates when obliged to stay in Washington. Like Michael Hayden with his Pittsburgh Steelers, or many agency underlings with the Washington Redskins, Panetta was a big football fan—of the San Francisco 49ers.

Some controversies were wastes of Panetta's political capital. One that consumed too much ink would be the fracas over whether Speaker of the House Nancy Pelosi had been briefed on CIA waterboarding in September 2002. Answering a question at a news conference, Pelosi denied it. Panetta made a distinction "between respect and subservience," he records, and would not "simply roll over." Aides showed him records of a September 4, 2002, briefing where Pelosi was listed as present. Director Panetta ordered preparation of a list of congressional briefings on the program, declassified it, and thought he had caught her.

Not that there weren't fires in the in-basket. Only a month later, operations officers told the director of Project Cannonball, the DO scheme to create a permanent standby murder capability like the ZR/Rifle unit of President Kennedy's day. Whether or not Pelosi had been told of waterboarding when the CIA claimed, the agency had *never* told Congress about Cannonball, including the fact that personnel of the private security firm Blackwater had been participants. Vice President Cheney reportedly ordered that Congress be kept in the dark. Project Cannonball remained on the books when Panetta learned of it. He immediately canceled it, despite Stephen Kappes's protests. Panetta went to tell the Hill the next day.

But Langley's defining experience came with the Senate intelligence committee's inquiry into the CIA torture program. On February 11, 2009, the Senate staffers who had looked at the CIA cables reporting on its videotapes were ready to brief on what they had seen. Daniel Jones and Alissa Starzak's record demonstrated major differences between what the cables described and the "enhanced interrogation techniques" of which Congress had been told. One chart in particular, detailing more than a fortnight during which Abu Zubaydah underwent the most intense "techniques," shocked the senators. On March 5, the SSCI voted 14–1 for an investigation. Chairperson Dianne Feinstein approached Director Panetta for agency documents. The Senate committee wanted everything—background information on Greystone decisions, details of interactions between the CIA's general counsel and the Department of Justice, the records on creation of the black sites, and claims for the effectiveness of the methods. Langley officials believed they were talking about hundreds of thousands of documents.

To some degree, Leon Panetta became the prisoner of agency secrecy hacks. They were the professionals. He was not. Panetta objected vociferously when Feinstein wanted access to a wide range of materials. Feinstein, just as angry, retorted that the CIA would face subpoenas otherwise. "Feinstein's staff had the requisite clearances," Leon Panetta recalls. "We had no basis to refuse her." Nevertheless, the CIA director wanted control mechanisms, so the sides met, corresponded, and negotiated access.

The spooks tried hard to obtain an arrangement similar to what the agency had enjoyed with the Church Committee in 1975: congressional investigators would have to come to the CIA, not have material delivered to them on the Hill. It didn't matter that the Senate intelligence committee had a "skiff"—a Special Compartmented Information Facility—the equal of anything at Langley. As a matter of fact, the SSCI staffers would not even be going to Langley. Rather, the agency furnished a "reading room" at a remote location in northern Virginia. There the CIA installed computers providing for a shared network, one side for the SSCI people, the other for the watchdog unit the agency set up to keep an eye on this investigation. The spooks called this the Rendition, Detention, and Interrogation Network, or RDINet.

The secrecy mavens tried to get Senator Feinstein and her colleagues to agree to a memorandum of understanding. They dressed this up as a big concession "to avoid protracted litigation over subpoenas and in a spirit of cooperation." On this basis, Langley wanted Senate acknowledgment that the computers, the documents, the work space, and everything else belonged to the spooks. After some arguments with SSCI on the requirements, the CIA proposed an understanding that investigators could create material on their portion of the shared network, but anything they took away from the reading room, including their own work, could be reviewed and censored by CIA officials. No agency material could leave at all. The reading room could be used only during business hours, Monday to Friday. No late nights or weekends. Langley wanted to limit access to ten persons at most and said that everyone should sign a CIA secrecy agreement.

No way was the Central Intelligence Agency going to get away with this in 2009. The torture program, already quite controversial, with obstruction-of-justice charges under investigation, would not have held up five minutes if the CIA went to court to quash Senate subpoenas. The litigation would not have been "protracted." At the end of it, Langley would have been under court order to hand over the material. Who knew where that might lead? Moreover, right after this proposal—an exercise in self-protection—the Cannonball hit-squad disclosure tarnished the CIA even more. The agency needed to deflect this outcome. Panetta saw that, even if his staff did not. There is no evidence that the "understanding" was even shown to the Senate committee.

Instead, on June 2, the SSCI chairwoman and her vice chairman sent a letter to Director Panetta laying out their own vision, covering some of the same ground. The SSCI wanted access for fifteen staff, *plus* all of its members, the staff directors and deputies, and their majority and minority counsels. Documents that Senate investigators created in the reading room would be SSCI property, and the CIA could not collect them, copy them, store them, or use them for any purpose.

The Senate committee agreed to forgo intelligence from sources *other than* the CIA documents, including espionage reports, electronic intercepts, and data from foreign spy services, even the contents of military prisoner debriefings. In its report, the Senate would use pseudonyms or otherwise protect nonsupervisory CIA officers, liaison partners, black sites, or cryptonyms on materials they took away from the reading room. There would be no special secrecy agreements.

Panetta replied immediately, accepting some points, disputing others. After more discussion, on June 8, the CIA sent a further reply stating that the main outstanding difference was the agency's continued demand for the right to review *all* notes, drafts, and final reports, wherever prepared, based upon its having given the SSCI operational records. Langley agreed that its employees would have no access to the reading room hard drive except for maintenance by information technology staff. The Senate committee continued to resist a CIA right of review. On June 12, Director Panetta sent the SSCI a letter acknowledging completion of final arrangements, reporting that a hundred thousand pages of documents were already waiting in the reading room.

Langley's boss thought he had a good deal. He did not bother referring it to the Obama White House. Suddenly he was summoned downtown. Panetta brought Stephen W. Preston, the CIA's newest gunslinger, for what quickly became a bitter confrontation. They met in the Situation Room. The group included Admiral Dennis Blair, the director of national intelligence, NSC staffers Tom Donilon, John O. Brennan, and Denis McDonough, and Obama staff chief Rahm Emanuel.

Emanuel expressed fury. "The president wants to know who the fuck authorized this release to the committees," he growled, pounding the table. "I have a president with his hair on fire, and I want to know what the fuck you did to fuck this up so bad."

Admiral Blair piled on. "If the president's hair is on fire, I want to know who the fuck set his hair on fire!"

Leon Panetta had known Rahm Emanuel a long time. A politician himself, he could read Emanuel's moods well. Panetta guessed that the chief of staff had played to his audience, that maybe President Obama had concerns, but that John Brennan and Denis McDonough were the real bogeymen.

Soon the CIA director clashed swords with Brennan, the NSC counterterrorism boss. They were still arguing when White House officials finally realized they were facing a done deal. Langley and the SSCI had an arrangement. No one could take that back.

Therefore the secrecy hacks at Langley put together another list of restrictions, eighteen points that would have severely limited the inquiry. Again there is no evidence that it was ever shown to anyone. Leon Panetta's reconciliation failed as badly as had George Tenet's exorcism.

INQUISITORS VERSUS COUNTERSPIES

Next came the actual investigation. Senator Feinstein asked Daniel Jones, reviewer of the videotape cables, to lead the team. That preliminary had mostly concerned the cases of militants Abu Zubaydah and 'Abd al-Rahim al-Nashiri. Jones's colleague in that heartwrenching work had been Alissa Starzak, who now stepped into the shoes of main assistant.

Jones had been an FBI terrorism analyst before joining the SSCI staff. Starzak had put in a couple of years in John Rizzo's CIA office. Their "dive" this time would be much deeper, covering the entire detainee program. Evan Gottesman and Chad Turner were other principal analysts. At various times, fifteen more researchers joined them. Senate committee staff director David Grannis supervised. The investigation kicked off on June 22, 2009. It goes unrecorded whether anyone noticed that that was the date of two invasions of Russia—Napoleon's of 1812 and Hitler's of 1941. An inauspicious date.

For its part Langley hastened preparations. Director Panetta issued an order requiring preservation of records for the interval between 9/11 and January 22, 2009, the day when newly inaugurated President Obama officially terminated the hostile interrogations by executive order. A CIA special review team (SRT) with shadowy functions filed regular reports on the proceedings. The RDINet team took care of the computers and watched what the Senate investigators were looking at. They, too, compiled reports, so-called weekly case reports (WCRs) updating Langley officials on what the investigators had examined. The SRT and WCR papers became central to the torture dispute.

Senior officials in the director's review group guided the response. A major part there went to the Office of General Counsel, the gunslingers. In October 2009, Daniel Jones and colleagues went to agency headquarters to interview people in the Inspector General's Office. They found top CIA lawyer Stephen Preston barring the hallway. Preston insisted on monitoring any conversation the Senate investigators had with agency personnel. Jones and company ended up back on the street, their mission a complete flub.

The general counsel controlled the machine interface too. Langley recruited people for Panetta's task forces under OGC direction. The computer whizzes for information technology were from the same contractor that served the Counterterrorism Center, and CTC officers wrote their efficiency reports. Substance experts were primarily agency retirees hired back for this investigation. Senate investigators encountered active hostility.

Key elements that would undermine the investigation were already in place. Panetta ordered that no one at CIA consent to be interviewed so long as the Justice Department continued its investigation of Jose Rodriguez for the tapes affair or other agency officers for abuses during interrogations. The order pleased Republican members of the intelligence committee.

The technology whizzes designed a system the CIA called Spartan Gate. So far as the Senate understood, Spartan Gate would be a two-sided database with the sides walled off from each other. The Senate committee's side would include the committee's summaries, notes, and reports, plus whatever documents investigators chose to copy. Langley's side contained the pool of documents, constantly refreshed, which SSCI investigators were permitted to see.

But that wasn't the whole story. The Spartan Gate firewall would not be impervious after all. The RDINet team's side of the system had more capability than the agency let on. The investigators' machines were modified standard agency workstations. For counterintelligence and other reasons—especially since the spy Aldrich Ames—system managers have access to monitor activity on any workstation. For another thing, Spartan Gate had software to track which documents in the CIA pool the Senate investigators actually accessed. That enabled the RDINet team to compile the weekly summaries for higher-ups. Langley's inspector general later found no evidence the Senate had been told of these features of their computers.

Between the special review team reports and the weekly case reports, agency analysts began speculating as to what a reasonable person might conclude based on the CIA documents the investigators consulted. Panetta says he didn't see any analysis in these summaries—eventually known as the Panetta Review—but there should be no doubt that the practice began well before the summer of 2011, when Leon left to head the Pentagon, because *the Senate investigators discovered the Panetta Review before then.* Analysis of what the Senate had been up to required more data from the SSCI side of Spartan Gate, so the CIA yielded to the temptation to breach the firewall to serve the interest of the director's review group and the CTC.

Another element of controversy entered the picture in the summer of 2009. The Department of Justice widened its inquiries to include individual cases of alleged torture. In mid-September a group of former CIA directors—including Hayden, Goss, and Tenet—sent Obama a joint letter objecting to the Justice Department action. On October 9, because Justice's reviews could conflict with the Senate investigation—again the Iran-Contra precedent—Director Panetta instructed CIA officers not to agree to Senate committee interviews. At the SSCI, the Republican minority withdrew from what had been a bipartisan investigation. Democrats carried on alone.

Nothing about the investigation retarded the CIA's secret war against terrorism. Director Panetta's White House appearances were most often for the purpose of participating in NSC principals meetings, which set strategy for the secret war. The first big hurdle was the air campaign. Bush had already stepped that up, but Obama wanted both a greater weight of attack and more precision to reduce collateral damage. The Air Force lacked the Predator capability the strategists wanted. Prodded by defense secretary Robert Gates, it eventually multiplied its force manyfold. Stephen Kappes, sitting on the Deputies Committee, chaired by White House counterterrorism czar John Brennan, helped make the operational decisions. Drone strikes increased exponentially.

In the middle of all this, with Counterterrorism Center mavens racking their brains for intel sources to replace detainee interrogations, the Jordanian General Intelligence Directorate told Langley of an agent in the Haqqani network. The opportunity seemed heaven-sent and, as related in our story of agency meteor Jessica Matthews, it was. The mission at FOB Chapman became a huge disaster. President Obama came to the agency. His previous visit to Langley had been to quiet a workforce in uproar over release of the Justice Department legal memoranda. The drone war over Pakistan escalated with calculated fury, starting days after the Chapman attack.

During Obama's first year, his political problem had sharpened, and not in the anticipated direction. He had managed to skirt calls for a truth commission, but the byplay had effectively created a new political pressure group. You could call it the "League of Former CIA Chiefs." Agency wags just called them the Formers. Their letter to Attorney General Holder marked a sort of founding event. Obama officials had already complained of the activities of this group. Then came the attack on Firebase Chapman, with its heavy toll providing ammunition to critics of Obama's CIA policy.

Leon Panetta considered it among his more important tasks to be "ridding ourselves of a destructive relationship with certain contractors." Some at Langley deplored breaking this tie. The Mitchell Jessen Associates consultancy would finally be terminated in mid-2009, to be closed out in 2010. By that time the psychologists had been paid $75 million. There were additional payments of $5 million for a legal indemnification agreement protecting Mitchell Jessen. Under this agreement the CIA is responsible for the torture shrinks' lawyer bills until 2021. The company immediately hired a high-powered firm when it came under scrutiny in 2007. By 2012 Mitchell Jessen had billed the CIA $1.1 million in legal fees. In all, the tab came to $81.6 million.

That was *before* October 2015, when the ACLU brought suit against Mitchell Jessen on behalf of three former CIA captives, Suleiman Abdullah Salim, Mohamed Ahmed Ben Soud, and Obaidullah, in the Ninth Circuit of the United States Court. Defense motions to dismiss failed in April 2016, and in June Mitchell and Jessen served subpoenas on the CIA for evidence in their defense. Naturally the government resisted, and the psychologists asked for an order to compel a response. Agency officers John Rizzo and Jose Rodriguez were deposed in the case. In October the court quashed parts of the subpoena but ordered the CIA to produce additional contract material. At this writing, the suit is headed for court, with the agency on the hook for the bill and on the slab for the secrets revealed at trial. The odds are high that this case, scheduled for June 2017, will be settled out of court. The lawyer bills have only begun. The firm Blank Rome represents defendants Mitchell and Jessen.

Properly speaking, the $40 million that Langley spent to restrict and inhibit the Senate intelligence committee investigation should be added to this bill.

Just to put some context around these figures, in its rebuttal to the Senate intelligence committee's report, the CIA specified that if it had exercised every option under the Mitchell Jessen contract, more than $180 million in charges would have accrued. However, the CIA also noted that its *total expenditures* for Project Greystone from 2001 to 2006 were $246.4 million. Put another way, the rampaging psychologists cost the CIA *one third of everything it spent* on the capture, rendition, detention, and interrogation of Al Qaeda suspects—and that was *before* the court trials. The money Langley spent to inhibit the Senate investigation represents another sixth *of the entire torture program*. If you don't think the nation got its money's worth, here's a number that should lift your eyebrow: Mitchell Jessen plus the never-used black prison in Morocco ($55 million) add up to *more than half* of the CIA's spending for torture and detention.

In 2015 the American Psychological Association repudiated the ethics guidelines under which all this had taken place—a factor in the ACLU's conclusion that the matter is ripe for adjudication. The psychologists adopted a resolution that its professionals should stay out of government interrogation programs in any form. James Mitchell and Bruce Jessen will not be able to do again what they did. Kafka would still not recognize this as one of his plots.

Meanwhile the pages were piling up in Spartan Gate. After the first hundred thousand came more, documents by the thousand and tens of thousands. The heap surpassed 4 million pages in 2010, and reached 6.2 million when the data dump ended in July 2012. And the data really were "dumped"; they arrived in tranches reflecting no more than the order in which the CIA considered items for access. The mass was not organized by date, subject, case, or in any other way. Naturally this hindered analysis. SSCI soon asked for a search tool.

The RDINet team installed a modified Google search program in November 2009 but made a key error. The tool, programmed to scan the file universe, listed items on *both* sides of the firewall. Senate investigators could discover files on the CIA side of Spartan Gate. Even when the system denied access, the URL addresses of documents could be pasted into a toolbar, and the documents would open, then could be saved in SSCI's cache.

But the shenanigans started on Langley's side of the firewall, not the Senate's. In January 2010, CIA system managers surreptitiously removed 874 items from the cache. In March Dan Jones's investigators began noticing that things they had accessed previously were missing. On March 12, Jones met with White House lawyers, who said they knew nothing about it. In May the RDINet team took out another fifty-two documents. They removed nearly ten thousand pages. This time Senate investigators reacted immediately. Agency staff at first denied that anything had been removed. Then they claimed the tech consultants had taken the stuff without orders or permission. Then the CIA switched to saying that the documents had been removed on White House instructions for a determination as to whether to claim executive privilege for them.

On May 12, senior Senate staff responded acridly: "Our understanding of the agreement we reached with you last year was that the computer system on which the Committee would be working would be accessed by CIA personnel for purely administrative, IT actions. CIA's actions in removing documents from our system are unequivocally *not* administrative." The SSCI argued that material made available, even if in error, had been handed over and should remain untouched, that the CIA ought not to unilaterally access documents on the committee side of Spartan Gate, and that it should not unilaterally remove or alter them. The reading room monitors from Langley answered this would never happen again.

Alerted by her investigators, Senator Feinstein went to the White House counsel. There Robert F. Bauer had replaced Greg Craig. Bauer, chief counsel to Barack Obama's 2008 campaign organization, knew the California senator. She had offered her good offices—along with her apartment with some Napa Valley wine thrown in—for the make-nice meeting where Obama smoothed Hillary Clinton's ruffled feathers, enlisting the presidential candidate he defeated for the 2008 nomination, to work for his own election and subsequently to become his secretary of state. Now Senator Feinstein wondered if she needed to call in the favor. Bob Bauer had no idea what she was talking about. White House counsel had issued no orders pertaining to executive privilege in the CIA documents. Of course, there were nearly fifty lawyers and staff in the counsel's office, so it could have been someone else. A mystery.

One obvious possibility is that Langley really *was* responsible for the deletions and tried to pass them off as a White House gambit. This seems unlikely. Director Panetta had too much riding on his relations with the Congress to permit a move like that, while the officials responsible for Greystone were retired and had no authority. E-mail messages exchanged during these events also point a finger. On May 13, a staff lawyer commented to acting top attorney Robert Eatinger, "The White House is not inclined at this point to ask CIA to categorically replace all the documents that were pulled, in large part because the mistake was clerical in nature." That's obvious nonsense for if the mistake was "clerical," what is the harm in returning items to the cache? Moreover, if the documents were removed in error, why did the White House then demand to see them to make executive-privilege determinations? Conversely, given the tight control of political interests exercised in the Obama White House, it is hard to conclude that its lawyers might be unaware of instructions to Langley to suppress documents. After a few days, the CIA's liaison apologized to the SSCI, but there were still no documents.

Nearly a month afterward, on June 7, a CIA lawyer noted,

> Occasionally in the course of the White House's review of EP [executive privilege] documents, they will come across a document they believe may already be in the reading room (as part of a different batch) and have asked us to check, so they don't assert EP over a document that has already been produced.

Prior to last month's events, the SOP was to check the reading room's holdings (electronically—not physically) and let the
White House know.

The attorney asked his superior if it was OK to continue that practice
and reminded him that several requests were pending. The answer would
be that searches should check only whether specified documents were
already in the reading room.

Disturbing aspects in this investigative crisis are apparent here. First,
the e-mails unveil the fact the RDINet team *did* access the Senate side
of Spartan Gate, and that they used it *routinely* to check for White
House–requested items. Second, they show that White House involvement
had been real, not fancied. Timing is still an issue. It may be that the
"White House's review" only followed Feinstein's complaint to Bauer. But
it could also be that the inquiries had been taking place all along. That fits
with the two bursts of document removal.

There is no evidence that the White House actually made any judgments
on executive privilege, *ever*. Ten thousand pages were removed from evidence, whereupon the White House sat on them. The most likely source of
pressure at 1600 Pennsylvania Avenue would have been the NSC staff and,
within it, John O. Brennan. During the early days of the torture program,
Brennan had sat at Tenet's right hand. He'd been CIA chief of staff, then
deputy executive director. In April 2003, when an interagency Terrorist
Threat Integration Center (now called the National Counterterrorism Center, distinct from the CIA's Counterterrorism Center) formed at President
Bush's behest, Mr. Brennan became its first director. That moment coincided with Abu Zubaydah's detention and the dawn of the black sites. Brennan has always admitted to having seen some papers on the project, but
insisted he was not in the chain of command, his knowledge incidental, and
he had opposed Greystone. Documents showing otherwise would be very
damaging. Papers showing him right? No reason they shouldn't come out.

The Senate intelligence committee, unaware of any posturing, tried to
forge ahead. Dianne Feinstein relied upon Bob Bauer to reach a modus
vivendi with Langley. The agreement reaffirmed the prohibition against
CIA access to the Senate side of the reading room and its material in Spartan Gate. Much of the agency's computer team acting as counterparts to
the investigators turned over that summer and the new people displayed
little of the hostility of their predecessors. Nobody enforced the rule about
working hours anymore.

In the fall of 2010, a Senate investigator discovered that the Spartan Gate search tool could show things on the CIA side of the firewall. Rooting about over there revealed some portion—we don't yet know how much—of the Panetta Review, the summary reports compiled on what Senate investigators were accessing. The first known access took place on November 9. Chief investigator Jones learned of the "review" immediately. According to the agency, Senate researchers jumped the firewall thousands of times before they switched to writing their report. Feinstein and her colleagues were stunned to discover that CIA officers drew the same conclusions they did, even while Langley brass maintained its front that its methods had been legal, responsible, and useful. That discrepancy gave the lie to agency explanations.

Langley's monitors discovered the penetration when an investigator asked for a certain videotape. RDINet people could not identify the material, whereupon the Senate researcher directed them to files in their own cache referencing the item. This revealed that the SSCI had been on the agency side of Spartan Gate. Langley denied the request; managers told RDINet that the responsible office had already inventoried its holdings and given the SSCI those portions deemed relevant. This demonstrated that officials were making spot decisions on what might be relevant to the Senate torture investigation. It also disclosed that videotapes existed other than the ones Jose Rodriguez conspired to destroy. Those bombshells might come out in a fracas over the firewall. Also the techies argued that the search tool could not easily be modified. For the moment, sleeping dogs were left to lie.

Meanwhile, agency officials repurposed Leon Panetta's order to ensure the preservation of agency records between certain dates. Langley subsequently maintained that Senate investigators were entitled to view *only* materials originated between those dates, a debatable proposition that would figure in a huge scandal.

THE DUTCHMAN HOVES IN SIGHT

As the Senate investigation proceeded, on the operational side, the CIA continued closing in on Osama bin Laden, uncovering intel that led them to suspect a compound in Abbottabad, Pakistan, as the terrorist's hideout. From what we know of Langley's efforts to prove its suspicions, which included renting a house down the road for an observation post, information collection was under way by the time SSCI investigators encountered the Panetta Review documents. The U.S. Special Operations Command had the time to build a replica of the Abbottabad house and rehearse a raid on it. John Brennan's NSC Deputies Committee was meeting two or three times a day during the final preparations. Vice Admiral William McRaven briefed his plan to President Obama and the NSC principals and demonstrated it in rehearsals. On May 1, 2011, a platoon of SEAL Team 6 attacked the Abbottabad compound in Operation Neptune Spear, killing bin Laden and seizing computers, documents, and other intelligence material.

The next day, newly promoted CIA deputy director Michael Morell led an agency team to brief Senator Feinstein's committee. On May 4, Director Panetta took the lead and met with both oversight committees. Langley continued to bask in the sun with additional briefings in the following days. This became important when current and former CIA officials began claiming that hostile interrogations yielded the intel that enabled the U.S. to kill bin Laden. The Senate committee held hearings and found that multiple streams of intelligence actually had contributed to Neptune Spear. This point of difference aggravated the SSCI investigators.

Leon Panetta left Langley not long after the raid. President Obama asked him to lead the Department of Defense when Bob Gates retired. For the CIA, the president named David Petraeus, famous for his generalship in Iraq and Afghanistan. Michael Morell continued to represent the agency on Brennan's NSC Deputies Committee. With Obama adopting a "surge" strategy in the Afghan hills similar to what Bush had done in Iraq, and with the CIA increasingly militarized from its role in the drone war, this seemed a good fit. But Petraeus lasted barely a year. He had recorded classified information in journals he let his girlfriend see. She authored an admiring biography of the general. Petraeus resigned in November 2012.

Drone attacks were being justified under secret legal memoranda of the same sort as backed the interrogations. The secrecy became especially painful in 2011, when a Predator deliberately targeted an American citizen and another drone killed his son a few weeks later.

Anwar al-Awlaki had been a popular Muslim cleric on both the East and West coasts. At some point he became radicalized, morphing from chat-room and social-media star to bombmaker and terrorist planner in Yemen. Regardless of misdeeds, however, the Constitution affords protections to American citizens, so legal arguments for extrajudicial killing are problematic. As the Bush administration had done with its torture memos, Obama's people did with the drone papers. Protests mounted. Officials tried to paint justifications in broad brush, avoiding any specifics about laws. The State Department's legal adviser gave speeches along this line. Then came John Brennan, who, as White House adviser atop the drone war, had the most credibility. Brennan gave a speech at the Wilson Center in 2012 that retailed a "lite" version of the legal arcana, emulated by State Department counselor Harold Koh. The administration contrived to leak a watered-down version of its brief excusing the Awlaki killing, then the State Department issued a white paper on the subject.

Senate investigators continued to plug away in the reading room. Gradually their focus changed from wading through the material to crafting the report. A first section rolled off the printer in October 2011. By the summer of 2012, writing was the main task. Into the fall they sat at the keyboard. As sections were finished, Feinstein distributed them to all the members of the intelligence committee, including the Republican rejectionists. No one would be blindsided here. In August, Attorney General Holder announced that he had halted further inquiries into criminal jeopardy for CIA interrogators. That November, an SSCI investigator noticed that the Spartan Gate search tool had been indexing *Senate* draft papers on both sides of the firewall, and the SSCI informed RDINet of this fact.

Michael Hayden's phone rang. George Tenet came on the line. He asked if Hayden knew about a Senate report. The ex–spy chief answered that he had heard of it but basically knew nothing. On November 8, a group of former CIA bigwigs gathered at Langley to hear about the Senate intelligence committee investigation. George Tenet, John McLaughlin, Porter Goss, and Michael Hayden all attended. Michael Morell, who had worked for all of them except Goss, gave the briefing, describing the draft report. "We were more than a little stunned," Hayden recalls. Angry too. They—the Formers—began to organize their response.

One more mystery here, by the way: *there was no SSCI report* on November 8, 2012. Dan Jones and his team were still putting finishing touches to the draft. That work presumably took place on computers in the reading room. The report wouldn't go to the committee for another month. It would not exist as a document until the SSCI approved it. *Where did the CIA obtain its early copy of the Senate report?* It is possible Langley got the report in sections from some friendly senator, or the agents may have put it together from the draft portions acquired via Spartan Gate.

— ✦ —

The fateful day came on December 13, 2012. The Senate Select Committee on Intelligence met to consider its report on the CIA detention and interrogation. Room 217 of the Hart Office Building is secure and shielded to permit conversations that cannot be bugged. Senator Feinstein wanted this vote right away. One Republican senator, Olympia Snowe of Maine, had been a supporter of the investigation, but she was retiring. Her vote would take the result beyond mere party line. Senate majority leader Harry Reid also attended and spoke to members. Reid told the SSCI and its staff that their work stood as the most important intelligence oversight action since the Pike Committee report of the 1970s. Minority leader Mitch McConnell, a Republican from Kentucky, who counted as an ex officio member of the SSCI, would be angry that he had not been invited, though how he could have kept Olympia Snowe in line was anybody's guess. She was famous for voting her conscience *and* she was headed out the door.

An executive summary with front matter plus three volumes of content made up the study. One volume dealt with the history and operation of Greystone. At 1,539 pages, it was the shortest. A second tome focused on "effectiveness" and tried to evaluate how much had been learned from each detainee, what the CIA had represented about that, and what contribution the data had made to Bush administration claims. The third volume concentrated on the treatment of the prisoners at the black sites and the agency's day-to-day management of the prisons. Altogether there were nearly 6,800 pages and a stunning 38,000 footnotes.

The senators cast ballots. By a 9 to 6 vote, they approved the SSCI report and put it out for comments. Senator Feinstein wanted all comments in hand within sixty days. The committee rounded that out to February 15, 2013. Republicans filed their individual views and minority report on time. The CIA did not.

With Petraeus gone, Mike Morell carried the water as acting director of the Central Intelligence Agency. He spent the weekend of December 15 at his Langley office, paging through SSCI's executive summary. Like Hayden reflecting on the briefing of the former directors, Morell used the word *stunned*. Later he remembered thinking, "If even half of this is true, this is awful." The first thing Deputy Director Morell did would be to task Langley's Center for the Study of Intelligence to produce a study of the interactions between the CIA and Congress on the detainee program. Both the scope and depth of the SSCI study were impressive and were going to require a major-league response. And the Senate committee wanted feedback in sixty days. Morell decided the best way to assemble a response would be on a dual track: the Senate committee had cast twenty key conclusions, so the agency would "drill down" on each one and critique it. But the larger effort would be to take apart SSCI's analysis of the actual intelligence provided, because the Senate's arguments regarding effectiveness and phony agency claims hinged on individual detainee cases.

Deputy Director Morell picked top-flight officers for his rebuttal squad. The requirements were that they be sharp analysts and had had nothing to do with torture. Officers were assigned narrow subjects—for example, one SSCI conclusion or a single detainee's case—and asked to trace that piece of the puzzle through all the Senate's material as well as any CIA documents they needed. As results began to come back, Morell took his chief of staff, Gregory Tarbell, off routine duties just to coordinate the response and scrub the reply. Tarbell prepared Langley's overview paper covering the two sections of substantive material. Though the deputy director considered Tarbell one of his most brilliant officers, even he needed to paper his office walls with large sheets to help keep track of the elements in the CIA's story.

Mr. Morell expressed dismay at the Senate report. His substance analysts agreed there were valid criticisms from Greystone's early days, but Langley viewed the majority of the Senate's conclusions as simply wrong. The agency objected most to rejection of the effectiveness of hostile interrogations, which officers insisted had furnished a host of intel treasures.

The CIA did not actually hand over its comments until the summer of 2013. Morell deliberately decided to digest the report and complete his review before engaging Capitol Hill. He faulted the Senate report on fact, logic, and context, and met with Dianne Feinstein to relate those objections, warning her the Senate's report was studded with examples of the kinds he described.

By then observers among the public were accusing Langley of foot-dragging to delay release of the Senate report. Meanwhile, the CIA had a new director, none other than John O. Brennan, who had earned Barack Obama's trust as early as the transition before his inauguration, and whom the president had previously been dissuaded from putting in charge of the agency because of his own links, however minor, to torture. Brennan met with SSCI officials on June 27 to give them the CIA rebuttal document. Subsequent encounters brought together his analysts with SSCI investigators to hash out evidence on various disputed items.

More than a dozen times, adding up to sixty hours, Dan Jones butted heads with agency defenders. To Brennan's distress, his champions hardly dented the Senate's account.

At one of these sessions, for example, Senate investigators displayed CIA photos of waterboards ready for action at the Salt Pit in Afghanistan (Site Cobalt in the report). The agency had kept every record of Cobalt secret, possibly because a detainee had died there of hypothermia. Jones had CIA pictures of a waterboard at another site where the CIA had not admitted to using them. Pails of pink liquid were on the floor next to the thing. Langley's experts could not account for the discrepancies.

The review meetings dragged on through August 2013 into September. The Senate did indeed amend its report where necessary, but Senator Martin Heinrich later said that the CIA caught his investigators in just *one* factual error, a minor one that the committee corrected. But in many more instances, SSCI examined the CIA's countervailing evidence, debunked Langley's claims, and affirmed its original account. A typical example concerned the hunt for bin Laden, which takes center stage in many agency claims for the efficacy of torture. Langley's rebuttal attributes key data that helped identify the Al Qaeda leader's courier to interrogations of Abu Zubaydah, and Khalid Sheik Mohammed later, using strong-arm methods. However, CIA records that the Senate examined revealed that no one questioned Zubaydah about the courier *until July 2003*, even though his name and cell phone number were in Zubaydah's notebook when captured in March 2002. On October 25, 2013, the agency confirmed in writing that the Senate report, not its response, had been accurate.

Hot under the collar, CIA officials time and again proclaimed their refutation authoritative only to admit time and again to error. The refutation document would be published in book form with the title *Rebuttal*. Nowhere did the CIA's response actually come close to a genuine rebuttal. Stephen W. Preston, Langley's gunslinger, reviewed the paper from his perch as general counsel. Preston's suggestions went mostly to presentation. As for substance, his evaluation was humble: "I see the response not as a rebuttal to the study or as any kind of counter-report [which is precisely how agency people represent it] but as comments on the study for the Committee's consideration." Langley's gunslinger expressly contradicts two rebuttal claims—that the agency kept Congress "fully and currently informed" and that it provided adequate notice of the Justice Department opinions. Preston *admits* that the agency *did* furnish the oversight committees with "inaccurate information related to aspects of the program of express interest to Members."

Langley's objections were a pastiche. Take Morell's criticisms of fact, logic, and context, for example. He objects to the statement that the CIA restricted information to Congress until September 2006, which it *did* do. So is it an error of *fact* for the Senate to say so? The agency's excuse that the blackout was ordered by the White House does nothing to answer the SSCI's consequent criticism—*that the CIA's circumscribed briefing practices obstructed intelligence oversight*. That *is* a fact. And that was the Senate committee's point.

Morell's charge of faulty logic revolves around the numbers thirty-nine and seven—thirty-nine being the number of detainees subjected to torture and seven the number who provided no intelligence. He reads that as thirty-two who talked, hence torture was *effective*. That argument is way too simplistic. A proper determination depends on individual cases, on reports before versus after strong-arm techniques, on the number and timing of fabrication notices filed about each prisoner. A better way to evaluate these numbers would conclude that torture had no effect at all on seven detainees and an indeterminate impact—unknowable except on the basis of documents the CIA keeps secret—on the others.

Readers of the SSCI report and CIA response will discover that the Senate document has at least dozens and more likely hundreds of footnotes debunking CIA statements about intelligence reporting to the oversight groups.

Morell's complaint about context revolves around the charge that Langley's original briefings, in the fall of 2002, impeded proper oversight. Here the CIA official explains that Congress had been on its summer recess and says that that context obviates the criticism. That might be true if the CIA had fully briefed the committees on Project Greystone and its legal authorizations at the next session, but *it did not*. That's a *context* that the senior agency official leaves out.

In each case, narrow elements are used to discredit whole texts. Honest intelligence analysts object to cherry-picked reporting, but that's exactly what these CIA objections are. That is only the beginning. Criticism of the Senate report's conclusions forms an entire section of the agency's rebuttal. A point-by-point comparison of the SSCI conclusions versus this part of the CIA response shows that Langley's experts *reordered* the Senate conclusions, *changed their sense and wording* as the foundation of their "analysis," *made up* "conclusions" they attributed to the Senate, and did not answer others.* The SSCI conclusions that the detainee program was inherently unstable and that it *damaged the national security of the United States* got no answer at all. A Senate conclusion that the CIA impeded even *presidential* oversight is juxtaposed with an alleged SSCI point about money. In fact, it does not appear that a single one of the Senate report's conclusions is matched by the corresponding item in Langley's response.

No detailed comparison of Senate versus CIA versions of the individual detainee cases will be attempted here. That would be a book in itself, and the data required have been kept secret by CIA, have been destroyed, or never existed in any real sense. As the Counterterrorism Center itself noted in its September 2005 blue-ribbon assessment of torture's effectiveness,

> There is no objective way to answer the question of efficacy. Because of classification, it is not possible to compare this program with other programs (e.g. law enforcement procedures) which derive information through interrogations. As such, there are no external standards for comparison. And there is the epistemological problem of internal measure[s] of effectiveness.

The CTC therefore confined itself to general observations based upon metadata supplied by Greystone's own program office. How objective was that? A year earlier, when the inspector general's report on Greystone circulated for comment, agency operations boss James Pavitt returned a critique backed by a study of several detainee cases. It credited hostile interrogation of Khalid Sheik Mohammed with saving "at least several hundred, possibly thousands, of lives." Those numbers were guesstimates with no basis in fact. Pavitt also assumed that detainees were not simply trying to impress their captors and that *they had the operational capability to carry out every plot mentioned.* Assessments of effectiveness were embroidered from metadata that based itself on guesstimates and faulty assumptions.

At the street level, some sleeper cells were busted, some solo operatives apprehended, and some plots neutralized, but the enemy remained nebulous. Claims about effectiveness are illusions.

---

* Additional commentary on this section of the CIA response appears as an endnote.

Deputy Director Morell, who retired in August 2013 as the frothing over the Senate report raged in full fury, rises above the weeds in his memoir to weigh in on the subject. Morell's six points there deserve comment. The first is a throwaway—that really there were two programs, one for incarcerating the enemy, the other for interrogation. From George Tenet's first written directives through the IG reports, until President Bush closed the black sites, the distinctions were minimal; both programs were *always* managed and reviewed as a single initiative, carried out by a single element of the CIA. Morell's point is a distraction.

Secondly, the former spook argues, Greystone never was a rogue operation. The president approved it and kept updated—by some process we have yet to hear of. Dianne Feinstein, Morell recounts, was surprised to learn of Bush's knowledge, in June 2013 when he and John Brennan together briefed her on Langley's rebuttal. But the existing declassified evidence *all* indicates a constant White House concern to keep the president away from contact with the CIA program. Unfortunately, this point, which the former agency person uses to lambast the senator for ignorance, actually reflects the inadequacy of CIA congressional briefings—exactly the point made by former gunslinger Stephen Preston.

From President Bush on down, everyone sat on the edge of their seat. The intel added up to "the longest period of sustained threat reporting that I experienced in my fifteen years of working the al Qa'ida issue." At one point, Morell thought a nuclear detonation in New York or Washington was a possibility and warned his wife, if that happened, to put the kids in the car and just head west. He and George Tenet would go to the White House speculating on whether today was the day of the next attack. This is without doubt an accurate reflection of the atmosphere of the time. And in that context, "professional intelligence officers . . . came to the leadership . . . and said, 'If we do not use these techniques, Americans are going to die.' This statement was not hyperbole. It was exactly what our officers thought, and there was good reason to think it." So the spooks *fear*—and then they torture.

This picture would be nicer if, after applying their "enhanced interrogation techniques," the CIA had developed a real, nuanced understanding of the terrorists, but that was never true. In 2007—just as in 2002—the NIEs pictured Al Qaeda as being on the march. In reality the adversary was a splintered collection of fragments with wildly disparate operational capabilities. Those NIEs had more to do with budgets, roles, and missions than with threats.

A third point Michael Morell makes is that the legality of the torture is open to debate. Amen. But not very much. On the one hand there is national and international law, on the other—what? A memo that says "torture" begins at the point of organ failure?

His fourth point veers back into the effectiveness morass, claiming that the strong-arm interrogations worked. I will leave the agency and its over-seers to their dispute about that, noting only that here, once again, a CIA person invokes torture as key to the bin Laden raid.

Fifth, the former deputy director asserts that historians *should* debate the necessity for the torture. From Morell's operational standpoint, its efficacy was unknowable—*except* that from the very first detainee, Abu Zubaydah, FBI interrogator Ali Soufan obtained very good results before the CIA ever applied torture, which gained no additional information from him. Here is a passage from Terrence DeMay, chief of the agency's Office of Medical Services, in his reflections on detainees and Zubaydah's case (OMS here is the acronym for the office and AZ that for the victim):

> In retrospect OMS thought AZ probably reached the full point of cooperation even prior to the August institution of "enhanced" measures—a development missed because of the narrow focus of questioning. In any event there was no evidence that the waterboard produced time-perishable information which otherwise would not have been obtainable.

This is the CIA's top doctor, in an official account, on CIA paper. It is no longer just the word of an FBI guy against the agency's. *Langley cut off a reasonable effort to apply conventional interrogation techniques in order to implement its strong-arm methods.*

Mike Morell punts with his last point, asking whether, other consider-ations aside, torture is moral, whether or not the Department of Justice said it was OK. Reasonable people can disagree, he notes, then lards the issue with the reverse case—the morality of *not torturing* if the result will be the death of Americans at terrorists' hands.

The former CIA person ought to have stayed away from that one. The answer is easy. Torturing a human being is morally wrong *of a certainty*. The death of Americans at terrorist hands in the reverse case is misapplied because it is indeterminate. This argument assumes the automaticity of American deaths *unless* torture is applied. It skirts past a whole series of variables: it *assumes* that each plot is authentic, that the terrorists' capability is in place and the assets ready, *and* that existing security measures will fail to stop the attack. It also assumes that the person about to be tortured actually knows things and can be made to divulge them. Even after that, the case assumes that attackers' weaponry will function properly. These postulates betray *moral relativism*. Moreover—not to draw this out very much longer—having obtained relevant intelligence through torture, there are further variables in the way of accomplishing successful preventive action. Not to mention the question of whether conventional interrogation would have yielded a similar result. *No one who talks about torture should be employing moral relativism.*

Like Mr. Morell, Langley's stalwarts defended their ramparts. Greg Tarbell *needed* paper-covered walls to keep track of the meandering rebuttal. Perhaps there is a lesson there—as with Dick Bissell and Tracy Barnes, back in the days of the Guatemala coup, covering the walls of their Station Lincoln with paper displaying the flow chart of how it needed to go. The lesson is, if you have to paper your walls to accomplish the mission, then the task has become fraught with unmanageable complexity. Cancel it.

As the spooks stuck to their denials, Senate investigator Daniel Jones became increasingly concerned. Agency officers had already destroyed videotapes; who knew what else they might be capable of? Jones determined to preserve the Panetta Review. One summer night, the inquisitor worked in the reading room until after one a.m., stuffed a copy of the document into his canvas bag, and left. Agency monitors merely asked if he had anything with him that contained names or cryptonyms. They didn't check the bag. Jones drove immediately to Capitol Hill, where he placed the document in the SSCI's secure safe in the Hart Senate Office Building.

Events proceeded. In October 2013, Stephen Preston left to assume a new position at the Pentagon. Acting in his stead would be Robert Eatinger, whose name or pseudonym appeared, we are told, more than 1,600 times in the Senate report. This gunslinger was up to his eyebrows in the torture program. Eatinger sat in the audience on December 17 when a new nominee for general counsel, Caroline Krass, went for her confirmation hearing. Senators pressed Krass repeatedly for news of the release of the SSCI report, and then reached toward something different, the Panetta Review. Both Senator Feinstein and Colorado Democrat Mark Udall referred to it. Before the hearing, investigator Daniel Jones had told an OGC attorney, Darrin Hostetler, that the Panetta Review confirmed the Senate's findings. Hostetler countered, "I'm done talking with you." Bob Eatinger rode a wave of rising anxiety.

THE SHUTOUT

In journalism, to succeed in suppressing a story, preventing publication, is to *spike* it. In 2005 President Bush, Jose Rodriguez, and others sought to get the *Washington Post* to spike the black prisons story. The CIA did its best to spike the Senate intelligence committee report. Langley's opening bid, which Michael Hayden tabled, had been to claim the daily cable traffic showed the detainee program in bounds, no investigation necessary. Then the agency agreed to an inquiry but tried to impose conditions. The third move had been to secretly monitor activity on Spartan Gate and to watch what the investigators were looking at. Then came the act of actually removing documents from the pool. Langley stalwarts can dispute whether the White House ordered that or if it happened at their own initiative, but the fact remains that their invasion of Spartan Gate obstructed the Senate inquiry. Once Langley could not prevent the Senate report, the next move would be to stall on its response. After the CIA rendered its reply and it fell flat, the spooks had a real problem.

No stoplights were left to prevent the Senate report's release. In theory the agency could demand to review it for classified material, but the Senate intelligence committee had the ability to release the documents on its own authority. (The Church Committee had actually done this with its report on CIA assassination plots.)

Gunslinger Robert Eatinger had had a box seat for every play in CIA's effort. As an OGC official, and then as acting general counsel, he'd been directly involved in many of them. In lawyerly fashion, it would have been appropriate for Eatinger to recuse himself, for he was heavily implicated in events the SSCI had investigated, and his conflict of interest seemed palpable. Instead, he took control.

Eatinger's excuse was that the counsel's office held responsibility for the security of the RDINet. At first the talk of a Panetta Review made him wonder what the senators were referring to, but he soon hit on those weekly case reports (WCRs) and the strategic review team (SRT) documents the monitors had assembled. By early January 2014, staff had reminded "Eatinger" (whose redacted name is ascertainable by comparing internal evidence in several documents, but who is not directly identified and will be accorded quotation marks here) of the incident when Senate inquisitors had caught the Spartan Gate software indexing their writing on the CIA side of the firewall. Choosing to interpret that as SSCI spying on the agency, rather than the other way around, "Eatinger" also convinced himself that the CIA-SSCI arrangement for computer access allowed the agency, but not the investigators, to breach the firewall. The gunslinger saw only that the CIA owned the computers, which were maintained in a CIA facility subject to agency regulations, including laws applicable to classified information. Between January 6 and 10—there are discrepancies as to timing—"Eatinger" had CTC techies probe the Senate computers looking for the Panetta Review. Subordinate Darrin Hostetler played go-between for the OGC with the Counterterrorism Center. Their action amounted to an information audit. They were to minimize their footprint by refraining from reading, altering, moving, or examining any contents. On January 9, one of the techies warned "Eatinger" that agency material indeed existed on the SSCI side of the firewall, both on shared caches and in the personal files of one user.

Another agency official, likely from the CTC, discussed these findings with Director Brennan and Deputy Director Avril Haines, Morell's successor. The response, "Eatinger" learned, was instructions to verify that the items in the Senate cache really were SRT reports. By the afternoon of January 10, the CIA had established that five different Senate investigators had peered over the wall. The gunslinger reported this to Brennan and top community bosses.

"Eatinger" told Brennan that they should establish all the facts before taking it outside the building. Brennan, the lawyer recounts, ordered him to use any means necessary to find out how the documents were on the SSCI side of Spartan Gate. The counsel reminded the boss that the OGC had no investigative capability, but he could ask the CTC computer experts to help. The next afternoon, Saturday the eleventh, "Eatinger" answered the phone at home to hear John Brennan on the line. The director said he had reached Denis McDonough at the White House and become more convinced than ever that they needed to talk to Dianne Feinstein as soon as possible. Brennan repeated the order to use any means necessary to clarify the intrusion.

"Eatinger" told the CTC computer staff to get cracking. Another attorney had three RDINet staffers help her and reported that several documents' first pages revealed them as SRT reports. After this an agency team apparently entered the reading room—January 11, 2014, was a Saturday, and they knew who was coming and going—took pictures, and viewed offending documents on a Senate staffer's computer screen. (The CIA intruders apparently had the Senate researcher's log-on information too.) The intruders reportedly spent twenty minutes in the Senate work spaces. Langley's Office of Security conducted a forensic analysis of log-ons and visits.

In these forays "Eatinger" came to the line he would use repeatedly. He already had a criminal investigation in mind. That might kick up so much dust, it could stop the SSCI report. The gunslinger warned Brennan and other seniors *not* to talk to the White House: "If the WH were to order the inquiry stopped, it could constitute an act in furtherance of obstruction of justice." Just speaking to McDonough put Brennan in a bad light, politicizing a potential criminal matter, and talking to Feinstein would result in the culprits having an opportunity to get their stories straight before being set upon by CIA security officers.

Breathtaking! A lawyer who had helped Jose Rodriguez arrange the destruction of the torture videotapes—the obstruction of justice that Obama's attorney general had refused to charge—argued that *avoiding* a criminal prosecution of the Senate staff would *be* obstructing justice.

Tuesday, January 14, became the critical day. Agency executive director Meroe Park called a morning meeting in the director's conference room. Senior officials at her confab included lawyer Eatinger, agency congressional aide Neal Higgins, and CTC officials. Everyone there knew the CIA had breached the Senate's side of Spartan Gate, now at least twice. Some of them had approved or participated. Techies apparently went so far as to reconstruct e-mails sent by Senate investigator Daniel Jones. One CIA officer emphasized that Mr. Brennan had repeatedly demanded a "go" on the affair.

That was the morning. That afternoon, same place, Director Brennan presided. He expressed surprise that counterintelligence would be involved and concern at the "bad optic" of counterspies investigating the Senate intelligence committee. He wanted nothing more done on the technical or forensic side but wanted to see Dianne Feinstein and offer to join forces for a combined forensic investigation. Eatinger prepared talking points. The gunslinger repeated his mantra of potential Senate criminal conduct. Brennan expected that his orders would lead to a CIA stand-down on intrusions into the Senate committee's reading room.

A showdown took place on Capitol Hill the next day. It began cordially, but Director Brennan soon showed his edge. He told Feinstein that CIA documents had been found in Senate hands, that the agency had logged all materials placed on Spartan Gate, and that these particular documents had never been given to the SSCI. He wanted the senators to discipline their staff—a veiled suggestion they fire Dan Jones—and to be fully aware before the CIA ordered further measures. Before starting a full forensic computer review, Brennan offered the alternative of a joint one, because he preferred a review conducted with SSCI consent. Feinstein did not agree. Brennan left, he told the agency's inspector general later, with the impression that the senator had not dismissed the suggestion but simply wanted to consult others. Senate colleague Martin Heinrich recalled, "I think she knew, after that meeting, that it was going to be a real battle to bring that report out."

On January 16, the SSCI's security officer notified Neal Higgins, CIA congressional liaison, that the agency should scrap any plans for a joint inquiry. He should expect a letter from Chairwoman Feinstein to Director Brennan. Meanwhile, the Cyber Blue Team of Langley's security office, created to identify vulnerabilities in agency computer systems, began *another* intrusion into the SSCI computer net, later claiming that they knew nothing of Brennan's stand-down order, although the official who initiated the intrusion told interviewers that he'd been consulted on an urgent basis the day Brennan saw Feinstein, i.e., the day *after* the stand-down order.

The Senate committee struck back with Senator Feinstein's letter, invoking separation of powers between Congress and the executive. She sent another missive, almost a week later, with a dozen probing questions that Langley never answered. Instead Brennan shot back his own message on January 27, thundering that "sensitive" CIA documents "may have been improperly obtained and/or retained." On February 7, acting general counsel Robert Eatinger filed a criminal referral with the Department of Justice against the Senate Select Committee on Intelligence.

Fighting the quicksand sank the CIA deeper. Inspector General David B. Buckley began an inquiry into the allegation that the agency had intruded into SSCI computers while senators and CIA officials traded barbed statements. Dianne Feinstein felt caught in the middle. More than a month earlier, she had intervened to shield Brennan when the CIA director refused senators' questions probing Langley's intent to intimidate the committee. Early in March, anonymous leaks—where could they have come from?—accused the *Senate* of hacking *CIA* computers. Senate majority leader Harry Reid warned Brennan the agency had nothing to gain from this tactic, that Feinstein had been a friend, and that Brennan should just say he'd been wrong. Instead, Brennan thundered about "spurious" SSCI allegations. This time Nevada senator Reid went to Feinstein. Dismissing her objections, Reid pointed out that the CIA had done the leaking, undercutting its overseers. At that point, Senator Feinstein reserved time to speak on the Senate floor.

On March 11, Dianne Feinstein stood up to address her august colleagues. She began with the leaks, said she spoke out reluctantly and had been trying to resolve the dispute discreetly. Feinstein revisited the committee's efforts to oversee the CIA detainee program, which had led to an investigation. She noted how the agency had previously intruded into SSCI computers and that therefore finding Panetta Review documents had led to fears that Langley would destroy or deep-six them. Most had disappeared from Spartan Gate, the committee thought, during 2010. Those that could be found needed protection. Feinstein noted that the Senate committee had the same security clearances as the CIA, that it had the same secret vaults, and that documents had been handled with identical safeguards. Agency claims of security breaches were bogus. The committee rejected Langley's efforts to intimidate.

Three requests for the Panetta Review documents had met only silence or CIA rejoinders that they fell outside the stipulated date range of the SSCI investigation. Here Langley pretended that Panetta's preservation order was a mutual agreement on the scope and range of the investigation. Feinstein demolished that ploy by pointing out that both the study and the CIA response devoted much attention to the case of Osama bin Laden, which, of course, climaxed in 2011. After her remarks, Dianne Feinstein went to a lunch of the Senate Democratic Caucus, where a standing ovation greeted her.

That day John O. Brennan happened to be on the same side of the Potomac, giving a speech at the Council on Foreign Relations. Attention to the CIA-Congress impasse was inevitable. Brennan tried to fend it off. "We have made mistakes, more than a few," the director said. "And we have tried mightily to learn from them." More than anyone, Brennan wanted to put this chapter of history behind them. He believed in congressional oversight, Brennan said.

Taking questions toward the end, the director added, "As far as allegations of, you know, CIA hacking into Senate computers, nothing could be further from the truth." He averred that once the facts emerged, the critics would be proved wrong. And he promised, "If I did something wrong, I will go to the president and I will explain to him what I did and what the findings are."

Director Brennan also dismissed the notion that the CIA was holding up release of the Senate torture report, saying that the SSCI had never submitted it (for declassification review). Brennan covered much of this same ground later that day in a message to the CIA workforce. There he added,

"We also owe it to the women and men who faithfully did their duty in executing this program to try and make sure any historical account of it is balanced and accurate."

So the latest excuse for spiking the SSCI torture report became ensuring that a "historical" account would be balanced and accurate. This, too, became a mantra. After the events of that day, Robert Eatinger later told a CIA Accountability Board, he *did* recuse himself from dealing with the torture report, that day. In other words, Eatinger recused himself *after* the agency's hacking of the Senate became public. As it happened, Caroline Krass won approval as CIA general counsel on March 13. Mr. Eatinger continued to act on this matter until the moment his replacement arrived.

Early in April, the Senate intelligence committee voted 11–3 to release the investigative report, but it did not take the nuclear option of unilaterally releasing the documents. Feinstein displayed a finer sensibility than Langley. Her committee adopted an intermediate course—sending the report to the White House. President Obama was on record numerous times favoring the report's release. To facilitate secrecy review, the SSCI agreed to confine the first release only to the executive summary and minority views. The report reached the White House on April 7. Presidential counsel Kathryn H. Ruemmler informed the Senate on the eighteenth that Obama had asked the CIA to perform the declassification review. The report languished for months.

Inspector General David Buckley, with the Senate's sergeant-at-arms, finally did do a joint inquiry on RDINet log-in data. They discovered that the data that would have revealed CIA users breaching the Spartan Gate firewall had been corrupted. The IG also found that several employees or contractors interviewed, to put it delicately, had not been forthcoming in their initial interviews. Two recanted when confronted with evidence of lying. One refused further contact. Under the "reforms" General Hayden had imposed on the inspector general, there was nothing Buckley could do about it. Mr. Brennan offered no help. The IG concluded that the charges that Senate computers had been hacked were correct.

Eatinger's criminal referral, the IG found, had been based on inaccurate information. Buckley recommended that a number of CIA officers be disciplined. Director Brennan's apology was a croak, compared to his booming denunciations of those who believed the Senate committee had been hacked. Brennan did set up an accountability board headed by Evan Bayh, who had previously served on the SSCI for a decade, retiring just before its computers were mined for "executive privilege" documents. Robert Bauer, the former White House counsel who had participated in that fracas, also sat on this board.

Completion of the inspector general's inquiry on the computer hacking coincided with three other major developments, all of them on August 1, 2013. In one, the Justice Department dismissed the CIA's criminal referral against the Senate. In another, Langley returned the torture report to SSCI with its deletions. Senators saw extensive redactions gutting their report. All references to Allah, all names of any detainees, and the entire interrogation of prisoner Khalid Sheik Mohammed were supposed to be too secret for public eyes. A "balanced and accurate" report, in Langley's view, required that the Senate's inquiry be stripped of substance.

This was on John Brennan. In the executive order (number 13526) that regulates the entire secrecy system, Section 1.7(a)(1)(2) explicitly provides that information cannot be classified, maintained as classified, or fail to be *de*classified for the purpose of concealing violations of law or preventing embarrassment of an agency. Brennan could dispute whether the CIA broke the law, but there can be no doubt that "balanced and accurate" was all about avoiding embarrassment. The Flying Dutchman showed his hand.

Langley kept another development under wraps, an *un*classified paper to which it gave no circulation, sat on for more than four months, and then prayed no one would notice—and no one did, for the better part of a year. This was the "Note to Readers of *The Central Intelligence Agency's Response to the Senate Select Committee on Intelligence's Study of the CIA's Detention and Interrogation Program*." Under that ponderous title, the CIA admitted that *its own response* to the Senate torture report contained more than a dozen mistakes. One was its claim that the secretary of state and the deputy secretary were aware of all black prisons from the moment they became operational (the CIA admitted that it had no records to show that). Worse, there were errors about attribution of claims for intelligence success, errors on the number of detainees tortured without authorization, and errors caused by inflating the number of inspector general investigations that supposedly kept the interrogations honest—all because the CIA had lumped Iraq War statistics with the data on the torture program. The actual number came in at less than half what had been advertised. Brennan was massaging the numbers just like Michael Hayden.

If you can't spike the report, discredit it. The final stage in this sorry story is the Senate's fight to get out its report in the face of those who lined up to knock it down. The declassification side is simpler and can be put in a few sentences. Senator Feinstein rejected the CIA's proposed deletions. That revived the possibility that the Senate might unilaterally release the documents, something the Obama administration wanted to avoid. After listening to Feinstein, the White House put chief of staff Denis McDonough in play as mediator. He spent the October holiday of Columbus Day in San Francisco conferring with the senator.

They cleared up a few items but broke on Feinstein's view that individuals were sufficiently protected by referring to them pseudonymously. This device—quite acceptable to Langley in CIA memoirs—suddenly became dangerous to national security. Feinstein offered to settle on forty or fifty key pseudonyms and delete hundreds of others. McDonough refused. The to-and-fro went on for another month, until late November.

One day McDonough visited Capitol Hill to engage legislators on immigration. He knew the torture report would come up, though. Senators had prepared remarks. Feinstein, Rockefeller, Heinrich, Wyden, and Udall all spoke. McDonough complained of being put on the spot. Resistance dissipated on both sides. The Senate committee gave up on its pseudonyms. The sides reached final agreement on December 3.

The administration's goal-line defense would be soothsaying, predicting that revelation of the torture report would trigger worldwide violence against Americans, troops and officials primarily, but even ordinary citizens. Some broadcasters lent themselves to this shabby maneuver, poking microphones in senators' faces and demanding to know why they would insist on a report that was going to get people killed.

Feinstein got a personal appeal from Secretary of State John Kerry. She stood her ground. Some committee members, Kerry's friends and colleagues from his years in the Senate, might have been tempted to go along, but at just this moment Director of National Intelligence James Clapper intervened with a shoddy intelligence estimate that represented the SSCI report falsely and used that misunderstanding to predict global violence and chaos. Senators were incensed. The Senate committee's report appeared on December 9, 2014. No violence occurred.

John Brennan was the top authority for deciding on pseudonyms and secrets in the Senate report. He and McDonough went back a long way. The latter's mediation was not so evenhanded, after all. Brennan, who had blathered about balanced and accurate studies, had to be a source for claims that violence would greet the torture report. How a "historical" study would lead to violence was left unsaid.

The fact that the secrecy ploys amounted to spin-doctoring became only too evident in this next deep game. It brings us back to the new CIA lobby of Formers. They had kept in touch since briefed on the SSCI draft report. Eager to see how they were portrayed in the final document, they wanted access. Director Brennan opened up the report for the most senior people before it was declassified and while still under negotiation between CIA and SSCI. It was a limited window, and not everyone got access. Michael Hayden complained that, what with summer travel and all, he had only four hours to peruse the document. Nevertheless Brennan chose to privilege these people.

Langley stalwarts had no intention of taking criticism of torture lying down. Bill Harlow, the agency's PR man back in George Tenet's day, built a website to showcase reactions, and later stocked it with dozens of media appearances where former officers denounced the Senate. That much was politics. More disturbing would be the CIA's lobby's presentation on its website of secret agency documents released to lobbyists. This is not about the evidence in the documents, which understandably shifts the spotlight onto the Bush White House, showing how the CIA acted with caution. Disturbing is the manner of the declassification, which involves Mr. Brennan.

Many, many people file Freedom of Information Act (FOIA) requests every day. At Langley there is a minimal staff serving these requests. As a matter of law and administrative regulation, FOIA requests are taken in the order received. As a matter of government secrecy and CIA reluctance, the waiting list is long and frustrating. Many requests have languished for a decade, some for two. The CIA lobby filed FOIA requests and had them met *almost instantaneously.*

On September 9, 2014, Langley released a first batch of documents that included a record of a George Tenet meeting and a notice from the Counterterrorism Center, among others. Exactly two months later came another tranche. This set included five general counsel records, still from the Tenet period, showing the agency trying to get the White House on board with its interrogation methods. Among them were PowerPoint slides for an NSC briefing, George Tenet conversation notes, and talking points for a meeting with the attorney general. The record of a meeting with National Security Adviser Condoleezza Rice was released on December 5. Three days later, the CIA declassified the historical study of interactions with Congress that Deputy Director Michael Morell had ordered created in November 2012.

Work could *only* have been accomplished on these FOIA requests at the expense of requestors who had been standing in line for years. Worse, Brennan's CIA *moved on the lobby's FOIA requests while stalling declassification of the Senate report.* Langley lobbyists got their material in time to stock their website *before the Senate report appeared.*

Equally instructive, the documents the CIA released to the Formers were remarkably complete. They were, in fact, redacted more lightly than the Senate report itself. Some of these same documents had previously been subjects of other FOIA requests the CIA had *denied.* For example, the American Civil Liberties Union had sued for a swath of material, including the Condi Rice meeting record. ACLU *won* its case, but the CIA declassified just a few lines of text, the rest blacked out. The Formers got a practically full record with only a few lines missing. They had not sued.

Langley's FOIA staff is part of a unit that works directly for the director. Preemption of the FOIA queue, as well as the light pen the censors applied in a case of this importance, had to have received Mr. Brennan's personal attention—the Flying Dutchman in action.

As for the hacking, SSCI staff investigator Alissa Starzak would be nominated for general counsel of the U.S. Army. Senate Republicans held up her nomination in the spring of 2015, effectively punishing her, even though she left the SSCI before investigators smuggled any documents. The record of the CIA accountability board stands in stark contrast. Supposed to make judgments on officers implicated in hacking the Senate's computers, the board reported out on January 15, 2015. It found *no one* accountable for the CIA hacking. This finding was based on the proposition that the Senate committee and the CIA had never reached a concrete agreement delimiting each of their roles. So the only person punished for any of this became a Senate staffer.

This astonishing outcome amounted to a complete rejection of the inspector general's investigation. David Buckley resigned. President Obama never recruited a new IG. He left office two years later. At the end of the day, there is the damage to America's standing in the world and hence its national security, which the Central Intelligence Agency wholly refused to acknowledge as flowing from its detainee and torture program.

The Flying Dutchman of lore is a sailing ship hidden in the mist. She emerges suddenly, perhaps nearly colliding, only to vanish like a puff of smoke or a leaf on the wind. So it was with John O. Brennan and accountability for the Central Intelligence Agency. Like others before him, the director had made all the desired promises of cooperation with Congress, showed the proper enthusiasm for oversight, and even voiced positive preliminary opinions about the Senate report and made statements about what he considered torture. But Langley's director was the Flying Dutchman. When the time came to deliver CIA accountability, he engaged in a full-court press to derail the investigation and suppress the report. Accountability became a chimera. By means of its actions the CIA has squirmed away from the last bonds of congressional oversight.

Agency acting inspector general Christopher R. Sharpley, meanwhile, informed the Senate intelligence committee in August 2015 that OIG's copy of the torture report *had been destroyed*—the computer discs were broken after it had been uploaded into a data bank. Officials then interpreted the attorney general's instruction that no one should open the report as an order to delete it. Sharpley could not obtain a new copy from Brennan's office. The Flying Dutchman again.

To this day, the Central Intelligence Agency maintains a disingenuous position, refusing to acknowledge the reality of these events. At Guantánamo Bay, where some of the former CIA detainees are on trial for their crimes, Brigadier General Mark S. Martins, the chief prosecutor, filed a legal brief stipulating that the Senate torture report is accurate. Reporters sought comment from Langley spin doctors. It came: "To be clear, although we did make a serious effort to respond [to the Senate torture report], we were not able to perform a comprehensive fact check. . . . [The agency] found that accuracy was encumbered as much by the authors' interpretation, selection, and contextualization of the facts as it was by errors in their recitation of the facts, making it difficult to address their flaws with specific technical corrections." The CIA pretends it wrote nothing in error and made no mistakes.

John Brennan never went to the president, confessed his sins, and begged expatiation. The beginning of wisdom would have been to acknowledge outrageous misbehavior. No organization that fails to recognize damage like this deserves the title of "intelligence" agency.

In the end, Langley evaded accountability for torture. The ghost of CIA's future, the Flying Dutchman, is John O. Brennan. The moment of challenge predictably came. During the 2016 presidential election Langley spooks began to see signs of suspicious contacts between Russian operatives and Republican political activists in the United States. Brennan briefed the congressional oversight committees, expressing his fears. While the FBI did not help him—at that stage the Bureau, though it had begun to investigate, had yet to reach any conclusions; Congress dismissed his concerns. At the SSCI, where Republican senator Richard Burr had demanded the return to him of all copies of the torture report, Brennan made headway only with committee Democrats. Ironic—to have stiffed the Feinstein committee on torture only to be thrown into the arms of its remaining members. Donald J. Trump, victor in the election, worried about the political implications of accumulating evidence that Russia had run an intelligence operation to benefit his campaign. He tried to deflect criticism by shooting back. Before being inaugurated, Trump attacked the spy agencies, accusing them of acting like "Nazis" and saying they needed extra time to cobble together their phony account—of a potentially true tale of Russian interference in the presidential election that put him in the White House. Furious, Brennan denounced the incoming president and his charges, reacting just the way he had with the Senate torture report. This time no one came to his aid.

COMES THE SHIP TO FOUNDER

The house that Allen built holds many secrets. Spirits inhabit the halls. Ghosts—from horseman to Dutchman—will shape the next era of CIA history. John Brennan completes the circle, for like George Tenet before him this director was a dreamer. He sought to bring back the agency, to refocus it on classic missions, to chip away at the militarization and ossi-fication. He had some success. The tragedy of the Dutchman is that what he did to evade the consequences of a shameful chapter of CIA history is quite likely to destroy those things he valued the most. That will be tragic for all of us.

Director Brennan helped turn the agency away from the drone war. During the last year for which there is a figure, 2015, CIA Predators made only two strikes in Pakistan. The center of gravity for agency drones has shifted to Yemen, where the situation is obscured by Langley's close cooperation with the U.S. Special Operations Command (SOCOM), whose Joint Special Operations Command serves as field unit for the secret war against terror. The CIA's paramilitary wing has had two main functions of late, support for military operations on battlefronts that now include Africa, Afghanistan, Syria, Yemen, and again Iraq, plus the Predator strikes. Shifting U.S. priorities have confused activity. Rules of engagement that dictate which insurgent groups are distinct enough from Al Qaeda to qualify for CIA arms and training have hampered paramilitary support in Syria. The bright spot is the Kurds—ironically, CIA allies in an anti-Saddam coup attempt during the Clinton years, and a paramilitary war nearly half a century ago. But on most of today's battlefronts, SOCOM wants the lead and protects its interests fiercely. John Brennan had an opening for narrowing Langley's involvement and used it. Then came President Donald Trump, who made Syria an early focus of his actions.

Brennan's major enterprise has been a wholesale refashioning of the Central Intelligence Agency. It is this initiative, the nature of Trump's leadership, plus the conditions the CIA has created by cutting free of oversight, that will lead to disaster.

The coming failure most likely will flow from the success of John Brennan's initiatives. Brennan sought to refashion the CIA as a coalition of "mission centers." The essential idea is to extend the fusion center formula to the entire agency, that is, use the model of the Counterterrorism Center (CTC) across the board. In the 1980s and 1990s, the CTC numbered among the first fusion centers. These units melded covert operations, traditional intelligence gathering, special intelligence (the term used for electronic eavesdropping), and analysis. George Tenet was a fan. He expanded the number and scope of the species. In the Counterproliferation Center and the CTC, the main function centered on operations, not intelligence. More traditional centers were formed for inquiries into foreign technology, ground weapons, and WMDs. At the turn of the millennium, these were all the rage.

John Brennan cut his teeth on the fusion center idea when he headed the precursor to the National Counterterrorism Center. That unit, at the level of the director of national intelligence, formed as an old-style fusion center, bringing together all-source data. President Bush needed a unit of that kind because the CTC no longer functioned in an analytical capacity.

In the war on terror, the CTC vision came down to a case approach —combating an organization like Al Qaeda or an individual like Osama bin Laden. Analysis became tied to planning operations. So far as the Central Intelligence Agency's vaunted analytical capability was concerned, no one minded the store. The idea of the fusion center was to break down walls, bridging operators with analysts and support people, plus personnel from other agencies, and focusing them on a particular mission. Once focused on the mission, of course, that is what they do. The vision narrows. This is one reason for the shortcomings in U.S. appreciation of the overall dimensions of the terrorist threat. Similarly, the predilection for viewing refugee flows into and across Europe entirely from the security perspective failed to detect the social and economic forces that led to the

British exit (Brexit) from the European Union and the election of Donald J. Trump.

Among the challenges today, the continental shifts wrought by such centrifugal forces are just one issue for intelligence. Resource scarcity, global climate change, unstable governments, cyberwarfare, revanchism, and nuclear proliferation are all problems that concerned Director Brennan in the summer of 2016. At an appearance before the Senate intelligence committee that June, Brennan tempered optimistic notes on the losses of the Islamic State of Iraq and the Levant (ISIL) with dark foreboding that "our efforts have not reduced the group's terrorism capacity and global reach." Though he denies climate change and resource scarcity, President Trump shares the fear of terrorists and in his election campaign promised even stronger efforts to eradicate the Islamist foe.

When Brennan's precursor unit formed during the Bush years, it sought to draw on CTC expertise. Robert Grenier headed the Counterterrorism Center then. Grenier and others feared entities like Brennan's would feed on their fusion centers. When the Flying Dutchman asked for the assignment of CTC analysts, Grenier offered to turn over the whole organization instead. He argued that other major agencies—the FBI, the NSA, the military, all the key ones—had counterterror units. Why not combine them all and make a true national agency? Grenier asked. Brennan seemed interested, but his questions became skeptical. He turned down the idea, fearing he wouldn't be able to count on all those officers pulled out of their home agencies. But he kept thinking about it, and when Brennan emerged as CIA chief in his own right, he started reorganizing the agency as a coalition of mission centers. Frank Archibald, the operations director, opposed this scheme and went into retirement in 2015. His replacement, Gregory Vogel, had been chief of the agency paramilitary division and led the internal review that endorsed Brennan's vision. Vogel got the DO job. For deputy he had Gina Haspel, the Batwoman of Greystone.

Besides the narrowness of the mission centers and the tenuous relationships with home divisions or agencies of officers assigned to the mission centers, another key problem is bifurcation of effort. The old regional divisions of the operations directorate—and, under John Brennan, that name came back, the awkward title National Clandestine Service dispensed with—were each responsible for one area of the globe. The barons have always been jealous guardians of turf. The baron "owns" the CIA stations in the region, the operations, the relationships with ambassadors. A CTC team coming in to execute an op needs approvals from the appropriate DO regional barons. So operations have to be staffed through both centers and divisions, an invitation for bureaucratic logjams.

Worse, the home agency or directorate of officers assigned to centers are still responsible for the employees, which means the regional baron writes the efficiency report for the officer at the center. That's a recipe to stifle initiative at the center level. Meanwhile all those mission centers work for the CIA director. He or she has to manage the agency directorates, four at last count, plus the multiplying centers. Handling that many administrative units is practically beyond the span of any person. The weak leadership exhibited by the director of national intelligence illustrates the problem.

More menacing still is the prospect of fresh orders from a new president. Donald J. Trump spoke of tortures *more* extreme than those reviewed here, of new fierceness in prosecuting the war on terror, of pulling back from cooperation with European and Asian allies, and of reneging on the agreement made with Iran to hold back Tehran's nuclear weapons program. Such decisions will dictate an even faster CIA "ops tempo." President Trump's early missile strikes in Syria will have no impact without a bigger ground game, and he depends on SOCOM and the CIA for that. Direct American involvement should be expected to increase.

Director Brennan joined the Formers. They have been stunned. Most have spoken out, cautioning Mr. Trump against his extreme propositions. Michael Hayden, who preferred that oversight be restricted to times when a single political party possesses the presidency and controls both houses of Congress, now achieved that condition. The powerlessness of congressional oversight investigating the Russian election caper reveals the craven nature of Hayden's position. Meanwhile the general now says that Trump the torturer will have to bring his own bucket—a Hayden reversal. John Brennan, the Flying Dutchman, who finally decoupled the CIA from accountability, has observed, "Without a doubt the CIA really took some body blows as a result of its experiences. I think the overwhelming majority of CIA officers would not want to get back into that business."

In the Trump presidential transition, a politico has been selected to lead the CIA. Congressman Michael Pompeo, formerly a member of the House intelligence committee, has no administrative experience and no leadership credentials other than service as a junior tank officer in the Army. Pompeo is regarded as a quick study and a smart fellow with book knowledge of national security, but he shares some of Mr. Trump's outlook and is unlikely to stand up to the chief executive. Director Pompeo seemed notably silent when Trump ordered attacks on Syria, where the cleavages and infighting among assorted rebel groups, the Kurds, the Turks, the Russians, Syrian government forces, and the ISIL terrorists have shifted so often and so much that escalating without deep deliberation is foolish. Press reports indicate that Gina Haspel, whom Pompeo has elevated to be his own deputy, substituted for the boss by videoconference at Trump's decision meeting on the missile strike.

The true results of the dispute that raged around the Senate torture report are three: First, the CIA showed that it regards oversight as a political convenience, a cloak to disguise operations, not a watchdog to which it is responsible. Second, the controversy defanged the inspector general system, leaving it bankrupt. Third, Langley's excesses, unanswered by presidential measures of discipline, make the agency unassailable. Donald J. Trump *likes* "strong." Add to these elements the fact that under Panetta the CIA broke free of the director of national intelligence, who failed in an attempt to assert control over the naming of station chiefs. As a result, you have Langley in position to run away at any time. Director Pompeo will be carried off with it. The rank-and-file officers John Brennan worries about have been exposed to danger by his own success at evading accountability. At this point, only the remaining tendrils of presidential control keep the CIA from becoming—in Frank Church's memorable phrase—a rogue elephant.

The CIA entered the heart of its darkness at a moment of trauma for all Americans. Langley's denizens let ignorance and revenge skew their approach to the real business of spying. The zealots disdained anyone who rejected such a course. From that moment, evasion of accountability became necessary. That has entailed turning the CIA into a "paper mill" generating false claims of success and specious arguments to game the laws and engineer the conditions under which investigations are conducted. It has led the agency to engage in conspiracy, obstruction of justice, perjury, manipulation of secrecy regulations, phony referrals to the Department of Justice, countersurveillance against congressional overseers, and many other crimes. The spooks didn't have to invent all this. They drew on CIA experience at handling outsiders stretching back to its origins. There was a degree of innovation, to be sure, but there were rich illustrations from the agency's past to show how this sort of thing can be done. And Langley succeeded. The agency cut what it considered the fetters of accountability.

The thing is, the world is still a dangerous place. The reasons the nation needed an intelligence agency in 1947 persist, different only in detail. The ultimate horror is that the CIA's escape from accountability sows the seeds for its coming failure. The specifics of that failure are not possible to foresee, but the fact of it is perfectly predictable.

One key feature will be the stewardship of Donald J. Trump. As candidate Mr. Trump talked about interrogation methods worse than waterboarding. He spoke of destroying the Islamist "caliphate" in Syria and of putting more of the clandestine service's officers into the field. As president-elect, Trump kicked up a feud with America's spies to protect his own political position, and brought in politicians both as director of national intelligence and as head of the CIA.

Any CIA director, of necessity at the very limit of his capacity to lead the broad organization, will have no effective inspector general as warning bell. In addition, there will be a thinned-out body of midlevel and senior management personnel, the people who could keep the CIA train on the tracks. Those are precisely the officers who, like Mr. Brennan, are troubled by President Trump's shoot-from-the-lip style, but they are leaving or going into retirement by the dozen. There was an exodus from CIA when the Cold War ended and another after the Guatemala and Aldrich Ames fiascoes. More seepage took place during the angst-ridden black-prison phase. The advent of Donald Trump has brought the latest departures. The net result will be a cadre of very junior officers left to cope with the demands of a president demanding miracles on his breakfast plate.

In addition, talented people from all directorates have been siphoned off to the mission centers. There they are focused on operations, not on understanding the larger meaning of events. Just as worrisome—as the talent leaves, perhaps the directorates will send only their poorest people to the centers. Meanwhile the mission centers and the DO's geographic divisions will be fighting each other every step of the way. The centers, with their tunnel vision, will almost inevitably foul up. As a senior CTC officer put it in the dawn before the darkness, this is a train wreck waiting to happen. Good time to get off.

The DO surge into the field that Mr. Trump has promised will leave headquarters support as thin as upper management. At the same time, the shift to the operations-heavy mission-center model will further reduce the potential input from intelligence analysis, while CIA's newly ordained presence on the National Security Council Principals Committee multiplies its exposure to badgering. Given hard-driving agents in the field, a challenged Director Pompeo, and the demands from President Trump, blunders are almost certain. That's where the Ghosts of Langley come into the picture.

The CIA director will have minimal direction from above. The president is a character completely without scruples or substantive knowledge. Phony congressional oversight will flow from a Congress completely controlled by the president's party, and Langley seldom heeds Congress anyway. There will be a host of gunslinging attorneys as enablers. At hand will be a menu of ready-made tactics to evade scrutiny. First, pretend all is well and oversight is splendid. Next, deny every charge. Laugh critics off the stage when possible. When it is not—as with Eerik Heine or Frank Snepp—slander them. Prevent insiders from speaking out of court. Control the release of secrets. Discipline agency personnel only as a last resort. Maneuver to neutralize investigations where they become inevitable. If inquisitors interview, say they ignored documents; if they do documents, claim the results are skewed for lack of interviews. If necessary, claim that the investigators are breaking the law. If reforms are demanded, say these will lead to excess caution, to risk aversion that will damage intelligence. It's a quiver full of arrows sufficient to defeat all but the most intense inquiry.

If perchance the spy chieftain is not prepared to stonewall, there is now a Langley lobby ready to pull strings and apply pressure to stiffen the CIA's backbone and induce the president to order the agency director to do whatever it deems necessary. The Formers may have opposed Trump the candidate, but they will most likely line up behind Trump the president.

The Ghosts of Langley teach that keeping perceptions of the threat at an intense level reduces pressures on the CIA to observe legal and political boundaries. Both President Trump and Mr. Pompeo have drawn a bleak picture of a hostile world. Bombing the terrorists back to the stone age is on Trump's list. Barack Obama must take a share of the blame here. Had Obama begun with a conscientious national look back at what had been wrought, any reversion to torture today would simply be impossible, and had President Obama brought the drone war within a constitutional war powers framework, America would have had the Great Debate that would have built a consensus around our national actions. Instead, Obama's successors think they can turn back the clock, perhaps as far as the Middle Ages, the Islamists' favorite era. The Trump administration will do nothing to turn back the Ghosts of Langley. And that leads to the Great Train Wreck. The challenge is clear.

NOTES

PROLOGUE

2 "shape the future" et seq.: CIA contract language quoted in Greg Miller, "How a Modest Contract for 'Applied Research' Morphed into the CIA's Brutal Interrogation Program," *Washington Post*, July 13, 2016, p. A1.

2 Swigert/Mitchell's previous experience: James E. Mitchell with Bill Harlow, *Enhanced Interrogation: Inside the Minds and Motives of the Islamic Terrorists Trying to Destroy America* (New York: Crown Forum, 2016), 46–47.

2–3 Terminology for CIA terms, techniques: Senate Select Committee on Intelligence (SSCI), *Committee Study of the Central Intelligence Agency's Detention and Interrogation Program* (hereafter cited as Senate torture report).

3 CIA agents detained, date selected for number, etc.: Senate torture report, Executive Summary, Dec. 13, 2012, declassified Dec. 3, 2014, passim.

5 "Detention Site Green": Ibid., p. 23.

6 "hard approach": Ibid., p. 26, cf. pp. 19–21.

7 "We need to hustle to come up with a strategy" and later, Bush's instructions to Tenet: Alberto Gonzales, *True Faith and Allegiance: A Story of Service and Sacrifice in War and Peace* (Nashville, TN: Nelson Books, 2016), 186–88, quoted p. 186.

7 "shift the dynamics": John Rizzo, *Company Man: Thirty Years of Controversy and Crisis in the CIA* (New York: Scribner, 2014), 183.

7 "mostly because a lot of what they were telling me" et seq.: Rizzo, *Company Man*, 184–88, Tenet quoted at 188.

7 Thailand money: The Senate investigation confirms that the Thais received CIA support but text that might have identified what has been deleted.

8 Threats made to Abu Zubaydah: Senate torture report, pp. 27–28. Also see John Kiriakou and Michael Ruby, *The Reluctant Spy: My Secret Life in CIA's War on Terror* (New York: Bantam, 2010).

10 Bybee and Yoo disavowals: Bybee cited in "Investigating the Interrogators," *Los Angeles Times* editorial, July 21, 2010, p. A16. Yoo in Andy Sullivan, "Author of Interrogation Memo Says CIA Maybe Went too Far," Reuters dispatch, Dec. 14, 2014.

10 "novel interrogation methods": CIA, Operational Update Memorandum for CIA Leadership, July 3, 2002, 1630 Hours; Senate torture report, p. 32.

10 Psychologist Shumate on Mitchell aircraft: Mitchell and Harlow, *Enhanced Interrogation*, 21.

10 Meeting with Tenet: Ibid., 49–51.

11 Swigert instructions: Ali H. Soufan with Daniel Freedman, *The Black Banners: The Inside Story of 9/11 and the War Against al-Qaeda* (New York: Norton, 2011), 393–96.

11 "One month or a little over a month": Abu Zubaida journal, Feb. [deleted], 2008, p. 3. Feb. [deleted], 2008, p. 14. Document released in discovery, December 20, 2016, in *Salim v. Mitchell*, U.S. District Court, Eastern District, Washington State, No. CV-15-0286-JLQ, Item 7B. (This bears a redacted date and was "declassified" although never secret—originated by a private individual with no classification authority. The document is marked "SECRET/NoForn" and the notations lined out, with "UNCLASSIFIED" substituted. Probably due to this odd handling it contains none of the usual declassification data.) Hereafter cited as Abu Zubaydah journal.

11 "CIA records do not support this assertion": Senate torture report, p. 31.

12 "TO ESTABLISH A RELATIONSHIP": CIA cable, EYES ONLY, "Interrogation Plan" (other details deleted), 120509Z, Apr. 2002 (declassified Dec. 20, 2016); *Salim v. Mitchell* Discovery, Bates numbers 001825–001829, quoted at 001825.

12 "DETAILED AND VERIFIABLE" and "HE HAD ALREADY PROVIDED": CIA cable (details deleted), 041559Z, Aug. 2002, declassified Dec. 20, 2016, Bates numbers 001755–001759, quoted at 001755. This dispatch also introduces the CIA terms for the psychologists referred to in the text. Other interrogation reports appear in the discovery documents at 001803–001806 (Aug. 6), 001942–001944 (Aug. 7), 001945–001948 (Aug. 8), and 001949–001954 (Aug. 9). The order "You know what to do" appears at 001951 and elsewhere in these cables, as well as at 001807–001808 (Aug. 18).

14 "The hood was lifted" : Abu Zubaydah journal, p. 14

14 "HIGHLY UNLIKELY" to "STRONGLY URGE THAT ANY SPECULATIVE LANGUAGE": Station Green and Jose Rodriguez e-mails, Aug. 12, 2002, reprinted in Senate torture report, p. 43. In December 2014, Rodriguez claimed through a spokesperson that he had had nothing to do with this message.

15 Soufan interrogation said to fail: Mitchell and Harlow, *Enhanced Interrogation*, 35–38.

15 "replacing our freedoms": Ibid., 127.

16 "even totally legal techniques will look 'ugly'" et. seq. : Joint Task Force 170, Notes, "Counter Resistance Strategy Meeting Minutes," October 2, 2002, printed in Senate Armed Services Committee (110th Congress, 2nd Session), *Hearings: The Treatment of Detainees in U.S. Custody* (Washington, DC: Government Printing Office, 2009), pp. 215–18, quoted at 217. The meeting is further discussed in the committee's *Report: Inquiry into the Treatment of Detainees in U.S. Custody*, released Nov. 20, 2008. The hearings and report make clear that Army Lieutenant Colonel Diane E. Beaver, who convened the meeting, by 2008 had no specific recollections of the discussion, including Mr. Fredman's contributions. Guantánamo's Interrogation Control Unit chief David Becker had written the notes while actively participating, so seems unlikely to have forgotten what transpired. As Jonathan Fredman insists, Becker's notes specified that he had paraphrased the remarks of participants. Mr. Fredman's overall denial appears as the enclosure to Office of the Director of National Intelligence, Letter,

Kathleen Turner–Senator Carl Levin, November 17, 2008 (www.slideshare.net/ guest93466b77/jonathan-fredman-to-the-senate-armed-services-committee). But the Fredman memorandum confirms he attended this meeting and, at a minimum, briefed the Guantánamo inquisitors on legal issues of interrogation.

17 Pavit instructions on tapes: CIA cable, Oct. 25, 2002, declassified Apr. 15, 2010, released by American Civil Liberties Union (hereafter cited as ACLU release), tranche no. 1.

17 *Washington Post* **story:** Dana Priest and Barton Gellman, "U.S. Decries Abuse but Defends Interrogations," *Washington Post*, Dec. 26, 2002, p. A1.

18 read and understood instructions: CIA cable, CTC-Station Bangkok, EYES ONLY, Dec. 3, 2002, declassified Apr. 15, 2010, ACLU release, tranche no. 1.

18 CIA lawyer: CIA, Office of the Inspector General, "Special Review: Counterterrorism Detention and Interrogation Activities (September 2001–October 2003)," 2003-7123-IG, May 7, 2004, declassified 2008, 2015. Other evidence indicates the lawyer was John McPherson.

19 "Endgame Facility" to "Just hope our myopic view": CIA, e-mail (details deleted), "RDG Tasking for IC Psychologists Jessen and Mitchell," June 16, 2003, 4:54 p.m. (declassified Sept. 30, 2016; C06552085), in ACLU court case 1:15-CV-09317-AKH, document 53-4. Content and context make clear that this e-mail is from the CIA's Office of Medical Services and was sent to either the Technical Services office, which controlled the psychologists' contracts, or the CTC, where the RDG was located.

19 "our interest in these techniques": CIA, e-mail (details deleted), "RDG Tasking for IC Psychologists Jessen and Mitchell," June 20, 2003, 2:19 p.m. (declassified Sept. 30, 2016; C06552086); ACLU case 1:15-cv-09317-AKH, document 53-5. Context and content are identical to the previous citation. Also, this language bears on the dispute over CIA's briefings to Congress. If in June 2003 the agency still held to its cover story that the waterboard was strictly a training device, that casts doubt on whether Congress had really been told of its use in interrogations during 2002.

19 "I learned early on": Al Kamen, "In the Loop: In Washington and Beyond, Disclosing a Few of Cheney's Locations," *Washington Post*, Oct. 5, 2007, quoted p. A19. Mr. Cheney made this statement in Grand Rapids, Michigan, at a September 2007 event.

19–20 Events of July 29, 2003, including "forcefully reiterated the view of the Department of Justice": Central Intelligence Agency, Scott W. Muller, "Review of Terrorist Program on 29 July 2003," OGC-FO-2003- 50078, Aug. 5, 2003, declassified Nov. 9, 2014, CIA CO6238939. The CIA's PowerPoint briefing for that meeting has also been declassified. For the NSC meeting, see Gonzales, *True Faith and Allegiance*, 189–91, 202.

21 "recommended that CIA move": CIA, e-mail, Scott M. Muller (OGC) to James L. Pavitt (DDO), "CIA Detainees at GITMO," 2004/02 [redacted], declassified June 10, 2016.

21 "some of our rules might be described as": CIA Office of Congressional Affairs, Memorandum for the Record, Nov. 30, 2004, declassified for *Amnesty International et al. v. CIA*, document 361, Feb. 22, 2010. Written retrospectively, the memo makes clear that it pertains to the May 10 briefing.

23 "I wanted to assure the people here": White House text, "President Thanks

CIA Employees," Central Intelligence Agency, Langley, Virginia, Mar. 3, 2005, copy in author's files.

23 "the false impression that US intelligence may have had a policy": Central Intelligence Agency, press release, "Statement by CIA Director of Public Affairs Jennifer Millerwise," Mar. 18, 2005, copy in author's files.

23 "I got nowhere": Rizzo, Company Man, quoted p. 242. Also see Paul Kane and Joby Warrick, "Cheney Led Briefings of Lawmakers to Defend Interrogation Techniques," Washington Post, June 3, 2009, which quotes McCain saying, "Torture is torture" (p. A4).

25 "CIA HOLDS TERROR SUSPECTS IN SECRET PRISONS": Dana Priest, Washington Post, Nov. 2, 2005, p. A1.

26 "I'd like to know if there is anything": Robert L. Grenier, 88 Days to Kandahar: A CIA Diary (New York: Simon & Schuster, 2015), quoted p. 402.

29 "This is a train wreak [sic]": CIA, CTC/RG e-mail, Jan. 22, 2003, 10:22 a.m., declassified June 10, 2016, C06541516, CIA Electronic Reading Room.

29 "We all knew it would": David Ignatius, "Revolt of the Professionals," Washington Post, Dec. 21, 2005, p. A31.

29 "We all knew the political wind would change": David Ignatius, "Slow Roll Time at Langley," Washington Post, Apr. 22, 2009, p. A25.

29 "The agency is glad to be out of it": David Ignatius, "A Sigh of Relief at the CIA," Washington Post, Aug. 26, 2009, p. A15.

1. THE HOUSE THAT ALLEN BUILT

33 "a pride of lions": James Srodes, Allen Dulles: Master of Spies (Washington, DC: Regnery, 1999), 20.

41 "the Agency shall have no police, subpoena or law enforcement powers": National Security Act of 1947, Section 103 (d) (1), in U.S. Congress, House of Representatives, Permanent Select Committee on Intelligence, Compilation of Intelligence Laws and Related Laws and Executive Orders of Interest to the National Intelligence Community, as amended through Jan. 3, 1998. (Washington, DC: Government Printing Office, 1998), 10. Hereafter this source will be cited as Compilation of Intelligence Laws 1998.

43 such other functions: Ibid., Sec. 103 (d) (5).

48 "subtly consultative and mutually enriching": George R. Urban, Radio Free Europe and the Pursuit of Democracy: My War Within the Cold War (New Haven: Yale University Press, 1997), 47.

49 "writing reports for the government": Allen Welch Dulles, The Craft of Intelligence (New York: New American Library, 1965), ix.

52 "Allen, you don't know how to run anything!": Burton Hersh, The Old Boys: The American Elite and the Origins of the CIA (New York: Macmillan, 1992), quoted pp. 314, 316.

52 "Allen isn't a bad administrator": Ludwell Lee Montague, General Walter Bedell Smith as Director of Central Intelligence, October 1950–February 1953 (University Park: Pennsylvania State University Press, 1992), quoted p. 92.

52 "You gave it to Allen Dulles?": Lincoln K. White oral history, in CIA, Studies in Intelligence, Winter 1999–2000, pp. 29–41, quoted p. 34.

53 **"The General was in fine form"**: Montague, *General Walter Bedell Smith*, 92.

60 **Israeli historians:** Yossi Melman and Dan Raviv, "The Journalist's Connections: How Israel Got Russia's Biggest Pre-Glasnost Secret," *International Journal of Intelligence and Counterintelligence,* vol. 4, no. 2, 1990, pp. 219–25. Even Melman and Raviv cannot come down to a single source. By their account, the speech came from Ben *or* through Amos Manor of the internal security service Shin Bet, from an agent in the Soviet bloc. Either way, Israeli prime minister David Ben-Gurion personally approved the handover to the CIA, and that was done late in April 1956, which matches the chronology from the U.S. side.

61 **"By golly, I'm going to make a policy decision"**: Ray Cline, *Secrets, Spies and Scholars: Blueprint of the Essential CIA* (Washington, DC: Acropolis Books, 1976), quoted p. 164.

62 **"scurrilous"** and **"He is in bad company"**: CIA, Minutes, Deputies Meeting (DIM-519), Oct. 31, 1956, declassified May 6, 2003, CIA -RDP80B01676R002300200014-2.

62 **"matter on the other side of the world"**: Allen to John Foster Dulles phone notes, Jan. 16, 1958, Dwight D. Eisenhower Library (hereafter DDEL), Dulles Papers: Telephone Series, box 8, folder "Memoranda of Telephone Conversations, General, February 1–March 31, 1958."

69 **"We sometimes thought he was trying"**: Richard Helms, "Address to CIA Retirees," *Central Intelligence Retirees Association Newsletter* (hereafter cited as *CIRA Newsletter*), vol. 22, no. 3, (Winter 1997–1998): 8.

70 **"Red, you have to have a cornerstone"** et seq.: Lincoln K. White, "Naming the HQ Buildings," *CIRA Newsletter,* Summer 1998, quoted p. 22.

71 **"I believe we get the same reports"**: *Time,* Sept. 28, 1959.

72 **"the work of this agency demands"**: CIA, "Presidential Reflections on U.S. Intelligence, President Eisenhower," September 7, 2010.

73 **"I was faced with a heads-he-wins, tails-I-lose proposition"** : Richard Nixon, "Cuba, Castro and John F. Kennedy: Some Reflections on United States Foreign Policy," *Reader's Digest,* November 1964, p. 288.

75 **"I have not commented"** et seq.: Allen Dulles, *The Craft of Intelligence,* 157, 175. The account that Dulles dismissed was in Haynes Johnson's book *The Bay of Pigs: The Leaders' Story of Brigade 2506* (New York: Dell, 1964).

2. ZEALOTS AND SCHEMERS

77 **"The social side was very important to Allen"**: Hersh, *The Old Boys,* 316.

79 **"Park Avenue cowboys"**: Hugh Wilford, *The Mighty Wurlitzer: How the CIA Played America* (Cambridge, MA: Harvard University Press, 2008), 27.

82 **"The operators are not going to decide"**: Hersh, *The Old Boys,* 298.

82 **"I don't care if they are blabbing secrets or not"**: Ibid., 301.

83 **"Kindly do not bring in here any more"**: Ibid.

90 **"Present governmental policy does not provide"**: CIA, Frank Wisner–Allen Dulles, Draft Memorandum, Policy Guidance for CIA Planning to "capitalize on and exploit new uprisings in the satellites," Jan. 8, 1954, in Douglas Keane and

Michael Warner, eds., *Foreign Relations of the United States, 1950–1955: The Intelligence Community, 1950–1955* (Washington, DC: Government Printing Office, repr. 2007, 469–71. *Foreign Relations* is the official historical documentary record of the U.S. government. Various volumes of this series will be quoted here. In subsequent citations, when a volume first appears, it will be given a full annotation so as to credit the editors, but in other appearances, only the form *FRUS*, with a brief volume identification and the relevant page number. Please note that within the *FRUS*, internal cross-references are to documents by number. Citations here, however, conform to publishing practice by referring to *page numbers* in all cases.

91 "I'd rather have Allen" et seq.: John Prados, *Presidents' Secret Wars: CIA and Pentagon Covert Operations from World War II through the Persian Gulf* (Chicago: Ivan R. Dee/Rowman & Littlefield, 1996), quoted p. 111.

91 "aggressive covert psychological, political" et seq.: Report of the Special Study Group (Doolittle Committee), "Report on the Covert Activities of the Central Intelligence Agency," n.d. (Oct. 19, 1954), *FRUS: Intelligence Community, 1950–1955*, p. 542.

93 "navigate, fly, drop the bomb": Robert A. Lovett testimony, May 11, 1961, p. 4, Paramilitary Study Group (Taylor Committee), Memorandum for the Record, 14th Meeting, May 11, 1961, John F. Kennedy Library (JFKL), Kennedy Papers, National Security File, Country File, box 61A, folder "Cuba: Subjects, Paramilitary Study Group, Part II Meetings 13–15" (hereafter cited as Lovett testimony).

94 "demonstrate the Communist technique": National Security Council, Operations Coordinating Board, Assistants Working Group, "List of Agreed Courses of Action to Implement NSC 174," Aug. 25, 1954, *FRUS, Intelligence Community 1950–1955*, pp. 531–39, quoted p. 532.

94 "detaching" countries, "soft" policies: National Security Council, Operations Coordinating Board, Working Group Report, "Analysis of the Situation with Respect to Possible Detachment of a Major European Soviet Satellite," Jan. 5, 1955 *FRUS: Intelligence Community, 1950–1955*, p. 592.

94 RFE paper: A. Ross Johnson, "Setting the Record Straight: Role of Radio Free Europe in the Hungarian Revolution of 1956," Woodrow Wilson Center, 2006.

97 "it's time we held Sukarno's feet": Joseph B. Smith, *Portrait of a Cold Warrior* (New York: Putnam's, 1976), quoted p. 205.

98 "No one was listening to Wisner": Thomas, *The Very Best Men*, quoted p. 152.

99 "disintegration" and "could not be described as an irrevocable revolt": Robert McMahon et al., eds., *Foreign Relations of the United States, 1955–1957*, vol. 22, *Southeast Asia 1955–1957* (Washington, DC: Government Printing Office, 1989), 655.

100 "Some CIA men": William Stevenson, *Birds' Nests in Their Beards* (Boston: Houghton Mifflin, 1963), quoted p. 29.

102 "intelligence," "crystally-clear facts" et seq.: Lovett testimony, 7.

104 leading CIA team to HPSCI briefing: Jose Rodriguez with Bill Harlow, *Hard Measures: How Aggressive CIA Actions after 9/11 Saved American Lives* (New York: Simon & Schuster, 2012), 64. At 2:52 p.m. on September 6, Rodriguez complimented a CIA lawyer on removing a sentence from the meeting record which noted congressional incumbents had legal doubts about the detention program. Senate torture report, p. 438 and fn. 2455.

105 "getting rid of some ugly visuals": Rodriguez and Harlow, *Hard Measures*, 193.

105 "I understand your lawyers chopped on it": Rizzo, *Company Man*, 18. "Chopped" is a term government officials use as slang for approving or approval.

106 "In my thirty-four years": Ibid., 19.

106 "Actually, it would be he, PG, who took the heat": CIA, e-mail to Executive Director Kyle D. Foggo, Nov. 10, 2005, 5:48 p.m., declassified, ACLU FOIA release, Apr. 15, 2010, part 3.

107 Walsh charges Adkins: U.S. Court of Appeals for the District of Columbia Circuit, Division for the Purpose of Appointing Independent Counsel, Division no. 86-6, Lawrence E. Walsh, *Final Report of the Independent Counsel for Iran/Contra Matters*, vol. 1, *Investigations and Prosecutions*, Aug. 4, 1993, pp. 309–11. Also see John Prados, *Safe for Democracy: The Secret Wars of the CIA* (Chicago: Ivan R. Dee, 2006), 558–60. (Hereafter cited as Walsh Report with volume and page numbers.)

108 "The anti-CIA mood in government": Christopher D. Costanzo, *My CIA: Memories of a Secret Career* (North Charleston, SC: Create Space Independent Publishing, 2013), 392.

109 Jose is "out on Business": Mark Mazzetti and Scott Shane, "Tape Inquiry: Ex-Spymaster in the Middle," *New York Times*, Feb. 20, 2008, quoted p. A12.

109 "We'll find something for you": Rodriguez and Harlow, *Hard Measures*, 30.

109 fifty-four nations that helped: *Globalizing Torture: CIA Secret Detention and Extraordinary Rendition* (Washington, DC: Open Society Foundation, Feb. 2013).

111 Vodaphone scandal: Greek investigators traced the purchase of telephones used in the surveillance to individuals at the U.S. embassy in Athens and later issued a warrant for the arrest of an individual said to have been employed by the NSA. The surveillance took place during the 2004 Olympics, when Rodriguez was point man for all U.S. agencies' security efforts. Rodriguez and Harlow, *Hard Measures*, 127.

111 "could resurface . . . given press speculations": Department of State, Memo, Robin Quinville–Ambassador Charles P. Ries, "Briefer for your Breakfast Meetings with John Bellinger," Apr. 14, 2008, sensitive but unclassified, declassified Jan. 28, 2009, State Department FOIA Reading Room.

113 Project Cannonball: Mark Mazzetti and Scott Shane, "After 9/11, CIA had Plan to Kill Qaeda's Leaders," *New York Times*, July 14, 2009, pp. A1, A14; Joby Warrick and Ben Pershing, "CIA Had Program to Kill Al-Qaeda Leaders," *Washington Post*, July 14, 2009, p. A2; David Ignatius, "The CIA's 'Hit Team' Miss," *Washington Post*, July 23, 2009, p. A21; Joby Warrick and R. Jeffrey Smith, "CIA Hired Firm for Assassin Program," *Washington Post*, Aug. 20, 2009, pp. A1, A4; Joby Warrick, "Blackwater Founder Says He Aided Secret Programs," *Washington Post*, Dec. 3, 2009, A6.

114 "Fuck you!" et seq.: Michael Morell with Bill Harlow, *The Great War of Our Time: The CIA's Fight Against Terrorism from Al Qaeda to ISIS* (New York: Hachette, 2015), 144–45.

114 **New York Police Department operation:** As his deputy leading the Intelligence Division, NYPD commissioner Raymond W. Kelly appointed David Cohen. A long-service CIA veteran who had actually started as an analyst, Cohen had been the deputy director for operations when Jose Rodriguez took charge of DO's Latin America Division in the 1990s. Now Rodriguez was CTC chief of operations. While Cohen had gone into retirement before the NYPD stint, he still needed the CIA for his security clearance and to facilitate NYPD activity. In April 2002, the CIA approved a concept for cooperation, and a couple of months later, agency analyst Lawrence Sanchez went to the NYPD as Director Tenet's representative. Two years later, Rodriguez approved as the CIA put Sanchez on extended leave so he could work for Cohen and the NYPD directly, full-time. In a related move, an NYPD detective trained for more than a year with the CIA. That, at least, cannot be traced to Director Rodriguez; Jose left the CIA in September 2007, but the NYPD detective arrived only in October 2008. CIA, David B. Buckley (IG)–David H. Petraeus (DCIA), Memorandum Report, "Review of the CIA-NYPD Relationship," Dec. 27, 2011, declassified June 24, 2013, C05999891, CIA Electronic Reading Room.

116 **"although I knew he believed":** Morell and Harlow, *The Great War of Our Time*, 260.

3. STARS AND METEORS

123 **"Don't think that just by pressing a button":** Joby Warrick, "The Reluctant Martyr," *Washington Post*, June 29, 2011, p. C3.

124 **"There's been an attack" and "This guy turned out to be a double agent"** et seq.: Leon Panetta with Jim Newton, *Worthy Fights: A Memoir of Leadership in War and Peace* (New York: Penguin, 2014), 262, 263.

125–130 **Robert Ames's Accomplishments:** The following discussion of CIA officer Bob Ames depends largely on Kai Bird's fine biography, *The Good Spy: The Life and Death of Robert Ames* (New York: Crown Publishers, 2014), passim.

135 **"You use my airfields, you take my orders":** Stephen Schlesinger and Stephen Kinzer, *Bitter Fruit: The Untold Story of the American Coup in Guatemala* (Garden City, NY: Doubleday, 1982), 193.

136 **"a man of Allen Dulles's imagination":** Richard Helms with William Hood, *A Look Over My Shoulder: A Life in the Central Intelligence Agency* (New York: Random House, 2003), 176.

138 **"It's none of your damn business":** Kenneth W. Thompson, ed., *Portraits of the American Presidency*, vol. 3, *The Eisenhower Presidency: Eleven Intimate Perspectives of Dwight D. Eisenhower* (Lanham, MD: University Press of America, 1984), 219.

140 **"Don't be too specific on briefing Adlai":** Thomas, *The Very Best Men*, 254.

142 **"With Rip you could never be sure":** CIA, *Official History of the Bay of Pigs Operation*, vol. 3, *Evolution of the CIA's Anti-Castro Policies, 1959–January 1961* (Jack Pfeiffer history), TS-795052, Dec. 1979, declassified in *Historical Review Program*, 1998, p. 24.

4. CRISES

145 "I am the responsible officer": *New York Times*, Apr. 22, 1961.

146 "Tears came to their eyes": Grayston L. Lynch, *Decision for Disaster: Betrayal at the Bay of Pigs* (Washington, DC: Brassey's, 1998), 148.

146 "The men in this force": *Operation Zapata: The Ultrasensitive Report and Testimony of the Board of Inquiry on the Bay of Pigs* (Frederick, MD: Aletheia Books, 1981), 160. Grayston Lynch, in the book cited above, outlines testimony (pp. 149–50) that corresponds to what is recorded here in Taylor's record. But the Taylor Committee recorded this statement on April 28 (Friday), and Lynch insists he testified on the Monday (May 1). According to its records, on May 1, the Taylor Committee took testimony from CIA mission chief Colonel Jack Hawkins. It heard Robertson and Lynch on April 28 and May 2. Nothing Lynch said on May 2 matches his written recollection, but the April 28 testimony does.

147 no "inquiry," no "investigation": Taylor Committee, Memorandum for the Record, Apr. 24, 1961. All references to Taylor Committee documents are to materials held at the JFKL, Kennedy Papers, National Security File, Country File, Cuba, box 19, folders: "Paramilitary Study Group" [with Annexes].

147 "I'm your man-eating shark": Peter Wyden, *Bay of Pigs: The Untold Story* New York: Simon & Schuster, 1979), 95.

150 "a man of high character": Arthur M. Schlesinger Jr., *A Thousand Days: John F. Kennedy in the White House* (Greenwich, CT: Fawcett, 1967), 226.

151 "It's in the air now" et seq.: Richard M. Bissell Jr., Columbia University, Center for Oral History Archives, Rare Books Collection, Oral History No. 138, June 5, 1967, pp. 43–44.

154 "The planning for this operation": Church Committee, Deposition of Richard M. Bissell, June 9, 1975, p. 21, quoted p. 23, National Archives and Records Administration, RG-246, Records of the Assassination Records Board, box 11.

155 "After the President" et seq.: Smith, *Portrait of a Cold Warrior,* pp. 323–24.

157 "Bissell's View": CIA, "Cuba," Feb. 17, 1961, declassified Apr. 19, 1996, attached to memorandum, McGeorge Bundy–John F. Kennedy, Feb. 18, 1961, declassified Aug. 23, 1977, JFKL, Kennedy Papers, National Security File, Country File, box 35, folder "Cuba, General, 1/61–4/61." In his memo, Bundy identifies the author of the CIA paper as Richard Bissell. He also appends a cover sheet to the paper with the title "Bissell's View."

157 "The Taylor Committee report was probably correct": Richard M. Bissell, "Response to Lucien S. Vandenbroucke, 'The "Confessions" of Allen Dulles: New Evidence on the Bay of Pigs,'" *Diplomatic History* 8, no. 4 (Fall 1984): 379. The Vandenbroucke paper, with that title, appears in the same journal issue at pp. 365–76.

158 "I know of no estimate": Allen Dulles, *The Craft of Intelligence*, 157–58.

158 "attempt to set up an acceptable alternative": Taylor Committee, Hearing Transcript, 19th Meeting, May 22, 1961, declassified Mar. 22, 2000, p. 2. JFKL, Kennedy Papers, National Security File, Country File, Cuba, box 19, folder "Paramilitary Study Group, Taylor Report, Part III, Annex 19."

159 "splintering" et seq.: Taylor Branch and George Crile, "The Kennedy Vendetta," *Harper's*, Aug. 1975, p. 50.

160 persons interviewed for IG report: Some uncertainty attaches to the number the Kirkpatrick staff interviewed. The body of the IG report states "about 125." In his cover letter of November 20, however, Kirkpatrick says 130 people plus the four named officials. I have used that figure because this cover letter addressed to the Director of Central Intelligence would have been most careful to be exact.

160 "one of the most painful episodes": Lyman Kirkpatrick, *The Real CIA*, 184.

160 "Rather than receiving": Ibid., 200.

162 "This was indeed part of the problem": CIA, Memorandum Lyman Kirkpatrick–Director John McCone, May 24, 1964 (declassified Dec. 6, 2015, LBJ Library, Johnson Papers, National Security File, Agency File, box 8, folder: "CIA v. I [1 of 2]"). The magazine did indeed run the article, and Mario Lazo later published the book *Dagger in the Heart: American Policy Failures in Cuba* (New York: Funk & Wagnalls, 1968).

165 "Sticks and stones may break my bones" et seq.: Walsh Report, vol. 3, *Comments and Materials Submitted by Individuals and Their Attorneys Responding to Volume I of the Final Report*, Washington, DC, Dec. 3, 1993, p. 51.

169 "no basis has been found": Senate Select Committee on Intelligence, "Report on the Casey Inquiry," Dec. 3, 1981, p. 6. Copy in author's files.

170 "Intelligence and counterintelligence capabilities": U.S. Congress, 97th Congress, 1st Session, Senate Foreign Relations Committee, *Hearing: Nomination of William J. Casey* (Washington, DC: Government Printing Office, 1981), 14.

170 "chronic inarticulateness": Jonathan Alter and Nicolas Horrock, "A Most Unlikely Superspook," *Newsweek*, Oct. 10, 1983, p. 40.

170 Flappy: Bob Woodward, *Veil: The Secret Wars of the CIA, 1981–1987* (New York: Pocket Books, 1988), 228.

170 "It's a tremendous advantage to Casey": James Conaway, "Spymaster: The File on Bill Casey," *Washington Post*, Sept. 7, 1983, p. B9.

172 I'M A CONTRA TOO: Personal observation.

173 "If the operation blew up": Duane R. Clarridge, *A Spy for All Seasons: My Life in the CIA* (New York: Scribner, 2002), 206.

176 Casey admitted, "We are": U.S. Congress, 98th Congress, 2nd Session, Senate Select Committee on Intelligence, *Report: January 1, 1983 to December 31, 1984* (Washington, DC: Government Printing Office, 1985), pp. 7–10.

176 "The CIA was directly involved": Barry M. Goldwater with Jack Casserly, *Goldwate* (New York: Doubleday, 1988), quoted pp. 304, 306.

176 "I am pissed off" et seq.: SSCI Report, repr., p. 8.

176 "can only be described as a domestic disinformation campaign": Robert Simmons as quoted by Daniel Patrick Moynihan, *Congressional Record*, Aug. 12, 1994, p. S11834.

177 "Moynihan was probably drunk" et seq.: Rizzo, *Company Man*, 84.

178 "grudging": L. Britt Snider, *The CIA and the Hill: CIA's Relationship with Congress, 1946–2004* (Washington, DC: Central Intelligence Agency, Center for the Study of Intelligence, 2008), p. 61.

180 "a personal repudiation": Rizzo, *Company Man*, 103.

181 "If such a story gets out": National Security Planning Group, Meeting

Record, June 25, 1984, reprinted in Peter Kornbluh and Malcolm A. Byrne, *Iran-Contra Scandal: The Declassified History* (New York: The New Press, 1993), 69–82.

183 "I didn't even know": Joseph E. Persico, *Casey: The Lives and Secrets of William J. Casey: From the OSS to the CIA* (New York: Viking, 1990), 410.

183 "I don't want you operating in Central America" et seq.: Walsh Report, vol. 1, *Investigations and Prosecutions*, 204.

186 "We were transfixed": James McCullough, "Coping with Iran-Contra: Personal Reflections on Bill Casey's Last Month at CIA," *Studies in Intelligence* 39, no. 2 (Summer 1995): 29.

187 "does have the authority to withhold prior notice" et seq. (all references to Casey testimony): House of Representatives, Permanent Select Committee on Intelligence, "Iran Briefing," stenographic transcript, Nov. 21, 1986, in U.S. Congress, 100th Congress, 1st Session, House Select Committee to Investigate Covert Arms Transactions with Iran and Senate Select Committee on Secret Military Assistance to Iran and the Nicaraguan Opposition, *Joint Hearings: Iran-Contra Investigation*, vol. 100–6 (Washington, DC: Government Printing office, 1988), 649–91, here quoted at pp. 659, 669–70, 674, 678. (Any reference to these hearings hereafter will be cited as Iran-Contra Hearings with the volume number.) Director Casey's reference to "successor general counsels" and DCIs is another obfuscation: right through the time of the January 1985 finding, there had been just one CIA general counsel during the Reagan administration, Stanley Sporkin, and one DCI, Casey.

190 "Boys, this will blow over": Jack Devine, *Good Hunting: An American Spymaster's Story* (New York: Farrar, Straus & Giroux, 2014), 85.

191 "Jim, I'll look at it": McCullough, "Coping with Iran-Contra," 43.

5. THE CONSIGLIERI

195 "Don't tell me it can't be done legally": Persico, *Casey*, 405.

196 "In a perfect world" et seq.: Iran-Contra Hearings, vol. 100–6, p. 124.

196 "partial non-notification" et seq.: Ibid., pp. 179–81.

196 "on the principle that notifying fewer": Iran-Contra Report, House vol. 100-433/Senate vol. 100-216, p. 585.

198 "I hadn't had my fill": Iran-Contra Hearings, vol. 100–6, p. 175.

200 "We reached a point" et seq.: Persico, *Casey*, 405.

201 "strictly a technical matter": Ronald Brownstein and Nina Easton, *Reagan's Ruling Class: Portraits of the President's Top 100 Officials* (Washington, DC: Presidential Acountability Group, 1982), 626.

202 Stanley Sporkin and Presidential Findings: U.S. Congress, 100th Congress, 1st Session, House Select Committee to Investigate Covert Arms Transactions with Iran and Senate Select Committee on Secret Military Assistance to Iran and the Nicaraguan Opposition, *Joint Hearings: Iran-Contra Investigation*, vol. 100-6, June 23–25, 1987 (Washington, DC: Government Printing Office, 1987), 122–90. Justice Department lawyer Charles Cooper's notes are in Joint Committee, *Appendix B: Depositions*, v. 7 (Washington, DC: Government Printing Office, 1988), 610–13.

202 **"prudential" and "this draft raises":** Theodore Draper, *A Very Thin Line: The Iran-Contra Affairs* (New York: Hill & Wang, 1991), 213.

202 **"the best advice anybody ever gave me":** Persico, *Casey*, 410.

207 **"pitchers should leak from the top":** Frank Snepp, *Irreparable Harm* (Lawrence: University Press of Kansas, 2001), 72.

210 **"Greaney's eyes almost popped out":** Philip Agee, *On the Run* (Secaucus, NJ: Lyle Stuart, 1987), 77–78. For the incident with Agee's father, see pp. 55–56.

212 **"This has become . . . essentially a work of fiction":** CIA Memorandum, Information Management Staff–Office of General Counsel, "Galley Proofs of 'Countercoup,'" Apr. 30, 1979, declassified July 31, 2013, MORI 6027365, National Security Archive, Electronic Briefing Book 468, May 12, 2014, item no. 17.

213 **"advisable in the interests of the United States":** National Security Act of 1947, Section 102 (c), CIA, Office of General Counsel, *Guide to Central Intelligence Agency Statutes and Law*, vol. 1, Sept. 1970, p. 3.

215 **"the absolute right to terminate any employee":** Ibid., 15, fn. 19.

215 **"to keep the CIA free of the law":** Snepp, *Irreparable Harm*, 55.

215 **father of intelligence law:** Gary M. Brenneman, "Father of Intelligence Law: Lawrence R. Houston," *Studies in Intelligence*, Summer 1974, pp. 37–41.

216 **"OSS had all kinds of people":** U.S. Congress, 102nd Congress, 2nd Session, Senate Select Committee on Intelligence, *Hearings: S.2198 and S.421 to Reorganize the United States Intelligence Community* (Washington, DC: Government Printing Office, 1992), 39.

216 **"Italy was not a very good example":** Ibid., 92–93.

217 **"Well, lieutenant, how to do you like your new assignment?" et seq.:** Ibid., 93.

217 **"He was a can-do lawyer":** Bart Barnes, "L. R. Houston Dies; CIA's First General Counsel," *Washington Post*, Aug. 17, 1995, p. B5.

219 **"commando type functions" et seq.:** Lawrence Houston, "CIA Authority to Perform Propaganda and Commando Type Functions," OGC-1, Sept. 25, 1947, declassified July 1990, MORI 17739, author's files.

219 **"legal basis for Cold War activities" et seq.:** CIA Memorandum, Houston–McCone, "Legal Basis for Cold-War Activities," OGC 62-0083, Jan. 15, 1962, declassified June 14, 1976, author's files.

219 **"Russian subversive action" et seq.:** Church Committee Transcripts, Testimony of Lawrence Houston, June 2, 1975, p. 78, NARA, RG-246, JFK Assassination Records Board Files, box 248-1.

220 **"Over the years":** Church Committee Transcript, Testimony of Lawrence R. Houston, Mar. 17, 1975, declassified July 2, 1993, Bates number 1696, NARA, RG-246, JFK Assassination Records Board Files, box 11.

220 **"many projects may have been discussed":** Church Committee Records, Timothy Hardy Memorandum for File, "Interview with John Warner, General Counsel of the CIA," Mar. 17, 1975, declassified June 12, 1998, NARA, RG-246, JFK Assassination Records Board Files, box 10, folder "CC-H [ii-B] Clark Clifford Interview."

220 **"executive privilege":** Lawrence Houston, "Executive Privilege in the Field of Intelligence," *Studies in Intelligence*, Fall 1958, pp. 61–74; Lawrence Houston,

"CIA, the Courts and Executive Privilege," *Studies in Intelligence*, Winter 1973, pp. 63–66.

221 discussion of *Heine v. Raus*: CIA, Office of General Counsel, *Guide to Central Intelligence Agency Statutes and Law*, Sept. 1970, vol. 1, pp. 16–18 and fn. 21; cf. *Heine v. Raus*, 261 F. Supp. 570, Dec. 8, 1966.

223 "If the CIA must defame someone": U.S. Court of Appeals for the Fourth Circuit, *Eerik Heine, Appellant v. Juri Raus*, 399 F.2d 785 (1968), James Craven Jr. dissenting.

6. THE SHERIFFS

225 "There were plenty of women": [Author's name deleted], "The Blind Men and the Elephant," declassified September 2, 2014, *Studies in Intelligence*, 36 (Winter 1992): 24.

226 "I think women have a very high place": Jacqueline [deleted] R[deleted], *The Petticoat Panel: A 1953 study of the Role of Woman in the CIA's Career Service*, Intelligence Monograph, CIA, Center for the Study of Intelligence, Mar. 2003, declassified Oct. 30, 2013, p. 1. Evidently women officers at the agency are not entitled to their full names even in declassified administrative histories of employment trends.

227 "No supervisor in this Agency" and "There is a constant inconvenience factor" et seq.: Ibid., 11.

227 "When I came in": CIA, "Divine Secrets of the RYBAT Sisterhood: Four Senior Women of the Directorate of Operations Discuss their Careers," declassified Oct. 30, 2014, p. 2. RYBAT is a cryptonym for the Directorate of Operations.

227 "Recruitment Division has had few specific directives": CIA, Memorandum "On the States of Women," July 6, 1971, declassified July 1, 2002, p. 1.

228 "I'm so sick of the deputization of women": Abigail Jones, "Not Your Daddy's CIA," *Newsweek*, Sept. 30, 2016, quoted p. 28

233 "I doubt I would have reported it": Paul Starobin, "Agent Provocateur," *George* magazine, Oct. 1997, p. 88.

233 "She had a drive, a persistence": Ibid.

234 "such functions as the Director of Central Intelligence may prescribe": Central Intelligence Agency Act of 1949, Section 20 (50 U.S.C. 403t), *Compilation of Intelligence Laws* 1998, p. 67. With creation of the Director of National Intelligence post, this language will have changed today to say the OGC works at the instruction of the director of the CIA, not the director of central intelligence.

234 "There are few who would argue": Scott Breckinridge, *CIA and the Cold War: A Memoir* (Westport, CT: Praeger, 1993), 94.

237 "appears not to have had the manpower, resources or tenacity": Iran-Contra Report, p. 425.

239 "heavy seas upon which the legislation sailed": U.S. Congress, 101st Congress, 2nd Session, Senate Select Committee on Intelligence, *Hearing: Nomination of Frederick P. Hitz* (Washington, DC: Government Printing Office, 1991), 36.

7. THE HEADLESS HORSEMAN

250 "We have to face the fact" et seq.: Helms and Hood, *A Look Over My Shoulder*, 105.

251 "I am sure his reluctance" et seq.: Richard M. Bissell with Jonathan B. Lewis and Frances T. Pudlo, *Reflections of a Cold Warrior: From Yalta to the Bay of Pigs* (New Haven: Yale University Press, 1996), 177.

252 "The wonder is he didn't throw me out": James E. Flannery, "Bay of Pigs," *Intelligencer: Journal of U.S. Intelligence Studies*, Fall–Winter 2006–2007, p. 52.

252 "In a parliamentary government": Thomas, *The Very Best Men*, 266.

254 "You're a natural": Helms and Hood, *A Look Over My Shoulder*, 31.

255 "The heat absorbed by the tin roof": Ibid., 73.

256 "In the preceding weeks": Ibid., 196.

258 "I work for only one president at a time": Powers, *The Man Who Kept the Secrets*, 201.

258 "just for the purpose of being briefed": CIA, John McCone, Memorandum for the Record, Apr. 30, 1964, declassified Aug. 26, 1999, LBJ Library, Johnson Papers, National Security File, John McCone Memoranda series, box 1, folder "Meetings with the President, 3 April 1964–20 May 1964."

258 "ideal method" et seq.: Memorandum, McGeorge Bundy–Lyndon Johnson, May 1, 1964, LBJ Library, Johnson Papers, White House Central File, General File, FG 11-1, box 55, folder "FG 11-2: CIA."

259 "I'm sick and tired of John McCone's tugging": Helms and Hood, *A Look Over My Shoulder*, 294.

259 "Dulles ran a happy ship": Central Intelligence Agency, David Robarge, *John McCone as Director of Central Intelligence, 1961–1965*, declassified Apr. 10, 2015, CIA Center for the Study of Intelligence, 2005, p. 416.

260 "Miami cocktail party chatter": Ibid., 98.

260 "I don't recall anything about any plans": Rockefeller Commission, Richard Helms Deposition, Apr. 23, 1975, declassified July 16, 1998, p. 151, NARA, RG-246, JFK Assassination Records Board Files, box 10, folder "S-M (IV-DD) Richard Helms."

260 "The business about the assassination of Castro" et seq.: Ibid., p. 160. Subsequent quotes and references are taken from this text up through page 169. The "any specific plan" language occurs on page 169.

261 "nutty idea" et seq.: Church Committee Records, Richard Helms Testimony, July 18, 1975 (declassified May 31, 1994). NARA: RG-246, JFK Assassination Records Board Files, box 25, folder "Edwards, Helms, Lewis, et al."

261 "There is something about the whole chain of episode": Ibid.

263 "one of my darkest days": Helms and Hood, *A Look Over My Shoulder*, 343.

265 "The pending exposé did not come as a total surprise": Ibid., 344.

265 "Well, aren't you the lucky one": Douglass Cater, "What Did LBJ Know and When Did He Know It?" *Washington Post*, July 19, 1987, p. C7.

266 "It would have been difficult to imagine": Helms and Hood, *A Look Over My Shoulder*, 345.

273 Senators Symington and Stennis: See, for example, Richard Helms, Luncheon Talk, May 1, 1995, *CIRA Newsletter* 20, no. 2 (Summer 1995): 5; Helms remarks at CIA 50th Anniversary, CIA, *What's News at CIA*, Oct. 1997, p. 15; Loch Johnson, "Spymaster Richard Helms: An Interview with the Former US Director of Central Intelligence," *Intelligence and National Security*, 18, no. 3 (Autumn 2003): 29.

273 "Because Senator Symington knew": Helms and Hood, *A Look Over My Shoulder*, 415.

273 "Did you try in the Central Intelligence Agency?" et seq.: Powers, *The Man Who Kept the Secrets*, 232.

277 HUGE CIA OPERATION: *New York Times*, Dec. 22, 1974, p. 1.

278 "You and I have known each other a long time" et seq.: White House, Memorandum of Conversation, Prresident Ford–Richard Helms, Jan. 4, 1975, declassified May 5, 1999, Gerald R. Ford Library, Ford Papers, National Security Advisers' Files, Memcon series, box 8, folder "January 4, 1975, Ford–Former CIA director Richard Helms."

279 "blackmailing people": Central Intelligence Agency, Cable Colby–Helms, 010332Z, Feb. 1975, declassified Mar. 2008, released in CIA, Center for the Study of Intelligence, *The Richard Helms Collection*, Washington, DC, 2012.

280 "ONE OF THE BASIC REASONS": Central Intelligence Agency, Cable, Bush–Helms, Mar. 1976, declassified Mar. 2008, paragraph 5, released in CIA, Center for the Study of Intelligence, *The Richard Helms Collection*, Washington, DC, 2012.

281 "of total conflict" et seq.: Richard Helms, "Statement of Richard Helms, n.d. [Nov. 1, 1977], Georgetown University Library: Richard Helms Papers, Part 1, box 10, folder 10.

281 "to disobey and ignore the laws of our land" plus the Carter quote, "A public official": *Washington Post* editorial, "No Right to Lie," Nov. 11, 1977, p. A16.

281 "obviously very drained by his experience": "Happiness Is Being with Friends," *CIRA Newsletter*, 3, no. 1 (Jan.–Mar. 1978): 3.

282 Walter Mondale: Interview with author, Mar. 30, 2015.

282 "have effectively shredded": *Washington Post* editorial, "No Right to Lie."

8. A FAILED EXORCIST

289 "one of the most remarkable people I have known": Tenet swearing-in remarks, July 31, 1997, copy in author's files.

290 "We will honor always the trust": U.S. Congress, 105th Congress, 1st Session, Senate Select Committee on Intelligence, *Hearings: Nomination of George J. Tenet to be Director of Central Intelligence* (Washington, DC: Government Printing Office, 1997), 57.

290 "We've put in place a system of command alertness": Ibid., p. 58.

292 "The ghost in the room": Loch K. Johnson, "The Aspin-Brown Intelligence Inquiry: Behind the Closed Doors of a Blue Ribbon Commission," *Studies in Intelligence,* v. 48, no. 3, 2004.

293 "the most down-to-earth" et seq.: Morell and Harlow, *The Great War of Our Time*, p. 7, quoted p. 10.

298 "risk-taking does not equate with recklessness": Tenet Nomination Hearing, p. 56.

298 "It should never be the last resort of failed policy": Ibid., p. 60

303 "It wasn't the last time on my watch": George Tenet with Bill Harlow, *At the Center of the Storm: My Years at the CIA* (New York: HarperCollins, 2007), 49.

303 "It is a delight to be away from Langley for a few hours" et seq.: John C. Gannon, "Remarks to the World Affairs Council, Washington, DC," June 4, 1998, copy in author's files.

309 "senior official": The news conference transcript makes clear that this person dealt at the very highest level of government and had authority to handle intelligence issues. Internal evidence indicates that Andrew Card, White House chief of staff, is this person. We have seen in conjunction with the Greystone project that Mr. Card served as an operative there also, so this text names Card here and in this connection.

311 "I would make it clear as well" et seq.: CIA, Memo, James L. Pavitt–John Helgerson, "Comments to the Draft IG Special Review, 'Counterterrorism Detention and Interrogation Program' (2003-7123-IG)," Feb. 27, 2004, DDO-0031-04, declassified June 10, 2016, C06566541, CIA Electronic Reading Room (on p. 357 in this text).

311 "I think it is going to be very difficult to publish a book": Quoted in the Associated Press story "New Rules to Govern Publications by CIA Officers," *USA Today*, Nov. 1, 2005.

312 "Lying is not something that I will ever tolerate": Tenet Nomination Hearing, p. 66.

9. JACOB MARLEY'S GHOSTS

314 "You have my word": Senate Select Committee on Intelligence, Porter J. Goss Nomination Hearing, Sept. 20, 2004, author's notes.

314 "I briefed both the HPSCI and the SSCI": Porter Goss, *"What* Must Never Happen Again," in Bill Harlow, ed., *Rebuttal*, p. 8.

314 "The truth is exactly what Director Goss said": CIA, Public Affairs Office, "Statement by CIA Director of Public Affairs Jennifer Millerwise," Mar. 18, 2005.

315 "We need to have the 7th Floor confront" et seq.: CIA, CTC/LGL e-mail, Apr. 25, 2005, 11:41 a.m., declassified June 10, 2016, CIA Electronic Reading Room.

315 "blue ribbon panel": CIA, CTC Report, "Blue Ribbon Panel: Response to Request from the Director for Assessment of EIT Effectiveness," Sept. 23, 2005, declassified June 10, 2016, C06541719, CIA Electronic Reading Room.

315 "This agency does not do torture": John Diamond, "CIA Chief: Interrogation Methods 'Unique' but Legal," *USA Today*, Nov. 21, 2005, p. 1-A.

315 "Successfully fighting": Porter Goss contribution to the *Rebuttal* collection, p. 7.

316 "It is true that specific sources and methods": Ibid., 8.

318 Gosslings, Kyle Foggo, Mary Graham: David Ignatius, How the CIA Came Unglued," *Washington Post*, May 12, 2006, p. A21; Stephen F. Hayes, "The CIA 1, Bush 0," *Weekly Standard*, May 22, 2006.

319 Goss versus Harman: Dafna Linzer, "A Year Later, Goss's CIA Is Still in Turmoil," *Washington Post*, Oct 19, 2005, p. A1.

319 "At CIA, we are improving how we do our business": CIA, Public Affairs Office, "Statement by Director of the Central Intelligence Agency Porter J. Goss on the WMD Commission Recommendations," June 29, 2005.

319 "After great consideration of this report": CIA, "CIA Director Porter J. Goss Statement on CIA Office of the Inspector General Report, 'CIA Accountability with Respect to the 9/11 Attacks,'" Oct. 5, 2005.

320 "field forward": CIA, Office of Public Affairs, "Statement by CIA Director Porter Goss," May 5, 2006.

321 "capture, detain and question" and "multiple pages in length": Rizzo, *Company Man*, 173–74.

323 "drip by drip": Ibid., 211.

324 "I have often wondered": Ibid., 17.

324 "FOR THE REASONS CITED THEREIN": CIA, Cable, Headquarters –Bangkok 081855Z Nov. 2005, declassified ACLU FOIA release, Apr. 15, 2010, part 3).

324 "It was an agency decision": Joby Warrick and Walter Pincus, "Station Chief Made Appeal to Destroy CIA Tapes," *Washington Post,* January 16, 2008, quoted p. A1.

327 "lethal force . . . is a concept" et seq.: Public Broadcasting System, WGBH-TV, *Frontline*, "Looking for Answers," p. 3, www.pbs.org/wgbh/pages/frontline /shows/terrorism/interviews/go.

328 "How many law professors have signed off?": Tara McKelvey, "Inside the Killing Machine," *Newsweek*, Feb. 13, 2011, quoted p. 3, www.newsweek.com /inside-killing-machine-68771.

328 "appointed from civilian life by the President": *Compilation of Intelligence Laws* 1998, p. 67. The 2003 and 2012 editions of this contain identical language, so the 1949 act was not amended in this respect. From this legal standpoint, the selection of John Rizzo for general counsel of the CIA appears to have been illegal. No one seems to have paid any attention.

329 "CIA courts disaster": U.S. Congress, 110th Congress, 1st Session, Senate Select Committee on Intelligence, *Hearings: Nomination of John A. Rizzo to Be General Counsel of the Central Intelligence Agency* (Washington, DC: Government Printing Office, 2008), 19.

329 "public flogging": Rizzo, *Company Man*, 252.

329 "There are no other opinions": Rizzo Nomination Hearing, p. 29.

330 Krongard airport incident: Luz Lazo and Greg Miller, "Former Top CIA Official Arrested at BWI for Allegedly Trying to Bring Gun Through Security," *Washington Post*, Aug. 7, 2015, p. A12.

330 versions of NSA's 9/11 story: General Michael V. Hayden, "Statement for the Record," Oct. 17, 2002, SSCI/HPSCI Joint Inquiry, typescript, p. 1, copy in author's files. The 2006 recitation is in General Michael V. Hayden, "What American Intelligence and Especially the NSA Have Been Doing to Defend the Nation," Speech at National Press Club, Jan. 22, 2006, Office of Director of National Intelligence Release, copy in author's files. The memoir version is in Michael Hayden, *Playing to the Edge: American Intelligence in the Age of Terror* (New York: Penguin, 2016), 29.

331 discussions of Trailblazer: This series of quotes, except where Hayden's nomination hearings are introduced, moves back and forth through the same sources used above. Rather than breaking it into separate entries, it will be better to list the items sequentially: "Our effort to revolutionize": SSCI/HPSCI Testimony, pp. 8–9; reporter about NSA whistleblowers: Press Club speech, p. 5; "Deltas" and "We overachieved" to "Moonshots": U.S. Congress, 109th Congress, 1st Session, Senate Select Committee on Intelligence, *Hearing: Nomination of Lieutenant General Michael V. Hayden, USAF, to Be Principal Deputy Director of National Intelligence* (Washington, DC: Government Printing Office, 2006), 14, 21–22; "What my memory tells me I said": p. 42. "We were also trying to do too much": Hayden, *Playing to the Edge*, 20.

333 "I have an order whose lawfulness has been attested": Hayden, National Press Club speech, p. 6.

333 discussion of NSA blanket eavesdropping: As above: "find the right balance": SSCI/HPSCI Testimony, p. 9; "It is not a driftnet": Press Club speech, p. 4; Wyden challenge: *DCIA Nomination Hearing*, pp. 40–41. Hayden noted under the congressional questioning—as a side example of his fabulism—that at the Press Club, in making his "Lackawanna-Fremont" remark, "I switched from the word 'communications' to the much more specific and unarguably accurate 'conversations.'" Put differently, the general used the assertion that contents of conversations were not being recorded to imply that no widespread surveillance was under way.

333 "He didn't answer *any* of the questions!": Hayden CIA Nomination Hearing, May 18, 2006, author's notes. This exclamation does not appear in the formal transcript, but it would have been on page 59 of that document.

333 "I'm sorry. I'm just not familiar": Ibid., p. 94. For General Hayden to say he was not familiar with a law with which he dealt every day amounted to a slap at congressional oversight.

334 "This was getting to be pointless bantering": Hayden, *Playing to the Edge*, 185. General Hayden's recounting of this story makes out his action of snapping shut the briefing book and daring the senators to make a judgment on his character to be his response to Ron Wyden's question posed below. But the hearing transcript shows that, far from issuing his challenge and clamming up, General Hayden went on for seventeen more paragraphs, more than a page of typeset text (pp. 40–41)—another example of Michael Hayden's fabulism.

334 "What's to say that, if you're confirmed to head the CIA, we won't go through exactly this kind of drill?": Hayden CIA Nomination Hearing, p. 40.

335 "The main point": Hayden, *Playing to the Edge*, p. 335. Italics in the original. Judging from U.S. drone strikes, which increased in 2007 but then multiplied by 700 percent in 2008, George W. Bush bought Hayden's argument. But it wasn't long until Leon Panetta, a successor, was saying that Al Qaeda had been reduced to a rump of just a few dozen individuals. What is disturbing in all this is Hayden's tendency to globalize the threat. All the attacks that took place after 2001 (Bali, Madrid, London, Nairobi, Paris, etc.) were conducted by locals, some with their own networks, who aspired to be recognized, not by some corps of Al Qaeda international commandos. This did not add up to a direct Al Qaeda threat to the U.S. homeland. The claim is much more like the assertion that Saddam Hussein's (nonexistent) nuclear weapons and drone aircraft were intended to attack the United States.

335 he "loved being a spymaster": Rizzo, *Company Man*, 246.

335 al-Masri case: CIA, Office of the Inspector General Report, "The Rendition and Detention of German Citizen Khalid al-Masri," 2004-7601-IG, July 16, 2007, declassified June 10, 2016, C06541725.

335 Bikowsky identified: Connie Bruck, "The Inside War," *New Yorker*, June 22, 2015, pp. 51–52. Director Hayden writes of Bikowsky without naming her in *Playing to the Edge*, pp. 223–24.

336 Bikowsky and Khalid Sheik Mohammed: Senate torture report, p. 85. Although CIA censors have deleted Bikowsky's name here, the text connects the incident to the deputy chief of Alec Station, which was Bikowsky's post at the time.

336 "the American intelligence business": Hayden CIA Nomination Hearing, p. 16.

336 "You should expect of me": Hayden ODNI Nomination Hearing, p. 22.

337 "played a bit back from the line": Hayden CIA Nomination Hearing, p. 88.

338 "If it is a fact": Aki Peritz, "What Did the CIA tell LBJ? Not Much," *Washington Post*, Feb. 21, 2016, p. C5.

338 "Here's an informal yardstick I use": General Hayden's Remarks at SHAFR Conference, June 21, 1997, p. 1, copy in author's files.

338 "The best way to strengthen the trust of the American people": Hayden CIA Nomination Hearing, p. 17.

339 "It didn't take long to realize": Hayden, *Playing to the Edge*, 187.

340 Hayden instructions to find a day when detainees numbered ninety-eight: Senate torture report, p. 476, fn. 2598.

341 "numerous verbal requests": Letter, Senator Jay Rockefeller (SSCI Chairman)–Director Michael Hayden, Oct. 29 2008, repr. CIA, Center for the Study of Intelligence, "Overview of CIA-Congress Interactions Concerning the Agency's Rendition-Detention-Interrogation Program," n.d., declassified Dec. 8, 2014, C06257473, p. 35.

341 "simply get a few things wrong": Michael Hayden, "Analysis: Flawed, Politicized . . . and Rejected," in Bill Harlow, ed., *Rebuttal*, 12.

342 "a more than adequate representation of the tapes": Senate torture report, p. 8.

10. THE FLYING DUTCHMAN

346 "If this was just theater, we would happily give him" et seq.: Hayden, *Playing to the Edge*, quoted 365, 366, 367.

347 "Criticize the program": Rizzo, *Company Man*, 281.

347 "It is my understanding that": U.S. Congress, 111th Congress, 1st Session, Senate Select Committee on Intelligence, *Hearings: Nomination of Leon Panetta to Be Director, Central Intelligence Agency* (Washington, DC: Government Printing Office, 2009), 129.

348 "Come on in, fellas": Panetta and Newton, *Worthy Fights*, p. 217.

350 "respect and subservience" et seq.: Ibid., 225.

350 **Pelosi briefing controversy:** I don't wish to break the narrative line in the main text with comment on whether Pelosi was informed of waterboarding or not on September 4, 2002, but this question is intrinsically important. Panetta devotes almost two pages to it in his memoir (pp. 225–27), and the matter deserves a note. Panetta continues to believe he was right, and Nancy Pelosi certainly backed away from her original position, later saying that she had been told of waterboarding as one of a menu of options, not as a method being employed.

The matter is not so clear cut, however. First of all, the CIA briefing list prepared for Mr. Panetta contains numerous errors of fact. In one place, Senator Rockefeller is listed as receiving a briefing he remembers months later. Senator Bob Graham is listed at meetings he did not attend. In another place, Porter Goss is named as being briefed when he was actually leading the CIA. There are instances where CIA officials—for example, John Rizzo—attended an event and are not listed, others where congressional staff are listed though they are known to have been excluded, and there are a number of briefings that do not appear at all. One entry lists a staff person who was no longer employed by the SSCI. Another is listed who had merely helped accommodate members.

The list marks data as "Not Available" for every briefing Vice President Cheney attended, which results in practically no record of briefings by Porter Goss.

Equally significant is a different, more contemporaneous document, which was only declassified a year later, that records Representative *Jane Harman*, not Pelosi, as attending the September 4, 2002, briefing. This record lists Harman, not Pelosi, as the ranking minority member that day; see CIA, Memo, Christopher J. Walker–Michael V. Hayden, Apr. 11, 2007, OCA 2007-00193, declassified 2010 to the Center for Constitutional Rights, CIA MORI C05470331.

Declassified documents are suggestive in another way also. A set of memoranda recording some briefings—unfortunately not including that of September 2002—appeared as a result of the ACLU lawsuit that is mentioned in the main text. Markings on these documents indicate that the records were created on November 30, 2004. If this is true of the recording memorandum for September 2002, its status as an authentic record is doubtful.

It is worth noting that the Center for the Study of Intelligence paper on agency information to Congress in connection with the detainee program has this to say about the CIA's *own* records: "We found gaps in the documentary record, particularly but not exclusively relating to briefings Agency officers gave to Congress in 2004 and 2005. The record . . . for the first two years is better, as it is for the period 2006 to 2008, but they are still only summaries of topics covered; we do not have anything approaching a verbatim record." (See CIA/CSI, "Overview of CIA-Congress Interactions," in "Scope Note" on page 1.)

Jose Rodriguez gave the September 4, 2002, briefing, and he insists that Pelosi attended and asked questions. He made these allegations about Pelosi's attendance in 2009 and repeated them in the memoir *Hard Measures*. His connivance to destroy the torture videotapes inevitably casts doubt on other Rodriguez assertions, including this one. He was, in fact, later reprimanded by a CIA accountability review board on Leon Panetta's watch.

Considering the liberties Dick Cheney took in dictating what Congress would and would not be informed of during this same period, it is impossible to reach a satisfactory conclusion on the Pelosi controversy.

Director Panetta was not a CIA professional, was not present—either at Langley or on Capitol Hill—at the events of 2002, and therefore has no special insight into these events.

351 **"Feinstein's staff had the requisite clearances"**: Panetta and Newton, *Worthy Fights*, 233.

351 **"to avoid protracted litigation"**: CIA letter on restrictions for SSCI, in CIA, Office of the Inspector General, "Report of Investigation: Agency Access to the SSCI Shared Drive," 2014-11718-IG, July 18, 2014, declassified Jan. 15, 2015, C06274838.

353 **"The president wants to know" et seq.**: Panetta and Newton, *Worthy Fights*, 233.

356 **"ridding ourselves of a destructive relationship"**: Ibid., 235.

358 **"Our understanding of the agreement"**: CIA, "Inspector General report on access to the SSCI Shared Drive," quoted on unnumbered page under heading "Other Related RDINet Events."

359 **"The White House is not inclined"**: CIA, e-mail, CIA Attorney–[Deleted], May 13, 2010, 5:36 p.m., in CIA, "Final Report of the Rendition, Detention, and Interrogation Network Agency Accountability Board Report," n.d. (c. Nov. 24, 2014), declassified Jan. 14, 2015, quoted fn. p. 10.

359 **"Occasionally in the course of the White Houses's review"**: CIA, e-mail, CIA Attorney– [Deleted], June 7, 2010, 10:53 a.m., in Ibid., quoted fn., p. 11.

363 **"We were more than a little stunned"**: Hayden, *Playing to the Edge*, 396.

364 **"If even half of this is true"**: Morrell and Harlow, *The Great War of Our Time*, 262.

366 **bin Laden courier**: The intelligence that led to the bin Laden raid became especially controversial after the movie *Zero Dark Thirty*, which received CIA help—including interviews with actual CTC personnel—and which implied strongly that the courier had been identified by means of torture. The Senate takedown of the CIA version of this story is in the Senate Intelligence Committee torture report, pp. 385–86, fn. 2182.

366 **"I see the response not as a rebuttal" et seq.**: U.S. Senate, 113th Congress, 1st Session, Armed Services Committee, *Hearings: Nominations of . . . Stephen W. Preston [et al.]* (Washington, DC: Government Printing Office, 2014). The hearing took place on July 25, 2013. This text is under "Questions for the Record for the Honorable Stephen W. Preston, CIA General Counsel, Nominated to be General Counsel of the Department of Defense," Aug. 9, 2013.

367 **CIA rebuttal of SSCI report**: This discussion is too detailed for the main narrative, but it is nevertheless important. My best guess as to why the denizens of Langley scrambled the SSCI conclusions the way they did is so readers would not notice the CIA sneaking in extraneous material and failing to respond to the Senate's points on national security and on presidential control. For example, one of the made-up conclusions (number 7) holds that the Senate objected that the CIA spent money and made cash payments. This enabled Langley to advance the general (and generic) proposition that it has the authority to make cash payments, special arrangements to do so, and does it all the time. This makes the SSCI look silly and its investigation unserious. The Senate *did* comment on the costs, as part of its conclusion no. 20, the main point of which was that the CIA program damaged the standing of the United States in the world. *The CIA did not respond to that conclusion at all.* And the Senate report made no specific complaint that the CIA spent money. Langley's document pretends that SSCI conclusion number 20 accuses the agency of using interrogation techniques not reviewed by the Justice Department (that is actually the Senate's conclusion number 14).

We could spend pages on an item-by-item comparison of the SSCI list and the CIA one that supposedly corresponds. Instead I will simply note that Langley avoided direct answers to Senate intelligence committee conclusions that: torture was not an effective means of gathering information (no. 1), that the CIA impeded White House oversight (no. 7), and that the torture program was "inherently unsustainable" (no. 19). In its direct answers to other SSCI conclusions or its deflection shots at purported Senate points that the CIA scrambled, the agency commented indirectly on some but not all of this, in particular avoiding the central argument that the torture program damaged America's standing all over the globe.

It is a mystery why the CIA did not confront the proposition that the CIA impeded White House oversight, since the available documents there appear to show an agency eager to obtain formal presidential approval, which presupposes oversight. That may be because the records show that White House officials tried to *avoid* putting George W. Bush in the position of direct knowledge of the CIA program, presumably for purposes of plausible deniability.

One Senate "conclusion" that the CIA made up (number 11)—that the agency did not warn policymakers and others that detainees under torture fabricated information anyway—appears to have been crafted simply so the CIA could bedazzle the reader with a string of examples of specific reporting cables in which it did circulate such warnings. This is a dangerous game, however, since it invites the question of why, if EITs were "effective," victims were able to fabricate at all. In addition, the "Note to Readers" of the CIA response, cited later, contains *the admission that the CIA response falsely represented* (in one instance due to a "sequencing error") the knowledge claimed to have been gained from torture *in its most important case* and some others as well. That must affect the judgment on "effectiveness."

368 **"There is no objective way"**: CIA, Memorandum, CTC–ODCIA, "Response to Request from Director for Assessment of EIT Effectiveness," Sept. 23, 2005, declassified June 10, 2016, C06541719, CIA Electronic Reading Room.

368 **"At least several hundred, possibly thousands"**: CIA Memorandum, "Successes of CIA's Counterterrorism Detention and Interrogation Activities," Feb. 24, 2004, attached to Memorandum, James L. Pavitt–John Helgerson, "Comments to Draft IG Special Review, 'Counterterrorism Detention and Interrogation Program' (2003-7123-IG)," Feb. 27, 2004, declassified June 10, 2016, C066566541, CIA Electronic Reading Room.

369 **"the longest period of sustained threat reporting"** et seq.: Morrell and Harlow, *The Great War of Our Time*, 267.

369 **Michael Morrell's six points**: Ibid., 265–74.

370 **"In retrospect OMS thought"**: CIA, "Summary and Reflections of Chief of Medical Services on OMS Participation in the RDI Program," date and identifying information redacted, declassified June 10, 2016, MORI C06541727, p. 41.

372 **"Eatinger"**: A top general counsel lawyer provided the account on which the following narrative relies. While the author's identity is deleted from the document, the internal evidence—of the author himself taking initiatives at the highest level of CIA, of phone calls at home from Director Brennan, of senior meetings—all points to this being Robert Eatinger. This individual is in the process of organizing the CIA's criminal referral to the Justice Department, and Mr. Eatinger

is on record as the attorney filing that paper. He will be so identified here. CIA, OGC Memorandum, "Memorandum for the Record re: Partial Timeline of Events Surrounding the Discovery of SRT Documents on RDI Net," Jan. 15–27, 2014, declassified Jan. 14, 2015, C06274838, attached to CIA, David B. Buckley, Inspector General, "Report of Investigation: Agency Access to the SSCI Shared Drive on RDINet," July 28, 2014, declassified January 14, 2015, C06274838, CIA Electronic Reading Room.

374 **"If the WH were to order the inquiry stopped":** Ibid.

374 **a "go" and "bad optic":** CIA, Accountability Board Report, 18–19. "Optic" is from the inspector general's report at page 11. It also occurs in the OGC memorandum cited above. A comparison between the various reports and the OGC memo suggests that Robert Eatinger made this remark. Mr. Eatinger puts the date of these events as January 13.

375 **"I think she knew, after that meeting":** Bruck, "The Inside War," p. 46.

375 **"may have been improperly obtained and/or retained":** CIA, Letter, John O. Brennan–Dianne Feinstein, Jan. 27, 2014, copy in author's files.

376 **"We have made mistakes" et seq.:** John Brennan, Council on Foreign Relations Speech, Mar. 11, 2014, *Washington Post* transcript, www.washingtonpost .com/world/national-security/transcript-cia-director-john-brennan-says-his -agency-has-done-nothing-wrong/2014/03/11/21d1dde8-a944-11e3-8599 -ce7295b6851c_story.html?utm_term=.b3cd53f78670.

377 **"We also owe it to the women and men":** CIA, John Brennan, Message to the Workforce, Mar. 11, 2014, copy in author's files.

382 **"To be clear, although we did make a serious effort":** Adam Goldman, "Military Prosecutor: Interrogation Report Correct," *Washington Post*, Feb. 11, 2016, quoted p. A9.

386 **Hayden and Brennan observations on Trump:** Matt Apuzzo and James Risen, "Plan to Revive Waterboarding Faces Obstacles," *New York Times*, Nov. 29, 2016, p. A1; and Gordon Corera, "CIA Chief Warns Trump: Scrapping Iran Deal 'Height of Folly,'" BBC News, Nov. 30, 2016, www.bbc.com/news/world-us -canada-38149088.

BIBLIOGRAPHY

Central Intelligence Agency

Clandestine Service History, Unnumbered, "Office of Policy Coordination, 1948–1952," (cover page, w/author NA), no date (declassified February 2005; the identical paper with very slight changes to the introduction appeared as an article in *Studies in Intelligence*, v. 17, no. 2-S, Summer 1973; declassified Apr 21, 2006; Section II, on "Enabling Directives," appears in the history but is entirely deleted in *Studies*. However the journal has an accompanying Ludwell Lee Montague paper that does not form part of the CSH).

CS HP 6. "The Hungarian Revolution and Planning for the Future, 23 October–4 November 1956, v. I (of II)." [author deleted], January 1958 (declassified March 2005; MORI 12003072, heavily redacted).

CSH 105. Record of Paramilitary Action Against the Castro Government of Cuba, 17 March 1960–May 1961," Colonel J. Hawkins, May 5, 1961 (declassified HRP 1997, substantially complete).

CS HP 323. "The Clandestine Service Historical Series: Hungary, v. I: [deleted]." May 1972 (declassified March 2005, MORI 1200373; heavily redacted).

Darling, Arthur B. *The Central Intelligence Agency: An Instrument of Government, to 1950*. University Park: Pennsylvania State University Press, 1990.

Ford, Harold P. *William E. Colby as Director of Central Intelligence, 1973–1976*. Washington, D.C.: CIA/Center for the Study of Intelligence, 1993 (declassified 2013).

Garthoff, Douglas F. *Directors of Central Intelligence as Leaders of the U.S. Intelligence Community, 1946–2005*. Washington, D.C.: Potomac Books, 2007.

Hathaway, Robert M., and Russel Jack Smith. *Richard Helms as Director of Central Intelligence, 1966–1973*. Washington, D.C.: Center for the Study of Intelligence, 1993 (declassified 2014).

Jackson, Wayne G. *Allen Welch Dulles as Director of Central Intelligence, 26 February 1953–29 November 1961*. 4 vols. Washington, D.C.: CIA History Staff, 1973 (declassified 1994).

Montague, Ludwell Lee. *Walter Bedell Smith as Director of Central Intelligence, October 1950–February 1953*. University Park: Pennsylvania State University Press, 1992.

Pfeiffer, Jack B. *Official History of the Bay of Pigs*. 5 volumes. Washington, D.C.: CIA/History Staff, 1979–1984 (declassified 1998, 2011, 2016).

Robarge, David. *John McCone as Director of Central Intelligence, 1961–1965*.

Washington, D.C.: CIA/Center for the Study of Intelligence, no date (declassified April 10, 2015).

Ruffner, Kevin C., ed. *Forging an Intelligence Partnership: CIA and the Origins of the BND, 1945–1949: A Documentary History.* 2 vols. Washington, D.C.: CIA History Staff/European Division, Directorate of Operations, 1999.

Steury, Donald P., ed. *Sherman Kent and the Board of National Estimates: Collected Essays.* Washington, D.C.: CIA History Staff/Center for the Study of Intelligence, 1994.

Warner, Michael, ed. *CIA Cold War Records: The CIA Under Harry Truman.* Washington, D.C.: Central Intelligence Agency, History Staff (CSI), 1994.

Studies in Intelligence.

Department of State

Foreign Relations of the United States (Series. Specific volumes are cited in Endnotes.)

McAllister, William B., Joshua Botts, Peter Cozzens, and Aaron W. Marrs. *Toward "Thorough, Accurate, and Reliable": A History of the* Foreign Relations of the United States *Series.* Department of State: Office of the Historian, 2015.

National Archives and Records Administration

Breitman, Richard, and Norman J. W. Goda. *Hitler's Shadow: Nazi War Criminals, U.S. Intelligence, and the Cold War.* Washington, D.C.: National Archives and Records Administration, n.d.

United States Senate Select Committee on Intelligence

U.S. Congress. Senate. Select Committee on Intelligence. *Committee Study of the Central Intelligence Agency's Detention and Interrogation Program,* 2014.

——. *Fact Check: Inaccurate and Misleading Assertions Related to the CIA Detention and Interrogation Program in the book, "Rebuttal: The CIA Responds to the Senate Intelligence Committee's Study of Its Detention and Interrogation Program,"* Vice Chairman Feinstein Staff Summary, September 9, 2015.

——. *Report: Legislative Oversight of Intelligence Activities: The U.S. Experience,* 103rd Cong., 2d sess., 1994. S. Prt. 103–88.

United States Senate Select Committee to Study Governmental Operations with Respect to Intelligence Activities (94th Congress, 1st Session)

U.S. Congress. Senate. Select Committee to Study Governmental Operations with Respect to Intelligence Activities. *Interim Report: Alleged Assassination Plots Involving Foreign Leaders,* 94th Cong., 1st sess., 1975.

——. *Covert Operations,* 94th Cong., 1st sess., 1976.

————. *Detailed Staff Reports on Intelligence Activities*, 94th Cong., 1st sess., 1976.

————. *Foreign and Military Intelligence, v. 1*, 94th Cong., 1st sess., 1976.

Books and Periodicals

Agee, Philip, and Louis Wolf. *Dirty Work: The CIA in Western Europe*. Secaucus, NJ: Lyle Stuart, 1978.

Allison, John M. *Ambassador from the Prairie, or Allison Wonderland*. Boston, MA: Houghton Mifflin, 1973.

Baer, Robert. *See No Evil: The True Story of a Ground Soldier in the CIA's War on Terrorism*. New York: Crown Publishers, 2002.

Baker, Peter. *Days of Fire: Bush and Cheney in the White House*. New York: Doubleday, 2013.

Bearden, Milt, and James Risen. *The Main Enemy: The Inside Story of the CIA's Final Showdown with the KGB*. New York: Random House, 2003.

Bell, P.M.H. *The World Since 1945: An International History*. London: Arnold, 2001.

Bergen, Peter. *Manhunt: The Ten-Year Search for Bin Laden from 9/11 to Abbottabad*. New York: Crown Publishers, 2012.

Berghahn, Volker R. *America and the Intellectual Cold War in Europe*. Princeton, NJ: Princeton University Press, 2001.

Berntsen, Gary, and Ralph Pezzullo. *Jawbreaker: The Attack on Bin Laden and Al Qaeda: A Personal Account by the CIA's Key Field Commander*. New York: Crown Publishers, 2005.

Bird, Kai. *The Good Spy: The Life and Death of Robert Ames*. New York: Crown Publishers, 2014.

Bissell, Jr., Richard M., with Jonathan E. Lewis and Francis T. Pudlo. *Reflections of a Cold Warrior: From Yalta to the Bay of Pigs*. New Haven, CT: Yale University Press, 1996.

Blum, William. *Killing Hope: U.S. Military and CIA Interventions since World War II*. Monroe, ME: Common Courage Press, 2004.

Breckinridge, Scott D. *CIA and the Cold War: A Memoir*. Westport, CT: Praeger, 1993.

Cabell, Charles P. *A Man of Intelligence: Memoirs of War, Peace, and the CIA*. Colorado Springs, CO: Impa Vide Publications, 1997.

Carle, Glenn L. *The Interrogator: An Education*. New York: Nation Books, 2011.

Castro, Fidel, and José Ramón Fernandez. *Playa Girón: Bay of Pigs, Washington's First Military Defeat in the Americas*. Edited by Steve Clark and Mary-Alice Waters. New York: Pathfinder Books, 2001.

Cavendish, Anthony. *Inside Intelligence*. *Granta* Magazine, no. 24 (1988).

Cline, Ray S. *Secrets, Spies and Scholars: Blueprint of the Essential CIA*. Washington, D.C.: Acropolis Books, 1976.

Coleman, Peter. *The Liberal Conspiracy: The Congress for Cultural Freedom and the Struggle for the Mind of Postwar Europe.* New York: Free Press, 1989.

Conboy, Kenneth, and James Morrison. *Feet to the Fire: CIA's Covert Operations in Indonesia, 1957–1958.* Annapolis: Naval Institute Press, 1998.

Copeland, Miles. *The Game of Nations: The Amorality of Power Politics.* New York: Simon and Schuster, 1969.

———. *The Game Player: Confessions of the CIA's Original Political Operative.* London: Aurum Press, 1989.

Corson, William R. *The Armies of Ignorance: The Rise of the American Intelligence Empire.* New York: The Dial Press, 1977.

Costanzo, Christopher D. *My CIA: Memories of a Secret Career.* North Charleston, SC: CreateSpace Independent Publishing, 2013.

Critchfield, James H. *Partners at the Creation: The Men Behind Postwar Germany's Defense and Intelligence Establishments.* Annapolis, MD: Naval Institute Press, 2003.

Crumpton, Henry A. *The Art of Intelligence: Lessons from a Life in the CIA's Clandestine Service.* New York: Penguin Press, 2012.

Cullather, Nick. *Secret History: The CIA's Classified Account of its Operations in Guatemala, 1952–1954.* Stanford, CA: Stanford University Press, 1999.

Cummings, Richard H. *Cold War Radio: The Dangerous History of American Broadcasting in Europe, 1950–1989.* Jefferson, NC: McFarland, 2009.

Devine, Jack, with Vernon Loeb. *Good Hunting: An American Spymaster's Story.* New York: Farrar, Strauss and Giroux, 2014.

Dreke, Victor. *From Escambray to the Congo: In the Whirlwind of the Cuban Revolution: Interview with Victor Dreke.* Edited by Mary-Alice Waters. New York: Pathfinder Books, 2002.

Drumheller, Tyler. *On the Brink: An Insider's Account of How the White House Compromised American Intelligence.* With Elaine Monaghan. New York: Carroll and Graf, 2006.

Dulles, Allen. *The Craft of Intelligence.* New York: New American Library, 1965.

———. *Germany's Underground.* New York: Macmillan, 1947.

———, ed. *Great True Spy Stories.* New York: Harper and Row, 1968.

———. *The Secret Surrender.* New York: Harper and Row, 1966.

Escalante, Fabián. *The Secret War: CIA Covert Operations Against Cuba, 1959–1962.* Melbourne, Aust.: Ocean Press, 1995.

Eveland, Wilbur Crane. *Ropes of Sand: America's Failure in the Middle East.* New York: W.W. Norton, 1980.

Firth, Noel E., and James H. Noren. *Soviet Defense Spending: A History of CIA Estimates, 1950–1990.* College Station: Texas A&M Press, 1998.

Gerolymatos, André. *Castles Made of Sand: A Century of Anglo-American Espionage and Intervention in the Middle East.* New York: St. Martin's Press, 2010.

Gleijses, Piero. *Shattered Hope: The Guatemalan Revolution and the United States, 1944–1954.* Princeton, NJ: Princeton University Press, 1992.

Gonzales, Alberto R. *True Faith and Allegiance: A Story of Service and Sacrifice in War and Peace*. Nashville, TN: Nelson Books, 2016.

Green, Fitzhugh. *American Propaganda Abroad from Benjamin Franklin to Ronald Reagan*. New York: Hippocrene Books, 1988.

Grenier, Robert L. *88 Days to Kandahar: A CIA Diary*. New York: Simon and Schuster, 2015.

Grey, Stephen. *Ghost Plane: The True Story of the CIA Torture Program*. New York: St. Martin's Press, 2006.

——. *The New Spy Masters: Inside the Modern World of Espionage from the Cold War to Global Terror*. New York: St. Martin's Press, 2015.

Grose, Peter. *Gentleman Spy: The Life of Allen Dulles*. Boston, MA: Houghton Mifflin, 1994.

——. *Operation Rollback: America's Secret War Behind the Iron Curtain*. Boston, MA: Houghton Mifflin, 2000.

Hagedorn, Dan, and Leif Hellström. *Foreign Invaders: The Douglas Invader in Foreign Military and US Clandestine Service*. Leicester, UK: Midland Publishing Limited, 1994.

Hagen, Louis. *The Secret War for Europe: A Dossier of Espionage*. New York: Stein and Day, 1968.

Harlow, Bill, ed. *Rebuttal: The CIA Responds to the Senate Intelligence Committee's Study of its Detention and Interrogation Program*. Annapolis, MD: Naval Institute Press, 2015.

Harvey, Barbara S. *Permesta: Half A Rebellion*. Cornell University: Modern Indonesia Project, Southeast Asia Program Monograph no. 57, 1977.

Hazard, Elizabeth W. *Cold War Crucible: United States Foreign Policy and the Conflict in Romania, 1943–1953*. Boulder, CO: East European Monographs, 1996.

Helms, Richard. *A Look over My Shoulder: A Life in the Central Intelligence Agency*. With William Hood. New York: Random House, 2003.

Hersh, Burton. *The Old Boys: The American Elite and the Origins of the CIA*. New York: Charles Scribners' Sons, 1992.

Higgins, Trumbull. *The Perfect Failure: Kennedy, Eisenhower, and the CIA at the Bay of Pigs*. New York: W.W. Norton, 1987.

Hitz, Frederick. *The Great Game: The Myths and Reality of Espionage*. New York: Vintage Books, 2005.

Hoffman, David E. *The Billion Dollar Spy: A True Story of Cold War Espionage and Betrayal*. New York: Doubleday, 2015.

Immerman, Richard. *The CIA in Guatemala*. Austin: University of Texas Press, 1982.

Janney, Peter. *Mary's Mosaic: The CIA Conspiracy to Murder John F. Kennedy, Mary Pinchot Meyer, and their Vision for World Peace*. New York: Skyhorse Publishing, 2015.

Johnson, Haynes. *The Bay of Pigs: The Leaders' Story of Brigade 2506*. New York: Dell Books, 1964.

Johnson, Loch K. *A Season of Inquiry: The Senate Intelligence Investigation*. Lexington: University Press of Kentucky, 1985.

Johnson, Ross. *Radio Free Europe and Radio Liberty: The CIA Years and Beyond*. Washington, D.C.: Woodrow Wilson Center and Stanford University Press, 2010.

Jones, Seth G. *Hunting in the Shadows: The Pursuit of Al Qa'ida Since 9/11*. New York: W. W. Norton, 2012.

Kahin, Audrey R., and George McT. Kahin. *Subversion as Foreign Policy: The Secret Eisenhower and Dulles Debacle in Indonesia*. New York: The New Press, 1995.

Kessler, Ronald. *Inside the CIA: Revealing the Secrets of the World's Most Powerful Spy Agency*. New York: Pocket Books, 1992.

Kinzer, Stephen. *The Brothers: John Foster Dulles, Allen Dulles, and Their Secret World War*. New York: Henry Holt, 2013.

Kirkpatrick, Lyman B., Jr. *The Real CIA*. New York: The Macmillan Company, 1968.

Korn, David A. *Assassination in Khartoum*. Bloomington: University of Indiana Press, 1993.

Kornbluh, Peter, ed. *Bay of Pigs Declassified: The Secret CIA Report on the Invasion of Cuba*. New York: The New Press, 1998.

———, ed. *The Pinochet File: A Declassified osier on Atrocity and Accountability*. New York: The New Press, 2004.

Langguth, A.J. *Hidden Terrors*. New York: Pantheon Books, 1978.

Lechuga, Carlos. *Cuba and the Missile Crisis: The Dramatic Inside Story*. Translated by Mary Todd. Melbourne, Aust.: Ocean Books, 2001.

Lukes, Igor. *On the Edge of the Cold War: American Diplomats and Spies in Postwar Prague*. New York: Oxford University Press, 2012.

Lulushi, Albert. *Operation Valuable Fiend: The CIA's First Paramilitary Strike Against the Iron Curtain*. New York: Arcade Publishing, 2013.

Lynch, Grayston. *Decision for Disaster: Betrayal at the Bay of Pigs*. Washington, D.C.: Brassey's, 1998.

Mahle, Melissa Boyle. *Denial and Deception: An Insider's View of the CIA from Iran-Contra to 9/11*. New York: Nation Books, 2004.

Mangold, Tom. *Cold Warrior: James Jesus Angleton: The CIA's Master Spy Hunter*. New York: Simon and Schuster, 1991.

Mayer, Jane. *The Dark Side: The Inside Story of How the War on Terror turned into a War on American Ideals*. New York: Doubleday, 2008.

Mazzetti, Mark. *The Way of the Knife: The CIA, A Secret Army, and a War at the Ends of the Earth*. New York: Penguin Press, 2013.

Mikelson, Sig. *America's Other Voice: The Story of Radio Free Europe and Radio Liberty*. New York: Praeger, 1983.

Mitchell, James E. *Enhanced Interrogation: Inside the Minds and Motives of the Islamic Terrorists Trying to Destroy America*. With Bill Harlow. New York: Crown Forum, 2016.

Morell, Michael. *The Great War of Our Time: The CIA's Fight against Terrorism from al Qa'ida to ISIS*. With Bill Harlow. New York: Hachette Book Group, 2015.

Mosley, Leonard. *Dulles: A Biography of Eleanor, Allen, and John Foster and their Family Network*. New York: Dell Books, 1979.

Murphy, David E., Sergei Kondrashev, and George Bailey. *Battleground Berlin: CIA vs KGB in the Cold War*. New Haven, CT: Yale University Press, 1997.

Naylor, Sean. *Relentless Strike: The Secret History of Joint Special Operations Command*. New York: St. Martin's Press, 2015.

O'Connell, Jack. *King's Counsel: A Memoir of War, Espionage and Diplomacy in the Middle East*. With Vernon Loeb. New York: W.W. Norton, 2011.

Osgood, Kenneth. *Total Cold War: Eisenhower's Secret Propaganda Battle at Home and Abroad*. Lawrence: University Press of Kansas, 2006.

Panetta, Leon. *Worthy Fights: A Memoir of Leadership in War and Peace.* With Jim Newton. New York: Penguin Press, 2014.

Paterson, Thomas G. *Contesting Castro: The United States and the Triumph of the Cuban Revolution*. New York: Oxford University Press, 1994.

Perry, Mark. *Eclipse: The Last Days of the CIA*. New York: William Morrow, 1992.

Persons, Albert C. *Bay of Pigs: A Firsthand Account of the Mission by a U.S. Pilot in Support of the Cuban Invasion Force in 1961*. Jefferson, NC: McFarland and Coy, 1990

Phillips, David A. *Secret Wars Diary: My Adventures in Combat, Espionage Operations and Covert Action*. Bethesda, MD: Stone Trail Press, 1989.

———. *The Night Watch: 25 Years of Peculiar Service*. New York: Atheneum, 1977.

Plame Wilson, Valerie. *Fair Game: My Life as a Spy, My Betrayal by the White House*. New York: Simon and Schuster, 2007.

Powers, Thomas. *Intelligence Wars: American Secret History from Hitler to Al Qaeda*. New York: New York Review Books, 2002.

———. *The Man Who Kept the Secrets: Richard Helms and the CIA*. New York: Alfred A. Knopf, 1979.

Prados, John. *The Family Jewels: The CIA, Secrecy, and Presidential Power*. Austin: University of Texas Press, 2014.

———. *Hoodwinked: The Documents that Reveal How Bush Sold Us a War*. New York: The New Press, 2004.

———. *How the Cold War Ended: Debating and Doing History*. Washington, D.C.: Potomac Books, 2011.

———. *Keepers of the Keys: A History of the National Security Council from Truman to Bush*. New York: William Morrow Publishers, 1991.

———. *Presidents' Secret Wars: CIA and Pentagon Covert Operations from World War II through the Persian Gulf*. Chicago: Ivan R. Dee Publisher, 1996.

———. *Safe for Democracy: The Secret Wars of the CIA*. Chicago: Ivan R. Dee, 2006.

——. *The Soviet Estimate: U.S. Intelligence Analysis and Soviet Strategic Forces.* Princeton, NJ: Princeton University Press, 1986.

——. *The US Special Forces: What Everyone Needs to Know.* New York: Oxford University Press, 2015.

——. *William Colby and the CIA: The Secret Wars of a Controversial Spymaster.* Lawrence: University Press of Kansas, 2009.

Rabe, Stephen. *Eisenhower: The Foreign Policy of Anticommunism and Latin America.* Chapel Hill: University of North Carolina Press, 1988.

Richelson, Jeffrey T. *Spying on the Bomb: American Nuclear Intelligence from Nazi Germany to Iran and North Korea.* New York: W.W. Norton, 2006.

——. *The US Intelligence Community.* 7th edition. Boulder, CO: Westview Press, 2016.

——. *The Wizards of Langley: Inside the CIA's Directorate for Science and Technology.* Boulder, CO: Westview Press, 2001.

Riedel, Bruce. *JFK's Forgotten Crisis: Tibet, the CIA, and the Sino-Indian War.* Washington, D.C.: The Brookings Institution, 2015.

Risen, James. *Pay Any Price: Greed, Power, and Endless War.* Boston, MA: Houghton Mifflin Harcourt, 2014.

——. *State of War: The Secret History of the CIA and the Bush Administration.* New York: Free Press, 2006.

Rizzo, John. *Company Man: Thirty Years of Controversy and Crisis in the CIA.* New York: Scribner, 2014.

Rodriguez, Jose A., Jr. *Hard Measures: How Aggressive CIA Actions after 9/11 Saved American Lives.* With Ball Harlow. New York: Threshold Editions, 2012.

Rodríguez, Juan Carlos. *The Bay of Pigs and the CIA.* Translated by Mary Todd. Melbourne, Aust.: Ocean Press, 1999.

Sanger, David E. *Confront and Conceal: Obama's Secret Wars and Surprising Use of American Power.* New York: Broadway Paperbacks, 2013.

Saunders, Frances Stoner. *The Cultural Cold War: The CIA and the World of Artists and Letters.* New York: The New Press, 2013.

Scahill, Jeremy. *Blackwater: The Rise of the World's Most Powerful Mercenary Military.* New York: Nation Books, 2007.

Schlesinger, Stephen, and Stephen Kinzer. *Bitter Fruit: The Untold Story of the American Coup in Guatemala.* New York: Anchor Books, 1983.

Schmitt, Eric, and Thom Shanker. *Counter Strike: The Untold Story of America's Secret Campaign Against Al Qaeda.* New York: Henry Holt, 2011.

Schroen, Gary C. *First In: An Insider's Account of How the CIA Spearheaded the War on Terror in Afghanistan.* New York: Ballantine Books, 2005.

Smith, Joseph B. *Portrait of a Cold Warrior.* New York: G. P. Putnam's Sons, 1976.

Soley, Lawrence C. *Radio Warfare: OSS and CIA Subversive Propaganda.* New York: Praeger, 1989.

Srodes, James. *Allen Dulles: Master of Spies.* Washington, D.C.: Regnery Publishing, 1999.

Storm, Morten. *Agent Storm: My Life Inside Al Qaeda and the CIA*. With Paul Cruickshank and Tim Lister. New York: Atlantic Monthly Press, 2014.

Talbot, David. *The Devil's Chessboard: Allen Dulles, the CIA and the Rise of America's Secret Government*. New York: HarperCollins, 2015.

Taubman, Philip. *Secret Empire: Eisenhower, the CIA and the Hidden Story of America's Space Espionage*. New York: Simon and Schuster, 2004.

Tenet, George J. *At the Center of the Storm: My Years at the CIA*. With Bill Harlow. New York: HarperCollins, 2007.

Thomas, Evan. *The Very Best Men: Four Who Dared: The Early Years of the CIA*. New York: Simon and Schuster, 1995.

Thomas, Hugh. *Armed Truce: The Beginnings of the Cold War, 1945–1946*. New York: Atheneum, 1987.

Thompson, Kenneth W., ed. *Portraits of the American Presidency, v. III: The Eisenhower Presidency, Eleven Intimate Perspectives of Dwight D. Eisenhower*. Lanham, MD: University Press of America, 1984.

Treverton, Gregory F. *Covert Action: The Limits of Intervention in the Postwar World*. New York: Basic Books, 1987.

Triay, Victor Andres. *Bay of Pigs: An Oral History of Brigade 2506*. Gainesville: University Press of Florida, 2001.

Troy, Thomas F. *Wild Bill and Intrepid: Donovan, Stephenson, and the Origin of CIA*. New Haven, CT: Yale University Press, 1996.

Tully, Andrew. *CIA: The Inside Story*. New York: William Morrow, 1962.

Twentieth Century Fund. *In from the Cold: Report of the Task Force on the Future of U.S. Intelligence*. New York: Twentieth Century Fund Press, 1996.

Urban, George R. *Radio Free Europe and the Pursuit of Democracy: My War within the Cold War*. New Haven, CT: Yale University Press, 1997.

Waldron, Lamar. *Ultimate Sacrifice: John and Robert Kennedy, the Plan for a Coup in Cuba, and the Murder of JFK*. New York: Carroll and Graf, 2005.

Wallace, Robert, and H. Keith Melton. *Spycraft: The Secret History of the CIA's Spytechs from Communism to Al-Qaeda*. New York: Penguin/Plume, 2009.

Warrick, Joby. *The Triple Agent: The Al-Qaeda Mole who Infiltrated the CIA*. New York: Vintage Books, 2012.

Weber, Ralph E., ed. *Spymasters: Ten CIA Officers in their own Words*. Wilmington, DE: Scholarly Resources, 1999.

Weiner, Timothy. *Legacy of Ashes: The History of the CIA*. New York: Doubleday, 2007.

Wilford, Hugh. *The Mighty Wurlitzer: How the CIA Played America*. Cambridge, MA: Harvard University Press, 2008.

Winks, Robin W. *Cloak and Gown: Scholars in the Secret War, 1939–1961*. New York: Morrow, 1987.

Wyden, Peter. *Bay of Pigs: The Untold Story*. New York: Simon and Schuster, 1979.

INDEX

Baltic States, 36, 42, 79–80, 81
Baltimore Sun, 332
Bámaca Velásquez, Efraín, 241–42
Bancroft, Mary, 32, 36
Bandar, Prince, 180
Bangkok Station, 10, 11–12, 18, 105, 324
Barnes, C. Tracy, 58, 96, 131–41, 147–49, 154, 160–63, 214, 235, 250–51, 255, 371; Cuba/Castro plot, 136–41, 147, 156–60, 161, 162–63, 251; Frankfurt post, 135–36; Latin America operations, 133–41; London Station post, 136; and OSS in Italy, 33, 131; PB/Success in Guatemala, 133–35; and the PSB, 90, 133; retirement, 163; and Taylor investigation, 147, 156–60
Barrow, Robert, 86
Batista, Fulgencio, 72, 156
Bauer, Robert F., 359–60, 377–78
Bay of Pigs invasion at Playa Girón (1961), 74–75, 137–43, 154–64, 218. *See also* Cuba operation (Project Ate or JM/Ate)
Bayh, Evan, 377
Becker, Loftus, 58
Beirut embassy truck bombing (1983), 124, 130, 181
Belarus, 81
Bellinger, John D., III, 7–8, 11, 12, 20, 111
Ben, Philip, 60
Ben Soud, Mohamed Ahmed, 357
Bennett, Gina, 228
Berger, Sandy, 299–300
Berlin Olympics (1936), 253
Bikowsky, Alfreda, 335–36
bin Laden, Osama, 113, 114, 299–300, 326, 361–62, 366; and CIA Alec Station, 112, 120–21, 299, 335; Tenet's planned raids, 284, 299–300, 327
bin Zeid, Sharif Ali, 123, 124
Bissell, Richard M., 58, 75, 142, 147–63, 218, 237, 249–55, 266, 371; and Barnes, 136, 148–49; and Cuba/Castro plot, 136–39, 140, 147, 154–63, 251–53; as Dulles's assistant, 150; forced resignation, 252–53; Guatemala coup against Arbenz, 136, 149–50; pre-CIA career, 147–49; Project Haik in Indonesia, 101; and U-2 spy plane missions, 101, 150–54, 218; World War II, 147–48
Black, Cofer, 4–5, 7, 8–9, 10, 109, 114

black prisons, xv, 110, 348; Afghanistan, 17, 335, 366; closure, 348; Project Greystone, 2–3, 5–18, 25–26, 27–28, 310, 316, 322–25, 340, 348, 378; Site Blue, 17, 20; Site Green in Chiang Mai, Thailand, 5–18, 105; Site Orange, 17. *See also* Project Greystone (CIA's detainee interrogation and torture program)
Blackwater, 113, 350
Blair, Dennis, 347, 353
Blakely, Yvonne, 126
Blank Rome (law firm), 357
Blanton, Thomas, 337
Blee, David, 274
Bocock, Natalie, 239
Boer War, 33–34
Bohlen, Chester, 89
Boland, Edward P., 174
Boland Amendment, 174, 180, 183, 202, 203
Bonk, Ben, 305
Boren, David, 286, 287, 345–46
Bosnia-Herzegovina, 283, 284, 300–302, 325
Bradley, Omar, 49, 84
Breckinridge, Scott, 235
Brennan, John O., 295, 299, 345, 353, 356, 360, 362, 373–89; and CIA accountability, 381–83; CIA response to Senate torture report, 365, 373–83; and drone program, 363, 383; fusion centers, 384–85; mission centers, 384, 385–86; and Trump administration, 383, 384, 388
Brewster, Kingman, 163
Brexit, 385
Bridge of Spies (film), 164
British Broadcast Corporation (BBC), 61
British Guiana, 102–3, 229, 235
Broe, William V., 237, 277
Brookner, Janine M., 232–34, 240
Bross, John, 136, 137, 148, 251–52, 270
Brown, Harold, 292–93
Bruce, David, 93, 170
Bruemmer, Russell, J., 205
Brugger, Fred, 108, 243, 297
Buckley, David B., 375, 377–78, 381
Buckley, William, 129, 181
Bundy, McGeorge, 159, 258–59
Bundy, William P., 59
Burke, Arleigh A., 143, 147
Burma (Myanmar), 73, 86
Burnham, David, 271
Burr, Richard, 383
Bush, George Herbert Walker, 131,

warfare and Southeast Asia strategy ("D-23"), 87; and 10/5 Panel, 58, 133
Publications Review Board (PRB), 212, 294–95, 311, 337

Al Qaeda, 4, 299–300; Alec Station and, 120; cruise missile strike against Afghanistan training camps, 284; and drone program in Afghanistan, 119–24; Hayden and Bush's war on terror, 335, 344; 9/11 terror attacks, 1–4, 284, 305–6; Rizzo's post-9/11 presidential finding authorizing capture and detention, 320–21; Tenet and Bush's war on terror, 305–10; Tenet and Clinton's war on terror, 298–300; U.S embassy bombings in Africa, 4, 8, 120, 284, 300; USS *Cole* attack (2000), 8, 120, 284, 305–6. *See also* Project Greystone (CIA's detainee interrogation and torture program); Zubaydah, Abu
QK/Broil (Romania), 81
QK/Droop (Soviet Union), 81
QK/Ivory, 48

Rabe, Stephen, 72
Raborn, William F., 223, 259–60
Radio Free Asia, 80–81, 218
Radio Free Europe (RFE), 46, 47–49, 51, 52, 57, 65, 80, 94–97, 218, 252, 258, 264, 266–67
Radio in the American Sector (RIAS), 90
Radio Liberty (RL), 47–49, 57, 90, 94–95, 252
Radio Warsaw, 63
Rahim, Muhammad, 28
al-Rahim al-Nashiri, 'Abd, 18, 353–54
Rahman, Gul, 19
Ramparts scandal, 262–67, 269, 279
Randolph, Jean Wellford, 216
Rastvorov, Yuri, 92
Raus, Juri, 221–24
RDINet (Rendition, Detention, and Interrogation Network), 351–52, 354–55, 358–61, 363, 372–73, 377
Reader's Digest, 162, 185
Reagan, Ronald: Casey as CIA director, 128, 167–93, 198–204; CIA operations in Afghanistan, 171–72; executive order on intelligence activities (E.O. 12333), 200; Iran-Contra Affair, 107, 129, 165, 179–93; Iran hostage crisis/rescue, 128, 169; and Israel-Palestine conflict, 129–30; and Lebanese civil war,

125; Nicaragua operation, 171–79, 203; "overt covert operations" and open-secret wars, 171–72; pushback against congressional oversight and covert operations approval laws, 169, 200–201
Red Brigades, 167
Regan, Don, 189
Reid, Harry, 364, 375
Rendition and Detention Group (RDG) of Counterterrorism Center, 15, 19
renditions, 4–18, 109–11, 322, 345–46. *See also* Project Greystone (CIA's detainee interrogation and torture program)
Rendon Group, 230
Reno, Janet, 289
Research Institute of America, 170
Reyes, Silvestre, 342–43
Rhodes, George S., 214–15
Rice, Condoleezza, 11–12, 19–20, 25–26, 28, 325, 341, 380
Richardson, John R., 97
Richardson, Wayne, 213–14
Richer, Robert, 318–19
Rindskopf, Elizabeth R., 232, 234, 241–42
risk aversion, 243–44, 317, 389
Rizzo, John A., 180, 190, 201, 320–30; and CIA drone program, 325–30; and Goss, 328; and Hayden, 335; nomination hearings to become general counsel, 328–29; and OGC Sporkin, 199–200; post-9/11 presidential finding authorizing capture and detention of Al Qaeda terrorists, 320–21; and Project Greystone, 7–12, 18–22, 27, 29, 104–6, 321–25, 329, 340–41, 346–49; and Rodriquez's destruction of the torture videotapes, 323–25
Robertson, William ("Rip"), 141–43; Cuba operation, 141–43, 145–47, 162–63; and PB/Success in Guatemala, 135, 142
Rockefeller, Jay, 342, 343, 379
Rockefeller, Nelson, 277–78
Rockefeller Commission (1975), 237, 260, 277–78, 280, 292
Rodriguez, Felix, 183–84
Rodriguez, Jose A., Jr., 103–17, 193, 316–19, 323–25, 334; accountability board review, 116, 240; and the CTC, 109–11, 112–14, 323–24; destruction of the torture tapes, 18, 28, 104–6, 115–16, 316–17, 323–25, 342–43, 349, 361, 374;

ABOUT THE AUTHOR

John Prados is a senior fellow of the National Security Archive, where he directs the CIA Documentation Project and the Vietnam Documentation Project and helps in other areas. He writes books on aspects of intelligence, diplomatic, military and national security. His recent works include *Storm Over Leyte: The Philippine Invasion and the Destruction of the Japanese Navy*, *Normandy Crucible*, and *Islands of Destiny: The Solomons Campaign and the Eclipse of the Rising Sun*. His books on the CIA—some of which have been on CIA recommended reading lists—include *Safe for Democracy*, *The Family Jewels*, *William Colby and the CIA*, *Presidents' Secret Wars*, and *The Soviet Estimate*. He has consulted on historical aspects of film projects and his papers, articles, and reviews have appeared widely. Prados also designs board strategy games.

Also available from Amberley Publishing

'It is impossible to imagine M. R. D. Foot's position as the pre-eminent historian of SOE ever being challenged.'

ANTONY BEEVOR

SOE
IN THE LOW
COUNTRIES

M. R. D. FOOT

FOREWORD BY NIGEL WEST